DISCARDED

COMPANION ENCYCLOPEDIA
OF ARCHAEOLOGY

COMPANION
ENCYCLOPEDIA
OF ARCHAEOLOGY

EDITED BY

GRAEME BARKER

Volume 1

London and New York

First published 1999
by Routledge
11 New Fetter Lane, London EC4P 4EE
29 West 35th Street, New York, NY 10001
© 1999 Routledge

Typeset in Ehrhardt by
RefineCatch Limited, Bungay, Suffolk
Printed and bound in Great Britain by
Butler and Tanner Ltd, Frome and London

British Library Cataloguing in Publication Data
A catalogue record for this book is available from the British Library

Library of Congress Cataloging-in-Publication Data
Companion encyclopedia of archaeology / edited by Graeme Barker
p.   cm.
Includes bibliographical references and index.
(alk. paper)
1. Archaeology – Encyclopedias.   I. Barker, Graeme.
CC70.C59   1999   98–7621
930.1 – dc21   CIP

ISBN 0–415–06448–1 (set)
0–415–21329–0 (vol. 1)
0–415–21330–4 (vol. 2)

CONTENTS

CONTENTS

LIST OF FIGURES

LIST OF TABLES

CONTRIBUTORS

GRAEME BARKER started his university training at Cambridge as a classicist, but graduated in prehistoric archaeology. He then took his Ph.D. at Cambridge on the prehistory of central Italy, with a spell at the British School at Rome as a Rome Scholar. Between 1972 and 1984 he was a Lecturer and then Senior Lecturer in prehistoric archaeology at the University of Sheffield, he was Director of the British School at Rome between 1984 and 1988, and since then has been Professor of Archaeology and head of the School of Archaeological Studies at the University of Leicester. His principal research interests have been in the archaeology of subsistence and agriculture, first with a special focus on archaeozoology but later in landscape archaeology. He has conducted fieldwork in Italy, Mozambique and the former Yugoslavia, and directed interdisciplinary field projects in Italy and Libya, and currently in Jordan. His publications include *Landscape and Society: Prehistoric Central Italy* (1981), *Archaeology and Italian Society* (1981, co-edited with R. Hodges), *Prehistoric Communities in Northern England* (1981), *Prehistoric Farming in Europe* (1985), *Beyond Domestication in Prehistoric Europe* (1985, co-edited with C. S. Gamble), *Roman Landscapes: Archaeological Survey in the Mediterranean Region* (1991, co-edited with J. Lloyd), *A Mediterranean Valley: Landscape Archaeology and* Annales *History in the Biferno Valley* (1985, with the companion volume *The Biferno Valley Survey: the Archaeological and Geomorphological Record*), *Farming the Desert: the UNESCO Libyan Valleys Archaeological Survey* (1996, two volumes with D. Gilbertson, B. Jones and D. Mattingly), and *The Etruscans* (1998, with T. Rasmussen). (Institutional address: School of Archaeological Studies, University of Leicester, Leicester LE1 7RH, UK.)

JOHN BINTLIFF took his first degree in Archaeology and Anthropology at Cambridge University, where he also completed his Ph.D. under the supervision of David Clarke and Eric Higgs. From 1977 to 1990 he taught Archaeology at Bradford University, and since 1990 has been Reader in Archaeology at Durham University. From 1978 to the present he has been co-director with Anthony Snodgrass of the Boeotia Survey Project in central Greece. Published books include *Natural Environment and Human Settlement in Prehistoric Southern Greece* (1977), *Mycenaean Geography* (1977), *Palaeoclimates, Palaeoenvironments and Human Communities in the Eastern Mediterranean in Later Prehistory* (1982, with W. van Zeist), *European Social Evolution* (1984), *Archaeology at the Interface* (1986, with C. Gaffney), *Extracting Meaning from the Past* (1986), *Conceptual Issues in Environmental Archaeology* (1988, with E. Grant *et al.*), *Recent Developments in Yugoslav Archaeology* (1988, with J. Chapman *et al.*), *The Annales School and Archaeology* (1991), *Europe Between Late Antiquity and the Middle Ages* (1995, with H. Hamerow), *Structure and Contingency in the Evolution of Life, Human Evolution and Human History* (1997) and *Mediterranean Landscape Archaeology 2: Demography and Regional Survey in Mediterranean Europe and Beyond* (1998, with K. Sbonias). (Institutional address: Department of Archaeology, University of Durham, South Road, Durham DH1 3LE, UK.)

PETER BOGUCKI completed his undergraduate studies in anthropology at the University of Pennsylvania and received his Ph.D. in 1981 from Harvard University. Since 1983 he has worked at Princeton University, first as director of studies of Forbes College and, beginning in 1994, as assistant dean for undergraduate affairs in the School of Engineering and Applied Science. He has also taught courses in archaeology and European prehistory. His research interests lie in the transition from foraging to farming and early agricultural societies in Europe. Since 1976, he has conducted archaeological fieldwork at sites in Poland, with a focus on settlement patterning and faunal remains. He is the author of *Early Neolithic Subsistence and Settlement in the Polish Lowlands* (1982) and *Forest Farmers and Stockherders: Early Agriculture and its Consequences in North-Central Europe* (1988) and the editor of *Case Studies in European Prehistory* (1993). (Institutional address: Office of the Dean, School of Engineering and Applied Science, Princeton University, ACE-23 Engineering Quadrangle, Princeton, New Jersey 08522–5263, USA.)

TONY BROWN trained as a physical geographer at UCL London and Southampton and wrote his Ph.D. on floodplain sediments and palaeoecology. This led to an interest in the geoarchaeological potential of alluvial sediments and to collaboration with archaeological projects in Britain and elsewhere. Following his appointment to the Department of Geography at the University of Leicester, he developed research into the alluviation and land use history of river valleys in the East Midlands, and following his appointment in 1991 to a joint lectureship at Leicester with the School of Archaeological Studies he expanded his interests to include changing riverine environments in the Mediterranean. In recent years he has worked as a geoarchaeologist with archaeological projects in the Midlands, northern England and at Lindisfarne (Holy Island) in Britain, and in central Italy and Tunisia, in tandem with theoretical research on palaeohydrology, alluvial processes, sedimentation and floodplain forests. Much of this work is combined in his *Alluvial Environments: Geoarchaeology and Environmental Change* (1997). (Institutional address: Department of Geography, University of Exeter, Amory Building, Rennes Drive, Exeter EX4 4RJ, UK.)

MARTIN CARVER was an army officer for fourteen years and a freelance field archaeologist for thirteen, before being appointed Professor of Archaeology at York. His main academic interest is early medieval Europe, and his initial research operations from 1972 onwards were mainly government-funded investigations of early towns in England, France, Italy and Algeria. The results led to the publication of *Underneath English Towns* (1987) and *Arguments in Stone: Archaeological Research and the European Town in the First Millennium* (1993). In 1983 he was appointed director of the new campaign of excavation at Sutton Hoo, which was completed in 1993 and is now ready for publication: interim studies appeared in *The Age of Sutton Hoo* (1992) and *Sutton Hoo: Burial Ground of Kings?* (1995) as well as in three feature films for the BBC. In the early 1970s he began to promote a staged approach to fieldwork, using the concept of predictive evaluation, which is convergent with archaeological practice in the USA. In addition to numerous papers on this theme, a major handbook on this approach to archaeological fieldwork is in preparation with Nan Rothschild. (Institutional address: Department of Archaeology, University of York, King's Manor, York YO1 2EP, UK.)

ANDREW T. CHAMBERLAIN studied Geology and Geophysics at the University of Liverpool and Archaeological Science at the University of Southampton, completing his Ph.D. in Palaeoanthropology at the University of Liverpool in 1987. After undertaking postdoctoral research with Professor Bernard Wood at Liverpool, he joined the Department of Archaeology and Prehistory at the University of Sheffield in 1990, where he is currently Senior Lecturer and co-director of the M.Sc. course in Osteology, Palaeopathology and Funerary Archaeology. He is the author of *Human Remains* (1994), and his research interests are in palaeoanthropology, biological anthropology and palaeodemography. (Institutional address: Department of Prehistory and Archaeology, University of Sheffield, Northgate House, West Street, Sheffield S1 4ET, UK.)

NEIL CHRISTIE studied archaeology at the University of Newcastle upon Tyne, where he wrote his Ph.D. thesis on *Byzantine and Longobard Northern and Central Italy*. In

1985–86 he held a Rome Scholarship at the British School at Rome, researching Byzantine Liguria in the sixth and seventh centuries AD, and then preparing for publication three British School excavation reports (published as *Three South Etrurian Churches: Santa Cornelia, Santa Rufina and San Liberato* in 1991). He held the Sir James Knott Research Fellowship (1988–91) at Newcastle upon Tyne and a British Academy Postdoctoral Fellowship (1991–93) at the Institute of Archaeology, University of Oxford, researching late Roman and early medieval Italy, before taking up his present appointment as a lecturer in medieval archaeology at the University of Leicester. He is the author of *The Lombards* (1995), editor of *Settlement and Economy in Italy 1500 BC–AD 1500: Papers of the Fifth Conference of Italian Archaeology* (1995), and co-editor of *Towns in Transition: Urban Evolution in Late Antiquity and the Early Middle Ages* (1996). (Institutional address: School of Archaeological Studies, University of Leicester, Leicester LE1 7RH, UK.)

JOHN COLLIS started excavating as a schoolboy in his native Winchester. Subsequently he did his first degree in Archaeology and Anthropology at Cambridge, continuing with his doctorate on the beginnings of urbanization in the Late Iron Age in central and western Europe, and studying in Czechoslovakia and West Germany. He was intimately involved in the change of direction of iron age studies in the late 1960s and 1970s, especially on the nature of iron age coinage. His first major excavation in the 1960s was of an iron age and Roman farming settlement at Owslebury near Winchester. In 1970 he took up a lecturing post at Exeter University, and carried out a major excavation in the Roman and medieval city. In 1972 he moved to Sheffield, where he is now Professor in the Department of Archaeology and Prehistory, teaching the European Iron Age and Techniques of Excavation. Since 1973 he has worked on iron age sites and survey in central France, but was also involved in surveys of bronze age field systems on Dartmoor with Andrew Fleming. His major publications are *The European Iron Age* and *Oppida: Earliest Towns North of the Alps*. At present he is preparing a book on the 'invention' of the Celts. (Institutional address: Department of Archaeology and Prehistory, University of Sheffield, Northgate House, West Street, Sheffield S1 4ET, UK.)

JAMES A. DELLE studied anthropology at the College of William and Mary, where he received his MA in 1989, and at the University of Massachusetts at Amherst, where he was awarded his Ph.D. in 1996. He has held teaching positions in archaeology and social anthropology at the University of Massachusetts in Amherst and New York University, and in social anthropology and international development at Clark University in Worcester, Massachusetts. Currently he is Assistant Professor of Anthropology at Franklin and Marshall College in Lancaster, Pennsylvania. He has published several articles based on field research conducted in the Netherlands Antilles, Ireland and Jamaica, and is the author of *An Archaeology of Social Space* (Plenum Press, 1998). (Institutional address: Department of Anthropology, Franklin and Marshall College, Lancaster, PA 17604, USA.)

ROBIN DENNELL first worked on an archaeological excavation when he was eleven. He specialized in the palaeolithic and human evolution for his BA whilst at Cambridge (1966–69), but focused on archaeobotany and the earliest farming settlements in Bulgaria for his Ph.D., which he completed in 1975 as part of the British Academy major research project into the early history of farming in Europe directed by Eric Higgs. In the 1970s his main fieldwork was in Iran and concerned with the origins of farming and patterns of land use. After the Iranian Revolution terminated this work, he wrote *European Economic Prehistory: A New Approach* (1983), since translated into Spanish and Japanese. His main fieldwork since 1981 has concerned the palaeolithic sequence of northern Pakistan; so far, ten seasons of fieldwork have resulted in one research monograph and about thirty research papers. In addition to working in Bulgaria, Iran and Pakistan, he has also undertaken archaeological fieldwork in Denmark, Germany, Israel, Italy, Tunisia and Turkey. He was appointed to a lectureship at Sheffield in 1973; after a four-year break between 1988 and 1992 as a Leverhulme Senior Research Fellow as director of the British Archaeological Mission to Pakistan, he now holds a personal chair in prehistory at Sheffield. (Institutional address: Department of Archaeology and Prehistory, University of Sheffield, Northgate House, West Street, Sheffield S1 4ET, UK.)

STEPHEN L. DYSON is Professor of Classics at the State University of New York at Buffalo. He received his BA from Brown University where he studied both classical and North American archaeology. At Oxford he took a diploma in classical archaeology with a speciality in Roman Britain. His MA and Ph.D. are from Yale, with a dissertation on the ceramics from Dura Europos. His fieldwork has focused on the rural archaeology of Roman Italy, first with villa excavations in southern Italy and then with survey and Roman rural settlement reconstruction in southern Tuscany. Most recently, he has been doing field research in Sardinia. The research on the Roman countryside resulted in his book *Community and Society in Roman Italy* (1992). In the area of Roman frontier studies he has published *The Creation of the Roman Frontier* (1985) and edited *Comparative Studies in the Archaeology of Colonialism* (1985). His most recent research has focused on the history of archaeology, with a book on classical archaeology in America, *Ancient Marbles to American Shores*, to be published in 1998. He is currently President of the Archaeological Institute of America. (Institutional address: Department of Classics, 712 Clemens Hall, SUNY Buffalo, NY 14260, USA.)

TIMOTHY EARLE is Professor and Chair of Anthropology at Northwestern University. He received his Ph.D. in Anthropology from the University of Michigan in 1973. His research interests include the evolution of pre-industrial societies, institutional finance and prehistoric economies. He has carried out research in the Hawaiian Islands and in Andean South America, and is presently involved in a long-term study of the Neolithic, Bronze and Iron Ages of Thy, Denmark. Earle is editor or co-editor of a number of volumes, including *Exchange Systems in Prehistory* (1977), *Modeling Change in Prehistoric Subsistence Economies* (1980), *Contexts for Prehistoric Exchange* (1982), *Specialization, Exchange and Complex Society* (1987), and *Chiefdoms: Power, Economy and Ideology* (1991). He is author of *Economic and Social Organization of a Complex Chiefdom: the Halelea District, Kauai, Hawaii* (1978, with A. Johnson), *The Evolution of Human Society* (1987) and *How Chiefs come to Power* (1997). (Institutional address: Department of Anthropology, Northwestern University, 1810 Hinman Avenue, Evanson, Illinois 60208–1310, USA.)

CHRIS GOSDEN studied for his BA and Ph.D. in the Department of Archaeology and Prehistory of the University of Sheffield (England), taking his Ph.D. on the production and exchange of pottery in iron age communities in central Europe in 1983. He then held the positions of Lecturer and Senior Lecturer in the Department of Archaeology at La Trobe University (Australia) from 1986 to 1993, before taking up his present position as Lecturer and Curator in Archaeology at the Pitt Rivers Museum of Oxford in 1994. His principal research interests include social theory and archaeology, the links between archaeology and anthropology, and the archaeology of colonialism. He has undertaken fieldwork in Papua New Guinea on sites ranging from the Pleistocene to the period of European contact, and in Turkmenistan, where he is part of a team interested in palaeolithic and neolithic sites, and he is also excavating iron age sites on the Berkshire Downs in southern England with Gary Lock. His publications include *Social Being and Time* and (with J. Allen) *Report of the Lapita Homeland Project*. (Institutional address: Pitt Rivers Museum, University of Oxford, 64 Banbury Road, Oxford OX2 6PN, UK.)

ANNIE GRANT has an MA and a Ph.D. in archaeology from the University of Cambridge. She has worked as a freelance archaeozoologist, and has held research posts at the Institute of Archaeology at the University of Oxford and in the Department of Archaeology at the University of Reading. Currently at the University of Leicester, she is both an Honorary Lecturer in the School of Archaeological Studies and Director of the university's Educational Development and Support Centre. Her research interests have centred around the role of animals in past societies. She collaborated with Barry Cunliffe for many years, with studies of the fauna from his excavations of sites such as Portchester, Mountbatten, Bath and Danebury. Her publications include two edited books – *The Countryside of Medieval England*

(Blackwell 1988, co-edited with G. Astill) and *Animals and Animal Products in Trade and Exchange* (L'Homme et L'Animal 1994) – and numerous papers on archaeozoological methodology, animal husbandry at sites in Britain, Spain and North Africa, and the social, religious and economic aspects of human/animal interrelationships. More recently, her interests have broadened to include landscape archaeology, and she is co-director (with Graeme Barker and Tom Rasmussen) of the Tuscania Archaeological Survey in central Italy. (Institutional address: School of Archaeological Studies, University of Leicester, Leicester LE1 7RH, UK.)

ANTHONY HARDING studied classics and archaeology at the University of Cambridge, taking his Ph.D. there in 1973. Since that time he has taught archaeology at the University of Durham, where he became Professor in 1990. He specializes in the archaeology of the Bronze Age in the Old World, and in particular the study of connections between the civilizations of the bronze age Aegean and those of west, central and northern Europe. His books include *The Bronze Age of Europe* (1979, jointly with J. M. Coles), *The Mycenaeans in Europe* (1984), *Henge Monuments of Great Britain* (1987), and *Die Schwerter im ehemaligen Jugoslawien* (1995). He has conducted field projects in Britain, Poland and the Czech Republic, and is particularly involved in collaborative work with local scholars on the archaeology of central and south-eastern Europe. (Institutional address: Department of Archaeology, University of Durham, South Road, Durham DH1 3LE, UK.)

FEKRI A. HASSAN is the Petrie Professor of Archaeology at the Institute of Archaeology, University College London. He was born in Cairo, Egypt, where he received his B.Sc. and M.Sc. in Geological Chemistry. In 1973 he took his Ph.D. at the Southern Methodist University in Dallas, Texas. Following an initial appointment at Wayne State University, Detroit, he was appointed Assistant Professor at Washington State University, Pullman, in 1975, became a professor in the same department in 1983, and took up his present position at UCL in 1994. His interest in demographic archaeology began with work on the origins of agriculture in the 1970s. He is the author of *Demographic Archaeology*, and is currently engaged in an examination of the relationships between cultural evolution and population change, and the population dynamics of the Egyptian civilization, to provide an archaeological perspective on contemporary population issues. He has published widely in geoarchaeology and the prehistory of Egypt, is currently involved in fieldwork in Egypt in the East Delta and at Farafra Oasis, and is coordinator of the Environment and Civilization Global Project (ECGP). (Institutional address: Institute of Archaeology, University College London, 31–34 Gordon Square, London WC1H 0PY, UK.)

SIMON HILLSON graduated from the University of Birmingham in 1974 with a joint degree in Geology and Archaeology, through which he was introduced to bones and teeth in the study of vertebrate palaeontology. He followed this interest into a Ph.D. supervised by Don Brothwell at the Institute of Archaeology, University College London, in which he studied the biology of ancient human populations from Egypt and Nubia, and developed a particular interest in teeth. In 1978 he took up a lectureship in archaeological science at the University of Lancaster, and returned to the Institute of Archaeology in London during 1987, where he is now a Reader in Bioarchaeology at University College London. Simon Hillson has written three textbooks: *Teeth* (1986) and *Dental Anthropology* (1996), both published by Cambridge University Press, and *Mammal Bones and Teeth* (1992), published by the Institute of Archaeology. (Institutional address: Institute of Archaeology, University College London, 31–34 Gordon Square, London WC1H 0PY, UK.)

MATTHEW JOHNSON was born in Texas and brought up in Britain. Having gained his BA in Archaeology and Anthropology at St John's College, Cambridge, he continued at Cambridge to research his Ph.D. on late medieval and early modern traditional houses in Suffolk, England. After holding posts at the University of Sheffield and St David's University College Lampeter, he has been Lecturer in Archaeology at the University of Durham since 1991, appointed Professor in 1998. His research interests include archaeological theory, architecture, and landscape history in England and Europe AD 1200–1800; he is currently researching in the field of later medieval castles. Matthew Johnson has published two books: *Housing Culture: Traditional Architecture in an English Landscape* (1993) and *An Archaeology of Capitalism* (1996). He is also the author of the forthcoming *Archaeological Theory: An Introduction*. (Institutional address: Department of Archaeology, University of Durham, South Road, Durham DH1 3LE, UK.)

KRISTIAN KRISTIANSEN studied prehistoric archaeology at the universities of Aarhus and Copenhagen in Denmark, obtaining his Ph.D. in 1975 and his D.Phil. in 1998. After working as a researcher from 1977 to 1979 at the University of Aarhus, from 1979 to 1994 he was Director of the Danish Archaeological Heritage in the Ministry of Environment. Since 1994 he has been Professor of Archaeology at the University of Göteborg in Sweden. He has edited several books on archaeological theory and method, as well as the *Journal of Danish Archaeology* and the *Journal of European Archaeology*, his most recent book (1998) being *Europe before History*. Until 1998 he was President of the European Association of Archaeologists. His main research interests are the Scandinavian Bronze Age, archaeological theory and method, the history of archaeology, and archaeological heritage management. (Institutional address: Institutionen for Arkeologi, University of Göteborg, S-412 Göteborg, Sweden.)

MARK P. LEONE received his Ph.D. in 1968 through the Department of Anthropology, University of Arizona. He has published on modern material culture and the historical archaeology of the Chesapeake. In 1981 he founded the Archaeology in Annapolis project in conjunction with the Department of Anthropology of the University of Maryland at College Park, and the Historic Annapolis Foundation, the city's principal private preservation organization. He has written extensively on the historical archaeology of the US, his publications including, for example, his edited volume with P. B. Potter *The Recovery of Meaning: Historical Archaeology in the Eastern United States* (1988). He produced *Invisible America* with Neil Silberman in 1995. Mark Leone has taught in the Department of Anthropology at the University of Maryland since 1976 and currently serves as chair of that department. (Institutional address: Department of Anthropology, University of Maryland at College Park, College Park, Maryland 20742, USA.)

STEVEN MITHEN studied archaeology at Sheffield University, and then acquired an M.Sc. in Biological Computation at York University in 1984 and a Ph.D. at Cambridge University in 1987. After a period of postdoctoral research and teaching at Cambridge, he moved to the Department of Archaeology at Reading, where he is now a Reader in Early Prehistory. His major fieldwork project has been concerned with reconstructing mesolithic settlement in the Hebridean islands of Scotland. Currently he is undertaking fieldwork in southern Jordan. He is the author of *Thoughtful Foragers: a Study in Prehistoric Decision Making* (1990) and *The Prehistory of the Mind* (1996), together with numerous papers concerning upper palaeolithic art, mesolithic society and the use of computer simulation in archaeology. (Institutional address: Department of Archaeology, University of Reading, Whiteknights, Reading RG6 6AA, UK.)

JOHN MORELAND received his Ph.D. from the University of Sheffield in 1990. He has taught at the University of Kent and Wesleyan University, USA, and since 1988 has been Lecturer in Medieval Archaeology at the University of Sheffield. He is involved in field projects in central Italy, southern Albania, and Derbyshire, England, as part of his research into the transition from the Roman Empire into the early Middle Ages. He is currently writing a book on *Reconstructing Ancient Economies* with Paul Halstead, Glynis Jones and Marek Zvelebil, and another on *Visions of a Monument: The Bradbourne Cross in History*. (Institutional address: Department of Archaeology and Prehistory, University of Sheffield, Northgate House, West Street, Sheffield S1 4ET, UK.)

PAUL R. MULLINS received a Masters in Applied Anthropology from the University of Maryland at College Park in 1990, and was awarded a Ph.D. in anthropology from the University of Massachusetts at Amherst in 1996. He teaches historical archaeology, archaeological theory, modern material culture, and popular culture as a Visiting Assistant Professor in the Anthropology Program of George Mason

University in Fairfax, Virginia. His research focuses on the relationship between racism and American consumer culture between the US Civil War and the 1930s; his fieldwork in Annapolis, Maryland, and Washington DC examines how African-Americans envisioned material consumption as a socio-political statement which critiqued anti-Black racism, yet secured the symbolic privileges of consumer citizenship. He is editor, with Paul A. Shackel and Mary S. Warner, of *Annapolis Pasts: Historical Archaeology in Annapolis, Maryland* (University of Tennessee 1998) and is the author of *Race and Affluence: an Archaeology of African America and Consumer Culture* (Plenum Press, forthcoming). (Institutional address: Anthropology Program, MSN-3G5, George Mason University, Fairfax, Virginia 22030 USA.)

ALASTAIR NORTHEDGE has been Maître de Conférences in Islamic Art and Archaeology at the Sorbonne in Paris since 1991. He trained in Islamic history at the University of Oxford, in Arabic at the University of Cambridge, and completed a Ph.D. in Islamic art and archaeology at the School of Oriental and African Studies in London. His main research interests lie in the archaeology of the eastern Islamic world, particularly in the early period. He has excavated at the Citadel of Amman in Jordan, at 'Ana and Samarra' in Iraq, at Tilbesar in Turkey, and in Kazakhstan and Turkmenistan in central Asia. His publications include *Excavations at 'Ana* (1988), *Studies on Roman and Islamic Amman I: History, Site and Architecture* (1993), and a series of articles on Samarra'. (Institutional address: UFR d'Art et d'Archéologie, Université de Paris-Sorbonne (Paris IV), 3 Rue Michelet, 75006 Paris, France.)

MARILYN PALMER is an Oxford-trained historian who developed an interest in industrial archaeology in the 1960s and has taught it at various levels ever since. She is currently Reader in Industrial Archaeology at the University of Leicester. Her fieldwork has been largely on metalliferous mining sites, but she also has a major interest in the archaeology of the textile industry. With her fellow editor of *Industrial Archaeology Review*, Peter Neaverson, she has written *Industrial Landscapes of the East Midlands* (Chichester: Phillimore 1992); *Industry in the Landscape 1700–1900* (London: Routledge 1994) and *Industrial Archaeology: Principles and Practice* (London: Routledge 1998). She represents the interests of industrial archaeology on several national bodies and is a Commissioner with the Royal Commission on the Historical Monuments of England. She is concerned to develop a more theoretical approach to industrial archaeology and to see it fully integrated into archaeological training. (Institutional address: School of Archaeological Studies, University of Leicester, Leicester LE1 7RH, UK.)

MIKE PARKER PEARSON is a Reader in the Department of Archaeology and Prehistory at the University of Sheffield. He studied archaeology at the universities of

Southampton and Cambridge. Between 1984 and 1990 he was an Inspector of Ancient Monuments for English Heritage, involved in the drafting of the government's planning policy guidance *Archaeology and Planning* and English Heritage's research strategy document *Exploring Our Past*. His major teaching and research interests include funerary archaeology, ethnoarchaeology, archaeological theory, and archaeological heritage issues. Since 1991 he has carried out fieldwork on funerary monumentality in southern Madagascar and on bronze age to medieval settlement on South Uist in the Scottish Western Isles. He is the author of *Bronze Age Britain* and co-author of *Between Land and Sea: Excavations at Dun Vulan*, and is editor, with T. Darvill, R. Thomas and R. Smith, of *New Approaches to our Past* (1978), with C. Richards, of *Architecture and Order* (1994) and, with T. Schadla-Hall, of *Looking at the Land* (1994). His next book will be *The Archaeology of Death and Burial*. (Institutional address: Department of Archaeology and Prehistory, University of Sheffield, Northgate House, West Street, Sheffield S1 4ET, UK.)

CHARLES L. REDMAN received his BA at Harvard University and his MA and Ph.D. at the University of Chicago, and having served as Chair and Professor of Anthropology at Arizona State University is currently Director of the Center for Environmental Studies there. He has directed numerous archaeological field expeditions in the Near East, North Africa, and the American Southwest. His research interests include the origins of complex society, human impacts on the environment, and archaeological research design. His authored and co-authored books include *The Rise of Civilization* (W. H. Freeman and Co.), *Explanation in Archaeology* (Columbia University Press), *Archaeological Explanation* (Columbia University Press), *Qsar es-Seghir: an Archaeological View of Medieval Life* (Academic Press) and *People of the Tonto Rim* (Smithsonian Press). He is currently completing the manuscript for a new book, *Human Impact on Ancient Environments*. (Institutional address: Center for Environmental Studies, Arizona State University, Box 872402, Tempe AZ 85287–2402, USA.)

ALAIN SCHNAPP trained in classical archaeology, taking his *doctorate de 3° cycle* at the University of Paris I (Panthéon-Sorbonne) in 1973. He then worked as a CNRS (Centre National des Recherches Scientifiques) researcher at the Centre Gernet et Institut d'Architecture Antique and at the University of Paris I, submitting a thesis on the anthropology of hunting in the classical Greek city in 1987, and is now Professor of Classical Archaeology at the same university. He has also been a visiting scholar at the universities of Princeton (USA), Cambridge (UK) and Naples (Italy), and at the Getty Foundation in Santa Monica, California. His research has focused on the anthropology and iconography of classical Greece, on the history of archaeology, and on the historical topography of Greek cities. His publications include *L'Archéologie Aujourd'hui* (Paris: Hachette 1980), *La Cité des Images* (Paris:

Nathan 1984), *La Conquête du Passé, aux Origines de l'Archéologie* (Paris: Carré 1993; Italian translation Milan: Mondadori 1984; English translation London and New York: British Museum Press 1996), *Le Chasseur et la Cité: Chasse et Érotique en Grèce Ancienne* (Paris: Albin Michel 1997), and *Préhistoire et Antiquité: Tome 1 de l'Histoire de l'Art Flammarion* (Paris: Flammarion 1997). (Institutional address: UFR d'Art et d'Archéologie, Université de Paris I [Panthéon-Sorbonne], 3 Rue Michelet, 75006 Paris, France.)

STEPHEN J. SHENNAN took his first degree in Archaeology and Anthropology at Cambridge and then completed his Ph.D. there on Bell Beakers in central Europe, supervised by David Clarke, who had a major influence on him as on many others. After moving to Southampton in 1975 to research on British prehistoric amber finds he was appointed Hampshire Archaeological Field Officer, when he carried out one of the first intensive fieldwalking projects in Britain. From 1978 to 1996 he was a member of the teaching staff of the Department of Archaeology at Southampton, becoming Professor in 1995; during this period his work was largely focused on the socio-economic prehistory of Europe and quantitative and computer methods; from 1985–89 he excavated a bronze age mining settlement in the Austrian Alps. Since 1996 he has been at the Institute of Archaeology, University College London, where he holds a Personal Chair in Theoretical Archaeology. His current interests are in the human impact of climatic change and Darwinian approaches to cultural evolution. His publications include *Quantifying Archaeology* (2nd edn, 1997), *Bronze Age Copper Producers of the Eastern Alps* (1995), *Prehistoric Europe* (co-author, 1984), *Archaeological Approaches to Cultural Identity* (editor, 1989) and *The Archaeology of Human Ancestry* (co-editor, 1996). (Institutional address: Institute of Archaeology, University College London, 31–34 Gordon Square, London WC1H 0PY, UK.)

ELIZABETH SLATER took her first degree in Natural Sciences, specializing in metallurgy and materials science, at a time when archaeologists were becoming increasingly concerned with the scientific examination of artefacts. Work on archaeological material prompted an interest in the history of metallurgy and the origins of processes and she remained in Cambridge to complete a Ph.D. on aspects of bronze age metallurgy, looking particularly at the interpretation of analytical data. In 1974 she became lecturer in Archaeological Sciences at Glasgow University and was appointed to the Chair of Archaeology at Liverpool in 1991. The use of scientific techniques in the study of artefacts has remained a prime focus of her research and she has completed extensive analytical programmes as part of major excavation projects on copper-based metals, ceramics, lithics and vitreous materials from sites in Britain, Italy, Germany, Cyprus, Egypt and Greece. Investigation of pyrotechnological processes, central to the interpretation of analytical and site data, has also been a major research interest and she has carried out detailed experimental projects from raw material through to final product. A wide-ranging book on artefact studies is in the process of publication, and a study of eastern Mediterranean and Egyptian ceramics, faience and metals, building on the Liverpool Museum collections, is in progress. (Institutional address: School of Archaeology, Classics and Oriental Studies, University of Liverpool, Liverpool L69 3BX, UK.)

NIGEL SPIVEY graduated in Classics at the University of Cambridge in 1980, subsequently studied at the British School at Rome and the University of Pisa, and then taught at St. David's University College Lampeter in Wales before taking up his present position as Lecturer in Classical Archaeology at Cambridge and Fellow of Emmanuel College. His previous publications include *The Micali Painter and his Followers* (Oxford: Oxford University Press 1987), *Etruscan Italy* (with Simon Stoddart, London: Batsford 1990), *Looking at Greek Vases* (edited with T. Rasmussen, Cambridge: Cambridge University Press 1991) and *Etruscan Art* (London: Thame and Hudson 1997). He is currently researching on the interpretation of Greek sculpture and excavating at the Etruscan city of Cerverteri. (Institutional address: Museum of Classical Archaeology, University of Cambridge, Sidgwick Avenue, Cambridge CB3 9DA, UK.)

SIMON STODDART graduated in 1980 from the University of Cambridge in Archaeology and Anthropology. He then studied in Rome and at the University of Michigan, before returning to Cambridge to write his doctoral dissertation on settlement organization and state formation in pre-Roman central Italy which he completed in 1987. After posts at the universities of York (lecturer) and Bristol (lecturer and senior lecturer), he is currently a University lecturer in the Department of Archaeology, Cambridge, and a Fellow at Magdalene College, Cambridge. He has undertaken fieldwork on state formation in the valley of Gubbio (Umbria, Italy) and at Nepi (Lazio, Italy), and on early complex society in Gozo (Malta). He is currently involved in a team engaged in the revision of the British School at Rome's South Etruria Survey north-west of Rome, originally undertaken in the 1950s to 1970s in a key area of Etruscan and Faliscan (pre-Roman) state formation. His major publications include *Etruscan Italy* (with Nigel Spivey, London: Batsford 1990) and *Territory, Time and State: the Archaeological Development of the Gubbio Basin* (co-edited with Caroline Malone, Cambridge: Cambridge University Press 1994). (Institutional address: Department of Archaeology, University of Cambridge, Downing Street, Cambridge CB2 3DZ, UK.)

JOSEPH A. TAINTER received his Ph.D. in anthropology from Northwestern University in 1975. He taught anthropology at the University of New Mexico, and is now Project Leader of Cultural Heritage Research, Rocky Mountain Research

Station, Albuquerque, New Mexico. Fieldwork and documentary research in North America, Polynesia, Europe, West Africa and the Near East have led to many journal articles, book chapters and monographs. His book *The Collapse of Complex Societies* (1988) develops a long-standing research interest in the evolution of socio-economic complexity. This work has been recognized in several fields, and has led to invitations to lecture to organizations as diverse as the Getty Center for the History of Art and the Humanities and the International Society for Ecological Economics. He is co-editor, with Bonnie Bagley Tainter, of the 1996 book *Evolving Complexity and Environmental Risk in the Prehistoric Southwest*. (Institutional address: Research Station, 2205 Columbia SE, Albuquerque, New Mexico 87106, USA.)

JULIAN THOMAS was educated at the universities of Bradford (B.Tech. 1981) and Sheffield (MA 1982, Ph.D. 1986). He was Lecturer in Archaeology at the University of Wales, Lampeter between 1987 and 1993, and he is now Senior Lecturer in Archaeology at the University of Southampton. His publications include *Rethinking the Neolithic* (Cambridge 1991) and *Time, Culture and Identity* (Routledge 1996). His archaeological fieldwork has included directing excavations on the neolithic to iron age ceremonial enclosure at the Pict's Knowe, Dumfries, in Scotland. He is Secretary of the World Archaeological Congress, and sits on the Council of the Royal Anthropological Institute. (Institutional address: Department of Archaeology, University of Southampton, Highfield, Southampton S17 1BJ, UK.)

PREFACE AND
ACKNOWLEDGEMENTS

The *Companion Encyclopedia of Archaeology* started life, like its predecessor the *Companion Encyclopedia of Anthropology* edited by Tim Ingold, on the initiative of Jonathan Price, at that time Senior Editor for Academic Reference Books at Routledge. As then befell Tim Ingold, succumbing to Jonathan's languid charm and infectious enthusiasm has resulted in almost ten years of somewhat rueful reflection on agreeing, in the words of Jonathan's original letter, 'to mastermind such an enterprise'! It was originally planned as a joint enterprise between Annie Grant and myself, but changes in her work circumstances sadly meant that Annie had to withdraw from the co-editorship after working with me on the structure of the volume, the selection and commissioning of authors, and the drawing up of guidelines and schedules.

As I describe in the General Introduction, whereas the *Companion Encyclopedia of Anthropology* has an explicit focus on what anthropology can tell us about human societies, rather than on how it is done, the *Companion Encyclopedia of Archaeology* attempts both. It is divided, in the best archaeological tradition, into three parts, the first covering the aims of the subject, its theoretical basis and remarkably diverse methodologies, the second a series of major cross-cultural themes to illustrate the essential interdisciplinarity of archaeological theory and practice, and the third the principal themes of our 'archaeological history' from human evolution to industrialization. It has often seemed a foolhardy enterprise to try to cover all of this in a single book, and there have had to be hard editorial choices about how to structure the chapters, what to include, what topics to subsume within a wider chapter, and what to omit. I have no doubt that there are many unintentional sins of omission as well, but I hope that readers will find on reading the chapters that most topics and issues of major significance in current archaeological theory and practice are included somewhere, somehow. In this respect I would like to emphasize that the main purpose of the book is that it should be *read*, not *consulted*. Contributors were asked to write authoritative but readable chapters, rather than the 'this is a summary of everything that everybody everywhere says' review or the 'this is what I think about my particular patch, anyway' essay. Editing the results has been a mountain to climb, both in terms of paper and intellectual stamina, but whenever I stopped for breath I was enormously pleased at how contributor after contributor had (to mix my metaphors) come up trumps. I hope that every reader, whether professional, student, or interested layperson, will find the same pleasure and profit that I have had in reading the contributions, from first to last.

I would like to acknowledge first and foremost the contributors to the *Companion Encyclopedia of Archaeology* for their enthusiasm, commitment and above all patience. I am ashamed to divulge the original schedule we drew up for author commissioning, production and circulation of synopses, writing of first drafts, initial editing, author revisions, and final editing, but suffice it so say that authors and editor sometimes wondered if the other side was still in business, and in the same world! Reading Tim Ingold's Preface to the *Companion Encyclopedia of Anthropology*, though, in which he says that the project was rescued by his good fortune in securing one whole year and two subsequent terms of research leave from his university, I don't feel nearly so bad about my own desultory progress: editing the *Companion Encyclopedia of Archaeology* has had to be fitted into chairing my department throughout the time-scale of the project, with my two terms of research leave in that period being devoted to writing up field projects in Italy and Libya. All the contributors, like the editor, were typically over-committed with other deadlines, and the original smooth and synchronized progress of the charabanc we had built all too frequently broke down. Despite all the hiccups in its progress, though, the passenger list is almost entirely as originally planned: only one author succeeded in dropping off entirely (though a few others tried to!), an intended joint chapter became two, a couple of joint authors were added, and an additional chapter was kindly added late in the day by Alastair Northedge (Chapter 27) at Neil Christie's request to widen the coverage of his own chapter on the medieval world (Chapter 26). The most striking testimony to the length of the road we have travelled together are the institutional addresses of the contributors – several of the authors have moved once since the project started, and a few have moved twice or even three times! I am profoundly grateful to all the contributors for not jumping off even when the charabanc occasionally seemed to be coming to a shuddering halt.

I would also like to thank the succession of staff at Routledge who have had to take on the *Companion Encyclopedia of Archaeology* after Jonathan Price's departure, especially Seth Denbo, Samantha Parkinson, Ben Swift (who shouldered the enormous burden of chasing permissions for the illustrations), Mina Gera-Price, and Sarah Hall, as well as Alan Fidler for taking on the other huge task of copy-editing the texts and doing it with such enthusiasm and care. If it has sometimes seemed to this editor that there could be nobody left at New Fetter Lane on the list of penitents to be punished with the management of the *Companion Encyclopedia of Archaeology*, I am all too aware of where the fault lies.

At Leicester, I would particularly like to acknowledge the help of Pam Thornett, Chief Clerk in the School of Archaeological Studies, both for moral support and for indefatigable photocopying of draft and edited chapters, done out of a spirit of loyalty despite all the far more important tasks she needed to be doing for the School's administration. I would also like to thank our draughtsperson Debbie Miles-Williams, for redrawing forty of the illustrations with her typical skill and commitment even on the eve of maternity leave when she could scarcely reach the computer.

It was a very great sadness to both Annie and myself that she felt obliged to withdraw from the co-editorship of the *Companion Encyclopedia of Archaeology* because of the demands of other publication commitments on the restricted research time available to her in her present senior position in Leicester's adminis-tration. I am especially grateful to her for undertaking the onerous task of translat-ing from French to English Alain Schnapp's original, complex – and lengthy – text of his contribution to Chapter 1, but most of all I would like to thank her for living with the *Companion Encyclopedia of Archaeology* these past years and supporting me through it. I wish she had let me put her name on the front alongside mine, given her direct contribution to the *Companion Encyclopedia*'s inception, development and character, and her continual support through the over-lengthy time it has taken me to bring it to fruition.

Graeme Barker
May 1998

GENERAL INTRODUCTION

Graeme Barker

THE NATURE AND SCOPE OF ARCHAEOLOGY

Archaeology is commonly defined as the study of past societies through their material remains, and history as the study of past societies through their written records. The difficulties of recovering, analysing and interpreting archaeological evidence are profound, but the principal strength of archaeology as a historical discipline concerned with trying to understand our past is that all human societies, from our earliest ancestors to most recent generations, have created archaeology. Hunter or farmer, emperor or slave, lord or serf – everybody uses material culture, and some of it has survived for us to discover and study. Even today huge numbers of the world's population are illiterate, and write no history about themselves – in a real sense, they are denied their history. Literacy in the past was even more restricted, so most historians have to try to understand the societies they study through the perceptions and biases of the small élite that wrote about them. Furthermore, for more than 99 per cent of human history there are no historical records. Thus the practice of archaeology is not restricted to any particular period of the past, or region of the world: whether we study early humans, or ancient Egyptians, or Incas, or a nineteenth-century shipwreck, or Second World War fortifications, we are all archaeologists, using archaeological methods to try to understand past societies through their material remains.

With the totality of the human past to study, though, there are of course many different kinds of archaeologies and archaeologists. Many archaeologists study a particular period of the past, and often by definition a particular region of the world (Egyptologists, for example). Prehistoric archaeologists are concerned with the immense periods of the human past that lie between the first appearance of creatures with recognizably human characteristics three or four million years ago and the development of writing. Writing was developed or adopted by ancient societies at different times, so the interface between prehistoric and historic archaeology varies widely in different parts of the world – the first systems of writing were developed in Mesopotamia *c.* 3500 BC and Egypt *c.* 3000 BC, but in Britain written records only begin with the Roman conquest, and many societies elsewhere in the world were effectively prehistoric until European contact in recent centuries. Most prehistorians specialize in particular segments of the enormous time-scale at their disposal, such as the stone age hunters of the Ice Ages, or stone age farmers 5–10,000 years ago, or later more complex agricultural societies that were metal-using and socially differentiated.

Even when writing appeared, many societies remained 'protohistoric' and scholars studying them need to rely heavily on the methods of prehistoric archaeology. For many early 'historic' societies, writing was in fact used for very restricted purposes and by a tiny segment of society, so most of the society was effectively prehistoric. The latter point applies also to many peoples adjacent to literate societies, such as the tribes bordering the Roman empire, whose 'history' – like that of the Etruscans who were the dominant power in central Italy before Rome – is seen through a Roman glass, darkly. The same is true of the American and African peoples along the expanding frontiers of European colonialism. There are other distinct archaeological communities concerned with the ancient civilizations of Mesopotamia, Egypt, China, India, the Levant, Greece and Rome, with the pre-Columbian states and empires of South and Central America, with the emergent states of medieval Europe, the spread of Islam, European colonialism in Africa, America and Australasia, the archaeology of the Industrial Revolution, and so on.

In addition to such chronological and regional groupings within the discipline, there are other distinct archaeological communities defined by the kind of material they study and the methods they use. In the case of artefact studies, for example, some archaeologists use techniques comparable to those of the art historian to elucidate information on style, chronology, and social context, whereas a very different group of science-based archaeologists uses techniques of physical and chemical analysis to study techniques of manufacture and (from the identification of the source of the material) systems of trade. Buildings and monuments can be studied by parallel groupings of humanistic and scientific archaeologists. For many periods of the more recent past, historical archaeologists have developed distinct methodologies for the analysis and interpretation of coins, inscriptions, maps and place-names as well as archival records. Much of the archaeological record consists of biological materials such as human skeletal remains, fragments of animal bone, seeds and other plant remains, as well as the sediments in which they are found, all of which have generated distinct specialisms within what is generally termed environmental archaeology; to this group can now be added molecular biologists investigating human, animal and plant remains from their ancient DNA. Other important schools of archaeological enquiry defined by method and material rather than by period or region include landscape archaeology and underwater archaeology; air photography is another distinct specialism. The role of archaeological scientists specializing in dating the past is fundamental. Yet another group are 'ethnoarchaeologists', archaeologists-cum-anthropologists who study present-day communities to try to understand better the relationship between material culture and human behaviour so as to improve our theories and methodologies for studying past societies.

One of the principal fascinations of archaeology as a methodology, therefore, is that it spans the humanities and sciences: archaeology needs an extraordinarily broad church of expertise to try to understand the total history of humankind from its material remains. I am writing this Introduction in the middle of a field project I am directing in the Wadi Faynan in southern Jordan. The project team is an example of modern interdisciplinary archaeology. There are five environmental archaeologists reconstructing how climate, landforms, flora and fauna have changed in the study area over the past 250,000 years. An ethnoarchaeologist is studying the Bedouin people living in the area today. A team of archaeological surveyors is reconstructing the development of settlement systems from prehistoric times to the present day, by mapping collections of surface artefacts and stone structures. Other field archaeologists are investigating the different kinds of irrigation systems (stone walls for diverting and trapping rainwater) that have been developed by farmers here over the past 5,000 years, in part using an initial study by an archaeological air photographer. An hydraulic specialist is studying modern rainfall and flooding behaviour to help two archaeologists who are using computer simulations to model how the different irrigation systems would have worked. There are four finds specialists classifying and dating the artefacts being collected by the field team, and others will be involved in laboratory studies of some of these artefacts later. The effects that ancient farmers and shepherds have had on the landscape in terms of deforestation are being examined by two palaeoecologists studying fossil pollen, charcoal and snails, and geochemistry is being used on human skeletons, animal bones and plant remains to monitor the extent to which ancient miners polluted their own and even the present-day environment. A variety of archaeological laboratories is dating samples of charcoal and sediment for us. A classical historian is examining inscriptions in the field, and integrating these with other documentary sources known for the area, and similar specialists will be involved in due course to look at the pre-Roman and Islamic evidence. Major structures will be studied by architectural specialists in terms of style, chronology, and construction techniques, and another specialist will need to be brought in to study the numerous rock carvings being found by the survey teams. As the Wadi Faynan team demonstrates, the answer to the perennial question about whether archaeology as a methodology is art or science is simply 'yes'.

APPROACHES TO UNDERSTANDING THE PAST

Methodology, though, is the means to the end, not the end itself, which is trying to understand our past. The latter, though, means different things to different archaeologists, and some of this diversity is reflected in the presentation of archaeology to the general public. One cluster of television programmes about archaeology, for example, is firmly within the tradition of 'archaeology is about finding wonderful things', the search for artistic treasures that fired the first antiquarians and archaeologists, whose discoveries form the centre-pieces of the world's great museum collections that enrich our lives today. Then there are the 'archaeology is about speculating about our mysterious ancestors' programmes, their directors automatically combining low-level camera shots of some fossil skull or standing stone or pyramid – preferably against a sunrise or sunset – with more-or-less the same soulful mood music. 'Archaeology as forensic science' is yet another strand of television archaeology with its own distinct style of test-tube and white-coat shots and computer visuals. Combining all three elements in some ways, but adding the critical component of 'archaeology is the most fun you can have with your trousers on' (to borrow the immortal if now politically incorrect phrase of the American archaeologist Kent Flannery) is a current series on British television with top viewing ratings called *Time Team*. In this, we watch a group of archaeologists sort out a specific archaeological field problem, like the layout and function of a buried building, by some frantic fieldwork over a weekend. The – highly experienced and skilful – archaeologists involved have achieved almost cult status in Britain, and their beards (sandals I am not sure about), horrible sartorial standards, wild hair and wilder enthusiasms for whatever pit, wall or bone is the subject of study have created the image of The Real Archaeologist for our aspiring first-year undergraduates against which most of their teachers fail dismally!

Curiosity about the past is of course what drives most archaeologists. Virtually none of us will ever find 'wonderful things' like Howard Carter's discovery of Tutankhamun's tomb, but I think that most archaeologists, for all their familiarity with the everyday act of discovery in fieldwork, will readily agree to suddenly finding themselves moved emotionally by the simple act of uncovering things made by people long ago, things which nobody else has seen or recognized for centuries or millennia. This engagement with 'touching our past' is surely also at the heart of popular interest in the subject, from viewing television programmes, reading popular archaeology books and attending exhibitions, to joining local archaeological societies and local archaeology classes.

The principal intellectual goal of archaeology, however, should surely be to write archaeological history, in the sense of the total history of humankind through its material remains. Just after the Second World War the French historian Fernand Braudel published a study of the Mediterranean world in the sixteenth century in which he argued that history had to be understood as the complex interplay between short-, medium-, and long-term processes. Short-term processes, *evéné-ments*, were the normal stuff of conventional political and military history (of the kind brilliantly caricatured for English readers in *1066 and All That*). Then there were what he termed *conjonctures*, medium-term processes that operated within a generation or an individual's lifetime, such as social, economic or demographic trends – in our own time, changes in the role of the family, in work patterns and gender roles in the industrial world over the past fifty years would be good examples. Lastly there were very long-term processes, the *longue durée*, such as the effect a particular landscape, and the technology to exploit it, could have on shaping the lives of its inhabitants over many centuries. In his Mediterranean study, for example, Braudel likened the changing relationship between lowlands and uplands, farmers and shepherds, to a 'slow-furling wave', ebbing back and forth. Another kind of long-term historical process hc cited was ideology and religion, *mentalité*. With this approach Braudel and his pupils founded a school of history in France known as the Annales school, and many archaeologists argue that ultimately we, too, should be attempting to use our material to write archaeological histories from the same standpoint as the Annales historians, but over the huge time-scales we are privileged to study.

In most archaeological situations it is difficult to recognize *evénéments* – the destruction of Pompeii by the eruption of Vesuvius in AD 79 is the exception that proves the rule. Searching archaeological data for evidence of such precise events has tended to produce pseudo-history: the burnt layer in an Italian farmstead dated by the pottery contained in it to somewhere in the last three centuries BC by circular reasoning becomes evidence that Hannibal's army destroyed it because we know from the written sources that he passed through the area in 216 BC – yet it could as easily be evidence for somebody leaving the bread in the oven too long one after-noon at any time over those three centuries. On the other hand, specific short-term actions by individuals or groups of individuals can often be detected by archaeologists, such as the painting of a motif on a rock face, the preparation of a stone tool, the decoration of a pot, or the alteration to a building, even though we may not know their names. Medium-term processes such as social, economic and demographic changes are certainly amenable to study by archaeologists, and in many ways are the prime focus of most archaeological enquiry, though our time-scales may be centuries or even millennia rather than Braudel's generational changes the further back in time we go. *Longue durée* history such as the evolution of subsistence systems, technologies, or ideological structures is also pre-eminently suited to archaeological study. Braudel was criticized by fellow historians for failing to demonstrate effectively exactly how different historical processes operating at different time-scales in fact interacted, and archaeologists face exactly the same problem in the evaluation of the competing roles of structure and agency, or process and individual actions, but we do the best service to our materials and time-scales by trying to meet that challenge and writing holistic archaeological history.

That may be the ultimate goal in terms of synthesis, but whatever the scale of process we are studying, our greatest challenge is undoubtedly the interpretation of archaeological data in human terms. What exactly is the link between the material culture we dig up and the people who discarded or lost it – not just how did they make and use it, but what wider significance or meaning did it have for them? A stone axe may look to our eyes like a useful tool or an effective weapon, but did it have the same function or meaning for the people who used it 100,000 years ago? In attempting to explain their material, archaeologists can have recourse to three principal sources of information. For the historical periods there are the documentary sources, though as mentioned before these may well give a highly selective perspective on the society in question. Experimental work may also yield useful insights in some cases: some archaeologists have replicated prehistoric stone tools, for example, then used individual tools on different materials such as wood, bone, meat, leather, and vegetable foods, and then compared the various microscopic abrasions and scratches produced on the replica tools with those on prehistoric tools to infer how the latter were used. The third, and most important, source of information is provided by anthropology, the study of present-day societies: studying modern San hunter-gatherers in the Kalahari desert, for example, should show not only how stone tools or rock carvings similar to the ancient ones found by archaeologists were made, but also their role in San social interactions; studying Masai cattle herders should show not just how cattle herding systems like theirs may produce the kinds of faunal samples we find on many British late prehistoric sites, for example, but also the central role of cattle on the hoof for Masai societies in terms of wealth accumulation, gift exchange, bridewealth, client relations and the like.

The obvious problem for archaeologists, though, is that whereas geographers can interpret ancient fluvial sediments in terms of what a river does today, Kalahari San are not Ice Age hunters, and Masai are not ancient Britons, and we have no modern Neanderthals or Etruscans to use as models for past Neanderthals and Etruscans. Archaeologists thus recognize both the central role of anthropology for the development of theories about the significance of their data – in the United States, archaeology is commonly taught as 'ancient anthropology' within an anthropology department – and also the problems of using the present as a straightforward guide to the past. It is in this context that ethnoarchaeologists are playing an increasingly vital role in their studies of present-day societies to establish the linkages between different kinds of activity today and the different kinds of residues that these activities will create. The most useful work has generally been on societies in more-or-less similar environments to the ancient societies under study: studies of Inuit hunting systems in Alaska, for example, have stimulated critical insights into how prehistoric hunters may have operated in glacial environments in Europe, and ethnoarchaeological studies of Mediterranean shepherds and Near Eastern Bedouin are providing similar help in studying the archaeology of pastoralist societies in these regions. We always have to remember, though, that simply to impose the present onto the past is to diminish the importance of the latter in terms of understanding the development of our own humanity.

In our theoretical approaches to explaining our data, therefore, just as in our methodologies, archaeologists generally admit that they have to combine human-istic and scientific approaches. In the classic procedure of scientific enquiry, the scientist makes observations about the natural world, formulates an hypothesis to explain them, and then devises a laboratory experiment to test independently whether or not the predictions of the hypothesis are verified. It may sometimes work like this in archaeology, as in the example of the stone tool experiments mentioned earlier, but in most cases our 'independent verification' has to be our understanding of the role of material culture in present-day societies, and in using anthropology to explain archaeology we always have to be aware of the oft-quoted phrase of L. P. Hartley that 'the past is a foreign country: they do things differently there' and not try to replicate it comfortably but simplistically in our own image.

The interaction between the discovery of our archaeological history and archaeologists' theorizing about its meaning is a central theme in the history of the subject, as the opening two chapters in this *Companion Encyclopedia* describe. Until recent decades most of this theorizing characterized prehistoric archaeology, historical archaeology developing very much in the shadow of history. (Happily neither of these 'subservient' relationships, either between prehistoric and historic archaeology, or between historic archaeology and history, exists any more.) In the nineteenth century the dominant theory was that the human past could best be viewed as an evolutionary sequence from primitive savagery eventually to civilization – a ladder of progress culminating implicitly if not explicitly in the Victorian age. In the first half of the twentieth century, the goal of much prehistoric research was to recognize what Gordon Childe defined as 'archaeological cultures', similar sets of material culture (settlement types, artefacts and so on) at a particular time and in a particular region that, it was assumed, probably related to some kind of present-day social unit such as a tribe. In Europe, the result was a 'chest-of-drawers' of archaeological cultures (Fig. 12.1), most of it only dated relatively, and with the overall structure tenuously bracketed by cross-dating to historically dated cultures in the eastern Mediterranean and Near East (Chapter 5). The inevitable effect of such linkages was that the main stimulus of culture change appeared to be contact with the Near East – neolithic farmers from there must have introduced agriculture to

Europe, bronze age smiths from there must have introduced metallurgy, and so on. It is easy now to criticize the kind of archaeology that produced successive maps of prehistoric Europe akin to those of the eastern front in the Second World War, but we have to remember that most prehistorians in the first half of the twentieth century had to put their main effort into trying to work out when things were (very many Ph.D. dissertations were on 'the chronology of the X culture'), not how and why things changed – as Mortimer Wheeler once remarked, the focus had to be on the timetables rather than the trains.

From the 1950s onwards, the development of radio-carbon dating and many other branches of archaeological science had a devastating impact on this kind of cultural archaeology. Together, they provided examples of different people living in different ways at the same time – hunters alongside farmers, for example, or metal-using peoples alongside stone-using peoples – and of episodes of rapid change contrasting with periods of great stability, raising serious questions about successive phases of invasion or cultural diffusion as explanations of cultural change. Through the 1960s and 1970s there were profound changes in archaeological theorizing generally referred to as the New Archaeology or processual archaeology, as archaeologists focused increasingly on trying to document processes of cultural change and to propose explanations for them. Many archaeologists felt that their discipline needed to be far more scientific than hitherto, not just in methodologies but in the theoretical procedures of theory-testing and model-building, as described earlier. Processual archaeology was concerned especially with explaining change in social and economic systems, frequently with a materialist and functionalist perspective such as in terms of adaptations to particular environmental, technological, or demographic circumstances. Its theoretical focus was therefore especially on long-term or diachronic change. (This focus had a significant impact on field methodologies, providing the stimulus for many regional studies of settlement that employed survey techniques to map settlement systems and trends.) At its most extreme, processual archaeology hoped to extract general laws of human behaviour from the archaeological record, though those that emerged were so general and unhelpful ('Mickey Mouse laws') that the expectation was short-lived.

Through the 1980s, also, many archaeologists became disillusioned with the focus of processual archaeology, arguing that it was de-humanizing the past, ignoring the role of the individual and concentrating on function at the expense of meaning. The British prehistorian Christopher Hawkes had once proposed that prehistorians were attempting to scale a 'ladder of inference' – in terms of increasing difficulty, they could study technology, then subsistence, then social organization, and only with the greatest difficulty ideology. In some ways processual archaeology worked to the same agenda, but many post-processual archaeologists argued from ethnoarchaeological studies of present-day societies that ideology commonly structured just about everything else, and that archaeological research should focus primarily on the broader meaning of their material culture for past societies. Most post-processualists have focused on detailed studies of individual societies, on statics rather than dynamics, and have invariably favoured idealist over functionalist explanations of what they observe. Whereas the theoretical basis of processual archaeology borrowed heavily from the natural sciences, post-processual archaeology has borrowed heavily from sociology and post-modernist philosophy, emphasizing for example the importance of understanding the role of the individual archaeologist's perception of the material under study in moulding the interpretation proposed. Probably the most striking example of the relationship between archaeologist and archaeology has been the dominant role of male archaeologists in writing most archaeological histories, in which women have often been all but invisible unless minding the children and weaving.

Reading undergraduate examination papers on archaeological theory these days gives a strong impression that processual archaeology is thoroughly bad and post-processual archaeology thoroughly good. However, rather than characterizing – or caricaturing – these approaches as mutually incompatible ways of thinking about the past, it is more helpful to see them as different ways of questioning the past, both of which have validity. Processual studies of long-term processes of change have been inclined to underestimate the importance of ideological structures and the significance of people's interpretation of the meaning of their own material culture for the reproduction or maintenance of society. Post-processual studies are inclined to forget that social reproduction must also function in relationship to environment, technology, demography and so on. Understanding the history of our species is at heart understanding the changing relationship between nature and culture, and neither processualist archaeologists nor post-processualist archaeologists can do that on their own: archaeology as long-term Annales history needs both.

So yes, archaeology should certainly lift the human spirit with its discoveries of the cultural and artistic achievements of past peoples; it should feed our curiosities with their mysteries; and it is certainly enormous fun to do – the principal thing I remember from my first ever archaeological supervision at Cambridge was the comment from the tutor – one of the contributors to this volume who probably prefers not to be identified! – that the most important side of archaeology was the social side. But at the same time I believe passionately that archaeology should also have important things to say about our past to help us understand ourselves and our place in the world which we now inhabit so uneasily. My own research interests have been primarily in relations between people and landscape over time, an interest I have pursued through interdisciplinary field projects especially in Italy, Libya and, currently, Jordan, an 'archaeology of sustainability' if you like, but our archaeological history is replete with big questions that remain entirely unresolved. How did the human species first evolve, and why? How did the scavengers and hunters of the Ice Ages manage eventually to people the globe – what, for example, were the respective roles of our peculiarly human mix of aggression and cooperation in that process? How can we explain the first appearance of artistic endeavour in the extraordinary cave paintings that were produced by the late glacial hunters who occupied Europe 20–30,000 years ago (especially now we know that the same species had been living elsewhere in the globe for tens of thousands of years previously sometimes producing rather similar things)? What factors caused many societies around the world to change from hunting to farming 10–5,000 years ago? How did stratification, and ultimately our state system of organization and city-life, develop in human societies? How, when and why have gender roles changed? To what extent has the growth of empire been characterized by cultural resistance or acceptance, and the collapse of empire by internal disintegration or external pressure? What can we learn from material culture about changing concepts of 'social belonging', of people's sense of identity and ethnicity? And so on. We do an enormous disservice to the archaeological record if all that archaeologists have to say – and expensively, compared with the historical disciplines – is that once upon a time people made houses, ate meat, sometimes decorated pots, and had a variety of relationships with molluscs or megaliths.

As Chapter 10 discusses, professional archaeologists share their subject with many other groups of people, and there has to be a lively debate about the ownership of the past: it belongs to all of us, not particular political or intellectual groups. The popular fascination with the subject has already been mentioned. Amateur or community involvement is a source of great research vitality in many countries, and a source of great irritation for those national archaeological authorities that try to deny or exclude it. The appropriation of a country's archaeology, and its rewriting to fit modern political agendas, is frequently most apparent in newly developing states, such as white-ruled Rhodesia's attempts in the 1960s to explain Great Zimbabwe as anything other than an indigenous black African achievement. Nazi Germany's misuse of its prehistory in support of its claims of racial superiority is also commonly cited in this respect. Yet there are related if much more subtle issues to be faced in the presentation of archaeology by national and regional archaeological authorities everywhere. Closest to home, English Heritage has the complex task of presenting the archaeology of England to a modern multi-cultural society, many members of which (the majority of people in my own university city, for example) look as much to Britain's ex-colonies as to Britain for their cultural roots. The numerous industrial archaeology 'heritage sites' springing up everywhere in Britain – including coal mines in regions devastated by politically contested mine closures only a decade or so ago – present an uneasy mix of political perspectives on the social and economic effects of modern capitalism. The movement to 'engender' archaeological interpretations for the public is also particularly active in the developed world.

The extreme position of the New Archaeology was that it could seek to understand the past, and extract general laws of human behaviour about it, with the detachment of the scientific observer. The extreme position of post-modern archaeology is that the past is unknowable, an intellectual game (mostly with taxpayers' money, it has to be said!): the individual archaeologist is engaged in his or her individual discourse with it, and will extract whatever individual meaning suits them best. In his introduction to the *Companion Encyclopedia of Anthropology*, Tim Ingold pointed to exactly the same tensions between detachment and engagement in anthropological theory, and the necessity to accept the challenge of both. We must, he writes, 'drop the pretence of our belonging to a select association of Westerners, uniquely privileged to look in upon the inhabitants of "other cultures", and recognize that . . . we are all fellow travellers in the same world'. Archaeologists face even harder challenges in seeking to understand the countless 'other cultures' that have journeyed the earth since humans first evolved three or four million years ago, but together with anthropologists, to adapt Tim Ingold's words, 'by comparing experience . . . can reach a better understanding of what such journeying entails, where we have come from, and where we are going'.

THE *COMPANION ENCYCLOPEDIA OF ARCHAEOLOGY*

Like most things in archaeology, the *Companion Encyclopedia* is divided into three parts: in essence, methods, approaches, and results. In his Introduction to the *Companion Encyclopedia of Anthropology*, Tim Ingold emphasizes that it is *of* the subject, not *about* it, in the sense that the focus throughout is on what anthropology can tell us about human societies, rather than on how it is done, but the *Companion Encyclopedia of Archaeology* attempts both. In drawing up the structure of the book, Annie Grant and I were clear that archaeological methodologies are so remarkably diverse, and that this diversity would not be readily apparent to many readers new to the subject, that methodologies needed to be addressed first, as well as research achievements later. Chapter 1 describes how modern archaeology has developed from what the British antiquarian William Camden famously called a 'backward-looking curiosity', and Chapter 2 builds on this to discuss the development of archaeological theory and the critical relationship there has always been and will always be, between discovering the past and trying to explain it, between the questions we ask and the kind of evidence we look for. Chapter 3 addresses the peculiar nature of archaeological evidence, and Chapter 4 the field techniques developed to investigate it, and each of the following chapters in the rest of the first section has a focus on major clusters of methodologies and Chapter 10 considers the ethical and political as well as practical issues in presenting the past to the public.

Whilst one of the fascinations of archaeology is that it is an extraordinarily broad church with a place for just about every kind of specialism, there is an inevitable danger of over-specialization amongst its practitioners, yet we are most effective as an *inter*disciplinary rather than simply a *multi*disciplinary subject. Hence the middle section of the volume addresses a series of general issues of common interest in archaeology to illustrate how very different kinds of archaeologies and archaeologists have to work together in their study, from reconstructing social systems, to lifeways, to population histories, to what people thought. The third section then addresses the principal themes of our 'archaeological history' from human evolution through the 'age of hunting' (or not, as Chapter 20 discusses) and the beginnings of farming to the emergence of increasingly complex societies, states, and empires, ending with the archaeology of European colonialism and industrialization.

To attempt to encapsulate in a single book the full gamut of archaeological techniques and approaches, and the full sweep of the archaeological history of humankind, is clearly impossible, and I am all too aware of gaps and omissions. There are certainly some specialisms or issues that some readers might have preferred to see as a separate chapter – as a landscape archaeologist myself, I am still rather bemused about how and why that ended up being subsumed into several chapters, and I have no doubt that reviewers will point out their own favourites that have ended up as similar casualties. However, I think that most significant topics get discussed in one chapter or another, or from different perspectives in more than one, but hard decisions had to be taken about the chapter structure to try to keep everything between two covers (and in the event, I failed!). The most important aspect of the book, as I have stated, is that it is designed to be *read*, not *consulted*. I asked the contributors to cover their individual topics treading a middle road between the detailed and dull literature review and the off-the-cuff polemical essay, to produce chapters that were both authoritative and readable. I must say that the contributors responded to the task splendidly. It has been a Herculean task editing the chapters, sometimes making savage cuts in length, building in linkages between chapters in different parts of the book, and so on; but in the process I have enormously enjoyed reading every chapter, finding each authoritative but still with the personal stamp of the author or authors, and highly readable. I have also learned an enormous amount, though I wish I could remember it all!

The *Companion Encyclopedia of Archaeology* is designed to be read by students, teachers and academics working within archaeology or related disciplines such as anthropology, history and geography, who are looking for an authoritative but accessible overview of current thought and practice and developing trends to supplement their existing specialist knowledge. However, I also hope that the book will enthuse and excite the general reader wanting to understand the nature of archaeology and what archaeology has to say about the totality of the human past. For this reason each chapter is fully referenced in the 'Harvard style' for the specialist reader wanting to check or follow up specific sources, with references to author and publication date in the text and the full list of references in alphabetical order at the end, but the chapter also concludes with a select bibliography to guide the more general reader to the key literature on the subject if they want to explore it further.

Whatever your background and interests, I hope that you will have the same pleasure that I have had, sitting down to read any chapter in its entirety with pleasure as well as profit. Archaeology is fun, and it is a hugely companiable subject, a team subject *par excellence*, but it also has serious things to say about our past and thus about ourselves. We should study the past to learn from it, not treat it as an escapist refuge – I find nothing more depressing than the succession of brown tourist signs down our motorways proclaiming post-industrial Britain as one enormous heritage site, or great houses filled with period furniture they never actually contained and then preserved in aspic, or historic towns blighted by mediocre and faint-hearted supermarket architecture aping the 'local heritage' in ways that the architects of those same medieval buildings would have thought completely daft. The past is more important than that. Whatever gaps and omissions it may have, the *Companion Encyclopedia of Archaeology* unashamedly proclaims not just the fascination and excitement of archaeology, but also its importance in helping us understand where we have come from and who we are.

Part I

ORIGINS, AIMS AND METHODS

1

DISCOVERING THE PAST

Alain Schnapp and Kristian Kristiansen

THE ANCIENT FOUNDATIONS OF A SCIENCE OF THE PAST

One of the oldest references to archaeological practice appears on the base of a statue found at Memphis in Egypt, of Ka Wab, one of the sons of the pharaoh Keops (*c.* 2700 BC): *c.* 1300 BC Khaemois, the son of the pharaoh Rameses II, had added an inscription in which he explained that, during work in the estate of Memphis of which he was in charge, the statue of a prince, precisely identified, had been found and honoured with cult status (Gomaà 1973). Another example comes from Mesopotamia, where German archaeologists found in one of the sixth-century BC levels of the palace of Babylon a group of statues including some that dated to the third millennium BC, and where Nabonid, the last king of Babylon, has left an extraordinary account of the excavation of the great sanctuary, the Ebabbar, carried out in order to recover traces of the constructions of his predecessors (Schnapp 1996: 13–17). These included the famous Hammourabi, to whom he attributed, probably correctly, a foundation tablet found during the work. In China, we have evidence from as early as the fifth century BC for the interest of scribes and emperors in collecting and identifying bronze age cult tripods.

Though latecomers to the world of writing, the Greeks knew that their modest alphabetical letters had a quality that no hieroglyph, no cuneiform inscription, nor ideogram possessed: they had an apprenticeship so easy that everyone could become master. In contrast to the writing systems of the ancient empires, the Phoenician discovery of alphabetical writing, completed by the Greek invention of the use of vowels, revealed a powerful tool for the preservation of memory, giving voice to those who dared to say 'I' where scribes for the reckoning of kings wrote 'we'. The birth of history – investigative history – is inseparable from that of the historian who began to speak, name himself, and assert his autonomy against the anonymity of the scribes: with the alphabet, writing is no longer servant. Thus, together with the sciences and philosophy, historical enquiry – *historié* – was born in classical Greece. Herodotus did not entrust to stone or mud-brick the recounting of a conquest or a victory: he set out for his readers the result of a personal enquiry, a confrontation of evidence, and offered his reader a text which transformed the arts of memory into history.

In order to create this new literary genre, it was necessary to use sources other than those of imperial chancelleries, to refer to models other than those of the rhetoric of the sovereign. It was necessary, like Herodotus, to combine seeing and hearing, to enquire about the mores, origins and customs of very diverse peoples. The sophist Hippias explains in Plato's *Hippias Major* (285) the reasons for his success, the fact that he mastered a new discipline which dealt with 'the genealogies . . . with the science of the past (*archaiologia*)'. For sure, this *archaiologia* is very different from what we now call 'archaeology', but the idea of a science of the past showed that monuments have their place beside documents. Ever since then, the observation of ruins and the collection of ancient objects became an integrating part of a vision of the past which claimed history as a knowable totality. *Archaiologia* in Greek and *antiquitates* in Latin designated a category of objects and of facts that a particular type of scholar sought to collect and interpret, as a way to systematize the evidence of the past.

A well-known text of Xenophon shows that the ancient philosophers had an intuition about the existence of fossils. On the origins of Egypt, Herodotus wrote, in support of arguments that Egypt had originally been a submerged gulf, 'I have seen shells on the hills and noticed how salt exudes from the soil . . . the soil is black and friable as one would expect of an alluvial soil formed of a silt brought down by the river from Ethiopia' (Herodotus *The Histories* II.10, 1954 Penguin translation by A. de Sélincourt). *Archaiologia* as a systematic observation of the traces of the past led naturally to the description of the varied marks of history on the earth. In the first century AD, when Pausanias visited the ruins of Tiryns and Mycenae, he was intrigued by the extraordinary architecture of the two sites and attempted to interpret them by establishing a chronology compatible with the myths of archaic history: 'there are parts of the ring-wall left', he wrote, 'including the Gate-with-Lions standing on it. They say that this is the work of Kyklopes, who built the wall of Tiryns for Proitos. In the ruins of Mycenae is a water source called Perseia, and the underground chambers of Atreus and his sons where they kept the treasure-houses of their wealth. There is the grave of Atreus and the graves of those who came home from Troy, to be cut down by Aigisthos at his supper party' (Pausanias *Guide to Greece* II.XVI.6, 1971 Penguin translation by P. Levi). His efforts to explain and interpret these remains distinguish him from the Assyrian and Egyptian scribes: he did not try to force a continuity, but to explain the reasons for

4

a break between what we now term the Mycenaean Bronze Age and Archaic and classical Greece. The weapons of Homer's heroes were still visible amongst the treasures of the temple; verification of the tradition was possible by inspection of their manufacture and material. It does not matter much that Pausanias gives us no information about the way in which the temples were able to make a collection of such weapons: what is important is that he established a relationship between tradition and material facts.

The philosophers and antiquarians of the Graeco-Roman world were able to establish the antiquity of man and a chronology which, even if it was not absolute, suggested a considerable time difference between men of these unknown times and those of mythical times. They sensed that natural phenomcna, such as the evolution of plants and animals, could unite to lay the foundations of a human prehistory. By elaborating a theory of stages – hunting, pastoralism, agriculture – they introduced for the first time a rationality in the development of ways of life and technology. They did not hesitate, as the Roman poet Lucretius suggested in the first century BC (*De Rerum Natura* V, 1283–7), to affirm that the progress of mankind was a progress in technology which, from stone to bronze and then to iron, was linked to the capacity of man to extract nature's minerals. However, we must not consider that this vision of the past was generally accepted: primitivist ideas of the decadence of man since the golden age, cyclical theories, of myth as explanation, all struggled against the rationalist explanations that our vision of the history of human science has confirmed. In its flashes of intuitive enlightenment, however, as in its original observations, the vision of the past that we have been bequeathed by Graeco-Roman antiquity constitutes for historians – and in particular for archaeologists – an appeal to humility, to doubt, and to the examination of the evidence.

What differentiated the Greeks and Romans from the Egyptians or Assyrians, therefore, was not their concern for the past but their way of being interested in it and of writing history. Within this newly established intellectual sphere, several types of history emerged. This diversity explains how it was possible for a descriptive history which sought to classify societies, institutions, and objects to blossom alongside a political history. The work of a historian such as Varro cannot be dissociated from the work of philosophers who, in trying to define the uniqueness of the human species, laid the foundations for a history of evolution in which mankind was the biological and social subject.

THE COLLAPSE OF THE GRAECO-ROMAN MODEL OF HISTORY

With the progressive break-up of the Roman empire, not only did institutions and social practices disappear, but also the framework of intellectual reference (Rodocanachi 1914). Even though, in the West, culture was going to merge with the

Graeco–Roman tradition for hundreds of years still, the intellectuals of the Middle Ages never exercised the liberty, time, or facilities of their classical predecessors in classical antiquity. The difficulties of these times, the wars, the consequences of multiple invasions, do not explain everything, however; the loss of the influence of the model of ancient education, together with the affirmation of a Christian culture which was suspicious of the idolatry manifested in the ancient texts, monuments, and objects, also had something to do with it. In the great disorder which ravaged the West, bishops and monks became the devoted guardians and the defenders of Letters. Clerics had to eradicate from the countryside the numerous traces of paganism, because the type of history that the new reigning dynasties reclaimed had to justify their rapid fortune and assert their affiliation with a prestigious past. Scholars writing saintly hagiographies not only undertook to expunge the ancient literature from the works which could threaten the sacred writing, but they scarcely sustained any interest in digressions on the origins of their species – they had enough to do to establish that the Franks, like the Romans, were the descendants of the Trojans and to reconcile the Revelation with Graeco–Roman history, the only history available (Beaune 1985; Kendrick 1950).

Everywhere were the remains of fortifications, works of art, gigantic monuments such as baths and aqueducts, but they did not arouse admiration or astonishment because people in the sixth and seventh centuries AD had neither the time nor the inclination to muse on their long history. What concerned them was to live with them by converting them, modifying them or (most frequently) destroying them: a ruin was not only a vestige of a vanished past, it was, according to circumstances, an object to be made useful or removed. For the people of the early Middle Ages, the rapport with the past became one of continuity: there was no sign of a rupture between the Roman empire and their own daily lives, so why should they make one? German chiefs set themselves up in the palaces of Roman governors; peasants took over abandoned villas; princes took the marble from great villas to cover the walls of their own residences; bishops salvaged columns, statues and sarcophagi to decorate their churches and tombs; and clerics in the unstable calm of their libraries hunted out quotations of ancient authors (Adhémar 1996; see also Mennung 1925 and Wright 1844). For all of them, their interest in the past was primarily utilitarian.

THE RECONSTRUCTION AND RECUPERATION OF THE PAST

In laying claim to the Western Empire, Charlemagne was better placed than his predecessors to inherit the grandeur of Rome, and his claim was not without cultural consequences, for Antiquity became again an inspirational source and model. With the reading of ancient texts, the taste for discovery of the sources of the Graeco–Roman culture spread. The great abbots of the eleventh and twelfth

6

centuries, such as those of Saint Benoît sur Loire, Cluny and Saint-Denis, made pilgrimages to Rome and experienced for themselves the monuments of antiquity (Adhémar 1996). The first accounts of journeys to Italy appeared at this time, and in Rome itself an interest in protecting its buildings emerged. In northern Europe, too, there is the first evidence for observations of the monuments of the past: thus in AD 1009 a Carthusian monk of Quimperlé tells us that Rudalt and Orscand, sons of the bishop of Vannes, gave a gift of land to the monastery of Saint Cado, land on which there were many heaps of stones, the first mention of the prehistoric mega-liths of Brittany (Mortet 1911). These were mentioned as topographical markers, though, not as a potential source of history – for the objects found in the earth to become historical signs it was essential that the vision of the observer should itself be a historical vision, a condition that was rarely fulfilled in the Middle Ages or in Antiquity.

It was in Italy that a new feeling for Antiquity emerged: at Modena, Pisa and soon in all the peninsula, people were no longer content just to recover remains but made use of them in architecture and the plastic arts. The emperor Frederick II embodied to perfection those princes of the Middle Ages who sought to use all means to establish the continuity between the ancient and medieval worlds (Weiss 1988). Elsewhere, however, the interest of other European nations in the Graeco-Roman past seemed to diminish. The eleventh and twelfth centuries witnessed the integration of barbarian invaders and Classical history: the English and French, for example, both laid claim to their Trojan origins, whilst some scholars spiced their accounts still further with a dash of Jewish history and *chansons de geste* (Adhémar 1996). Over time, the Romans became confused with Charlemagne, the Graeco-Roman divinities with the Islamic demons of the *chansons de geste*: theatres, amphi-theatres, temples became the towers of Roland, the palace of Pepin the Bref, the gates of Ganelon. In the middle of the thirteenth century all ruins were essentially Saracen, and the crusades replaced the German invasions in the popular imagina-tion. With urban expansion, the destruction of Roman monuments reached a scale never before known – the chronicles record massive demolition of the amphitheatre of Trèves, the murals of Poitiers and the arenas of Nîmes and Le Mans, for example (Adhémar 1996). The rural and urban landscape was profoundly changing, and with it regional history.

In the cities of northern Italy at this time, scholars such as Petrarch, the most celebrated editor of Livy and Cicero, embarked on writing treatises on Roman history; his taste for the ruins of Rome marked the rediscovery of the town. The work of such scholars established the break between the present and the past and dictated that Antiquity should be treated as a historical object, investigated by visits, descriptions, and studies of objects such as inscriptions and coins. The Italian scholars of the fourteenth and fifteenth centuries laid out the path of humanism by preparing a return to Antiquity which was not merely a purely literary experience, or even the rediscovery of certain plastic forms, but the systematic comparison between the monument and the text (Weiss 1988). The fifteenth-century antiquarian Cyriaque of Ancona was one of the first people since Varro to tackle the question of the truth of the written sources: monuments, coins and inscriptions were now *sigilla historiarum*, 'seals of history'.

RENAISSANCE ROME, THE CAPITAL OF HISTORY

If the intellectual movement that was to overturn history (and the sciences!) in Europe was Italian, it was because the Italians found themselves at the confluence of two movements which were like the poles of the Renaissance: they were the best placed to supply themselves with Latin and Greek manuscripts, and to discover in their towns and countryside the clear presence of Antiquity (Weiss 1988). The description and study of antiquities in fifteenth-century Rome was not only a speculative and disinterested activity: it was necessary for the development of the town, with possibilities for profit, for the ancient monuments provided cheap material for the construction of residences for princes or cardinals – some building contracts specified the reuse of materials found on site. Surveys and excavations had an economic function devolved to a particular type of builder, the *cavatore*, who exploited the soil of Rome on such a scale that the Popes tried to limit the destruction and to reserve for Papal finances at least a part of the profits. In 1515, Leo X entrusted the construction of St Peter's to Raphael, expressly commanding him to control the antiquities which were to be used to decorate or build the monument and to avoid any destruction that was not decided by himself.

The Italian antiquarian of the Renaissance thus took after Archimedes as much as Herodotus, because he was essential to every architectural project – in Italy at this time there was no architecture without archaeology. The very rapid changes that affected the treatment of ancient monuments, with the development of techniques of excavation, survey, and the critical evaluation of monuments and written texts, paralleled the revolution which overturned the knowledge and editing of ancient texts. The antiquarians, through the ties which they maintained with the scholarly world because of the necessity of interpreting coinage and restoring and interpreting inscriptions, became familiar with the methods of textual criticism, of *emendatio*, correction and *recensio*, and the verification and comparison of manuscripts. The clerks of the Roman court coexisted with the artists and builders responsible for the construction of the new Rome.

8

EARLY ANTIQUARIANISM NORTH OF THE ALPS

Nicholas Fabri of Peiresc, who was born in 1580 at Beaugensier in Provence and died at Aix in 1637, was unanimously acknowledged both by his contemporaries and by tradition for being the greatest antiquarian of France, at least until Montfaucon (Gassendi 1641). He published nothing, and is known for a correspondence which radiated across the whole of Europe. He collected books and rare and exotic objects, but he brought to his collection a preoccupation with knowledge and the desire to explain and to know, in pursuit of which he sought the help of Rubens, Galileo, Camden and many others. He showed to the scientific world that, if there had been a country of choice for all the antiquarians, antiquity was found everywhere where men of curiosity wished to discover it. The lesson was heard, far from Roman palaces, but in close communion with the most ardent humanism: from the fjords of Norway to the banks of the Thames, from the plains of Moravia to the canals of Holland, people began to scrutinize the earth and the countryside, trying, like Peiresc, to understand them (Sklenar 1983).

Amongst those that he knew well was William Camden, author in 1586 of a historical and geographic description of the British Isles called *Britannia* (Daniel 1964, 1967; Daniel and Renfrew 1986). Its original character and the quality of its observations (Fig. 1.1) quickly made this book the bible of British archaeology, repeatedly republished, added to, and enriched from the time of his death to the present day. Camden was not the first British antiquarian, but because his work was easily accessible he became, even more than Peiresc, an example and a model for others. His technique was topographic, departing from Roman geography to construct a local history of each English town, but his aim was not limited to high Antiquity: the ancient geography had to be the foundation for a history that considered the Saxon and medieval periods as a part of the history of a kingdom which asserted its place in the world of letters. Camden's two imperatives were precision of time and of place, and for these he invented the rules of historical cartography: the linguistic study of place-names to distinguish between Roman, Gaulish, and Saxon contributions; and reconstruction of historical territories through tradition and the study of coinage. He was the first to establish the existence of indigenous coinage in Roman Britain and to decipher the inscriptions on the coins to identify the towns from which they originated. In the face of the Trojan legends and Roman tradition, he emphasized the Anglo-Saxon character of the British population.

As far as we can tell from the sources, Nicolaus Marschalk (1460/70–1525) of Thuringia was the first scholar to use excavation to try to resolve a historical question (Stemmermann 1934; see also Abramowicz 1983). He asked himself about the difference between megalithic alignments and tumuli and, as a good reader of the Latin writers on the Germans, he attributed one to the 'Heruli' and the other to the 'Obétrites'. Not content to study the monuments, he remarked that nearby

Figure 1.1 Drawings of ancient British coins from William Camden's *Britannia* (1600). Reproduced with permission of Curtis Brown Ltd, London on behalf of Copyright © Glyn Daniel 1967, Glyn Daniel and Colin Renfrew 1988.

vessels with cremations had been found which he considered to be the graves of servants of the chiefs buried in the funerary monuments. Like 'thunder-stones' (which we now know as palaeolithic handaxes – Figure 1.6), megaliths and tumuli, prehistoric cremation cemeteries formed an element of the 'archaeological landscape' of medieval and modern Europe, but the presence of immense 'urn-fields' on the plains of central Europe was now an additional element of curiosity. Not everyone accepted this view, however: the 'cosmography' of Sébastian Münster which appeared a few years later took up again the myth of vases 'spontaneously born in the ground' (Schnapp 1996) – like the thunder-stones, the urns (which we know as vessels of the late bronze age Lausitz culture) were considered as objects of curiosity which it was appropriate to place in royal cabinets of rare objects (*Wunderkammer*).

Though the mythological identification of thunder-stones was traced back to ancient authors such as Pliny and Varro, the tradition was maintained right up to the eighteenth century and beyond. However, Michael Mercati (1541–93), the director of the Vatican's botanical garden, had already in the sixteenth century presented an alternative to the majority view that claimed them as manufactured by lightning (Mercati 1719). He saw the similarities between the objects being found in the countryside by Italian peasants and the Vatican's growing collection of American Indian and Asiatic artefacts being brought back by Italian and other voyagers. Professional historians, he wrote (*Metallotheca* XII), believed that before the use of iron, blades were detached from hard flint for use as knives.

What is striking in the history of these interpretations of flint, pottery, megaliths and tumuli is the perfect parallelism of the interpretations: in contrast with the mythological traditions, a small number of scholars produced convincing theories, but they were never completely accepted by the scientific world. This duality between knowledge and tradition was the basis of the archaeology of the sixteenth century. Certainly there were differences between one country and another: Britain was notable for archaeological cartography, in the tradition of Camden; the antiquarians of central Europe were more active in excavation, and in attempts at ethnic interpretation following the writings of Tacitus; the French, with the notable exception of Peiresc, were more concerned with collecting and cataloguing thunder-stones, coins and inscriptions than travelling the countryside. Meanwhile, in Scandinavia, a new way of practising archaeology was born where, for the first time in European history, the states were not only concerned with legislating on the preservation of the past but with the creation of archaeological institutions.

SCANDINAVIA: THE ARCHAEOLOGICAL SCIENCE OF THE NATION

At the end of the twelfth century Saxo Grammaticus had already pointed out the presence of strange monuments in the Scandinavian countryside, enormous artificial hills or blocks of stone that he attributed to the giants of the past, but systematic collection of Nordic antiquities did not begin until the end of the sixteenth century (Klindt-Jensen 1975). Johannes Bureus, the son of a pastor of Uppsala, was

11

educated in the strict humanist discipline, knowing Latin and Greek, but also Hebrew, which he taught himself. In the passionately intellectual and nationalist climate of the Swedish court, his interest soon turned towards the decipherment of rune stones. He established an accurate alphabet, suggested rules for transcription and proposed a dating system, and above all undertook a systematic survey of all the inscriptions in Sweden. Accompanied by two assistants, from 1599 onwards he organized regular archaeological and topographical expeditions. In comparison with Camden's, his method was not an original one, but it was distinguished by the care taken over drawings and the attention devoted to the epigraphic material, whose collection was the principal objective of his excursions: in a few years, his team collected a quarter of the inscriptions known today from Sweden. The kingdom of Sweden was thus the first state to have an archaeological service, whose work anticipated many of the features of our modern antiquities services. The achievement of Johannes Bureus has also to be understood in the context of the political and diplomatic rivalry between Swedes and Danes at this time: the two double monarchies (Denmark–Norway and Sweden–Finland) intended to create an image of their past that matched their political and diplomatic role in a Europe torn apart by wars. History thus constituted a formidable ideological stake between the two kingdoms, and in Scandinavia archaeology was from its inception a critical part of history.

The exploration of the earth is a voyage in time; in order to undertake it, there is no need for Latin and Greek sources, but one must have at one's disposal an inclination to be curious, an eye always on the lookout, and a taste for the country-side and for drawing. Johannes Bureus and Ole Worm (1588–1654) were the founders of an archaeology of the landscape which is the ancestor of our modern surveys: their innovation did not only consist of the inspection, cataloguing and surveying of sites, but in their topographic approach and their interest in accurate recording and publication. From site to publication, Worm (who was antiquarian to the king of Denmark) controlled a sequence of complementary operations which could no longer be undertaken by an isolated individual, but which demanded collaboration to facilitate his knowledge, functions and international relations. Worm's researches (Worm 1643) also showed the way to those such as Olaf Rudbeck (1630–1702), who moved from observation to excavation (see pp. 13–14). The Scandinavian antiquarians, perhaps because they were more in a hurry than others to find new historical sources, were the first to attempt the synthesis of collection and interpretation.

'COMPARATIVE ANTIQUITY': JOHN AUBREY

Peiresc, Camden and Worm opened the way for the epigraphists, numismatists and all those who were engulfed in the vast movement of curiosity that came from the Renaissance and its consequences on the intellectual life of Europe. However, in order for the study of antiquities to progress, it needed the addition of fieldwork to the knowledge not only of literary sources but also of local customs, place-names and regional linguistics. It was a Briton, John Aubrey (1626–97), who was to succeed in this synthesis (Daniel 1964, 1967; Legg and Fowles 1980; Powell 1963). An admirer of Francis Bacon and Descartes, Aubrey was an active member of the Royal Society of London, a friend of Thomas Hobbes and William Harvey, a colleague of Newton and Locke, in short a man at the centre of British intellectual life, a physician and naturalist as well as a folklorist and antiquarian. His major antiquarian work *Monumenta Britannica* remains unpublished in Oxford's Bodleian Library, but the manuscript was circulated, read, and admired as one of the most important treatises on archaeology in the seventeenth century.

Aubrey's method consisted of combining observation of the present and the past, ethnology with textual tradition, the analysis of the landscape and the anatomy of its monuments. He is distinguishable from Worm by the larger scope of his interests and methods, but also by his rejection of description for its own sake and by his willingness to establish rules of interpretation which governed observation. In order to restore these antiquities 'of an age so long ago that no book can reach them', he invented a method of 'comparative antiquity': he was certainly not the first to envisage the comparison of monuments with each other as a way of identifying them, but he can be regarded as the inventor of the typo-chronological method, the systematical classification of archaeological types, as is shown in his *Miscellanea*. To arrange objects and monuments according to a chronological order, to identify the variables which decided their order, and to compare the types that emerged one with the other – this was the method proposed by Aubrey, and it seemed like the programme of a new science. Aubrey did not confine himself to a palaeontological restitution of the past, he suggested to the antiquarian that his final goal should be to recover the form of life, the behaviour, even the psychology of vanished populations. 'Comparative antiquity' is a speculative method which attempts to elucidate the language of the monuments.

THE GERMAN AND SCANDINAVIAN SEARCH FOR THEIR ORIGINS

In Scandinavia, Olaf Rudbeck (1630–1702), doctor, philologist and student of myths, was the most active and the most visionary of seventeenth-century archaeologists, bringing not only topographic survey to excavation but also, in his excavation of the tumuli of Uppsala, the stratigraphic section (Klindt-Jensen 1975). A curiosity for local antiquities was also as strong in a troubled Germany, constantly seeking its origins: here too, doctors and pastors were the first actors of a new history that was as attentive to the countryside as to texts. Christian Detlev Rhode and Andreas Albert Rhode personified this new generation of antiquarians who dared to descend from the saddle to excavate the soil with their hands. Both ministers, both from the region of Hamburg, C. D. Rhode (the father, 1653–1717) and A. A. Rhode (the son, 1682–1724) combined a solid classical education with a taste for the earth, much like the contemporary British antiquarians, but they owed to German erudition an experience of excavation that was scarcely found anywhere in Europe.

The goal of A. A. Rhode, who took on the collections and excavations of his father in 1717, was the more ambitious: he wished to share with the curious the concrete experience of contact with the past, using the results of excavations as a way of understanding local history. In order to achieve this he published a weekly magazine, *Cimbrisch-Holsteinische Antiquitäten Remarques*, which is one of the most entertaining publications in the history of archaeology (Rhode 1720). Rhode brought to his discoveries a freshness of first amazement and a naïvety – but also the precision – of a man of the soil. Excavation was not considered as a manual task for a subordinate, but as a technique of exploration which obeyed a set of rules. J. D. Major had already proposed several techniques for excavating tumuli to avoid the destruction of the funerary structures within them. Like the other pioneer excavators Rudbeck and Major, Rhode was a meticulous observer of detail. This curiosity was not limited to observation, but also led to interpretation: he asked himself about the functions of flint in the daily life of the ancient peoples of Germany, himself working on modern flints in order to reconstruct the techniques of the ancients. Rhode did not possess the extraordinary intuition of an Aubrey in matters of typology, nor did he give the same attention to topographical survey of his excavations as Rudbeck, but more than either of these he typified, in his many interests, the field archaeologist of the Age of Enlightenment. For these men, the knowledge of the past was inextricably linked to their religious convictions. The thirst for knowledge of the pastors of northern Germany was inseparable from their desire to apply their reason to religion, and in this they are similar to those in Britain who went out to find the Druids in order to rescue a new type of Anglicanism.

DRUIDS AT THE SOURCE OF HISTORY: WILLIAM STUKELEY

Everything began, however, under the auspices of a serene positivism. William Stukeley (1687–1765) was born in Lincolnshire and began his studies of medicine at Cambridge at a very young age. There, and afterwards at St Thomas's Hospital in London, he formed connections with everyone in England who was respected as a scientist at the time, including Isaac Newton, the astronomer Edmond Halley, and Richard Mead, the director of the hospital and one of the most brilliant doctors of his time. In this scientific milieu, where a taste for antiquities was linked with a passion for botany, astronomy and mathematics, Stukeley – aided by his gift as an artist – showed himself as an outstanding observer (Daniel 1975, 1981; Kendrick 1950). He was not the first to discover Stonehenge, but his description and surveys were momentous, and his visit to the neolithic site of Avebury was to enter into the annals of British archaeology. He combined the description of the landscape with excavation, and his vision was that of a modern archaeologist, paying attention to the layers in the earth. Because he complemented his discoveries with precise survey (Fig. 1.2), Stukeley is without doubt one of those who made the greatest contribution to the foundation of field archaeology (Piggott 1976, 1985, 1990).

His contribution, though, was not limited to the development of topographical analysis or to the inclusion of excavation within the range of tools of scientific verification available to the antiquarian. His researches led to a chronological analysis of the past which threw to the winds the interpretation of megalithic structures as Roman or Saxon in favour of a Celtic origin. However, without the means of establishing a chronology which showed the existence of a history before history, Stukeley came to consider all pre-Roman monuments as Celtic. The consequences would not have been so dramatic for science if Stukeley had not linked enigmatic sites such as Stonehenge and Avebury with the Druids, whom he considered as Phoenician colonists and as the civilizers of Britain – a kind of silent Christianity which well before the Revelation had tried to introduce to Europe the early symptoms of civilization. For this was the central question. If the scholars of the Rennaisance had succeeded in expelling the fable of Trojan origins from the scientific history of Europe, the theologians of the seventeenth century were not emancipated from biblical chronology. In consequence, the beginnings of history in Europe had to be mixed with holy history. It is not, then, surprising to find that Stukeley built his druidic revelation on such sources. It is a strange irony that this admirable scientist who began his enquiry with excavations should have ended it with the maddest reveries!

QUESTIONS OF BIBLICAL REVELATION

Why did not the most passionate and curious of the antiquarians of the seventeenth and early eighteenth centuries try to relate what they observed in the ground to a chronology that was longer than commonly accepted? Part of the answer lies in the

Figure 1.2 William Stukeley's illustration of Stonehenge from his *Stonehenge, a Temple Restored to the British Druids* (1740). Reproduced with permission of Curtis Brown Ltd, London on behalf of Copyright © Glyn Daniel 1967, Glyn Daniel and Colin Renfrew 1988.

emblematic history of Isaac Lapeyrère (1594–1676), a scholar who, if not the most learned of his generation, was certainly the most obstinate defender of a long human history, 'du noir abîme du temps' to use the poetic definition of Buffon (1776). Lapeyrère was the author of a work published secretly in 1655: *Preadamitae, sive exercitatio super versibus duodecimo, decimotertio et decimoquarto, capitiis quinti epistolae D. Pauli ad Romanos* ('The Préadamites, or an essay on verses twelve, thirteen and fourteen . . . . of the epistles of Paul to the Romans'). This book was not a surprise to the scientific world (Popkin 1987). The notoriety of its author

16

and the passionate character of its subject made it a sought-after and awaited manuscript, published in five editions simultaneously, three by a single publisher, Elsevier, in Amsterdam.

At the edge of Protestantism and Catholicism (indeed also of Judaism, as some authors saw him as a Christianized Jew), Lapeyrère appeared literally obsessed by the narrowness of the historical and geographical boundaries imposed by the Jewish Revelation. Contrary to the accusations of his innumerable (and fascinated) critics, Lapeyrère did not attempt to undermine the basis of the holy scriptures, but sought more modestly – but just as dangerously – to distinguish in biblical text that which was human from that which was divine. Doing this, he resumed an ancient tradition that allowed for mankind a history that was much longer than that authorized by the biblical Revelation. That humanity had a long history of tens of millennia was an idea common to the Greeks, and before them to the Egyptians and to the Assyro-Babylonians, but the reading of the Bible, from the moment when it became accessible to the Greeks and Romans through the translation of Septantes, offered a much shorter chronology and a story of the creation of the world which was to become an essential point of Christian orthodoxy.

From the time of St Augustine in the fifth century AD, all reference to a history of the world which was longer than the few millennia of biblical history became suspect and heretical. The discovery of America, however, came to disturb these certainties because, first, it posed to scholars the question of the origin of the American people and, second, because much evidence attested that these peoples used a chronology much longer than the biblical tradition (von Hohenheim 1929). Even if Christopher Columbus had never considered that the Americans could be different from the Indians that it was normal to encounter on the journey to Asia, his immediate successors soon confronted the problem of the ethnic and racial nature of the Amerindians. It took some effort for the missionaries and conquistadors to admit that it was men and therefore souls that they conquered. Once the human identity of the Amerindians was admitted, speculation over their origins was wide: lost tribes of Israel, Phoenicians, Arabs and even Norwegians were invoked to explain the peopling of America (Popkin 1987).

Lapeyrère had to wait a long time before the scientific world would accept the evidence of men before Adam. The reason for this was undoubtedly the fact that the antiquarians of the period regarded the proposition of the existence of pre-Adamite man only as a philosophical suggestion. However, in his *Relation de l'Islande*, Lapeyrère showed that, although he was not an antiquarian by profession, he knew well how to develop a geographical and historical argument. Did he not at the time of his stay in Copenhagen debate with the master of Scandinavian antiquities, Ole Worm, and visit his museum? It was Worm himself who told him about the first inhabitants of Greenland and Iceland, and it was due to him that he was able to contest Grotius's theory that the Americans were the descendants of Vikings that had established themselves on the American coast from Greenland. To the Scandinavian and British surveyors, the German excavators, and the Italian and French collectors, Lapeyrère made a gift of the long antiquity of man, but they were hardly inclined to accept it, because, in displacing the question of the origin of man from a descriptive to an interpretive sphere, he had transformed a chronological question into a philosophical one.

Certainly others before him such as Fracastoro, Leonardo da Vinci and Bernard Palissy had suggested that the world was very much older than it appeared and that fossils were not the result of some spontaneous phenomenon by which the mineral imitated the animal, but were once living creatures petrified and buried deep in the earth. Furthermore, G. Owen, and after him N. Steno, suggested a stratigraphic theory of the formation of the earth that also required a long time-scale (Rossi 1984); but none of them addressed the crucial dogma of Adamism. Even if some, such as Robert Hooke in his *Micrographia* (1665) and his *Lectures and Discourses on Earthquakes* (1669), had discrete doubts about the necessity of the biblical Universal Flood, it was better to separate the history of mankind from the history of the world. For the naturalists, the history of the world paralleled that of humankind, but the different lines of evolution never intersected. Natural history should have everything to gain by borrowing its methods from the secular history of the antiquarians. Shells and fossils were the

> medals, the urns and the monuments of nature, they are the biggest and the most durable monuments of history which in all probability are distant precedents of the most ancient monuments of the world, more than the authentic pyramids, mummies, hieroglyphics and coins and they offer more information on natural history than all the latter put together on civil history.
>
> (Hooke 1705: 355)

These comments by Robert Hooke illustrate well the paradox of the era – the naturalists agreed with their colleagues to construct a history of the natural world on the model of antiquarian history, but did not ask the opposite question: whether antiquarian history could benefit from natural history. For sure, the idea of the vastness of natural history and of its relationship with the history of humankind was in the air, but precisely because he made a manifesto of this idea, Lapeyrère created about him a vast halo of distrust. He had to wait two centuries before his theories found an echo amongst antiquarians, with the discovery of the immensity of prehistoric time in the mid-nineteenth century. Thus the men of the Enlightenment provided the tools necessary for archaeological observation: numismatism, epigraphy, field observation, topography, and, in some cases, as we have seen, a sense of the landscape, and an interest in the relationship between what appeared on the surface of the earth and the layers that formed it. With this, there were also regional and national traditions. The taste for ruins and for exploration of the Scandinavians, the taphonomic passion of the central European antiquarians, the

British attachment to the description of local antiquities, the more traditional preoccupation of the French and Italians with the collection of Roman and Greek antiquities, together painted an archaeological landscape that had very little in common with that of the Renaissance. It was necessary next to provide some order for all this.

TOWARDS A SCIENCE OF MATERIAL CULTURE: THE ENLIGHTENMENT

Bernard de Montfaucon (1655–1741) represented the great tradition of the Benedictines of Saint-Maur: like Mabillon, he was both a palaeographer and a philologist, but he had the idea, during a visit to Italy (1698–1701), of devoting a part of his religious texts to antiquities (de Broglie 1891). Montfaucon's project, as is revealed explicitly in its title *L'Antiquité Expliquée* (Montfaucon 1719–24), was to attempt to explain the monuments of Antiquity by illustrating them with as full documentation as possible – and he suggested to the reader to devote two years to the systematic study of his manual. The work was structured functionally (and here again we find the Varronian plan): first there are the gods, then cults, then the customs of life (the private mores) to which correspond the public mores – 'wars, vehicles, roads, bridges, aqueducts, navigation' – with the last part devoted to funerals, tombs and mausolea. Rather than by simple curiosity, Montfaucon was driven by a historical ambition to reconstruct the past from a global perspective: to the antiquarian, texts suggested ideas, notions, the functioning of institutions, whereas objects and monuments offered knowledge of another kind, their analysis subject to the eye of the expert and the hand of the artist. The ancient Platonic distinction between the world of ideas and the world of the senses led him to consider that archaeology was the image and history the text. *L'Antiquité Expliquée* was a methodological effort to assign to each object a text which gave it meaning; in this way Montfaucon theorized the reciprocal movement between text and image that underpins historical archaeology today.

In opposition to the classic *descriptio* and *interpretatio*, the Count of Caylus proposed the replacement of the philological model by an experimental paradigm, making the antiquarian a sort of physicist of the past. Born in 1692, he accompanied the ambassador of France to Constantinople and visited the coast of Asia Minor, before beginning, from 1718, the life of a dilettante and friend of the arts. An excellent engraver himself, he was interested in the techniques of drawing and painting, past and present. His fortune allowed him to be the patron of Parisian artists, and also to acquire antiquities from a network of devoted correspondents which spread as far as Alexandra or even Syria (Rocheblave 1889). However, he was not a collector in the narrow sense: once the boxes of antiquities had been unpacked, he thought of nothing but letting the scientific world know about them. His contribution to archaeology stands in a number of memoirs published by the Académie des Inscriptions, but his masterpiece remains his *Recueil d'Antiquities Egyptiennes, Erusques, Grecques, Romaines et Gauloise*, published in seven volumes in Paris between 1752 and 1768.

No one before him (and very few after him) explicitly criticized the philological interpretation that the scholars of the Renaissance had applied to monuments: if the study of antiquities had something to do with an experimental method, the paradigm of textual interpretation would no longer suffice, and the diagnosis of the archaeologist, like the reasoning of the physician, was open to proof. As much as it was possible, it was necessary to establish laws: if every object could be assigned to a place and a period by virtue of a cultural determinism that was observable and quantifiable, the antiquarian thus had a logical instrument capable of ordering series of objects. Caylus's double principle of evolution and cultural distinction laid the foundations of the descriptive typology which is at the heart of modern archaeology.

In 1711, at the same time that Montfaucon completed the writing of *Antiquité Expliquée*, a colonel in the Austrian army, the Prince of Elbeuf, who owned a small property near Portici in southern Italy, discovered there at the bottom of a well statues and inscriptions of an exceptional quality (Zevi 1987). In 1738 the King of Naples ordered the resumption of these explorations under the direction of a Spanish engineer, Rocco Joachim Alcubierre. Beginning from the wells and the galleries of the Prince of Elbeuf (happily situated in the centre of the theatre of Herculaneum), the excavators found a treasure house of inscriptions, bronze and marble statues, and above all – unique in the history of the Graeco-Roman world – paintings which the disaster which struck the town had rapidly buried and thus protected. Ten years later, under the direction of the same Alcubierre, the king ordered similarly spectacular excavations to begin on the site of Pompeii (Fig. 1.3). It is difficult for us today to imagine the passions and the interest that these excavations released at a time when they constituted practically the only royal archaeological site in the whole of Europe.

These discoveries impacted on the collection of antiquities in the Kingdom of France. First, the great construction programmes of roads and fortifications of the age of Louis XIV revealed numerous buried monuments. The fortifications constructed by Vauban led to the discoveries at Metz and Besançon of Roman amphitheatres. The bridge builders encouraged by Trudaine, director of 'Ponts et Chaussées' (Bridges and Roads), sent Caylus wonderful surveys of their discoveries, which provided a number of illustrations and commentaries for *Recueil d'Antiquités* – the idea of a survey of French antiquities was born. There was even systematic excavation, subsidized by the royal government. In 1750 the bridge engineer Legendre had identified at the site of Châtelet, between Saint-Dizier and Joinville

Figure 1.3 Early excavations at Pompeii. Reproduced with permission of Michael Holford Photographs.

in Champagne, an important Gallo-Roman site, and in 1772 Grignon, a master blacksmith of the neighbouring village of Bayard, decided to undertake excavations there with the support of the Académie des Inscriptions et Belle-Lettres and of the king. He published his discoveries in 1774 in two volumes of the *Bulletin des Fouilles Faites par Ordre du Roi d'une Ville Romain, sur la Petite Montagne du Châtelet*. Grignon was one of those practical minds that contributed to archaeology the techniques of a man of the land: survey and topographical analysis, drawing and description of the finds, attention to the variations in the ground and the conditions of discovery.

Throughout the eighteenth century, intellectuals attempted to make intelligible the mass of discoveries which kept accumulating, but it was Johann Winckelmann (1717–68), the son of an obscure shoemender of Stendal in Prussia, who completely renewed Western awareness of the works of the Graeco-Roman world (Fig. 1.4). There were indeed already many scholarly works on ancient art, but in his *Histoire de l'Art de l'Antiquité* (1781) Winckelmann proposed an order in the learned jumble of knowledge, daring to establish a stylistic chronology where his predecessors had contented themselves with iconographic commentary. From his perspective, Greek art was not the bearer of a particular awareness, determined historically, but the ideal of a perfect and absolute beauty, embodied in the works of Phidias; stylistic analysis was not, as with Caylus, a technical instrument, but the key to the knowledge of an aesthetic. He gave to the social world of dilettanti, writers, artists, and antiquarians a framework of reference and a philosophy of art, with both practical and intellectual consequences.

From the middle of the eighteenth century, the Grand Tour (first to Italy, and soon to Greece and Turkey) became a mode of social distinction and cultural exploration. The travellers of the eighteenth century, like the antiquarians who preceded them, were collectors, but they showed a technical curiosity and a willingness to imitate that was new. Ambassadors put their resources at the service of the collectors. Richard Worsley, British ambassador to Venice, Choiseul-Gouffier, French ambassador to Constantinople, Lord Elgin, British ambassador in the same town, Sir William Hamilton in Naples: all these had their 'antiquarians', their draughtsmen and their mould-makers. In London, the Society of 'Dilettanti' founded in 1733 was the soul of these undertakings, the place to meet for English gentlemen, the most resolute and numerous of the travellers. Their curiosity combined with the necessity to finance their journeys to make looting economic sense (Constantine 1984; Pomian 1987).

The incredible and unsurpassed success of Winckelmann can be explained within the context of the Enlightenment, when a taste for, and a knowledge of, Graeco-Roman antiquities was at the heart of European culture (Gaetghens 1986). Where Europe only knew taste, however, Winckelmann offered an aesthetic of Greek art: his *History of the Art of Antiquity* is not a series of comments on art, but a

Figure 1.4 Johann Joachim Winckelmann (portrait by Angelika Kauffmann, 1764) whose *History of Art* (1763–68) renewed Western awareness of the works of the Graeco-Roman world. Reproduced with permission of Kunsthaus Zurich.

well-ordered account which laid out, in his inimitable style, the works in their historical context. Generations of antiquarians had sought to explain objects, but Winckelmann claimed to explain culture through objects, a formidable change of perspective that appealed to scientists as much as to artists. Even better, he was not content only to talk to the princes of Germany, the scholars of Holland and the cardinals of Italy in revealing the charms of the sublime: he addressed the men of the Enlightenment to tell them that if Greek art had attained such a degree of perfection (as he put it: 'by no people has beauty been so highly esteemed as by the Greeks') it was because it developed in the most liberal society that humanity was to have known: beauty was the sister of liberty. To the gifts of his pen Winckelmann added those of the connoisseur, travelling from one collection to another, from Rome to Paestum via Herculaneum, on the lookout for all the new archaeological discoveries of his time. Winckelmann imposed on the society of his time a new image of Greece, an aesthetic which was to be considered for decades as the key to the understanding of ancient art. The sublime and freedom were the two poles of Winckelmann's view of Greek art, though later writers did not always interpret it thus: for some – Herder, Lessing, Humboldt and of course Goethe (Franz 1945) – the mystery of Greek art constituted the heart of Winckelmann's heritage, whereas for others, particularly for the revolutionaries, the Ancients' message of freedom found in Winckelmann its modern incarnation.

BETWEEN THE MIST AND THE FLOOD

The discovery in 1685 in Normandy of the tomb of Cocherel provides a good example of the difficulties which the antiquarians of the eighteenth century confronted when they tried to interpret monuments outside the classical tradition. This megalithic tomb, carefully described by the gentleman who excavated it, comprised a burial chamber in which around twenty corpses were buried with unusual objects: flint axes, worked bone, arrow heads: 'it seems that these barbarians had no use of either iron, copper or any other metal' (Montfaucon 1719: vol. 2). This first burial was associated 'on ground raised eight inches above' with a cremation burial. Montfaucon favoured an ethnic interpretation of these different means of burial: 'without doubt these are the burials of two nations of the most distant Antiquity'. However, he was wary of chronological interpretation, contenting himself with joining to his description a letter of an antiquarian from Bâle, Jacques Christophe Iselin, which gave full details of similar burials found in Germany and the Nordic countries. In this letter, Iselin suggested a simple classification of these types of burial according to the weapons and tools discovered in the excavations, a succession from stone to copper and thence iron. It was a fundamental paradigm inherited from the Greek and Latin authors, but which hitherto no antiquarian had explicitly used to classify archaeological finds.

Other antiquarians had already experienced the malaise of discovering, or at least intimating, a time longer than biblical history. In *Les Epoques de la Nature*, for example, Buffon (1779) argued that there was no solution of continuity between the history of humankind and the history of nature:

as in secular history, one consults the titles, one pursues the medals, one deciphers the ancient inscriptions, in order to determine the period of human revolutions, and notes the dates of events; just as in the history of nature, one must search through the archives of the world, draw from the entrails of the earth the ancient monuments, gather their fragments and reassemble in a body of evidence all the indices of the physical changes that can reconstruct the different ages of nature. It is the only way to fix some points in the immensity of space and to place a certain number of valuable stones on the eternal road of time [our translation].

With the prudence of someone who knew he was treading on dangerous theological ground, Buffon suggests throughout this essay that what he had proposed for the history of the world and of animal species, others might undertake for human history.

Pierre Legrand d'Aussy (1737–1800) was another antiquarian who found himself contemplating a 'deep antiquity' beyond the classical and biblical chronologies (Laming-Emperaire 1964). Typological reasoning suggested that megaliths could not be monuments built by the Gauls, constructed a few centuries before Caesar, but 'tombs of the first times of the nation', which went back to an 'immeasurable succession of years'. However, although he had an intuition of the long duration of history, he did not understand the existence of prehistoric times because, like his contemporaries in France, his approach remained purely theoretical: during the early decades of the nineteenth century, French antiquarians, in contrast to those of Germany and Britain, hardly ever excavated. In Britain, on the other hand, an interest in the observation of the soil and excavation had continued since Stukeley: men such as the Reverend Brian Fausset (1720–76) and the officer-engineer James Douglas (1753–1819) were the pioneers of a primarily funerary field archaeology (Marsden 1983). They were early examples of the English nobility's romantic passion for opening tombs (Fig. 1.5).

Two characters linked by such a passion embody this new British archaeology: William Cunnington (1754–1810) and Sir Richard Colt Hoare (1758–1838). For them, barrow digging was a collective exercise, a professional undertaking supported by documents, plans and sections (Daniel 1967). Their curiosity was not confined to funerary archaeology: it was the beginnings of landscape archaeology as well. The work on the ground was prepared by preliminary prospection, the excavation then supervised by Cunnington and his team. In 1808 Colt Hoare undertook the editing of a comprehensive monograph, *A History of Ancient Wiltshire*, which was published from 1810 to 1812. Colt Hoare wanted to be a real historian – as he commented, 'we speak from facts not theory. I shall not seek among the fanciful regions of Romance an origin of our Wiltshire barrows.' However, for all their passionate endeavours, antiquarians such as Legrand d'Aussy, Colt Hoare, and Cunnington could not make the logical relationship between their material and the layers of the earth because of the short chronology of biblical history – the accepted

Figure 1.5 The English nobility's romantic passion for barrow-digging, as illustrated by the *Gentleman's Magazine* (1852). Reproduced with permission of Curtis Brown Ltd, London on behalf of Copyright © Glyn Daniel 1967, Glyn Daniel and Colin Renfrew 1988.

chronology calculated by Bishop Ussher dated the beginning of the world in the first book of Genesis to 4004 BC. As the Danish antiquarian Rasmus Nyerup commented in 1806, 'everything which has come down to us from heathendom is wrapped in a thick fog: it belongs to a space of time which we cannot measure. We know that it is older than Christendom, but whether by a couple of years or a couple of centuries, or even by more than a millennium, we can do no more than guess.' Where did the border which separated the ancient from the very ancient begin?

Already by the seventeenth century, the pioneers of fossil research Nicolaus Steno and Agostino Scilla had shown that the history of the earth was made up of a long process of geological formation. The most curious antiquarians could not fail to note the discoveries which, like Cocherel, demonstrated the existence of a worked stone industry associated with the evidence of the great antiquity of man. In 1715, a librarian from London, John Bagford, described a flint point discovered in a gravel pit in London as like a Breton weapon made from a point of flint driven into a long handle (Daniel 1975). In 1797, John Frere, high sheriff of Suffolk and later Member of Parliament, discovered a series of worked flints (Fig. 1.6) associated with animal remains several feet below the ground in undisturbed deposits in a brick quarry in Suffolk; he wrote to the Society of Antiquaries (in a letter published in their journal *Archaeologia* for 1800) that 'they are, I think, evidently weapons of war, fabricated and used by people who had not the use of metals . . . the situation

Figure 1.6 The 'weapons of war, fabricated and used by a people . . . even beyond that of the present world', illustrated by John Frere in *Archaeologia* (1800). Reproduced with permission of Curtis Brown Ltd, London on behalf of Copyright © Glyn Daniel 1967, Glyn Daniel and Colin Renfrew 1988.

in which these weapons were found may tempt us to refer them to a very remote period indeed, even before that of the present world'. However, his spectacular discoveries did not at the time provoke any particular debate – the Society recorded that 'thanks were returned to our worthy member Mr Frere for this curious and most interesting communication'. After all, without directly questioning the biblical chronology, scholars had long been trying to identify men contemporary with the Great Flood or Universal Deluge of the Bible. Thus in 1774, a pastor of Erlangen, Johan Friedrich Esper, discovering fossil animals, worked flints and human remains in the caves of Bayreuth, claimed that he had found in the earth physical traces of the Flood (Esper 1774).

Such debates characterized the first half of the nineteenth century. In France, Cuvier (1787–1832) collected and described as many animal fossils as possible, assigning them to well-defined strata and thus laying the foundations for a general stratigraphy of extinct species and associated geological features (Cuvier 1801). In Britain, the geologist and theologian Dean Buckland (1784–1856) made extensive studies of cave stratigraphies (Daniel 1967). Paradoxically, however, though their researches opened the way to a rigorous study of the association between human remains and fossil animals, both Cuvier and Buckland challenged the idea of con-temporaneity between man and extinct mammals, explaining their discoveries in terms of biblical floods, as the sub-title of Buckland's *Reliquiae Diluvianae* (1823) indicates: *Observations on the Organic Remains Contained in Caves, Fissures and Diluvial Gravels and in Other Geological Phenomena Attesting the Actions of an Universal Deluge*. In contrast, Marcel de Serres, a pupil of Cuvier and a friend of Buckland, in collaboration with the naturalist Jules de Christol and pharmacist Paul Tournal, discovered and published remains of fossil animals associated with stone tools in central France, and argued for their great antiquity (Grayson 1983). Doctor Schmerling (1791–1836) of Liège published documents with similar findings, as did Boucher de Perthes (1788–1868) on his discoveries in the Somme gravels (Cohen and Hublin 1989). However, such conclusions went against the opinions of most geologists, naturalists, and antiquarians. It was only after geologists accepted uniformitarianism, the basis of modern geology advocated by Charles Lyell in his *Principles of Geology* (1830–33), that occurrences of stone tools associated with extinct animals could be recognized as indisputable evidence for the antiquity of man (Daniel and Renfrew 1986). As John Evans reported to the Society of Antiquaries in his lecture of 2 June 1859, 'this much appears to be established beyond doubt, that in a period of antiquity remote beyond any of which we have hitherto found traces, this portion of the globe was peopled by man'.

THE RISE OF MUSEUMS AND OF COMPARATIVE ARCHAEOLOGY

A number of factors distinguish the pre-modern from the modern development of archaeology. While some of them were already present in the period prior to 1850, as we have seen, it was their contribution to a new organizational and ideological framework, spurred by a remarkable quantitative increase in archaeological finds, which made possible the development of archaeology as a scientific and public discipline.

The formation of numerous museum collections during the first half of the nineteenth century in Europe, closely paralleled in America, was in the context of three major processes (Kristiansen 1985): as described in the previous section, history and natural science, including archaeology, replaced popular myth and religion as the dominant expressions of human origins; the landscape was transformed as the western world changed from static mercantile–agrarian societies to dynamic industrialized societies; and nationalism rose to dominance as a political and historical framework (Trigger 1989). In this ideological climate, the first museum collections appeared as exhibitions of the origin of nations.

The formation of museum collections and the destruction of the archaeological heritage were interrelated phenomena, not as cause and effect but as alternative responses to social and economic developments (Kristiansen 1985, 1996a, 1996b). The rapid destruction of archaeological monuments in the late eighteenth and early nineteenth centuries led to the uncovering of thousands of burial finds and hoards and a growing desire to preserve the archaeological heritage. As has been demonstrated in many studies, a graph of museum acquisitions over time, divided into ten-year intervals, reveals a recurring trend: all over Europe finds from non-professional contexts (levelling of barrows, drainage and so on) boom during the nineteenth century, while professionally excavated finds start to increase only during the latter part of the century. During the twentieth century, non-professionally uncovered finds decline, while professional excavations become the main source (Fig. 1.7). This pattern can be explained by the effects of agrarian intensification, land reclamation and so on, which brought forth thousands of finds as well as destroying a similar number of monuments in the process. Museums arose in part as a response to this development, in order to save at least the movable part of the archaeological heritage. Only the increased archaeological activity in the latter part of the nineteenth century, in combination with increased pressure to protect the surviving monuments in the landscape, changed the picture.

During the early nineteenth century, museums were mainly passive receivers of finds, whereas later they became increasingly involved in classification and excavation, and in developing conservation policies for the non-movable part of the archaeological heritage. The critical change came with the development of comparative archaeology as a framework for classifying objects. For over a century, above all since Aubrey and Caylus, scholars had seen that it was possible to classify the remains of the past by using their intrinsic characteristics to arrange them chronologically. This method, as common to antiquarians as to geologists, had not only overturned geology at the beginning of the nineteenth century but had also led to considerable progress in historical, classical, and then oriental archaeology.

In the early nineteenth century, archaeological curiosity not only affected geologists and palaeontologists, it spread throughout the eastern Mediterranean. The fight for independence in Greece mobilized European opinion, enflamed by the ideas of Winckelmann, the poems of Goethe, Hölderlin and Byron, and the public's

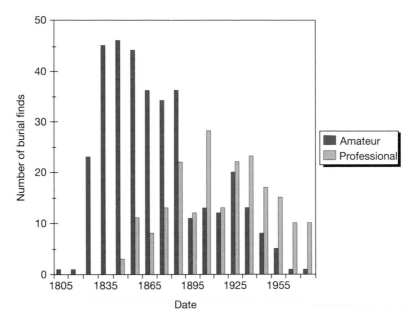

Figure 1.7 Number of amateur and professional burial finds of the Early Bronze Age on Zealand, Denmark; in most cases, barrows levelled for cultivation yielded the finds. © Kristian Kristiansen.

enthusiasm for antiquities such as the Parthenon frieze purchased by Lord Elgin and displayed in the British Museum (Fig. 1.8). The taste for Greece was matched by that for Egypt, in part stimulated by Bonaparte's expedition to Egypt (1798–99), on which he was accompanied by many scientists. The many resultant publications, in particular Edme Jomard's lavish *Expedition to Egypt* (1809–22), were the originators of the 'Egyptian style' which affected both architecture and the plastic arts. The decipherment of the Egyptian hieroglyphic script on the Rosetta Stone by Champollion (1790–1832) further stimulated the taste for Egypt, and the parallel deciphering of the cuneiform inscriptions of Assyria by Rawlinson (1810–95) produced similar interest in the ancient civilizations of the Near East (Larsen 1997).

However, it was in northern Europe where the model emerged that was to revolutionize archaeology. Christan Jürgensen Thomsen (1788–1865), Curator of the National Museum in Copenhagen, was the first archaeologist to construct a museum on the succession of stone, bronze and iron (*Aarbøger Nordisk Oldkyndighed* 1988; Hildebrandt 1937; Jensen 1992). He argued for the necessity of comparing the technologies of archaeological and ethnographic objects (Thomsen 1836): 'experience shows that similar conditions and in particular an equivalent cultural level lead to equivalent tools'. In giving such concise expression to the law

Figure 1.8 The Elgin Marbles displayed in the British Museum in 1819. © The British Museum.

of cultural similarity, Thomsen added to the typological rules of Caylus a way of analysing objects that was not only descriptive but also technical. He laid the foundations for a prehistory that was no longer dependent on texts. Also, he was able to construct a picture of prehistoric Europe before writing that coincided with the revelation of the prehistory of humanity. The originality of Thomsen was not only in the justification of the old model of the Three Ages of Stone, Bronze and Iron which had inspired philosophers, historians and antiquarians ever since classical Antiquity: it was also in the practical consequences that it brought with it – the establishment of a chronology which could be the basis of an explanation that was accessible to everyone. Thomsen published his guide to Nordic antiquities in 1836, but his system had already been elaborated and applied when he used it to organize his collections. In fact, Thomsen's museum methodology is perhaps his most important contribution to archaeology (*Aarbøger Nordisk Oldkyndighed* 1988; Jensen 1992).

The many museums that swiftly followed his lead differed from the earlier 'cabinets of antiquities' in two important aspects: they were all based upon systematic classifications and recordings of objects in their original find context, and they had as their main objective the presentation of this new evidence to the public in an orderly manner, according to period, find context, and type. Museums were thus anchored both in a new scientific tradition of recording and classification and in a new tradition of public display, based upon the history of the nation-state and its cultural origins. In the expanding industrial and colonial states of the United States, France, Germany and England, this inevitably included the cultural heritage of the Near East (Larsen 1997) and the eastern Mediterranean and Greece, whereas in central and northern Europe, and in Latin America, the focus was on the national archaeology (Trigger 1984). By the mid-nineteenth century, therefore, the new concept of public, national, museums – later to expand to regional and local museums – had become formalized, with the aim of collecting, recording and presenting the movable past, including archaeology, to the public.

CONTEXT, EXCAVATION AND STRATIGRAPHY

Alongside the development of his classification system, C. J. Thomsen had laid down the principles for recording museum collections according to find circumstances, finder, the context of the find, and descriptions of individual objects that were numbered. He established the methodological principle of the 'closed find', the context of objects found in association being the starting point for analysis and interpretation. He also established the basic methods of museum registration, as expressed, for example, in a letter to a colleague in 1822: 'no less important is that the antiquarian should observe which objects are found together – we have been neglectful in this respect. I hope that the careful inventory we keep on everything that comes into our Museum will be of some help' (Kristiansen 1985: 21).

J. J. A. Worsaae (1821–85), Thomsen's brilliant successor, consolidated and expanded his mentor's work by adding a new methodological practice to archaeology, that of systematic excavation according to the principles of stratigraphy – what the American archaeologist Rowe called 'Worsaae's Law' (Fig. 1.9). He established a more precise chronology for Danish prehistory, a particularly important contribution being his study of shell middens first discovered on the coast of Jutland in 1848: aided by the zoologist Steenstrup and the geologist Forchammer, he demonstrated that they were the food refuse of stone age hunter-gatherers – what we now know as the Ertebølle Mesolithic (Fischer and Kristiansen in press). He also published his results in a readable and accessible way, beginning with *Danmarks Oldtid oplyst ved Olsager og Gravhoje* in 1843 (when he was only 22), published in English in 1849 as *The Primeval Antiquities of Denmark*. Other Scandinavian prehistorians followed his lead, integrating acute observation of the evidence from the ground with the application of evolutionary theory, producing important syntheses of their prehistory such as Sven Nillson's *Skandinaviska Nordens Urinvånare* (1837), published in English in 1868 as *The Primitive Inhabitants of Scandinavia*.

The second half of the nineteenth century witnessed the gradual emergence of archaeology as a discipline with its own philosophy and field methodology (Daniel 1975; Trigger 1989). In America this period has been called the Classificatory–

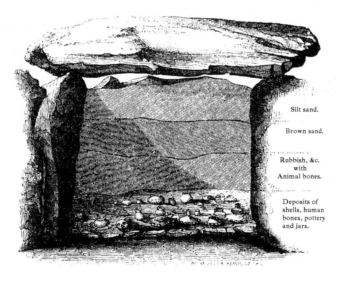

Silt sand.

Brown sand.

Rubbish, &c. with Animal bones.

Deposits of shells, human bones, pottery and jars.

Figure 1.9 An illustration by J. J. A. Worsaae of a section through a megalithic tomb. Reproduced with permission of Curtis Brown Ltd, London on behalf of Copyright © Glyn Daniel 1967, Glyn Daniel and Colin Renfrew 1988.

Descriptive period by Willey and Sabloff (1974). In both Europe, America, and the Near East, it was the great period of explorations and early excavations of prime sites: in North America the great Mississippian mounds; in Central and South America the great Maya and Inca ruins; in the Near East, Troy, Nimrud, Nineveh and Babylon. In Europe, excavations of stone age caves, for example of the Dordogne in central France by Edouard Lartet and Henry Christy, of the lake dwellings of Switzerland, 'kitchen middens' of Denmark, and of thousands of prehistoric barrows and cemeteries all over Europe, uncovered a hitherto unknown rich prehistoric past. To these researches must be added the work described earlier by archaeologists such as Boucher de Perthes and the geologists and zoologists who collaborated with them to establish a new scientific understanding of the antiquity of man.

The decade 1855–65 in particular revolutionized the classical, biblical, perceptions of the antiquity of man, and laid the foundations for not only the modern world-view, but also for its science-based foundations in geology, zoology, and archaeology. The pioneering works published by Darwin and Lyell in England, Lartet and de Perthes in France, and Worsaae and Steenstrup in Denmark, all had several things in common: they were all based upon field investigations and carefully documented observations, including principles of stratigraphy, find context, and typological change, establishing a new scientific practice that in time eclipsed the initial scepticism that usually greeted their publication. They were also based upon interdisciplinary work, which was to remain a dominant feature in archaeological practice until this day. These ground-breaking works established the basic methodological principles of archaeological excavation and observation, and the use of natural science.

As described in Grayson's (1983) study of this pioneering phase, the results were immediately applied and discussed on both sides of the Atlantic, but the scientific network that linked the main actors is no less interesting. Both Lartet and Boucher de Perthes refer in their works to the first results of the Danish Kitchen Midden Commission from 1851 as supporting evidence. Worsaae visited Boucher de Perthes in Abbeville, and refers to both the French and English results in an 1859 article in which he noted that 'entirely independent observations have been made in England and France, which are in almost verbatim agreement with the reasons given here for my proposed distinction between an early and a late Stone Age' (Worsaae 1859, our translation). The small band of early archaeologists was well connected, and travelled widely with the new modern means of transport, steam boats and trains. From the 1860s onwards, the network of this new international archaeological research community found its formal forum in international archaeological congresses that helped to speed up the distribution of new results, as well as the development of archaeological methods and principles of interpretation (Fig. 1.10). The formation of archaeological societies throughout Europe during this

Figure 1.10 Participants in the international archaeological congress in Copenhagen 1869, posing for the photograph at a shell midden under excavation at Sölager, northern Zealand. Reproduced with permission of the National Museum, Copenhagen.

period helps to explain the great similarity of excavation methods and reports that were published during the later half of the nineteenth century by some of the pioneering figures in archaeological excavation, such as Schliemann in Germany, Pitt-Rivers in England, Sophus Müller in Denmark, and Max Uhle in America. However, though by 1870 archaeology had been established as a discipline in its own right, it still lacked its own interpretative methodology, beyond that of find context and stratigraphy. This was to follow in the decades at the end of the nineteenth and beginning of the twentieth centuries.

CHRONOLOGICAL SYSTEMS AND EARLY INTERPRETATIVE FRAMEWORKS

The late nineteenth century and the early twentieth saw the development of chronological systems based upon the principles of typology. A major figure behind this was the Swede Oscar Montelius (Gräslund 1987), and the French Gabriel de Mortillet (for the early Stone Age: de Mortillet 1872). During the 1870s, at work in the National Museum in Stockholm, where all new finds were brought in, Montelius observed how objects changed gradually. By ordering the artefacts in so-called typological series, he was able to demonstrate in great detail the direction of typological change (Figs 1.11 and 5.2). By adding the evidence of closed find association and the stratigraphy of barrows, he could then prove his typological series to be chronological. A new method had been born, by combining existing methods with a new principle of typological change.

On this basis, Montelius was able in 1885 to subdivide the Nordic Bronze Age into six periods instead of the previous simple division between an Early and Late Bronze Age, a scheme further developed in his later publications (Montelius 1895a, 1895b, 1900, 1904). An important aspect of the new method was the plotting of all finds on a distribution map, to distinguish between spatial and chronological change. These maps established the first documentation of archaeological cultures that could be relatively dated against each other. Montelius also developed absolute dating by cross-dating down into the safe chronological harbours of the ancient civilizations in the East Mediterranean (Eggers 1959; and see Chapter 5). Later he applied his method to the bronze and early iron age cultures of Europe and the Near East (Montelius 1903 – which includes a description of the principles of typology that still reads as a methodological masterpiece). We should note, however, the practical background to these early methodological developments in Scandinavian archaeology and their later international spread. The National Museums in Copenhagen and Stockholm were the first to acquire a large representative sample of finds from the main periods that could be subjected to comparative and typological analyses. This explains the validity of many of the old chronological systems:

36

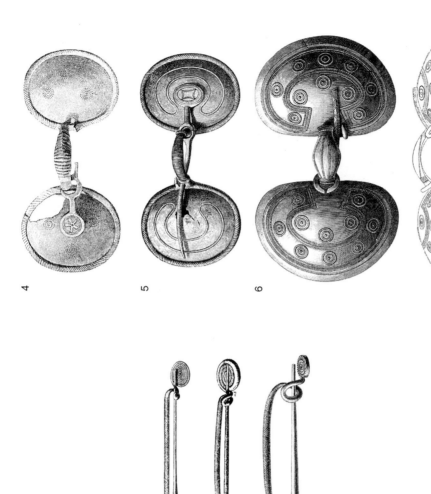

Figure 1.11 The typological method: the development sequence of bronze fibulae (safety-pins) postulated by Oscar Montelius for the Scandinavian Bronze Age. Reproduced from O. Montelius, *Die typologische Methode*, 1903. (See also Fig 5.2.)

chronological and cultural systems of comparable detail could not be established in many parts of Europe until the regional collections reached a similar level of find representativity during the first half of the twentieth century. We may, however, distinguish between an early phase lasting until the Second World War, and a later phase lasting into the 1960s. The latter was characterized by a more developed use of combination statistics and other quantitative methods, linked to demands for objectivity formulated by researchers such as Mats Malmer in Sweden, François Bordes in France and Waterbolk in the Netherlands, and culminating in David Clarke's *Analytical Archaeology* (1968).

Similar developments took place in America, although slightly delayed compared with Europe, and with a stronger emphasis on stratigraphy and the definition of culture areas (Willey and Phillips 1958; Willey and Sabloff 1974). This approach was applied systematically from 1915 onwards. The early classification period up to 1940 was mainly concerned with developing seriation, a quantitative typology that could be employed at the many settlement sites without good stratigraphies. Alfred Kroeber formulated elegantly the principle of order in civilization as exemplified by changes in fashion (Kroeber 1919), and archaeologists such as Irwin Rouse, Alex Krieger and James Ford refined and formalized the method during the 1930s and 1940s (summarized by Ford 1962; see also Meltzer *et al.* 1986). The culmination of the methodological framework of the culture area tradition was the publication in 1958 of the standard work by Willey and Phillips, *Method and Theory in American Archaeology*. With its complex mixture of methodological principles and principles of interpretation, it also represented the termination of this tradition.

Thus in the decades after 1900, the progressive application of the typological method meant that the archaeology of Europe and America came to be peopled with cultures and culture areas, horizons and traditions of all periods, which formed the background to the first interpretative endeavours (see Chapter 2). The increasing sophistication of the cultural prehistory that could be established in Europe by the typological method is well illustrated in the successive editions of Vere Gordon Childe's *Dawn of European Civilization* between 1925 and 1961. (Childe's profound contribution to the development of European prehistory through the twentieth century is explored in detail in Chapters 2, 5, 11 and 12.) In America, Julian Steward's *Handbook of South American Indians*, issued in six volumes between 1946 and 1950, is similarly illuminative.

Although the reconstruction of the past always had its place in archaeology since the early settlement excavations, the many new cultures represented an interpretative challenge that had to be met. In Europe this was most clearly seen by Gustav Kossina, who in a series of papers in the years shortly before 1900 formulated theoretical principles for the interpretation of cultures and cultural traditions (see Chapters 11 and 12). They were summarized in two interlinked propositions: 'clearly demarcated cultural provinces always correspond to specific peoples or tribes' (translated after Eggers 1959: 211). This was followed by another proposition, that continuity in archaeological cultures over time also implied ethnic continuity of a specific people or tribal group. These propositions were probably inspired by the European tradition in ethnography, which in similar ways defined 'cultural areas' and linked them to population movements, and to the diffusion of specific cultural traits. Such interpretative principles were widely applied in European archaeology to trace the history of historically known peoples such as Germans, Celts and Illyrians, although not without critical discussions (Jacob-Friesen 1928). When no names existed, in the case of the people of earlier prehistory, they were named by the archaeologists. In America a related interpretative practice developed, under the influence of the so-called Boas school in ethnography, which had many similarities to the European *Kulturkreislehre* (cultural area tradition). Culture was defined as ideas which were transmitted through generations and which might spread through diffusion. Society was perceived as consisting of multiple layers that were the result of the spread and acculturation of new cultural traits and ideas over time, which led to increasing cultural and social complexity (see also Chapters 11 and 12).

Thus in the period after 1900 archaeology developed a descriptive chronological-culture historical basis, with historical interpretations of cultural distributions, diffusions and traditions as the theoretical superstructure rooted in the theoretical framework of the Boas school in America and the *Kulturkreislehre* in Europe, but applied to a historical–philological tradition in Europe. After the Second World War disillusion and dissatisfaction with this theoretical framework led to its abandonment.

The development and refinement of the methods of typology represented the final step in the development of archaeology as an independent and scientific discipline. A new theoretical framework was not to emerge until after 1960, stimulated in the 1940s and 1950s, especially by Gordon Childe and Grahame Clark in Europe and Julian Steward and Leslie White in America. These developments were accompanied from the early 1960s by a series of methodological battles which drew up the borderline between good and bad archaeology, between history and archaeology, and between amateurs and professionals (see Chapter 2). Alongside these changes in interpretation and method, however, the period between the 1930s and 1960s was also characterized by a stronger emphasis on the importance of the cultural heritage, and of the role of settlement archaeology in it.

FROM NATIONAL SURVEYS TO NATIONAL HERITAGE

During the latter part of the nineteenth century, the global destruction of monuments led to a growing recognition among archaeologists and nation-states that new measures needed to be taken to preserve the archaeological heritage *in situ*.

Museums had preserved the movable heritage, while at the same time the unmovable heritage – monuments and sites in the landscape – were being destroyed at an accelerating pace. Although large-scale campaigns of barrow excavation were initiated all over Europe, it soon became clear that this only accounted for a fragment of the lost knowledge. More extensive and systematic methods of documentation had to be applied in order to preserve a record of the full range of archaeological monuments and sites before it was too late.

Thus the decades around the turn of the century were characterized by systematic efforts to make inventories of archaeological monuments and sites, and to restore and protect (either by voluntary action or through legislation) a portion of the remaining monuments, mostly the more visible ones such as, in northern Europe, barrows, hill-forts, and standing ruins. In Denmark, work started as early as 1873, whilst in England the Royal Commission on Historical Monuments was founded in 1911. By the beginning of the twentieth century, regional and national registers were emerging in many countries, corresponding to the national and regional museums. The new registers were recorded on the modern topographical maps that were being produced in the second half of the nineteenth century, often at scales as detailed as 1:20,000 (Larsen 1992).

From the turn of the century onwards, the mapping of this vast material formed the basis for the first archaeological analyses of settlement patterns. In Denmark, for example, the mapping of more than 60,000 barrows and several thousand megaliths allowed Sophus Müller to document the basic layout of neolithic and bronze age settlement structures (Müller 1904), and there were similar studies in many other countries. This new emphasis on settlement patterns based on the visible monuments naturally led on to a new emphasis on settlement sites, their discovery, and excavation. New excavation methods were developed to uncover large settlement sites, such as by Mortimer Wheeler at Maiden Castle in England and Mohenjo-Daro in India (Wheeler 1954), and by Gudmund Hatt on the early iron age villages in Denmark (Hansen 1984), but it was only after 1960 that the potential of settlement excavations was realized with the use of machines for open-area excavation and the application of the techniques of natural science (see Chapter 4). By the 1960s in both Europe and America, regional settlement projects based on the concept of systematic field surveying were setting new standards for archaeological work, expanding the principal focus of fieldwork from the archaeology of the dead to the archaeology of the living (see Chapter 13). Major contributors to this movement were, in northern Europe, Therkel Mathiassen's Northwestern Jutland project (Mathiassen 1948), and in America, Gordon Willey's Viru Valley project (Willey 1953). In Germany, Kossina's approach was replaced after the Second World War by a new *Siedlungsarchäologie*, explicitly formulated in the new journal *Archaeologica Geographica*, with leading figures such as Herbert Jahnkuhn, Georg Kossack and Rolf Hackmann. However, it reflected a general trend that was paralleled in England by J. G. D. Clark (for example: Clark 1952), in Czechoslovakia by B. Soudsky (Audouze and Leroi-Gourhan 1981) and in Holland by A. E. van Giffen (Waterbolk 1981).

The fact that these theoretical and methodological developments only became dominant in the second half of the twentieth century was due to several factors. One of them was the development of new protective legislation (see Chapter 10), which formed the basis for the expansion of rescue archaeology. In fact, from the late nineteenth century, strategies for conservation had stimulated developments in the compilation of monument inventories and in field surveying that had gradually opened up new avenues of archaeological information and interpretation. Another contributing factor were developments in the natural sciences, for example in pollen analysis, with the possibilities this opened up for reconstructing vegetational and environmental history, and in the study of bones and seeds, with similar importance for the investigation of subsistence (see Chapters 6 and 14). Major questions such as the introduction of farming could now be addressed from an ecological perspective, as exemplified in the influential work of Johannes Iversen using pollen analysis to identify the *landnam* or land colonization of early farmers (Iversen 1941) and the interdisciplinary excavations of the early farming village of Jarmo in Iraq directed by Robert Braidwood during the 1950s (Braidwood and Howe 1960), as well as Grahame Clark's classic investigation of a mesolithic hunter-fisher-gatherer site at Star Carr in northern England (Clark 1954). The rapid development of such techniques in the second half of the twentieth century, and over the same period of all the other techniques of archaeological science for analysing artefacts (Chapter 9) as well as organic remains, and to date them (Chapter 5), revolutionized the practice of archaeology – a comparison of the range and content of the papers in the 1963 and 1969 editions of *Science and Archaeology* (Brothwell and Higgs 1963, 1969) exemplifies how archaeological science was being transformed in the 1960s. These developments were also intimately associated with the profound impacts on the discipline of the successive theoretical frameworks described in the next chapter.

However, along with these dramatic transformations in methods and theories there have been developments as powerful in the whole organizational framework of archaeology and in its role in society (Cleere 1984, 1989; Kristiansen 1996b). It is paradoxical that it is only during the last decade that archaeology is beginning critically to examine and understand the deep historical connections between national heritage, national ideology, and archaeological practice (Atkinson *et al.* 1996; Diaz-Andreu and Champion 1996; Kohl and Fawcett 1995; Schnirelman 1996). It suggests that archaeology still has a long way to go before it is able to interpret and understand not only the past but also its own foundations in the present (Graves-Brown *et al.* 1996; Pinsky and Wylie 1989; Vargas and Sanoja 1993; see also Chapter 10). The development of archaeology as a historical discipline has been determined by its role at the interface between science and the humanities, history and prehistory, knowledge and interest, past and present, nationalism and internationalism, management and research. Each of these relationships deserves to be studied from a historical perspective; only then will a more complete understanding of archaeology's own history emerge.

REFERENCES

Aarbøger Nordisk Oldkyndighed (1988) Anniversary collection of articles on Christian Jürgensen Thomsen.

Abramowicz, A. (1983) *Dzieje Zainteresowan starozytniczych w Polsce* (*History of Antiquarianism in Poland*), two volumes, Wroclaw: Zaklad Narodowy Imiena Ossolinskich.

Adhémar, J. (1996) *Influences antiques dans l'art du moyen-age français* (2nd edition), Paris.

Arce, J. and Olmos, R. (eds) (1991) *Historiografia de la Arqueologia y de la Historia Antigua en Espana (siglos XVII–XX)*, Madrid: Ministerio de Cultura, Instituto de Conservacion y Restauracion de Bienes Culturales.

Atkinson, J., Banks, I. and O'Sullivan, J. (eds) (1996) *Nationalism and Archaeology*, Glasgow: Cruithne Press.

Audouze, F. and Leroi-Gourhan, A. (1981) 'France: a continental insularity', *World Archaeology* 13 (2): 170–89.

Beaune, C. (1985) *Naissance de la Nation France*, Paris: Gallimard.

Berghaus, P. (ed.) (1983) *der Archäologe*, Münster: Graphische Bildnisse aus dem Porträtarchiv Diepenbroick, Landschaftsverband Westfalen-Lippe.

Braidwood, R. and Howe, R. (1960) *Prehistoric Investigations in Iraqi Kurdistan*, Chicago: University of Chicago Press.

Brattli, T. (1993) 'Evolusjonismen og det Moderne. Ein Analyse av Tilkomten av Arkeologien som Vitskapleg Disiplin', Tromsø: University of Tromsø, unpublished Ph.D. thesis.

Brothwell, D. and Higgs, E. S. (eds) (1963) *Science in Archaeology*, London: Thames and Hudson.

Brothwell, D. and Higgs, E. S. (eds) (1969) *Science in Archaeology* (2nd edition), London: Thames and Hudson.

Buckland, D. (1823) *Reliquiae Diluvianae*, London: John Murray.

Buffon, G. L. de (1776) *Les Epoques de la Nature, Tome XXIX de l'Histoire Naturelle Générale et Particulière*, Paris: Imprimerie Royale.

Caylus, Compte de (1752–68) *Recueil d'Antiquities Egyptiennes, Erusques, Grecques, Romaines et Gauloise*, Paris: Saillant.

Chamberlain, R. (1983) *Loot. The Heritage of Plunder*, London: Thames and Hudson.

Chang, K. C. (1986) *The Archaeology of Ancient China*, New Haven: Yale University Press.

Childe, V. G. (1925) *The Dawn of European Civilization*, London: Routledge and Kegan Paul (six editions up to 1961).

Christenson, A. L. (ed.) (1989) *Tracing Archaeology's Past. The Historiography of Archaeology*, Carbondale: Southern Illinois University Press.

Clark, J. G. D. (1952) *Prehistoric Europe – the Economic Basis*, London: Methuen.

Clark, J. G. D. (1954) *Excavations at Star Carr*, Cambridge: Cambridge University Press.

Clarke, D. (1968) *Analytical Archaeology*, London: Methuen.

Cleere, H. (ed.) (1984) *Approaches to the Archaeological Heritage*, Cambridge: Cambridge University Press.

Cleere, H. (ed.) (1989) *Archaeological Heritage Management in the Modern World*, London: Unwin Hyman, One World Archaeology 9.

Cohen, C. and Hublin, J.-J. (1989) *Boucher de Perthes, 1788–1868 et les Origines Romantiques de la Préhistoire*, Paris: Belin.

Colt Hoare, R. (1810–12) *A History of Ancient Wiltshire*, London.

Constantine, D. (1984) *Early Greek Travellers and the Hellenic Ideal*, Cambridge.

Cuvier, G. L. C. F. D. (1801) 'Extract d'un ouvrage sur les espèces de quadrupèdes . . .', *Journal de Physique* LII: 253–57.

Daniel, G. E. (1964) *The Idea of Prehistory*, Harmondsworth: Penguin.

Daniel, G. E. (1967) *The Origins and Growth of Archaeology*, Harmondsworth: Penguin.

Daniel, G. E. (1975) *150 Years of Archaeology*, London: Duckworth.

Daniel, G. E. (1981) *Toward a History of Archaeology*, London: Thames and Hudson.

Daniel, G. E. and Renfrew, C. (1986) *The Idea of Prehistory*, Edinburgh: Edinburgh University Press.

de Broglie, E. (1891) *La Société de l'Abbaye de Saint Germain des près au XVIII° siècle. Bernard de Montfaucon et les Bernardins*, Paris.

Diaz-Andreu, M. and Champion, T. (eds) (1996) *Nationalism and Archaeology in Europe*, London: University College London Press.

Eggers, H. J. (1959) *Einführung in die Vorgschichte*, München: R. Piper and Co. Verlag.

Esper, J. F. (1774) '*Descriptions des zoolithes . . .*', Nürnberg.

Etienne, R. and Etienne, F. (1990) *La Grèce Antique. Archéologie d'Une Découverte*, Paris: Gallimard.

Fischer, A. and Kristiansen, K. (eds) (in press) *The Birth of Ecological Archaeology*, Sheffield: Sheffield Academic Press.

Ford, J. A. (1962) *A Quantitative Method for Deriving Cultural Chronology*, Technical Manual 1, General Secretariat, Organization of American States, Washington, DC: Pan American Union.

Franz, L. (1945) *Goethe und die Urzeit*, Innsbruck: Innsbrück Universitäts Verlag.

Frere, J. (1800) 'An account of flint weapons discovered at Hoxne in Suffolk', *Archaeologia* 13: 204–5.

Gaetghens, T. W. (ed.) (1986) *J. J. Winckelmann, 1717–1768*, Hamburg.

Gassendi, P. (1641) *Viri illustris Nicolai Claudii Fabricii de Peiresc senatoris aquisextiensis vita*, Paris.

Gomaà, F. (1973) *Chaemwese, sohn Ramses II und hoher priester von Memphis*, Wiesbaden.

Grafton, A. (1993) *Rome Reborn. The Vatican Library and Renaissance Culture*, Washington: Library of Congress.

Gräslund, B. (1987) *The Birth of Prehistoric Chronology. Datings Methods and Dating Systems in Nineteenth Century Scandinavian Archaeology*, Cambridge: Cambridge University Press.

Graves-Brown, P., Jones, S. and Gamble, C. (eds) (1996) *Cultural Identity and Archaeology. The Construction of European Communities*, London: Routledge.

Grayson, D. K. (1983) *The Establishment of Human Antiquity*, New York: Academic Press.

Greene, K. (1996) *Archaeology: an Introduction*, London: Batsford.

de Grummond, N. T. Thomson (ed.) (1996) *An Encyclopedia of the History of Classical Archaeology*, Westport: Greenwood Press.

Guidi, A. (1988) *Storia della Paletnologia*, Rome: Laterza.

Gummel, H. (1938) *Forschungsgeschichte in Deutschland, Die Urgeschichtsforschung und Ihre*

Historische Entwicklung in der Kulturstaaten der Erde herausgegeben von Karl Hermann Jacob-Friesen, Berlin: Walter de Gruyter.

Hansen, S. S. (1984) 'Gudmund Hatt – the individualist against his time', *Journal of Danish Archaeology* 3: 164–69.

Hildebrandt, B. (1937) *C. J. Thomsen och hans lärda förbindelser i Sverige 1816–1837, bidrag till den Nordiska forn-och Hävdaforskingens Historia*, 2 volumes (*C. J. Thomsen and his Scholarly Relations in Sweden, 1816–1837. Contribution to the History of Nordic Archaeology and the History of Research*), Stockholm: Wahlström and Widstrand.

Hooke, R. (1665) *Micrographia*, London: Martyn and Allestry.

Hooke, R. (1669) *Lectures and Discourses on Earthquakes*, London: Martyn and Allestry.

Hooke, R. (1705) *The Posthumous Work of Thomas Hooke* (edited by R. Waller), London: Smith and Walford.

Hunter, M. (1975) *John Aubrey and the Realm of Learning*, London: Duckworth.

Iversen, J. (1941) 'Land occupation in Denmark's Stone Age', *Danmarks Geologiske Undersøgelse* 2 (66): 1–68.

Jacob-Friesen, K. H. (1928) *Grundfragen der Urgeschichtsforschung. Rassen, Völker und Kulturen*, Hildesheim: August Lax.

Jenkins, I. (1992) *Archaeologists and Aesthetes*, London: British Museum Press.

Jensen, J. (1992) *Thomsens Museum. Historien om Nationalmuseet*, Copenhagen: Gyldendal.

Jomard, E. (1809–22) *Receuil des Observations et des Recherches Qui Ont Étés Faites en Egypte Pendant l'Expedition de l'Armée Française*, Paris.

Kendrick, T. D. (1950) *British Antiquity*, London: Methuen.

Kenrick, J. (1850) *Ancient Egypt under the Pharaohs*, London.

Klindt-Jensen, O. (1975) *A History of Scandinavian Archaeology*, London: Thames and Hudson.

Kohl, P. and Fawcett, C. (eds) (1995) *Nationalism, Politics and the Practice of Archaeology*, Cambridge: Cambridge University Press.

Kristiansen, K. (ed.) (1985) *Archaeological Formation Processes. The Representativity of Archaeological Remains from Danish Prehistory*, Copenhagen: The National Museum Press.

Kristiansen, K. (1996a) 'The destruction of the archaeological heritage and the formation of museum collections. The case of Denmark', in W. D. Kingery (ed.) *Learning from Things. Method and Theory of Material Culture Studies*, Washington, DC: Smithsonian Institution Press: 89–101.

Kristiansen, K. (1996b) 'Old boundaries and new frontiers. Reflections on the identity of archaeology', *Current Swedish Archaeology* 4: 103–22.

Kroeber, A. (1919) 'On the principle of order in civilizations as exemplified by changes of fashion', *American Anthropologist* 21 (3): 235–63.

Kühn, H. (1976) *Geschichte der Vorgeschichtsforshung*, Berlin: Walter de Gruyter.

Laming-Emperaire, A. (1964) *Origines de l'Archéologie Préhistorique en France*, Paris: Picard.

Lapeyrère, I. (1655) *Preadamitae, Sive Exercitatio super Versibus Duodecimo, Decimotertio et Decimoquarto, Capitiis Quinti Epistolae D. Pauli ad Romanos*, Amsterdam: Elsevier.

Lapeyrère, I. (1663) *Relation de l'Islande*, Paris: Jolly.

Larsen, C. U. (ed.) (1992) *Sites and Monuments: National Archaeological Records*, Copenhagen: National Museum of Denmark.

Larsen, M. T. (1997) *The Conquest of Assyria. Excavations in an Antique Land*, London: Routledge.

Legg, R. and Fowles, J. (eds) (1980) *John Aubrey, Monumenta Britannica*, Milborne Port: Dorset Publishing Company.

Lundbech-Culot, K. (in press) 'Influence de l'archéologie danoise sur la préhistoire française au XIXe siècle', Paris: Centre Alexandre Koyré Histoire des Sciences et des Techniques: Ecoles et Styles Nationaux de Recherche dans l'Archéologie Préhistoire Européenne (Journée d'etude 22.11.94).

Lyell, C. (1830–33) *Principles of Geology*, London: John Murray.

Malina, J. and Vasicek, Z. (1990) *Archaeology Yesterday and Today*, Cambridge: Cambridge University Press.

Marsden, B. (1983) *Pioneers of Prehistory, Leaders and Landmarks in English Archaeology (1500–1900)*, Ormskirk: Heskett.

Mathiassen, T. (1948) *Studier over Vestjyllands Oldtidsbebyggelse*, Copenhagen: National Museum of Denmark.

Meltzer, D., Fowler, D. and Sabloff, J. (eds) (1986) *American Archaeology, Past and Future: a Celebration of the Society for American Archaeology 1935–1985*, Washington, DC: Published for the Society for American Archaeology by the Smithsonian Institution Press.

Mennung, A. (1925) *Über die Vorstufen der Prähistorischen Wissenschaft im Altertum und Mittelalter*, Schönebeck a. Elbe: Veröffentlichung der Gesellschaft für Vorgeschichte und Heimatkunde des Kreises Calbe.

Mercati, M. (1719) *Metallotheca Opus Postumum*, Rome: Vatican Archive.

Montelius, O. (1885) 'Sur la chronologie de l'Age du Bronze, spécialement dans la Scandinavie', *Matériaux*.

Montelius, O. (1895a) *Les Temps Préhistoriques en Suede et dans les Autres Pays Scandinaves*, Paris.

Montelius, O. (1895b) *La Civilisation Primitive en Italie depuis l'Introduction des Métaux*, Stockholm: Imprimerie Royale.

Montelius, O. (1900) *Die Chronologie der ältesten Bronzezeit in Nord-Deutschland und Skandinavien*, Brunswick.

Montelius, O. (1903) *Die Typologische Methode. Die älteren Kulturperioden im Orient und in Europa*, Stockholm: Im Selbstverlage des Verfassers.

Montelius, O. (1904) *La Civilisation Primitive en Italie depuis l'Introduction des Métaux*, Stockholm: Imprimerie Royale.

Montfaucon, B. de (1719–24) *L'Antiquité Expliquée et Représentée en Figures*, 15 volumes, Paris: Delaune.

Mora, G. and Diaz-Andreu, M. (eds) (1997) *La Cristalizacion del Pasado: Génesis y Desarrollo del Marco Institucional de la Arqueologia en España*, Malaga: Servicio de Publicaciones della Universidad de Malaga.

Mortet, V. (1911) *Recueil de Textes Relatifs à l'Histoire de l'Architecture et à la Condition des Architectes en France au Moyen Age*, Paris: Picard.

Mortillet, G. de (1872) 'Classification des diverses périodes de l'age de la pierre', *Revue d'Anthropologie*: 432–35.

Müller, S. (1904) Vei og Bygd i Sten-og Broncealderen. *Aarboger for Nordisk Oldkyndighed og Historie*, Copenhagen: Royal Danish Society of Antiquities.

Nillson, S. (1837) *Skandinaviska Nordens Urinvanarg*, Lund.

Nillson, S. (1868) *The Primitive Inhabitants of Scandinavia*, London: Longman.

Nora, P. (1984–92) *Les Lieux de Mémoire*, 7 volumes, Paris: Gallimard.

Piggott, S. (1976) *Ruins in a Landscape: Studies in Antiquarianism*, Edinburgh: Edinburgh University Press.

Piggott, S. (1985) *William Stukeley, an Eighteenth Century Antiquary*, London: Thames and Hudson.

Piggott, S. (1990) *Ancient Britons and the Antiquarian Imagination. Ideas from the Renaissance to the Regency*, London: Thames and Hudson.

Pinon, P. (1991) *La Gaule Retrouvée*, Paris: Gallimard.

Pinsky, V. and Wylie, A. (eds) (1989) *Critical Traditions in Contemporary Archaeology. Essays in the Philosophy, History and Socio-Politics of Archaeology*, Cambridge: Cambridge University Press.

Pomian, K. (1987) *Collectionneurs, Amateurs et Curieux, Paris-Venise XVIe–XVIIIe Siècle*, Paris: Gallimard.

Popkin, R. H. (1987) *Isaac Lapeyrère*, Leiden: Brill.

Powell, A. (1963) *John Aubrey and his Friends*, London: Heinemann.

Reich, J. (1979) *Italy Before Rome*, London: Phaidon.

Renfrew, C. and Bahn, P. (1996) *Archaeology: Theories, Methods and Practice*, London: Thames and Hudson.

Rhode, C. D. (1720) *Cimbrisch-Holsteinische Antiquitäten Remarques*, Hamburg: Piscator.

Rocheblave, S. (1889) *Essai sur le Comte de Caylus*, Paris.

Rodocanachi, E. (1914) *Les monuments de Rome après la chute de l'empire*, Paris: Hachette.

Rossi, P. (1984) *The Dark Abyss of Time: The History of the Earth and the History of Nations from Hooke to Vico*, Chicago.

Schnapp, A. (1996) *The Discovery of the Past*, London: British Museum Press.

Schnirelman, V. A. (1996) *Who Gets the Past? Competition for Ancestors among Non-Russian Intellectuals in Russia*, Baltimore: Johns Hopkins University Press.

Settis, S. (ed.) (1984) *Memoria dell'Antico nell' Arte Italiana*, 3 volumes, Rome: Einaudi.

Sklenar, K. (1983) *Archaeology in Central Europe: The First 500 Years*, Leicester: Leicester University Press.

Stark, C. B. (1880) *Systematik und Geschichte der Archäologie der Kunst*, Leipzig: Engelmann.

Stemmermann, P. H. (1934) *Die Anfänge der Deutschen Vorgeschichtsforschung. Deutschlands Bodenaltertümer in der Anschauung des 16ten und 17ten Jahhundert*, Heidelberg: C. Trute.

Steward, J. (1946–50) *The Handbook of South American Indians*, 6 volumes, Washington, DC: Bureau of American Ethnology.

Street-Jendsen, J. (1985) *Christian Jürgensen Thomsen und Ludwig Lindenschmit. Eine Gelehrtenkorrespondenz aus der Frühzeit der Altertumskunde (1853–1864)*, Monographien Band 6, Mainz: Römisch-Germanisches Zentralmuseum.

Stukeley, W. (1740) *Stonehenge, a Temple Restored to the British Druids*, London: W. Innys.

Svestad, A. (1995) *Oldsakenes orden. Om tilkomsten af arkeologi*, Oslo: Universitetsforlaget Oslo.

Thomsen, C. J. (1836) *Ledetraad til Nordisk Oldkyndighed*, Copenhagen, Royal Danish Society of Antiquities.

Trigger, B. (1984) 'Alternative archaeologies: nationalist, colonialist, imperialist', *Man* 19: 355–70.

Trigger, B. (1989) *A History of Archaeological Thought*, Cambridge: Cambridge University Press.

Vargas, I. and Sanoja, M. (1993) *Historia, Identidad y Poder*, Caracas: Fondo Editorial Tropykos.

von Hohenheim, T. (1929) *Sämtlichewerke*, I, 12, Berlin.

Waterbolk, H. T. (1981) 'Archaeology in the Netherlands: delta archaeology', *World Archaeology* 13 (2): 240–54.

Weiss, R. (1988) *The Renaissance Discovery of Classical Antiquity*, Oxford: Blackwell.

Wheeler, R. E. M. (1954) *Archaeology from the Earth*, Oxford: Oxford University Press.

Wiell, S. (1996) '4. internationale Antropologi – og Arkaeologikongres i København 1869 bag kulissen (4. internationaler Antropologie – und Arkäologiekongress in Kopenhagen 1869 – hinter den Kulissen)', *Aarbøger for Nordisk Oldkyndighed og Historie*: 113–48.

Willey, G. R. (1953) *The Viru Valley Project*, Washington, DC: Bureau of American Ethnology, Bulletin 155.

Willey, G. R. and Phillips, P. (1958) *Method and Theory in American Archaeology*, Chicago: University of Chicago Press.

Willey, G. R. and Sabloff, J. (1974) *A History of American Archaeology*, London: Thames and Hudson.

Winckelmann, J. J. (1781) *Histoire de l'Art de l'Antiquité*, 4 volumes, Leipzig: J. G. I. Breitkopf, Huber translation.

Worm, O. (1643) *Danicorum Monumentorum, Libri Sex*, Copenhagen: J. Molkte.

Worsaae, J. J. A. (1843) *Danmarks Oldtid oplyst ved Olsager og Gravhøje*, Copenhagen.

Worsaae, J. J. A. (1849) *The Primeval Antiquities of Denmark*, London: Parker.

Worsaae, J. J. A. (1859) 'Om en ny Deling af Sten- og Broncealderen', in *Oversigten over De Kongelige Danske Videnskabernes Selskabs Forhandlinger i Aeret 1859*: 93–117, Copenhagen: Bianco Luno.

Wright, T. (1844) 'On antiquarian excavations and researches in the Middle Ages', *Archaeologia*: 438–57.

Zevi, F. (1987) 'Gli scavi di Ercolano e le antichità', *Le Antichità di Ercolano* (Napoli), pp. 9–38.

SELECT BIBLIOGRAPHY

A general survey of the beginnings of antiquarianism and the history of archaeology is given in Schnapp (1996), though the best comprehensive history is still by Daniel (1975). There are useful introductory pieces in Greene (1996) and Renfrew and Bahn (1996), and Berghaus (1983) is valuable for its iconography. For classical archaeology the sources are collected in Stark (1880) and Thomson de Grummond (1996), for medieval archaeology by Adhémar (1996) and Wright (1844), and for the Renaissance by Weiss (1988). Regional syntheses are given for America by Meltzer *et al.* (1986) and Willey and Sabloff (1974), for Britain by Piggott (1976, 1990), for China by Chang (1986), for central Europe by Sklenar (1983), for France by Pinon (1991), for Germany by Gummel (1938) and Stemmermann (1934), for Greece by Etienne and Etienne (1990), for Italy by Settis (1984), for Poland by Abramovicz (1983), for Scandinavia by Gräslund (1987) and Klindt-Jensen (1975), and for Spain by Arce and Olmos (1991) and Mora and Diaz-Andreu (1997). Detailed discussions include those by Christenson (1989), Daniel (1964, 1967, 1981), Eggers (1959), Grayson (1983), Guidi (1988), Kühn (1976), Malina and Vasicek (1990), Svestad (1995) and Trigger (1989); of these, Eggers provides a classical introduction to archaeology organized as a history of the discipline up to 1955, Kühn gives a detailed descriptive account, Guidi and Malina and Vasicek present the background to modern archaeology, and Trigger presents a more philosophical and theoretical overview. There is still a notable lack of books on the history and philosophy of the archaeological heritage.

2

THE DEVELOPMENT OF ARCHAEOLOGICAL THEORY

Explaining the past

Charles L. Redman

INTRODUCTION

As long as people have sought to know more about themselves, they have tried to understand and explain the past. In various cultures this enquiry has taken idealist forms, such as myth, religion, or tradition, while in other contexts the pursuit has been more empirical as exemplified by the study of history and archaeology. As is outlined in the previous chapter on the history of archaeology, the Western approach to knowing the past has taken many forms, but in a general sense has become increasingly empirical.

In trying to assess the approaches used to know the past, it is impossible to separate the study itself from the individuals pursuing the study and the social context within which these studies are undertaken. The critical awareness of the active role of the researcher into the past has led to a necessary evaluation of biases influencing attempts to know the past, while at the same time leading some scholars to be cynical of our ability to know the past in an objective sense. Recognizing full well the potential biases that personal and societal values may introduce into the study of the past, this chapter takes the optimistic position that the past can satisfactorily be known through archaeology and that it has been achieved with varying degrees of success by researchers of many persuasions.

The first half of this chapter will organize its review according to four major interpretive approaches that have dominated the work of most modern archaeologists: evolutionary; reconstruction of cultural histories; economic–ecological; and social–ideological (see also Trigger 1989; Willey and Sabloff 1980). While it is useful to examine each of these approaches separately, it will quickly become evident that most researchers adopt only one or the other but work with aspects of more than one.

The second half of this chapter reviews the development of archaeological theory from cross-cutting perspectives: that throughout its history, archaeologists have sought to become increasingly empirical (sometimes within a scientific framework), as well as the fact that our discipline is strongly influenced by the political and social context within which the research is conducted. The historical trends for these developments were largely covered in the previous chapter, so this chapter will briefly review the history of thinking and focus on the situation as it has evolved since 1960. Many of the following chapters expand on the issues dealt with here, for example the discussion of how archaeologists have approached the establishment of chronologies (Chapter 5), the study of culture (Chapter 11) and of forms of social organization (Chapter 12).

THE EVOLUTIONARY APPROACH

Three major intellectual currents reached fruition in the middle of the nineteenth century, setting the conceptual basis for archaeological interpretation. First, in his *Principles of Geology* (1836) the geologist Charles Lyell proposed his principle of superimposition, or uniformitarianism, that provided the framework for a scientific understanding of stratigraphy and a rational means to ascertaining the relative age of archaeological objects already being discovered. Second, Thomsen and Worsaae proposed the three-age system (Stone, Bronze and Iron Ages) as a chronological framework for classifying and displaying archaeological discoveries from northern Europe (see Daniel 1962). Third, Charles Darwin published his *Origin of Species*, outlining the evolution of living species and suggesting possible mechanisms for change. These conceptual innovations allowed a rational context to be formulated to explain the increasing number of archaeological discoveries, such as those of extinct fauna associated with tools of obvious human manufacture.

Contrary to the religious doctrine of the time, this revolution in thinking and the archaeological discoveries of the era were indicating a very long period of human and cultural development. Moreover, this record of the past included an unexpected diversity of societies awaiting fuller explanation. Many scholars of the late nineteenth century and the early twentieth therefore adopted an evolutionary perspective to explain the development of these many cultures over what was now appearing to be very long spans of time. This clearly was initially thought of as a parallel to biological evolution, where societies changed and evolved into new forms over time according to rational, but yet to be discovered, rules. As biological evolution could be interpreted as leading through a welter of lower life forms towards more complex forms, and eventually the human species, so cultural evolution could be taken to indicate that simpler societies eventually evolve into more complex societies or become extinct. Hence, the many societies of the past, and seemingly simpler societies of the ethnographic present, could be organized along an evolutionary trajectory leading to what was seen as the pinnacle of the evolutionary tree: modern western civilization.

Scholars from many countries adopted an evolutionary perspective, but it was in the United States that it gained greatest popularity. Archaeology there had grown with the expansion west and its academic marriage to the anthropology of American Indians. Because US archaeologists saw no historical connection between their society and that of the Indians they were studying, an evolutionary perspective gave value to what they were doing more than relying on normal social concerns with one's origins. In addition, by assuming an evolutionary perspective, there is an implicit notion that a society's position along this evolutionary trajectory related to how advanced or backward it was, with the expanding western civilizations being perceived as far above indigenous Indian cultures.

Best known of the early American evolutionists was Lewis Henry Morgan, who wrote *Ancient Society* in 1877. Based primarily on ethnographic information and what was then known archaeologically of house forms, community size, and technology in use, Morgan posited a three-stage sequence of Savagery, Barbarism, and Civilization. Although this was a very general framework, it provided a conceptual approach to the diverse American Indian evidence as well as being used in many other parts of the world. The implication was that people in many, if not all, parts of the world had been and were still moving through a uniform sequence of cultural development. This sequence had evolved through its full trajectory in parts of the Old World, while European discovery of the Americas and elsewhere had revealed societies at various positions along this trajectory. This perspective gave scientific value to studying the 'simpler' societies of the Americas, because they in some ways represented what may have happened during earlier epochs on the trajectory to western civilization.

Vere Gordon Childe can be credited with integrating more than one perspective into his monumental works on prehistory, but it is clear that evolutionism was of special interest to him. In his book *Social Evolution* (1951), he adopts Morgan's three stages and adds his own strongly materialistic ideas, which clearly were influenced by Marxist writings. Childe sees parallels in the beginnings and ends of the developmental sequences he examines, but divergences in the paths taken to civilization. He also suggested that the differences in the sequences of social institutions were greater than those observed in the economic systems. He concluded that his empirical observations of the evidence of archaeology 'vindicated' the use of cultural evolution as an interpretive framework for the past.

Cultural evolution was to find opponents as well as advocates and went out of fashion in the period between the two world wars. However, evolutionary ideas were to re-emerge in American archaeology and their renaissance can be traced to the works of Julian Steward and Leslie White (for example: Steward 1955; White 1959). Steward's overall objective was to discover regularities among cultures. His approach focused originally on seeking similar adaptations to similar environments and then observing whether regularities existed in other aspects of the society. This led Steward to combine evolutionism with the observation that there were similar cultural responses to similar environments in widely separated geographical situations. He identified the most important elements of these cultures with respect to their adaptations as being their technology, economic system, and the social institutions that comprised their 'culture core'. Seeing parallel, historically distinct, trajectories towards complex society he posited a multilinear evolutionary scheme as at the heart of culture change.

At roughly the same time, Leslie White was promoting the use of an evolutionary perspective for anthropologists. Unlike Steward, who based his work on observed regularities, White's focus was on causation of development and, in particular, on a society's use of energy. He saw that the trajectory from what had been identified as simple to complex societies was paralleled by its increasing per capita consumption of energy. This was a strongly materialist perspective that focused on changing technology and the operation of integrated cultural systems rather than individuals.

A new generation of American archaeologists emerged who had been influenced by the ideas of Steward and White: they believed that the evolutionary perspective would allow them to attack the general issue of culture change from an empirical perspective. Betty Meggars, for example, actively defended evolutionary theory in her writings (1954), suggesting that archaeologists could accomplish more if they adopted this perspective than if they worked with competing paradigms. Robert Braidwood was not as outspoken an advocate of evolutionism, but organized much of his influential research and writing according to an implicit acceptance of this perspective. His most explicit article, 'Levels in prehistory' (1960), sought to order our knowledge of different regional sequences as the results of the combined influence of evolutionary and diffusionary forces. However, throughout his writings on the cultural stages that led from hunting and gathering through agricultural villages to urban societies, there is a clear, but seldom enunciated, reliance on cultural evolutionism.

More outspoken advocates of the neo-evolutionary perspective were Marshall Sahlins and Elman Service whose book *Evolution and Culture* (1960) redefined the contemporary Americanist approach to the subject. Drawing heavily on ethnographic evidence, the authors suggested that developments could be best understood if we separated concepts about culture change into 'General' and 'Specific' evolutionary processes. This biologically based model suggests that at a very broad level (hence the term 'General'), societies throughout the world seem to experience similar changes and to develop in a basically parallel form. However, the familiarity with both the ethnographic and archaeological record demonstrated that the actual trajectories of culture change in each region often were significantly different in response to environmental, social, or historical factors. Looking at the survival and failure of numerous societies, Sahlins and Service proposed that two 'laws' could be used to predict the behaviour of societies. First, the Law of Cultural Dominance indicates that societies with more effective adaptive systems spread geographically. Second, the Law of Evolutionary Potential suggests that those societies that retain a greater range of adaptive alternatives within their cultural inventory have a greater chance of survival, while conversely those who become very specialized are more likely to fail over time.

Service went on to define what he perceived as the four basic forms of community organization in his book *Primitive Social Organization* (1962; see also Service 1975). Although the evolutionary mechanisms that would lead one form to evolve into the next were not the subject of the book, this typology of community forms has formed the basis of many subsequent studies from an evolutionary perspective, such as Colin Renfrew's treatment of chiefdoms in Britain (1974) and Sanders and Price's book *Mesoamerican: The Evolution of a Civilization* (1968).

An evolutionary perspective was one of the fundamental elements in Lewis Binford's early reformulations of archaeological theory that has come to be known as New Archaeology (Binford 1962, 1964, 1965). He referred directly to Leslie White and made a strong point about how archaeologists should seek to understand the evolutionary processes 'behind' culture change and not simply the regularities in the products these processes produced. Kent Flannery (1972a) and Fred Plog (1974) put forward two compelling examples of evolutionary formulations within the New Archaeology paradigm, although they adopt quite distinct positions.

Flannery conceptualizes the rise of the state as a process of increased segregation and centralization within a society. Segregation is the internal differentiation and specialization of sub-systems of the society, while centralization is the linkage between the sub-systems and the highest-order controlling apparatus in the society (1972a: 409). Flannery outlines where he sees many archaeological and ethnographic societies belong on an evolutionary trajectory according to these measures. He then points out that an adequate explanation of the rise of the state would carefully distinguish between the *processes* of segregation and centralization, the *mechanisms* by which they take place, and the *socio-environmental stresses* that select for those mechanisms. Flannery adopts two evolutionary mechanisms from systems theorists to explain many of the changes that took place during the rise of the state, particularly in Mesoamerica. The first is promotion, by which a low-level special-purpose institution becomes a higher-level institution serving a more general purpose, often during a time of stress. The second mechanism is linearization, by which low-level controls are permanently by-passed by higher-level controls.

Plog formulates what he calls a 'dimensional model of change' by isolating the critical elements of change and describing their interrelationships (1974). He believes that 'certain variables critical to individual instances of change are also important to change in general' (Plog 1974: 10). Plog focuses on the Basketmaker to Pueblo transition in the American Southwest, that he suggests exemplifies the world-wide cultural transition called the Neolithic. He identifies 'growth' as the process at issue and empirically examines four dimensions: population, differentiation, integration, and energy. By seeking archaeologically observable measures of each of these dimensions and then evaluating their interrelationships statistically, Plog was able to posit which factors were associated with this major cultural change.

In order to explain the causes of changes such as these, Plog (1973) suggests that we should examine how cultures deal with variations. Following more basic evolutionary theory, he points out that variety is continually being generated in every human population: in fact, if left on its own, the natural trend would be toward greater and greater variety in the world. However, processes of selection are also acting within every population to limit the generation of variety and to produce a modal pattern of behaviour. Some selective pressures are related to the environment, others emanate from our biology, while many are culturally created. For Plog, an explanation of an evolutionary culture change would be based on an understanding of the special forces that govern variety generation and selection within a particular culture and how they operate, particularly in the face of a changing environment.

Robert Dunnel is a strong advocate of an evolutionary perspective, but he urges archaeologists to abandon the tenets of cultural evolutionism and return to a more directly biological version (Dunnel 1971, 1980). He believes that within each society there is a great store of variability with respect to key issues facing that society and that some equivalent of natural selection acts to select among that variability. Implicit in this approach is a minimization of the role of conscious choice and an avoidance of dealing with symbolic systems as important to our understanding. An example of this approach is David Rindos's theory on the origin of domestication, where the process is seen as mutualistic wherein the plants and animals are equally responsible as the humans (1984). The advocacy of biological evolutionary principles is an important movement, but has not attracted the majority of archaeologists who adhere to an evolutionary perspective away from the cultural evolutionary framework.

THE CULTURE–HISTORY APPROACH

Archaeology was born out of an attempt to extend our knowledge of the past beyond the frontier of history. This is especially true for the Mediterranean world, where biblical and classical writings provided an awareness of the precursors of western civilization, but few details of those societies. Hence, European and American scholars set off on a quest for their 'origins' on European soil and in the classical and biblical lands of the Mediterranean and Near East. Austin Layard sought the Assyrians of the Old Testament, Heinrich Schliemann searched for a historical basis for the Homeric poems, and Flinders Petrie was one of many who contributed to uncovering the origins of Egyptian greatness. More than anything, these early archaeologists can be thought of as explorers who found sites, objects, and sometimes written documents that informed directly about episodes of the past.

This newly found source of evidence on the distant past resulted in some trial syntheses of the prehistoric sequences of regions, but probably the most notable cultural historian of his era was V. Gordon Childe. Although a field archaeologist himself, Childe's greatest accomplishments came through a series of books and articles in which he synthesized what was known of world prehistory, with particular emphasis on the rise of civilization in the Near East (1934) and the growth of European societies (1925). The key to Childe's success was his ability to bring together the variety of archaeological evidence available with a powerful logic based on an understanding of human history and behaviour. He wrote with a broad brushstroke, treating broad areas and vast spans of time, while pointing to particularly crucial episodes in the human career, such as the 'agricultural' and 'urban' revolutions – terms he coined (Childe 1936, 1942, 1951; see also Chapters 21 and 23). His works were logical and interesting, although sometimes short on empirical underpinnings. However, many of his reconstructions, speculative at the time, still appear to be reasonable even in the face of a half century or more of additional research.

Many other European scholars focused on the prehistory of their own continent, a subject with a huge audience, both lay and scholarly. Some, like Stuart Piggott (1965), sought to explain history from a technological/economic basis, while others like Colin Renfrew (1973) have defended Europe's independent development from those who saw all innovations coming from the Near East. Others, like David Clarke (1972), who are best known for their theoretical writing, spent most of their energies on historical studies and reconstructions.

The rationale for archaeology as a means of reconstructing history has always been strongest among European scholars, but it attracted many adherents in America as well. The origin of interest in the prehistory of the United States may have involved a bit of antiquarianism and perhaps even some racial ideas; but as the amount of information on local sequences mounted, scholars developed an intrinsic interest in knowing the past better. The key discoveries that stimulated greater interest in a systematic approach to the pre-European history of North America came from evidence of a very long Indian presence there, the fact that there were geographically delimitable cultural manifestations, and that the archaeological record could not be simply explained by one group replacing another.

54

As early as the 1890s, the anthropologist Franz Boas argued for more detailed ethnographic studies at the local and regional level as part of what he was defining as the historical method (Boas 1896). Particularistic studies that eschewed evolutionism or any other integrating theory came to dominate American anthropology during the early twentieth century. In the absence of any theory that would explain the extant variability in the ethnographic record or how societies developed greater complexity, observed geographic differences were assumed to represent different positions on a developmental trajectory. This had a major impact on archaeological interpretation in that, following this approach, ethnographic examples of 'simpler' societies were taken as models for prehistoric predecessors of known historic societies.

A. V. Kidder (1924) and others had been conducting extensive fieldwork in the American Southwest, combining excavation evidence with interpretive insights gained from observations of contemporary Indian groups. Kidder proposed a regional synthesis identifying local cultural traditions and developmental periods that eventually was codified by regional archaeologists at a meeting held at Pecos pueblo. Scores of subsequent researchers have applied themselves to refining our understanding of these cultures, their accomplishments, and their chronology.

In the midwestern United States, a parallel approach to classifying the rapidly growing amount of archaeological material was taken under the leadership of McKern (1939). It was based on the straightforward assumption that differences in collections of objects from the same region should be attributed to different time periods. Furthermore, the system was hierarchical, allowing that differences through time and across space could exhibit differing degrees of similarity. With a methodological basis for handling diverse information from across broad regions, archaeologists set about reconstructing local histories in earnest.

Probably the culmination of historical reconstruction is reflected in Gordon Willey and Philip Phillips's *Method and Theory in American Archaeology* (1958). The authors suggested that historical reconstructions were an essential element of American archaeology, but as a stepping stone to the recognition of cross-cultural regularities and the eventual explanation of culture change. Focusing on the eastern half of the country, Willey and Phillips proposed five basic stages of development. They saw periodic influences entering these regions from Mesoamerica to the south, but they also credited the local societies with much of the impetus behind observed culture changes.

As with most Americanist archaeologists, Willey and Phillips emphasized historical reconstruction, not as an end in itself but rather as a stepping stone toward broader generalizations about human behaviour. To others, especially in Europe, historical reconstruction was the ultimate objective of archaeology. The subjects often were seen as direct ancestors and, hence, of unique interest to scholars and lay-people alike. In fact, most European scholars were trained in historiography and recognized the false dichotomy that American archaeologists had constructed between history and science. David Clarke in particular represented a British archaeologist who was concerned both with generalizing from archaeological data and with the explanation of complex historical situations (Clarke 1968, 1978).

The focus on the value of historical reconstructions based on archaeology has also led to two developments treated later in this chapter: post-processualism and national archaeologies. Post-processualism involves many elements, but key among them is a concern for the specific historical context of archaeological materials and the social context of the investigators. With the explosion of new nations from former colonies, there has been a parallel growth in interest in their indigenous heritages. This often involves cultures and periods that were not emphasized by the colonial archaeologists and have opened new domains of inquiry (as discussed in particular in Chapter 10).

ECONOMIC AND ECOLOGICAL APPROACHES

Economic and ecological approaches to explaining the past were direct responses to the nature of archaeological data and expectations about the lifeways of the past. Tools, containers for food, and food itself, were the most common items found by archaeologists. In addition, techniques were developing quickly to monitor the ways food resources were utilized and the nature of the ancient environment. Identifying different human adaptations to their environment became the central objective of many scholars, which led to a largely functionalist approach to explanation. For some, functionalism had proved too limiting and they sought to interpret their findings through the perspective of ecological systems.

Although intertwined with the two previous approaches, this perspective attained an identity of its own from its focus on subsistence strategies, human–land relationships, and exchange systems. The name most closely associated with bringing this perspective to modern archaeology is Grahame Clark. His basic premises were that archaeological findings should be studied in their environmental context and that reconstructing economic activities was a first step in studying the broader society. Clark assembled his views in his influential book *Archaeology and Society* (1939). In it, he argued that the primary function of a culture was to ensure the survival of a society; hence, virtually all aspects of a society would have some adaptive value that might be discovered by the archaeologist. Clark was also a field archaeologist and sought new methods for improving archaeological data recovery. He is best known for his excavations at the waterlogged mesolithic site of Star Carr (England), where he actively sought out organic material as well as stone artefacts; his work there is often cited as the paradigm for environmental archaeology. At roughly the same time, Clark published *Prehistoric Europe: the Economic Basis*

(1952), in which he summarized existing archaeological data on the economic development of Europe. The result of these studies and of Clark's efforts at training many talented students was that laboratory study and interpretation of biological remains from archaeological sites became a focus of activity. This was part of his larger effort to get archaeologists to broaden their focus beyond typologies and artefacts to the broader economic and social aspects of society.

Clark's pioneering work encouraged many others to focus their efforts on discovering prehistoric subsistence patterns and information on the broader economic realm. At Cambridge, this developed directly into a major project to explain the early history of agriculture, as well as the formulation of a 'site catchment' approach to interpretation (Higgs 1972, 1975; Vita-Finzi and Higgs, 1970; see also Chapter 13). The agriculture project emphasized the improved recovery and study of the residues of plant and animal foods as the key to understanding. Site catchment analysis involved the careful study of the micro-environments surrounding a site and the resources that would be available from each.

Among American archaeologists, the focus on environment and economy took many forms. In 1948 Walter Taylor had called for a conjunctive approach to archaeological interpretation that highlighted the functional relationship between many aspects of a society. This approach did not attract many adherents immediately, but was fundamental in the initial formulations of New Archaeology twenty years later. Building on Steward's and Childe's emphasis on the importance of irrigation agriculture for the rise of urban societies, Robert McC. Adams (1966) and William Sanders (1968) proposed new multi-variable theories. Sanders' idea rested on the productive advantage afforded by irrigation agriculture and the tendency for producers in different localities to specialize in the crops they produced, leading to an intra-regional exchange system. Adams saw the same factors at work, but also believed that irrigation agriculture would exacerbate the differentials in wealth and power among landholding groups and that control of long-distance trade would reinforce the emerging economic differences.

Control of trade and the establishment of artificially high values for particular goods was seen by some scholars as a key element in establishing the surplus value to support élites within a society. Flannery had pointed to the possibility that the exchange of élite goods to less developed groups in return for access to valuable raw materials might be a powerful factor in the growth of hierarchy among Central Mexican groups (Flannery 1972b, 1976). Some scholars adopted this idea of the importance of élite exchange, while others pointed to trade in more basic subsistence goods as the prime mover (Rathje 1971). Various combinations of local and long-distance trade, as well as movement of élite goods or basic commodities, have come to form the basis of many ideas on the operation of advanced societies in prehistory (Earle and Ericson 1977; Peacock 1977; see also Chapter 15).

Other environmental perspectives used by scholars in America include what Karl

Butzer has called 'contextual archaeology' (1980) and David Thomas's simulation of Great Basin subsistence strategies (1972). Butzer's approach focuses on the environmental context of a society and the ecological relationships it establishes. Availability of resources, possible climatic changes, and human impact on their surroundings all become central forces in understanding the growth and decline of particular societies. Thomas relied heavily on ethnographic observations of a historical situation to set up a very detailed model of a series of procurement strategies that prehistoric hunters and gatherers in the Great Basin may have utilized. These are defined in terms of the micro-environmental locale and the impact one has on the conduct of the other. The implications of this model were then compared to the actual archaeological data to provide insight into its validity.

THE SOCIAL ORGANIZATIONAL APPROACH

A fourth perspective includes those studies whose primary objective has been the reconstruction of prehistoric social organization. The close association of prehistoric archaeology with social anthropology in the United States has made that a logical objective for Americanists, but it also gained popularity with some Europeans as an effort to move beyond largely technological and economic explanations (see, for example, Bender 1978; James 1993; Renfrew 1984; and Chapter 12).

A focus on social organization can be seen as early as Lewis Henry Morgan's attempt at correlating changes in social organization with changes in house forms as the key markers in the overall evolution of society (1881). The rough equation of successive social forms (that is, kinship, residence practices, and community organization) with the evolution of prehistoric and early historic societies can be seen in the works of many of those adhering to an evolutionary perspective (Fried 1967; Service 1975; Steward 1955; White 1959).

The social organizational perspective took a new turn when it became adopted by a number of young archaeologists who would soon be called New Archaeologists. Their initial concerns were with explicit testing of ideas about prehistoric behaviour primarily by using what were interpreted as stylistic differences in ceramics. The origin for this school of 'ceramic sociology', as I have named it, probably can be most directly traced to the work of Constance Cronin (1962) in the American Southwest. An art historian and social anthropologist by training, she was employed to study the designs found on prehistoric ceramics from a variety of sites in Arizona. Her inference was that there were uniformities in design that were associated with each site, even over periods of time. This contrasted sharply with the idea that ceramic designs changed uniformly with the passage of time, and it led to the possibility that there might have been identifiable ceramic traditions that were very localized and passed on even within single sites.

This insight was picked up by various students at the University of Chicago, who under the influence of Lewis Binford were attempting to be more explicit about testing ideas in the archaeological record and utilizing statistics to test these ideas. Freeman and Brown (1964) demonstrated the statistical differences between ceramic assemblages from different rooms and room floors and fills. William Longacre, in his 1963 dissertation, attempted to show a correlation between ceramic design elements and possible social organizational patterns at a pueblo in east-central Arizona (1963, 1970). His fellow student James Hill further systematized this approach by using sampling procedures to select rooms to be excavated, multivariate statistics to examine ceramic distributions, and a more detailed testing procedure (Hill 1965, 1970).

Archaeologists studying regions outside of the American Southwest also began to look at ceramic evidence as potentially revealing aspects of prehistoric social organization. James Deetz (1965) argued that the increasing diversity of ceramic designs among neighbouring villages could be traced to a breakdown in traditional social relations due to the entry of Europeans into the middle Missouri River region. Similar changes were observed among upstate New York villages by Robert Whallon (1968).

These social organizational studies were built upon by some young scholars (Graves 1982; Leone 1968), praised by others (Aberle 1968; Watson *et al.* 1971), and criticized by some ethnographers (Allen and Richardson 1971; Friedrich 1970; Stanislawski 1969) and archaeologists (Dumond 1977; Muller 1973; Plog 1980; Schiffer 1976). The criticisms ranged from pointing out the problems with defining social residence rules, to questioning the statistics being used, to suggesting that the context of discovery of the ceramics may not represent meaningful prehistoric units. The overall impact was to discourage further efforts to discover prehistoric social organization, at least in so far as it meant kinship types and residence rules, particularly as they operated at individual sites.

The social organizational perspective survived the criticisms, but largely by taking somewhat different approaches. Studies of inter-community organization and interaction have thrived in the American Southwest (Hantmann and Plog 1982; Watson *et al.* 1980), as well as in Mesoamerica (Flannery 1976; Haviland 1970), and the Near East (Johnson 1972; LeBlanc and Watson 1973). Other scholars have productively focused on the nature of households and household production within communities as a key to understanding the past (Binford 1978; Kent 1984; Yellen 1977). Another perspective that is attracting widespread interest is the attempt by certain scholars to discern gender relations and gender-based activities within prehistoric communities as a way to improve our insight into major processes in the prehistoric record (Bender 1978; Conkey and Spector 1984; Gero and Conkey 1991; Wylie 1992; also see Chapter 12).

For others, the criticisms of the early residence studies did not dissuade a broad approach to examining social organization at all levels (see authors in Redman *et al.* 1978). Colin Renfrew publishing a collection of his own works gives it an overall title of *Approaches to Social Archaeology* (1984). To Renfrew and others who now pursue this approach, it has come to mean a broad concern with issues beyond technology, economics, and chronology in isolation; rather, the social forms that have governed societies and driven culture change are the ultimate objective of study.

THE NEW ARCHAEOLOGY AND ITS AFTERMATH

In the 1960s what was to become known as the New Archaeology emerged in the United States under the leadership of Lewis Binford. Related developments occurred in Britain and elsewhere and the discussion of archaeological theory was elevated to centre stage in almost every forum. From its localized beginnings, people appearing to be 'new archaeologists' were doing and claiming many things during the 1970s. By the 1980s, much of the theoretical literature of archaeology is devoted to bashing the 1970s and the target often turns out to be the so-called New or Processual Archaeology. While many of the attacks come from recent theorists who are attempting to replace it with post-processual archaeology (Hodder 1982b, Shanks and Tilley 1987), some criticism comes from within what was New Archaeology, even from the hand of its original champion, Lewis Binford (1983). If scholars from both outside and inside the theoretical developments of the 1970s are rejecting the New Archaeology, why do I focus the remainder of this chapter on it? The answer is very simple: for better or worse, it is *us*!

As Alison Wylie has said (1989), the New Archaeology of the 1960s quickly became everybody's archaeology in the 1970s. Most of today's faculty members and senior archaeologists were the people who, in one way or another, adopted the teachings of New Archaeology. Although most archaeologists did not claim to agree with all aspects of New Archaeology, nor could more than two or three people agree on what it was, virtually no one rejected it outright. Typically, each one presented her or his version, often using a New Archaeology text as a starting point for pedagogical purposes. Few wanted to be left out of the exciting new theoretical movement of those years, and New Archaeology was passed on to the succeeding generation of students who reached maturity in the 1980s and who are today's young professionals.

Criticisms now levelled against the New Archaeology of the 1970s do have merit, but by discounting that era as misguided, critics have overlooked its crucial importance. New Archaeology had an important historical role in the development of the field we have today, and it has continuing importance because it is still guiding archaeology's trajectory into the future. Equally troubling is that some critics ask us to reject the basic tenets of New Archaeology and to replace them with a system often called *Post-Processualist Archaeology*. I believe this is rhetoric which not only misrepresents the achievements of the New Archaeology of the 1970s, but also does not successfully articulate the potential contributions of its own position.

To put the New Archaeology into perspective, it is important to review the social context of the decades leading up to its development (something post-processualists would certainly advocate). In the first years following the Second World War, archaeology was still a small field, but by the 1950s and 1960s it was expanding rapidly and taking itself quite seriously. With the launching of Sputnik in 1957 there emerged a frenzy in the United States and western Europe to make all disciplines more 'scientific'. Great strides were made in bringing science into archaeology through new dating techniques, a multidisciplinary approach, early experiments with the use of statistics, and devoting substantial attention to increasing the precision of artefact classification. The 1960s provided the United States with both the optimistic Kennedy years, with an emphasis on science and the conviction that we were capable of accomplishing wondrous things, and the cynical Vietnam era. Coming on the heels of a decade of civil rights unrest, the widespread dissatisfaction with the Vietnam conflict in the late 1960s moulded a generation of young Americans who were distrustful of established authority. In academic life, there was an increasing emphasis on the environment, other cultures, and people-orientated disciplines. Anthropology and archaeology grew markedly because of these trends. Archaeologists were urged to become concerned with sociological issues: the people behind the artefacts.

It was during these decades of rapid change that many of the core concepts of the New Archaeology entered the literature. However, they were not, at first, assembled into a programme for action that attracted a solid following. Walter Taylor (1948) advocated the conjunctive approach with little effect, while Leslie White's evolutionism (1959) and Julian Steward's cultural ecology (1955) attracted some attention, though largely among cultural anthropologists. Albert Spaulding led a one-man campaign to bring science and statistics into archaeology (1953, 1960). But the individual whose work catalysed the New Archaeology movement was Lewis Binford, who incorporated these earlier lines of thinking, together with an explicit concern for scientific methods and field research designs. Much of Binford's thinking probably crystallized while he was at the University of Michigan, but it was during his relatively few years at the University of Chicago that he changed the direction of modern archaeology (see Binford 1972).

Among the keys to Binford's success was that he attracted a talented group of students who, under his direction, carried out innovative research projects. Binford himself wrote a series of powerful methodological articles setting the guidelines for the New Archaeology (1962, 1964, 1965, 1968), and his students filled in with substantive examples (Hill 1965; Longacre 1963; Whallon 1966). The publication in 1968 of the book *New Perspectives in Archaeology* (Binford and Binford 1968) marked the crossing of a threshold. New Archaeology was discussed and debated by an ever-increasing proportion of the field. Binford's New Archaeology caught on because its advocation of a scientific approach was timely and because it represented a major advance over the way things had previously been done. It should be noted, however, that the political climate of the late 1960s and early 1970s was important in fostering its widespread acceptance as well. There were three important 'political' elements to the New Archaeology that were right for the times: first, it was explicitly scientific; second, it demanded social relevance; and third, it rejected arguments based on authority alone, thereby providing a means for junior people to assail the establishment on an equal footing.

The advocates of the New Archaeology created their own momentum. Binford's writing became clearer, making his message accessible to more readers. Binford's students wrote compelling articles and got teaching positions at important universities, where they could directly influence a second generation of New Archaeologists. The attractiveness of an explicitly scientific approach and the teaching of New Archaeology by this cohort led new scholars to conduct further research re-examining the results of earlier investigations. In this way early studies laid the intellectual groundwork for later studies. This cumulative aspect to several lines of enquiry followed by New Archaeologists gave the field a special momentum that made it appear as if real interpretive progress was being made. Nowhere was this more clear than in studies of decorated ceramics, the 'Ceramic Sociology' that I referred to earlier (Cronin 1962; Deetz 1965; Graves 1981; Hill 1965, 1970; Leone 1968; Longacre 1963, 1970; Tuggle 1979).

If New Archaeology had all this going for it, why was it not universally accepted and why is it now out of style? There were, unquestionably, useful innovations in New Archaeology, but it was not entirely clear how a researcher operationalized it to achieve the desired results. The early emphasis in New Archaeology on seeking general laws of cross-cultural applicability set our sights high, considering the relatively mundane set of substantive accomplishments. This grand goal led to cynicism from outsiders and active debate among New Archaeologists themselves about how realistic their objectives were (Clarke 1973; Flannery 1973a; Isaac 1971). Exacerbating these reservations about the New Archaeology was the aggressive manner in which it was promoted, leading to a defensive reaction from many established scholars. Because of this, in its early years the New Archaeology was not taught, and I doubt if it was even discussed, at many of the most prestigious universities.

Despite doubts and opposition, there were relatively few articles opposing New Archaeology during its heyday, and those that did offered an olive branch by acknowledging some of its contributions (Trigger 1973). Especially among younger archaeologists, there were few who were not attracted to the New Archaeology. Most criticized a few aspects of it and claimed to be following their own version. In this way, they could adopt many of the convincing tenets of the new programme, yet they did not have to claim to be following Binford, who may have offended their senior faculty members.

In America one of the central tenets of New Archaeology was a rejection of culture history as the primary goal of the field; history was pejoratively associated with idiosyncratic details and regional chronology building. These activities were still valued, but only as means to a greater end – processual explanations. In Britain, however, those who appeared to accept many of the 'scientific' principles of New Archaeology did not reject history as their primary objective. This is probably due to the fact that archaeologists in Britain were trained in a modern historical approach based in the social sciences, and the connection of their prehistory to their history was quite obvious. David Clarke published *Analytical Archaeology* (1968) in the same year as Binford's *New Perspectives in Archaeology*, and it was taken by many as the outline of a sort of British new archaeology. Clarke himself clearly recognized the differences and in his own work kept to a strong trajectory of historical reconstruction. What he did emphasize in this masterwork was that up to this point archaeologists had failed to assemble a real body of method and theory that would allow their discipline to advance. He looked to sister disciplines for methods and associated theories that might set archaeology on the right path. Cultural geographer Peter Haggett (1965), numerical taxonomists Sokal and Sneath (1963), and system theorist Ross Ashby (1956) were repeatedly cited in Clarke's work and formed the methodological basis for his strongly functionalist approach. Although extremely influential through his writing and mentorship, Clarke died at a tragically early age in 1976 before he was able to react fully to the rapid theoretical developments of the era. His substantially revised second edition to *Analytical Archaeology* was published posthumously.

Few scholars today would still call themselves New Archaeologists, but much of the New Archaeology's programme has survived and has become the mainstream conduct of our field. Perhaps above any other influence, the New Archaeology's demand for rigorous archaeological methodology, both in formulating research designs for the field and analytical strategies for interpretation of results, has been fully accepted by almost all practitioners today. Which philosophical model is most appropriate is either ignored or a matter of quiet controversy, but it is without argument that researchers must be able to explain and support the methods chosen. There is now a universal expectation that explicit questions are to be formulated and a research design established before archaeological work is carried out. Also attributable to the New Archaeology is the recognition of the diversity of material needed to support an interpretive proposition and the resultant use of sampling in many aspects of field and laboratory work. Another enduring outcome of the increasing scope and precision desired for our observations has been the growing reliance on statistical procedures.

Related to the methodological changes brought by New Archaeology was the emphasis on the systemic view that culture is a series of interrelated sub-systems and on the importance of ecological relationships. This dovetailed nicely with the diverse datasets defined and sampled through extensive research designs. Emphasis on examining variability among datasets led many scholars to supplement traditional artefact typologies with attribute-based analytical systems, experimentation with artefact classes, data from allied sciences, and an understanding of the operation of material culture in a systemic context, which has, in turn, encouraged the pursuit of 'middle range theory' (see below, p. 65) and ethnoarchaeology.

I believe that New Archaeology also had an important impact on the professional structure of our discipline. New Archaeology's emergence coincided with a period of great growth in numbers of practitioners and university departments offering anthropology graduate degrees in America. Earlier, archaeological training was available in a limited number of universities where senior professors comprised the acknowledged establishment. Access to the establishment required training and apprenticeship under a senior scholar with an established reputation. This system, which is still dominant in many European countries, restricts access to professional positions and in some situations may inhibit intellectual innovations. The New Archaeology position, that new knowledge is validated through explicit testing rather than reference to authority, opened the doors for young unknown scholars to make significant contributions to the field. Such contributions became the major means of attaining credibility for young scholars and for programmes at universities without an established tradition in graduate anthropology.

Twenty-five years have passed since the heyday of the New Archaeology debates. Despite the shake-up that the new programme caused, New Archaeologists who were the *outsiders* of the 1970s now make up much of the establishment. Few people today are beating the drums of New Archaeology, but where have they all gone and what are they pursuing? Many of the people who matured professionally in the 1970s during the New Archaeology era are now involved in public archaeology, either through positions with government agencies or in conducting fieldwork for these units. Their methodological and philosophical focus has been on developing data recovery strategies and management principles. The New Archaeological emphasis on research design and hypothesis testing is fundamental in much of public archaeology today.

There also has been an expansion in the substantive domains pursued by anthropologically trained archaeologists. For some of us, it has meant carrying out fieldwork in countries that heretofore had not received much attention (McIntosh and McIntosh 1984; Redman 1986), or by expanding the study of complex societies where other disciplines have focused on only the élites to a more balanced, holistic treatment (Cowgill 1983; Fritz 1986; Marcus 1973; Wright 1969). Further developments have involved ethnoarchaeology, experimental studies, and other ways to gain insight into the meaning of the archaeological record, a series of approaches often called 'middle range theory' (Binford 1978; Raab and Goodyear 1984; Schiffer 1976). There has also been a renewed interest in the material of the archaeological record. Chemical and physical studies of ceramics are once again common after receiving little attention in the United States for forty years since their introduction by Anna Shepard (1955). These supplemental sources of information, combined with the objective of discovering differing sub-systems of behaviour, have prompted a re-evaluation of how artefacts and other information are analysed. The typological approach that yielded easily interpreted nominal sets of units is being supplemented by integrated, attribute-based systems that allow for multiple, over-lapping sets of interpretive results. This is also true of distribution studies, in which models and mathematical techniques are being borrowed from geography and ecology to allow for a richer description of the patterns that we discover.

If so much of modern archaeology is peopled with graduates of the 1970s, each with her or his own brand of New Archaeology, why is there so much commotion about Post-Processual Archaeology? And why do these theorists identify what they are doing as *replacing* 'processual' or New Archaeology? Who are these post-processualists?

POST-PROCESSUALISM

In America, for the most part, the post-processualists come from the ranks of the New Archaeologists of the 1960s and 1970s. There have always been members of the New Archaeology cadre who felt that the rejection of psychological and sym-bolic factors was too strong and that the workings of the mind and the style of the way people do things were inadequately treated in most New Archaeological works. James Deetz (1977), John Fritz (1978), Mark Leone (1982), and Margaret Conkey (1982), among others, believed that the New Archaeology agenda, as most often portrayed, did not do justice to the archaeological record and often misrepresented what could be accomplished. These scholars often derived their concern from having backgrounds in history, art, or belief systems. With their additional insights, these post-processualists saw how non-material domains of societies, downgraded by many New Archaeologists, were crucial in deciphering the past.

The birthplace of post-processualism, as well as the area of its greatest intensity today, is Britain. Just as Binford crystallized and led New Archaeology, Ian Hodder at Cambridge has been the central figure in post-processual studies (Hodder 1982b, 1986). Interestingly, Hodder's early contributions to archaeology were in the domain of quantitative methods and locational analysis (Hodder and Orton 1976). Hodder himself has said that he was led to the new way of thinking out of a frustration with the accomplishments of archaeology as it was practised (by which

65

he meant the version of New Archaeology defined by David Clarke). He found himself able to devise sophisticated quantitative methods to describe the distribution of archaeological artefacts or phenomena accurately, but he still did not have a solid idea about what those phenomena represented. This led Hodder in two directions: first, to investigate generalities about human existence; and second, to embark upon ethnoarchaeological studies in order to put the objects being investigated into a richer context.

Hodder soon attracted a substantial number of young British archaeologists to his way of thinking, as well as some Americans. There has been some ambiguity about who might acknowledge being a post-processualist, but for at least some time this programme appealed to some among those who were concerned with such diverse topics as Marxist archaeology, world systems approaches, critical theory, gender studies, and ethnoarchaeology. Each of these domains has found some support in Hodder's approach, but I believe that for the most part, each of them has maintained themselves as separate, although sometimes overlapping, pursuits. What one must recognize then is that the term 'post-processualism' does not represent a monolithic approach, but has come to signify a wide range of practices and that even the views of its primary advocate have evolved over time (Hodder 1987b).

The post-processual approach to archaeology has attracted a growing and very credible following. As much as I like New Archaeology, I concede that it has some significant shortcomings and that the post-processualists offer some worthwhile alternatives. I prefer to use the more descriptive title of Contextual Archaeology, as does Hodder (with due respect to Karl Butzer [1980], who previously used this term to refer to an environmental approach). Critical, symbolic, or structural archaeology are also useful terms to identify other varieties of what have more often been tied together under the single title of post-processual archaeology. I do not think processualism deserves a *post*, and I agree with Colin Renfrew (1989) who suggests that, if taken at their word, some would more properly be called *anti*-processualists.

Some of the more vocal adherents to this new movement disagree with archaeologists who view interpretation as a rational and objective method. They perceive New Archaeologists as focusing on objectivity and validation of things in the past, while practising their profession in the present. Hence, they argue, there is no objective archaeological record. Facts can be observed only via living individuals; therefore, facts about the past cannot be separated from the biases of the present-day observers. This relativistic position leads to historical pluralism in archaeological reconstructions and asserts that politics will inevitably enter archaeological interpretations (Shanks and Tilley 1987).

The essential point of these writers who emphasize the relativistic nature of data is that we must recognize the importance and the inseparability of the present–past dialectic that can also be seen as a subject–object dialectic. Their goal is to establish a *situated discourse* which, with appropriate respect for the gulf between the archaeologist and the past, attempts to consider the objects and events of the past in their full context. The most successful examples of these 'situated discourses' are with historical societies where many social and ethical linkages to the present can be brought to bear on evidence of the past (Hodder 1987a; Leone and Potter 1988). These relativists believe that the possibility for interpretive richness and the control of subjective intrusions offered by their approach are unobtainable via New Archaeology.

Having highlighted the importance of the perspective of the investigator, the more relativistically minded among the contextual archaeologists view the way that archaeologists interact with the archaeological record as an active interplay that is often manipulated and hence must be understood in order to be controlled. In this way, archaeological method can be seen as a 'style' that may involve politics, power, rhetoric, and perhaps even aesthetics. At its most extreme, these contextualists maintain that we are so bound up by our own perspective and style that we cannot know the past at all, but merely present our own views of the present as if they were an interpretation of the past (Miller and Tilley 1984).

There are numerous articles by contextualists that reinterpret an already-collected dataset from their perspective (Hodder 1982a, 1982b, 1986). They often begin by seeking a recognizable structural patterning in the archaeological data. In early studies, this often took the form of demonstrating spatial or typological 'polarities' in the dataset. The second step would be to relate these patterns to causes that are not normally cited by New Archaeologists. The source for these explanations often, but not necessarily, was from anthropological literature or ethnoarchaeological studies that the contextualist had been doing among nearby peoples. The final step might be to draw on information derived from the historical context and various general anthropological ideas that would enrich the original explanation and give it more plausibility. The principles and procedures of post-processualism should not be seen as an isolated phenomenon. It has parallels with approaches advocated by social anthropologists who focus on meaning or 'thick description' (Geertz 1973; Rabinow and Sullivan 1979; Sahlins 1981).

Contextualists are, despite their condemnation of it, descendants of the New Archaeology of the 1970s. Their own political agenda requires them to claim they are *post*-processualist, but their programme is in fact a logical offshoot of processualism. Moreover, many developments happening at about the same time within New Archaeology, including middle range theory as advocated by Binford and others, show how some of our trajectories are at least parallel (Watson 1986). The post-processualists' continuity with New Archaeology can be demonstrated in numerous areas.

First, post-processualists call for a *reflexive archaeology*, in which archaeologists must be concerned with how their *style* affects their conclusions. The New

Archaeology's first rule, however, was to have an explicit concern with methods and how conclusions were reached because data collection and interpretation were recognized to include subjective elements. Ironically, many of the original critiques of New Archaeology accused it of being over-reflexive (Clarke 1973).

Second, post-processualists say that it is essential to put the archaeological object in its context of ancient meaning. New Archaeologists could not agree more, but were less certain how to best achieve this. Contextualists have made some interesting new contributions in this area by seeking contextual relations more broadly, but their ideas are not different in kind, or in the intensity of their application, from the New Archaeology. Primary among the efforts of the New Archaeology was to see objects, features, and sites within their systemic and ecological contexts. Unfortunately, many examples of New Archaeology models reflected a rather simple, materialist–functional viewpoint. The key contribution of the contextualists is to expand their definition of systemic context to include broader symbolic and social domains, while attempting to avoid the pitfalls of a naïve application of functionalism.

Third, post-processualists say that knowledge comes from a dialogue between subject (us) and object (the archaeological record). Some see this as a dialectic involving an unbridgeable gap, whilst others see the subject and object as being inseparable. Both views do not believe that an objective interpretation of the past can exist. In the place of objective interpretations are politically or rhetorically motivated 'critiques' that reflect the investigator more than the object. For many years, some New Archaeologists have also been concerned about the use of archaeological data for political agendas (Ford 1973; Leone 1981). It is something to be sensitive to and to be made explicit in one's writings, but not something to inhibit moving forward.

Belief in the lack of objective reality is often diminished once an archaeologist spends substantial time doing fieldwork: archaeological objects are a lot more real out there in the dirt than they are when thought about from an armchair! However, as the contextualists rightly observe, fieldwork sometimes can lead to delusions in the other direction, fostering the belief that the work is extremely objective just because precise measures are used during fieldwork or laboratory analysis.

Fourth, an acceptance of the contextualist position that archaeologists cannot attain objectivity in their interpretations undermines the very basis of our research. At the extreme, some contextualists believe there is little chance of obtaining an objective view of the past with available approaches (see Miller and Tilley 1984). Because archaeological excavation is necessarily destructive of contextual relationships, if we do not have an effective method for understanding these relationships, it could be argued that all excavations should stop. Despite these relativist claims, the generation of systematically collected and carefully reported data has mushroomed in recent decades. The consistency of much of this material has led most scholars to accept it as a sufficiently objective set of data to serve as the basis for interpretations and further research.

Fifth, and probably the most important divergence between the approaches, is that some contextualists believe the New Archaeology's primary failing is its over-emphasis on validation and efforts to be objective (Shanks and Tilley 1989). Even if not espoused by all contextualists, I believe that this is a useful point for current New Archaeologists to ponder. In the early years of the New Archaeology, major concern with idea generation was explicitly rejected: the focus was on confirmation as the method of science. Ironically, in the same book about the New Archaeology in which Patty Jo Watson, Steven LeBlanc, and I (1971) heralded Carl Hempel's (1966) positivist focus on confirmation, we lauded Norwood Hanson's (1958) and Thomas Kuhn's realist (1962) treatments of the complexities of idea generation in the history of science. By presenting both, we overtly recognized the distinction between context of discovery and context of validation, without providing a means for integrating the first with the second. More energy should be devoted by scientific archaeologists to generating ideas and perceiving contextual relationships, but we should not reject efforts at validation and a systematic approach to being objective, replacing them with uncontrolled story-telling, as has been said of some extreme examples of contextual archaeology.

THEORETICAL PERSPECTIVES AND PROSPECTS

I would prefer to transfer this debate to the well-worn format of Science versus Humanities. What troubles me most about the current argument, as well as many earlier ones on this theme, is that it is not really a conflict; I believe the best possible solution would be integration, but the more likely resolution is coexistence (see Spaulding 1988). These approaches, each encompassing great diversity, are essentially complementary aspects of the study of the human condition. One of these approaches does not have to replace the other: I see them as *alternative systems of knowing*, each with its own contributions.

Among the reasons that New Archaeology emerged was to dispel a widespread belief that archaeology could advance as a science solely by achieving more precise measurement and not revising its faulty interpretive ideas. Another major reason for New Archaeology's formation was to combat the acceptance of plausible stories as the truth, as long as they were put forward by distinguished scholars. The need was seen for careful consideration and explicit justification of methods of enquiry and the results that were obtained: a scientific approach. A scientist assumes that the world is knowable, and that it operates in an orderly manner, which can be understood by reference to widely accepted rules or laws. Whether human phenomena are amenable to general laws, similar to those that explain the physical properties of the world, is yet to be demonstrated, but the pursuit of general principles, statistical as well as universal, remains the cornerstone of a social scientific approach. For archaeologists this has meant, among other things, a general acceptance of uniformitarian principles, not a preoccupation with precision.

There is a perfectly acceptable alternative path to knowledge, however, which for simplicity I will call humanistic knowledge. Acknowledging that there are extremely diverse approaches followed by those who call themselves humanists, I shall attempt only to characterize the practices of a substantial portion of the field. Like scientists, most humanities scholars also believe that there is a real world, but usually acknowledge the relativists' position that we come to know it only through the present. In fact, their explicit objective is often to enrich the present through perspectives generated by studying the past. Some post-processualists claim that this type of mixing of the past and the present while making interpretations is an inherent shortcoming of archaeology. To the contrary, I view this as the essential relevance of archaeology.

Many humanists do not seek a precise answer to what went on in the past, but rather are interested in opening a *dialogue* with the evidence we have of it. That dialogue is clearly reflexive, being between the evidence in the past and the scholar in the present, analogous to the situated discourse of the post-processualists. Testing, replication, and rigorously argued evidence are not requisite methods to many in the field of humanistic knowledge. This does not undermine the possibility of knowing the past, but it puts the work of many humanists in a perspective of not seeking a final truth, but rather seeking what is most convincing or stimulating. To the extent that humanists, too, claim to know the past as it was, they tacitly use interpretations that rely on uniformitarian principles.

The essential frustration many of us have had with the New Archaeology of the 1970s is that it raised our hopes for grand interpretive breakthroughs that have not occurred. The rigour, scientific method, and explicit approach of the New Archaeology were orientated towards verification, not creation of new ideas. In the earliest New Archaeological publications, science was explicitly defined as a verification procedure, not a hypothesis generation procedure (Binford 1968; Watson *et al.* 1971). Concern was not with the origin of an idea, only with its confirmation. Lacking a methodology for generating stimulating ideas and applying them to our data, New Archaeologists looked to other fields where there were already established laws, or at least promising ideas being applied. Once again, this was disappointing.

One solution to this problem was offered by the philosophers Wesley and Merrilee Salmon (1979), who had devised a new viewpoint on how social science operates. As one of their test cases, they observed what New Archaeologists were actually doing, rather than what they said they were doing. The Salmons called their perspective the 'statistical relevance' model of scientific explanation. This approach allowed for building up confidence in ideas through an examination of the probative quality of all relevant information. Hypotheses are informally rated by archaeologists on their prior probabilities for being true, and the most likely are pursued. The difficulty of rigorously assigning prior probabilities to information, as well as other inferential pitfalls, has kept many in the science camp of the New Archaeology from accepting the Salmons' approach.

I believe that many of the best ideas in archaeology have emerged from studies that lack scientific rigour or extensive documentation. Gordon Childe's work (1936 and others) is a perfect example. Relying on only the scantiest of empirical information, he promulgated the most insightful, sweeping, views of the human career to date. More recently, Kent Flannery has made several of the greatest contributions to new ideas in archaeology. In articles that are among his most exciting – on the origins of agriculture (1969, 1973b), archaeological systems theory (1968), house forms (1972b), and the evolution of civilization (1972a) – he engages in what I would call a *dialogue* with the data. Although his propositions are surely prompted by the empirical record, Flannery gives these dialogues substance and importance by his personal insight, not by rigorous use of evidence in a process of scientific validation.

The Hodder school has rightly recognized the simplifying assumptions and lack of interpretive progress in New Archaeology and has tried to correct it by advocating a contextual approach. However, I believe that some contextualists have erred in the other direction by focusing their major effort on documenting the formulation of their idea, with little systematic effort devoted to further validation. This has led some contextualist studies to be ignored by most archaeologists because of a lack of testing, while other contextual studies rigorously document a boring pattern, something that New Archaeologists did quite well without them!

The obvious solution to archaeology's malaise would be to amplify the interpretive, idea-generating aspect of scientific approaches as has been suggested by Earle and Preucel (1987) or to systematize and firm up the evaluative efforts of the postprocessualists as is attempted by Hodder in his more recent works (1986, 1987a, 1987b). There is great promise in both of these efforts, and what might very well emerge is an 'ideal' combination of the best of the two approaches. It is my belief, however, that although there may be a few cases where this marriage succeeds, it will not work out for the field at large. There are real differences in beliefs concerning appropriate knowledge that cannot be easily bridged. Hence, even though I hold out hope for the emergence of a newly unified archaeology, I think it is neither realistic nor necessary for our advancement. Rather, I would like to see a diverse, but more cooperative, discipline, with shared goals and results but distinct approaches.

I suggest that, as a discipline, we encourage those who are gifted in creative dialogue to think great thoughts: to brainstorm unconstrained by the rigour of normal scientific methodology; to look at the world from all angles, both the obvious and the less obvious; and to put forward interesting propositions, providing enough information for others to determine whether a dialogue should be pursued. I certainly would not hope to turn the entire discipline into story-tellers, but we need our share! The key is that they recognize that the pursuit of knowledge is not over once they have promulgated their story.

The majority of us in archaeology should do what we can with generating new ideas, but stick to scientific verification as our primary activity, seeking new ways to measure behavioural processes with evidence from the past (Watson *et al.* 1984). Read widely, expose ourselves to the ideas of the new thinkers, but bring them and their ideas back to earth! Be aware of the possible pitfalls that contextualists have identified, because surely there is culture-bound contextual meaning to all we study and to ourselves. To the extent that ideational factors that may have been contingent on specific cultural traditions played a substantial role, we must apply uniformitarian ideas with appropriate caution. But we must not let that be a hindrance to progress in understanding the past. As scientists, we should continue to proceed under the banner of the general validity of uniformitarianism. This does not mean that we have to constrain ourselves to projecting present patterns into the past, but at least we should use them as starting points or building blocks for a new view of the past: there is no other way. Yes, we may misinterpret some things, but looking back from our culture-bound present over the past hundred years of scholarship, archaeologists have developed many ideas about the past that have withstood careful scrutiny for generations. There *are* patterns in the past, and these patterns *are* reminiscent of things we can understand in the present: *uniformitarianism does work*!

I do not claim that we can know all of the past, or even know any particular piece of it with absolute certainty. At some level, however, there are shared elements to being human: to perceive opportunities, to categorize, to elaborate, and to cooperate for a common good. These are among the factors that have led to our position of pre-eminence in the animal kingdom, and it is what is most likely to be knowable through uniformitarian studies. If we were to reveal only those ideas to the world, archaeology would truly be a worthwhile endeavour.

CONCLUSION

I would like to conclude this discussion by departing from archaeology in isolation and say a few words about our present-day political context: how it may have led many post-processualists to reject New Archaeology and how at the same time it is creating new opportunities for our discipline. New Archaeology was born as part of the optimism of the 1960s. All was possible: racial tensions could disappear, the Cold War could thaw, the poor could be made wealthy, and archaeologists could devote themselves to testing general laws that had social significance. Unfortunately, in the broader world, as in archaeology, the problems proved too difficult to be solved at that time.

The 1980s in the United States can be generally characterized as an era of economic expansion and getting on with your work. There were more of us, more jobs, and more research money, at least in cultural resource management. In Europe, however, growth did not spread to the academic ranks, and the restrictive, hierarchically controlled university system has remained largely in place. The era of New Archaeology in Britain saw innovations in thinking, but not the massive structural shift in the discipline that accompanied it in the United States. Because of this, anti-establishment feelings are still active, and the subject of their acrimony now focuses on New Archaeology and some who once championed the British version of it, such as the legacy of David Clarke. Young scholars who are seeking to break into the establishment are more inclined to emphasize the distinctiveness of their approach, rather than its continuities with what came before.

Now in the 1990s we find ourselves in a profoundly different and rapidly changing world situation. There must now be a shift in our energies from conflict to cooperation just as there is in the broader political scene. New political alignments are forming, material goods are flowing over old barriers, and global interaction is intensifying. The ultimate resolution of these processes is difficult to foresee, but it is certain that a new world order is emerging. What do these changes mean for the course of archaeology? It can mean business as usual, or it can mean responding to a rare opportunity. I believe that people in many parts of the world are ready to embrace new world perspectives on world history and certainly a new explanation of the world order. As Binford and many others have said, we as archaeologists are especially well suited to view long-term change and to view it within a perspective unavailable to the textual historian, the ethnographer, or the sociologist (Binford 1968; Plog 1973; Watson 1973). This is an enormous challenge and fraught with difficulties. To achieve this lofty objective, archaeologists must cultivate the renewed humanistic focus on idea generation and accept the value of thoughts stimulated by the past but written in the present. At the same time, I believe that real progress can only be made if this more free-wheeling individualistic approach to knowledge is carried forward in cooperation with others who pursue the continued growth of rigour and validation. Whether we call it New Archaeology, Post-Processualism or even a New Processualism is of little importance. The essential element is that we encourage serious scholars to do what they are best at doing and to coordinate diverse thinking to form a loose but lasting alliance for new knowledge of the past and present.

ACKNOWLEDGEMENTS

I am grateful for the many scholars I have had the good fortune to work with and observe; I hope I have represented their work fairly. Some sections of this chapter derive from a Distinguished Lecture in Archaeology which I delivered at the American Anthropological Association.

REFERENCES

Aberle, D. F. (1968) 'Comments', in S. R. Binford and L. R. Binford (eds) *New Perspectives in Archaeology*, Chicago: Aldine Publishing House: 353–59.

Adams, R. McC. (1966) *The Evolution of Urban Society*, Chicago: Aldine Publishing House.

Allen, W. L. and Richardson, J. B. (1971) 'The reconstruction of kinship from archaeological data: the concepts, the methods, and the feasibility', *American Antiquity* 36: 41–53.

Bender, B. (1978) 'Gatherer-hunter to farmer: a social perspective', *World Archaeology* 10: 204–22.

Binford, L. R. (1962) 'Archaeology as anthropology', *American Antiquity* 28: 217–25.

Binford, L. R. (1964) 'A consideration of archaeological research design', *American Antiquity* 29: 425–41.

Binford, L. R. (1965) 'Archaeological systematics and the study of cultural process', *American Antiquity* 31: 203–10.

Binford, L. R. (1968) 'Archaeological perspectives', in S. R. Binford and L. R. Binford (eds) *New Perspectives in Archaeology*, Chicago: Aldine Publishing House: 5–23.

Binford, L. R. (1972) *An Archaeological Perspective*, New York: Seminar Press.

Binford, L. R. (1978) *Nunamiut Ethnoarchaeology*, New York: Academic Press.

Binford, L .R. (1983) *Working at Archaeology*, New York: Academic Press.

Binford, S. R. and Binford, L. R. (eds) (1968) *New Perspectives in Archaeology*, Chicago: Aldine Publishing House.

Boas, F. (1896) 'The limitations of the comparative method of anthropology', in F. Boas *Race, Language and Culture*, New York: Macmillan: 271–304.

Braidwood, R. (1960) 'Levels in prehistory: a model for the consideration of the evidence', in S. Tax (ed.) *Evolution after Darwin*, Volume 2, Chicago: University of Chicago Press: 143–51.

Butzer, K. (1980) 'Context in archaeology: an alternative perspective', *Journal of Field Archaeology* 7: 417–22.

Childe, V. G. (1925) *The Dawn of European Civilization*, London: Kegan Paul.

Childe, V. G. (1934) *New Light on the Most Ancient East: the Oriental Prelude to European Prehistory*, London: Kegan Paul.

Childe, V. G. (1936) *Man Makes Himself*, London: C. A. Watts and Co. Ltd.

Childe, V. G. (1942) *What Happened in History*, Harmondsworth: Penguin.

Childe, V. G. (1951) *Social Evolution*, Cleveland: World.

Clark, J. G. D. (1939) *Archaeology and Society*, London: Methuen.

Clark, J. G. D. (1952) *Prehistoric Europe: the Economic Basis*, London: Methuen.

Clarke, D. L. (1968) *Analytical Archaeology*, London: Methuen.

Clarke, D. L. (1972) 'A provisional model of an iron age society and its settlement system', in D. L. Clarke (ed.) *Models in Archaeology*, London: Methuen: 801–69.

Clarke, D. L. (1973) 'Archaeology: the loss of innocence', *Antiquity* 47: 6–18.

Clarke, D. L. (1978) *Analytical Archaeology* (2nd edition, revised by R. Chapman), New York: Columbia University Press.

Conkey, M. (1982) 'Boundedness in art and society', in I. Hodder (ed.) *Symbolic and Structural Archaeology*, Cambridge: Cambridge University Press: 115–28.

Conkey, M. W. and Spector, J. D. (1984) 'Archaeology and the study of gender', *Advances in Archaeological Method and Theory* 7: 1–37.

Cowgill, G. L. (1983) 'Rulership and Ciudadela: political inferences from Teotihuacan architecture', in R. M. Leventhal and A. L. Kolata (eds) *Civilization in the Ancient Americas: Essays in Honor of Gordon R. Willey*, Cambridge: University of New Mexico and Harvard University Press: 313–43.

Cronin, C. (1962) 'An analysis of pottery design elements, indicating possible relationships between three decorated types', in P. S. Martin, J. B. Rinaldo, W. A. Longacre, C. Cronin, L. G. Freeman, Jr and J. Schoenwetter (eds) *Chapters in the Prehistory of Eastern Arizona*, Volume 1, Chicago: Chicago Natural History Museum: 105–14.

Daniel, G. (1962) *The Idea of Prehistory*, Baltimore: Penguin Books.

Deetz, J. F. (1965) *The Dynamics of Stylistic Change in Arikara Ceramics*, Illinois Studies in Anthropology, No. 4, Urbana: University of Illinois Press.

Deetz, J. F. (1977) *In Small Things Forgotten: the Archaeology of Early American Life*, New York: Anchor Press/Doubleday.

Dumond, D. E. (1977) 'Science in archaeology: the saints go marching in', *American Antiquity* 42: 330–49.

Dunnel, R. (1971) *Systematics in Prehistory*, New York: The Free Press.

Dunnel, R. (1980) 'Evolutionary theory and archaeology', in M. B. Schiffer (ed.) *Advances in Archaeological Method and Theory*, New York: Academic Press: 35–99.

Earle, T. K. and Ericson, J. E. (eds) (1977) *Exchange Systems in Prehistory*, New York: Academic Press.

Earle, T. K. and Preucel, R. W. (1987) 'Critique', *Current Anthropology* 28 (4): 501–38.

Flannery, K. V. (1968) 'Archaeological systems theory and early Mesoamerica', in B. Meggers (ed.) *Anthropological Archaeology in the Americas*, Washington, DC: Anthropological Society of Washington: 67–87.

Flannery, K. V. (1969) 'Origins and ecological effects of early domestication in Iran and the Near East', in P. J. Ucko and G. W. Dimbleby (eds) *The Domestication and Exploitation of Plants and Animals*, London: Duckworth: 73–100.

Flannery, K. V. (1972a) 'The cultural evolution of civilizations', *Annual Review of Ecology and Systematics* 3: 399–426.

Flannery, K. V. (1972b) 'The origins of the village as a settlement type in Mesoamerica and the Near East: a comparative study', in P. J. Ucko, R. Tringham and G. W. Dimbleby (eds) *Man, Settlement and Urbanism*, London: Duckworth: 23–53.

Flannery, K. V. (1973a) 'Archaeology with a capital S', in C. L. Redman (ed.) *Research and Theory in Current Archaeology*, New York: Columbia University Press: 47–53.

Flannery, K. V. (1973b) 'The origins of agriculture', *Annual Review of Anthropology* 2: 271–310.

Flannery, K. V. (ed.) (1976) *The Early Mesoamerican Village*, New York: Academic Press.

Ford, R. I. (1973) 'Archaeology serving humanity', in C. L. Redman (ed.) *Research and Theory in Current Archaeology*, New York: Columbia University Press: 83–93.

Freeman, L. G., Jr. and Brown, J. A. (1964) 'Statistical analysis of Carter Ranch pottery', in P. S. Martin, J. B. Rinaldo, W. A. Longacre, L. G. Freeman Jr., J. A. Brown, R. H. Herly and M. E. Cooley (eds) *Chapters in the Prehistory of Eastern Arizona, II, Volume 55*, Fieldiana: Chicago Museum of Natural History: 126–54.

Fried, M. H. (1967) *The Evolution of Political Society: An Essay in Political Anthropology*, New York: Random House.

Friedrich, M. H. (1970) 'Design structure and social interaction: archaeological implications of an ethnographic analysis', *American Antiquity* 35: 332–43.

Fritz, J. M. (1978) 'Paleopsychology today: ideational systems and human adaptation in prehistory', in C. L. Redman (ed.) *Social Archaeology: Beyond Subsistence and Dating*, New York: Academic Press: 37–59.

Fritz, J. M. (1986) 'Vijayanagara: authority and meaning of a South Indian capital', *American Anthropologist* 88: 44–55.

Geertz, C. (1973) 'Deep play: notes on the Balinese cockfight', in *The Interpretation of Cultures, Selected Essays*, New York: Basic Books, Inc.: 181–223.

Gero, J. M. and Conkey, M. W. (eds) (1991) *Engendering Archaeology: Women and Prehistory*, Oxford: Basil Blackwell Ltd.

Graves, M. W. (1981) 'Ethnoarchaeology of Kalinga Ceramic Design', Phoenix, University of Arizona, Unpublished Ph.D. dissertation.

Graves, M. W. (1982) 'Breaking down ceramic variation: testing models of White Mountain Redware design style development', *Journal of Anthropological Archaeology* 1: 305–54.

Haggett, P. (1965) *Locational Analysis in Human Geography*, London: Edward Arnold.

Hanson, N. R. (1958) *Patterns of Discovery: An Inquiry into the Conceptual Foundations of Science*, London: Cambridge University Press.

Hantmann, J. L. and Plog, S. (1982) 'The relationship of stylistic similarity to patterns of material exchange', in T. Earle and J. Ericson (eds) *Contexts for Prehistoric Exchange*, New York: Academic Press: 237–63.

Haviland, W. A. (1970) 'Tikal, Guatemala and Mesoamerican urbanism', *World Archaeology* 2 (2): 186–99.

Hempel, C. G. (1966) *Philosophy of Natural Science*, Englewood Cliffs, N.J.: Prentice-Hall.

Higgs, E. S. (ed.) (1972) *Papers in Economic Prehistory*, Cambridge: Cambridge University Press.

Higgs, E. S. (1975) *Palaeoeconomy*, Cambridge: Cambridge University Press.

Hill, J. N. (1965) 'Broken K: A Prehistoric Society in Eastern Arizona', University of Chicago, Unpublished Ph.D. dissertation.

Hill, J. N. (1970) *Broken K Pueblo: Prehistoric Social Organization in the American Southwest*, Anthropological Papers of the University of Arizona, No. 18, Tucson: University of Arizona Press.

Hodder, I. (1982a) *Symbols in Action*, Cambridge: Cambridge University Press.

Hodder, I. (1982b) *The Present Past*, New York: Pica Press.

Hodder, I. (1984) 'Burials, houses, women and men in the European Neolithic', in D. Miller and C. Tilley (eds) *Ideology, Power and Prehistory*, Cambridge: Cambridge University Press: 51–68.

Hodder, I. (1986) *Reading the Past: Current Approaches to Interpretation in Archaeology*, Cambridge: Cambridge University Press.

Hodder, I. (1987a) *Archaeology as Long-term History*, Cambridge: Cambridge University Press.

Hodder, I. (1987b) 'Comment on processual archaeology and the radical critique by Timothy K. Earle and Robert W. Preucel', *Current Anthropology* 28 (4): 516–17.

Hodder, I. and Orton, C. (1976) *Spatial Analysis in Archaeology*, Cambridge: Cambridge University Press.

Isaac, G. (1971) 'Whither archaeology?', *Antiquity* 45: 123–29.

James, S. R. (1993) 'Variation in Pueblo Household Use of Space: A Processual Approach to Prehistoric Social Organization', Arizona State University, Unpublished Ph.D. dissertation.

Johnson, G. A. (1972) 'A test of the utility of Central Place Theory in archaeology', in P. J. Ucko, R. Tringham and G. W. Dimbleby (eds) *Man, Settlement and Urbanism*, London: Duckworth.

Kent, S. (1984) *Analyzing Activity Areas: An Ethnoarchaeological Study of the Use of Space*, Albuquerque: University of New Mexico Press.

Kidder, A. V. (1924) *An Introduction to the Study of Southwestern Archaeology*, New Haven: Phillips Academy No.1, Papers of the Southwestern Expedition.

Kuhn, T. S. (1962) *The Structure of Scientific Revolutions. International Encyclopedia of Unified Science*, Volume 2, No. 2, Chicago: University of Chicago Press.

LeBlanc, S. A. and Watson, P. J. (1973) 'A comparative statistical analysis of painted pottery from seven Halafian sites', *Paleorient* 1 (1): 117–33.

Leone, M. P. (1968) 'Neolithic economic autonomy and social distance', *Science* 162: 1150–51.

Leone, M. P. (1981) 'The relationship between artifacts and the public in outdoor history museums', *Annals of the New York Academy of Sciences* 376: 301–14.

Leone, M. P. (1982) 'Some options about recovering mind', *American Antiquity* 47: 742–60.

Leone, M. and Potter, P. Jr. (eds) (1988) *The Recovery of Meaning: Historical Archaeology in the Eastern United States*, Washington, DC: Smithsonian Institution Press.

Longacre, W. A. (1963) 'Archaeology as Anthropology: A Case Study', University of Chicago, Department of Anthropology, Unpublished Ph.D. dissertation.

Longacre, W. A. (1970) *Archaeology as Anthropology: A Case Study*, Anthropological Papers of the University of Arizona, No. 17, Tucson: University of Arizona Press.

McIntosh, S. K. and McIntosh, R. J. (1984) 'The early city in West Africa: towards an understanding', *The African Archaeological Review* 2: 73–98.

McKern, W. C. (1939) 'The midwestern taxonomic method as an aid to archaeological culture study', *American Antiquity* 4: 301–13.

Marcus, J. (1973) 'Territorial organization of the Lowland Classic Maya', *Science* 180: 811–16.

Meggers, B. J. (1954) 'Environmental limitations on the development of culture', *American Anthropologist* 56 (5): 801–24.

Miller, D. and Tilley, C. (eds) (1984) *Ideology, Power and Prehistory*, Cambridge: Cambridge University Press.

Morgan, L. H. (1877) *Ancient Society*, New York: Holt.

Morgan, L. H. (1881) *Houses and House-life of the American Aborigines*, Contributions to North American Ethnology IV, Washington: U.S. Department of the Interior.

Muller, J. (1973) *Structural Studies of Art Styles. Ninth International Congress of Anthropological and Ethnological Sciences*, The Hague: Mouton.

Peacock, D. P. S. (ed.) (1977) *Pottery and Early Commerce: Characterization and Trade in Roman and Later Ceramics*, London: Academic Press.

Piggott, S. (1965) *Ancient Europe, from the Beginnings of Agriculture to Classical Antiquity: A Survey*, Chicago: Aldine.

Plog, F. T. (1973) 'Diachronic anthropology', in C. L. Redman (ed.) *Research and Theory in Current Archaeology*, New York: Columbia University Press: 181–98.

Plog, F. T. (1974) *The Study of Prehistoric Change*, New York: Academic Press.

Plog, S. (1980) *Stylistic Variation in Prehistoric Ceramics: Design Analysis in the American Southwest*, Cambridge: Cambridge University Press.

Raab, M. and Goodyear, A. (1984) 'A review of middle-range theory in archaeology', *American Antiquity* 498: 255–68.

Rabinow, P. and Sullivan, W. (eds) (1979) *Interpretive Social Sciences*, Berkeley: University of California Press.

Rathje, W. L. (1971) 'The origin and development of Lowland Classic Maya civilization', *American Antiquity* 36 (3): 275–85.

Redman, C. L. (1986) *Qsar es-Seghir: An Archaeological View of Medieval Life*, New York: Academic Press.

Redman, C. L., Berman, M. J., Curtin, E. V., Langhorne, W. T. Jr., Versaggi, N. M. and Wanser, J. C. (eds) (1978) *Social Archaeology: Beyond Subsistence and Dating*, New York: Academic Press.

Renfrew, C. (1973) *Before Civilisation, the Radiocarbon Revolution and Prehistoric Europe*, London: Cape.

Renfrew, C. (1974) 'Beyond a subsistence economy: the evolution of social organization in prehistoric Europe', in C. B. Moore (ed.) *Reconstructing Complex Societies*, Baltimore: Bulletin of the American Schools of Oriental Research, No. 20: 69–85.

Renfrew, C. (1984) *Approaches to Social Archaeology*, Cambridge, Mass.: Harvard University Press.

Renfrew, C. (1989) 'Comments on archaeology into the 1990s', *Norwegian Archaeological Review* 22 (1): 33–41.

Rindos, D. (1984) *The Origins of Agriculture: An Evolutionary Perspective*, New York: Academic Press.

Ross Ashby, W. (1956) *An Introduction to Cybernetics*, London: Methuen.

Sahlins, M. (1981) *Historical Metaphors and Mythical Realities: Structure in the History of the Sandwich Islands Kingdom*, Ann Arbor: University of Michigan Press.

Sahlins, M. and Service, E. (1960) *Evolution and Culture*, Ann Arbor: University of Michigan Press.

Salmon, M. H. and Salmon, W. C. (1979) 'Alternative models of scientific explanation', *American Anthropologist* 81: 61–74.

Sanders, W. T. (1968) 'Hydraulic agriculture, economic symbiosis, and the evolution of states in Central Mexico', in B. J. Meggars (ed.) *Anthropological Archaeology in the Americas*, Washington, DC: The Anthropological Society of Washington: 88–107.

Sanders, W. T. and Price, B. J. (1968) *Mesoamerica: The Evolution of a Civilization*, New York: Random House.

Schiffer, M. B. (1976) *Behavioral Archaeology*, New York: Academic Press.

Service, E. R. (1962) *Primitive Social Organization*, New York: Random House.

Service, E. R. (1975) *Origins of the State and Civilization: The Process of Cultural Evolution*, New York: Random House.

Shanks, M. and Tilley, C. (1987) *Social Theory and Archaeology*, Cambridge: Polity Press.

Shanks, M. and Tilley, C. (1989) 'Archaeology into the 1990s', *Norwegian Archaeological Review* 22 (1): 1–54.

Shepard, A. O. (1955) *Ceramics for the Archaeologist*, Washington, DC: Carnegie Institute of Washington.

Sokal, R. R. and Sneath, P. H. A. (1963) *Principles of Numerical Taxonomy*, San Francisco: W. H. Freeman and Company.

Spaulding, A. C. (1953) 'Statistical techniques for the discovery of artifact types', *American Antiquity* 18: 305–13.

Spaulding, A. C. (1960) 'The dimensions of archaeology', in G. E. Dole and R. L. Carneiro (eds) *Essays in the Science of Culture in Honor of Leslie A. White*, New York: Thomas Y. Crowell: 437–56.

Spaulding, A. C. (1988) 'Distinguished lecture: archaeology and anthropology', *American Anthropologist* 90: 263–71.

Stanislawski, M. (1969) 'The ethno-archaeology of Hopi pottery making', *Plateau* 42: 27–33.

Steward, J. H. (1955) *Theory of Culture Change: The Methodology of Multilinear Evolution*, Urbana: University of Illinois Press.

Taylor, W. W. (1948) *A Study of Archaeology*, American Anthropological Association Memoir No. 69, Menasha, Wis.: American Anthropological Association.

Thomas, D. H. (1972) 'A computer simulation model of Great Basin Shoshonean subsistence and settlement patterns', in D. L. Clarke (ed.) *Models in Archaeology*, London: Methuen: 671–704.

Trigger, B. G. (1973) 'The future of archaeology is the past', in C. L. Redman (ed.) *Research and Theory in Current Archaeology*, New York: Columbia University Press: 47–53.

Trigger, B. G. (1989) *A History of Archaeological Thought*, Cambridge: Cambridge University Press.

Tuggle, H. D. (1979) 'Prehistoric Community Relations in East-Central Arizona', University of Arizona, Department of Anthropology, Unpublished Ph.D. dissertation.

Vita-Finzi, C. and Higgs, E. S. (1970) 'Prehistoric economy in the Mount Carmel area of Palestine: site catchment analysis', *Proceedings of the Prehistoric Society* 36: 1–37.

Watson, P. J. (1973) 'The future of archaeology in anthropology: cultural history and social science', in C. L. Redman (ed.) *Research and Theory in Current Archaeology*, New York: Columbia University Press: 113–24.

Watson, P. J. (1986) 'Archaeological interpretation, 1985', in D. Meltzer, D. Fowler and J. Sabloff (eds) *American Archaeology, Past and Future*, Washington, DC: Smithsonian Institution Press: 439–57.

Watson, P. J., LeBlanc, S. A. and Redman, C. L. (1971) *Explanation in Archaeology: An Explicitly Scientific Approach*, New York: Columbia University Press.

Watson, P. J., LeBlanc, S. A. and Redman, C. L. (1980) 'Aspects of Zuni prehistory: preliminary report on excavations and survey in the El Morro valley of New Mexico', *Journal of Field Archaeology* 7: 201–18.

Watson, P. J., LeBlanc, S. A. and Redman, C. L. (1984) *Archaeological Explanation: The Scientific Method in Archaeology*, New York: Columbia University Press.

Whallon, R., Jr. (1966) 'The Owasco Period: A Reanalysis', University of Chicago, Department of Anthropology, Unpublished Ph.D. dissertation.

Whallon, R., Jr. (1968) 'Investigations of late prehistoric social organization in New York State', in S. R. Binford and L. R. Binford (eds) *New Perspectives in Archaeology*, Chicago: Aldine Publishing House: 223–44.

White, L. A. (1959) *The Evolution of Culture: The Development of Civilization to the Fall of Rome*, New York: McGraw-Hill.

Willey, G. R. and Phillips, P. (1958) *Method and Theory in American Archaeology*, Chicago: University of Chicago Press.

Willey, G. R. and Sabloff, J. A. (1980) *A History of American Archaeology* (2nd edition), London: Thames and Hudson.

Wright, H. T. (1969) *The Administration of Rural Production in an Early Mesopotamian Town*, Anthropological Papers, No. 38, Ann Arbor: University of Michigan Museum of Anthropology.

Wylie, A. (1989) 'A Proliferation of Archaeologies: Skepticism, Processualism, and Post-Processualism', Unpublished manuscript, on file at Arizona State University.

Wylie, A. (1992) 'The interplay of evidential constraints and political interests: recent archaeological research on gender', *American Antiquity* 57 (1): 15–35.

Yellen, J. E. (1977) *Archaeological Approaches to the Present*, New York: Academic Press.

SELECT BIBLIOGRAPHY

In order to capture the full sweep of human prehistory and the development of archaeological science at the same time, I would recommend starting with something like V. Gordon Childe's *Man Makes Himself* (1936) if you can forgive him the title and balance it with Grahame Clark's solid *Archaeology and Society* (1939). As more fieldwork was conducted, the syntheses got better too, and I still view Robert McC. Adams's *The Evolution of Urban Society* (1966) as one of the best, and Kent Flannery's edited volume *The Early Mesoamerican Village* (1976) as a good attempt at bringing together new archaeology and results of field investigations. To get a grasp of theoretical developments over the past few decades it would be best to start with Lewis Binford's first major article 'Archaeology as anthropology' (1962), continue with the book he edited with Sally Binford, *New Perspectives in Archaeology* (1968), and check out one of his more recent books like *Working at Archaeology* (1983). For a view of parallel developments in Britain one need only look at David Clarke's tome *Analytical Archaeology* (1968, or posthumously 1978), or Colin Renfrew's *Approaches to Social Archaeology* (1984). For a continuation of the debate on archaeological theory one must not miss the writings of Ian Hodder that exhibit a range of viewpoints from *The Present Past* (1982) to *Archaeology as Long-Term History* (1987). The best overall summary of theoretical developments in the subject is by Bruce Trigger (1989) *A History of Archaeological Thought*.

3

THE NATURE OF ARCHAEOLOGICAL EVIDENCE

John Collis

INTRODUCTION

In this chapter I wish to explore the nature of archaeological data – what is fact, what is interpretation, or what is plain fantasy; to discuss the limits of our knowledge; and how archaeological information is used and abused. It is about the nature of archaeological knowledge, and how it can be ordered. We can never know, nor do we want to know, all that happened in the past. There is too much of it, it is too complex, much was very banal, nor do we really understand it. It is also always changing shape and perspective as our own viewpoint changes. Thus we must make a selection, and it is the results of this selection which form the database of archaeological information. The nature of that database depends on three factors. First, what do we want to know? What do we consider important? This is our paradigm, the framework of thought which we use to order the past, and the framework within which we collect data. Second, what has actually survived? There are many things which we would like to know about, but the evidence may have simply disappeared, or was not recorded by the person who made a find. In other cases it may have never existed, but we may only be able to approach it indirectly from other forms of evidence. Third, what is the technology available to us to find the evidence? This is always improving, and includes a number of methods which can be grouped under remote sensing and survey, excavation, and scientific analysis. This chapter is mainly concerned with the second question, but it is very much influenced by the first and third; indeed, the first set of questions are fundamental to the whole study of the past, as I describe in my next section.

PERSPECTIVES OF THE PAST

The archaeological database, as it exists today, consists of the accumulation of the observations and finds gathered by previous generations of archaeologists and antiquarians, in some countries stretching back several hundred years. As the discussions here and in Chapter 1 emphasize, each generation has its own perspective of the past, different aims, and different levels of understanding and technology. Even in a country with a long tradition such as England, the database is still fundamentally affected by the activities of individual antiquarians from the nineteenth century, such as Colt Hoare and Cunnington in Wiltshire (Annable and Simpson 1964; Colt Hoare 1812–21), Bateman in Derbyshire (Bateman 1861; Howarth 1899), and Mortimer (1905) and Greenwell (Greenwell 1877; Kinnes and Longworth 1985) in Yorkshire. Other areas which lacked such individuals, or, where the recording was poor for the period, are under-represented.

Different paradigms, different perspectives of the past, affect not only the sort of information which is collected, but also the methodology employed and the sorts of sites chosen for excavation. They also reflect the interest of the individuals who are engaged in archaeology at any one time, and this in turn reflects the social structure of their contemporary society. Thus, in nineteenth-century Europe, archaeology was largely in the hands of rich landowners and clerics. Their interests included art, élite architecture, and warfare, and one of the defining characteristics of their social class was their education, which included a knowledge of the Classics. Antiquarian interest therefore naturally concentrated on their interests – such as the architecture of castles and churches – and on collections of art objects especially from Greece and Rome, but also local artefacts, for display in their 'cabinets' (Daniel 1964, 1967, 1975). To gather local objects, an efficient collecting policy was developed, which consisted largely of digging holes in the middle of ancient burial mounds where success was virtually guaranteed.

With the rise of the leisured middle classes in the later nineteenth century, these interests continued to be aped as indicators of education and status. However, the middle classes brought their own concerns, especially an interest in technology and science. The Three Age System developed by Christian Thomsen was itself based on technology (Daniel 1964, 1967), and this extended into the use of types of artefact to characterize each period. Scientific approaches were dominated by Darwin's concept of evolution, not only for the antiquity and evolution of Mankind itself, but also for social evolution, in the works of Marx, Morgan and Engels. Evolution could also be linked with technology in the form of 'typology', the evolution of artefacts into evermore functional and efficient forms, an approach developed by the Swede Oscar Montelius (1903) which gave a means of refining chronology (Chapter 5). For these new demands on the archaeological database, more detailed recording was needed, especially of associated groups of finds in graves and hoards. The latter were usually chance finds made outside the control of the archaeologist, but the late nineteenth century and early twentieth century saw a great period of cemetery excavation (Hodson 1968, 1991; Wilson 1970). The paradigm of social evolution also had its impact on excavation method, producing attempts at large-scale excavation of settlements, such as the Roman towns of Pompeii (Corti 1951; Grant 1971; Maiuri 1970) and Silchester (Boon 1974), or more prosaic farmsteads excavated by Pitt-Rivers on Cranborne Chase in southern England (Bowden 1991; Pitt-Rivers 1887, 1888, 1892, 1898), or the numerous cave excavations in western France. In this way the increasing complexity of social organization could be illustrated.

The late nineteenth and early twentieth centuries were also the period of the European nation-state, not merely the traditional powers of Spain, France, Russia and Britain, but also new major European states such as Germany and Italy, as well as a plethora of smaller states, especially in the aftermath of the collapse of the Austro-Hungarian Empire. Archaeology and History were harnessed for the ideology and aims of these states, initially by seeking out heroes, mythical or historical, such as Siegfried in Germany or Vercingetorix in France, but subsequently in the development of the 'Culture-Historical' paradigm (Trigger 1989). The concept of the 'Culture' as a group of associated artefacts regularly occurring together and equating with an ancient people, was a concept developed especially by Gordon Childe (1929) for ordering European prehistory. In Europe and America it became the dominant paradigm from the 1930s to the 1960s, and as late as 1959 in the standard German textbook *Einführung in die Vorgeschichte* Eggers could claim that the two main aims for the prehistorian were dating and ethnicity (1959: 199).

Though this approach relied on the previous achievements of Montelius and his successors, Reinecke ([1903–9] 1963) and Déchelette (1908, 1910, 1913, 1914), in providing a chronological framework for prehistoric Europe, it made new demands on the archaeological database. 'Cultures' did not only have a chronological range, they also had a geographical distribution, and the distribution map of different artefact types and cultures became one of the standard tools used by the culture-historical school, and they are now a standard feature of all archaeological books. Even stray finds became useful for such an approach, and were used for such purposes as defining the origins and spread of prehistoric cultures as well as historical peoples such as 'Celts', 'Germans' and 'Slavs'; or the invasions of peoples from the steppes, 'Thrako-Cimmerians', Scythians, Huns and Hungarians; or the movements of Franks, Lombards and Anglo-Saxons during the migration period. Invasion was the main explanation for the replacement of one culture by another, as indeed for most change and innovation (Trigger 1989).

Thus, what was required from controlled excavation was a sequence to demonstrate the succession of cultures replacing one another. This in its turn required close stratigraphical control, with finds clearly assigned to a specific archaeological stratum. This led to an abandonment of the sort of area excavation pioneered by Pitt-Rivers and his contemporaries. Rather, excavation consisted of narrow trenches or boxes divided by 'baulks' with sections in which the superimposed layers were visible and so could be recorded in graphical form, as a 'section drawing' (Wheeler 1954). Alternative methods existed, such as that devised by the German archaeologist Gerhard Bersu, who used a system of alternating trenches (Bersu 1940, 1977; Evans 1989), or Sir Cyril Fox, who used a moving sequence of sections to slice systematically through barrows (Fox 1959: 1–11). Less emphasis was placed on the nature of settlement, so the site plan was less important than the section. Wheeler's excavation of Maiden Castle in Dorset demonstrates this clearly (Fig. 3.1), with much of the campaign concentrating on the ramparts and gateways, but relatively little time expended on excavation of the interior (Sharples 1991; Wheeler 1943).

The period after the Second World War saw a widening of interest in archaeology to encompass the working classes, as new educational opportunities in many

Figure 3.1 Maiden Castle, England. This aerial view shows the iron age hill-fort during the excavations by Sir Mortimer Wheeler. Typically for excavations carried out within the culture-historical model, the emphasis is on discovering sequence by the use of trenches. Reproduced with permission of the Society of Antiquaries of London.

countries saw the rise, first of an amateur, and later of a professional group drawn from a wide range of society. The more egalitarian countries of Scandinavia had fostered a society in the 1930s interested in settlement archaeology, dealing with the investigation of ordinary farming settlements and peasant economies (Hatt 1957; Kristiansen 1992), and after the war the political ideology of the communist areas of central and eastern Europe also encouraged extensive settlement archaeology, though still within a culture-historical framework (Sklenář 1983). The style of excavation was also still that of the 1930s, with an élite groups of scholars employing untrained labourers, who actually did the digging.

The post-war changes were most marked in Britain: excavations in the late 1950s and 1960s drew mainly on a labour force of volunteers, especially from the new class of students benefiting from wider access to state education, and these were the people who became the new professionals of the 1970s; but this period was associated with a major paradigm shift, to interests in social and economic matters. Patterns of structures could only be understood, if at all, when large areas were cleared, so excavations shifted to 'open area' methods (Barker 1977), assisted by the use of the mechanical excavator to clear large areas cheaply. This revolution hit both rural archaeology (Beresford and Hurst 1990) and urban archaeology (Biddle 1973). Excavations were no longer confined to the investigation of élite residences or ecclesiastical structures, but encompassed the merchants, craftsmen, and the poor. Questions shifted to matters such as diet, disease, housing and organization of industry. Under the previous paradigms finds such as animal bones had generally just been discarded; now they became central to the sorts of questions asked. Cunliffe's excavation at Danebury, with large-scale clearance of the interior, epitomizes this shift in interest and forms an interesting contrast with the techniques employed by Wheeler a generation earlier (Fig. 3.2).

Settlements do not exist in isolation, they are part of regional and international systems. Already in the 1950s and 1960s ambitious survey projects were started looking at the increasing complexity of society following the introduction of farming, for instance, MacNeish in the valley of Tehuacán in Mexico (Byers 1967–72), or Braidwood in Iraqi Kurdistan (Braidwood and Howe 1960). Since the 1970s, however, the 'socio-economic' paradigm, using models such as 'central place theory' and the 'world economy' (Wolf 1982), has promoted more ambitious projects looking at the political, social and economic structures of regions – for instance relating cities to their hinterlands, and using concepts derived from geography and from anthropology (Christaller 1935; Smith 1986; Wagstaff 1986). Chance finds made in uncontrolled circumstances were no longer adequate, and new methods were applied, including the systematic walking of fields and intensive aerial photography to locate a wide range of different types of settlements drawn from representative samples of the environments under study.

The 1980s and early 1990s have also seen changes, though driven more by social

Figure 3.2 Danebury, England. In contrast to Maiden Castle, Barry Cunliffe's excavations had a socio-economic aim, and so concentrated on plan, on function, and the nature of the inhabitants, so were primarily open area. Copyright © Danebury Trust.

and political factors and by technology rather than by paradigm. Legislation in many countries includes protection of sites and monuments, and anyone destroying sites is legally obliged to have them recorded; paradoxically, in some countries such as Britain can potentially lead to less excavation and on a smaller scale. The major technological innovation of this period has been the advance of the computer, which has had an enormous impact on excavation techniques, allowing much greater detail of recording and of manipulation of the data. More ambitiously, in some countries the detailed recording of the archaeological database in electronic form is well underway. In Britain this takes the form of Sites and Monuments records developed and maintained by local planning authorities who deal with requests for development. This in turn links in with a national database and archive, the National Monument Record, developed by the Royal Commission on Historical Monuments. The full academic exploitation of these databases still lies in the future.

The requirements of the archaeologist have thus changed enormously over the last 150 years. It is not just a matter of us becoming better archaeologists – the early antiquarians were extremely efficient in achieving their aims of building up collections. In part it has been due to a change of the technology available – aeroplanes for photography, mechanical excavators for clearing large areas cheaply, computers for storing data. Our nineteenth-century predecessors hardly envisaged that little scraps of charcoal might hold a solution to the dating problems which perplexed them. Nor is it simply a matter of methodology – for instance, our ability now to recognize timber buildings and other ephemeral structures. The major driving force has been the paradigm, the questions which we pose of the data, which then demand new solutions to the discovery, recording and analysis of information.

Every generation must use the data that were acquired by the previous generation, and this by very definition is inadequate for the new aims because it was collected for other purposes. Poor quality data is still being acquired as not all finds and excavations are made under ideal conditions – the finds of treasure hunters, for instance, are often of no better quality than those of the early antiquarians, and their motives in hunting for finds are not dissimilar; nor are professional excavations necessarily of good quality. All of these data are available for our use, and have to be used, but they require evaluation in terms of their quality, both of what they tell us and what they are incapable of telling us. Better recorded data can be used as a control, but databases such as that of the British National Monument Record require care in their use, and a clear understanding of the source of the information if we are not to make fundamental mistakes in interpretation. All data are biased: they have to be used and 'read' with care, and we cannot accept them at face value. It is this problem which is the major theme of this chapter.

The same is also true, however, for written sources. An extremist might claim that History is only an adjunct to Archaeology, dealing as it does with at most the last 5,000 years of human existence and, in most areas of the world, much less than that. It is based on a limited range of artefacts; that is, documents on which symbols have been written. True, these symbols are more easily read than the symbolism which exists in other types of artefact, and are much more informative about events in the past, of people, and their thoughts and motivation. However, they are as biased as the rest of the archaeological record as someone had an interest in writing them in the first place, and then of preserving them. Such information has to be treated with the same scepticism as the rest of the archaeological record, and cannot form the basis of archaeological research. There are too many gaps in this written record, information left out by the chances of individual interest or of survival, or simply not recorded because it was deemed of no interest. We can give no precedence to the written document over the archaeological information; the two sources are simply complementary to one another.

FACT, FICTION AND INTERPRETATION

What is an archaeological 'fact'? The basic building block for archaeological interpretation is that a certain object was found in a certain context or stratum. But we ourselves cannot be present at every find. Even if we find it ourselves, can we always be sure that we have observed it correctly, or that someone has not played a trick on us and buried it the night before, or that it is not in a secondary position, having been redeposited by some human or natural process such as erosion? Immediately we are having to make value judgements. What, and whom, can we trust?

First, there is the quality of the person reporting the find. There are good and bad archaeologists, and we can only judge the quality of the find from the quality of the report; for instance, details of the methodology used, and the standards of excavation, based on the details of the report and our judgement of photographs of the excavation, preferably with work in progress. Archaeologists have been known to falsify their evidence: the mythical story of the archaeologist who gambled away the funds for a rescue excavation and wrote a report without ever setting a spade in the soil; or more infamously the Piltdown forgery, which was finally disproved by the use of a battery of scientific techniques to prove the antiquity, or otherwise, of the find (Weiner 1955). Early antiquarians, without the use of modern maps, were often a bit vague about the location of a find; modern treasure hunters may deliberately lie to protect their site from rivals, or because they were trespassing when the find was made. In these cases we can only judge from the consistency of the individual, or how much their work is confirmed by other workers and finds.

Reports of discovery are more acceptable if they fit in with the framework of prevailing thought or previous experience. The Piltdown find was considered genuine because it coincided with the theories of the time, but as further finds were made it became more and more anomalous. It has been claimed that Archaeology is not a 'Science' because every 'experiment', every find or excavation is unique, and can never be repeated. This is only half true, because over time consistent patterns of association appear. Thus, red-slipped Samian pottery occurs with early Roman coins, and is found on sites with a distinctive form and layout which from documentary evidence we can recognize as Roman military forts. This combination is now so commonplace that it excites no comment, and would be accepted by all archaeologists as a 'fact'.

The problems start with combinations or discoveries which are unexpected, unusual, rare, or even unacceptable. A Roman coin from a stone age settlement on Tasmania would be considered unlikely to the point of impossibility. An Egyptian scarab from a site in central America might be acceptable by Hyperdiffusionists such as Thor Heyerdahl who sought the origin of American pyramids in Egypt, but it would be unacceptable to all 'serious' scholars. The occurrence of Chinese porcelain of the thirteenth and fourteenth centuries associated with the construction of stone buildings at Great Zimbabwe in central Africa was not accepted by white colonialists, who preferred to see its origin with the Queen of Sheba or some such fanciful theory, simply because they could not conceive that native Africans could build such structures; but it is entirely acceptable to archaeologists who see the rise of Zimbabwe as an indigenous reaction to the Arab trade system along the coast of East Africa (Garlake 1973). A Christian fundamentalist might accept an archaeologist's identification of the collapsed walls of Jericho, but not the discovery of early hominids from Olduvai Gorge.

Some discoveries take time to be accepted: for example, the occurrence of tin-glazed pottery in medieval contexts in Britain was largely dismissed as 'contamination' from material that had fallen in from higher levels, until it was realized that 'lustre wares' from Arabic Spain were being imported; suddenly several such finds were reported (Dunning 1961). Similarly, lead-glazed pottery from Roman contexts can still be discarded as medieval contamination, though such finds are now fairly common. Other finds which were totally unexpected have been accepted immediately partly because they are so unexpected that they are unlikely to be faked, like the Barbary ape from the iron age Navan Fort in Ireland (Raftery 1994).

So far we have been dealing with positive evidence, but a major problem is negative evidence. There are periods of deposition, and periods when nothing appears in the archaeological record. Evidence can consist of burials, settlements, religious sites, hoards and so on – it is rare in prehistory for all these classes to occur together, and certain types of material may never be deposited at all. When is absence of evidence, therefore, evidence of absence? If we have two periods when we find both brooches and swords, but a period in between when we have neither, it is likely that brooches and swords continued in use but were simply not deposited. Often 'culture-historical' interpretations fail to take this into account; for instance, the 'expansion' of 'Celts' into central and western France is supposed to be marked by a spread of new brooch and ceramic types, when in fact all we are seeing is a gap in the archaeological record when burials are not readily identifiable, so the brooches and pottery which are deposited in them do not occur (Collis 1984).

So, who are the wise persons, the experts, who can pass judgement on the archaeological record? What do we do if those experts are seen to disagree among themselves, or change their minds from one generation to another? Who is to say that religious fanatics are not correct in their rejection of archaeological data; or that extra-terrestrial beings have not influenced our development; or that Egyptians were not a master race who developed and disseminated civilization? Like all sciences, archaeology has been developing 'rules of the game', which are part of the logic of western European thought. These rules can be overturned, but this can only be done by scientific knowledge, and that includes the sceptical approach to, and reinterpretation of, the database.

THE LOGIC OF DEPOSITION

Unlike the pure sciences, archaeology has few 'laws' which are of universal application, and most of these are of such a banal nature that they take us but little along
the road to interpretation. There is the law of 'superimposition', which is the basis
of archaeological stratigraphy and chronology, that states that a stratum which
overlies another is logically later (Harris 1989). There is also the belief that man-
made objects from the past can be logically ordered and placed in chronological
sequence, and be used to reconstruct human activity in the past. But to go one step
further and apply the geological principle of Uniformitarianism, which states that
deposits laid down in the past were laid down by forces similar to those laying down
similar deposits today, is a principle which can only partly be followed, and then
only as a working hypothesis.

There are three problems. First, archaeological finds may have been deposited by
activities which have no modern correlates – for example, there is no animal similar
to the early hominids or to early species of *Homo* – and activities are also governed
by ideology and belief systems, so deliberate deposition of material can reflect
religious beliefs which we can never comprehend. Second, different types of activity may produce the same archaeological record: thus, 'social' exchange systems
such as 'redistribution' may produce the same type of distribution of traded goods
as 'market' exchange. Third, even where direct correlates exist, the link between
present and past activities has to be made, often using the anthropological record,
and this may not be easy, given the partial preservation and recording of archaeological data – this is what Louis Binford has termed 'Middle Range Theory' (1977,
1983).

However, our first attack in the interpretation of archaeological data must be an
attempt to apply 'normative' logical principles, and this can be most successful in
the areas of subsistence or domestic activities. Successful examples of such an
approach include:

1 The hunting of large animals. The capture of animals and the processing of their
  carcasses will lead to different sorts of sites – hunting sites, butchering sites,
  storage sites, consumption sites, and home bases. Each should be distinguishable
  by different sorts of artefacts and animal waste.
2 Crop processing. Cereals are harvested, threshed, winnowed, cleansed of impurities such as weed seeds, stored, and finally sown or consumed. Each of these
  phases produces a different sort of residue, though different methods of processing and different types of crops can affect the nature of those residues. A failure
  to recognize these different phases of processing can lead to misinterpretation.
  Thus, a high incidence of weed seeds has been seen as evidence of collecting as
  against cultivation, when in fact it may merely be the residue from the cleaning

out of weed seeds from the harvest (Hole and Flannery 1967: 169). By observing present-day methods of crop processing using traditional methods, archaeological samples can be directly compared with modern samples (Hillman 1984; Jones 1984).

3   Rubbish disposal. When a pot is broken, the small pieces will not be picked up, and will often become part of the archaeological record near where the accident happened. Large pieces will be removed to some distance for deposition where they will be out of the way, in middens or pits. The larger the fragments, the further they are likely to be transported (Schiffer 1976).

4   Settlement location. Settlements will be located at optimum siting for their function – hunting sites where game is likely to pass, farms on the best agricultural soils. Pasture and arable fields will be organized to keep travelling down to the minimum ('least effort' models). Similar models can be developed for the plans of individual settlements, for instance, Sjoberg's 'Pre-Industrial City' (1960), or for regional systems, for instance, Christaller's 'Central Place Theory' (Wagstaff 1986).

Even where these forms of logic seem to work, we must be aware that other less logical factors may be at play. The sorts of 'rubbish' found on neolithic and iron age sites in Britain, for instance, are obviously 'peculiar', with unusual associations of animal bones, and complete or partial skeletons of both humans and animals (Cunliffe 1983, 1995; Hill 1995). In the Iron Age in southern Britain, many settlements are on hill-tops, not the best siting for subsistence farming. They have ramparts around them, and social factors, especially the need for defence, seem the obvious reason. All these sites were subject to the same type of warfare, and presumably would need the same size of ramparts. So why do big sites have big ramparts, and smaller sites have smaller ramparts (Collis 1996)? Clearly there is another logic, perhaps social display, which is playing a part (Bowden and McOmish 1987).

SAMPLING

It is impossible for archaeologists to excavate everything. On occasion archaeologists have attempted the 'complete' excavation of 'sites', but this is self-deception – often all that is excavated is the area of most concentrated activity. On agricultural sites this may be relatively easy to define because most activities – living, cooking, processing of crops and meat – all take place at one point in the landscape. In contrast, in hunting groups these activities are dispersed at various locations. So, what does a 'site' consist of? Is it just the farm with its farmyard, or does it encompass the pens for livestock, the arable fields, areas of enclosed pasture, and shared areas of common pasture? The settlement alone will not tell us how the farm functioned (see Chapter 14). At all levels the archaeologist is forced to reconstruct the past on the basis of samples, and we must be aware of what biases enter each stage of that sampling process.

To show the nature of this problem I will take the example of Roman coinage. What is the significance of an individual coin, and what is its relationship to the total production of coinage in the Roman empire (Collis 1988)? The questions that have to be asked include:

1 How typical is the coin of the feature or stratum in which it was found? Is it a coin which has just come into circulation, or has it been circulating for a long time, or is it 'rubbish survival' (for instance, redeposited from another context)?

2 How typical is the feature or stratum of the part of the site in which it is located? Finds from a pit are likely to be different from those from occupation levels on floors. Individual deposits may have only a limited chronological range, and several periods may be represented on the site.

3 How typical is the part of the site of the whole site? Different sorts of activities will produce different patterns of coin loss, and on a major complex site such as a town there will be differences between commercial, religious, habitation and administrative areas, or between rich and poor quarters of the town (see Curnow 1988 for a good example).

4 What is the relationship between the coins lost on the site and the coins found by the archaeologist? What excavation methods were employed? Unless sieving took place, there will be a bias towards larger coins, and very small coins such as third and fourth century *minimissimi* may be under-represented if not totally missed.

5 How typical is the site of the region? The coins circulating on the site will depend on its function – market, fort, villa, peasant farm – and/or on the wealth and social status of its inhabitants.

6 Are there differences between different regions in a single province caused by different sorts of activity which could have affected coin distribution – for instance, between military and civil areas?

7 Were there differences between different provinces connected with imperial activity, such as the date of conquest or abandonment of the province, the construction of public works, or the conduct of military campaigns? There may be varying patterns of wealth, taxation and spending, and between military and civil provinces.

8 What was the imperial policy for coin production? The amount of coinage struck, the purity of the metal, its denomination, patterns of withdrawal and demonetarization, indeed the reasons for striking coinage, varied considerably from one period to another.

An understanding of the total picture is essential if we are to interpret our site finds correctly. A coin in mint condition in a deposit in which it is unlikely to have been redeposited, and of a type only in circulation for a small number of years, has more value for dating the deposit than a worn example of a common type which was minted and circulated for many years. It is even more important for the interpretation of negative evidence. Is the absence of a specific coin type due to it being small and difficult to find, of a type which is rare and therefore unlikely to occur; or if it is a type common in circulation and easy to find, does it mean the site had either stopped using coins, or even been abandoned? Does an increase in the number of coins mean that there was greater activity and wealth on the site, or simply that the supply of coins in circulation had increased dramatically, as was the case in the late third century AD?

An example of the way in which interpretation can progress is shown on Figure 3.3. Such bar charts became familiar in the 1970s, claiming to demonstrate coin 'loss' for sites and areas (Casey and Reece 1988), but they actually represent coin 'finds' – indeed, in some cases coins 'collected' or 'preserved', where they are in museums or derive from private collections; they are even further from representing the coins which may have been in circulation on a site. The charts also show the date when a coin was minted, not when it was lost, and recent work on pre-Roman coinage in Britain has shown that often means a thirty-year timelag, which can have important implications when one is trying to tie in archaeological evidence with historically dated events (Haselgrove 1987). The time period on the bar charts can range from ten to over forty years; to reduce the distorting effect of percentages, and so to allow one chart or period to compare more directly with the others, the bars show the average number of coins per year for each time period.

The first chart tries to show the general pattern over southern England, based on the thirteen sites, ranging from towns to temples, listed by Richard Reece (1972). It clearly shows how there were certain periods when there was a massive surge in coin loss. Richborough is left out, because it has an exceptionally large collection which distorts the overall pattern, and also has some anomalies compared with the other sites. Its pattern is shown on Figure 3.3(b); against the general pattern, two periods show up as different, AD 330–48 and especially the final phase of coin-using in Britain, AD 388–402, suggesting that Richborough's role as one of the major ports of entry into Britain was of exceptional importance in those periods, and that it had some special status. The third chart shows the overall pattern for the Roman town of Verulamium (St Albans), which generally follows the provincial pattern, except for the final period AD 388–402 when coin-using seems to have dropped, despite evidence we have, both documentary and archaeological, that the settlement was still important (Frere 1983). The fourth chart is taken from one site at Verulamium which was left outside when the defences were constructed in the late second century AD (Reece 1989); the area was virtually deserted and this is reflected in the coin finds. These comments, however, only touch on a complex and fascinating line of approach which can be used to investigate the rise and fall of settlements, their

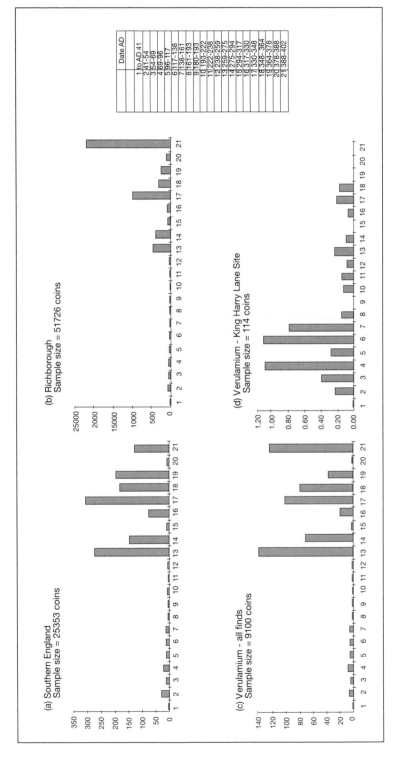

Date AD
1 to AD 41
2 41-54
3 54-69
4 69-96
5 96-117
6 117-138
7 138-161
8 161-193
9 180-193
10 193-222
11 222-238
12 238-259
13 259-275
14 275-294
15 294-317
16 317-330
17 330-348
18 348-364
19 364-378
20 378-388
21 388-402

(a) Southern England
Sample size = 25353 coins

(b) Richborough
Sample size = 51726 coins

(c) Verulamium - all finds
Sample size = 9100 coins

(d) Verulamium - King Harry Lane Site
Sample size = 114 coins

Figure 3.3 Coin finds from Britain. The first graph (a) gives the overall pattern of coin finds in southern England, as averaged from thirteen major settlements. The second graph (b) comes from Richborough, which was especially important in the late Roman period as the major point of entry from the continent. The third (c) shows the pattern from the Roman town of Verulamium (St Albans), and the fourth (d) from the King Harry Lane site at St Albans. Based on data in Reece 1972 and 1989, redrawn by D. Miles-Williams.

role in the wider provincial and imperial pattern, and economic and social questions like the integration of rural settlements into the money-using economy (Reece 1987).

This example covers a group of material which is extremely diagnostic, so comparison between sites and regions is relatively easy (though the statistics can get quite complex, and depend on the questions being asked), but the sampling processes are similar for all archaeological material.

SURVIVAL OF THE EVIDENCE

Like any form of history, what we can glean from archaeology is very much dictated by what actually survives. In the example of coinage examined in the previous section, it was assumed that nothing had happened to the coin between deposition and discovery to make it unusable or inaccessible to the archaeologist. But even with something as solid as a coin, processes can go on which will destroy the coin. In an acidic situation, the coin will be attacked chemically, and by the time it is excavated, all the archaeologist may have is a mass of corrosion products, perhaps not even identifiable as a coin, let alone to a type or ruler.

Survival depends on three related factors: the material of which the evidence is made (stone, bone, wood, and so on); the conditions under which it was deposited (soil type, location of the site, climatic conditions, speed of deposition); and subsequent processes to which the object or deposit was subjected (such as erosion or chemical change).

Burial and deposition

For much archaeological material, and for archaeological sites generally, survival will depend especially on the speed of burial, or indeed, if it is buried at all, the process known to geologists and archaeologists as 'taphonomy' (Schiffer 1987). In the recent geological record, most deposits have been laid down under wet conditions – sediments in seas and lakes, silts in river basins, or peats forming on moorland. None of these are normal habitats for the human species and, if archaeological finds do occur, they are usually redeposited, or they represent unusual occurrences (for instance, shipwrecks), or atypical communities, such as the 'lake dwellings' which occur around the world in various forms. The majority of our species has lived in dry environments, often on higher ground where visibility is better and well-drained soils occur, but where erosion is more likely than deposition.

On sites exposed to erosion by wind and rain, only the most resilient materials, such as stone, will survive, and even those are unlikely to remain at their original point of deposition, but will be moved around by heavy rain, or by animal or human activity on the site. Soft organic remains will quickly be scavenged by birds, animals, and insects, and carcasses and other waste spread around the nearby countryside. Bones and pottery will be shattered by frost or eroded by the wind; metals will corrode and disintegrate. Even in high ground situations where deposits are subsequently covered by peat, or in the lowlands by alluvium and colluvium, the process of burial may have been so slow that little survives intact.

The amount of information that is lost when the living surface of a settlement is lost is obviously huge. Hints of how much are given by sites such as the so-called 'lake-villages' of the Alpine area (Drack 1969, 1971), or the iron age settlements of Glastonbury and Meare in the Somerset Levels of southern England (Coles 1987; Coles and Minnitt 1995). These sites are generally rich in the numbers of finds that they produce, not merely the organic materials which drier sites will not produce, but also in pottery and metalwork, or traces of industrial production. Is it merely that living surfaces have survived and show us what sort of material was normally lying around on settlement sites, information which is normally destroyed by erosion? Or is there something special about deposition caused by the unusual location of these sites in damp conditions which caused items to be lost or discarded in a way which would not be normal on dry sites, such as an axe or sword being dropped into the water or lost under a raised floor and not recovered? Or are these unusually wealthy sites exploiting a rich environment with lake resources such as fish, and the potential of using boats for trading over long distances? Or are they special-purpose sites? Each interpretation gives us a very different view of the prehistoric societies and their organization.

Only rarely do natural causes provide a quick burial of an archaeological find or settlement. Water is the most common agent in the form of flooding, from the flash flood which caught a group of early hominids at Hadar in Ethiopia 3.5 million years ago (Johanson et al. 1994; Radesovich et al. 1992) to the iron age bridge at Cornaux les Sauges in Switzerland (Schwab 1989). In the latter case, the bodies of some of the inhabitants of the nearby village were caught in the collapsed remains of the bridge, along with some of their possessions (Fig. 3.4). Mud slides and avalanches also can seal over complete settlements, especially in mountainous areas. An exceptional case was the so-called Ice Man from the South Tyrol, whose body was covered by snow which subsequently turned to ice and preserved his body for 5,000 years (Spindler 1994).

The most spectacular sites caught by such acts of nature are whole communities buried by volcanic activity. Sites such as the Mycenaean settlement of Akrotiri on the island of Thera in the Aegean (Doumas 1978), or the Roman towns of Pompeii and Herculaneum in Italy (Corti 1951; Grant 1971; Maiuri 1970) provide spectacular centres for tourism because their masonry buildings have been left standing to exceptional heights. Buried sites with less imposing methods of construction,

Figure 3.4 Cornaux les Sâuges, Switzerland. The finds from this site have been interpreted as the results of a flash flood which destroyed a bridge dated by construction between 120 and 116 BC over the river Thielle, and drowning at least twenty inhabitants of a nearby settlement whose bodies were trapped under the collapsed timbers. Source: Schwab 1989.

perhaps of timber, clay and thatch, are also known throughout the world, such as deserted Viking farmsteads on Iceland, or the sixth-century farming village of Kuroimine north-west of Tokyo in Japan (Hiroshi 1992; Niiro 1993). The importance of such sites is twofold. The fall of ash is sufficiently fast to preserve buildings and artefacts *in situ*, but without the disruption caused by a flood or landslide; the settlements were sealed at a moment in time, and then left undisturbed until excavated by the archaeologist. Also, they tend to be fairly typical settlements of their period, so that the insights and details of daily life that they reveal can often be extrapolated to a wide range of other less well-preserved sites.

Occasionally wind-deposited sand can have the same effect. At Gwithian in Cornwall, a bronze age farm and its fields were engulfed by sand dunes, so that even the individual marks left by spades and plough furrows were still recognizable (Megaw *et al.* 1961; Thomas 1970). In coastal areas with unstable sand dunes, such occurrences are not unusual, and dunes may have stratified sequences of such sites; but the sites are equally prone to destruction by the wind. More normally, burial by sand is a relatively slow process, leading to gradual rather than sudden abandonment. One thinks of some of the trading oasis cities of central Asia (Mongait 1961), but it is equally true, for instance, of the whole of the Tiber estuary west of Rome, which was slowly engulfed by coastal dunes in the post-Roman period (Meiggs 1960). At sites such as Ostia, the buildings themselves may survive to a remarkable degree, but, unlike at Pompeii, Ostia's inhabitants had time to remove anything worth taking.

However, the majority of the archaeological record is preserved because of the activities of humans themselves. On sites which suffer erosion, 'artefact traps' are set up which cause archaeological deposits to build up. The most common are pits, post-holes, ditches and cellars dug into the subsoil. Defensive ramparts, house walls and fences act as physical boundaries against which material may accumulate. The problem with these man-made contexts is that they introduce an additional bias into deposition. Why and when are pits dug? Where does the material filling them originate from? This fill may reflect the purpose for which the pit was dug (for instance, rubbish pits, pottery kilns, graves, or cesspits), or it may have nothing to do with the original purpose. Unwanted cellars, grain silos, subterranean work-shops and sunken dwellings such as Anglo-Saxon *Grübenhäuser* were just filled in with whatever was at hand when they were no longer needed. The fill may represent seasonal activity: for instance, when pits for seed grain are emptied in the spring, the pits are likely to be filled in soon after; or quarries are dug only when houses have to be constructed. Possibly the material has been gathered from above-ground middens, or it has been deliberately deposited for ritual purposes (Cunliffe 1983, 1995; Hill 1995). Thus the finds from such sub-surface contexts may bear little relationship to the deposits which have been eroded away.

From the earliest times, people have introduced materials from elsewhere on to their living areas – food to eat, stone and organic tools, bedding, housing materials – thus causing an accumulation of objects, but also concentrations of chemicals such as phosphates. On many sites the process of erosion is quicker than the accumulation. As society became more complex, settlements more permanent, and especially with the arrival of wheeled transport, transporting bulky material around was made easier, and on certain types of site accumulation started to outstrip erosion. Anyone standing at the gates of a pre-industrial city would have seen much more entering the gate than leaving it. Even the rubbish tended to stay within the enclosed area, in cesspits, rubbish pits and middens or, if it was removed, it would only be for a short distance. In some societies, such as those of medieval Europe, even the dead would be buried within the city.

The major component of this build-up would be from building materials, such as sand and gravel for streets, floors and foundations; sand and lime for mortar; clay, stone, timber and bricks for walls; timber, thatch, tiles and slates for the roofs. In areas such as the Near East where sun-dried brick was used, it was easier simply to demolish the old building and build on top of it with new bricks brought in from outside. The result are the *tells*, often many metres high, which form such a distinctive feature of, for instance, the floodplains of the Tigris and Euphrates. Though such sites represent an extreme case, the characteristic of rapid accumulation is common elsewhere in the world. In western Europe the process is often disguised partly by the location of sites in terrain where the contours will mask the build-up, partly by the presence of modern towns and suburbs on and around the accumulation. None the less, excavations in the centre of towns reveal the accumulations; in major towns in Roman Britain, about a metre per century is quite normal, though the rate of accumulation is often directly proportional to the city's importance and prosperity.

The result is that excavation in urban centres, while extremely expensive because of both the depth of stratigraphy and the complexity of the deposits, is very much more productive for certain aspects of research (such as the construction of a detailed chronology of artefact types) than on rural settlements, where accumulation is usually limited or non-existent. In the past thirty years such deeply stratified sites have tended to attract greater attention than less spectacular poorly stratified sites. They also allow better analysis of the function and layout of buildings, as floors and living surfaces tend to survive, buried under later deposits, whereas on minor sites they are commonly destroyed by erosion and ploughing. In some areas such as the Near East, because of the need for a chronological framework, our knowledge of the archaeology was largely confined to the major sites, producing a major bias in the archaeological record.

The influence of deposition and survival of evidence is even more apparent when we consider matters such as religious belief and ritual. One way to divide prehistory is into 'periods of living' and 'periods of dying'; that is, periods when we can find plentiful evidence of settlement sites, but no trace of burials, and vice versa (Collis 1977). At certain periods, monuments are built either as containers for the dead, such as pyramids, barrows, and mausolea, or as a focus for burial (for instance, medieval churches). Burials in holes in the ground (graves), especially inhumations in a non-acidic soil, will attract notice and comment from even lay people not otherwise interested in archaeology. But from many periods and places we have no such data. What was happening to the dead? Were they exposed on platforms or in trees, floated down rivers, or cremated and scattered, or simply exposed to the elements and to excarnation by animals and birds? In Britain today we are entering a period when we are shifting from inhumation on centralized cemeteries, to scattered cremation, often on secular sites following the wish of the deceased individual, in contrast with other western European countries such as Spain or Italy where multi-storey blocks are sometimes constructed to accommodate the dead.

POST-DEPOSITIONAL TRANSFORMATIONS

We have already discussed how surface sites can be transformed, if not totally destroyed, by processes such as erosion. Even sites which are deeply buried are not exempt from destruction, both from natural processes such as erosion by the sea or by rivers or, in the case of sites on light sandy soils, by the wind. Increasingly, we humans are becoming the main force for the destruction of our own heritage, by urban development, quarrying, road construction and deep ploughing. In considering settlement distributions, all these forms of development which destroy the archaeology, or render it invisible, must be taken into account. Most transformations of the archaeological record are, however, not of this drastic nature, but are due to natural processes of change which affect virtually all archaeological sites.

Few soils are static and free from chemical or microbial activity. It is essential for archaeologists to understand these processes of change in the soil itself if we are to maximize our use of the archaeological record. In fine-grained soils such as clays, the mechanical movement of the grains, due, for instance, to the expansion and contraction of the soil as it dries or becomes wet, can erode even tough materials like pottery. Rising groundwater or percolating rain may move chemicals up and down the soil profile, most clearly visible in processes such as the formation of iron panning on acidic soils.

The chemistry of the soil itself has a profound effect on what survives. Acid soils will attack bones and completely destroy them within a few years, whereas in alkaline soils they will survive better. But even on strongly alkaline soils such as chalk and limestone, local conditions such as patches of clays with flints will lead to very localized acidic conditions which will cause differential survival. This is most clearly visible when complete skeletons are excavated: in one grave all the bones may be completely preserved, in a neighbouring grave only the larger ones such as the skull and long bones may survive, and then probably in a very friable state. Often such contrasts of preservation are visible in the same grave (Fig. 3.5). Studies of the fills of ditches on chalk sites have shown how small bones do not survive in the upper fill of ditches, but do in the lower fills. A jaw of a sheep in the upper fill may only survive as a collection of eroded teeth, but be completely preserved in the lower fill (Maltby 1996: 19). What might at first sight seem to be a change from a sheep-dominated economy to one dominated by cattle may thus simply be due to factors of preservation.

Changes in water content can have a disastrous effect on metals, and accelerate the process of decomposition. The combination of plentiful oxygen, an acidic soil, and water, quickly reduces bronze objects to piles of corrosion, and is even more disastrous for iron. If preservation of bones and cultural artefacts tends to be better in alkaline soils, these produce their own problems. Organically they are much more active, not only in microbial activity but also because larger creatures living in the

Figure 3.5 Wigber Low, Derbyshire, England. The skeletons of a man and a woman, buried around AD 700 with a number of weapons and other material, show the typical differential preservation on alkaline soils. Though generally the long bones have been preserved, some of the ribs and smaller bones have already decayed, but others have not, demonstrating different local soil conditions within a few centimetres of each other. Photograph: J. Collis.

soil can have a major disrupting effect on the stratigraphy. Chief among these creatures is the humble earthworm, whose ability to turn over many tonnes of soil per year has been recognized ever since Darwin's pioneering study in which he observed the speed with which earthworms could 'bury' a stone (Atkinson 1957). In fact the burying process is caused by the object sinking, as it is systematically undermined by the removal and redeposition of the finest grains of soils. The effects of this are clearly visible in soil profiles, with a fine stone-free loam forming on top of a layer of 'pea grit' mixed with larger stones and artefacts at the bottom of the worm-affected profile. The impact on the archaeological record is twofold: first, it has the effect of mixing objects which may have been deposited over a considerable period of time, and which all gradually sink to the level of the pea grit; second, worm activity causes objects which might not have been incorporated into the archaeological record to be buried. They will tend to be concentrated in areas where the soil profile is deepest, and so worm activity is at its maximum, for instance, above pre-existing pits and ditches but also occasionally in the upper filling of natural features. Such finds can be an indicator of a period of inactivity on that part of the site, with pasture replacing cultivation, rather than a period of increased activity as the number of finds might imply. On the negative side, this movement of the soils through the gut of the worm is one of the factors which can destroy other evidence such as pollen grains, as well as mixing the soils.

A HIERARCHY OF PRESERVATION

The survival of evidence from the past can be envisaged as a continuum from, at one end, inorganic materials which are virtually indestructible, to actions and beliefs, which at the most can only leave indirect traces on other materials.

Inorganic remains

Material objects made from inorganic remains are by far the most resistant. Our earliest records of human existence consist largely of stone objects, flint, quartz, obsidian and other rocks which have been turned into artefacts. Under normal circumstances they will remain intact, perhaps with little change other than the formation of a surface patina. Traces of wear from the use of the artefact, even traces of the substances on which it was used (for instance, blood traces from the cutting of meat), can survive. Only physical erosion can destroy the surface; only heavy pounding, for instance from the waves on a seashore, can totally destroy the object. Softer stones may lose their form: for example, shale used as bracelets and other jewellery, which can be worked like wood when fresh, will crack and disintegrate when exposed to a dry environment. Generally, however, stone stands at the top of the survival hierarchy.

Metals form their own hierarchy, from the 'noble' to the 'base'. Gold is virtually unaffected by chemical activity, and physical pressure or melting will only cause it to change its shape. Silver, tin, lead and the numerous alloys of copper are resistant to varying degrees. Under benign alkaline conditions a patina will form which will protect the underlying metal, and preserve surface detail such as the inscription on a coin. Under poor conditions such as in an acidic soil, all of them can be reduced to oxide powders. Iron represents the other extreme: it will rust and corrode under almost all conditions, especially where it is exposed simultaneously to both damp and oxygen. The surface rarely survives intact.

Man-made organic materials are generally resistant. Highly fired clay is almost as durable as soft stone, but poorly fired ceramics are prone to destruction from natural forces such as frost and abrasion. Thus, in field walking, post-medieval pottery, Roman Samian pottery and porcelain will survive under conditions in which prehistoric pottery disintegrates. Ancient glass is variable – surfaces can oxidize and flake on exposure to air and sunlight, while glass made from potash, like medieval glass in Europe, simply disintegrates even under normal preservation conditions.

Organic materials

Soft tissues of either plants or animals rarely survive, and generally it is only the skeletal structure which is resistant. Bones of animals will survive under alkaline conditions, but are attacked by acidic soils. In sandy soils only the most resistant parts such as the enamel of teeth may be found, though the outline of not only the skeleton but of the whole body may be traced as a 'ghost' of darker staining; the same may be true for wood, for instance the outline of the boat from Sutton Hoo (Bruce Mitford 1972, 1975). Bones of birds and fish are prone to destruction. In the latter case even under conditions where animal bone and shell are preserved, fish may only be represented by otoliths, the compact bony structure of the ear (Mellars and Wilkinson 1980). On the other hand, the silica structures of plant and tree pollen, and phytoliths (silica which fills cells in the leaves of plants, especially grasses) are resistant to acidic soils, but less so to abrasion such as occurs in soils subject to animal and microbial activity.

Soft tissues will only survive under the exceptional conditions of cold and damp, described in the next section. Otherwise, many organic remains need to undergo some form of chemical change, such as the replacement of tissue with some more resistant material which happens with the fossilization of bone and shell. For softer tissues this can mean being in contact with a metal whose corrosion products will produce salts which infiltrate and preserve the structure. A common example of this is traces of clothing (textiles, fur, and so on) in contact with copper salts from objects such as belt fittings or brooches. This happened in the iron age burial of Hochdorf in south-western Germany, where fibres included some silk-like threads, presumably imported from the east Mediterranean, and also the hairs from the pelts of badgers, with even some of the pine needles caught in their hair (Biel 1985).

The most common chemical change which leads to preservation of organic material is from burning. Under slow-burning conditions in which not enough oxygen is present to form carbon dioxide, plant remains will simply be carbonized, and wood charcoal, carbonized seeds and even chaff will be preserved, but these can only be recovered systematically by a carefully thought-out strategy of sampling, sieving and flotation. Moreover, the formation of charred remains is heavily biased towards those activities which involve fire, for instance drying cereals, heating them to assist de-husking, and especially cooking. Accidents in cooking occasionally provide us with complete loaves and residues inside pots, which, other than the stomach contents of preserved bodies, or of coprolites, are our only hints at eating habits and cuisine. The charring and cremation of bone will also lead to it surviving in acidic soils in which bone is not normally preserved.

Actions and beliefs

It is one of the basic tenets of modern archaeology that we can go beyond the actual objects themselves, and by careful observation of location and context of objects and debris we can get at the intangibles of the past, such as belief systems and activities. Occasionally this can be the single action, often of a prosaic nature, but which by its utter banality can give us a feeling of being close to our ancestors: the group of early hominids who left their footprints in the silts at Laetoli as they crossed the mud flats (Leakey and Harris 1987); a glass wine bottle in a pit in Winchester with the stone that smashed it resting on the broken pieces; the violent death of a defender at Maiden Castle with the Roman ballista bolt still embedded in his spine (Wheeler 1943). All these bring back vivid events which link us as humans to our human past, though the circumstances which surrounded these isolated events can only be conjectured.

It is the regularity of actions that it is most useful for the archaeologist to identify. An example is the regularity of movement of humans across or within space. Thus, at Wroxeter, wear on the stone rubble of collapsed early Roman buildings identified the positions of paths between the timber buildings of the fourth and fifth centuries AD (Barker 1969, 1977). Potentially worn areas in the floors of rooms may indicate movement around the house, and so how space was used; conversely, unworn areas may indicate the position of bedding or of furniture. It is such subtleties of the archaeological deposits that earlier archaeologists, intent on discovering objects or chronological sequences, failed to identify.

The examples just quoted are cross-cultural phenomena. Regular movement by humans, animals, and wheeled vehicles will produce wear at any time anywhere in the world. But at what point do such 'natural' laws give way to another logic of culturally influenced results? Ploughing a hillside will cause the soil to be eroded. Careful ploughing following the contours will conserve moisture and minimize erosion; ploughing across the contours, whether through ignorance or through greed in obtaining a quick return with no concern on the long-term effects on the environment, can cause major erosion and degradation. In this case the natural process of erosion is influenced by the cultural choice of the farmer.

The effect of cultural ideology on the archaeological record is most obvious in the realms of religion and funerary rites. Anthropologists are sceptical about the extent to which beliefs are translated into regular activity, as observations in the field generally show there is great variety (Ucko 1969). In a case quoted by Ucko, the Ashanti supposedly bury their dead facing the village; in fact not much care is taken in ensuring the body is actually facing in the right direction, as they also believe that the body itself will turn over and face in the right direction. So how can an archaeologist identify these beliefs? The anthropologist is usually making observations over only a short period of months, at most years, during fieldwork. By contrast, an archaeologist excavating a cemetery may be looking at decades, perhaps centuries, of activity, and long-term trends and norms are more easily identifiable, even if much of the detail of the ceremony and the beliefs surrounding the actions is unknown. A number of factors may influence the homogeneity of the burial rite: the nature of the belief systems; how much deviation from the norm is tolerated; how familiar the group carrying out the burial was with the norms of the burial rite. This latter will be influenced by the time that has elapsed between one burial and the next, and whether there was a group within the society which specialized in giving advice or actually conducting the ceremony. Many of our distribution maps of objects are influenced by the basic factors in the disposal of the dead.

The burial of objects with the dead may occur for many reasons: to accompany the dead person in the after-life; as a display of destruction of wealth to demonstrate power; due to taboos about using objects belonging to someone dead; or simply sentimentality, like the woman recently in Chesterfield in Derbyshire (England) who buried her husband's beer mug with him! The deposition of grave-goods is something 'understood' cross-culturally, even among societies where it is not practised, though its actual meaning may not be understood. The deliberate destruction of wealth for religious or prestige purposes (for instance, a potlatch) are less 'understood'. As a coroner in Guildford said, summing up for his jury for them to decide whether a group of gold and silver coins was buried with or without intent of recovery (and so whether it was treasure trove, and thus according to English law the property of the Crown): 'what person in their right mind deliberately throws away gold and silver?' For capitalist westerners, such an act is folly and incomprehensible; for a Kwakiutl chieftain it would have been a potent sign of power and prestige.

Even less obvious is the boundary between 'natural' and 'cultural' in a 'domestic' context. The case of clearing away large fragments of pottery from the living area and depositing them elsewhere where they were out of the way may seem logical, but is such logic always followed? Hodder has discussed cases where the attitude towards 'rubbish' can be very different even among adjacent and contemporary societies with similar economies and technologies, one systematically removing it, the other disguising it but leaving it on the settlement (Hodder 1982). On neolithic and iron age settlements in Britain, archaeologists have generally assumed that pits and ditches were filled with 'rubbish', but once the basic proposition was questioned, it was found that the contents of pits by no means conformed to the 'rubbish' that a settlement might logically be expected to produce (Cunliffe 1983, 1995; Hill 1995). So, is iron age 'rubbish' simply different from 'rubbish' in other societies, or was the deposited material something radically different with ritual overtones, or is the whole concept of 'rubbish' false in such societies, and merely imposed though our own cultural bias?

These are direct examples where ideology and belief impose themselves directly on the archaeological record; they can also do so indirectly. Artefacts and ecofacts survive usually because they are buried, and they are more likely to become buried if there are holes for them to become buried in. As an example, why do some societies enclose settlements, fields, houses, with ditches? It can be for defence, to define areas with different functions, to prevent animals from straying, for display and prestige, or simply as a symbol of a boundary (Collis 1996). Whatever the reason, these ditches will subsequently fill up with 'natural' or 'cultural' deposits, but it is the very presence of the ditch that allows this material to become incorporated within an archaeological deposit, making such sites easier to locate, for instance through aerial photographs. Thus, sites and periods with ditches are likely to be over-represented and better understood than those without. They will also bias distributions of objects against those areas where ditch digging was not the norm, so one type of object may be commonly found in one area and never in another, even though both areas were using the same objects.

Thus the recognition of such norms and regularities of belief systems are an essential first task for the archaeologist wishing to interpret the archaeological record. But we have to adjust our thinking away from our own cultural bias if such regularities are to be identified. We in our turn may be able to identify regularities of which the practitioners themselves may have been unaware.

SPECIAL CASES OF PRESERVATION

So far we have generally been dealing with 'normal' conditions under which the vast majority of artefacts and debris produced by a society disappeared through the natural process of decay. There are, however, exceptional circumstances in which this process is arrested.

Preservation through desiccation

One immediately thinks of the valley of the Nile as the supreme example of preservation in desiccated conditions – the wooden ships of the pharaoh Cheops at Giza, the tomb of Tutankhamun, the mummies which grace almost every large museum in Europe. Much of our knowledge of early literature is derived from such sources, Egyptian papyri such as those from Oxyrhinicus, the Dead Sea scrolls (Allegro 1956), or the texts from the caves of Tun Huang in central Asia (Renfrew 1987: 64–5). Desert conditions in the south-west of the United States have preserved a rich range of finds, mainly from caves, made by the early Indian 'Basket Maker' cultures – not only the basketry and other woven containers which give their name to the culture, but a range of wooden artefacts and less attractive material such as coprolites which give us a detailed insight into the diet. The timbers of Pueblo Indian villages have allowed the construction of a dendrochronological sequence for the south-western United States, and with it details of the major drought in the fourteenth century which decimated the rich cultures of the area (Douglass 1919, 1928, 1936). The desert areas of Peru have also produced preserved finds, especially bodies, from caves.

But such conditions are not as rare as we may think, though finds may not be so old or as spectacular as those already mentioned. Anywhere where damp is unable to penetrate and the microbial organisms responsible for decay are unable to survive, organic remains are likely to survive. Timbers in many churches and castles in Europe have survived for a thousand years or more, and wood in domestic buildings several hundred years old is not uncommon. Finds such as leather shoes and dead animals are regularly found under floors or in chimneys, sometimes deliberately deposited. Stone-built tombs in cathedrals can preserve wooden coffins and textiles, as in the tomb of St Cuthbert in Durham; some of the objects such as the decorated coffin itself date to a couple of years after the saint's death in AD 687 (Cronyn and Horie 1985), others to the date of his reburial in 1104. Preservation is greater where deliberate efforts at conservation are made, in libraries and treasuries.

Waterlogged conditions

When organic material is permanently under water, and oxygen is unable to penetrate, microbial activity is likewise inhibited. This is the most common form of preservation in temperate Europe, both in natural and man-made situations. Bogs may not have been entirely congenial conditions in which people could live, but they do preserve sequences of natural vegetation, both in the form of macroscopic plant remains, and as pollen grains and spores. But such conditions did attract early people, with their resources of fish, wildfowl, reeds for basketry and thatching (Coles 1992). Sometimes trackways were constructed to provide access to these resources, or simply the bog may have been in the way and had to be traversed, giving rise to the sorts of trackway found in the Somerset Levels dating to as early as the fifth millennium BC (Coles and Coles 1986).

However, the degree of preservation is also dependent on the mineral content of the soil. Textiles are preserved under some circumstances, like the clothing in the coffin burials of Egtved, Muldbjerg, Bornum Eshøj and Skrydstrup in Denmark (Glob 1974). Leather is more common, in the form of shoes, belts, caps, and cut-offs from leather working, largely because it has undergone a tanning process which makes it more resilient to decay. The famous 'bog' burials of Denmark and northern Germany ostensibly seem perfectly preserved, even to the wrinkles on Tollund Man's face (Glob 1969). The stomach and other internal organs also survive, but this is largely due to the tannin derived from oak trees growing in the vicinity which has naturally 'tanned' the skin. Despite this the bones generally do not survive as they have been dissolved by the acid conditions. The softer tissues disappear, both of plants and animals, or rather they collapse as the water content is dried out, but the harder materials such as the husks of seeds, the epidermis of insects, parasite eggs, pips and stones from fruits, commonly survive under waterlogged conditions.

Wood is the most resilient of the organic materials to survive by waterlogging, often in exquisite detail. To name only some of the more spectacular examples, there are the 5,000 fragments of votive offerings from the early Roman shrine at Chamalières in central France (Provost and Mennessier-Jouannet 1994: 57–61; Fig. 3.6). Many are simply rough-hewn arms and legs, but there are also schematic representations of internal organs such as lungs and intestines, as well as breasts and eyes, presumably a request to the divinity for these parts of the body to be healed. One or two are high quality portraits like the bust of a woman, or goddess, shown wearing a torc. Both in terms of scale and quality of artistic content, the most spectacular find is the Viking ship from Oseberg in Norway, perhaps the burial of a queen who died around AD 800 (Brøgger and Shetelig 1951; Wilson 1970; Fig. 3.7). The ornate carving of the prow is among the finest surviving examples of Viking art, but other finds loaded on to the boat included vehicles such as sledges, and household furniture and containers, pillows, and decorative items such as peacocks' feathers. The oldest surviving wooden artefacts are the pointed stick or spear from waterlogged contexts at Clacton-on-Sea in England, dated to about a quarter of a million years ago, and the newly discovered finds from Schöningen in Germany dated to about 380,000 years ago (see Chapter 20).

Shipwrecks too often produce plentiful wood remains, but only if the timbers have been buried in silt, and so preserved both from attack by sea creatures and from currents (for instance, see Bass 1996). The presence of a wreck is often only betrayed by inorganic finds such as wine amphorae or iron cannon, and there is a natural bias in discovery towards periods when ships were carrying such visible items. If the boat has sunk in an upright position, usually only the keel and the lower part of the hull are preserved, but many boats keel over, so preserving one side of the boat. Two almost new boats whose sinking was recorded historically have been located and raised for preservation, the Swedish man-of-war, the *Vasa*, lost in

Figure 3.6 Chamalièrcs, Puy-de-Dôme, France. Some 5,000 wooden objects, depicting mainly legs, arms, but also breasts, intestines, busts, and images of animals, were deposited in a shallow lake, presumably as votive offerings. Source: Provost and Mennessier-Jouannet 1994.

1698 (Landstrøm 1988), and the *Mary Rose*, which sank on 20 July 1545, destabilized by the simultaneous firing of its cannons (Rule 1983). In both cases they have produced a wealth of ship's instruments, personal belongings and stores, including weapons such as bows and arrows. The early medieval ships displayed in the boat museum at Roskilde were deliberately sunk to protect the entrance of the harbour from attack, and though not so informative in terms of contents, they do show a range of the different vessels in use at the period (Olsen and Crumlin Pedersen 1967; Wilson 1970).

Frozen finds

Even in the Arctic it is only under special circumstances that remains will become frozen. Normally settlements are on the surface, so subject to thawing and freezing

Figure 3.7 Oseberg, Norway. A view of the ship burial as found; it is dated to around AD 800. It had been preserved by burial in a damp environment, and by being sealed with clay. © Universitetets Oldsaksamling.

with the seasons, and only in conditions of permafrost will organic material survive, for instance in pits or shelters, or where a settlement has been buried in an avalanche. Thus, some burials and settlements have been preserved, for instance at Utqiagvik (Barrow) in Alaska (Dekin 1987; Lobdell and Dekin 1984) and at Qilakitsoq on the western coast of Greenland (Hart Hanson *et al.* 1985, 1991), and, in the latter case, also the Viking settlement which was wiped out by worsening climatic conditions in the fourteenth century AD.

The Austrian 'Ice Man' was a freak preservation (Spindler 1994). Bodies incorporated into glaciers normally come out at the bottom within a century or two. He died in a natural hollow protected from glacial action, but also his body must have been buried quite quickly, again under worsening weather conditions. The famous burials from Pazyryk only survived because water condensed on the stones of the cairns and dripped into, and flooded, the underlying timber chambers (Rudenko 1970). In the winter the ice froze, but during the summer in the cases

110

where the cairn was sufficiently large, it acted as insulation, and the tombs remained permanently frozen; this did not occur under the smaller cairns.

In all these cases the material is exceptionally well preserved, including the soft tissues. In all three cases, Eskimos, the 'Ice Man', and at Pazyryk, tattoos could be identified on the skin, in the last case with elaborate animal art. At Pazyryk, dated to around 400 BC, felt clothing, a wagon canopy, carpets and silk textiles, saddles and harness, along with the horses' bodies, and equipment for inhaling hemp, all survived intact.

Mineral preservation

Fills of cesspits often survive in exceptional condition, due to the process of waterlogging followed by desiccation which can mineralize the contents, thus preserving seeds, and eggs of internal parasites such as tapeworms.

An unusual case of preservation due to carbonic acid from a volcanic spring occurred in the Roman cemetery of Les Martres-de-Veyre in central France (Provost and Mennessier-Jouannet 1994: 182–86; Fig. 3.8). Not only were the wooden coffins preserved, but also the plaited hair-dos of the women. In one case a body was buried wearing shoes, woollen stockings and a woollen dress and belt. Small plates and cups are common in Roman burials, but only at Les Martres have the contents been preserved – small tarts, raisins, plums and coriander seeds.

The salt mines at Hallstatt in Austria have also produced numerous organic remains preserved in the salt (Barth 1983). Much of it is prosaic, such as coprolites and the charred ends of the pine torches used to light the galleries. Wooden tools such as handles, mattocks and wedges are also known, and the haversacks made of wood and skin used to transport the salt out of the mine. In the eighteenth century the preserved body of a miner was found, but unfortunately reburied without any scientific study. He was interred at the local church in the modern town of Hallstatt, but outside the consecrated ground, because it was thought that he might not have been 'a true Catholic'!

THE ARCHAEOLOGICAL RECORD

We are now in a position to review the nature of the archaeological record, what it can and cannot tell us, and how potentially it can be misunderstood and abused. As with the case of the Roman coin, it is useful if we do this as a sort of hierarchy, working from the single individual find and building up to inter-regional comparisons. At all levels there are potential pitfalls in interpretations and misunderstanding.

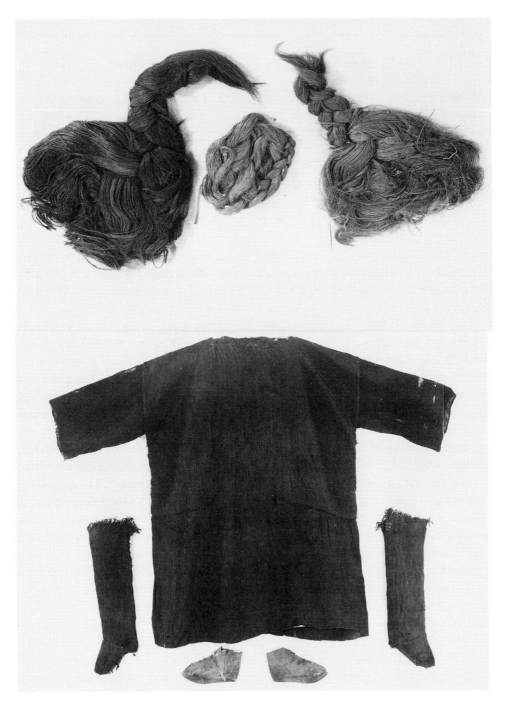

Figure 3.8 Les Martres-de-Veyre, Puy-de-Dôme, France. Better known for its Samian pottery kilns, the site has also produced Roman burials with exceptional preservation due to mineral springs. Not only are the clothes and hair of the dead preserved, but also the food offerings in the cups and bowls which are normal accompaniments of Roman burials elsewhere. Reproduced with permission of the Centre Regional de Documentation Pedagogique, Clermont-Ferrand.

The individual, the artefact and the ecofact

At the lowest level, there is the individual find, be it a potsherd, a bone, a person, or a pollen grain.

At all levels of the hierarchy we must face the significance of absence as much as presence. At the lowest level it is a question of what has not survived; in other words, post-depositional transformations. On most sites this will be the majority of the material culture, everything made out of organic material such as wood, tissues and leather; on acidic soils it may also include bones and metal objects as well. Considering absence does help to concentrate the mind on maximizing the value of the evidence which does survive. Thus, a skeleton may not survive as bone in a grave, but its presence should be looked for, either in the form of a silhouette, or a few pieces of tooth enamel, or simply as a concentration of phosphate in the grave. Suitable strategies can then be prepared to recognize and record such evidence as may exist.

For objects which are found, there are two immediate questions which pose themselves; the first is, when was it deposited and is it contamination? It may have been brought down from a higher level by a burrowing animal or by worm action, and it could have slipped down through a crack in the soil, or even been introduced in the mud on the excavator's boot. The resolution of this depends on maintaining a clean digging environment. If it is a genuine find in its proper context, there is the second related question of how it was deposited. Is it in its primary position, a potsherd or group of potsherds with unworn breaks, dumped soon after the pot was broken, or is it a worn and highly fragmented sherd which has been lying around for some time, perhaps even deposited from another context? This question of 'residuality' is a major problem on deeply stratified and long-lived sites. It is relatively easy to recognize with intrinsically dated objects like pottery or coins, but less easy to identify with undated material like bones. In the case of bones, are the fragments fresh, with little sign of erosion and gnawing? Perhaps they are even in articulation with other bones, or dumped as a group of bones derived from a single carcass. Though it is best to be treating the group of finds as a sample, dating is provided by the latest object in the group, for instance the latest coin, and this provides the *terminus post quem* – that is, the earliest date that the deposit could have formed (see Chapter 5).

Material can be deposited due to entirely natural processes, pollen rain for example. At the other extreme, objects can be deliberately placed in position by humans, and that positioning may be highly significant, like the orientation of a corpse or the location of a pot or other object in the grave. In these cases the archaeologist will need to record the details with care. Most deposition falls between these two extremes: material that has been thrown into a pit as part of rubbish disposal; rubbish that had been dumped nearby and was finally deposited through erosion; an animal that had fallen into a pit and died. These are the subtleties of deposition which need to be understood if a deposit, indeed a site, is to be properly interpreted.

The context

The context is a term used by field archaeologists to describe the location of a group of finds. Normally it is synonymous with a layer in a pit or a ditch, or a floor, or a wall of a building, and so on: it is the matrix in which archaeological finds are found, and so it is a means of grouping finds into meaningfully associated groups. In theory such a group of finds in a context is contemporary, but this is only true to the extent that they were deposited at the same time, or during the period of time in which the soil which forms the matrix of the context was accumulating. The context could contain 'residual' finds, material accidentally dug up when a pit has been cut through earlier deposits, a common problem on deeply stratified sites. It may also contain material that has been 'stored' for some time, like rubbish on an above-ground midden or, in the case of human remains, a body that had been excarnated by exposing it to the elements, and only buried after the flesh had been removed by animals and natural processes of decay. It may contain material that was in use at the same time, but which included items which had been in circulation for some time, such as family heirlooms or coins which were a century or more old but which still had a value and were still in use.

Such a group of finds represents a 'sample', partly a sample of what was actually in use and circulating at the time of deposition, partly a sample of all the rubbish that had already accumulated on the site. Deciding which category individual finds belong to is not always easy. One way is to look at the fragmentation patterns, distinguishing between primary deposition (large, fresh fragments) and secondary deposition (small, worn, fragments derived from elsewhere), but such distinctions depend on the nature of the deposit. In a pit, contemporary sherds are likely to be large, whereas in a floor level they are likely to be small and highly fragmented.

As at the artefact level, a distinction needs to be made between 'deliberate' and 'natural' deposition. The latter will include the effects of erosion, but may also include deposits which have taken a long time to develop, such as a 'turf line' which may have been subject to worm sorting over a considerable length of time. In contrast, deliberate dumping of material is often something which happens over a very brief span of time, though the material used may have been gradually accumulating somewhere else. This distinction between material that has accumulated *in situ*, and material which has been brought from elsewhere and dumped, is important if we are to identify 'activity areas', as dumping can distort the spatial pattern.

114

Seasonality is also an important factor. Most hunter-gatherer sites are of a seasonal nature, and even in sedentary agricultural societies there may be seasonally occupied sites, connected with activities such as transhumance, salt-making, or fairs, all of which involve part of the population moving away from the permanent settlement for a period of time. But even on sites which are occupied throughout the year, there are activities which will lead to seasonal deposits forming, such as the filling up of storage pits in which the seed grain was stored over winter. In this case, infilling will take place in late spring and early summer, though the actual fill may be derived from above-ground middens formed throughout the year. Effects of heavy rain or frost on newly excavated ditches and pits may also lead to more rapid build-up in specific seasons, and again introduce the bias that material from certain seasons is more likely to be buried and be over-represented. Such seasonal bias has to be tested for against a model of what might be expected, and seeing if, for instance, certain stages of eruption of animals' teeth are over-represented, and looking at the presence of migratory birds, or of shed and unshed antlers of deer.

The feature

A feature can be defined in several ways. It may be an individual hole dug into the ground: a pit, a post-hole, a ditch, or an oven. Or it may be part of a larger structure: a room of a building, an enclosure in a farmyard complex, or a field, or a trackway. Each of these is a separate functional unit, with activities which may be special to it, and therefore associated with different sorts of finds. Within a house, separate rooms will have different functions: kitchen, entrance hall, dining room, bedrooms, storage, dairy, though in a simpler and poorer house one room may perform many of these functions. Rooms may be used by different categories of people, with differentiation by class (owners and servants), by sex (male and female quarters as in Roman public baths), by age (the children's nursery), or by occupation (outdoor and indoor servants, doorkeeper). Each in theory should leave behind a distinctive group of finds, like the hairpins which appear in the drains of the female bath establishments in the Roman period.

The reality is, of course, more complex, one of the problems being the relationship of context and finds to the feature. In houses, rubbish will not usually start accumulating until it has been abandoned, though some items reflecting the original use may be left if they are not worth recovering. It is only in the case of uncontrolled abandonment, through flood, avalanche, volcanic eruption, plague, or some such disaster, that the finds may be genuinely those used in the room; such cases are important, as they allow us to extrapolate to less well-preserved situations. But many mistakes have been made in the past by assuming too readily that finds in a feature reflect its use. Carbonized grains from the post-hole do not mean that it was part of a granary, and carbonized grain in a storage pit is unlikely to have been burnt *in situ*. Sunken-floored houses (*Grübenhäuser*) of the Anglo-Saxon period in England are often assumed to have had an industrial function, especially for weaving, so occurrences of loomweights are carefully recorded, but they are often just amongst the rubbish dumped to level up the hole when it was abandoned and may have nothing to do with the original use.

Ditches and storage pits, or tanks used for industrial purposes like tanning and dyeing, are kept clean until they are no longer needed. Thus the finds in a ditch date to the period when it was going out of use, and may reflect neither the period when the ditch was first dug, nor the activities which went on in the adjacent enclosures. A corn silo is only filled when it has turned sour, or the sides have become too degraded for it to be used. Only in some cases was the pit made deliberately to be filled with its contents – foundation trenches for stone walls, graves, rubbish and cesspits.

The structure

Features are parts of larger entities. Rooms, courtyards and gardens make up house compounds; byres, stables, dairies and livestock enclosures form farmyards; arable fields, pastures and trackways make field systems. At this level, too, it is easy to pick up functional and social differences: the residences of the rich and the poor; domestic houses; workshops and factories; cult buildings. Even so, the outward form may not necessarily reflect function; indeed function can change, like the conversion of the courtyard houses at Pompeii into industrial buildings, or redundant churches into barns and offices.

The site

Even in the simplest social systems, sites have different sorts of function: the base camp, the hunting stand, the kill site, or sites occupied seasonally to exploit special resources. Such sites will have their distinctive range of tools associated with those activities. In more complex sites there may be functional hierarchies: city, town, village, farm; or special sites: ports, cult sites, industrial centres, forts. These too will possess special types of architecture, finds, and industrial waste, reflecting their role.

However, it is not always easy to define a site. In normal archaeological terminology a site is represented by a concentration of finds, but when we consider a farm, it consists of farm buildings, stock enclosures, arable fields, pasture, and trackways to give access both to the field and to neighbouring sites. A town could be supposed to consist only of the built-up area, but in Roman times, for instance, the town also included a *territorium*, which included fields and allotments belonging to the inhabitants, as well as the cemeteries of the town, which by law had to be outside the built-up limits. Such sites consist, then, of a complex of zones with different functions. In discussing the functioning of the rural estate, von Thünen in the nineteenth century defined the areas in terms of concentric circles of exploitation – dairy, arable, woodland, pasture – each with their own distinctive activities (Chisholm 1962). Geographers have attempted similar analysis of urban centres (Haggett 1965), like Sjoberg's concept (1960) of the 'pre-industrial city', with its core dominated by religious and administrative buildings; around this were the houses of the élite land-owning class who controlled the religion and administration, and in the outer core of the city were the poorer areas, themselves fragmented into separate zones. These different quarters could be defined in terms of occupation (butchers, leather workers, merchants, weavers), or by wealth, or by ethnicity (for instance, the Jewish quarters in medieval towns).

But archaeologists also deal with time. Settlements expand and contract, and the pattern of occupation in one part of the settlement may be very different from that in another. A good example is the Roman town of Verulamium (St Albans, Herts.), which started around a Roman fort, at first expanding along the primary through-routes, then along secondary parts of the street grid (Frere 1983). At various times defences and boundaries were established. Wheeler's excavations in the 1930s suggested that the town was in general decline by the early fourth century, based on his excavation in the southern part of the walled area (Wheeler and Wheeler 1936). Frere's excavations in the 1950s in the centre of the town produced wealthy houses constructed towards the end of the fourth century (Frere 1983: 20–25). In contrast, the western suburb of the town was isolated from the main part of the town by the construction of a new defensive wall, and it was already in decline in the third century (Curnow 1988; Stead and Rigby 1989). Excavations in different parts of the town therefore have given very contrasting pictures about the origin and the final abandonment of the site.

The region

In comparing one settlement with another, for instance the relative occurrence of imported pottery compared with local wares, or the ratio of different animal species, it is obviously important to be comparing like with like. If one wishes to compare two settlements in terms of access to fine pottery or glass, it is pointless if the sample for one comes from an élite part of the town and for the other from a low-class or industrial area. Adequate sampling strategies need to be in place both for individual settlements and at a regional scale. With caution, for some categories of finds, regional 'norms' can be established, even using chance finds as has been done for coins in various parts of the Roman empire, and the occurrence of coins on a particular site can be compared with the norm (Casey 1988; Reece 1972, 1988). The relative rarity of first- and second-century coins in Britain would mean that their absence on a site would not be particularly significant, whereas the absence of common third- and fourth-century coins would. The sort of mistake that has been made in the past is claiming, for instance, a great upsurge of activity on a site in the mid-third century because coin numbers increase dramatically, when in fact this simply reflects the regional norm.

In looking at a region, potential biases must first be investigated. An active museum can encourage finds to be reported in its close proximity; the activities of individual fieldworkers can increase densities of finds; some sorts of sites show up better on aerial photographs and some soils and crops are more susceptible to such methods. Settlements may be completely masked by woodland, pasture, or modern conurbations; they may have been completely eroded, or be buried under deep deposits of colluvium or alluvium. Even where attempts are made to overcome these biases by systematic field walking (Haselgrove *et al.* 1985; Shennan 1985), certain periods, for instance with an abundant lithic technology or with more durable pottery, may be better represented than those without. If a certain period is poorly represented, some independent confirmation should be looked for before it can genuinely be interpreted as a drop in population: one thinks of the Dark Ages in both Greece (Morris 1987; Snodgrass 1971) and western Europe, when in part the lack of sites is due to a drop in the production of pottery, though a drop in the population is certainly part of the explanation. In parts of Poland, at the end of the Lausitz period in the Early Iron Age (the sixth century BC), the lack of sites seems to be confirmed by evidence from pollen cores, which show considerable forest regeneration, implying abandonment (Buch and Gramsch 1986).

Inter-regional comparisons

The distribution map is a common archaeological tool, a method of quantifying archaeological data visually. Usually all such maps show are the positive occurrences of the traits plotted, and rarely are symbols used to show a genuine lack of evidence, for instance, where there are pottery assemblages which lack the type being plotted. Blank areas on maps may reflect either a lack of fieldwork, or a genuine gap. They can also mean that the trait being plotted is not actually the one that it is claimed to be plotted: the distribution of Roman coins and bronze vessels in Figure 3.9, for example, is not one of Roman trade contacts but of local burial rites. Thus, a distribution map of a sword type may not show where such swords were in use but simply where they were deposited in graves or in votive offerings at

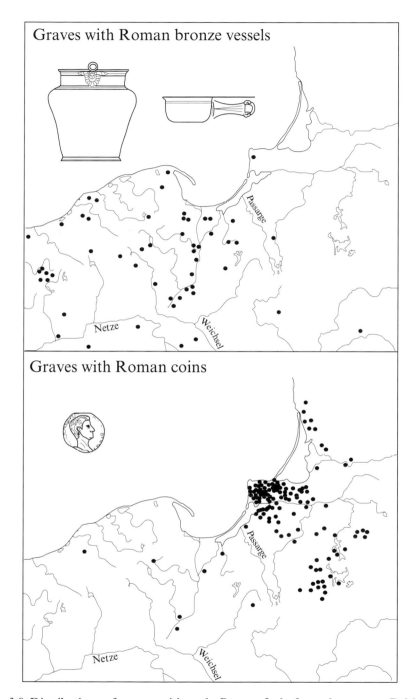

Figure 3.9 Distributions of graves with early Roman finds from the eastern Baltic. The distribution does not show the intensity of trade contact, but simply two areas with different burial rites, one employing imported Roman bronze vessels, the other Roman coins. © Piper Verlag GmbH, Munich 1959. Redrawn by D. Miles-Williams.

religious sites or in rivers. In inter-regional comparisons, it is usually two things that are being plotted, field activity, and deposition. Rarely do such maps show genuine distributions of the use of objects.

CONCLUSION

Like any historical document, archaeological data can tell us a great deal about the past as long as we are aware of the biases that are inherent in them. They form a document that has been written by many people, most of whom were not conscious that someone later would try to 'read' what they had left on the landscape. They are a document written in many languages, some of which we think we can read, some of which we may be misled by, and some of which is in a language nowadays totally incomprehensible. Much of the document has been destroyed and defaced and will never be reconstructed, and we need to preserve as much of it as we can until our reading becomes more proficient, though for many sites time is short as we are destroying the archaeological record at an alarming rate. Each of us has our own reading built on our own experience, and none of us will read the document in precisely the same way; each generation will see the document differently, but this is one of the attractions of archaeology.

The archaeological record is a complex tool, full of the knowledge accumulated by generations of archaeologists. It is constantly being improved as more sophisticated questions are asked of it, as more and more archaeologists are employed, and as our means of data storage and manipulation develop with better technology. With due caution, we can use areas which have been intensively investigated to give us clues about areas where less work has been done; large-scale and skilful excavations of selected sites can inform us about the many sites it is not possible to dig; and chance discoveries of exceptional quality in terms of preservation can tell us much about what does not normally survive in the archaeological record. But we must also be aware of the negative aspects of the record, and how it has become biased and distorted, due to the processes by which it came into existence. Archaeological data have enormous potential for interpretation, and even more possibilities for misinterpretation.

REFERENCES

Allegro, J. M. (1956) *The Dead Sea Scrolls*, Harmondsworth: Penguin Books.
Annable, F. K. and Simpson, D. D. A. (1964) *Guide Catalogue of the Neolithic and Bronze Age Collections in Devizes Museum*, Devizes: Wiltshire Archaeological and Natural History Society.

Atkinson, R. J. C. (1957) 'Worms and weathering', *Antiquity* 31: 219–33.

Barker, P. A. (1969) 'Some aspects of the excavation of timber buildings', *World Archaeology* 1: 220–30.

Barker, P. A. (1977) *Techniques of Archaeological Excavation*, London: Batsford.

Barth, F. E. (1983) 'Prehistoric salt mining at Hallstatt', *Bulletin of the Institute of Archaeology* 19: 31–43.

Bass, G. (1996) *Ships and Shipwrecks in the Americas*, London and New York, Thames and Hudson.

Bateman, T. (1861) *Ten Years' Digging in Celtic and Saxon Grave Hills in the Counties of Derby, Stafford, and York from 1848–1858*, London: Privately printed.

Beresford, M. and Hurst, J. G. (1990) *Wharram Percy: Deserted Medieval Village*, London: English Heritage/Batsford.

Bersu, G. (1940) 'Excavations at Little Woodbury, Wiltshire. Part I: the settlement revealed by excavation', *Proceedings of the Prehistoric Society* 29: 206–13.

Bersu, G. (1977) *Three Iron Age Round Houses in the Isle of Man: Excavation Report*, Glasgow: Robert MacLehose and Co.

Biddle, M. (1973) 'Winchester: the development of an early capital', in J. Jankuhn, W. Schlesinger, and H. Stewer (eds) *Vor- und Frühformen der europäischer Stadt im Mittelalter*, Göttingen, Vandenhoeck and Ruprecht: Abhandlungen der Akademie der Wissenschaft in Göttingen: 229–61.

Biel, J. (1985) *Der Keltenfürst von Hochdorf*, Stuttgart: Konrad Theiss Verlag.

Binford, L. R. (1977) *For Theory Building in Archaeology*, New York: Academic Press.

Binford, L. R. (1983) *In Pursuit of the Past*, London and New York: Thames and Hudson.

Boon, G. C. (1974) *Silchester: the Roman Town of Calleva*, Newton Abbott: David and Charles.

Bowden, M. (1991) *Pitt-Rivers: the Life and Archaeological Work of Lieutenant Augustus Henry Lane-Fox Pitt-Rivers, DCL, FRS, FSA*, Cambridge: Cambridge University Press.

Bowden, M. and McOmish, D. (1987) 'The required barrier', *Scottish Archaeological Review* 4: 76–84.

Braidwood, R. J. and Howe, B. (1960) *Prehistoric Investigations in Iraqi Kurdistan*, Studies in Ancient Oriental Civilisation, No. 31, Chicago: Oriental Institute of the University of Chicago.

Brøgger, A. W. and Shetelig, H. (1951) *The Viking Ships, their Ancestry and Evolution*, Oslo: Dreyers.

Bruce Mitford, R. L. S. (1972) *The Sutton Hoo Ship Burial: a Handbook*, London: British Museum.

Bruce Mitford, R. L. S. (1975) *The Sutton Hoo Ship Burial: Vol. 1, Excavations, Background, the Ship, Dating and Inventory*, London: British Museum.

Buch, D.-W. and Gramsch, B. (eds) (1986) *Siedlung, Wirtschaft und Gesellschaft während der jüngeren Bronze- und Hallstattzeit in Mitteleuropa*, Berlin: Museum für Ur- und Frühgeschichte, Potsdam.

Byers, D. S. (ed.) (1967–72) *The Prehistory of the Tehuacán Valley*, Vols 1–5, Austin: University of Texas Press.

Casey, J. (1988) 'The interpretation of Romano-British site finds', in J. Casey and R. Reece (eds) *Coins and the Archaeologist* (2nd edition), London: Seaby.

Casey, J. and Reece, R. (eds) (1988) *Coins and the Archaeologist* (2nd edition), London: Seaby.

Champion, T. C. and Collis, J. R. (eds) (1996) *The Iron Age in Britain and Ireland: Recent Trends*, Sheffield: J. R. Collis Publications.

Cherry, J., Gamble C. and Shennan, S. (eds) (1978) *Sampling in Contemporary British Archaeology*, Oxford: British Archaeological Reports, British Series 50.

Childe, V. G. (1929) *The Danube in Prehistory*, Oxford: Clarendon Press.

Chisholm, M. (1962) *Rural Settlement and Land Use*, London: Hutchinson.

Christaller, W. (1935) *Die zentralen Orten in Süddeutschland*, Jena.

Clarke, D. L. (1968) *Analytical Archaeology*, London: Methuen.

Coles, B. (ed.) (1992) *The Wetland Revolution in Prehistory*, Exeter: Prehistoric Society and Wetland Archaeological Research Project.

Coles, B. and Coles, J. (1986) *Sweet Track to Glastonbury*, London: Thames and Hudson.

Coles, J. M. (1987) *Meare Village East: the Excavations of A. Bulleid and H. St. George Gray, 1932–1956*, Somerset Levels Papers 13, Exeter.

Coles, J. M. and Minnitt, S. (1995) *Industrious and Fairly Civilised: the Glastonbury Lake Village*, Exeter: Somerset Levels Project and Somerset County Museums Service.

Collis, J. R. (1977) 'Pre-Roman burial rites in north-western Europe', in R. Reece (ed.) *Burial in the Roman World*, London: Council for British Archaeology: 1–12.

Collis, J. R. (1983) *Wigber Low, Derbyshire: a Bronze Age and Anglian Burial Site in the White Peak*, Sheffield: University of Sheffield, Department of Prehistory and Archaeology.

Collis, J. R. (1984) *The European Iron Age*, London: Batsford.

Collis, J. R. (1988) 'Data for dating', in J. Casey and R. Reece (eds) *Coins and the Archaeologist* (2nd edition), London: Seaby: 189–200.

Collis, J. R. (1996) 'Hill-forts, enclosures and boundaries', in T. C. Champion and J. R. Collis (eds) *The Iron Age in Britain and Ireland: Recent Trends*, Sheffield: J. R. Collis Publications: 87–94.

Colt Hoare, R. (1812–21) *The Ancient History of South (and North) Wiltshire*, London: W. Miller.

Corti, E. G. (1951) *The Destruction and Resurrection of Pompeii and Herculaneum*, London: Routledge and Kegan Paul.

Crawford, O. G. S. and Keiller, A. (1928) *Wessex from the Air*, Oxford: Clarendon.

Cronyn, J. M. and Horie, C. V. (1985) *St. Cuthbert's Coffin: the History, Technology and Conservation*, Durham: Durham Cathedral.

Cunliffe, B. W. (1983) *Danebury: Anatomy of a Hillfort*, London: Batsford.

Cunliffe, B. W. (1995) *Danebury: an Iron Age Hillfort in Hampshire. 6: A Hillfort Community in Perspective*, Research Report 102, London: Council for British Archaeology.

Curnow, P. (1988) 'Coin lists: some problems of the smaller site', in J. Casey and R. Reece (eds) *Coins and the Archaeologist* (2nd edition), London: Seaby: 57–72.

Daniel, G. (1964) *The Idea of Prehistory*, Harmondsworth: Penguin Books.

Daniel, G. (1967) *Origins and Growth of Archaeology*, Harmondsworth: Penguin Books.

Daniel, G. (1975) *A Hundred and Fifty Years of Archaeology*, London: Duckworth.

Déchelette, J. (1908) *Manuel d'Archéologie Préhistorique, Celtique et Gallo-Romaine. I: Archéologie Préhistorique*, Paris: Librairie Alphonse Picard et fils.

Déchelette, J. (1910) *Manuel d'Archéologie Préhistorique, Celtique et Gallo-Romaine. II-1: Age du Bronze*, Paris: Librairie Alphonse Picard et fils.

Déchelette, J. (1913) *Manuel d'Archéologie Préhistorique, Celtique et Gallo-Romaine. II-2: Deuxième Age du Fer ou Époque de Hallstatt*, Paris: Librairie Alphonse Picard et fils.

Déchelette, J. (1914) *Manuel d'Archéologie Préhistorique, Celtique et Gallo-Romaine. II-3: Deuxième Age du Fer ou Époque de La Tène*, Paris: Librairie Alphonse Picard et fils.

Dekin, A. A. (1987) 'Sealed in time: ice entombs an Eskimo family for five centuries', *National Geographic* 171 (6): 824–36.

Douglass, A. E. (1919) *Climatic Cycles and Tree Growth*, Vol. 1, Washington, DC: Carnegie Institution of Washington.

Douglass, A. E. (1928) *Climatic Cycles and Tree Growth*, Vol. 2, Washington, DC: Carnegie Institution of Washington.

Douglass, A. E. (1936) *Climatic Cycles and Tree Growth*, Vol. 3, Washington, DC: Carnegie Institution of Washington.

Doumas, C. (ed.) (1978) *Thera and the Aegean World*, London: Thera Foundation.

Drack, W. (ed.) (1969) *Ur- und Frühgeschichtliche Archäologie der Schweiz: Band II. Der jüngere Steinzeit*, Basel: Verlag schweizerische Gesellschaft für Ur- und Frühgeschichte.

Drack, W. (ed.) (1971) *Ur- und Frühgeschichtliche Archäologie der Schweiz: Band III. Der Bronzezeit*, Basel: Verlag schweizerische Gesellschaft für Ur- und Frühgeschichte.

Dunning, G. C. (1961) 'A group of English and imported medieval pottery from Lesnes Abbey, Kent and the trade in early Hispano-Moresque pottery in England', *Antiquaries Journal* 41: 1–12.

Eggers, H.-J. (1959) *Einführung in die Vorgeschichte*, Munich: Piper Verlag.

Evans, C. (1989) 'Archaeology and modern times: Bersu's Woodbury 1938 and 1939', *Antiquity* 68: 436–50.

Fleming, A. F. (1988) *The Dartmoor Reaves: Exploring Prehistoric Land Divisions*, London: Batsford.

Fox, C. (1959) *Life and Death in the Bronze Age: an Archaeologist's Field Work*, London: Routledge and Kegan Paul.

Frere, S. S. (1983) *Verulamium Excavations*, Vol. 2, Reports of the Research Committee of the Society of Antiquaries of London, no. 12. London: Society of Antiquaries of London.

Garlake, P. S. (1973) *Great Zimbabwe*, London: Thames and Hudson

Glob, P. V. (1969) *The Bog People: Iron Age Man Preserved*, London: Faber and Faber.

Glob, P. V. (1974) *The Mound People: Danish Bronze Age Man Preserved*, London: Faber and Faber.

Grant, E. (ed.) (1986) *Central Places, Archaeology and History*, Sheffield: Sheffield University, Department of Prehistory and Archaeology.

Grant, M. (1971) *Cities of Vesuvius: Pompeii and Herculaneum*, London: Michael Grant Publications.

Greenwell, W. (1877) *British Barrows: a Record of the Examination of Sepulchral Mounds in Various Parts of England*, Oxford: Clarendon Press.

Haggett, P. (1965) *Locational Analysis in Human Geography*, London: Edward Arnold.

Harris, E. C. (1989) *Principles of Archaeological Stratigraphy* (2nd edition), London and New York: Academic Press.

Hart Hanson, H. P., Medgaard, J. and Nordqvist, J. (1985) 'The mummies of Qilakitsoq', *National Geographic* 167 (2): 190–207.

Hart Hanson, H. P., Medgaard, J. and Nordqvist, J. (eds) (1991) *The Greenland Mummies*, London: British Museum Press.

Haselgrove, C. C. (1987) *Iron Age Coinage in South-East England*, Oxford: British Archaeological Reports, British Series 174.

Haselgrove, C., Millett, M. and Smith, I. (eds) (1985) *Archaeology from the Ploughsoil: Studies in Collection and Interpretation of Field Survey Data*, Sheffield: J. R. Collis Publications.

Hatt, G. (1957) *Norre Fjand: an Early Iron Age Village Site in West Jutland*, Copenhagen: Ejnar Munskgaard.

Hill, J. D. (1989) 'Rethinking the Iron Age', *Scottish Archaeological Review* 6: 16–23.

Hill, J. D. (1993) 'Hillforts of Iron Age Wessex', in T. C. Champion and J. R. Collis (eds) *The Iron Age in Britain and Ireland: Recent Trends*, Sheffield: J. R. Collis Publications: 95–116.

Hill, J. D. (1995) *Ritual and Rubbish in the Iron Age of Wessex: a Study on the Formation of a Specific Archaeological Record*, British Archaeological Reports, British Series 242, Oxford: Tempus Reperatum.

Hillman, G. (1984) 'Interpretation of archaeological plant remains: the application of ethnographic models from Turkey', in W. van Zeist and W. A. Casparie (eds) *Plants and Ancient Man*, Rotterdam: Balkem: 1–41.

Hiroshi, T. (1992) 'Kuroimine', in R. J. Pearson (ed.) *Ancient Japan*, New York: George Braziller Inc.: 223–25.

Hodder, I. (1982) *The Present Past: an Introduction to Anthropology for Archaeologists*, London: Batsford.

Hodson, F. R. (1968) *The La Tène Cemetery of Münsingen-Rain*, Berne: Acta Bernensia 5.

Hodson, F. R. (1991) *Hallstatt: the Ramsauer Graves*, Bonn: Habelt.

Hole, F. and Flannery, K. (1967) 'The prehistory of south-western Iran: a preliminary report', *Proceedings of the Prehistoric Society* 32: 147–206.

Howarth, E. (1899) *Catalogue of the Bateman Collection of Antiquities in the Sheffield Public Museum*, London: Dulau.

Johanson, D., Johanson, L. and Edgar, B. (1994) *Ancestors: in Search of Human Origins*, New York: Villard.

Jones, G. E. M. (1984) 'Interpretation of archaeological plant remains: ethnographic models from Greece', in W. van Zeist and W. A. Casparie (eds) *Plants and Ancient Man*, Rotterdam: Balkem: 43–61.

Kinnes, I. A. and Longworth, I. H. (1985) *Catalogue of the Excavated Prehistoric and Romano-British Material in the Greenwell Collection*, London: British Museums Publications Ltd.

Kristiansen, K. (1992) ' "The strength of the past and its great might": an essay on the use of the past', *Journal of European Archaeology* 1: 3–32.

Landstrøm, B. (1988) *Regalskeppet Vasan (The Royal Warship Vasa)*, Stockholm: Interpublishing.

Leakey, R. and Harris, J. M. (1987) *Laetoli: a Pliocene Site in Northern Tanzania*, Oxford: Clarendon Press.

Lobdell, J. E. and Dekin, A. A. (1984) 'The frozen family from the Utqiagvik site, Barrow, Alaska', *Arctic Anthropology* 21 (1): 1–154.

Maiuri, A. (1970) *Pompeii*, Rome: Instituto Poligrafico dello Stato.

Maltby, M. (1996) 'The exploitation of animals in the Iron Age; the archaeozoological evidence', in T. C. Champion and J. R. Collis (eds) *The Iron Age in Britain and Ireland: Recent Trends*, Sheffield: J. R. Collis Publications: 17–27.

Megaw, J. V. S., Thomas, A. C. and Wailes, B. (1961) 'The bronze age settlement of Gwithian, Cornwall: preliminary report on the evidence of early agriculture', *Proceedings of the West Cornwall Field Club* 2: 200–15.

Meiggs, R. (1960) *Roman Ostia*, Oxford: Clarendon Press.

Mellars, P. A. and Wilkinson, M. R. (1980) 'Fish otoliths as evidence of seasonality in prehistoric shell middens: the evidence from Oronsay (Inner Hebrides)', *Proceedings of the Prehistoric Society* 64: 19–44.

Mongait, A. L. (1961) *Archaeology in the USSR*, Harmondsworth: Penguin Books.

Montelius, O. (1903) *Die typologische Methode: die älteren Kulturperioden im Orient und Europa*, Vol. 1, Stockholm: Privately printed.

Morris, I. (1987) *Burial and Ancient Society: the Rise of the Greek City-State*, Cambridge: Cambridge University Press.

Morris, I. (1992) *Death, Ritual and Social Structure in Classical Antiquity*, Cambridge: Cambridge University Press.

Mortimer, J. R. (1905) *Forty Years' Researches in British and Saxon Burial Mounds of East Yorkshire*, London: A. Brown and Sons Ltd.

Niiro, I. (1993) 'The formation of complex society in Japan and the surrounding area', Pre-circulated paper for the Congress of The Urban Origins in Eastern Africa, Mombasa, Kenya 1993.

Olsen, O. and Crumlin Pedersen, O. (1967) 'The Skuldelev ships', *Acta Archaeologica* 38: 73–174.

Pitt-Rivers, A. H. Lane-Fox (1887) *Excavation on Cranborne Chase*, Vol. 1, Privately printed.

Pitt-Rivers, A. H. Lane-Fox (1888) *Excavation on Cranborne Chase*, Vol. 2, Privately printed.

Pitt-Rivers, A. H. Lane-Fox (1892) *Excavation on Cranborne Chase*, Vol. 3, Privately printed.

Pitt-Rivers, A. H. Lane-Fox (1898) *Excavation on Cranborne Chase*, Vol. 4, Privately printed.

Provost, M. and Mennessier-Jouannet, C. (1994) *Carte Archéologique de la Gaule: 63/2 Le Puy-de-Dôme*, Paris: Fondation Maison des Sciences de l'Homme.

Radesovich, S. C., Retallack, G. J. and Taieb, M. (1992) 'Re-assessment of the palaeo-environment and preservation of hominid fossils from Hadar, Ethiopia', *American Journal of Physical Anthropology* 87: 15–27.

Raftery, B. (1994) *Pagan Celtic Ireland: the Enigma of the Irish Iron Age*, London: Thames and Hudson.

Redman, C. L. (1974) *Archaeological Sampling Strategies*, Reading, Mass.: Addison-Wesley Modular Publications in Anthropology, no. 55.

Redman, C. L. (1986) *Qsar es-Seghir: an Archaeological Overview of Medieval Life*, London and New York: Academic Press.

Reece, R. M. (1972) 'Roman coins found on fourteen sites in Britain', *Britannia* 3: 269–76.

Reece, R. M. (ed.) (1977) *Burial in the Roman World*, Research Report no. 22, London: Council for British Archaeology.

Reece, R. M. (1987) *Coinage in Roman Britain*, London: Seaby.

Reece, R. M. (1988) 'Clustering of coin finds in Britain, France and Italy', in J. Casey and R. Reece (eds) *Coins and the Archaeologist* (2nd edition), London: Seaby: 73–85.

Reece, R. M. (1989) 'The Roman coins and their interpretation', in I. M. Stead and V. Rigby, *Verulamium: the King Harry Lane Site*, London: English Heritage, Archaeological Excavation Report no. 12: 12–15.

Reinecke, P. ([1903–9] 1963) *Mainzer Aufsätze zur Chronologie der Bronze- und Eisenzeit*, Bonn: Habelt.

Renfrew, C. (1987) *Archaeology and Language: the Puzzle of Indo-European Origins*, London: Jonathan Cape.

Renfrew, C. and Bahn, P. (1996) *Archaeology: Theory, Methods and Practice* (2nd edition), London: Thames and Hudson.

Rudenko, S. I. (1970) *Frozen Tombs of Siberia: the Pazyryk Burials of Iron Age Horsemen*, London: J. M. Dent and Sons.

Rule, M. (1983) *The Mary Rose: the Excavation and Raising of Henry VIII's Flagship* (2nd edition), London: Conway Maritime.

Schiffer, M. B. (1976) *Behavioural Archaeology*, London and New York: Academic Press.

Schiffer, M. B. (1987) *Formation Processes of the Archaeological Record*, Albuquerque: University of New Mexico Press.

Schwab, H. (1989) *Archéologie de la 2ᵉ Correction des Eaux de Jura. Vol. 1. Les Celtes sur la Broye et la Thielle*, Fribourg: Editions Universitaires Fribourg.

Sharples, N. (1991) *Maiden Castle*, London: English Heritage/Batsford.

Shennan, S. (1985) *Experiments in the Collection and Analysis of Archaeological Survey Data: the East Hampshire Survey*, Sheffield: J. R. Collis Publications.

Sjoberg, G. (1960) *The Pre-Industrial City, Past and Present*, New York: Free Press.

Sklenář, K. (1983) *Archaeology in Central Europe: the First 500 Years*, Leicester: Leicester University Press.

Smith, B. D. (ed.) (1978) *Mississippian Settlement Patterns*, London: Academic Press.

Smith, C. A. (ed.) (1986) *Regional Analysis*, London: Academic Press.

Snodgrass, A. M. (1971) *Dark Age Greece: an Archaeological Survey of the Eleventh to the Eighth Centuries BC*, Edinburgh: Edinburgh University Press.

Spindler, K. (1994) *The Man in the Ice: the Preserved Body of a Neolithic Man Reveals the Secrets of the Stone Age*, London: Weidenfeld and Nicolson.

Stead, I. M. and Rigby, V. (1989) *Verulamium: the King Harry Lane Site*, London: English Heritage, Archaeological Excavation Report no. 12.

Steponaitis, V. P. (1978) 'Location theory and complex chiefdoms: a Mississippian example', in B. D. Smith (ed.) *Mississippian Settlement Patterns*, London: Academic Press: 417–54.

Thomas, A. C. (1970) 'Bronze age spade marks at Gwithian, Cornwall', in A. Gailey and A. Feston (eds) *The Spade in Northern and Atlantic Europe*, Belfast: Institute of Irish Studies: 1–9.

Trigger, B. G. (1989) *A History of Archaeological Thought*, Cambridge: Cambridge University Press.

Ucko, P. J. (1969) 'Ethnography and the archaeological interpretation of mortuary remains', *World Archaeology* 1: 262–90.

van Zeist, W. and Casparie, W. A. (eds) (1984) *Plants and Ancient Man*, Rotterdam: Balkema.

Wagstaff, M. (1986) 'What Christaller really said about Central Places', in E. Grant (ed.) *Central Places, Archaeology and History*, Sheffield: Sheffield University, Department of Prehistory and Archaeology: 119–22.

Weiner, J. S. (1955) *The Piltdown Forgery*, London: Oxford University Press.

Wheeler, R. E. M. (1943) *Maiden Castle, Dorset*, Reports of the Research Committee of the Society of Antiquaries of London, no. 12, Oxford: Oxford University Press.

Wheeler, R. E. M. (1954) *Archaeology from the Earth*, Harmondsworth: Penguin Books.

Wheeler, T. V. and Wheeler, R. E. M. (1936) *Verulamium: a Belgic and Two Roman Cities*, Reports of the Research Committee of the Society of Antiquaries of London, no. 12, Oxford: Oxford University Press.

Wilson, D. (1970) *The Vikings and their Origins: Scandinavia in the First Millennium*, London: Thames and Hudson.

Wolf, E. R. (1982) *Europe and the People without History*, Berkeley: University of California Press.

SELECT BIBLIOGRAPHY

Roman coinage forms one of the best examples of the problems of sampling, survival of the evidence and interpretation. Several of the chapters in Casey and Reece (1988) can be read with profit, as can Reece (1987). For more statistical approaches to archaeological sampling, Redman (1974) lays out the various options, and the problems of implementing them. These techniques are applicable both to field survey and to excavation, but his excavation of Qsar es-Seghir (Redman 1986) is virtually unique in applying strict sampling (both statistical and judgement) to an excavation. There are many books on the methodology of field survey, but the edited volumes by Haselgrove *et al.* (1985) and Cherry *et al.* (1978) are two which can be recommended, and Shennan's *East Hampshire Survey* (1985) is a classic of the genre. Renfrew and Bahn (1996) give many examples of survival of data, but for distribution maps they are more concerned with their potential rather than their limitations. A good sceptical approach to the use of burial evidence can be found in Morris (1987) and (1992).

4

FIELD ARCHAEOLOGY

Martin Carver

INTRODUCTION

Field archaeology is both an art and a science: an art because it requires imagination, creativity and flair; and a science because it requires the systematic recording and analysis of data. It is thus either an unusually imaginative science or an unusually disciplined art, and in practice requires both kinds of thinking to be successful.

The purpose of field archaeology is to detect and define every kind of trace left by people in the past, whether buildings or midden heaps, pottery or pollen, whether solid or ephemeral, and whether visible or invisible to the naked eye. These traces of human material culture are mapped in plan and chronicled in sequence, using both non-invasive and invasive methods ('survey' and 'excavation'). The targets of field archaeologists are principally *sites*, such as cemeteries or settlements, where cultural remains are concentrated, and *landscapes*, where they are more widely dispersed. From the records made during their interventions in the field, archaeologists make interpretations of the economy, social organization, ideology and the environment of ancient communities and examine how and why these changed.

PRINCIPLES

Formation processes

As discussed in the previous chapter, the buildings, artefacts and natural resources used by ancient people do not survive intact but are subject to a battery of natural and human agencies which modify their character sometimes beyond the powers of modern recognition (Rapp and Hill 1998; Fig. 4.1 Schiffer 1976, 1987). The primary factor in this transformation is the particular form of the ancient material culture itself. Communities who built pyramids, or stone triumphal arches, or buried their dead deep under earth mounds, have successfully ensured the memory of their culture, while those who built in timber and used mainly organic materials in their daily lives have left a more vulnerable legacy. Groups of finds ('assemblages') or groups of structures and activities ('sites') begin to be changed as soon as they are abandoned: the occupants may take away their choice possessions, and later people may remove, disturb or scramble what remains. The abandoned site or 'deposit' may lie very shallow, as many prehistoric settlement sites do on gravel or chalk, or very deep, as do settlements of long duration built over streams or valleys. Both kinds are immediately subject to physical attrition, shallow sites by ploughing or quarrying, and the deep sites, often in living towns, by continuous occupation and the construction of new buildings.

Most decisive of the natural agencies in the formation process is the chemistry of the subsoil itself. High acidity and the free circulation of oxygen, such as

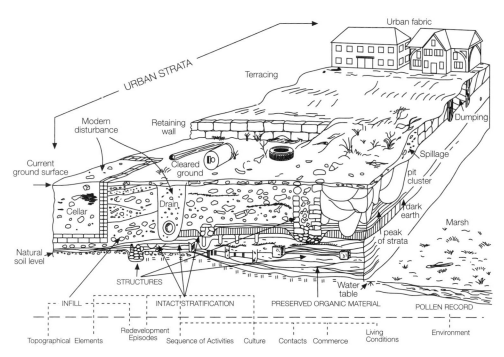

Figure 4.1 A slice of urban strata, broken down into its components and what they can tell us. Source: Carver 1983.

characterize sands and gravels, make a corrosive combination which can reduce timber structures, bones, metals and even certain types of pottery to little more than discoloured smears. If the terrain is very dry, very cold or starved of oxygen (anaerobic) it will by contrast result in a high degree of preservation, since these conditions inhibit the bacteria which cause organic decay. The site is further modified by the climate it has endured: it may be eroded or buried by wind, flood or volcanic ash. Under the sea or in a river, the remains of a ship and her cargo may be remarkably preserved, or dispersed by the agencies of current and looting. The character of the sites and deposits encountered by the field archaeologist is therefore immensely varied.

Theoretical platforms

The practice of field archaeology still grows wild from a number of different roots, in spite of the attempts of archaeological theorists to cultivate and tame it. People have long been excited by buried treasure, which was sought by early grave-robbers and is pursued more energetically than ever in the popular hobby of treasure hunting, whose adherents may be formed into clubs and equipped with technically advanced metal detectors.

Those with greater curiosity about the past, wondering whose treasure it was, and why it was deposited, broaden their enquiries to the documented people of the past, and this remains a traditional goal. In the nineteenth century archaeologists working in the Middle East, like Sir Austen Layard, took the Bible as their historical framework, and Heinrich Schliemann in the Aegean took the writings of Homer as his: he declared his chosen site, the *tell* or mound settlement at Hissarlik, to be the Troy of the *Iliad*, and went on to identify Agamemnon's Mycenae and the palace of the Minotaur at Knossos on Crete, later excavated by Sir Arthur Evans. Other ancient texts, those of classical Greece and Rome, of Egypt, of China, of the Maya, of the early Christians, and of Islam, continue to provide historical frameworks in which field archaeologists have worked.

Buildings and groups of artefacts (assemblages) present cultural signatures ('a culture') for a documented people, and in the 1920s and 1930s Gordon Childe, following German methodology, logically attributed an equal cultural identity to material which, being prehistoric, had no documentary references (see Chapter 12). Ever since, the goal of many archaeologists has been to write history from cultural sequence, and cultural sequence from sites and assemblages. The provenance of diagnostic, dated finds, plotted on a map allows the cultures to be tracked and equated with migrating and settling peoples and their 'culture-zones' (for example, Syedov 1982). In this approach, it may be deemed sufficient to excavate small parts of monuments to characterize the cultural history, a procedure adopted with

130

famous precision, for example, by Sir Mortimer Wheeler equally in the hill-forts of late iron age Britain (1943) or in Mohenjo-Daro, an abandoned town of the Indus civilization some 3,000 years older (1945, 1946, 1976). Within this approach, the culture sequence is sampled mainly by 'sections', vertical profiles cut through the deposits which can be seen to be divided into layers. The finds recovered from each layer during the digging define the culture.

Much field archaeology has been influenced by anthropological goals. In the late nineteenth and early twentieth centuries, the ethnicity of peoples became a popular explanation for the apparent success or failure of cultures: A. L. F. Pitt-Rivers, the first Inspector of Ancient Monuments in England, excavated sites of all periods on his private estate at Cranborne Chase in Dorset, determining changes in the form of objects, the form of sites and the form of the human skull as being symptomatic of wider evolutionary forces (Bradley 1983; Pitt-Rivers 1887–1905). Other examples of ethnicity-driven research were studies of the mound builders of Ohio (Willey and Sabloff 1974) or the graves of Anglo-Saxon England (Leeds 1945).

Later anthropological directions have been more influential still. Steward and Willey saw a major area of explanation in the interaction of humans with their environment (Willey 1953), and fieldwork targets henceforward included the sequence of natural vegetation and the landscape which contained it, derived from pollen analysis (Godwin 1956; Dimbleby in Brothwell and Higgs [1963] 1969) and environmental survey (Vita-Finzi 1978). Binford (1972) and Clarke (1968) urged that the material culture sequence be studied as a *process*, in which society is expressed as a network of intersecting environmental, economic and social *systems*. Fieldworkers revealed these systems by taking *samples* of sites and landscapes, and constructing explanatory models of how and why systems change (Cherry *et al.* 1978; Mueller 1975). Another fruitful branch of anthropology, drawn from studies of modern traditional peoples, has shown that the organization of human society and its material culture were both strongly influenced by the mental structure shared by a community – its beliefs and mythology. The material culture actually found, therefore, was not only dependent on the environment but on the ideological decisions of the community concerned (Hodder 1986). Specific fieldwork targets are here more difficult to define, although new agendas for recording and interpretation have been suggested by studies of cult sites and cult practices (Carver 1993; Renfrew 1985; Richards 1987).

Practical approaches to fieldwork

While all these approaches have greatly enlarged the expectations of field archaeology, it has remained in practice an activity in which the empirical has dominated over the theoretical. Archaeologists working in the field are often divided into those

131

doing excavation and those doing survey. Survey is seen as a group of operations that are generally non-destructive and on a large scale, while excavations destroy the archaeological deposit and are usually applied to a smaller area of deposit or site. This division is in fact rather artificial (Scholfield 1991): survey, for example, is employed during excavation – and can be destructive – as when pottery is taken from the ploughsoil. Both excavation and survey are employed at most stages of the research procedure (see below). Further divisions are sometimes made between archaeologists working mainly with buildings and those working underwater. These divisions are generated by the varied practicalities concerned, including (in many countries) different legal frameworks and academic communities. However, the principles of research procedure apply equally to all, and shared approaches and practices are becoming more common (NAS 1992; Wood 1992, 1994).

In survey, much attention has been given to mapping the archaeological resource with the aim of making the inventory of known sites as full as possible. In nineteenth-century England, for example, the Victoria County History devoted the first chapter for each county to a synthesis of pre-Norman evidence as known at the date of publication; while the Royal Commission on Historical Monuments set out to complete an inventory of all visible monuments. These provisions have had their analogues in many countries, sometimes managed by governments and sometimes the result of scholarly initiative, such as Stephens and Catherwood's survey of Maya sites (Stephens [1841] 1969), or Gsell's survey of sites in Algeria (1901). Since the mid-twentieth century, these initiatives have been supplemented by the creation of regional 'Sites and Monuments Records' (the term used in Britain), in which all kinds of sightings of known or suspected archaeological sites are routinely recorded. More recently, methods have been developed for mapping the buried archaeological evidence of a region rapidly. This is achieved by a sampling strategy in which sample areas distributed across the region are examined (Redman 1987; Renfrew and Wagstaff 1981).

Archaeological excavation, the oldest branch of fieldwork, has developed in a series of approaches, sometimes rather dogmatically promoted by their practitioners. The *trench* is a simple rectangular area excavated to the natural subsoil, leaving the sequence of layers excavated in sections on all four sides. The trench is still commonly used for sampling in pursuit of cultural, historical and processual goals, or for *evaluation* (see pp. 142–50). Wheeler extended the method by digging a number of square trenches side by side, the earth baulks between them providing a network of sections from which the sequence could be read (Wheeler 1954). Danish archaeologists, working in opaque soils with little visible strata, dispensed with these baulks and opened large areas in order to better understand the character of settlements which leave only earth traces, such as post-holes and pits. This 'open area' excavation was further developed in England by Hope-Taylor at Yeavering (1977), Biddle at Winchester (1975) and by Barker, whose excavations at Hen

Domen and Wroxeter set new standards for the definition of ephemeral structures and activities (Barker 1969, [1977] 1982). Vanished post-Roman timber buildings on these sites were indicated by soilmarks or patterns in stone rubble which were visible only in large areas viewed from above.

The objectives of excavation are to record activities both in plan and in sequence, and excavation strategy is usually a compromise between the two. The British school of archaeology has always championed *stratigraphy*, the art of reading sequence from archaeological strata, as the dominant contribution to excavation methodology. Stratigraphic recording was practised in the eighteenth century by Thomas Jefferson, who used it to investigate the sequence in Indian burial mounds, before he embarked on a second career as President of the United States. The method was used by Schliemann at Troy (Schuchhardt 1891) and was greatly influenced by Charles Lyell, whose *Principles of Geology* (1830–33) inspired Pitt-Rivers, who in turn inspired Wheeler. Most excavators read their stratigraphy from sections, until in the 1960s open-area excavation was employed in town sites with their long and complex sequences. Sequence models were then developed which showed the interrelationship of all the layers in the deposit (Harris 1975, 1989).

A large modern open-area excavation can employ about forty persons, and as the scholarly and technical demands have risen, so the team of excavators has become increasingly professional. Excavation is thus expensive, and its cost has become an increasingly important factor in its development. Excavation is also destructive, often totally so; rarely can much new information be expected from a second excavation in the same place. An equally formative influence on field methods, therefore, has been the development of archaeological ethics.

Ethics

The archaeological resource, comprising all the remains of previous ages, is largely buried and invisible and therefore vulnerable to unwitting destruction by the modern community who quarry it and build in it. Archaeologists have long been aware of this problem, but the pace and extent of modern building operations raised new consciousness in the 1960s. Rapid survey methods developed under the impulse not only of research hunger but of the imminent destruction of the landscape, for example by quarrying for gravel for the construction of a motorway. Heritage managers have often seen excavation as an extension of their conservation strategy, the excavation record being seen primarily as a substitute for the archaeological deposit itself. This approach received a great boost in Europe and the United States during the second half of the twentieth century, when archaeologists began to sense the losses of information due to the intensive and competitive use of land, in comparison with their new expectations from technique. Known as 'rescue' in the

UK, and 'salvage' in the USA, these field interventions were usually justified as providing a 'preservation by record' of the threatened deposit. The goals of 'preservation by record' implied that the recovery of the evidence should be as full as possible so as to compensate for the loss. 'Total excavation', as expounded by Barker ([1977] 1982), required the recovery of every detail, a laudable edict which initially had the effect of promoting more meticulous observation and recording. However, 'total excavation' is conceptually impossible, since the anomalies observed and the records made of them require acts of recognition, definition and ultimately of choice. In other words, the excavator decides that one group of stones is more significant than another, and thus worth drawing or keeping on the basis of imagination and prior knowledge, rather than from objective observation. A further paradox comes from the fact that total excavation is most ethically appropriate to 'rescue' situations, where it is most difficult to apply due to constraints of time and money. On unthreatened sites, such as monuments in public care, total excavation is more practical, but less ethical, since total excavation is total destruction, and the site cannot be reinvestigated to answer new research questions in the future.

Access to the archaeological resource is regulated in many countries by a state archaeological service, a group of experts who make decisions on the basis of their laws and regulations; while in others, the fate of the resource is decided by open competition between the different values championed by different sections of society: amenity value, commercial value, sentimental value and so forth (Lipe 1984). *Archaeological value* has to compete with these, but a competition cannot take place unless archaeologists know the value of that resource in advance and how to define it. Archaeological value can be defined as the product of a research agenda and a deposit model: what we need to know with what we can know at a given time (Carver 1996). Archaeological value is assigned by field archaeologists during a process known as *evaluation* (see pp. 142–50). Modern field archaeology is therefore a compromise between theory-led research objectives, practicalities imposed by terrain, and the ethics of contemporary society: a compromise between what archaeologists would like to know, what they are capable of discovering, and what society will allow them to investigate.

A FRAMEWORK FOR FIELD ARCHAEOLOGY

A modern approach attempts to construct a framework for field archaeology by combining these theoretical, practical and ethical imperatives into a single procedure (Carver 1989, 1990). The procedure is divided into a series of stages in one of which at a given moment every archaeologist in the field is knowingly (or unknowingly) engaged (Figs 4.2 and 4.3).

Reconnaissance is the act of exploring the archaeological resource without a

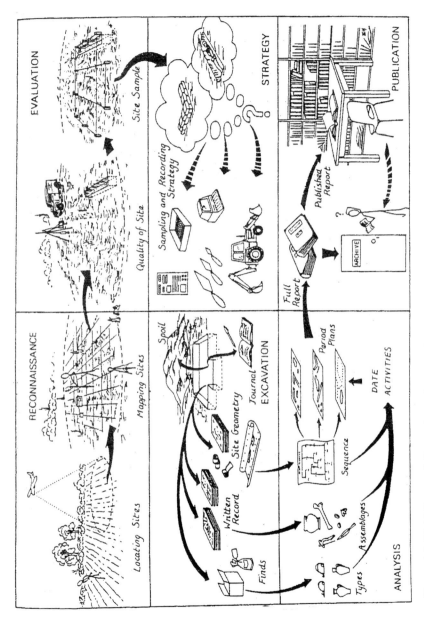

Figure 4.2 Field Research Procedure, the staged approach to fieldwork. Source: Carver 1987.

cemeteries. Most effective in ploughed soils or in deserts, surface collection consists of mapping (not necessarily collecting) visible archaeological materials and from their distribution inferring the presence of archaeological sites (see discussion and illustrations in Chapter 13). The archaeologist normally lays out 'transects' which may be in the form of regular parallel lines 5–500 metres apart, depending on which stage the reconnaissance has reached. For terrain about which virtually nothing is known, 'random samples' of quadrats or transects may also be used to avoid the bias of preconceived ideas about where a settlement ought to be.

A third level of intensity in reconnaissance is achieved by attempting to see below the surface of the soil, a type of *remote sensing* relying on scientific techniques of detection. There are chemical methods, such as measuring the concentration of phosphate in the topsoil: most human activities involve the life and death of animals, and these in turn produce insoluble phosphates amongst their decay products. Where human activity has been concentrated, the phosphate is also concentrated. The amounts of insoluble phosphate present in the topsoil are measured by taking a sample of soil at regular intervals, say every 10 metres over a grid. The phosphate is extracted as P_2O_5 and measured in ppm (parts per million) (Craddock *et al* 1985).

The most intensively used methods of remote sensing at ground level, however, are the group of techniques known as geophysical survey (Clark 1990; Gaffney and Gater 1993; Weymouth 1986; Fig. 4.5). Geophysical instruments, which were developed during and after the Second World War for detecting sub-surface anomalies, rely on three basic phenomena: the passage of electric current through the ground which varies according to the resistivity of the soil, the ability of sub-surface features to distort the earth's magnetic field which is measured by magnetometry, and the ability of sub-surface interfaces to reflect radio waves, which is detected by means of pulse radar. Each of these methods functions differently on different kinds of terrain. In spite of nearly fifty years' experience, however, it is still difficult to predict which, if any, is capable of making sub-surface features visible within a particular terrain. It appears that resistivity works the best at detecting 'dry' features, such as walls and roads, but it has also performed well on gravel where it has found boundary ditches and other large negative features. Those methods which rely on magnetic anomalies are particularly good at searching out burnt clays, such as those found in hearths and burnt-out buildings. Magnetic susceptibility locates buried pedological and/or cultural zones. Radar has been, and is being, extensively tested both in rural and urban sites, but has yet to find a reliable place in the routine geophysical repertoire (Addyman and Stove 1989; Atkin and Milligan 1992; Carver 1986; Imai *et al.* 1987; Scollar *et al.* 1990; Weymouth 1986). Geophysical methods, like aerial, perform in the reconnaissance, evaluation and data acquisition stages (cf. Gaffney and Gater 1993: 'levels I, II, III').

Other methods of looking beneath the ground's surface are less technical. Lerici, one of the pioneers of archaeological remote sensing, began his experiments by

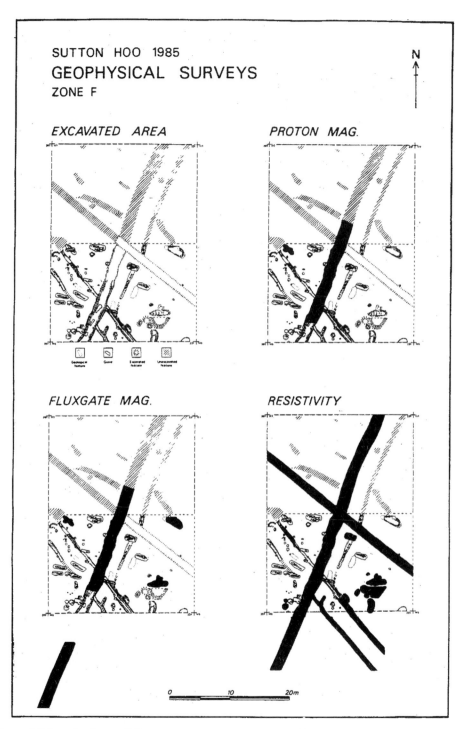

Figure 4.5 Results from different types of geophysical survey at Sutton Hoo, showing the powers of three different gadgets to detect underground features in an area that was subsequently excavated (top left) – their success is marked in black. Source: Carver 1986.

driving a periscope down through the roof of Etruscan tombs, photographing the interior and resealing the hole, thus achieving a non-destructive entry (1960). Bore-holes drilled with an auger are routinely used by the Lerici Foundation, among others, to map the extent and depth of deposits. A variety of surface collecting methods, where the surface is unbroken or obscured, involves 'shovel-testing' – lifting the surface at intervals to recover the pottery and other artefacts lying in the topsoil.

The principal target of *underwater reconnaissance* is the ancient wreck, although submerged harbour-works and settlements are known, and likely to become an increasingly large component of the archaeological resource during global warming. The location of historic sites may be predicted by documentary references to known shipping lanes or known ships, as in the case of the *Mary Rose*, lost in 1585 (Rule 1982). More often, sites are discovered by chance, or by the hunch of divers inspecting the sea bottom. Sonar can be used to detect the presence of ancient wrecks, just as it can for submarines. The sub-bottom profiler picks up anomalies under the silt, which can then be investigated further by divers. Visibility, current and mobility of deposits conspire to make the reconnaissance particularly challenging on the sea-bed, and it is here too that the competition with unregulated treasure hunting is at its most intense (Muckelroy 1978; NAS 1992; Throckmorton 1987).

EVALUATION

Evaluation is the process of assigning 'archaeological value'. Some attempts have been made to equate 'value' with the archaeological quality of a deposit, defined as its legibility for research purposes (for example, Carver 1983). Others have provided a rationale for management selectivity by ranking sites according to their relative rarity, diversity of content, clustering and so on (for example, Darvill 1988; Darvill *et al.* 1987; Startin 1993). A third approach, more theoretically correct but harder to implement, defines archaeological value in terms of both the known deposit and current research interests (Groube and Bowden 1982). The most recent definitions accept that the deposit-model and the research agenda are both constructs of their own time and should be given equal weight: 'value' is computed by matching the two (Carver, in Arup 1991; Carver 1990). This view also enshrines the political principle (following Lipe 1984) that the objective is to enable archaeological resources to compete with other social demands, not with each other.

In all cases, the fieldwork component of evaluation is largely dedicated to mapping deposits and assessing their quality. Evaluation has to be clearly distinguished from both the reconnaissance stage which precedes it and the data acquisition stage that follows it, although it can look like them and uses many of the same techniques and field methods. What distinguishes evaluation is its purpose, which is to anticipate the result of a fieldwork programme, whether the programme is predominantly conservation, survey or excavation. Such anticipation requires the archaeologist to know as much as possible about a deposit without actually removing it. Obviously, it would be pointless to destroy the deposit in an attempt to establish its value, since there would then be nothing of value to defend or research. Evaluation therefore relies heavily on the power of archaeology to predict the character of deposits while they are still invisible, an ability which is by no means highly developed.

The earliest recorded evaluation is probably that of Claudius J. Rich at Babylon (1839), where the objective was to make as full an account of the ancient city as was possible without putting a spade in the ground. Others have used and developed the evaluation stage in their projects, without publishing the fact or, in many cases, recording it. The most intensive and large-scale mapping of a deposit has probably been that by Millon and his team at Teotihuacan (Cowgill *et al.* 1984). In the UK, Martin Biddle's study of London (Biddle and Hudson 1973) was a report on the archaeological implications of modern building construction in the city. This report also contained some predictive mapping, and this technique, and the concept of evaluation itself, was more explicitly developed in the West Midlands urban campaign of the same decade (Carver 1987; Fig. 4.6). In 1983, evaluation moved to the countryside where it was applied to the site of the Anglo-Saxon burial mounds at Sutton Hoo, and preceded the research programme there (Carver 1986).

In 1988 mandatory 'impact assessment', which had long been a fact of life in the USA, became law in the European Community. Under Article 5(1) of the 1988 Act, member states are required to ensure that the sponsor of a development project produces a description of 'the aspects of the environment likely to be significantly altered by the proposed project' (including the architectural and archaeological heritage) and does so 'having regard inter alia to current knowledge and methods of assessment'. The current professional interest in developing evaluation – and the techniques of deposit-mapping in particular – comes not a moment too soon.

What is measured? The parameters to be sought are the extent and depth of the deposit, its quality of preservation for artefacts and biota (seeds, animal bones and other organic materials), its legibility (the ease with which layers can be distinguished from each other) and its status (whether the layers are *in situ* or have been redeposited) (Fig. 4.7). Notice that the results of deposit-mapping do not add up to any kind of historical or prehistoric sequence, and it would be misleading to claim as much. The quality assessment is limited to inspection of the surface, or at the most of a cut section. The temptation to over-interpret is always at the evaluator's elbow, but the temptation must be fought. Evaluation is not only intended for other archaeologists, who can be relied on to take their colleagues' assertions with a pinch of salt, but for planners, developers and public representatives, who are inclined to take other professionals at their word.

When fighting for access to land in the value-forum, archaeologists would be well advised to stick to what is measurable. An imaginary example might run as follows:

143

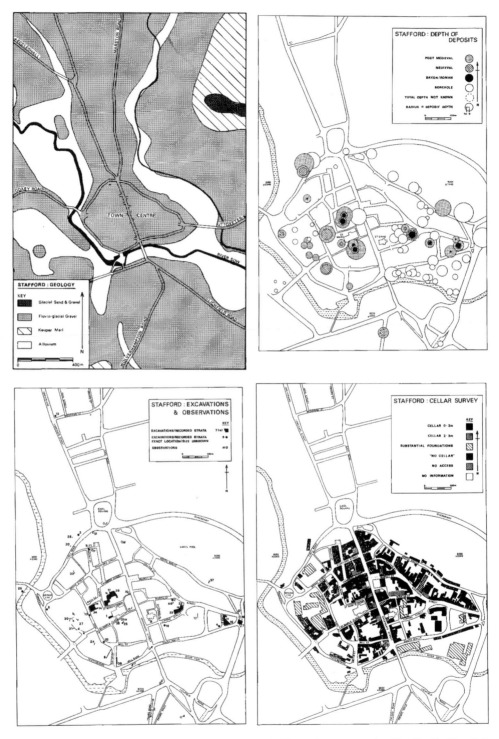

Figure 4.6 Four contributions to the deposit modelling of an urban site (Stafford). Top left: the position of the interventions. Top right: cellar survey, showing the depth of strata destroyed by cellaring. Bottom left: the base geology determined by stripping off the modern town. Bottom right: the depth of strata that survives. Source: Carver 1987, after research by J. Glazebrook.

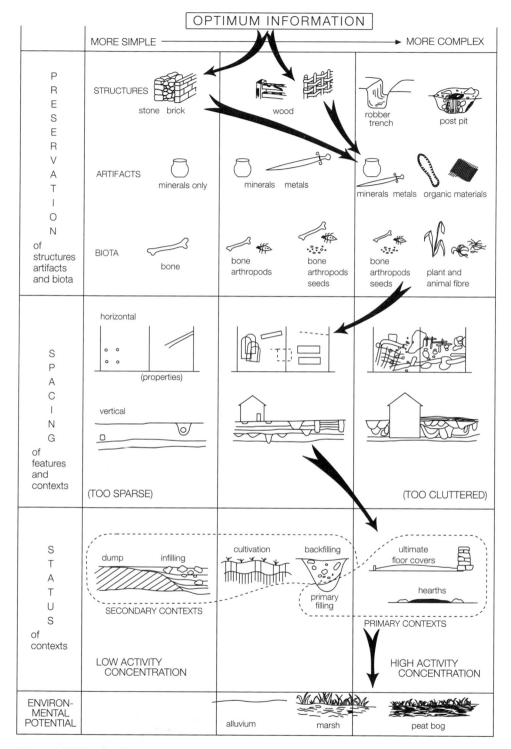

Figure 4.7 The quality of a deposit, based on what it can tell us: a 'good site' follows the arrows. Source: Carver 1983.

- *Deposit model*: the deposit in question extends to 0.25 ha; its depth varies from 1–3.5 m; it is anaerobic and preserves leather and other organic materials from 2.5 to 3.5 m deep; the top metre is thoroughly disturbed and is of low archaeological value.
- *Research agenda*: the site is predicted to be a late Roman tannery reoccupied in the late Saxon period, possibly by an ecclesiastical community (documentary evidence); the lowest metre of deposit is of immediate relevance to questions on Roman manufacture posed by the recent review of research priorities in Roman Europe.

The measurements of the deposit are here separated from its likely historical context, allowing the rival exploiters of land to see that, whatever the site turns out to be, there is nevertheless a deposit of some kind there. This is, strangely enough, often the hardest thing for the non-archaeologist to accept. To produce positive evidence of the existence, size and quality of a deposit is far more persuasive to other professionals than imaginative tableaux about its possible contribution to world history. On the other hand, these last are necessary to win public support.

In the countryside, archaeological deposits are often spread thin and shallow and relatively unencumbered by modern buildings, so a deposit located by reconnaissance can be evaluated by concentrating many of the same techniques upon it. The extent of the deposit is most readily mapped from surface collection of flint or pottery or phosphate, but since this material can also arrive in the topsoil through ancient manuring and modern cultivation and dumping, it would be important to test the validity of the distribution with test trenches sited over predicted boundaries. If there is coincidence between the surface patterns and the feature patterns, the former is likely to be a useful indication of the occupied area. Aerial photographs provide a powerful mapping technique (see above), but the ground may not offer the right conditions at the time the evaluation is needed. Unploughed grass surfaces suspected of containing earthworks, however slight, may be mapped by three-dimensional topographic survey or by photography under enhanced lighting. 'Grass-mark survey', the pattern given by the flora after mowing, may also indicate the degree of disturbance by revealing the pits of early robbers and former burrows of animals. Sub-surface mapping of features also helps to establish the extent of the deposit, though since the effectiveness of different types of geophysical instrument varies markedly with terrain, it is important to evaluate the techniques themselves (Fig. 4.5): a portfolio of instruments is set to map the same small area (approx. 10×10 m) which is then excavated, the instrument which 'saw' most then being selected not only in the evaluation phase but for a role in the subsequent data acquisition strategy (see below).

The results of a rural evaluation project are presented as a deposit model which shows, first, the extent and depth of the deposit, second, its quality, and third, its

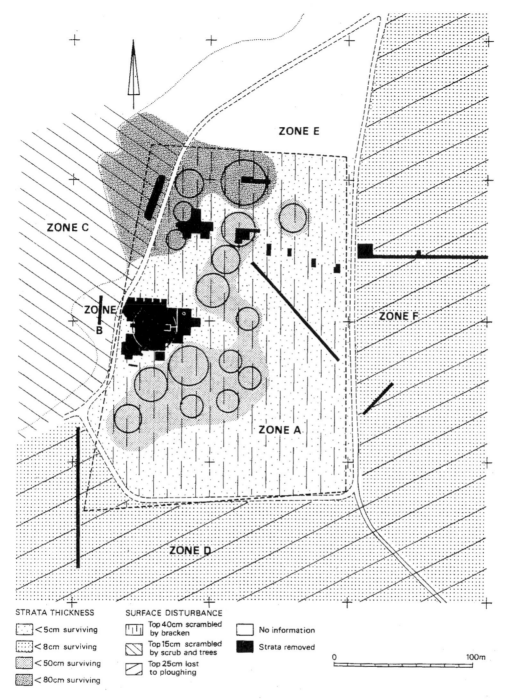

ZONE E

ZONE C

ZONE B

ZONE F

ZONE A

ZONE D

STRATA THICKNESS

- <5cm surviving
- <8cm surviving
- <50cm surviving
- <80cm surviving

SURFACE DISTURBANCE

- Top 40cm scrambled by bracken
- Top 15cm scrambled by scrub and trees
- Top 25cm lost to ploughing

- No information
- Strata removed

0   100m

Figure 4.8 Deposit model for a rural site: Sutton Hoo. The black areas have already been excavated. The stippling shows the depth of strata, and the hatching the depth to which they have already been scrambled by ploughing and roots. Table 4.1 shows the different sizes of features and finds that could be found over this area by different intensities of intervention. Source: Carver 1986.

Table 4.1 The 'visibility template' at Sutton Hoo

Method	Potential yield						
	Features >1.5m	Features >1.0m	Features >0.5m	Graves	Finds >2cm	Finds >1cm	Finds >1mm
Non-destructive							
AP	×						
Field walking					×		
Surface mapping	×						
Metal detector					×	×	
Resistivity	×	×	×				
Magnetometer	×						
Fluxgate	×	×					
Radar	×						
Phosphate							
Contour	×						
Destructive							
Level A	×						
Level B	×	×			×		
Level C	×	×	×		×	×	
Level D	×	×	×	×	×	×	×
Level E	×	×	×	×	×	×	×

Note: This visibility template prepared for Sutton Hoo shows the size and kind of archaeological evidence that can be detected by different methods, both non-destructive (like topographical survey) and destructive (shown as five levels of excavation).

degree of disturbance. In the example shown as Figure 4.8, the model concentrates on the extent and depth of the deposit and the damage it has sustained. Note that, in Zone F, the post-war ploughing has removed all earthworks and the features are covered by 25 centimetres of ploughsoil, which can be read for pattern from surface collection. The 'scheduled monument' (Zone A), covered in grass and without potential for surface collection mapping, has retained traces of earthworks, but they have been disturbed to a depth of 40 centimetres by bracken roots and rabbit burrows. This predictive map shows the limits of Anglo-Saxon burial and where the prehistoric site has been best preserved, and it was used in the strategy (see below). The site given as an example had had a number of earlier excavations, but, even so, additional test trenches were necessary; it is nearly always necessary boldly to cut such trenches in support of a rural evaluation programme.

These procedures can be extended to evaluate a whole landscape. If this seems an impractical proposition at present, that is because the time allowed by impact assessment (which usually provokes the work) is far too short. There is a case, therefore, for investing in pre-emptive evaluation for whole regions as part of a management programme for the curation and conservation of the archaeological heritage.

Abandoned towns, such as Teotihuacan (Cowgill *et al.* 1984), may be treated under the rural procedures, but the stratigraphic situation in living towns is different, in that deposits often lie deep and their surface is thoroughly obscured by buildings, roads, pavements and car parks (Fig. 4.1). On the other hand, in towns occupied during the last three centuries there have usually dwelt archaeologists and antiquaries who were curious about them and have recorded their encounters with the deposits underground. In most cases these sightings, kept in scrapbooks, letters and newspaper cuttings in the local city library, are perfectly usable by the modern evaluator. They can and should be supplemented by test sections which give firsthand views of the strata. Such test sections can often be achieved with the minimum damage to the deposit by removing the walls of cellars and recording the section in the vertical earth face which lies behind them. The more technical methods of mapping buried strata are occasionally effective in towns. Photogrammetric aerial survey has been employed by Meeson at Tamworth to reveal the square platform of the Anglo-Saxon palace (Carver 1987: 118). Resistivity survey has been carried out on tarmac car parks at La Charité-sur-Loire by flooding the surface with water (Bossuet 1980). Georadar has been claimed as an effective instrument for the mapping of deep urban strata, but has still to develop a successful protocol for regular use and reliable interpretation.

Urban evaluation therefore relies heavily at present on direct observations of the deposit, whether ancient or modern. From these observations, predictive maps can be compiled, which show the extent, depth and quality of the deposit, and the degree to which it has already been removed or disturbed by cellars and other buildings (Fig. 4.6). Arising from the deposit model, other maps can be generated for management and research purposes. One may show the areas of particular archaeological interest and vulnerability; another the template used to sample the urban activities relating to a particular period. The exploration of a town's records for evaluation purposes can lead to some interesting discoveries. At Worcester, a large area of open ground, now allotments, which characteristically produced prehistoric pottery and flint, turned out to be an area of dumped dredging, including the remains of an ancient ford, taken out of the River Severn. This prehistoric material lay, misleadingly, *on top of* a Roman watercourse (Carver 1980: 23).

Although the character of deposits varies from site to site within a town, offering different management problems and different research opportunities, each town preserves a general 'personality' in its deposits below ground, as it does in its buildings above street level. A surprising amount of information about this buried resource can be drawn from the town simply by walking around it: a half-buried medieval church doorway or Roman arch, a line of houses echoing the line of a buried amphitheatre – such occurrences give hints of unseen deposits and monuments. The deposit-character which distinguishes town from town is determined, on this scale too, by basic topography and geology, the most important factor in deposit-formation. High rocky sites tend to shed their deposits in a lens at the base; towns built around a river or stream creep out across them in periods of expansion, sealing, often in anaerobic strata, the debris of that age. In towns equipped with a thick and permanent wall, deposits tend to rise inside the wall – the so-called 'belting effect'. Towns of different topographic circumstances thus give rise to different kinds of strata-capture. Just as the comparison between site and site within a town can provide the basis for research and conservation planning, so comparison between towns can allow the programming of the urban project on a regional or a national scale (Carver 1983).

Urban archaeological evaluation was developed in Britain in the 1970s (Carver 1987) and is currently receiving notable development in France (CNAU 1990–). The evaluation of York (Arup 1991) broke new ground, both technically by introducing the computer-mapping of the underground deposit (Richards 1990), and conceptually by insisting on the relevance of the current research agenda for both curation and intervention strategy.

Evaluation is thus the linchpin of a scientific field archaeology, the basis for all management and research programmes and the ticket to the public debate on social value. With the model of the buried riches of a particular site or landscape in mind, the field archaeologist can go on to formulate programmes of formal intervention designed to answer questions and push forward society's enquiry into the past. This is the strategy stage.

STRATEGY

The aim of this stage is to turn the predicted model of an archaeological site as defined by evaluation to good account by devising a plan for its management and its research. Strategies may emerge in a number of written forms. A *research design* is specifically directed to a data-acquisition programme intended to meet research objectives. A *management plan* is directed rather at the conservation and/or presentation of a site. A *project design* refers to a combination of the two.

Each of these components of strategy may be applied to either a site or its territorial analogue, a landscape. Published fully developed strategies for landscapes are uncommon, although they are implicit in many a successful survey project. The reason for this is that landscape evaluation is rarely sufficiently thorough to allow a full programme to be stated at the outset; more usually a strategy for data acquisition over a landscape is followed by research strategies for individual sites, often as a result of survey. Management plans follow at several removes, or are developed independently, sometimes by a different group of archaeologists. This stage, like those of reconnaissance and evaluation, may therefore be revisited several times in the course of a single project.

A *research design* will include a statement of the present understanding of the past culture and the questions to be addressed. The choice of territory is justified, and reasons are given why it is likely to offer the answers, drawn from the evaluation. The data selected to be recorded are defined, and how they are to be analysed, with what expected result. A recording system appropriate to these data forms part of the same design. A *management plan*, similarly springing from the evaluation, provides both short- and long-term protection for the archaeological asset that has been located. Where damage from other exigencies of society cannot be resisted, a 'mitigation strategy' (which may include rescue excavation) is included in the plan. For sites that are to survive contemporary excavation, 'presentation' – the management of public access to a comprehensible monument – is an important component (see Chapter 10). It can be argued that, in many countries, presentation is the most effective way of winning public support for the fossilization as 'heritage' of land which might be much in demand for other purposes: presentation is in this case the ally of conservation. A *project design* which incorporates both these aspects must also report on their cost, duration, staff and viability. Major factors in all branches of archaeology, they are fundamental in excavation.

Examples of field projects incorporating some or all of these concepts have been seen in many countries in recent years. A famous and exemplary project, which combined research-driven ecological and settlement survey with selective excavation and was subsequently presented in an entertaining and instructive manner, was conducted in the Oaxaca Valley, Mexico, by Kent Flannery (Bahn and Renfrew 1991: 446–54; Flannery 1976). At Dancbury in England, Barry Cunliffe designed a model project which showed the role of this iron age hill-fort in its territory, combining large-scale excavation of the interior with intensive survey of its hinterland; fieldwork was followed by publication at several levels and a management plan for the monument (Cunliffe 1993; Cunliffe *et al.* 1984–91). At St Catherine's Isle (Georgia), off the south-east coast of the United States, Hurst Thomas set himself the problem of locating and excavating the Spanish mission station of Santa Caterina. Treated as a single site, the island was surveyed in parallel transects, using surface collection. Of 135 sites located, only five threw up sixteenth- and seventeenth-century Spanish ceramics. These were then mapped more intensively with a power-auger (used normally for digging fence posts), which narrowed the search to an area one hundred metres square. Geophysical survey was then used to map the buried buildings, and a choice could be made where to apply the more costly and unrepeatable measure of excavation (Hurst Thomas 1989: 227–36). At Qsar es-Seghir, a ninth-century Islamic city in Morocco, Redman began by exploring the circular walled area by random quadrants – the equivalent of the reconnaissance and evaluation stages, but as the geography of the buried town became clearer, he was able to develop his data acquisition strategy, targeting excavation areas so as to address research questions on the society and economy of the citizens (Redman 1986; Fig. 4.9).

At Sutton Hoo in Suffolk (south-east England), evaluation produced a map of a prehistoric (Beaker period) settlement underneath the famous Anglo-Saxon cemetery. The 'visibility template' (Table 4.1) indicated that the prehistoric field system could be mapped by remote sensing, whereas the prehistoric structures had survived comprehensively only beneath Anglo-Saxon burial mounds. The research

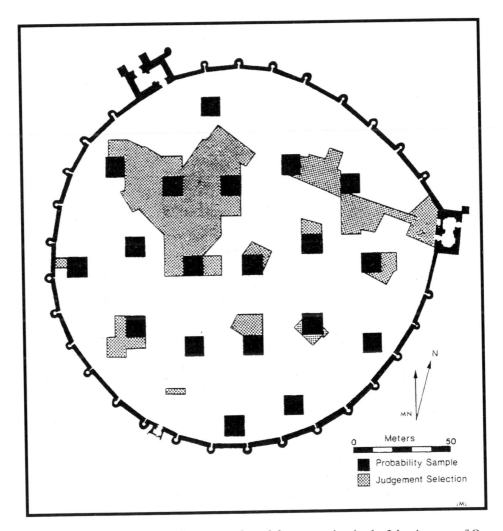

Figure 4.9 Strategy at a town site: areas selected for excavation in the Islamic town of Qsar es-Seghir, Morocco. Source: Redman 1986.

agenda required the sequence of burial rites to be determined and mapped, on the theoretical grounds that this sequence would reflect the changing ideology of the Anglo-Saxon community during the period that their historical kingdom was being formed, the seventh century AD. This sequence could only be ascertained through excavation, since the graves had proved impossible to detect by the currently available remote-mapping technology. The strategy for intervention, therefore, comprised the excavation of a cruciform transect and an adjacent area for remote mapping (Fig. 4.10). Subsequent excavations showed the excavation sample to have been the right size for the questions asked. The excavated site was subsequently returned to grass, with one mound reconstructed to its seventh-century height to aid presentation. Simultaneously, the Deben Valley (in which the site lay) was mapped by field survey, this being one of six sample regions to be surveyed in the known kingdom of East Anglia.

A large-scale evaluation carried out in the 1960s in Northamptonshire, in the English Midlands, provided the material for a management plan for the whole of that county, and a similar exercise for Dorset resulted in the publication of an explicit strategy in which the surviving archaeological assets were matched with a research agenda (Groube and Bowden 1982). In the latter work a system of scoring was introduced which ranked the problems seen as crucial to each period, the scarcity of the deposits likely to solve them, and the threats from farming and other forms of disturbance likely to inhibit or prevent their solution. The management of the resource was therefore here combined with research priorities which targeted named areas and sites for survey and excavation.

Some final examples may be offered from the specially challenging situation in living urban sites, which vary no less than rural in what they have to offer to research, but where the archaeologist rarely has a free hand to choose where to excavate. In the Winchester campaign of 1961–71, the opportunities presented by redevelopment were combined with those allowed by conserved monuments to give an intensive array of research-directed interventions which has rarely been matched in a living city (Biddle 1975). At Stafford, a full evaluation of the small county town (Fig. 4.6) was followed by four area excavations targeted on the early medieval borough. At York, twenty years of intensive investigation of the city within the rescue framework were followed in 1991 by the construction of a deposit model and a research agenda to match it (Arup 1991).

In the 1990s, as European countries follow the American lead and deregulate their archaeological management from the centre, strategies are certain to become more explicit: the well-known question 'Why did you dig there?' is no longer merely the casual enquiry of a bystander. In an age of intensive demand on land and money, society as a whole requires a reasoned, convincing, and indeed competitive public answer to this question.

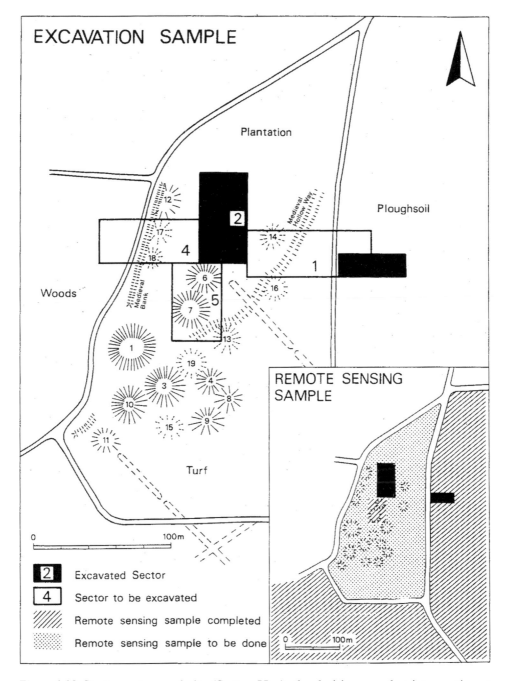

Figure 4.10 Strategy at a rural site (Sutton Hoo): the decision on what interventions to undertake expressed as an area for excavation and an area for remote mapping. Source: Carver 1986.

DATA ACQUISITION: SURVEY

The non-destructive acquisition of data for research purposes is carried out routinely by archaeologists world-wide (Redman 1987). The techniques employed are shared with *reconnaissance* and *evaluation* (see pp. 137–42 and 142–50) and survey is often used as a prelude to excavation or combined with it in the same strategy. Although survey can map settlements (for example by aerial photography) and retrieve finds by surface collection, occasionally in the same place, the lack of secure stratigraphic context, obtainable only by digging, often means that sequence and dating remain imprecise.

Settlements, field-systems, dykes and other features captured by survey can, however, be classified by their shape and a few dated examples are then often sufficient to determine the pattern of settlement and land use (Edis *et al.* 1989). Settlements can also be ranked from their size, and occasionally by the type of surface find: in some cases the use of the metal detector has proved decisive here, providing metalwork finds diagnostic of status from the ploughsoil. In areas of extensive and shallow ploughsoils, aerial photography can provide comprehensive accounts of land boundaries (Riley 1980) using interruptions in the pattern to determine their sequence. In lands rich in pottery and obtrusive monuments, such as those bordering the Mediterranean, ground survey has been able to confront major questions without excavation (Adams 1981; Barker and Lloyd 1991; Keller and Rupp 1983). Leveau's survey of the territory of Iol Caesarea (Cherchell) in northern Algeria in the Roman period, distinguished villa sites from native sites from their building materials and showed how affluence moved between the town and its hinterland as the economy and society changed (Leveau 1984). In the Guadalquivir Valley, Spain, the geography of olive oil production was mapped from extant olive presses, centuriated olive groves, and kilns producing amphora to transport the oil (Mattingly 1988). In southern Etruria north of Rome, surface collection over many years allowed the mapping of settlement patterns from the neolithic to the medieval periods (Potter 1974; Fig. 25.2).

As in the reconnaissance and evaluation stages, ground survey is usually conducted in systematic transects or quadrats (Fig. 4.11), although total coverage is always preferred and sometimes attempted (Bahn and Renfrew 1991: 454). Within a transect, a group of field-walkers, say four to six persons, walk slowly along the axis of the transect in a line abreast, each having the responsibility for searching a strip 2–3 metres wide. Recent developments in surface collection such as the analysis of assemblages for their representivity (Bintliff 1985; Millett 1991; Scholfield 1991) promise new levels of sophistication. A parish survey at Witton conducted over twenty-five years mapped not only the changing size and location of settlements during the first millennium AD, but also the amount of land under the plough, on the assumption that freshly broken pottery could be attributed to a buried

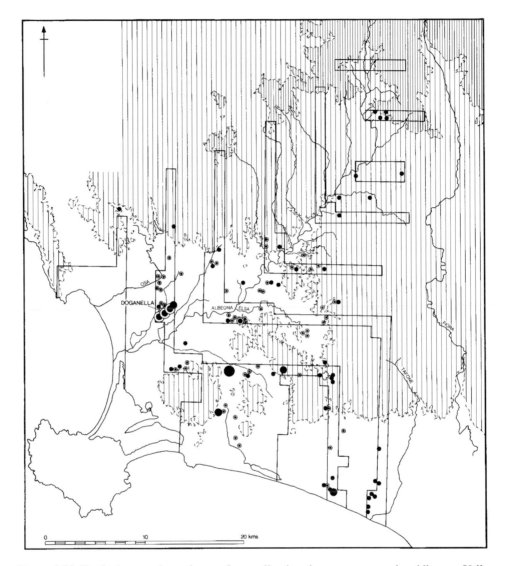

Figure 4.11 Exploring territory by surface collection in transects – the Albegna Valley survey, Italy. The circular symbols represent different-sized assemblages of Etruscan amphorae. Source: Barker and Lloyd 1991.

settlement and smaller, abraded, sherds to the practice of manuring ancient fields with household rubbish (Wade 1983). From the resulting model it was argued that land dedicated to arable farming had doubled in size every 200 years, and with it the population.

Detailed questions about natural resources, preferred economic strategies and the use of land are also in reach of environmental studies or palaeoecology: as

Chapter 6 describes, organisms such as pollen (Dimbleby 1985; Faegri *et al.* 1989) and land snails (Evans 1972, 1978), and the sediments themselves (Courty *et al.* 1990; Limbrey 1975; Rapp and Hill 1998), can be read for the sequence of local vegetation: woods, pasture or arable farming.

Survey projects therefore deploy a parcel of techniques which, when harnessed together, can write the history of extensive landscapes over considerable stretches of time. The changing character of the landscape itself, its exploitation by people and the geography of settlement are all within reach of survey, which is moreover a mainly non-destructive form of study. Although excavation has traditionally enjoyed pride of place in field archaeology, it can now be argued to be the junior partner in the enterprise: survey provides not only the backdrop, the *longue durée* of the human experience, and the basic human strategies of existence, but the basis of the archaeologists' strategic choice of which sites merit the more penetrating and more final measure of excavation. Nevertheless, it is only through excavation that the most intimate and significant questions of past human behaviour can be addressed.

DATA ACQUISITION: EXCAVATION

Archaeological excavation is the systematic dissection of a cultural deposit. An appropriate modern term would be 'deconstruction', since the principal objective – to determine the way the deposit was put together – is achieved by taking it apart. In this case, however, it cannot be reassembled: excavation is always partially, and often totally, destructive. There is therefore only one chance to excavate a given deposit, and since the operation usually takes place outside and in public, a high degree of organization, both in precept and in practice, is essential.

Preparation and management

The location and size of the area to be excavated are selected by the strategy, as discussed above. Around this chosen area are arranged the facilities which will support the excavation process without inhibiting it: the area where excavated soil is to be dumped (the 'spoil-heap'), the offices, and the viewing platform for the visiting public. In the countryside, the excavation team will usually have to be accommodated, often on the site itself. One site office will serve for the processing of finds, another for the cataloguing of drawings and photographs, another for the checking of written records and the entry of data on computer file. In the toolshed, trowels, hand shovels, spades, wheelbarrows, finds trays, sprays, and surveying equipment await the signal to begin.

The assembled team will include a director responsible for planning and coordinating the operation, supervisors responsible for managing certain areas or tasks, and excavators who may be professionals, amateurs, labourers or students. Supervisors share responsibility for managing artefacts, biological material, survey, photography, drawings, and for the written record, each of which must be treated consistently throughout the operation. The excavation area is demarcated with nails and string, or a white line, and its condition before excavation is recorded photographically. This is for legal reasons, since excavation always takes place on someone's land, the character of which is about to be altered irreversibly. Faced with a piece of blank ground, excitement is intense and the responsibility formidable, but though neither the excitement nor the responsibility ever quite vanish, a modern excavation is not a hunt for the unexpected: if the evaluation was effective and the strategy well thought out, the course run by the excavation should be quite precisely known in advance.

Stratigraphic units

Thanks to this preparatory work, moreover, the excavator can also imagine the components of the unexcavated deposit in some detail, and has already decided the measures necessary to define and record them. These components have largely entered excavation practice through tradition and consensus. For the early excavators, they were 'layers', 'walls', and 'pits', each of which would be numbered separately (pit 1, wall 2, etc.). In modern systems, the site is divided into 'contexts', which are layers, walls, and all other sets of materials seen as being homogeneous, discrete and individually definable together with their interfaces (Harris 1977). These are the basic 'stratigraphic units' of which the physical stratification of the deposit is composed. For some excavators, the 'context' is the only stratigraphic unit used, apart from 'find'. Others prefer a hierarchical system, where *additional* higher entities of interpretation are also defined, recorded and numbered separately (Carver 1979; Fig. 4.12). Thus a 'structure' (a building) is a set of 'features', and a feature (a post-hole) is a set of 'contexts', and a context (a layer) is a set of components, which may be anything from grains of sand to fragments of charcoal, bricks or stones. A 'find' is simply a component which is kept. This system maybe acknowledges that each entity requires an act of definition and is not strictly a fact to be observed.

The ability to define finds, contexts and the higher-order stratigraphic concepts depends, of course, on how far they can be seen, and this depends in turn on the terrain that contains them and the effort made to make them visible. So here, too, the controlling influence is provided by the excavator and the excavator's strategy. A midden heap or a rubbish pit may have contained several hundred acts of dumping and discard; but the number of layers into which the excavator can divide it on

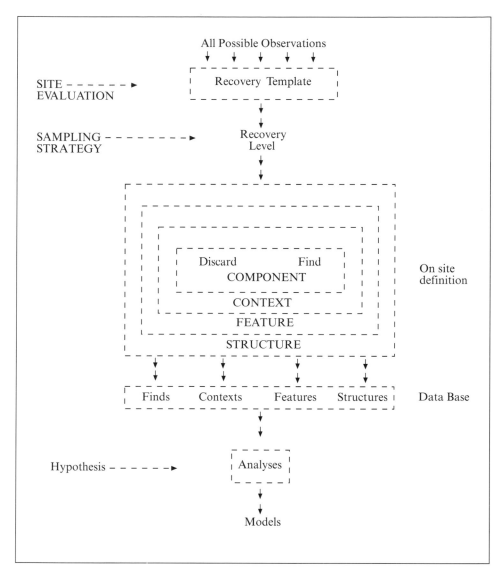

Figure 4.12 A hierarchical system of stratigraphic units. The smallest definable entity is known as a 'component', which might be a pebble or a potsherd. The components that are kept are the 'finds'. A group of components which is defined as forming a set is called a 'context'. A group of contexts which forms a set is called a 'feature'; and a set of features is called a 'structure'.

rediscovery will depend on the degree of preservation and the excavation method applied. Dug with a shovel, it will be resolved into only two or three major episodes and only the larger finds recovered; the remainder will end up on the spoil heap.

Dissected with a spatula, and analysed in a laboratory, it can risk being divided into more layers than there actually were, but the traces of macroscopic plant remains recovered will greatly enrich the assemblage. Plainly, not every cubic centimetre of a site will be excavated with a toothpick, or offered for microanalysis in the laboratory, nor would there be any point in doing so in a research-driven procedure. Selectivity of recovery is therefore inevitable. It is logical to impose selectivity, but still more essential to make the selectivity explicit and record it. This can be done using the device of information recovery levels (Table 4.2), which allows the excavator to match the levels of the precision of digging to those of recording, and both to the data demanded by the strategy. The system provides the excavator with a series of 'gears' with which to control the pace and intensity of the excavation.

The techniques of excavation applied are those appropriate to the recovery level. Thus the topsoil might be removed by a mechanical excavator (level A) and the surface of the site then cleaned with a shovel (level B); the contexts contained by an earthwork might be defined with a trowel (level C), but those expected to contribute more detail, for example, graves, dissected as level D or E. Extremely fragile groups of finds, or contexts containing organic traces, might be lifted in a block and examined in the laboratory as level F.

Recording

What to record is also decided by the recovery levels, and a recording system will be devised to suit the particular terrain (DUA 1990; *Lattes* 1986). The first essential of any recording system is a grid from which to locate every recorded entity in space. A local grid is established by setting wooden pegs or iron rods at regular intervals beside the excavation area to provide permanent points of reference, tied into the national geographic system. The grid is often extended across the excavated area itself, so that every find and context can be located with reference to the nearest line of pegs running east (easting) and north (northing). This generates the location to the nearest 10 metres, 1 metre or 1 centimetre, depending on the precision required. For locations more precise than a metre, a planning frame is placed over a known metre square and the target located by the mini-grid of parallel strings. The third dimension, height, is measured with a level and staff, and related to a temporary benchmark. The inconvenience of a grid of pegs, which must be lowered continually with the excavation, has been partially overcome with the use of electronic distance measurers (or total station theodolites) which record all three dimensions working from a point of reference on an offsite grid.

With the grid established, the records made can be conveniently managed in five parts: the *written record* (Hirst 1976) consists of pro formas, such as context cards,

Table 4.2 Guide to information recovery levels

Level	Operation	Find	Component	Context	Feature	Structure
A	Machining	PLOT 2-D	(not recovered)	OUTLINE PLAN	OUTLINE PLAN	OUTLINE PLAN
	Fieldwalking	PLOT 2-D	(not recovered)	(not recovered)	Inferred from density plot	Inferred from density plot
	Geophysics	(not recovered)	(not recovered)	(not recovered)	Inferred from density plot	Inferred from density plot
	Topographics	(not recovered)	(not recovered)	(not recovered)	Inferred from map	Inferred from map
B	Shovel scraping (definition)	PLOT 2-D	(not recovered)	SHORT DESCRIPTION, OUTLINE PLAN	SHORT DESCRIPTION, OUTLINE PLAN	SHORT DESCRIPTION, OUTLINE PLAN
	Shovel excavation	Recover by context	Optional sampling	SHORT DESCRIPTION, OUTLINE PLAN	SHORT DESCRIPTION, PLAN and PROFILE	SHORT DESCRIPTION, PLAN and PROFILE. PHOTOGRAPH (PostX)
C	Coarse trowelling (definition)	PLOT 2-D	(not recovered)	DESCRIPTION, OUTLINE PLAN	DESCRIPTION, OUTLINE PLAN	DESCRIPTION, OUTLINE PLAN
	Excavation	Recover by context	Optional sampling	FULL DESCRIPTION, OUTLINE PLAN	FULL DESCRIPTION, PLAN, SECTION. PHOTOGRAPH (PostX)	FULL DESCRIPTION, PLAN, SECTION. PHOTOGRAPH (PostX)
D	Fine trowelling (definition)	PLOT 3-D	(not recovered)	FULL DESCRIPTION, DETAILED PLAN. PHOTOGRAPH	FULL DESCRIPTION, DETAILED PLAN. PHOTOGRAPH	FULL DESCRIPTION, DETAILED PLAN. PHOTOGRAPH
	Excavation	PLOT 3-D SAMPLE SIEVING	Selective sampling	FULL DESCRIPTION, DETAILED PLAN, SECTION. PHOTOGRAPH (PreX)	FULL DESCRIPTION, DETAILED PLAN, SECTION. PHOTOGRAPH (PreX/PostX)	FULL DESCRIPTION, DETAILED PLAN, SECTION. PHOTOGRAPH (by phase)
E	Detailed excavation	PLOT 3-D DESCRIBE ATTITUDE. SIEVE ALL	KEEP ALL	(as LEVEL D) Optional colour plan/section	(as LEVEL D) Full photographic record	(as LEVEL D) Full photographic record
F	Block removal for controlled dissection	(as above) PHOTOGRAPH and DRAW in situ	(as above)	(as LEVEL E) Full photographic record	(as LEVEL E)	(as LEVEL E)

which give the number of the context, describe the materials which compose it, its stratigraphic relationships, its location and its recovery level. The *drawn record* consists of maps, plans and sections: maps show a number of contexts and their relationship in the horizontal plane; plans show the outline of individual contexts and features; and sections show the relationship of contexts in the vertical plane. The *photographic record* includes photographs of individual finds, contexts and features, and of the methodology employed during the excavation. Photography is now also used for planning, especially on sites of low stratigraphic visibility. A camera is used from a tower, or suspended from a quadrapod. Some excavations now use videocameras to record both maps and plans, inserting the taxonomy and descriptive commentary by sound.

The *finds record* includes an inventory of the finds recovered, their location, their recovery level and description, often supported by a drawing and photograph. The finds record includes not only the finds recovered from the site, but also the details of their processing: washing, drying, marking, and cataloguing. The 'finds' also usually include samples taken for palaeoenvironmental analysis or dating, though most samples on excavation will be taken from 'anthropogenic' contexts, where they represent material gathered and deposited by or because of human activity, rather than those which have accumulated naturally. The extraction of this material is achieved by sieving: dry sieving for animal bones, and fine mesh assisted by water flotation for seeds and other plant remains (plant macrofossils) and by paraffin flotation for insects.

The final part of the recording system is the *notebook*, essentially the logbook of the excavation, which records the decisions and the progress made. The recording system is mainly dedicated to recording the data required by the strategy to serve the analytical itinerary, but it must also serve two other functions required by the special and unrepeatable nature of excavation. The first of these is that the recording itself must be monitored, by stating what was recorded and why, at all times. This monitoring of the records made is clearly allied to the second additional obligation: that of recording all chance observations. Although the recording agenda has been set by the strategy and looks forward to the analysis, it must be emphasized that excavators will remain constantly on the alert for new anomalies and previously unrecognized signs of past activity. The excavator is here acting as evaluator, and although it is unlikely that a new concept can be quickly included in the current enquiry, it is certain that it will help to construct the framework for future projects. It is in this way that the excavator may reconcile the obligation to follow a research-driven programme with the obligation to record everything that could conceivably be useful to the scientific community during a unique trip below ground.

In practice, the excavation technique and the recording system vary markedly with terrain and more particularly with stratigraphy. Stratigraphic excavation is by far the most powerful method of reading a deposit, and the stratigraphic sequence is the most fundamental information that an excavator can provide. The opportunities for applying the stratigraphic method do vary, however, and sites which have virtually no visible stratification are common but play an important role in research programmes. Many rural sites are covered by a thin layer of topsoil and the remains of the ancient site consist of a number of holes cut into the subsoil, not necessarily related to each other. Here, the topsoil (which contains most of the finds disturbed from floors or midden heaps) is examined by surface collection, and then removed with a mechanical shovel or toothless backhoe (at level A). Each feature is subsequently investigated at higher recovery levels. On some types of terrain, for example sand, even these features are difficult to define and may not penetrate the subsoil. The clean surface is therefore recorded before excavation, generally as a 'horizon map' or a 'horizontal section' to locate anomalies which are most visible from above. In the struggle to improve visibility on such sites, methods of chemical mapping have been developed which locate traces of skeletons, detritus or timber which the taphonomic trajectory has rendered undetectable to the naked eye (see, for example, Conway 1983 for phosphate mapping; and Bethell 1991 for mapping vanished bodies with ICP). The recording system in this case emphasizes the spatial relationships given by these maps and the characteristics of individual features.

By contrast, many deep deposits, particularly under towns, contain stratification which is readily legible (Fig. 4.1). Contexts can be individually defined even at low recovery levels and provide the main target for both digging and recording. The recording system emphasizes the stratigraphic relationships which are presented in stratigraphic sequence diagrams (Figs 4.14, 4.15), by entering the stratigraphically related contexts on the context card or, more reliably, by planning each context separately and using the 'single context plans' to generate a diagram.

Other types of site offer deep deposits, but with little stratigraphic legibility. It is here that the section proves useful: in the excavation of burial mounds, for example, layers in light soils are difficult to distinguish in plan, but the horizons between them may be visible in section. For some investigators, this vertical sequence is decisive, which is why burial mounds have often been examined by cutting a trench through them. In the rescue excavation of the enormous (100-metre diameter) mounds of the Kurgan culture, the trenches were cut through the centre, initially with a box grader, and a sequence of secondary burials read from the exposed section (Ministry of Education, Ukraine 1986). On the other hand, it is normally important that relationships in plan are not sacrificed for those in section; the mound may therefore be examined in successive vertical slices, advancing towards the centre as in early excavations in the United States, or divided into quadrants. The reconciliation of visibility in plan and section can also be achieved by creating 'running sections' along a profile maintained at the same axis, but demolished at drawable intervals, so as to pause and examine the site in plan.

163

The stratigraphy of buildings requires a specially subtle reading, since walls, windows and other features can be added and subtracted from above, from beneath, or from the side (see Chapter 8). The principle for stratigraphic ordering in buildings is not so much 'superposition' (as in soft deposits) as 'post-position', where the later feature may be underpinning from below, or an inserted panel or opening. These are detected by signs carried on mortar or timber, and by the fabric, form and style of the newer material.

How to dissect and what to record are therefore the result of decisions made before the operation starts and modified during it. These decisions depend on the evaluation, which predicts what can be seen, and the strategy, which proposes how the research targets can be met. The recording system is dedicated to the consistent recording of the data destined for analysis, but must also monitor itself, and include all the other observations that modern techniques allow to be made. Even if electronic data capture takes part of the load, the records of an excavation are bulky: ring binders full of context cards, rolls of drawings, sheaves of photographic negatives and slides, numerous notebooks, and boxes of potsherds, animal bones, human bones, fragile metal objects, and biological samples. A fairly modest excavation can produce a truckload of these records which, of course, may compose all that remains of the site. The next task is to analyse and curate them.

ANALYSIS

The analytical phase of a field project, sometimes called rather vaguely 'post-excavation', is a crucial part of the scientific journey which takes an archaeologist from the first result of a quest to its publication. It is unfortunate that so much of this procedure tends to remain hidden, a kind of black box from which the interpretation eventually emerges. If the analytical stages are explicit, as they should be, it is not only the present generation which benefits, but the next.

The post-excavation process begins with the organization and management of the *field records*. The data generated in a survey or excavation project, together with its log, are indexed and archived in a *site file*. The site file may be accompanied by a *project file*, which contains management records, and a *research file* which contains research notes and a record of all analyses and experiments undertaken, whether or not they led to a result. The 'raw data' must then be worked into a *field report*, which gives a full account of the archaeological discoveries and their significance. Parts of this report, suitably edited, may merit circulation in multiple copies as a *research report* (see Frere 1975, where the field records, field reports and research report were termed Levels II, III and IV respectively).

The production of the field report from the records made in the field is achieved by carrying out a series of analyses which may be broadly grouped as follows:

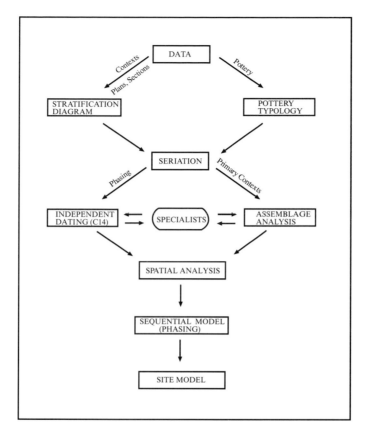

Figure 4.13 The 'analytical itinerary': all the data recovered on an excavation should be destined for a particular analysis; the analyses form a sequence or itinerary which leads to the site model. Source: Carver 1990.

establishing the sequence; defining the activities; providing a chronology; and placing the discoveries in their cultural context. The different operations of a typical itinerary are shown in Figure 4.13. Before the analytical programme begins, it is sensible to evaluate it (and cost it) in the light of the results of the fieldwork, especially the harvest of finds actually retrieved (English Heritage 1992). Then the sequence of operations must be managed so that the stages which depend on each other occur in the right order. Thus the process of ordering the contexts to give the *sequence model* can begin at once and may even have been completed on site. The sequence model may not depict the complete sequence, especially on sparsely stratified sites. Hence a *seriation* analysis is usually required, which shows the order of deposition of a dated species of find (such as flint or pottery). For the seriation analysis, a *typology* of pottery (or flint) is required. The sequence model and seriation taken together offer a rectified sequence, showing which groups of features

165

are likely to have been contemporary. These features can then be mapped together to give a statement of the geography of the site at a particular time, variously called an 'event', a 'horizon', or – more commonly – a 'phase'.

The activities which characterize each phase are derived from another suite of analyses. Once it is established which contexts and features may have been contemporary, the records are searched for evidence that they formed *structures* which were not recognized on site. The *assemblages* of finds, both artefacts and biota, are the main source of evidence for *activity*. The activities relevant to a particular phase will be signalled by finds in use during that phase; but only a small fraction of the material recovered falls into this category: the grave-goods in a grave, for example, or the contemporary rubbish dumped in a rubbish pit, or the fragments of crucible left in a bronze-worker's hearth. These are 'primary contexts'. 'Secondary contexts' consist of material transported or displaced from an earlier phase: the packing for a post-hole, for example, or the soil and turf quarried to build an earthwork. Many, if not all the finds in a secondary context belong to an earlier phase of occupation and are said to be 'residual'. In deeply stratified sites residuality is a major problem, one being confronted by seriation analysis. The seriation produces a 'residuality threshold', which shows which pottery is likely to be residual in each context, and which contexts, having no residual pottery, are likely to be primary. Since secondary contexts contain the displaced pottery of earlier eras, it follows that they will also contain displaced animal bone, plant remains and insects too. The assemblages in primary contexts are therefore the key to absolute dating and the key to interpreting activity.

The contemporary activities can then be examined by *spatial analysis*, which studies their relationships in plan; and the last step on the itinerary is to assemble the sequence of phases and the changes that occurred between them. It should be recalled here that when comparing the variation of an activity through time, only assemblages gathered at the same recovery level are eligible. For example, if animal bone is being used as an indication of diet, the animals represented will depend on the sieves which were used (Payne 1972), which depend in turn on the recovery level (see Table 4.2) decided: a group of large mammal bones recovered with a shovel from a pit may suggest that the pit-diggers ate beef; but only sieving with the appropriate mesh will show whether they also ate fish and fruit. The sequence of phases provides the basic framework for the *site model*, which is the principal method of presenting the results of fieldwork. Some of these analyses can be briefly described.

The most commonly used form of *sequence model* is that developed and promoted by Harris (1975, 1989), in which each context number is placed in a box and the relationships between them shown by vertical and horizontal lines (Fig. 4.14). Another procedure (Carver 1979) begins by ordering the contexts in the same way, but then groups the contexts into their interpreted sets – features and structures –

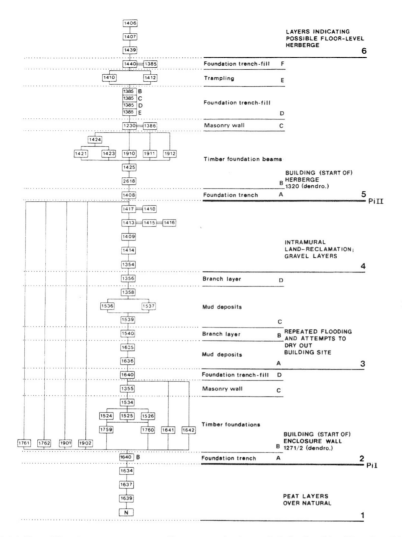

Figure 4.14 Stratification or sequence diagrams: the 'matrix' devised by Harris which uses contexts only, compared with the stratification diagram which uses contexts and features. Source: Bibby 1993, fig 7.10.

to provide a more 'narrative' model (Fig. 4.15). The second type of diagram can therefore be viewed as an interpretive version of the first. On large urban excavations where contexts can run to many thousands, these more summary diagrams, which carry a higher level of interpretation, can be easier to use for presenting the stratification in a publication and for supporting the synthesis. All contexts in the sequence model which can be grouped into features can be replaced by a feature signalled as a vertical arrow. This also indicates the 'life' of a feature, such as a wall

DURHAM CITY, SADDLER STREET 1974
STRATIGRAPHY, SITE D

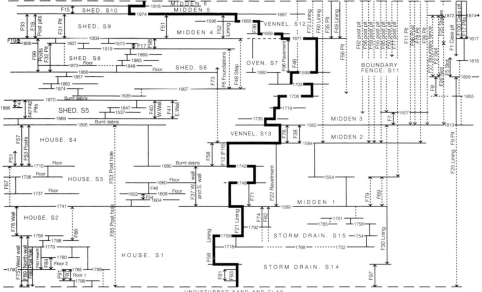

Figure 4.15 Stratification or sequence diagrams: stratification diagram for a complete site. The bold black line shows the train of contexts used in seriation. Dotted lines show where the stratified position was uncertain. The activities on site began at the bottom of the picture, and finished at the top. Source: Carver 1979.

or post, which may endure during the deposition of many contexts. Other ways of presenting the stratification which match the physical sequence with the researchers' model of events are under continual development – for two recent examples see Paice (1991) and Hammond (1991). All types of stratification diagram can be 'rectified' – that is, redrawn to show their phasing and dating – following the seriation analysis.

Seriation is used to order contexts and features by virtue of the finds contained in them. Where a site is sparsely stratified, seriation can be the sole method of sequencing, as in the studies by Petrie (1904) of Egyptian pre-dynastic graves and by Hodson (1968) of iron age cemeteries in Europe described in the following chapter. In well-stratified sites, seriation is used in a slightly different way. A species of artefact is selected which runs right through the sequence – in Roman and later urban sites this will generally be pottery. Both the stratification and the typological sequence will be known, but in both cases imperfectly. The objective of the seriation analysis is to match the order of context deposition to the order of the manufacture of pottery types, in order to model the best order for each. The stratified contexts are placed along one axis of the diagram, and the pottery types

168

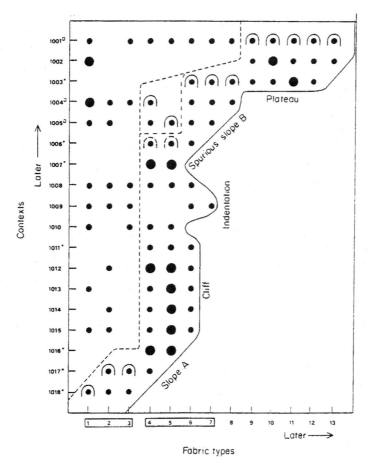

Fabric types

Figure 4.16 Seriation diagram for pottery assemblages in an urban sequence. The contexts are arranged in their best stratified order on the vertical axis of the diagram, and the quantity of pottery is given by the size of the spot. The different pottery fabrics are numbered along the horizontal axis. The interpretation of these diagrams is still being developed. A 'cliff' should mean that the contexts concerned are contemporary. A 'plateau' implies that some of the site has been removed by levelling. Slope A shows that one context is following another; but Slope B is spurious in that the contexts concerned can still be contemporary. Pottery fabrics in use at the same time are enclosed in a rectangle. The dashed line is the 'residuality threshold' connecting the 'fade points' for each fabric. Pottery to the left of this line is residual. Source: Carver 1985.

along the other; the quantities of pottery of each type in each context being indicated by a symbol (Fig. 4.16). The order of both parameters is then adjusted within the limits permitted by the stratification (context) or chronology (pottery) to give the best fit – usually a jagged diagonal. The rewards of the exercise are several. The shape of the diagonal shows which context, and which types of pottery, were in

169

contemporary use on site. It also indicates episodes of levelling, where the strata have been removed. The diagram also indicates where residual pottery is present, and which contexts may be primary. Certain types of context may also be identified: for example, a layer containing small quantities of many different types of pottery ('high diversity') is likely to be a ploughsoil. The potential of seriation analysis for assisting in the interpretation of long stratified sequences is very great and invites further development (Carver 1985).

Before the *finds* can be used for the interpretation of on-site activities, they must be identified, dated, and placed in their cultural context. The different kinds of material recovered during excavation can be very numerous, and their examination will usually require the deployment of a large number of specialists. The management of collaborative finds analysis programmes is therefore a major component of the analysis as a whole. The majority of artefacts may be classified by their fabric, form and style, which can offer details of where they were manufactured, for what purpose and at what date (see Chapter 9). The *biological component* of the assemblage is similarly deployed to different specialists – experts in identifying and interpreting animal bones (Davis 1987), human remains (Brothwell 1986), plant remains (Keeley 1978; Renfrew 1973), insects (Kenward 1978) and sediment samples (Courty *et al.* 1990; Limbrey 1975). Other specialists will treat material for dating, for example by radio-carbon, thermoluminescence or dendrochronology (see Chapter 5).

Reading activity from an *assemblage*, even when all its components are primary and have been successfully identified, is by no means straightforward and is an important area for development. Much interpretation of activity relies on knowledge of the observed culture, or on experiments or on analogies drawn from cultures which can then be validated (for example, Bonnichsen 1973; Reynolds 1979). *Structures and activities* can be partially read from the features and finds identified in a particular phase; but a still more powerful indication is given by their relationship in plan (Hietala 1984; Blankholm 1991). The search for pattern in the distribution of features and finds is therefore a major component in the analytical itinerary. On large flat rural sites with sparse stratification, such distributions may be decisive for determining the phasing. Many of these patterns will be recognized during excavation. An array of post-sockets, for example, may already have been designated as a building and recorded as such (Fig. 4.17a). Pits of similar structural type, or containing similar assemblages, can be clustered into occupation areas. Such spatial analyses can be carried out even with materials now invisible, such as the chemical map of a vanished body (Carver 1990: 85). Areas exploited for particular purposes can also be derived from distribution patterns of finds, such as flint waste, iron slag and pottery. On thinly stratified sites, secondary finds are spatially useful: patterns can be discerned in the ploughsoil which covers the site, and the ploughsoil finds, although no longer in context, have often not moved far and still

WEST STOW
ALL PERIODS

Figure 4.17 (a) The Anglo-Saxon settlement at West Stow. Plan showing excavated features.

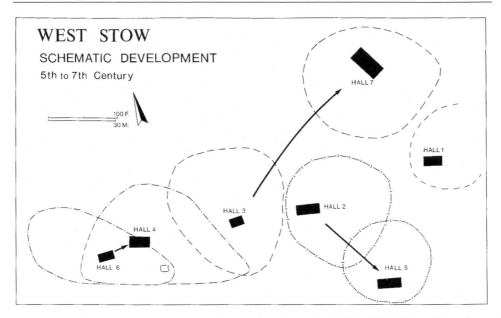

Figure 4.17 (b) Spatial analysis: phases of the settlement determined from the pottery found in the buildings. Copyright © Suffolk County Council.

represent the use–pattern beneath (Scholfield 1991). For this reason, the horizontal patterns given by dated material can also be used to indicate the phasing (Fig. 4.17b). Spatial analyses normally make use of three parameters, two of them the coordinates giving the location. The third parameter will be varied: height in the case of a topographical survey; parts per million for a phosphate survey; nano-teslars for a magnetic survey; grammes or vessel-equivalents for a pottery distribution plot. The third parameter may be presented in the form of contours, dot density, symbols or other devices.

Both modern surveys and excavations generate an immense quantity of data to be managed and analysed; and in field archaeology, as in other complex operations, the computer is playing an increasingly decisive role (Reilly and Rahtz 1992; Richards and Ryan 1985). Although much computer usage on site is unstructured, the computer being used as a large electronic notebook, it is widely recognized that the most appropriate use of computers is in handling data: that is, something measurable which has an analytical destiny. Many of the records made on site, for example the context records and finds records, fall into this category. These records may be carried in a *database management system*, written especially for archaeology, or adapted from one of the many proprietary brands.

Some field archaeologists have developed procedures for capturing data on site using battery-driven hand-held computers. Others are experimenting with digital mapping, which uses three-dimensional coordinates taken from the edge of a context, captured on site (for example by a total station theodolite) to construct an approximate plan. Many other analytical routines, which use the computerized data processing of site data, are in the course of being developed. Routines for enhancing contour surveys, geophysical maps and aerial photographs can bring structural and other use-patterns out of 'fuzzy' data (for example, O'Brien *et al.* 1982; Scollar 1978). Prototype software for constructing sequence models and seriation tables has been devised, but the most rapid progress is in the field of spatial analysis. Three-parameter maps can be generated by standard software (such as GINOSURF or Uniras), and the possibility of multi-parameter mapping using Geographic Information Systems will play an increasingly important role in field archaeology projects, particularly survey (Allen *et al.* 1990; Gaffney and Stančič 1991; Kvamme 1989; Peuquet and Marble 1990; Richards 1990).

SYNTHESIS AND PUBLICATION

The analytical stage generated a sequence of dated phase-plans, each phase with its varied activities, structures and use of space. This sequence is now presented in the form which is most accessible and attractive for the user, one which simultaneously demonstrates how the questions posed in the first place have been answered by the fieldwork.

The traditional method of presenting these conclusions is in phase- or period-plans, supported by a commentary in prose. Just as the prose commentary may imaginatively embellish the factual sequence to provide a lively narrative (famously, for example, in Wheeler's 1943 report on Maiden Castle), so the elements of each phase may be brought to life by imaginative, if authenticated, reconstruction or re-enactment (Fig. 4.18). Such creative hypotheses of the human attributes of the sequence and its place in history are necessary for a discipline which undertakes to serve human society; but they must be kept separate from the analysis and cross-referenced to it. The reader can thereby distinguish analysed data from imagination, while recognizing the need for both.

It is an axiom of field archaeology in most countries that it is conducted not in the private but in the public interest, so the records of fieldwork are therefore to be regarded as public documents. However, there are some difficulties here in both centralized and deregulated communities: in countries with a centralized state archaeological service (the majority), the project records may be owed to the state and access restricted to its officers; in deregulated societies, where the fieldwork is sponsored not by the state but by private clients, the project records may be owed to the client, who may have reasons for keeping them confidential. These are serious matters for field archaeologists, since free public access to their discoveries is the main criterion which distinguishes their activity from that of treasure hunters. In

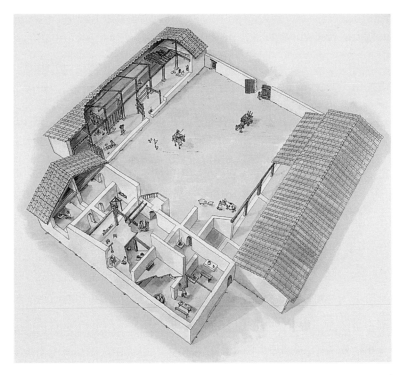

Figure 4.18 A site model: part of the sequence excavated at Monte Barro, northern Italy. Source: Brogiolo and Castelleti 1991, with permission.

societies which no longer have a centralized state archaeological service, therefore, professional organizations such as (in Britain) the Institute of Field Archaeologists or (in the USA) the Society of Professional Archaeologists are engaged in providing their own regulations for the protection of the profession's and the public's interests. Ideally, field records and field reports, however sponsored, should be placed in the public domain where they become part of the national heritage.

Full publication, the traditional method of providing public access, is usually now neither practical nor desirable, given the enormous increase in data generated by modern field projects. Since field projects are considered as primarily a vehicle for research – and this remains their necessary justification – it is logical to reassess the field reports produced from the analysis and publish selectively according to the demands of current research. Publication is therefore not a single goal, nor – as was once thought – an obligation: it is rather, as in many sciences, a range of options by which access may be managed. Thus the project records may be deposited in a museum, to be visited by the scholar, student or specialist. The field reports may be produced in a small number of copies, for the local heritage manager, for the national archive, and for appropriately specializing universities, libraries or archives. An account of the synthesis, or of particular finds, or of particular analyses, may be selected for publication in nationally and internationally distributed monographs or journals.

But publication does not end even there. A project which has created wide public interest will be promulgated also in other media: museum displays, on television, in the press. And if the site itself has survived, its consolidation, curation and presentation also form part of the publication programme; for the fresh images of the past created by field archaeologists in the name of the public are destined to be enshrined not only in prose and pictures, but in the range of monuments and landscapes bequeathed to the generations which follow (see Chapter 10).

REFERENCES

Adams, R. Mc. (1981) *Heartland of Cities: Surveys of Ancient Settlement and Land Use on the Central Floodplain of the Euphrates*, Chicago: University of Chicago Press.

Addyman, P. V. and Stove, G. C. (1989) 'Ground-probing impulse radar: an experiment in archaeological remote sensing at York', *Antiquity* 63: 337–42.

Allen, K. M., Green, S. W. and Zubrow, E. B. W. (eds) (1990) *Interpreting Space: GIS and Archaeology*, London: Cambridge University Press.

Alvisi, G. (1989) *La fotografia aerea nell' indagine archeologica*, Rome: La Nuova Italia Scientifica.

Arup (1991) = Ove Arup and Partners and Department of Archaeology, University of York, *York Development and Archaeology Study*, London: English Heritage.

Atkin, M. and Milligan, R. (1992) 'Ground probing radar in archaeology – practicalities and problems', *The Field Archaeologist* 16: 288–91.

Bahn, P. and Renfrew, A. C. (1991) *Archaeology: Theories, Methods and Practice*, London: Thames and Hudson.

Barker, G. and Lloyd, J. (eds) (1991) *Roman Landscapes: Archaeological Survey in the Mediterranean Region*, London: British School at Rome, Archaeological Monographs 2.

Barker, P. A. (1969) 'Some aspects of the excavation of timber buildings', *World Archaeology* 1: 220–30.

Barker, P. A. ([1977] 1982) *Techniques of Archaeological Excavation*, London: Batsford.

Bethell, P. H. (1991) 'Inorganic analysis of organic residues at Sutton Hoo', in P. Budd, B. Chapman, C. Jackson, R. Janaway and B. Ottoway (eds) *Archaeological Sciences 1989*, Oxford: Oxbow: 316–18.

Bewley, R. H. (1993) 'Aerial photography for archaeologists', in J. Hunter and I. Ralston (eds) *Archaeological Resource Management in the UK: an Introduction*, Birmingham: Institute of Field Archaeologists: 197–204.

Bibby, D. L. (1993) 'Building stratigraphic sequences on excavations: an example from Konstanz, Germany', in Harris, Brown and Brown (eds): 104–21.

Biddle, M. (1975) 'Excavations at Winchester, 1971. Tenth and final interim report', *Antiquaries Journal* 60 (2): 96–126, 295–337.

Biddle, M. and Hudson, D. (1973) *The Future of London's Past*, Worcester: Rescue.

Biddle, M. and Kjolbye-Biddle, B. (1969) 'Metres, areas and robbing', *World Archaeology* 1: 208–17.

Binford, L. R. (1972) *An Archaeological Perspective*, London and New York: Seminar Press.

Bintliff, J. L. (1985) 'The Boeotia survey', in S. Macready and F. H. Thompson (eds) *Archaeological Field Survey in Britain and Abroad*, Occasional Paper no. 6, London: Society of Antiquaries: 196–216.

Blankholm, H. P. (1991) *Intra-site Spatial Analysis in Theory and Practice*, Aarhus University Press.

Bonnichsen, R. (1973) 'Millie's Camp: an experiment in archaeology', *World Archaeology* 4: 277–91.

Bossuct, G. (1980) *La Reconnaissance Archéologique des Milieux Urbains par les Méthodes de Prospection Géophysique: L'Exemple de la Charité-sur-Loire*, Paris, Université de Paris VI, Mémoire du Diplome d'Études Supérieures de Sciences.

Bradley, R. (1983) 'Archaeology, evolution and the public good: the intellectual development of General Pitt-Rivers', *Archaeological Journal* 140: 1–9.

Brogiolo, G.-P. and Castelletti, L. (1991) *Archeologia a Monte Barro I*, Lecco: Editrice Stefanoni.

Brothwell, D. R. (1986) *The Bogman and the Archaeology of People*, London: British Museum Press.

Brothwell, D. R. and Higgs, E. S. (eds) ([1963] 1969) *Science in Archaeology* (2nd edition), London: Thames and Hudson.

Carver, M. O. H. (1979) 'Notes on some general principles for the analysis of excavated data', *Science and Archaeology* 21: 3–14.

Carver, M. O. H. (ed.) (1980) *Medieval Worcester*, Worcester: Worcestershire Archaeological Society.

Carver, M. O. H. (1983) 'Forty French towns: an essay on archaeological site evaluation and historical aims', *Oxford Journal of Archaeology* 2 (3): 339–78.

Carver, M. O. H. (1985) 'Theory and practice in urban pottery seriation', *Journal of Archaeological Science* 12: 353–66.

Carver, M. O. H. (1986) *Project Design for the Sutton Hoo Project*, Bulletin of the Sutton Hoo Research Committee 4, Woodbridge: Sutton Hoo Research Committee.

Carver, M. O. H. (1987) *Underneath English Towns*, London: Batsford.

Carver, M. O. H. (1989) 'Digging for ideas', *Antiquity* 63: 666–74.

Carver, M. O. H. (1990) 'Digging for data: archaeological approaches to data definition, acquisition and analysis', in R. Francovich and D. Manacorda (eds) *Lo Scavo Archeologico: dalla Diagnosi all' Edizione*, Florence: Insegna del Giglio: 45–120.

Carver, M. O. H. (ed.) (1993) *In Search of Cult: Investigations in Honour of P. A. Rahtz*, Woodbridge: Boydell Press.

Carver, M. O. H. (1996) 'On archaeological value', *Antiquity* 70: 45–56.

Cherry, J. F., Gamble, C. and Shennan, S. (eds) (1978) *Sampling in Contemporary British Archaeology*, Oxford: British Archaeological Reports, British Series 50.

CIRA (1982) *Photographie Aerienne et Prospection Géophysique en Archéologie*, Brussels: Centre Interdisciplinaire de Recherche Aerienne.

Clark, A. (1990) *Seeing Beneath the Soil*, London: Batsford.

Clarke, D. L. (1968) *Analytical Archaeology*, London: Methuen.

CNAU (1990-) *Documents d'Evaluation du Patrimoine Archéologique des Villes de France*, Paris: Centre National d'Archéologie Urbaine, Ministère de la Culture (individual volumes published from 1990 onwards, e.g. Angers, Douai).

Conway, J. S. (1983) 'An investigation of soil phosphorous distribution within occupation deposits from a Romano-British hut group', *Journal of Archaeological Science* 10: 117–28.

Courty M.-A., Goldberg, P. and Macphail, R. (1990) *Soils and Micromorphology in Archaeology*, Cambridge: Cambridge University Press.

Cowgill, G. L., Altschuhl, J. H. and Sload, R. S. (1984) '1. Spatial analysis at Teotihuacan', in H.-J. Hietala (ed.) *Intrasite Spatial Analysis in Archaeology*, Cambridge: Cambridge University Press: 154–95.

Craddock, P. T., Gurney, D., Pryor, F. and Hughes, M. J. (1985) 'The application of phosphate analysis to the location and interpretation of archaeological sites', *Archaeological Journal* 142: 361–76.

Cunliffe, B. (1993) *Danebury; Anatomy of a Hill-fort*, London: Batsford.

Cunliffe, B., Palmer, R. and Poole, C. (1984–91) *Danebury: an Iron Age Hillfort in Hampshire*, London: Council for British Archaeology (Research Reports, continuing: five volumes to date).

Darvill, T. (1988) *Monuments Protection Programme: Monument Evaluation Manual Part I/ II*, London: English Heritage.

Darvill, T., Saunders, A. and Startin, W. (1987) 'A question of national importance: approaches to the evaluation of ancient monuments for the Monuments Protection Programme', *Antiquity* 61: 393–408.

Davis, S. (1987) *The Archaeology of Animals*, London: Batsford.

Dimbleby, G. (1985) *The Palynology of Archaeological Sites*, London and New York: Academic Press.

DUA (1990) *Site Manual* (2nd edition), London: Department of Archaeology, Museum of London.

Edis, J., Macleod, D. and Bewley, R. H. (1989) 'An archaeological guide to the classification of cropmarks and soil marks', *Antiquity* 63: 112–26.

English Heritage (1992) *The Management of Archaeological Projects*, London: English Heritage.

Evans, J. G. (1972) *Land Snails in Archaeology*, London: Seminar Press.

Evans, J. G. (1978) *An Introduction to Environmental Archaeology*, London: Granada.

Faegri, K., Ekaland, P. and Krzywinski, K. (eds) (1989) *Textbook of Pollen Analysis* (4th edition), Chichester: Wiley.

Flannery, K. (ed.) (1976) *The Early Mesoamerican Village*, London and New York: Academic Press.

Frere, S. S. (1975) *Principles of Publication in Rescue Archaeology*, London: Department of the Environment.

Gaffney, C. and Gater, J. (1993) 'Practice and method in the application of geophysical techniques in archaeology', in J. Hunter and I. Ralston (eds) *Archaeological Resource Management in the UK: an Introduction*, Birmingham: Institute of Field Archaeologists: 205–14.

Gaffney, V. and Stančič, Z. (1991) *GIS Approaches to Regional Analysis: a Case Study of the Island of Hvar*, Ljubljana: Research Institute Faculty of Arts and Science, University of Ljubljana.

Godwin, Sir Harry (1956) *The History of the British Flora: A Factual Basis for Phytogeography*, Cambridge: Cambridge University Press.

Groube, L. M. and Bowden, M. C. B. (1982) *The Archaeology of Rural Dorset: Past, Present and Future*, Dorchester: Dorset Natural History and Archaeological Society Monograph 4.

Gsell, S. (1901) *Les Monuments Antiques de l'Algérie*, Algiers and Paris: Hachette.

Hammond, N. (1991) 'Matrices and Maya archaeology', *Journal of Field Archaeology* 18: 29–42.

177

Harris, E. C. (1975) 'The stratigraphic sequence: a question of time' , *World Archaeology* 7 (1): 109–21.

Harris, E. C. (1977) 'Units of archaeological stratification', *Norwegian Archaeological Review* 10 (1): 84–106.

Harris, E. C. (1989) *Principles of Archaeological Stratigraphy*, London and New York: Academic Press.

Harris, E. C., Brown, M. R. and Brown, G. J. (eds) (1993) *Practices of Archaeological Stratigraphy*, London and New York: Academic Press.

Hietala, H.-J. (ed.) (1984) *Intrasite Spatial Analysis in Archaeology*, Cambridge: Cambridge University Press.

Hirst, S. (1976) *Recording on Excavations: the Written Record*, Worcester: Rescue.

Hodder, I. (1986) *The Present Past*, London: Batsford.

Hodson, F. R. (1968) *The La Tène Cemetery at Münsingen-Rain*, Bern: Acta Bernensia 5.

Hope-Taylor, B. (1977) *Yeavering: an Anglo-British Centre of Early Northumbria*, London: HMSO.

Hunter, J. and Ralston, I. (eds) (1993) *Archaeological Resource Management in the UK: an Introduction*, Birmingham: Institute of Field Archaeologists.

Hurst Thomas, D. (1989) *Archaeology*, Fort Worth.

Imai, T., Sakayama, T. and Kanemori, T. (1987) 'Use of ground-probing radar and resistivity surveys for archaeological investigations', *Geophysics* 52 (2): 137–50.

Keeley, H. C. M. (1978) 'The cost-effectiveness of certain methods of recovering macroscopic organic remains from archaeological sites', *Journal of Archaeological Science* 5: 179–83.

Keller, D. R. and Rupp, D. W. (eds) (1983) *Archaeological Survey in the Mediterranean Area*, Oxford: British Archaeological Reports, International Series 155.

Kenward, H. K. (1978) 'The analysis of archaeological insect assemblages: a new approach', *The Archaeology of York* 19/1, York: York Archaeological Trust.

Kvamme, K. L. (1989) 'Geographic informity systems in regional archaeological research and data management', in M. B. Schiffer (ed.) *Archaeological Method and Theory* I (University of Arizona Press): 139–203.

Lattes (1986) *Enregistrer la Fouille Archéologique: la Système Elaboré pour la Site de Lattes (Hérault)*, Lattes: Association pour la Recherche Archéologique en Languedoc Oriental.

Layard, A. (1849) *Nineveh and its Remains*, London: John Murray.

Leeds, E. T. (1945) 'The distribution of the Angles and Saxons archaeologically considered', *Archaeologia* 91: 1–106.

Lerici, C. M. (1960) *Alla Scoperta delle Civiltà Sepolte I Nuovi Metodi di Prospezione Archeologica* Milan: Lerici editori.

Leveau, P. (1984) *Caeserea de Mauretanie: une ville Romaine et ses Campagnes*, Rome: Ecole Française de Rome.

Limbrey, S. (1975) *Soil Science and Archaeology*, London and New York: Academic Press.

Lipe, W. (1984) 'Value and meaning in cultural resources', in H. Cleere (ed.) *Approaches to the Archaeological Heritage*, Cambridge, Cambridge University Press: 1–11.

Lyell, C. (1830–33) *Principles of Geology*, London: Murray.

Mattingly, D. J. (1988) 'Oil for export' and 'Olea Mediterranea', *Journal of Roman Archaeology* 1: 33–56 and 153–61.

Maxwell, G. S. (1983) *The Impact of Aerial Reconnaissance on Archaeology*, Research Report 49, London: Council for British Archaeology.

Millett, M. (1991) 'Pottery: population or supply patterns? The Ager Tarraconensis approach', in G. Barker and J. Lloyd (eds) *Roman Landscapes: Archaeological Survey in the Mediterranean Region*, Archaeological Monographs 2, London: British School at Rome: 18–26.

Ministry of Education, Ukraine SSR (1986) *Metodicheskie Recomendatsi po Issledovaniyu Kurgannih Pamyatnikov* (Methods Recommended for Excavating Kurgan-Type Monuments), Kiev.

Muckelroy, K. (1978) *Maritime Archaeology*, Cambridge: Cambridge University Press.

Mueller, J. W. (1975) *Sampling in Archaeology*, Tucson: University of Arizona Press.

NAS (1992) *Archaeology Underwater: The NAS Guide to Principles and Practice*, London: Nautical Archaeology Society.

O'Brien, M. J., Beets, J. L., Warren, R. E., Hotrabhavananda, T., Barney, T. W. and Voigt, E. E. (1982) 'Digital enhancement and grey-level slicing of aerial photographs: techniques for archaeological analysis of intrasite variability', *World Archaeology* 14: 173–90.

Paice, P. (1991) 'Extensions to the Harris matrix system to illustrate stratigraphic discussion of an archaeological site', *Journal of Field Archaeology* 18: 17–28.

Payne, S. (1972) 'Partial recovery and sample bias: the results of some sieving experiments', in E. S. Higgs (ed.) *Papers in Economic Prehistory*, Cambridge: Cambridge University Press: 49–64.

Petrie, W. F. (1904) *Methods and Aims in Archaeology*, London: Macmillan.

Peuquet, D. J. and Marble, D. F. (eds) (1990) *Introductory Readings in Geographic Information Systems*, London: Taylor and Francis.

Pitt-Rivers, A. L. F. (1887–1905) *Excavations in Cranborne Chase*, London: Privately published, five volumes.

Potter, T. W. (1974) *The Changing Landscape of South Etruria*, London: Elek.

Rapp, R. and Hill, C. (1998) *Geoarchaeology. The Earth Science Approach to Archaeological Interpretation*, Yale University Press.

Redman, C. L. (1986) *Qsar es-Seghir: an Archaeological View of Medieval Life*, London and New York: Academic Press.

Redman, C. L. (1987) 'Surface collection, sampling and research design: a retrospective', *American Antiquity* 52 (2): 249–65.

Reilly, P. and Rahtz, S. P. Q. (1992) *Archaeology and the Information Age: a Global Perspective*, London: Routledge.

Renfrew, A. C. (1985) *The Archaeology of Cult: the Sanctuary at Phylakopi*, London: British School at Athens.

Renfrew, A. C. and Wagstaff, J. M. (eds) (1981) *An Island Polity: the Archaeology of Exploitation on Melos*, Cambridge: Cambridge University Press.

Renfrew, J. (1973) *Paleoethnobotany*, London and New York: Methuen.

Reynolds, P. J. (1979) *Iron Age Farm: the Butser Experiment*, London: Colonnade.

Rich, C. J. (1839) *Narrative of a Journey to the Site of Babylon*, London: Longman, Hurst, Rees, Orme and Brown (Paternoster Row), and J. Murray (Albemarle Street).

Richards, J. D. (1987) *The Form and Significance of Anglo-Saxon Cremation Urns*, Oxford: British Archaeological Reports, British Series 166.

Richards, J. D. (1990) 'Terrain modelling, deposit survival and urban archaeology', *Science and Archaeology* 32: 32–38.

Richards, J. D. and Ryan, N. S. (1985) *Data Processing in Archaeology*, Cambridge: Cambridge University Press.

Riley, D. N. (1980) *Early Landscape from the Air: Studies of Cropmarks in South Yorkshire and*

North Nottinghamshire, Sheffield: Sheffield University, Department of Archaeology and Prehistory.

Rule, M. (1982) *The Mary Rose*, London: Conway Maritime Press.

Schiffer, M. B. (1976) *Behavioural Archaeology*, London and New York: Academic Press.

Schiffer, M. B. (1987) *Formation Processes of the Archaeological Record*, Albuquerque: University of New Mexico Press.

Scholfield, A. J. (ed.) (1991) *Interpreting Artefact Scatters: Contributions to Ploughzone Archaeology*, Oxford: Oxbow Monograph 4.

Schuchhardt, K. (1891) *Schliemann's Excavations: an Archaeological and Historical Study*, London: Macmillan.

Scollar, I. (1978) 'Computer image processing for archaeological air photographs', *World Archaeology* 10: 71–87.

Scollar, I., Tabbagh, A., Hesse, A. and Herzog, I. (1990) *Archaeological Prospection and Remote Sensing: Topics in Remote Sensing 2*, Cambridge: Cambridge University Press.

St Joseph, J. K. (ed.) (1977) *The Uses of Air Photography* (2nd edition), London: J. Baker.

Startin, W. (1993) 'Assessment of field remains', in J. Hunter and I. Ralston (eds) *Archaeological Resource Management in the UK: an Introduction*, Birmingham: Institute of Field Archaeologists: 184–96.

Stephens, J. L. ([1841] 1969) *Incidents of Travel in Central America, Chiapas and Yucatan*, New York: Dover.

Syedov, V. V. (1982) *Vostochnie Slavyanie v VI–XIII vv*, Moscow: Nauka (in the series 'Archaeology of the USSR').

Throckmorton, P. (ed.) (1987) *History from the Sea*, London: Mitchell Beazley.

Vita-Finzi, C. (1978) *Archaeological Sites in their Setting*, London and New York: Thames and Hudson.

Wade, K. (1983) 'The archaeology of Witton, near North Walsham', *East Anglian Archaeology* 18.

West, S. E. (1985) 'West Stow: the Anglo-Saxon Village', *East Anglian Archaeology* 24.

Weymouth, J. (1986) 'Geophysical methods of archaeological site surveying', *Advances in Archaeological Method and Theory* 9: 311–95.

Wheeler, R. E. M. (1943) *Maiden Castle, Dorset*, Research Report, London: Society of Antiquaries.

Wheeler, R. E. M. (1945) 'Technical section: recording and stratigraphy', *Ancient India* 3: 133–40.

Wheeler, R. E. M. (1946) 'Technical section: recording and stratigraphy', *Ancient India* 4: 311–21.

Wheeler, R. E. M. (1954) *Archaeology from the Earth*, Oxford: Clarendon Press.

Wheeler, R. E. M. (1976) *The Indus Civilization* (3rd edition), Cambridge: Cambridge University Press.

Whimster, R. P. (1989) *The Emerging Past*, London: RCHME.

Willey, G. R. (1953) *Prehistoric Settlement Patterns in the Virú Valley, Peru*, Washington, DC: US Government Printing Office.

Willey, G. R. and Sabloff, J. A. (1974) *A History of American Archaeology*, London: Thames and Hudson.

Wilson, D. R. (ed.) (1975) *Aerial Reconnaissance for Archaeologists*, London: Council for British Archaeology.

Wilson, D. R. (1982) *Air Photo Interpretation for Archaeologists*, London: Batsford.

Wood, J. (1992) 'Building on recording: the analysis and interpretation of buildings', *The Field Archaeologist* 16: 293–303.

Wood, J. (ed.) (1994) *Buildings Archaeology. Applications in Practice* Oxford: Oxbow.

SELECT BIBLIOGRAPHY

The principles given in this summary article follow my papers 'Digging for Ideas', *Antiquity* 63 (1989), 666–74, and 'Digging for Data' in R. Francovich and D. Manacorda, *Lo Scavo Archeologico: dalla Diagnosi all'Edizione* (Florence 1990), 45–120. Since early field archaeology books tend to reflect their authors' experience and research culture, they remain useful over unexpectedly long periods, in spite of the effort they sometimes make to displace one another. Thus W. F. Petrie's *Methods and Aims in Archaeology* (London 1904) remains an inspiring work, containing prophetic accounts of systematic evaluation, photogrammetry, block-lifting of finds, seriation and other techniques of fieldwork and management combined with a stirring and by no means outdated ethical message. R. E. M. Wheeler's *Archaeology from the Earth* (Oxford 1954) and *Still Digging* (London 1956) are also essential reading for research-driven fieldworkers. J. Coles' *Field Archaeology in Britain* (London 1977) is full of good sense. P. A. Barker's *Techniques of Archaeological Excavation* (London 1977) emphasized stratigraphic recording, but was most notable for its empirical approach ('the only valid question to ask of an archaeological deposit is what is there') and its advocacy of large open area excavations such as he was conducting at Wroxeter and Hen Domen. These ethics were popular with fieldworkers and governments alike, although for rather different reasons. By the time of the publication of his *Understanding Archaeological Excavation* (London: Batsford 1986), however, there was more than a nod towards research-selectivity. An important European multi-authored work, incorporating evaluation, excavation, analysis and publication, is the aforementioned volume by R. Francovich and D. Manacorda, *Lo Scavo Archeologico: dalla Diagnosi all'Edizione*. In the USA, the wisdom and humour of Kent Flannery's comments on field methods (particularly survey) in *The Early Mesoamerican Village* (1976) have inspired a generation. A fine descriptive overview of staged field archaeology in the service of research is R. Sharer and W. Ashmore, *Fundamentals of Archaeology* (Menlo Park: Benjamin Cummins 1979). A fieldwork classic in its seventh edition is T. N. Hester, H. J. Shafer and R. F. Heizer, *Field Methods in Archaeology* (Palo Alto 1997). D. Hurst Thomas's *Archaeology* (Instructors Edition, Forth Worth 1989) is an exuberant and often stimulating textbook. M. Joukowsky's *A Complete Manual of Field Archaeology* (New Jersey: Prentice-Hall 1980) contains many useful practical details. *Archaeology: Theories, Methods and Practice* by P. Bahn and C. Renfrew (London and New York: Thames and Hudson 1991, 2nd edition 1996) treats many aspects of field research and is particularly good for the reconnaissance and analysis stages. S. Wass, *The Amateur Archaeologist* (London: Batsford 1992) offers a sympathetic reception to the part-timer who wants a chance to join in.

Articles, anecdotes and asides on the theory and practice of field archaeology will be found in reports on excavation and survey projects, and in mainstream journals such as *Antiquity*, *American Antiquity*, *World Archaeology*, *Journal of Archaeological Science*, *Helinium*, *Norwegian Archaeological Review*, *Nouvelles d'Archéologie*, *Archeologia Medievale*, and so on. Dedicated series are *Journal of Field Archaeology* (Boston, USA), *Archaeological Method and Theory* (Tucson) and *The Field Archaeologist* (Institute of Field Archaeologists, Reading, UK).

5

ESTABLISHING ARCHAEOLOGICAL CHRONOLOGIES

Anthony Harding

INTRODUCTION

All archaeologists are required to know something about the sequence of artefacts, cultures and sites which are their stock in trade, but most of them, most of the time, take the framework for the chronology of a given period or civilization for granted, on the grounds that it has been carefully built up over many years, and the foundations cannot constantly be questioned. But the ways in which that framework has been constructed may be many and various, not all of equal reliability. In this chapter the main sources for the construction of archaeological chronologies are presented, and some examples of reliable – and unreliable – chronologies discussed.

To those brought up in the Judaeo-Christian tradition, the genealogical lists in the early books of the Old Testament serve as a vivid reminder of how time-depth could be expressed in the ancient world. This indeed was the basis for the calculation that has made James Ussher, Archbishop of Armagh between 1625 and 1656, famous to generations of archaeologists: that the Creation occurred in the year 4004 BC. The details of his calculation are unimportant, and the result itself merely of historical interest, but the method is significant. By assuming that a generation was of X years, and that there had been Y generations prior to defined historical events as recorded in the Bible, the years elapsed were X times Y, an absolute number of years that can be related to historical and thence to modern times.

The writings of the biblical genealogists and of Archbishop Ussher represent two quite separate aspects to the establishment of a chronology. On the one hand, the chronicler of ancient times was concerned to record the events of his or previous ages, in relation to certain fixed points, in a way which other people of his own or later generations could understand. On the other hand, the historian of later times needs to be able to 'read' the chronicle, and to reconstruct both the fixed points and the system of reference which alone will guarantee success in arriving at 'dates' – periods of time elapsed since the events in question. These two activities are quite different, though they are often collated or even confused in writings on the subject. If all ancient chronicles were immediately intelligible in their chronological aspects, the problem would hardly arise, but in fact archaeologists and historians have to spend much time simply in reconstructing the nature and meaning of ancient chronological systems before they can move on to matters of greater significance for the understanding of ancient societies.

The importance of exact dating varies considerably from period to period. For recent history, the exact day on which an event occurred is important, even the exact time or minute, mainly because international communications now mean that events occurring in one place are known of as they happen everywhere else on the globe. Prior to the advent of such simultaneous transmission of news, the speed of non-local reaction to events depended on the speed of transport, usually that of the horse, unless signals could be sent by other means. In such cases, the resolution with which events can be viewed is somewhat coarser: weeks and months, typically even years; only exceptionally days. Naturally the strength or otherwise of the written record plays an important part here. Where historical records, or artefacts such as coins or inscriptions, are available, archaeologists and historians demand a fine resolution to their dating. In the Roman period, for example, where the records are excellent, it is frequently possible to date events to an exact day, though it is more usual to deal in months and years (depending on area and period). In Archaic and classical Greece, written histories may give a chronicle of events in which things are recorded at the level of weeks or months, but archaeological artefacts are more likely to be referable to decades or quarter-centuries.

Before written history, the resolution available declines dramatically. In the European Iron Age, contemporary with the world of Classical Athens, the resolution is further reduced: where Greek imports are involved, a dating corresponding to that in Greece may be obtained, but otherwise the resolution may be down to anywhere from quarter-centuries to centuries. In the Bronze Age we are usually lucky to be able to deal in centuries, in the Neolithic in centuries to half-millennia; while before that, in the Mesolithic and Upper Palaeolithic, the millennium will be the usual time-bracket employed. As one goes further back still, tens or even hundreds of millennia become the closest approximations one can achieve, and at the dawn of human activity, several million years ago, the available methods only allow a chronological resolution at the level of hundreds of thousands of years. In each period of the past, therefore, very different possibilities and expectations prevail (Fig. 5.1).

It can be seen from this that different periods have different requirements as far as the construction of chronologies is concerned. A chronology that set out the

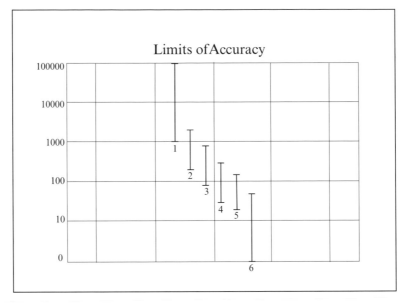

Figure 5.1 Limits of accuracy of dates for particular periods of the past (see text). Note the logarithmic scale: 1. Palaeolithic; 2. Mesolithic; 3. Neolithic; 4. Bronze Age; 5. Iron Age; 6. Egypt, Greece, Rome. Source: A. Harding.

events of the Neolithic to an accuracy of ±50 years (an accuracy that is now attainable) would be regarded as highly satisfactory, though for a period with good historical evidence, for instance the Roman period, it would be regarded as barely worth having, and for the Lower Palaeolithic much too precise to be meaningful. In other words, archaeological chronologies depend for their usefulness on their context as much as if not more than on their potential precision. Deciding whether an attainable resolution is appropriate for the purposes of understanding the period under investigation will be a matter for each archaeologist to decide in the light of the context of the datable material.

THE APPRECIATION OF TIME-DEPTH IN THE ANCIENT PAST

The Greek and Roman historians realized that their nations had an ancient past, though they had no means of putting a precise date on distant events of which they were only vaguely aware. Thucydides, for example, writing around 400 BC, referred to the ancient past of Greece, though the main points of reference for him were events – such as the Trojan War – which were legendary rather than demonstrable historical fact. Many Greek and Roman writers used rough and ready systems of dating events in the past, and some (the Roman writer Censorinus, for example) were deeply interested in reconstructing the chronology of the historical past. The poets Hesiod and Lucretius both imagined a gradual progression through a remote antiquity to the times recorded by the historians known to them, and the same may be said for Chinese historians, who developed a lively sense of their own history from earliest times. The medieval period in Europe produced scholars who were concerned with chronological aspects of the human past, but on the whole these were seen within the theological framework of the Creation. Even the start of antiquarianism after the Renaissance brought with it little appreciation of time-depth, though the revival of interest in classical Antiquity did bring with it some understanding of the progress of history back to 500 BC.

The story of the development of an understanding of the true time-scale of the past is one that is interlinked with the story of discovery (Daniel 1975; see also Chapter 1). In Britain, antiquaries such as William Stukeley (1687–1765) had to glean what they could about the world of 'the ancient Britons' from classical sources. The gradual realization of a very long time-scale of the ancient past gathered steam in the early nineteenth century. Until then, belief in the literal truth of the Bible meant that the Flood was generally accepted as a, if not the, cause of landforms being what they were (the 'diluvial' theory), but observations by geologists, notably Charles Lyell (1797–1875), gradually led to an acceptance of 'uniformitarianism'; that is, that physical processes observable at present were the same ones which had caused changes to the earth's surface in the past as well, and had therefore taken place over a very long time-scale. *How* long was still very uncertain, and no one was really prepared to hazard a guess, so overlain was the topic with religious and philosophical implications, but uniformitarianism clearly had profound implications regarding the antiquity of stone tools associated with extinct faunas of the kind that were being widely reported from gravels and caves.

At the same time as such evidences of human antiquity were being produced, others had noted structure in the archaeological finds themselves, a process which had its best-known outcome in the invention of the Three Age system (Daniel 1943; Gräslund 1987). C. J. Thomsen is generally credited with the first formalization of such a scheme, though others were experimenting with it around the same time, and a general awareness of successive 'ages' can be found going back to classical Antiquity, to Lucretius for example. But a clear statement, and acceptance, that a Stone Age preceded a Bronze Age, which in turn preceded an Iron Age, helped engender a realization that different artefacts were of very different ages.

The missing link, which completed the conceptual framework for an understanding of prehistoric chronology, and enabled chronologists to advance with confidence, was the assertion of the evolutionary principle. Darwin's *Origin of Species* (1859) did two things for archaeology: it brought about a realization that humans were not always as they are today, but had developed physically over very long time-spans; and it enabled people to realize that evolutionary development was not confined to biology, but could also be discerned in the works of our own species. In other words, progress was the natural state of things; objects changed over time, and the rate of change was in principle measurable.

In the latter part of the nineteenth century, detailed archaeological chronologies were provided by scholars such as the Swede Oscar Montelius (1843–1921), to whom we owe one of the first and still one of the best archaeological chronologies that exist (Montelius 1886; Fig. 5.2). The method adopted was a combination of *typology* and *association*, of which we shall have more to say below. *Typology* – literally the study of types – involved the recognition and definition of variant forms of the same functional class of object, *association* the occurrence of these objects with each other in collective finds (typically in graves). By this means, a series of steps or stages could be identified, characterized by groups of objects of particular types that regularly occurred together. Montelius's most famous application of the method was to the Scandinavian Bronze Age, but he worked on and produced schemes for other areas and periods as well. The success of Montelius's work can be judged from the fact that his six-part division of the Bronze Age, known as Periods I–VI, is still used today and is regarded as largely correct in its definitions.

The schemes that Montelius and others like him produced were *relative* schemes: they provided a chronology that defined the position of each stage relative to all the others. When Montelius came to put actual dates on his stages, he had to adopt a different method. For the Iron Age, he was able to refer to objects that linked in with known Roman material, or to Celtic coins, in order to provide an absolute chronology. For periods earlier than that, he developed the technique of *cross-dating* – seeking analogies for objects in northern Europe in areas where a dating system already existed, such as Italy, Greece and Egypt (Table 5.1; Fig. 5.3). In Italy, for instance, dates as far back as the Etruscan period could be arrived at through historical means; beyond that, things were in the realm of guesswork, and an estimate of 1500 BC for the start of the Bronze Age was made. Close comparisons were evident north and south of the Alps in the period covered by the great cemetery of Hallstatt in Austria, so that a dating could be arrived at for that area too; and enough similarities existed between northern Europe and central Europe for the entire northern chronology to be tied in to the Mediterranean world. This, together with the assumption that the Nordic stages or periods each lasted between 100 and 200 years, enabled Montelius in 1885 to set the start of the Scandinavian Bronze Age at 1500 BC, the same as in Italy.

But there was another source of chronological comparison: Egypt. The progress of discovery and research that culminated in the decipherment of the hieroglyphic script by Champollion in 1822, combined with detailed examination of textual material (for instance the writings of the Jewish scribe Manetho), brought about the production of a more or less complete Egyptian chronology as far back as the

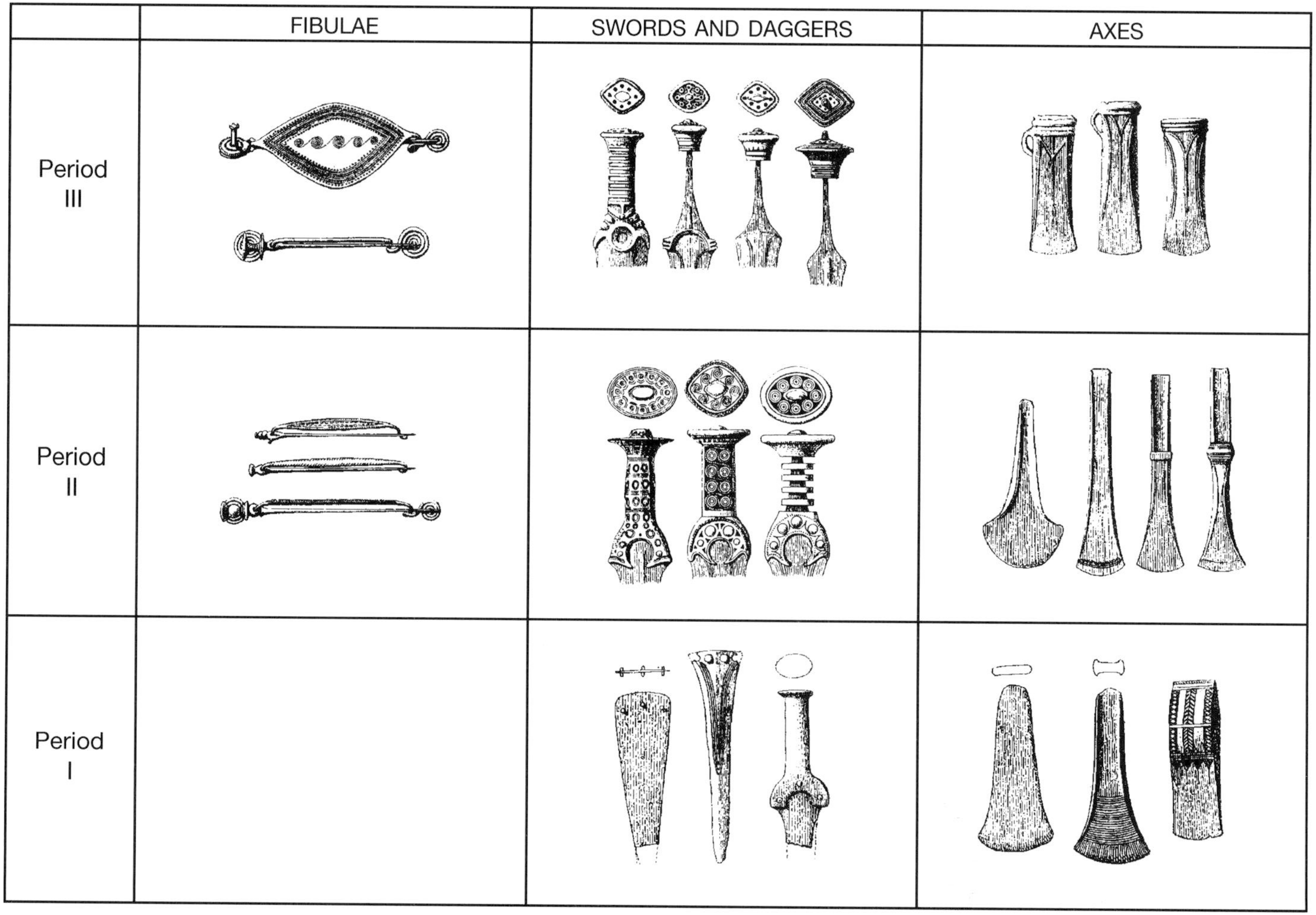

	FIBULAE	SWORDS AND DAGGERS	AXES
Period III			
Period II			
Period I			

Figure 5.2 Typology as a means of constructing chronologies. The same functional types in each column develop in form from bottom to top. From their development, Oscar Montelius was able to distinguish succeeding periods of the Bronze Age in Scandinavia. Reproduced with permission of The Royal Swedish Academy of Letters, History and Antiquities.

Table 5.1 Cross-dating by means of artefacts: the reigns of Egyptian pharaohs; and correlations for the Aegean area by means of exported artefacts

Egypt			Aegean correlations
18th Dynasty pharaohs	Reign length (Manetho)	Dates (Helck 1987)	
Ahmose	25y 4m	1530–1504	
Amenophis I	20y 7m	1504–1483	
Tuthmosis I	12y 9m	1483–1470	
Tuthmosis II	3y	1470–1467	
Hatshepsut	21y 9m	1467–1445	
Tuthmosis III	30y 10m	1445–1414	Late Minoan IB pot at Abydos
Amenophis II	25y 10m	1414–1388	
Tuthmosis IV	9y 8m	1388–1379	
Amenophis III	37y 7m	1379–1340	Scarab in Knossos tomb of Late Minoan IIIA1
Amenophis IV	16y 1m	1340–1324	⎫
Smenkhare	5y 5m	1324–1319	⎬ Late Helladic IIIA2 pottery at El Amarna
Tutankhamun	9y	1319–1309	⎭
Ai	4y 1m	1309–1305	
Horemheb	12y 3m	1305–1293	
Ramesses I	1y 4m	1293–1291	
Seti I	11y	1291–1279	
Ramesses II	66y 2m	1279–1213	LH IIIB pottery at Gurob tomb with his scarab

beginning of the Pharaonic period (about 3000 BC) (see p. 198). The correlation of Egyptian phases with Greek ones meant that dates could be derived for areas outside Egypt by the cross-dating technique via Greece to other areas of Europe. Comparable chronological systems were developed in the Near East. During the course of the nineteenth century, therefore, an Old World chronology that was roughly correct over the last 5,000 years came into being; the work of the twentieth century has largely been an enlargement and refinement of that chronology.

BUILDING UP CHRONOLOGICAL FRAMEWORKS

The evidence used to build up chronological frameworks can be either *internal* or *external*. Internal evidence is that deriving directly from the archaeological material, for instance its form, appearance, historical content (such as in an inscription), or its physical and chemical properties. External evidence is that deriving from its context, its find-spot and position, from its relationship to other material, or from its relationship to known outside events.

188

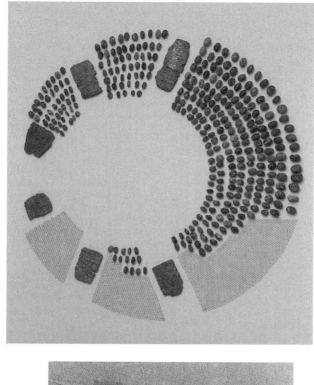

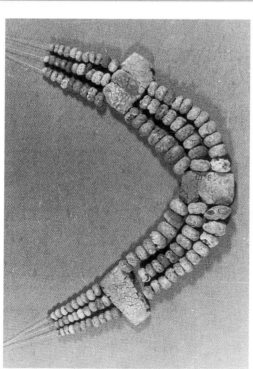

Figure 5.3 Cross-dating by means of artefacts: amber beads of identical form found in the Shaft Graves of Mycenae (left) and a burial mound in southern England (right), providing a chronological fixed point for the English material. Left: photograph of a recent reconstruction by K. Demakopoulou, appearing in O Mykinaikos Kosmos, *The Mycenean World*, catalogue no. 280 (Athens, National Archaeological Museum); right: reproduced with permission of Wiltshire Archaeological and Natural History Society.

Under the heading of internal evidence, it is possible to distinguish between *typological* evidence, which considers the form and appearance of an artefact, in whole or in part; *direct historical* evidence, where for instance an aspect of an artefact can be related directly to known historical events (for instance the head of an emperor on a coin, or an inscription on a building or tombstone); or *physical* evidence, such as the carbon-14 content of an object, or its luminescence properties. External evidence includes first and foremost *positional* evidence, referring to the context in which an object occurred – whether in a given stratigraphic layer, on a particular site, in a region or even a country. Positional evidence is heavily dependent on taphonomy, and depositional and post-depositional transformations critically affect its validity. There is also a category of *indirect historical* evidence, where known historical events may relate to archaeological phenomena, such as the possible identification of burning layers at Colchester with the sack of the town by Boudicca, queen of the Iceni, in AD 61.

RELATIVE CHRONOLOGIES

Relative chronologies place archaeological phenomena, and by implication events, in a particular relationship to each other: that is, before, contemporary with, or after. In some cases, such as stratigraphic succession, indications of priority or posteriority are all that can be determined, but with some classes of evidence, *terminus* dates are obtained (*terminus* meaning the end-point, the position beyond which an event cannot go). There are two sorts of *terminus* date: the *terminus ante quem* and the *terminus post quem*.

A *terminus ante quem* is a point *before* which something must be placed, or something occurred. If, for instance, a site is known to have been abandoned at a particular date and not reoccupied (such as Pompeii in AD 79), then all the material on that site must date prior to the abandonment, even if only by a few days. Such materials will probably have been manufactured at various times prior to this, however, but all that can be said in dating terms is that the abandonment date is the latest possible date when they could have been made: 24 August AD 79 thus represents a *terminus ante quem* for all the material found under the volcanic ash at Pompeii.

A *terminus post quem*, by contrast, represents a point *after* which an event must have occurred. Coins, and coin hoards in particular, are good examples of this: coins can remain in circulation for considerable lengths of time, and the finding of a coin in a given layer only tells us that the layer was laid down after the minting of the coin, but not by how much. Every coin in a coin hoard gives a *terminus post quem*, but only that of the latest issue in the hoard is really significant for establishing the date of deposition. A good example of this is the hoard of 1,925 silver *denarii* found near Falkirk, southern Scotland (Reece 1987: 49–61). Of these, a few dated to the

190

Republican period (before 27 BC), rather more to the early principate, large numbers to the Flavian period (69–96) and the second century AD, with a relatively small number belonging to the earlier third century – the latest is of Severus Alexander, who died in AD 235. This long time-span – well over 200 years – presents a problem for establishing dates, and to pin down a year of deposition a lot of unknowns need to be quantified, including frequency of minting in each year, purpose and destination of minted coins, value in metal terms of the coinage of different periods, distance from place of minting, and other factors. In this case it has been plausibly demonstrated that the bulk of the hoard is close in composition to a series of hoards buried in the period 193–217, and quite different to those of the period 222–38, suggesting that it had accumulated as a hoard destined for recycling in the former period, the time of the Emperor Septimius Severus. But it was not finally deposited then: it had some extra coins of the next period added and was eventually deposited after 235. What is important about this example is not the absolute dates involved, but their relative placing, and the demonstration that the deposition date was not necessarily the date of most interest.

Dating by typology

The principle of typological dating is that functionally identical artefacts vary in form over time. There are of course other aspects to this variation, most notably that variation in artefact form reflects geographical factors, for instance place of manufacture, or intentional variation on the part of the maker; that is, style – variation in style is as much a cultural trait as a temporal one. The crucial concern is to recognize meaningful variations of form; that is, variations that correspond to real variations of either time or production in Antiquity. In other words, typologies that are created by archaeologists must bear a real relationship to the intentions of the makers if spurious conclusions are not to be drawn.

Typology is the study of types, but 'types' are not a universally constant concept, and a famous article by Julian Steward (1954) was entitled 'Types of types' (see also Brown 1982; Hill and Evans 1972). His 'morphological', 'historical–index', 'functional' and 'cultural' types are of varying importance for chronological studies: 'morphological' types ('descriptive' in other workers' terminology) are defined in accordance with external appearance (that is, form) and are basically a descriptive means of reducing a given population to manageable categories. On the other hand, 'historical–index', or chronological, types also use form but in a chronological sense: form can change over time; analysis of the change enables the passage of time to be recorded. Distinguishing between change that occurs over time and diversity for other reasons, such as functional or cultural factors, is one of the weaknesses of the typological method.

Typology can be practised on any category of artefact, provided only that it shows enough variation for differences between artefacts to be studied (Fig. 5.4). It is not merely the shape or form of the object that is of interest, but also the material and its properties (for example, hardness, or chemical characteristics), the technology involved, and the context in which it occurred. Typological analysis treats objects as collections of traits or attributes (Clarke 1968) – length, colour, curvature, fabric and so on. The only elements which are not suitable are those that are common to all objects of the class; that is, are essential to an object being referred to a given functional class. For instance, we could not use the material 'clay' as a suitable attribute on which to base a typology of a pot, since all pots will be of clay, but we could take the type of temper, the treatment of the clay, or the inclusions in the clay, as being relevant to a typological analysis.

In theory a typological sequence can be constructed using almost any of these variables, but in practice it is usually the shape and decoration of an object which are used to construct a typology. In this it is important to take functionally identical objects so that, for example, plates are compared only with other plates, and not with saucers or bowls. Clarke's classic analysis of the prehistoric European pottery known as Beakers, for instance, relied partly on the change from sinuous S-shaped profile to the creation of a long neck on the vessel, and partly on the zonation and form of the decoration (Clarke 1970). A study of palaeolithic handaxes by Roe (1968) used both visual and statistical techniques to produce a series of groups and

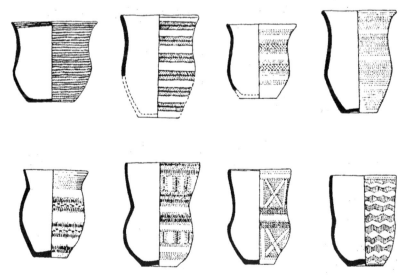

Figure 5.4 Typological series. The development of British Beaker pottery, twenty-eighth to seventeenth centuries BC. Source: Clarke 1970.

192

sub-groups of handaxes which had both internal consistency and chronological validity, and enabled both old and new finds to be placed in a likely chronological order.

It is reasonable to ask how types used for ordering (whether for chronological or other purposes) are recognized (Spaulding 1953; Whallon 1972). It would appear that the human eye picks out certain features that it regards as significant, and discards what it regards as incidental. Since humans vary, one can expect that typologies of identical artefact groups will also vary, and of course two people will not necessarily create identical typologies; but enough similarity exists for one to imagine that certain common pattern recognition traits exist in humans, so that the process of typologizing is not entirely a subjective art. An interesting experiment conducted by Hodson (1970) tested this suggestion: a group of archaeologists and a biologist were asked to place in order a series of Iron Age fibulae (safety pins). Although the results differed, both in detail and in basic approach, there were enough similarities between the different orderings of the material for the assumption of an in-built mechanism for pattern recognition to be reasonable.

A group of objects may be arranged so as to form a sequence of types, but without external information this cannot be dated, nor can the sequence be confirmed or modified in the light of other factors, principally stratigraphical position. This is the next step in the process of arriving at a typological dating framework. In itself, a typological sequence may be internally consistent, but it has no external reference points; one may not even know in which order the sequence goes. Comparison with contextual information may then enable such uncertainties to be resolved, though in practice it is likely that the creation of a typological sequence would have taken such information into account from the start. The incorporation of stratigraphic information into the typological sequence can thus provide a check and a calibration on the results of visual inspection.

Dating by seriation

Typology acquires an added importance when it can be combined with the techniques collectively called *seriation*, since by this means groups of individual typologies can be used together (Brainerd 1951; Cowgill 1972; Dempsey and Baumhoff 1963; LeBlanc 1975; Marquardt 1978; Robinson 1951). Seriation is the process of creating series, in this case type series, and its origin in an archaeological context is usually traced back to the Egyptologist Flinders Petrie, in his attempts to deal with the large quantities of pottery and other material found in Egyptian tombs of the prehistoric periods at sites such as Nagada and Abydos (Petrie 1899, 1901).

The method Petrie adopted was to create slips of paper a quarter of an inch wide and seven inches long, ruled in nine columns (one for each 'kind', or fabric type, of pottery), and to write the number of each form (or shape) of pot in the relevant fabric column for each grave, so that the whole of the pottery found in a given grave could be quickly compared with that from any other grave. He then arranged the slips into a 'seriated' order. Starting with a pot type (W, or wavy-handled vases) for which a typological sequence had already been established, those examples which occurred in graves together with another type (L, late) known to survive into later times were first segregated, and then the examples with each of the other contemporaneous types (B, black-topped; P, polished-red; and R, rough-faced), so that every example of W pottery was accounted for. Then in order to go back in time, the associations of a sixth type, C (white-cross lines), was correlated with B, P and R. Gradually more and more types were brought into play, until all 900 slips were sorted into an order that Petrie was convinced was the right one; at this stage Petrie divided all the material into fifty equal groups, and assigned to each a 'sequence date' or position in the seriated sequence.

Petrie had effectively discovered one of the main methods by which seriation of archaeological assemblages works: 'contextual seriation', which depends on the accompanying material of a given type rather than the frequency with which it is found. The alternative approach, sometimes called 'frequency seriation', depends on the principle that a given artefact type has a certain lifespan: when first introduced it is quite rare, then it gradually becomes commoner, until it reaches a peak of popularity, after which it declines and eventually dies out. If frequency is plotted on a graph against time, the resulting curve will be semi-lenticular, or lenticular (battleship-shaped) if one makes the frequency bars symmetrical about the axis on which they lie. From the succession of such frequency curves for different types, one can estimate the order and chronological position of deposits containing different pot types, and therefore make statements about the lifespan of each individual type. Naturally such a procedure will only work if there is sufficiently varied and copious material with which to work, but good success has been had especially on urban sites, where the volume of material is great and the number of closed-find deposits sufficiently large (Carver 1985; Crummy and Terry 1979).

Nowadays, of course, seriation is performed by computer analysis, but the principles which are involved are little different from those enunciated by Petrie (Ascher and Ascher 1963; Graham *et al.* 1976). There are many published examples of seriated sequences of finds data in European archaeology, ranging from the Bronze Age (Goldmann 1979) to the medieval period (Palm and Pind 1992). A typical example demonstrating the strength of the method is the work of Hodson on the Hallstatt cemetery in Austria (Hodson 1990) and the Münsingen-Rain cemetery in Switzerland (Hodson 1968); in both of these cases, a good overall sequence for the material was arrived at by judicious use of seriation, including the definition of 'horizons', and by an analysis of the horizontal stratigraphy of the cemeteries. Although these studies cannot be regarded as having established the definitive order

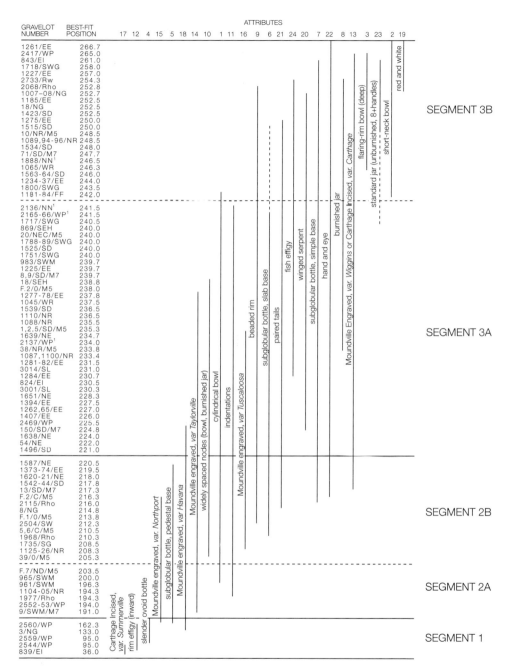

Figure 5.5 A seriated sequence of artefact attributes (pot decoration elements) from the Moundville cemetery, Alabama, the time-span of each attribute shown as a vertical line bracketing a series of graves. Source: Steponaitis 1983.

of the graves in them – that is, their real position in time – they are none the less extremely useful in pointing the way to how such things may be done in future.

A good example of seriation applied to pottery typology is the work done on the pottery from the Mississippian (pre-colonial) site at Moundville, Alabama, by Steponaitis (1983). From a detailed study of pot shapes, decoration, motifs and other features, twenty-four chronologically sensitive traits were chosen, and eighty-seven grave-groups were identified in which at least two of the traits were represented; the traits had to be present in not less than five grave-groups. Seriation was then carried out, first by calculating the 'distance' between the midpoints of each pair of traits, and then by using the technique of multi-dimensional scaling to arrange them into a relative sequence by taking the chronological 'distances' and fitting them to produce a 'map' which shows the approximate relative positions of the midpoints of the traits (Fig. 5.5). After this, the seriating or sequencing of the actual grave-groups was done by calculating a probable or best-fit position for each on the basis of the traits represented; the result was an incidence matrix of traits against graves. This was then compared with stratigraphic and radio-carbon results to produce a real chronology for the phases of the site.

ABSOLUTE DATING

The nature of the exercise of obtaining absolute dates, that is, dates fixed in time relative to the present day, is quite different from that involved in relative dating, even though as discussed above absolute dates are really only a special form of relative date. There are specific techniques and devices used for this process, which can be broadly divided into those based on calendars and those based on independent dating methods, usually those derived from the natural sciences.

Calendars

Calendars, formal devices for measuring the passage of time and fixing events in relation to each other past, present and future, must have had their origin in very simple methods of observation of natural events. Granted the need of all societies to adapt successfully to the environment so that subsistence and shelter requirements could be met, knowledge of daily, seasonal and annual natural events was essential. In many ancient societies, such natural events were early on associated with religious observations, which marked particular recurrent events in a highly formalized way. The observance of such religious focal points often became important in itself and was divorced from the natural events that gave rise to them; calendars thus provided a framework within which such observations could be carried out.

The apparent movement of sun, moon, planets and stars was for many societies an object of enduring fascination and a good guide to the seasons. A number of ancient societies acquired a good understanding of them and used them as crucial elements in calendrical systems; few ancient calendars, for instance, did not make use of lunations (the lunar cycle), and most reckoned on a system of twelve lunar months of twenty-nine or thirty days, plus a number of extra or intercalary days to make the year up to 365 days, in ancient times the commonest estimate of the length of the solar year. The advantage for modern scholars is that movements of the heavenly bodies in the past can be reconstructed, and where ancient sources record specific astronomical events such as eclipses, fixed points in the calendrical systems of the period can be obtained. Our own calendar owes its origin to the Roman, Greek and Egyptian calendars, and has evolved in unbroken succession since ancient times. In order to understand how dates are obtained for the ancient past, therefore, it is necessary to look briefly at some of the calendrical systems of the ancient world, and how they relate to our own usage.

The Christian calendar, Rome and Greece

The calculation of the date of Christ's birth was carried out by a seventh-century monk, Dionysius Exiguus, who knew that the crucifixion happened late in the reign of the Roman emperor Tiberius (died AD 37) and that Jesus must have been in his thirties at the time. He therefore set the incarnation (*Anno Domini* 1) fourteen years before the death of Augustus, 753 years from the date of the foundation of the city of Rome (see below). In fact we now know that Herod the Great died in 4 BC, so that Jesus must actually have been born in 5 or 6 BC. From the point of view of calendrical reckoning, however, what is important is the fact that all dates, ancient and modern, are calculated with reference to this point, no matter that it is incorrect and regardless of the fact that it is irrelevant to other faiths.

The birth of Christ is therefore fixed to Roman chronology, which depends partly on the Roman calendar and partly on the Roman dating system (Bickerman 1980; Michels 1967; Samuel 1972). According to tradition, the calendar originated in Rome itself soon after the city's foundation. It was based on months and therefore basically a lunar calendar, but until the Julian reform of 46–45 BC the rules for intercalating days were arbitrary, and the seasons increasingly liable to displacement from their expected position in the year. The rules adopted by Julius Caesar, which lasted until the reform under Pope Gregory XIII in 1582, also fixed the number and names of the months. The system by which the Romans fixed events in time was twofold: from early times the highest office at Rome was the consulship, held for a year at a time; the names of the consuls were recorded and gave a reference point to the historian for tying in other events. There is a complete list of consuls from 509

BC, regarded as the beginning of the Republic, compiled in definitive form during the reign of Augustus. Along with these lists there was a fixed point to which they were tied, by long tradition the founding of the city of Rome. There were various ways of reckoning this, but the consensus by the first century BC was that it fell in year 3 of the sixth Greek Olympiad, which equates with the year we call 753 BC – though some ancient authors preferred other dates.

Mention of the Greek Olympiad, the festival of Zeus held at Olympia every four years, brings further correlations. The list of victors at the Olympic Games was drawn up by the philosopher Hippias at the end of the fifth century BC. Since later authors referred datable events to Olympiad years, it was possible to reckon back-wards to establish the first Olympiad at 776 BC. The fourth-century historian Eusebius, for instance, informs us that the fifteenth year of the Emperor Tiberius fell in the fourth year of the 201st Olympiad (that is, shortly before the 201st festival, in the fourth year after the 200th festival). Tiberius, we know by other means (see above) ruled from 14 AD to 37 AD, so that his fifteenth year is AD 28; 4 × 200 is 800 plus 4 is 804; 804 years before AD 28 is 776 BC (comparable figures may be obtained from other calculations), which ties the Greek reckoning system into the Christian calendar. Like the Romans, some Greek cities had lists of officials, notably the Athenian archon lists which are fragmentary for the seventh and sixth centuries, but complete for the fifth and fourth centuries. Events tied in to the names of archons, as many recorded in the writings of ancient historians are, can thus be securely dated.

Egypt and the Ancient Near East

(Hornung 1964; Kitchen 1987; Neugebauer 1957, 1975; Parker 1950, 1978)

Although the origins of the Egyptian calendars are obscure, the basic elements appear to go back beyond the limits of recorded history. There were three different calendars in use: one (the civil calendar) based on day-counting and related to the annual flooding of the Nile; one based on lunar movements and regulated by the seasonal appearance of the star Sirius (Sothis); and a third, which was lunar but based on the civil calendar and used solely for religious purposes. Because of the different year-lengths involved in the civil and lunar calendars, there was a regular displacement between them. The civil year was 365 days long, divided into three seasons (Inundation, Spring or Going Forth, and Summer or Deficiency), each with four months of thirty days; five extra or intercalary days were added to make up the full year. The lunar year was, on the other hand, fixed by the appearance of the star Sirius (the 'heliacal rising': its appearance just before sunrise) which corresponds closely to the true astronomical or solar year of 365.25 days. The displacement of a quarter of a day per year, or one day in four years, led to a cycle of 1,460 years over which a given day in the civil calendar would go right through the year of the lunar calendar before returning to its original position. This is the so-called 'Sothic cycle', and it is of interest because heliacal risings of Sirius were often recorded by the Egyptians, though the cycle itself was not of such importance as was once thought. The Roman writer Censorinus records that civil New Year coincided with a heliacal rising of Sirius in the second year of the emperor Antoninus Pius, AD 139–40; this gives comparable coincidences in *c.* 1321 BC and 2781 BC (a cycle earlier, 4231 BC, falls in the prehistoric period and may well predate the system itself).

The calendars were used by the Egyptians in conjunction with record-keeping involving the regnal years and reign lengths of the kings. Three main sources inform us about these: monuments, such as a great inscription of Seti I at Abydos, where the king is shown making offerings to seventy-six of his ancestors (Fig. 5.6); papyri, of which much the most informative is the so-called Turin Canon which covers the kings of the Old Kingdom in the third millennium BC; and the writings of the third-century BC priest-scribe Manetho, preserved in the works of later writers. The combination of these sources, along with numerous shorter and more specific documents, is what leads to the establishment of the sequence of Egyptian history as we know it. Tying the sequence in to our own chronological system is a matter of some uncertainty. Two main methods are used: dead reckoning (reconstruction back from known points on the basis of reign lengths), and astronomical fixes.

The earliest securely fixed historical date that can be confirmed by independent sources is 664 BC, the accession date of the pharaoh Psammetichus I, founder of the 26th dynasty. Dead reckoning is then used to go back in time through the Early Iron Age into the Late and Middle Bronze Age, and even – with many uncertainties – the Early Bronze Age. There are numerous points in this system where for various reasons the record of regnal succession is unclear or was actually rewritten in ancient times, but for the first and second millennia BC a reasonable framework can be arrived at, which can vary only within certain fixed limits. Onto this system can be added the evidence of astronomical observations. The recording of a lunar date in the 52nd year of Ramesses II is usually regarded as reliable, and this indicates that he acceded to the throne in either 1304 or 1290 or 1279 BC; on historical grounds the first is very unlikely, and the last the most likely. Similar arguments apply to the accession of Tuthmosis III exactly 200 years earlier; and a heliacal rising of Sirius in the seventh year of Sesostris III can be pinned down to either 1872 or 1830 BC – depending on where one believes the observations were made (northern or southern Egypt).

Scepticism is expressed from time to time about the validity of this reconstruction, and it is true that it undergoes revisions from time to time; but these are

Figure 5.6 Part of the king list in the temple of Seti I at Abydos, Egypt; each cartouche shows one king. © The British Museum.

generally fairly minor in nature and small in effect. It is interesting and important that available radio-carbon determinations, while not completely unambiguous, can be used perfectly satisfactorily to confirm this historical chronology. Its correctness – at least in general terms – is extremely important, as the chronology of much of the East Mediterranean area depends on it, including Bronze Age Greece where there is no independent dating system (Warren and Hankey 1989). This has led to considerable debate about the dating of certain major events.

Unlike Egypt, Mesopotamia never had a unified calendrical system; different cities had different systems, which themselves varied over time. Basically all calendars were in origin based on lunar months and solar years, with various subdivisions into seasons, which were frequently marked by festivals. Since for administrative purposes concepts such as 'harvest season' were inconvenient, years consisting of twelve months of fixed length were introduced, with a great variety of devices for intercalating days. Calculation by regnal years was also used, as were astronomical observations; the movements of the planet Venus, for instance, were a source of great fascination, and some headway has been made in reconstructing the calendar to which it gave rise, though reliable sequences back into the Bronze Age are hard to come by.

The Near East is also the part of the world where Islam originated, and the journey of the prophet Mohammed from Mecca to Medina in AD 622 (the Hegira) provides the origin point for the Muslim chronological system in just the same way as the birth of Christ does for the Christian system: thus AH (*Anno Hegirae*).

Central America

The most famous and best understood of the American calendars is the Mayan (Lounsbury 1978); other Mesoamerican civilizations had variants of the basic structure of the Mayan calendar, notably the Aztec. The Inca calendar was based on astronomical observation, but too little is known about it for any meaningful discussion to be possible here.

The Mayan calendar consisted of a ritual cycle of 260 named days, and a year of 365 days divided into eighteen named months of twenty days each. The days of the ritual cycle (*Tzolkin*) are marked by a combination of number (1–13) and name (from a sequence of twenty). The cycle and the year ran concurrently, forming a longer cycle of 18,980 days or fifty-two years called a Calendar Round. A day would be designated by its numeral and name in the ritual cycle, along with the name of the month and the position within the month (a number from nought to nineteen, indicating days elapsed since the start of the month). Such a date occurs once in each Calendar Round. For longer periods – and the Maya were extremely interested in their past – the so-called 'Long Count' was established, using a series of periods of increasing size: one day (*kin*) – twenty days (*uinal*) – 360 days (*tun*) – 7,200 days *(katun)* – 144,000 days *(baktun)*. Counts of these period units were then fixed to a base date, four Ahau eight Cumku, which marked the end of a round of thirteen *baktuns* in the remote past, and which can be tied in to the modern calendar to give a date of 13 August 3113 BC. The earliest date in the Mayan area, from Stela 29 at Tikal, can thus be expressed in our calendar as 6 July AD 292 (Fig. 5.7). The correlation with the Christian calendar is itself a matter both of importance and of uncertainty, the latter because notation by the time of the Spanish Conquest had changed, so that it can only be assumed and not known for sure that the sequence of *katuns* in the colonial period was continuous with that of earlier times. It is recorded that the *katun* 13 Ahau ended shortly before the foundation of Mérida in the

Figure 5.7 Stela 29 from Tikal, Guatemala, showing the date of 6 July AD 292. Reproduced with permission of University of Pennsylvania Museum (neg. #61–4–267).

Yucatan, and it is believed by many that this corresponds to 14 November 1539 in the Christian calendar. Even allowing for such uncertainties, it is in principle possible to derive dates for historical events far back in the Mayan past by such means.

China

Calendars were established in China early, as inscriptions on 'oracle bones' of the Shang period (Bronze Age, sixteenth to eleventh centuries BC) show (Needham and Ling 1959). Both the solar year of 365.25 days and the lunar month of 29.5 days were established by this period, and a calendar based on seasons and phases of the moon with intercalary months was in use. Later, the 'meteorological cycle' was established, containing twenty-four points of seasonal significance and measured by the apparent movement of the sun through the stars. The means by which the passage of time was commonly computed was the day-count system, based on a sixty-year cycle. In this system, the Ten, or Celestial, Stems are combined with the Twelve, or Terrestrial, Branches: the Stems are repeated six times and the Branches five times (total sixty in each case), to give a unique two-character designation to each year in the cycle. This system has been in use since the Han period (206 BC–AD 200), and was combined by annalists with other indicators such as regnal years. Just as in Egypt, historiographic traditions divide rulers into groups, or dynasties, but unlike in Egypt these dynasties have continued into modern historical times, so that problems of correlation with the Christian calendar are less acute. There are many historical texts that enable this chronological system to be extended back in time. For example, the *Qian Han Shu* (History of the Former Han Dynasty) deals with the events of the last two centuries BC, and the *Spring and Autumn Annals* is the title of a chronological treatise covering major events in the eastern state of Lu between 721 and 475 BC, part of the Eastern Zhou (Chou) Dynasty (771–221 BC). There can be no more tangible example of the success of the Chinese chronological system than the way in which the mausoleum of Qin Shihuang, discovered in 1974, could immediately be correlated with its owner, who died in 210 BC.

As well as the dates in the sixty-year cycle, chronologies were also built up by 'year-periods' (*nianhaw*), basically subdivisions of an emperor's reign according to the occurrence of important events. The time elapsed since the inception of a *nianhaw* was indicated, along with the date in the sixty-year cycle, so that a double check on the absolute date is possible. Chinese historical texts regularly provide this information, so that reconstruction of chronologies is in principle quite straightforward.

Dating by historical methods

While calendars form the basis for the recording of the passage of time and therefore for the writing of histories, it is the application of histories and their accompanying calendars to archaeological material that is of greatest concern here. Dating by 'historical' methods is only possible where there is sufficient, and sufficiently precise, textual or other historical evidence with which to illuminate the archaeological material. These can include historical texts themselves – where the obvious problem is the lack of unambiguous association with archaeological contexts – or datable archaeological sources, such as coins and inscriptions.

Although there are problems associated with the use of coin dating in archaeology, there are many cases where the presence of a single closely datable object such as a coin can bring an element of chronological precision into a site or period that would otherwise be extremely hard to tie down. The medieval castle site of Hen Domen (Fig. 26.1), Montgomery (Powys) produced a single coin, a half-penny of King John (1199–1216), but the pottery indicates a wide span of time, from Romano-British (one sherd, presumably residual), through late eleventh-century Stamford ware to late thirteenth-century wares (Higham 1982). In such a wide span the coin does no more than confirm thirteenth-century occupation. On the other hand, a study of the iron age and Roman fort at Hod Hill, Dorset, shows that the sixty-two coins found on the site date mainly to the reigns of Gaius (AD 37–41) and Claudius (41–54), with no later coins associated with the occupation of the fort (Todd 1982). While this might indicate an entirely early use of the site, caution is necessary because the emperor Nero struck no bronze coins until AD 64, with earlier issues forming the main currency up till that date; some of the pottery may indeed date later than the Claudian period. Nevertheless, granted that the Claudian invasion of Britain occurred in AD 43, the coins undoubtedly represent material brought to Hod Hill at the time of the early construction and garrisoning of the fort soon after the invasion; their only drawback is that they give no end date for this phase of occupation.

Inscriptions offer a less ambiguous source of dating, at least if they are reasonably complete: many of the difficulties associated with this area of study come from the uncertainties associated with fragmentary evidence. In the best cases, as with those

Figure 5.8 The Arch of Septimius Severus in Rome (left), with inscriptions datable from their contents to AD 203. Reproduced with permission of M. Millett.

204

Figure 5.9 Lead waterpipe from Chester, datable from the consular years to AD 79. Photograph: copyright Grosvenor Museum, Chester.

emanating from the Roman period, monuments can be dated precisely to their year of construction or inauguration by epigraphic evidence. Good examples may be seen in many Roman towns and cities, for instance on the several imperial arches in Rome: the Arch of Severus in the Forum (Fig. 5.8) bears on both sides inscriptions in honour of the emperor and his sons, and can be dated to AD 203 (Keppie 1991: 49–51). A less glorious but still very precisely dated example is that of a lead waterpipe from Chester (Fig. 5.9), bearing the legend 'Imp(eratore) Vesp(asiano) VIII T(ito) imp(eratore) VII co(n)s(ulibus) Cn(aeo) Iulio Agricola leg(ato) Aug(usti) pr(o)pr(aetore)': 'In the ninth consulship of the emperor Vespasian and in the seventh of Titus, Agricola being legate of the emperor with rank of propraetor' (Keppie 1991: 27). This inscription is datable by the references of the consulships to an actual year (AD 79), and with its further reference to Agricola represents a significant point in the consolidation of Rome's hold over Britain in the first century AD.

DATING BY METHODS FROM THE NATURAL SCIENCES

The range of techniques now available to the archaeologist for absolute dating is considerable. Most of these techniques have been developed since the Second World War, though a few were in existence before: dendrochronology, for instance, was pioneered by A. E. Douglass in the 1910s and 1920s in the south-western United States, though its applicability to archaeology has only been exploited fully in more recent years. In practice, scientific dating techniques began in earnest with the invention of the radio-carbon dating technique by W. F. Libby between 1946 and 1950. This was soon followed by oxygen isotope dating (Emiliani 1955), archaeomagnetic dating (Thellier and Thellier 1959), thermoluminescence (Grögler *et al.* 1960), potassium–argon dating (Evernden and Curtis 1965), and a series of other methods whose value to everyday archaeology is rather less. Many introductory and advanced textbooks cover the details of these methods, and only a general outline will be provided here (Aitken 1990; Brothwell and Higgs 1969; Fleming 1976; Michael and Ralph 1971; Michels 1973; Zimmerman and Angel 1986).

Two general remarks need to be made about 'scientific' dating techniques. First, not all give absolute dates, since they themselves require some external reference point, often provided by archaeological or historical methods: archaeomagnetic dates, for example, depend on the construction of a reference curve which itself requires a chronology derived from dated contexts. Second, there is in many instances a discrepancy between the event being dated and the archaeological context under consideration. This is most obvious with radio-carbon dating, where the technique dates the point at which carbon-14 stopped accumulating in the material (typically wood), whereas what the archaeologist wishes to know is usually the date of the layer or construction in which the wood was found; the discrepancy involved can easily amount to scores or hundreds of years, or occasionally even more. This is in contrast to an 'inherent' technique such as thermoluminescence which depends on the setting of the relevant clock when the object of interest – typically pottery – was fired; this can usually be assumed to be close enough in time to the date of deposition for no difference to be discernible in practice, though in extreme cases it is possible that objects could be used for long periods, or re-deposited in much later layers, or refired.

For scientific dating techniques to be independent and absolute, they must contain the ability to be referred to an inherent 'clock', that is, a process occurring over time at a known rate, and if possible referable to terrestrial years and therefore a calendrical time-scale. One type of clock is that based on isotopic decay, the process by which unstable isotopes convert to other isotopes, stable or unstable, measured in terms of half-life (the time taken for half the original radioactivity to be achieved). Since this half-life is expressed in terrestrial years, absolute dates referable to human history may be obtained. Another type is cumulative, by which a given process on repetition brings about an increasing quantity or intensity of some phenomenon: patina or layering, for example, on the outside of some materials, or electron-trapping in the case of luminescence or electron spin resonance dating techniques. Provided that the amounts can be accurately assessed and the rate of increase is known, age estimates are possible, as in both cases the condition of the dating clock is proportional to age.

Dendrochronology

The principles of dendrochronology or tree-ring dating (Baillie 1982, 1995; Becker *et al.* 1985; Eckstein *et al.* 1984) are well-known and easily understood: most trees lay down a growth ring every year, the thickness of which depends on environmental factors prevailing at the time (principally temperature and precipitation). A series of year-rings thus constitutes a 'signature', and the greater the number of rings (that is, the longer the period), the less likely it is that the signature could be repeated by chance. By building up a series of overlapping signatures, a complete sequence has been established for a number of locations in western Europe and

North America, going back between 7,000 and 10,000 years, depending on region. When wood of the appropriate species (in Europe usually oak), and with not less than 60–100 rings, is found in archaeological contexts in areas where a master curve exists, it can be tied in to the established sequence, often giving exact dates for the felling of the trees involved. The technique has shown its worth in a number of studies, for instance the analysis of Tsegi phase sites in north-eastern Arizona, in many studies of medieval buildings and artefacts, and in the chronological definition of the prehistoric sequence in the sub-Alpine region of Europe (see pp. 214–15).

Radio-carbon dating

The technique of dating using the radioactive isotope of carbon, carbon-14, is so much the most widespread of all scientific dating techniques in use today that it must inevitably take pride of place in any discussion of methods (Bowman 1990; Gillespie 1984; Gowlett and Hedges 1986; Libby 1955/1965; Mook and Waterbolk 1985; Taylor 1987). Although much depends on quality of context and suitability of samples, it is possible to obtain results that are fully satisfactory in terms of precision and accuracy for many periods of the past. The highest precision currently obtainable is usually quoted at ±0.25 per cent of age or better, though dates of this precision involve relatively large samples and long counting times, and are not carried out on routine archaeological samples. Such error terms are satisfactory for many periods, but not of course those where historical dating allows a more refined chronology, or where the calibration curve (see below) is very flat. In fact the uncertainties deriving from the archaeological context are often very much greater than the error terms on the date itself, and high precision dating is for this reason most often carried out on samples whose local context is not in doubt, for instance on the rings of sub-fossil trees as part of the process of establishing the radio-carbon time-scale (see below). Nevertheless, error terms of ±50 years in the radio-carbon age at the 68 per cent probability level provide perfectly acceptable dates for many periods of the past, especially the prehistoric and early medieval periods.

Carbon-14 is produced in the upper atmosphere as a result of the interaction of neutrons produced by cosmic rays with nitrogen-14. Thereafter it becomes mixed with ordinary carbon, carbon-12, and with carbon-13, and behaves chemically in a very similar way, so that it is taken up by all living organisms at a fixed proportion of the total carbon. Because the half-life of carbon-14 at 5,730 years is much greater than the lifespan of the organisms themselves, its decay back to nitrogen-14 provides an effective means of estimating the time elapsed since the formation of the organism, and by a fortunate chance, a half-life of around 5,000 years means that the method is well suited to estimating ages for the later prehistory and the historic periods of both Old and New Worlds – in other words, the last 20,000–30,000 years. In the laboratory, the amount of radioactive carbon is measured, either directly by means of atom counting using accelerator mass spectrometry, or indirectly by detecting the emission of beta particles, themselves a reflection of the amount of the unstable isotope C14 remaining in the sample. Since this in turn bears a fixed relation to age, an age estimate can be obtained.

Because the production of carbon-14 in the upper atmosphere has not been constant over time, the amount taken up by living organisms has also varied slightly and so the age estimates obtained are somewhat at variance with true calendrical ages, as known from tree-ring data. A correction, or rather calibration, therefore has to take place before the age can be used in conjunction with other sources of dates. Recent work on the radio-carbon technique has concentrated above all on refining the calibration curve, particularly by means of the high-precision dating of tree-ring samples (Pearson and Stuiver 1986; Stuiver and Pearson 1986). As a result, computer-based calibration programmes are now available so that, for at least the last 7,000 years, radio-carbon age estimates can be converted into historical age ranges at stated probability levels (Fig. 5.10). It is important to realize that radio-carbon dates produce age ranges and not absolute fixed dates, since the process of radioactive decay is a random one and the counting of beta emissions is therefore subject to statistical uncertainty. The process of calibration can also produce more than one possible age range, because the calibration curve is far from straight: it is 'wiggly', and in some periods where the wiggles are particularly pronounced a given radio-carbon age can provide several possible calendrical ages. An example is the period from 800 to 400 BC: any radio-carbon age of between about 2,500 and 2,400 years can only give a historical date within the 400-year time bracket 800–400 BC, a serious drawback for using the method in that period (the end of the Bronze Age and the first half of the Iron Age in Europe).

On the other hand, the very fact that the calibration curve is 'wiggly' means that where the samples to be dated can be placed in a fixed relationship to each other, the technique of 'wiggle-matching' can be used. For instance, if a piece of timber, whose absolute age cannot be determined dendrochronologically, is used to obtain radio-carbon ages, the resulting curve of plotted dates can then be fitted to the master calibration curve in the position where the wiggles best fit against each other. The same process can be carried out by dating samples from each phase of a long-lived site and making estimates of the length of the phases (Manning and Weninger 1992).

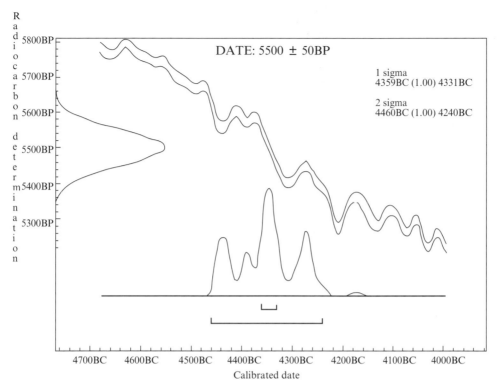

Figure 5.10 A segment of the radio-carbon calibration curve, illustrating the calibration of an age 5500 ± 50 BP, according to the OxCal calibration programme. The calibration curve is represented by the double meandering line running top left to bottom right; on the left is the distribution of values obtained during the counting process, centring around 5500; at the bottom is the probability distribution of the calibrated date ranges indicated; below that, the bars represent 1 and 2 sigma standard deviation curves respectively, with the values they indicate shown top right. After M. Stuiver, A. Ling and R. S. Kra (eds) (1993) 'Calibration 1993', *Radiocarbon* 35 (1). Redrawn by D. Miles-Williams.

Luminescence dating

Luminescence dating (Aitken 1985; Fleming 1979) depends on the fact that minerals in archaeological materials, such as pottery, are exposed to a weak flux of nuclear radiation emitted by radioactive impurities in the materials themselves and in the surrounding soil. Electrons thus liberated within the crystal structure by the action of ionizing radiation are trapped in the crystal lattice of the material. If the material is then heated rapidly, a weak emission of light results – the so-called *thermoluminescence* (TL), which is proportional to the cumulative radiation dose and the sensitivity of the minerals in acquiring TL. In cases where one can assume that the TL 'clock' was set to zero by a previous heating, for instance the firing of the pot, burning of stone and so on, an estimate of age for an archaeological event can then follow. The eviction of electrons, zeroing the clock, can also be achieved by exposure to light such as sunlight, which means that the technique can be used on unburnt materials in certain circumstances, such as sediments (*optically stimulated luminescence*, or OSL).

This brief sketch does not do justice to the complexities of the technique, which are considerable. Over the last thousand years, however, the accuracy is comparable with radio-carbon, and beyond the limit of radio-carbon calibration (*c.* 10,000 years) the technique gives an absolute age estimate, which radio-carbon cannot. A good example of this is the series of dates for the Middle Palaeolithic which have allowed at any rate a partial solution to the chronological problems of that period (see pp. 213–14). One might also hope that for periods where the radio-carbon calibration curve allows several possible ages, luminescence dating will step into the breach, for instance the Early Iron Age in Europe. Notable success has been achieved in the dating of medieval pottery, notoriously difficult to pin down in terms of archaeological and historical context and lifespan.

The related technique of *electron spin resonance* (ESR) (Grün 1989) relies not on the eviction of electrons from traps in the crystal lattice, but on their response to high-frequency electromagnetic radiation in the presence of a strong magnetic field, which is slowly changed. For a given frequency the electrons resonate (and absorb electromagnetic power) at a certain value of magnetic field. The greater the absorption, the greater the age. Good results have been obtained by this method on flint, tooth enamel, bone, and stalactite and related material.

Magnetic dating

Magnetic dating (Eighmy and Sternberg 1990; Tarling 1983; Wolfman 1984) depends on the fact that archaeological materials such as clay contain iron oxides as impurities; these become weakly magnetized by the earth's magnetic field at the time of their last zeroing; that is, when last heated – in an archaeological context, this usually means firing or burning. Since the direction of the magnetic field changes slowly over time, a curve of varying direction can be built up and dates assigned to archaeological objects depending on where on the curve the magnetic direction of objects falls.

The technique does not produce absolute age estimates, but depends on the existence of an archaeologically calibrated curve, based on a series of closely dated samples. Unlike radio-carbon, the technique is geographically limited, so that a separate curve has to be built up for each separate area (1,000 kilometres is usually taken as the geographical limit of the method). It also suffers from the disadvantage that the same value can be obtained from samples of widely different age as the curve can cross back on itself. Nevertheless, in many instances good results have been obtained. It will be evident that, in order for a sample to be dated, its exact position during heating must be known, so that the magnetization acquired at that time can be assessed. This means that pots cannot themselves usually be used, since neither the inclination nor the declination of firing (that is, the angle or position in which the pot was put in the kiln) can be known. Instead, fixed installations such as kilns or hearths must be used, assuming that their bases and walls have remained intact since deposition. A series of kiln sites from the Iron Age to the medieval periods in Europe has been dated in this way, sometimes to a high degree of precision. Sediments also become magnetized in the same manner, though it will be evident that here it is much more difficult to obtain an independent dating framework to calibrate the curve of magnetic change. There have also been applications to coinage and other materials.

Other methods

A considerable number of other scientific dating methods have been utilized in the service of archaeology, but their details will not be presented here as for the most part they are either insufficiently reliable or insufficiently widely used for a detailed presentation to be worth while (Aitken 1990). Exceptions, where good results have been obtained even though the archaeological applicability is somewhat limited, include uranium-series dating, ice-core dating (preserving climatic data and records of volcanic eruptions, tephrochronology (Thorarinsson 1970), and varve and lake sediment dating, where the annual deposition of glacial meltwater or particulates from spring floodwater lead to the possibility of long datable sequences. Only rarely are archaeological materials directly associated with these phenomena, but they have been found to be useful in conjunction with other methods, particularly radio-carbon, for building up a detailed cross-correlated sequence.

APPLICATIONS, PROBLEMS AND SOLUTIONS

The various techniques outlined have enabled various long-standing problems to be solved, though others remain. In some cases, radical revisions of traditional chronologies have led to controversy, which only the discovery of fresh data is likely to resolve. Four important examples are illustrated below.

The peopling of the Americas

(Fiedel 1987: 47–81)

Since the 1930s it has been known that hunters of big game were present in what is now the southern United States at a time that was contemporaneous with the latest period of the last Ice Age, when continental ice sheets covered the land further north. The finds from Blackwater Draw near Clovis in eastern New Mexico were regarded as typical of the cultural complex of these hunters of bison and mammoth, and no find complexes could be shown to be earlier, stratigraphically or otherwise. With the advent of radio-carbon dating, the start of sites of this complex could be attributed to the period between 12,000 and 11,000 before present – very late in global terms for the peopling of a huge continent, when much of the rest of the world had been occupied for hundreds of thousands, or even millions, of years. In general it is not in doubt that humans arrived in the Americas overland via the Bering Strait at a time when there was a land bridge between Siberia and Alaska. The question is, when? Since sea levels have fluctuated with climate, and the land bridge would have been present in glacial periods previous to the last one, why should the colonization not have taken place much earlier?

Over the years, a number of excavators have found remains that they have claimed to represent evidence of human presence earlier than the Clovis period. Of these, some are not very plausible and others can definitely be discounted, but the work at Meadowcroft rock shelter in south-west Pennsylvania is a different matter (Adovasio *et al.* 1990; Carlisle and Adovasio 1982). The site is well stratified and has been carefully excavated, yielding a sequence of radio-carbon dates in correct stratigraphical order. Dates for layers earlier than the first occupation are in the region of 31,000 BP, and those for the Palaeoindian layers with definite cultural associations lie shortly after 13,000 BP. Discussion centres on a small number of dates that fall earlier than this last date, going back to around 21,000 BP. Critics have remarked that the scarce material associated with these layers looks very like that found in much later layers, and have expressed surprise at the lack of big game bones that one would expect from a late Pleistocene site. Plant remains are also of types that grow in temperate areas, even though the ice sheet was no further away than 75 kilometres.

Another site that has been regarded as a likely candidate for an early presence of humans in the Americas is Monte Verde in southern Chile (Dillehay 1984), an open-air residential site with a series of huts. The upper layers seem to contain evidence of human habitation at about 13,000 before present, while the deeper layers contain possible artefacts dated at 33,000 BP. Needless to say, this association has attracted as much scepticism as all others of comparable age, and all that is safe to say is that Monte Verde and other sites like it have produced clear evidence of a pre-Clovis presence in South America.

The problem in these cases is not the accuracy or otherwise of the techniques being used: the only methodological doubt relates to the possibility of contamination of the samples involved by natural processes. What is at issue is the relevance of the dates to the layers and artefacts involved, and indeed the appropriateness of the artefact suites to the ages and cultures concerned. Establishing an archaeological chronology in these cases thus depends on the progress of excavation and discovery, though even then it is easier to see how the matter can be resolved positively than negatively: either undisputed early layers and artefacts will be found, in which case doubt will be removed; or they will not, and doubt will continue. In such a case it is up to archaeologists to ensure the maximum possible chance of unambiguous results being obtained through choice of site and efficiency of digging techniques.

The Middle Palaeolithic of France

The classic sequence of stone industries in France in the Middle Palaeolithic has been a matter of intense debate for a number of years (see Chapter 20). The various industries called Mousterian were originally defined by Bordes, and divided into the Ferrassie, Quina and Mousterian of Acheulian Tradition (MTA) industries, to which can be added 'typical' and 'denticulate' Mousterian. In the opinion of Laville (1973), these different aspects of the Mousterian were produced concurrently throughout the Mousterian and are to be attributed to the presence of different human groupings living in south-western France during the period, while the chronology of the period is to be reconstructed on the basis of 'chronostratigraphic' correlations using mainly sedimentological and other palaeoclimatic data. Mellars (1988), on the other hand, believes that there is a high degree of separation and chronological patterning in the occurrences of the three variants: in other words, that one succeeds another in chronological succession with relatively little overlap. The two interpretations imply radically different views of the Middle Palaeolithic, and strong arguments have been adduced on both sides. Which is correct?

Absolute age determinations using thermoluminescence have been obtained on the long sequence from the lower cave at Le Moustier, covering the whole of the period in question. The dates are internally consistent and agree closely with the stratigraphic sequence from which the samples came. They show that a relatively rapid deposition of sediments occurred, with MTA industries preceding the 'typical' Mousterian. In particular, they contradict the alleged evidence of sedimentological and palaeoclimatic data which purported to show that the main sequence of Ferrassie and Quina Mousterian industries at Combe Grenal was synchronous with the long sequence of MTA industries at Le Moustier. In fact, they agree well with the long stratigraphic sequence at Combe Grenal, with clear indications that the three Mousterian variants were stratigraphically separated. TL has thus been used to provide what seems to be a clear solution to a long-standing source of controversy.

Dendrochronology of the European Neolithic and Bronze Age, and of the Tsegi phase of Arizona

The rapid advances made in dendrochronology in recent years mean that a complete tree-ring sequence for central and western Europe has been developed back to 10,000 BP. With the finding of numerous timbers on sites of the Neolithic and Bronze Age, an accurate and agreed chronological framework is now possible (Becker *et al.* 1985). Some uncertainties remain, especially in periods from which few timbers emanate, but in general the picture is reasonably clear. This is due above all to work on sites in the sub-Alpine region, especially Switzerland and south-west Germany, where shallow lakes preserve hundreds of prehistoric settlements; good results have also been obtained from Ireland and Britain. The earliest Neolithic cultures in Switzerland were the Cortaillod in the west, Pfyn in the east. Felling dates for trees used in settlements of this period are between 3867 and 3507 BC, with an early and a late phase clearly distinguishable. The Late Neolithic Horgen culture falls between 3405 and 2958 BC, the Corded Ware culture between 2705 and 2499 BC, the Early Bronze Age (a late phase of it, according to the pottery) between 1665 and 1499 BC, and the Late Bronze Age between 1068 and 847 (divisible into an early phase, 1068–1033, and a late phase, 910–847).

These crude divisions may be seen in rather more detail when one looks at an individual site, where constructional phases may be assigned to close date ranges, or even individual years. At Zürich-Mozartstrasse, for instance, the early neolithic houses were constructed in 3661 BC, the Late Neolithic in 2883, the first Corded Ware houses in 2700, and a large number of such houses in 2697–2673, 2617, and 2604–2599. In the last case, none of the timbers was over fifty years old; presumably mature oaks were no longer available in the immediate vicinity of the site. At Auvernier on Lake Neuchâtel in west Switzerland it has also been possible to distinguish separate building phases according to the results of the dendrochronological analysis.

This type of work was pioneered in the USA, and a study by Jeffrey S. Dean (1969) is rightly seen as an example of what can be achieved in the building-up of site chronologies by this means. The extraordinary 'cliff dwellings' of the Tsegi Canyon of Arizona have much wood preserved; at Betatakin Cave, several hundred wood samples were taken and nearly three hundred were analysed dendrochronologically. As a result, it was possible to show that individual clusters of rooms were constructed in particular years: AD 1267–68, 1275, 1276, 1277, 1278, and after 1280. The phased plan thus shows that initially two concentrations of rooms existed, at either end of the site, perhaps as colonizer groups established occupancy at the cave; in 1269, much timber was felled but not used immediately; and then in the later 1270s the site was greatly enlarged and the stock-piled timber utilized. What tree-ring data cannot tell us is when the site was abandoned, but here other sources come to our aid, and a desertion date of around 1300 is likely to be close to the truth. These and other comparable examples have introduced an extraordinary degree of clarity into discussions of prehistoric and ahistoric settlement archaeology.

The dating of classical Greek archaeology

Classical archaeology depends more than most other forms of the art on the interrelationship between known and datable historical events and art styles, often those of an individual artist. The progress of research over many years has painstakingly built up valuable sequences for such differing artistic media as sculpture, architecture and vase painting. As Greece emerged into the historical Iron Age, a sequence of styles was created. Thus the Geometric style had given way to Protocorinthian by *c.* 725 BC, and to Corinthian by 625 BC. At the same time, the technique of Black Figure began to be used in Athens, lasting down to the first quarter of the fifth century BC. By around 530 BC the Red Figure technique was developed, and held sway throughout the fifth and into the fourth centuries. A comparable sequence is known for other art forms.

What is the basis of this chronology? It depends on a number of fixes provided by known historical events, such as the founding of Greek colonies, political events, or the creation of specific buildings. For many years one of the mainstays of the traditional scheme was the evidence of the great mound in the plain of Marathon in Attica, traditionally assumed to be the mound erected by the Athenians over their dead after the great battle with the Persians in 490 BC (Herodotus, *Histories* Book 6, 117.1). Excavation in the mound produced, along with ashes and human bones, Black Figure vases and a single Red Figure sherd, stylistically not among the earliest examples: 490 BC must be a *terminus ante quem* for these finds, assuming that they are undisturbed (not an altogether safe assumption). Another linchpin in the chronology is the foundation of the Siphnian Treasury at Delphi, which we know from Herodotus must have occurred around 525 BC. The architectural elements and finds of this building ought, if the building has been correctly identified (epigraphic evidence does not help with this), to date to the years before this.

That these matters are not foregone conclusions can be seen from the fact that

215

through the 1980s controversy over the very foundations of classical chronology has raged, with the publication of a series of articles challenging these assumptions (Cook 1989; Francis and Vickers 1983, 1988). Although the consensus of opinion is that the traditional chronology is more likely to be correct than the revisionist (Biers 1992), it is none the less salutary to be reminded how flimsy the evidence for some parts of the dating really are. Even for so well known a period historically as fifth-century BC Greece, the evidence of typological dating is always capable of refinement; and unless there are secure synchronisms, for instance by means of coins or inscriptions, few absolute dates can be regarded as certain.

CONCLUSION

Establishing chronologies is considered a natural, indeed an indispensable, activity for an archaeologist, but as this chapter has described, is often far from being a straightforward matter. Depending on period and area, there are many potential methods that can be used, singly or in combination. What is essential for the creation of a durable chronology is not only luck in the discovery of appropriate material, but also a sufficient understanding of the methodological underpinning of the various techniques. The progress of research in recent years has meant that many previously impenetrable periods are now brightly illuminated. Although 'chronologizing' is still not a precise art, it is nevertheless a technique with sufficient ground rules and sufficient available independent sources of evidence for rapid progress to be possible wherever suitable material is found. One can expect many of the chronological problems of today to be solved quite quickly tomorrow as material becomes available for study. At that point, the study of chronology should assume its proper place – as a means to an end, not an end in itself.

REFERENCES

Adovasio, J. M., Donahue, J. and Stuckenrath, R. (1990) 'The Meadowcraft Rockshelter radiocarbon chronology 1975–1990', *American Antiquity* 55: 348–54.

Aitken, M. J. (1985) *Thermoluminescence Dating*, London: Academic Press.

Aitken, M. J. (1990) *Science-based Dating in Archaeology*, London: Longman.

Ascher, M. and Ascher, R. (1963) 'Chronological ordering by computer', *American Anthropologist* 65: 1045–52.

Baillie, M. G. L. (1982) *Tree-ring Dating and Archaeology*, London: Croom Helm.

Baillie, M. G. L. (1995) *A Slice Through Time*, London: Batsford.

Becker, B., Billamboz, A., Egger, H., Gassmann, P., Orcel, A., Orcel, Chr. and Ruoff, U. (1985) *Dendrochronologie in der Ur- und Frühgeschichte. Die absolute Datierung von Pfahlbausiedlungen nördlich der Alpen im Jahrringkalender Mitteleuropas.* Basel: Verlag Schweizerische Gesellschaft für Ur- und Frühgeschichte.

Bickerman, E. (1980) *Chronology of the Ancient World* (2nd edition), London: Thames and Hudson.

Biers, W. R. (1992) *Art, Artefacts and Chronology in Classical Archaeology*, London: Routledge.

Bowman, S. (1990) *Radiocarbon Dating*, London: British Museum Publications.

Brainerd, G. W. (1951) 'The place of chronological ordering in archaeological analysis', *American Antiquity* 26: 301–13.

Brothwell, D. R. and Higgs, E. S. (eds) (1969) *Science in Archaeology* (2nd edition), London: Thames and Hudson.

Brown, J. A. (1982) 'On the structure of artifact typologies', in R. Whallon and J. A. Brown (eds) *Essays on Archaeological Typology*, Evanston: Center for American Archaeology Press: 176–89.

Carlisle, R. C. and Adovasio, J. M. (eds) (1982) *Meadowcroft Rockshelter: Collected Papers on the Archaeology of Meadowcroft Rockshelter and the Cross Creek Drainage*, Pittsburgh: Department of Anthropology, University of Pittsburgh.

Carver, M. O. H. (1985) 'Theory and practice in urban pottery seriation', *Journal of Archaeological Science* 12: 353–66.

Clarke, D. L. (1968) *Analytical Archaeology*, London: Methuen.

Clarke, D. L. (1970) *Beaker Pottery of Great Britain and Ireland*, Cambridge: Cambridge University Press.

Cook, R. M. (1989) 'The Francis–Vickers chronology', *Journal of Hellenic Studies* 109: 164–70.

Cowgill, G. L. (1972) 'Models, methods and techniques for seriation', in D. L. Clarke (ed.) *Models in Archaeology*, London: Methuen: 381–424.

Crummy, P. and Terry, R. (1979) 'Seriation problems in urban archaeology', in M. Millett (ed.) *Pottery and the Archaeologist*, London: Institute of Archaeology: 49–60.

Daniel, G. (1943) *The Three Ages. An Essay on Archaeological Method*, Cambridge: Cambridge University Press.

Daniel, G. (1975) *150 Years of Archaeology*, London: Duckworth.

Dean, J. S. (1969) *Chronological Analysis of Tsegi Phase Sites in Northeastern Arizona*, Papers of the Laboratory of Tree-Ring Research 3, Tucson: University of Arizona Press.

Dempsey, P. and Baumhoff, M. (1963) 'The statistical use of artifact distributions to establish chronological sequence', *American Antiquity* 28: 496–509.

Dillehay, T. D. (1984) 'A late ice–age settlement in southern Chile', *Scientific American* 251: 106–19.

Eckstein, D., Baillie, M. G. L. and Egger, H. (1984) *Handbook for Archaeologists No. 2 – Dendrochronological Dating*, Strasbourg: European Science Foundation.

Eighmy, J. L. and Sternberg, R. S. (eds) (1990) *Archaeomagnetic Dating*, Tucson: University of Arizona Press.

Emiliani, C. (1955) 'Pleistocene temperatures', *Journal of Geology* 63: 538–78.

Evernden, J. F. and Curtis, G. H. (1965) 'The potassium–argon dating of Late Cenozoic rocks in East Africa and Italy', *Current Anthropology* 6: 343–85.

Fiedel, S. J. (1987) *Prehistory of the Americas*, Cambridge: Cambridge University Press.

Fleming, S. (1976) *Dating in Archaeology: a Guide to Scientific Techniques*, London: Dent.

Fleming, S. (1979) *Thermoluminescence Techniques in Archaeology*, Oxford: Clarendon Press.

Francis, E. D. and Vickers, M. (1983) '"Signa priscae artis": Eretria and Siphnos', *Journal of Hellenic Studies* 183: 49–67.

Francis, E. D. and Vickers, M. (1988) 'The Agora revisited: Athenian chronology c. 500–453 BC', *Annual of the British School at Athens* 83: 143–67.

Gillespie, R. (1984) *Radiocarbon User's Handbook*, Oxford: Oxford University Committee for Archaeology.

Goldmann, K. (1979) *Die Seriation chronologischer Leitfunde der Bronzezeit Europas*, Berliner Beiträge zur Vor- und Frühgeschichte Neue Folge Band 1, Berlin: Verlag Volker Spiess.

Gowlett, J. A. J. and Hedges, R. E. M. (eds) (1986) *Archaeological Results from Accelerator Dating*, Oxford: Oxford University Committee for Archaeology.

Graham, I., Galloway, P. and Scollar, I. (1976) 'Model studies in computer seriation', *Journal of Archaeological Science* 3: 1–30.

Gräslund, B. (1976) 'Relative chronology: dating methods in Scandinavian archaeology', *Norwegian Archaeological Review* 9: 69–126.

Gräslund, B. (1987) *The Birth of Prehistoric Chronology*, Cambridge: Cambridge University Press.

Grögler, N., Houterman, F. G. and Stauffer, H. (1960) 'Über die Datierung von Keramik und Ziegel durch Thermoluminescenz', *Helvetica Physica Acta* 33: 595–96.

Gross, E. *et al.* (1987) *Zürich 'Mozartstrasse'. Neolithische und bronzezeitliche Ufersiedlungen*, Band 1, Berichte der Zürcher Denkmalpflege, Monographien 4, Zürich: Orell Füssli Verlag.

Grün, R. (1989) *Die ESR-Altersbestimmungsmethode*, Heidelberg: Springer.

Helck, W. (1987) 'Was kann die Ägyptologie wirklich zum Problem der absoluten Chronologie in der Bronzezeit beitragen?', in P. Åström (ed.) *High, Middle or Low? Acts of an International Colloquium on Absolute Chronology held at the University of Gothenburg 20th–22nd August 1987*, Gothenburg: Paul Åströms Forlag, Part I: 18–26.

Higham, R. (1982) 'Dating in medieval archaeology: problems and possibilities', in B. Orme (ed.) *Problems and Case Studies in Archaeological Dating*, Exeter: University of Exeter: 83–107.

Hill, J. N. and Evans, R. K. (1972) 'A model for classification and typology', in D. L. Clarke (ed.) *Models in Archaeology*, London: Methuen: 231–73.

Hodson, F. R. (1968) *The La Tène Cemetery at Münsingen-Rain: Catalogue and Relative Chronology*, Bern: Stämpfli, Acta Bernensia 5.

Hodson, F. R. (1970) 'Cluster analysis and archaeology: some new developments and applications', *World Archaeology* 1: 299–320.

Hodson, F. R. (1990) *Hallstatt: The Ramsauer Graves. Quantification and Analysis*, Monographien Band 16, Bonn: Habelt, Römisch-Germanisches Zentralmuseum Mainz.

Hornung, E. (1964) *Untersuchungen zur Chronologie und Geschichte des Neuen Reiches*, Ägyptologische Abhandlungen, Band 11, Wiesbaden: Harrassowitz.

Keppie, L. (1991) *Understanding Roman Inscriptions*, London: Batsford.

Kitchen, K. A. (1987) 'The basics of Egyptian chronology in relation to the Bronze Age', in P. Åström (ed.) *High, Middle or Low? Acts of an International Colloquium on Absolute Chronology held at the University of Gothenburg 20th–22nd August 1987*, Gothenburg: Paul Åströms Forlag, Part 1: 37–55.

Laville, H. (1973) 'The relative position of Mousterian industries in the climatic chronology of the early Würm in the Perigord', *World Archaeology* 4: 323–29.

LeBlanc, S. A. (1975) 'Micro-seriation: a method for fine chronologic differentiation', *American Antiquity* 40: 22–38.

Libby, W. F. ([1955] 1965) *Radiocarbon Dating*, Chicago: University of Chicago Press.

Lounsbury, F. G. (1978) 'Maya numeration, computation and calendrical astronomy', in

C. C. Gillispie (ed.) *Dictionary of Scientific Biography*, volume 15, supplement 1, New York: Charles Scribner's Sons: 759–818.

Manning, S. W. and Weninger, B. (1992) 'A light in the dark: archaeological wiggle matching and the absolute chronology of the close of the Aegean Late Bronze Age', *Antiquity* 66: 636–63.

Marinatos, S. (1939) 'The volcanic destruction of Minoan Crete', *Antiquity* 13, 425–39.

Marquardt, W. M. (1978) 'Advances in archaeological seriation', *Advances in Archaeological Method and Theory* 1: 257–314.

Mellars, P. (1988) 'The chronology of the south-west French Mousterian: a review of the current debate', in *L'Homme de Néandertal, vol. 4, La Technique*, Liège: Service de Préhistoire, Université de Liège: 97–119.

Michael, H. N. and Ralph, E. K. (eds) (1971) *Dating Techniques for the Archaeologist*, Cambridge: Mass.: MIT Press.

Michels, A. K. (1967) *The Calendar of the Roman Republic*, Princeton: Princeton University Press.

Michels, J. W. (1973) *Dating Methods in Archaeology*, New York: Seminar Press.

Montelius, O. (1886) *Dating in the Bronze Age, with Special Reference to Scandinavia*, Stockholm: Kungl. Vitterhets Historie och Antikvitets Akademien.

Mook, W. G. and Waterbolk, H. T. (1985) *Handbook for Archaeologists No. 3: Radiocarbon Dating*, Strasbourg: European Science Foundation.

Needham, J. and Ling, W. (1959) 'Astronomy', Chapter 20 in *Science and Civilisation in China*, volume 3, Cambridge: Cambridge University Press: 171–461.

Neugebauer, O. (1957) *The Exact Sciences in Antiquity* (2nd edition), Providence, R.I.: Brown University Press.

Neugebauer, O. (1975) *A History of Ancient Mathematical Astronomy*, Berlin and New York: Springer-Verlag, three volumes.

Orme, B. (ed.) (1982) *Problems and Case Studies in Archaeological Dating*, Exeter Studies in History No. 4; Exeter Studies in Archaeology No. 1, Exeter: University of Exeter.

Palm, M. and Pind, J. (1992) 'Anglian English women's graves in the fifth to seventh centuries AD – a chronological analysis', in L. Jørgensen (ed.) *Chronological Studies of Anglo-Saxon England, Lombard Italy and Vendel Period Sweden*, Arkæologiske Skrifter 5, Copenhagen: University of Copenhagen: 50–80.

Parker, R. A. (1950) *The Calendars of Ancient Egypt*, Studies in Ancient Oriental Civilisation 26, Chicago: Chicago University Press.

Parker, R. A. (1978) 'Egyptian astronomy, astrology and calendrical reckoning', in C. C. Gillispie (ed.) *Dictionary of Scientific Biography*, volume 15, supplement 1, New York: Charles Scribner's Sons: 706–27.

Pearson, G. W. and Stuiver, M. (1986) 'High-precision calibration of the radiocarbon time scale, 500–2500 BC', *Radiocarbon* 28: 839–62.

Petrie, W. M. F. (1899) 'Sequences in prehistoric remains', *Journal of the Royal Anthropological Institute* 29: 295–301.

Petrie, W. M. F. (1901) *Diospolis Parva. The Cemeteries of Abadiyeh and Hu 1898–9*, London: Egypt Exploration Fund.

Reece, R. (1987) *Coinage in Roman Britain*, London: Batsford.

Robinson, W. S. (1951) 'A method for chronologically ordering archaeological deposits', *American Antiquity* 16: 293–301.

Roe, D. A. (1968) 'British Lower and Middle Palaeolithic handaxe groups', *Proceedings of the Prehistory Society* 34: 1–82.

Rouse, I. B. (1967) 'Seriation in archaeology', in C. L. Riley and W. W. Taylor (eds) *American Historical Anthropology*, Carbondale: Southern Illinois University Press: 153–95.

Samuel, A. E. (1972) *Greek and Roman Chronology. Calendars and Years in Classical Antiquity*, Munich: Beck.

Spaulding, A. C. (1953) 'Statistical techniques for the discovery of artifact types', *American Antiquity* 18: 305–13.

Steponaitis, V. P. (1983) *Ceramics, Chronology and Community Patterns. An Archaeological Study at Moundville*, New York: Academic Press.

Steward, J. (1954) 'Types of types', *American Anthropologist* 56, 54–57.

Stuiver, M. and Pearson, G. W. (1986) 'High-precision calibration of the radiocarbon time scale, AD 1950–500 BC', *Radiocarbon* 28: 805–38.

Tarling, D. H. (1983) *Palaeomagnetism*, London: Chapman and Hall.

Taylor, R. E. (1987) *Radiocarbon Dating: an Archaeological Perspective*, Orlando: Academic Press.

Thellier, E. and Thellier, O. (1959) 'Sur l'intensité du champ magnétique terrestre dans le passé historique et géologique', *Annales Géologiques* 15, 285–376.

Thorarinsson, S. (1970) 'Tephrochronology and medieval Iceland', in R. Berger (ed.) *Scientific Methods in Medieval Archaeology*, Berkeley: University of California Press: 295–328.

Todd, M. (1982) 'Dating the Roman Empire: the contribution of archaeology', in B. Orme (ed.) *Problems and Case Studies in Archaeological Dating*, Exeter, University of Exeter: 35–56.

Warren, P. and Hankey, V. (1989) *Aegean Bronze Age Chronology*, Bristol: Bristol Classical Press.

Whallon, R. (1972) 'A new approach to pottery typology', *American Antiquity* 37: 13–33.

Whallon, R. and Brown, J. A. (eds) (1982) *Essays on Archaeological Typology*, Evanston: Center for American Archaeology Press.

Wolfman, D. (1984) 'Geomagnetic dating methods in archaeology', *Advances in Archaeological Method and Theory* 7: 363–458.

Zimmerman, M. R. and Angel, J. L. (eds) (1986) *Dating and Age Determination of Biological Materials*, Beckenham: Croom Helm.

SELECT BIBLIOGRAPHY

A useful book with chapters on various aspects of dating in archaeology is *Problems and Case Studies in Archaeological Dating*, edited by Bryony Orme (1982). Although not now the most up-to-date book on the various techniques, the four contributors offer exemplary analyses of their various special areas: the use of radio-carbon dates; dating in the Roman period, and specifically for Hadrian's Wall; and dating in medieval archaeology. A number of recent conference publications have dealt with specific chronological problems and the various ways of approaching them, including the three volumes of *High, Middle or Low?*, edited by Paul Åström (Gothenburg 1987) and the two volumes of *Chronologies du Proche Orient, Chronologies in the Near East, Relative Chronologies and Absolute Chronology 16,000–4,000 B.P.* (British Archaeological Reports International Series 379, 1987). Much more problematical, though at the same time with a much higher profile, is the book *Centuries of Darkness* by Peter James in collaboration with I. J. Thorpe, N. Kokkinos, R. Morkot and J. Frankish (London: Jonathan Cape 1991). The book proposes a radical down-dating of Egyptian chronology between 1300 and 800 BC, though these proposals have not found much acceptance in the scholarly world. Biers (1992) provides a very useful (if overly concise) introduction to the chronology of classical Greece and Rome, and see also Bickerman (1980) and Samuel (1972). Aitken (1990) is an excellent recent general guide to science-based dating techniques in archaeology, though simpler texts are those published by the European Science Foundation and the British Museum, such as Bowman (1990). Whallon and Brown (1982) provide a good collection of essays that discuss the principles behind the typologizing. Seriation techniques have mostly been presented in articles, but the accounts in chapter 5 of J. E. Doran and F. R. Hodson, *Mathematics and Computers in Archaeology* (Edinburgh: Edinburgh University Press 1975) and chapter 12 of S. Shennan, *Quantifying Archaeology* (Edinburgh: Edinburgh University Press 1988), provide convenient accounts in book form.

6

RECONSTRUCTING THE ENVIRONMENT AND NATURAL LANDSCAPE

Tony Brown

INTRODUCTION

The natural landscape is a relative concept: not only do cultures and individuals have differing views of what is natural and what is not, but these views have changed over time. The way we see our place in the 'natural order of things' is also culturally determined, as is demonstrated by differing views of calamity (Hewitt 1983). Although this affects how we conceptualize past nature–culture relationships, it does not prevent us from utilizing a battery of techniques derived from the natural sciences in order to reconstruct the physicality of past landscapes. This chapter aims to outline the many methods currently used in the reconstruction of natural landscapes and illustrate their archaeological application. Because this is a vast field of research, which includes many different disciplines, it is impossible to be comprehensive, either globally or temporally, so examples will be restricted to north-west Europe, the Mediterranean basin and North America.

An arbitrary but workable distinction between the natural and the cultural is that the natural is that which is not predominantly a human creation and which is not dependent upon human activity for its functional continuation. If we apply this definition in a temperate environment, heather moorland should be classified as cultural because it was created by human activity and requires regular management for its continuation, whereas most salt marshes would generally be regarded as natural. Although it can be argued that all environments have to some extent been influenced by human activity, the continuation of heather moorland, the salt marsh, and even the arable field, is also dependent upon ecological processes. This is why the techniques described in this chapter are not only useful for reconstructing past natural landscapes, but also past cultural landscapes: the argument is elaborated in

222

Chapter 14 (Food and Farming), where the focus is more on the relationship of culture to nature, of human interactions with environment and landscape, but where the contribution of techniques developed from the natural sciences is again profound.

The traditional Western model of the nature–culture 'dichotomy' is evolutionary, with *Homo sapiens* evolving from a natural world; it is epitomized by our views of 'wilderness' as something outside and to be conquered (Ingold 1986). The gatherer-hunter is often portrayed as being in harmony with the natural landscape, with the development of agriculture often assumed to represent a retreat of the natural and an expansion of the cultural, the process further exaggerated by urbanization. Thus it needs to be appreciated that 'ecofacts', the data of environmental archaeology, just like other facts, do not speak for themselves: they have to be interpreted and related to paradigms of the past.

SITE POTENTIAL: ASKING ANSWERABLE QUESTIONS

Any attempt to reconstruct natural landscapes has to begin with two questions. First, what do we wish to know about the past, given that we cannot know everything? All reconstructions are partial, so we need to decide which parts of the natural landscape have most archaeological importance; the answer to this will depend upon our archaeological interests and models. Second, given the present or near-future state of technology, and the nature of the site or landscape, what *can* we reconstruct? Sites and landscapes have different potential for environmental reconstruction. The answers to these two questions will vary from generation to generation as archaeology changes and as new techniques become available. (The term 'site' is used here, and throughout this chapter, to refer to any location where geoarchaeological techniques have been, or could be, used which may or may not contain artefacts.)

The origins of environmental work in archaeology lie in Quaternary geology and biology, particularly interest in glaciation and climate change (West 1977). The significance of techniques such as macrofossil analysis, pollen analysis, molluscan analysis and so on was not widely appreciated by archaeologists until the 1950s and 1960s and the work of Zeuner, Butzer, Godwin, Dimbleby, Troels-Smith and others. From the late 1960s onwards, we can see a parallelism between environmental science and the New Archaeology through the emerging use of systems theory (Clarke 1972). The role of geography, including human geography, is important here, as it was one of the main stimulants to the uptake of quantification and pursuit of process that characterized the New Archaeology (Haggett 1965; Hodder and Orton 1976).

It is worth while looking at the reasons for undertaking work on environmental reconstruction. The first is to predict (*sic* retrodict) past environmental controls (which may be geological, biological or climatic) on human activity. The second is to describe the impact of past peoples on their landscapes. The two reasons are obviously not independent, since it is the manipulation of natural resources that changes human environments and creates landscapes. It is important to take a wide view of what constitutes a resource, and to include space (that is, land), plants and animals, soils, water and minerals. This presents a problem, because it is difficult to think of any natural substance that has not, at one time or another, been used by human beings for something – even hazards are best conceptualized as negative resources which affect human living conditions.

Ideally archaeologists would like to reconstruct most, or all, of the important resources available to a population at any one 'time–place'. This would include aspects of the geological/geomorphological environment, the flora and fauna, and the local climate – what Butzer (1982) has termed the 'primary study components of geoarchaeology'. This involves an understanding of site formation and destruction processes (Vita-Finzi 1978) and the reconstruction of local vegetation and faunal history. No site, or even set of sites, is ever likely to allow such a comprehensive approach, because the conditions favouring the survival of some evidence will invariably destroy other categories of evidence. There are three reasons for this: natural taphonomy, variations in the ecological information-content of species, and archaeological uncertainty. If we have no direct evidence of use, we can only reconstruct potential resources: a butchered reindeer carcass at a site is evidence of a resource, but a spring near a site is only a potential resource, as resources are 'subjective, relative and functional' (Zimmerman 1951).

In order to understand the potential of any site, the preservation potential (or taphonomic potential) of different data types must be known. This is of most relevance to biological materials. The norm is of course for organic matter not to be preserved, but to be continually broken down as part of biogeochemical cycles. Organic matter suffers physical destruction through abrasion and crushing, most commonly in high energy environments such as steep gravel-bed rivers, least commonly in low energy environments such as a lake or tar pit. However, many high energy environments are also very changeable and so if the item is large enough (a tree-trunk, for example) it may be preserved if burial is rapid. Thus tree trunks and dugout boats may be relatively common in river gravels, but fragile plant remains are rare except in low-energy traps such as abandoned channels.

All organic materials will decompose if the conditions are suitable, and after enough time. The process is accomplished initially by macro-organisms, and subsequently by micro-organisms such as bacteria and fungi. The result is the breakdown of complex organic molecules such as cellulose and proteins to simpler substances, a process called mineralization. Therefore the sites of particular value for environmental reconstruction are those where for some reason mineralization has been slowed down or effectively stopped. There are four major limits on microbiological activity: extreme cold, desiccation, waterlogging, and unfavourable chemical conditions.

As the frozen mammoths from Siberia illustrate, freezing can preserve carcasses for thousands of years, whilst the discovery of the prehistoric 'Ice Man' preserved in a glacier on the Italian/Austrian border shows how valuable a rather atypical combination of circumstances and environment may be (Spindler 1993). Since micro-organisms cannot survive without some water, desiccation also preserves organic matter. It is not accidental that most of the desiccated material that has been recovered had been naturally buried or hidden in tombs, such as human remains (see Chapter 7), or crop remains: the physical forces of destruction are also strong in these environments, and aridity produces low biological productivity. The most important processes for most archaeologists are those caused by waterlogging and to a lesser extent unfavourable soil/sediment chemistry. The preservation power of waterlogged environments has led to an explosion of interest in wetland archaeology in many countries during the last two decades (Coles 1992).

THE GEOMORPHOLOGICAL ENVIRONMENT: SEDIMENTS AND SOILS

Excavation uncovers the stratigraphy of the site, and while the geological law of superimposition forms the basis of our sequencing (phasing), many geomorphological environments and archaeological sites are rather more complicated than geological stratigraphy. Lateral accretion of sediments by rivers and coastal processes produces vertical rather than horizontal time-lines (Fig. 6.1). Stratigraphy is also complicated by processes such as burial, tree-throws, other bioturbation processes (Brown and Keough 1992a; Stein 1983) and wind deflation/deposition.

In order to tackle the complexity of sediments and the interpretation of their depositional environments, we use the *facies* concept. A facies is a regular set of deposits which are related together and controlled by systematic relationships between micro-environments. The alluvial facies, therefore, contains sediments formed by several micro-environments: cut-off, levee, backswamp, scroll-bars and point-bars (Fig. 6.2). A non-rocky coastal facies may include sediments deposited in the lower, middle or upper beach, a storm beach, mobile foreshore dunes, a lagoon or slack, mudflats, a fossil cliff and raised beach. The different sediments that make up the facies are produced by a set of micro-environments which are linked in together by the transfer of mass and energy. The mapping of the geomorphology around a site not only produces a standardized description of the terrain but also indicates the spatial distribution of processes which may have affected site formation or destruction. For the full interpretation of archaeological

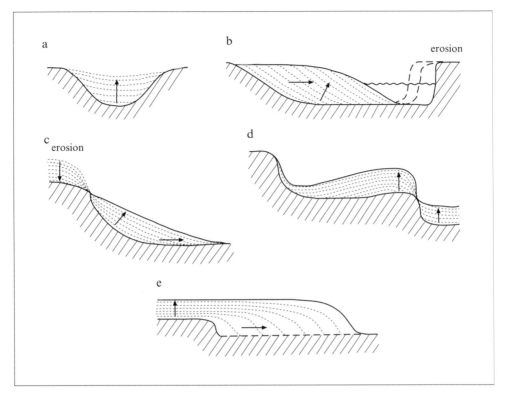

Figure 6.1 Time-lines in different geomorphological systems. Dotted lines are isochrones: (a) lake, pond or cut-off; (b) migrating river; (c) erosion of a scarp and colluviation; (d) overbank deposition on a floodplain and in-channel deposition; and (e) a prograding delta. Source: A. Brown.

sites which are interstratified with natural sediments, a genetic interpretation of the lithostratigraphy is essential (Butzer 1982).

Earth surface processes are classified according to the energy involved and the transporting medium, both of which effect sediment texture, structure and architecture (Fig. 6.3). There is a wide variety of geomorphological agencies responsible for site destruction and burial, related to the climatic and geological regime. In wet temperate, tectonically stable, environments, for example, alluviation, colluviation and bog formation predominate, whilst in semi-arid environments alluvial fan formation, gully erosion and deflation are more important. Tectonically active areas are generally of greater relief, so mass-movements (such as landslides, mudslides and mudflows) are more common, as is coastal change, earthquake and volcanic activity. The identification of sedimentary processes is not always easy, especially with slope-related sediments (colluvium), where the processes may be alluvial (Newtonian flow), mudflow (non-Newtonian flow), or dry mass movements (gravity

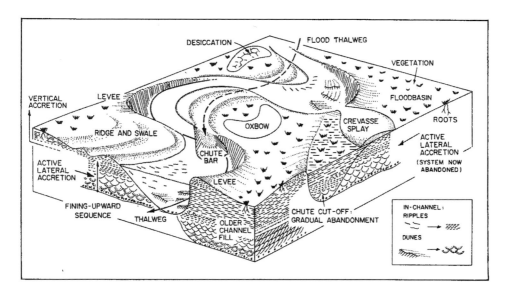

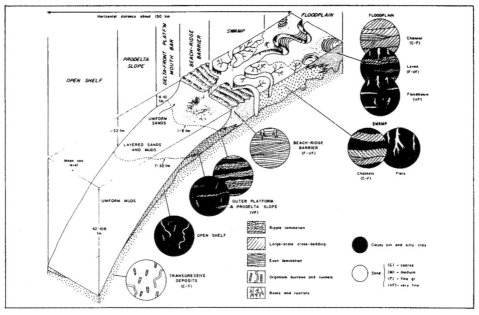

Figure 6.2 Facies: (above) floodplain of a meandering river; (below) a delta edge. Source: Walker, 'Facies models', *Geoscience Canada*, 2nd edition (Toronto: Geological Association of Canada, 1984). Copyright © Geological Association of Canada.

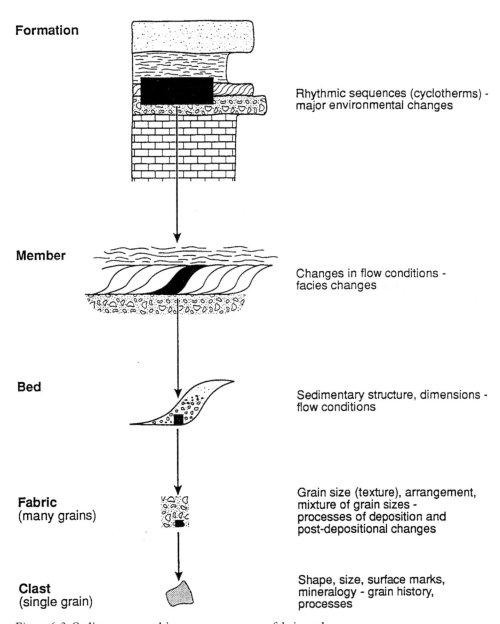

Formation

Rhythmic sequences (cyclotherms) -
major environmental changes

Member

Changes in flow conditions -
facies changes

Bed

Sedimentary structure, dimensions -
flow conditions

Fabric
(many grains)

Grain size (texture), arrangement,
mixture of grain sizes -
processes of deposition and
post-depositional changes

Clast
(single grain)

Shape, size, surface marks,
mineralogy - grain history,
processes

Figure 6.3 Sedimentary architecture: structures, fabric and texture.

slides). In most alluvial and coastal contexts the lithostratigraphy can be highly informative in terms of the environmental constraints and resources available to human societies. Archaeologists must therefore be familiar with the morphological, locational, and sedimentary aspects of typical facies: it is essential that they 'get out of the trench' in order to appreciate the local and regional context.

Facies analysis is also applicable to culturally modified sediments. An example is the work by Hunt *et al.* (1986) on the infill of Wadi Mansur in Tripolitania, which is closely related to the development of a system of intensive floodwater farming which may have triggered-off accelerated erosion. The facies equivalent in the urban archaeological context, if related to human rather than environmental processes, is the Harris Context Model (see Chapter 4).

The lithostratigraphy of the sediments can also be used to identify sediment provenance. Although colour can indicate provenance, it is most sensitive to reducing/oxidizing conditions in the soil and iron mineralogy. Lithology can be traced using clast analysis of coarse deposits, heavy mineral analysis, thin section analysis, and analytical methods such as X-ray diffraction and X-ray fluorescence. As a general rule, finer sediments are more susceptible to post-depositional changes such as the loss of constituents through weathering and leaching, and the formation of new minerals (Table 6.1). The use of sediment magnetic signatures to identify source rocks is an extension of provenancing using sediment mineralogy (Thompson and Oldfield 1986). In addition, topsoil is magnetically enhanced by soil processes while subsoil and sediment is not, a phenomenon used to distinguish between contemporary and archaeological arable-field erosion and river-bank erosion (Brown 1992; Foster *et al.* 1990).

Although complicated by the conditions of the bed, grain shape and grain density, the grain size of a deposit is mathematically related to the power of the transporting flow (flow competence) as indeed is the volume of material that can be transported (flow capacity). Equations which relate grain size to flow parameters can be used to estimate past river discharges, a procedure known as palaeohydraulic modelling. While archaeologists rarely require quantitative estimates of this kind of environmental parameter, they do need to distinguish between different processes and this can be done using sediment architecture, sedimentary structures, sedimentary fabric and particle size and shape. Grain or particle size, which is relatively easy to measure by a variety of methods (Table 6.2), has frequently been used for this purpose through the comparison of the frequency distributions of particle sizes in deposits including contemporary sediments. The analytical methods include moment statistics, bi-variate (CM) plots (Brown 1985), log-hyperbolic models (Bagnold and Barndorf-Nielson 1980), and the log-skew Laplace model (Fieller *et al.* 1992). This last method has proved valuable in detailing the infill history of the harbour at Lepcis Magna in Libya, which involved both shoreline and lacustrine or lagoonal deposition (Fieller *et al.* 1990). Polymodal sediments can be analysed by

Table 6.1 Common minerals formed in soils and unconsolidated sediments

Mineral	Chemical formula	Environment of formation
Calcite	$CaCO_3$	Precipitation from bicarbonate rich water, biomineralization, oxidation of acid sulphates – particularly in arid climates
Gibbsite	$Al(OH)_3$	Oxidation/reduction cycles in wet tropical soils
Greigite	cubic Fe_3S_4	Waterlogged sediments (transitional)
Gypsum	$CaSO_4$	Precipitation in arid and semi-arid soils and in acid sulphate soils
Haematite	αFe_2O_3	Inherited and formed under oxidizing conditions (especially in lateritic soils): weakly ferrimagnetic
Halite	$NaCl$	Precipitation in arid soils
Jarosite	$KFe_3(OH)_6(SO_4)_2$	Oxidation of waterlogged sediments and soils, especially estuarine
Lepidocrocite	$FeO(OH)$	Formed in reduced (gley) soils and sediments
Limonite	$Fe_2O_3.H_2O$	Oxidation/reduction cycles in temperate soils
Mackinawite	Fe_9S_8	Waterlogged sediments (transitional)
Maghemite	γFe_2O_3	An alteration product of magnetite and formed in soils due to oxidation/reduction cycles, burning and possibly microbial activity: strongly ferrimagnetic
Magnetite	Fe_2O_3	Inherited
Natrojarosite	$NaFe_3(OH)_6(SO_4)_2$	Oxidation of waterlogged sediments and soils
Pyrite	cubic FeS_2	Waterlogged sediments (reduction phase)
Pyrrhotite	FeS_{i+x}	Waterlogged sediments bacterial
Vivianite	$Fe_3(PO_4)_2.8H_2O$	Waterlogged sediments and soils

separating out the Gaussian components (Middleton 1976), or by multivariate similarity/difference methods (Brown 1985).

The sedimentology literature, combined with archaeological experience, suggests the need for some caution with grain size analysis, as many of these techniques seem to 'under-perform' in archaeological contexts. The reasons for this are probably threefold. First, grain size below the competence of the transporting medium is a function of grain type, availability and geomorphic history: as Burrin and Scaife (1984) have shown, the silt content of valley fills in southern England is high not only because silt is selectively transported as suspended load by rivers, but also because the Holocene soils of southern Britain were rich in loess (windblown silt: Catt 1986). Second, archaeologically related deposits have frequently been disturbed and mixed, and contain components transported by completely different media. Third, there do seem to be some fundamental particle sizes and shapes determined by crystal size and fracturing (Pettijohn 1949). While it is certainly possible to distinguish between extreme environments using shape and particle surface features, more subtle within-facies discrimination is often not possible,

Table 6.2 Methods of grain-size analysis

Methods applicable	Microns	Phi	Classification (Wentworth)
CC, SG, CF	0.24	12	
CC, SG, CF	0.49	11	
CC, SG, CF	1.00	10	Clay
CC, SG	1.26	9.6	
CC, SG	1.58	9.3	
CC, SG	2.00	9.0	————————
CC, SG	2.52	8.6	
CC, SG	3.17	8.3	Fine silt
CC, SG	4.00	8.0	
CC, SG	5.04	7.6	————————
CC, SG	6.35	7.3	
CC, SG	8.00	7.0	
CC, SG	10.08	6.7	Medium silt
CC, SG	12.70	6.3	
CC, SG	16.00	6.0	————————
CC, SG	20.16	5.6	
CC, SG	25.4	5.3	
CC, SG	32.0	5.0	Coarse silt
CC, SG	40.4	4.6	
CC, SG, WS	50.8	4.2	
CC, SG, WS	64.0	4.0	————————
CC, SG, WS, DS	80.6	3.5	Very fine sand
CC, SG, WS, DS	125	3.0	————————
WS, DS	180	2.5	Fine sand
WS, DS	250	2.0	————————
WS, DS	355	1.5	Medium sand
WS, DS	500	1.0	————————
WS, DS	710	0.5	Coarse sand
WS, DS	1,000	0.0	————————
DS	1,400	−0.5	Granules
DS	2,000	−1.0	(grit or pea
DS	2,800	−1.5	granules)
DS	4,000	−2.0	————————
DS	5,600	−2.5	Fine pebbles
DS	8,000	−3.0	————————
DS	11,200	−3.5	Medium pebbles
DS	16,000	−4.0	
DS	22,400	−4.5	————————
DS	32,000	−5.0	Coarse pebbles
DS	48,000	−5.5	
DS	64,000	−6.0	————————
DS, CA	128,000	−7.0	Cobbles
CA	256,000	−8.0	————————
T	512,000	−9.0	
T	1,024,000	−10.0	Boulders
T	2,048,000	−11.0	

CC	Coulter counter	WS	wet sieving	CA	calipers
SC	Sedigraph (X-ray)	DS	dry sieving	T	tape measure
CF	centrifugation				

largely due to the reworking of sediments, especially in temperate slope-river systems.

An understanding of soil processes is essential in order to interpret local environmental conditions (Barham and Macphail 1995; Cornwall 1958; Limbrey 1975) and to explain site formation (Quine 1995). Soils, and sediments, display degrees of internal order in the arrangement of particles in relation to each other, their sedimentary or pedological 'fabric'. This can be analysed using impregnated thin sections and optical microscopy, electron microscopy and also the investigation of magnetic properties. In sedimentary studies, any 'anisotropy' or preferred particle orientation can indicate current strength and even direction or other sorting processes such as ground freezing (Ellis and Brown 1998; Kemp 1985).

The terminology of soil micromorphology is complex (Brewer 1976; Bullock *et al.* 1985; Courty *et al.* 1989; Fitzpatrick 1984; Kemp 1985), but the major characteristics that are investigated are: void spaces – the distribution, size and shape of soil pores; S-matrix – the matrix type, from matrix to clast supported (edge to edge contact of the large particles); organic components – organic residues, root material and so on; the composition and thickness of coatings; and pedofeatures such as concretions, depletions, crystal growth and slickensides. Soil micromorphology has been particularly valuable in investigating soil disturbance and history in relation to agriculture (French 1990) and rather enigmatic deposits such as the so-called 'dark earth' found in many urban contexts (Macphail 1981).

Soil and sediment geochemistry has always been important in relation to taphonomy and artefact conservation, but some of the more persistent elements and compounds in soils and sediments can also be useful in environmental reconstruction. Phosphorus has received by far the most attention from archaeologists because of its association with human and animal activity. It is concentrated in the soil by the addition of faecal matter, bone, refuse and organic matter and it can be depleted in the topsoil principally by surface erosion. Modern humans excrete around 6 g per person per year, which can add to the soil phosphorus by as much as 10 per cent annually (Briggs and Courtney 1989). Phosphorus (P) is held in the soil in several forms (Fig. 6.4): available, organic, and inorganic or mineral. Because of its high affinity with oxygen, phosphorus is mostly found as phosphates (PO_4, also called the orthophosphate ion). The techniques used to measure soil P vary from a qualitative field test, such as the Schwartz spot-test (Schwartz 1967), to laboratory methods for total P extraction (Page *et al.* 1982). As Keeley (1981) warns, the technique does not always work due to unfavourable soil conditions (very acidic or waterlogged conditions), insufficient concentrations, or modern contamination. It is very important to record the background concentration as well as the concentrations of the site, although this can be difficult especially in urban sites. The normal range in soils is 0.02–0.5 per cent. More particular human activities, such as site formation and metallurgy, can be investigated using trace elements

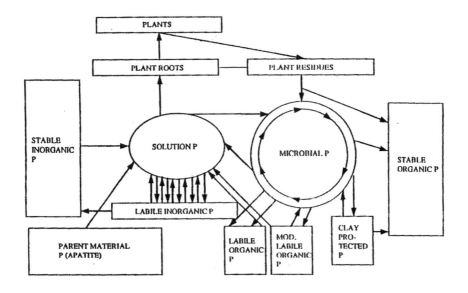

Inorganic Compounds
Apatite group $(Ca_2Ca_3(PO_4)_3(OH,F))$
Aluminium phosphate $(Al\ PO_4)$
Iron phosphate $(Fe\ PO_4)$
Calcium phosphate $(Ca\ PO_4)$

Organic Compounds
Phospholipids
Sugar phosphates
Inusitol phosphates

Figure 6.4 Soil phosphorus phases and common natural phosphorus compounds. Adapted from Mansell, Selim and Fiskell 1977, with permission from Waverly and Wilkins.

such as lead (Pb), zinc (Zn), copper (Cu), silver (Ag) and tin (Sn) (Bintliff *et al.* 1992).

ALLUVIAL IMPACTS: ALLUVIAL CHRONOLOGIES AND ARCHAEOLOGY

One area of particular interest in the last thirty years has been alluvial environments, largely because floodplains that have undergone aggradation usually contain thick sequences of alluvial deposits: the latter, if they can be dated, can provide information on both floodplain conditions and catchment conditions, especially erosion (Brown 1997; Needham and Macklin 1992). Dating is generally by radio-carbon assay of organics, but recent methods that are emerging from the experimental stages include optical stimulation luminescence (Bailiff 1992) and palaeomagnetics (Batt and Noël 1991; Ellis and Brown 1998). A complete and accurate sedimentary budget approach is only possible with extremely good dating control. Studies on the Duck river, Tennessee, for example, have revealed alternations between periods of stability coinciding with early, middle and late Archaic artefacts, and periods of aggradation by vertical suspended-load accretion on channel banks and channel bars (Brackenridge 1984). The middle Archaic artefacts were *in situ* on a fossil floodplain surface, along with evidence of hearths, and pollen evidence from the same horizon suggested a drier climate than present *c.* 4400 BC. The result of this alternating regime is an episodically deposited stratigraphy dominated by vertical deposition but in spatially distinct units, creating complex sub-lateral time-lines and preserving archaeology of different periods at very similar levels (Fig. 6.5).

This stratigraphy is similar to the 'parcel' stratigraphy of the lower Thames (Needham 1989), and the sedimentological model is essentially the same as the stable-bed aggrading-banks model of floodplain evolution proposed by Brown *et al.* (1994). In a small lowland catchment in southern England, radio-carbon dating and pollen and diatom analysis show that deforestation and cultivation of the slopes in the Late Bronze Age/Early Iron Age produced a lagged sedimentary response which represented over a fivefold increase in erosion within the basin (Brown and Barber 1985; Fig. 6.6). An upper silty-clay unit found throughout lowland England can be regarded as the result of the widespread increase in deforestation and intensification of arable cultivation in Roman and medieval times (Lambrick and Robinson 1988; Shotton 1978). While there is undoubtedly a climatic signal in the record (Macklin and Lewin 1994), it is blurred in the lowlands by changes in the availability of sediment and catchment hydrology resulting from land-use change (Burrin and Scaife 1988; Robinson and Lambrick 1984). This means that individual basins have their own sedimentary history, but in time all underwent a metamorphosis of their channels and floodplains, often from an anastomosing system (one with multiple stable-channels) to a stable meandering pattern. The Trent, which is slightly more powerful than the majority of lowland British rivers, seems probably to have gone through a period of braiding, caused by climate but exacerbated by deforestation, before reverting to a single channel (Buckland and Dinnin 1992; Salisbury 1992). This metamorphosis also changed floodplain physiography, ecology and land-use capability (Brown and Keough 1992b).

The situation in the Mediterranean basin (and other semi-arid zones) is rather more complicated due to the semi-arid climate, its strong seasonal contrasts and its inter-annual variability, which combined with the effects of grazing, fire and rather erodible lithologies produces a high erosion potential. Recent work has built upon the pioneering studies of the Younger Fill by Vita-Finzi (1969) and shown that both climatic and land-use controls are important (Woodward *et al.* 1995).

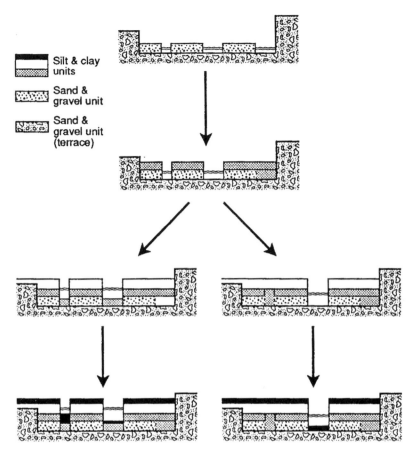

Silt & clay units

Sand & gravel unit

Sand & gravel unit (terrace)

Figure 6.5 Low-energy floodplain evolution: (above) the SBAB model of floodplain aggradation. (Redrawn after Brown *et al.* 1994.) (over) the stratigraphy of the Duck river, Tennessee, USA. From 'Alluvial stratigraphy and radiocarbon dating along the Duck river Tennessee: implications regarding floodpath origin', *Bulletin of the American Geological Society*, No. 95: 9–25 (1984), Brackenridge. Reproduced with permission of the publisher, the Geological Society of America, Boulder, Colorado USA. Copyright © 1984 Geological Society of America.

RECONSTRUCTING CLIMATE

The earth's climate has constantly changed when viewed over a variety of time-scales. The last 2.3 million years have been dominated by marked and abrupt oscillations of climate, especially in the high latitudes, causing major expansions and contractions of land and sea ice. It is generally believed that the fundamental cause has been variations in the earth's orbit and tilt, known as the Milankovitch

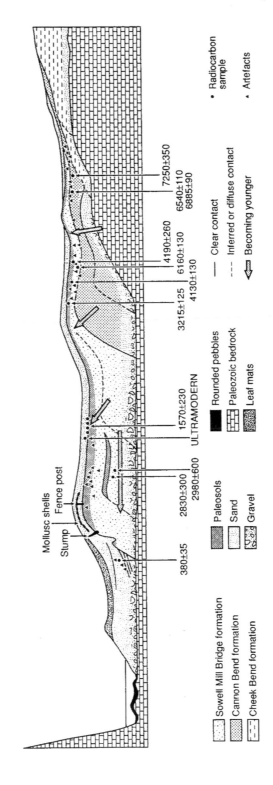

Figure 6.5 (continued)

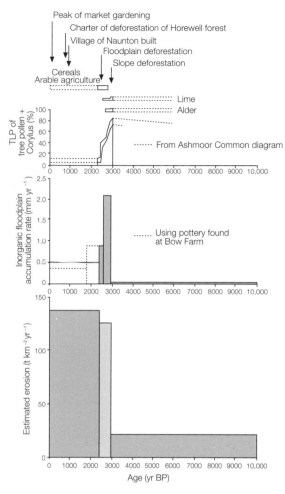

Figure 6.6 Alluvial response to land-use change in a small subcatchment of the river Severn in central England. Source: Brown and Barber 1985.

theory. Since this does not explain all the periodicities seen in the climate record, other factors such as sun-spot activity and feedback mechanisms have also been implicated. The best record of these oscillations has come from the ocean floor sediments such as from core V28–238 in the Pacific Ocean (Bell and Walker 1992; Jones and Keen 1993; Lowe and Walker 1984). Unfortunately the ocean record, whilst providing a fundamental climatic yardstick, cannot tell us much about the effects of these global changes on regional climates and more subtle changes in magnitude and frequency. An important emerging technique is the analysis of the humic acid signal from speleothems luminescence, which has the potential to provide high-resolution climatic records (Baker *et al.* 1993).

Methods of climatic reconstruction which are appropriate in the landscape context can be grouped into two categories: sedimentary and biological. Both produce what is now referred to as proxy climate data (Frenzel 1991), such as the estimation of past river discharges from bed material and from palaeochannel form (Baker 1974; Cheetham 1976; Starkel *et al.* 1991). This methodology has been employed in archaeological contexts such as studies of Romano–Libyan farming systems in Tripolitania, where Gale *et al.* (1986) have used the Darcy–Weisbach flow equation to estimate the carrying capacity of a floodwater channel. Other palaeohydrological methods include studies of past flood heights from flood–slack deposits (Baker 1989) and more traditional studies of lake sediments and lake-level fluctuations (Street-Perrott *et al.* 1989).

Biological proxy methods of climatic reconstruction range from the inference of climatic regime from vegetation type or assemblage through to quantitative estimates from tree rings. In theory the best methods for natural vegetation would be eco-physiological, such as the estimation of past primary productivity, but unfortunately this is not possible from the partial evidence we have on land such as macrofossils, pollen or phytoliths. Instead, contemporary relationships between the fossil assemblage and climatic parameters are projected into the past, such as past ranges, regression equations and transfer functions. This seems to work well for coleoptera (beetles), which are highly temperature-sensitive and mobile, but is more problematic in vegetation studies. In fact, even the estimation of past rainfall from the annual wood increment of trees (dendroclimatology), which is based upon primary productivity, requires robust statistical models of the productivity/climate relationship (Fritts 1976). This method has the potential to provide estimates as far back as the tree-ring chronology extends in any region.

Barber (1981) has shown that the humification and species composition of raised peat bogs can indicate wet and dry surface conditions and so provide a high-resolution climate record (Barber *et al.* 1994) which can be correlated with historical records. At present there are international projects in most zones of the globe established with the object of deriving proxy climate data as inputs to general circulation models, which are then being used to simulate climate change in the past and future (for example: Pilcher 1996).

RECONSTRUCTING VEGETATION

The most obvious and functional element of any landscape is vegetation cover, so it is not surprising that floral palaeoecological methods have traditionally formed the backbone of environmental archaeology. The identification and interpretation of Pleistocene plant remains have a long history, forming the basis of early nineteenth-century vegetation histories such as Clement Reid's classic *The Origin of the British*

238

Flora (1899) and similar work in Scandinavia. The use of databases and the Internet are now providing a valuable tool in the reconstruction of prehistoric food plants and ecology (Tomlinson and Hall 1996). Plant macrofossils range in size from tree trunks to small seeds, but the most common division is into woody and non-woody macrofossils.

Non-woody plant macrofossils

The preservation of non-woody macrofossils depends upon both the resistance of the fragment and environmental conditions. It is generally the structural elements of plants, along with organs that are adapted to withstand dormancy such as rhizomes and seeds, that are most easily preserved. The preservation potential of environments varies from peat bogs, where most of a rather restricted flora may be preserved, through waterlain deposits which have very variable preservation potential, to soils where only resistant fragments may persist. Permanently waterlogged alluvial sites such as palaeochannels can preserve a wide range of organics, including leaves, stems, seeds and nuts, and they share the same transporting processes as small lakes. On dry sites, preservation mechanisms are different and include desiccation, carbonization, seed impressions in pottery and daub, and silica skeletons (Pals *et al.* 1992).

While plant macrofossil sampling and extraction procedures will vary with the conditions and resources available, the most common method is the collection of bulk samples (5 kilograms or more) from a range of contexts, or the collection of monolith tins from exposures. The material may be sieved, or a flotation system used, either on-site or in the laboratory (Pearsall 1989). Identification is fundamentally reliant on the botanical knowledge of the analyst, aided by reference collections, atlases of macroscopic remains and some dichotomous keys. Because of the difficulty of equating different fragments from different plants, the most common form of data presentation is a taxa list, but extra information can, in appropriate circumstances, be gained from semi-quantitative analysis ('rare', 'occasional', 'frequent') or quantitative analysis using percentage sum of fragments or slide/dish cover from a known volume (Dickson 1970; Grosse-Brauckmann 1986).

Because most macrofossils are of local origin, there is a bias to the ecology of the preserving environment, which is often a *hydrosere* (succession of wetland plants). Although ecologists still recognize the existence of a tendency towards the systematic progression of plant communities (seres) from open water to dry land, work on both successional processes and macrofossils sequences themselves has shown us how variable is this process: not only do the pathways and sere types vary spatially, but retrogressive succession is common and the end-point is both temporally and spatially variable. On the north-west European seaboard the 'climax community' (assuming it can be identified) would probably be sphagnum bog rather than mixed oak forest (Walker 1970). Likewise in peat stratigraphy the replacement of the cyclic theory of bog-growth by the phasic theory (Barber 1981) has changed our perceptions of the environmental potential of these studies: in the raised bog in north-west England that became Lindow Man's grave, important changes in bog wetness and traversability occurred both before and after his death (Barber 1986). In the case of *ombogenous* (entirely rain-fed) bogs these changes were *allogenic* (externally forced), caused by changes in the precipitation/evapotranspiration ratio, but for hydroseres they can be due to *autogenic* (internally regulated) changes in the system (such as channel change or debris damming) and thus not be related to external variables.

We see the same problem of separating local/autogenic changes from wider environmental changes in studies of ditch fills, but, if this is allowed for, these sediment traps can provide excellent information on landscape change. An example is Lambrick and Robinson's (1988) study of the development of a floodplain agricultural landscape in the upper Thames valley in southern England. They grouped the seeds and other plant remains recovered from a series of waterlogged ditches of iron age to medieval date into pastureland species and hay meadow species. It was clear from the macrofossil diagrams that grassland areas had existed on the floodplain since clearance of the former alder woodland in places as early as *c.* 3000 BC; most of this pastureland could be described as *mesotrophic* (moderately mineral-rich) using the National Vegetation Classification for the British Isles (Rodwell *et al.* 1991–96) and much was similar to present-day unimproved pasture. Botanically rich hay meadows, however, had probably only existed since Roman times, as they were associated with seasonal flooding and deep alluvial profiles produced by Roman and post-Roman alluviation. Lambrick and Robinson (1988) suggest that the history of this grassland reflects a combination of management practices and changes in the natural environment.

Whilst plant macrofossils are less common in dry environments, van der Veen has recovered a considerable number of crop plants, predominantly by sampling trenches in middens, from the pre-desert region of Tripolitania (van der Veen *et al.* 1996). An extreme example is that of the packrat middens of the arid south-west US: these rodents collect all sorts of vegetation from a radius of about thirty metres to add to their middens, where it is preserved because it is cemented by their urine (Spaulding *et al.* 1983). This work shows that the Sonoran and southern Mojavi desert supported conifers, including pygmy pine, during the Late Pleistocene *c.* 20,000 years ago.

Wood and charcoal

Wood can also be preserved in a variety of ways, including waterlogging, desiccation, carbonization as charcoal, association with corrosion, and as impressions and stains (Taylor 1981). Wood is composed of two basic constituents: lignin, which is preserved; and cellulose, which is easily lost by conversion to sugars. In waterlogged environments, the cells are filled with water which must be replaced after excavation (using carbowax or polyethylene glycol) if shrinkage is not to occur on drying out, although improvements in freeze-drying have helped.

Wood and charcoal identification is based upon the internal structure or anatomy, which is controlled by the size, shape arrangement of vessels used for transporting water, salts, sugars and proteins. The wood is thin sectioned using a microtome revealing the anatomical features. Some conifers (such as pine) have resin canals, others (such as yew) do not, and hardwoods are divided into those which are ring-porous, where the spring vessels are larger that the summer vessels (such as oak) and those which are diffuse-porous, where they are more uniform (such as beech). (For more detail, see standard manuals and identification works such as Cutter *et al.* 1987 and Schweingruber 1978; computerized keys are also now available such as GUESS 1986.) The detailed recording of wood *in situ* can provide valuable information on the population dynamics and patchy structure of ancient woodlands (Lageard *et al.* 1995).

The ecology of trees is relevant not only to the interpretation of wood remains but also for pollen analysis, since we often want to infer the origin of the wood and past environmental conditions. Care is needed since most trees are more catholic than one might expect, but there are gradients based on preferred habitats. Three of these are: pioneers/non-pioneers – early colonizers, fast growing, infertility tolerant/opposite; boreal/thermophilous – typical of the boreal zone/warm-loving; and wetland/dryland – non-rotting, often nitrogen-fixing/waterlogging intolerant. There are much more sophisticated ordinations and classifications based upon phytosociological studies and to a lesser extent upon autecological studies, but as mentioned earlier, caution needs to be exercised. Beech, for example, although often regarded as a tree of alkaline soils, can under both natural and managed conditions grow on acidic soils, as it does in the New Forest in Hampshire, England (Tubbs 1968). The species distribution in the 'wildwood' (*sensu* Rackham 1980) was not static because of differential migration rates, the location of refugia, disturbance, and competition.

The analysis of wood and charcoal can also provide unique information on early forest practices. The reinvestigation of the timbers at the mesolithic site of Star Carr in northern England suggested a close association between beaver activity and human activity (Legge and Rowley-Conwy 1988). Although coppicing and pollarding can occur naturally, there is strong evidence for human agency from the early

Neolithic in the Somerset Levels in south-west England (Coles and Coles 1986). The concentration of archaeological and palaeoecological interest on a normative model of deforestation has to some extent hidden the importance of forest practices such as woodland grazing, the collection of dead timber, the prevention of regeneration, coppicing, pollarding and later charcoal production. Wood was not only the prime structural and energy resource in Antiquity: it also provided dyes, medicines and in some circumstances food (such as bark-bread from elm). Woodland was therefore a primary and multi-faceted resource, completely different to the modern concept of 'forestry'.

Plant microfossils

The distinction between plant macrofossils and microfossils is pragmatic: macrofossils are generally visible to the naked eye, whereas microfossils require the use of high-power microscopy. There are many types of plant microfossil now being used in archaeology but only the most popular will be discussed here. Although the principles of interpretation, including the uniformitarian assumptions and death assemblage concepts, hold true for all the different microfossil types, their detailed interpretation does not, and so they will be discussed separately.

Phytoliths

Phytoliths are the microscopic moulds of opaline (or biogenic) silica (Si) from certain plant cells, which because they can be associated with plant species, or more commonly with groups of plants and environmental conditions, are an increasingly important palaeoecological tool. Plants take up silica from soil water and store it in special cells, thereby increasing plant rigidity. Ancient plants tended to store it on the outside of their stems, but it is more commonly stored in internal cells and in cell walls (it is this silica that produces a use-gloss on harvesting implements); although this is particularly associated with grasses, most other species also store silica.

The importance of phytoliths for archaeologists lies in their high preservation potential in sandy and aerobic soils and sediments where pollen is rare. Extraction procedures are in theory relatively easy, involving the removal of organic matter by burning or wet oxidation and density separation (Powers and Gilbertson 1987). The most common problem is low concentration, but concentration itself may be indicative of land-use processes. High concentrations (up to 10^6 phytoliths per gram of sediment) occur in middens, cultivation deposits and animal faeces, while wind-blow sand concentrations are below 2^5 phytoliths per gram of sediment

242

and often very much lower. The rudimentary typologies of the 1960s (Rovner 1971; Smithson 1958) have been refined (Brown 1984; Piperno 1988; Powers and Gilbertson 1987), although species identification is rarely possible and some form of association analysis is required to define the palaeoenvironment. Powers *et al.* (1989) have shown how phytoliths may be used to identify the origins and land use associated with sand dunes and machair sediments in northern Britain. Absolute analysis and the application of correspondence analysis can help distinguish aspects of human activity, including the contributions of cut peat, plant and animal wastes, and possibly the character of grazing systems.

Pollen and spores

The analysis of pollen and spores has probably been the single most important technique for the reconstruction of natural landscapes during the last forty years. Classic early studies were undertaken by Godwin, Iversen, Troels-Smith, Dimbleby and others of sites closely associated with archaeological excavations. Discussion here will be concerned with interpretation and use, rather than methodology, the latter being covered well in a number of texts (Berglund and Ralska-Jasiewiczowa 1986; Faegri and Iversen 1991; Moore *et al.* 1992). In brief, the most common extraction process involves disaggregation and the removal of carbonates; oxidation of organic matter (acetolysis); and removal of silicates using hydrofluoric acid. Recent innovations include micro-sieving, density separation, and the use of microwave digestion. Spikes can be added to a known sample volume to give concentration values, although most routine work still uses relative counting.

In order to interpret the results, whether a type/taxa list or a diagram, notice must be taken of the 'three-differentials' of pollen analysis. The first is the differential pollen productivity of plants. Gross variations correspond with mechanisms of pollen dispersal, so aerophilous (wind-pollinated) plants produce large amounts, while entomophilous (insect-pollinated) plants produce much smaller quantities. Correction factors have been produced by several palynologists including Anderson and Erdtman (Moore *et al.* 1992); their application has, for example, changed our model of the Atlantic forest composition in central and eastern England from one dominated by oak to one dominated in many areas by lime (Greig 1982). The second factor is differential preservation. Although the exines (external walls) of pollen and spores are constructed from a tough natural polymer (sporopollenin), the classic experiments of Sangster and Dale (1964) have shown that some are more resistant than others and that this varies with the chemistry of the environment. Certain types are known to be particularly resistant, such as the ferns and some of the daisy family, and so high quantities of these and a reduced diversity indicates poor preservation – this is a problem in many archaeological contexts such as buried soils, sandy contexts, cave deposits, pits, latrines and ditches. The third factor is differential transport: just as the transport vector may vary, so will the average distance travelled by grains. Several palynologists have produced models of pollen transport, two of which are the Tauber model (Tauber 1965), which distinguishes between different transportational pathways (such as rainout, canopy, trunk-space and local components), and the Jacobsen and Bradshaw (1981) model, which relates site size to the pollen-contributing area. This has been further developed by Sugita (1994), who has shown that sites over 1,500 metres above sea level show little site-to-site variation and inevitably indicate homogeneous vegetation.

These models can be adapted for small ponds, oxbow lakes (Fig. 6.7) and archaeological sites (such as ditches), illustrating that such sites should provide an

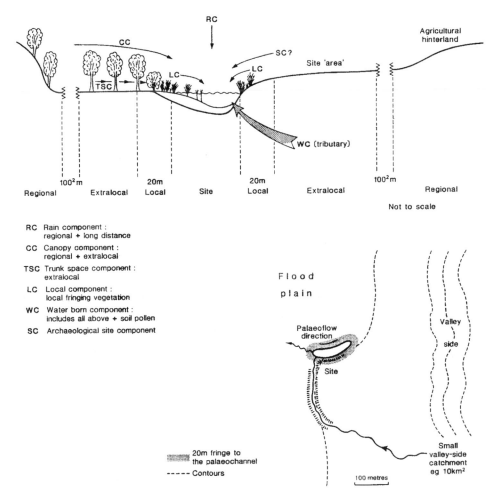

Figure 6.7 A pollen recruitment model for an oxbow lake or small pond. Source: A. Brown.

244

accurate picture of the local and extra-local vegetation 50–300 metres from the site (Brown forthcoming). However, on-site palynology has additional problems in the many types of input. These can include digger bees, fodder, food remains and coprolites, making cave sites and urban sites particularly problematic. Archaeologists who want to reconstruct the natural resource-base using pollen analysis therefore need to be aware of the chain of inferences involved from the original pollen rain to the inferred ecology, with the evidence becoming progressively more ambiguous. There is also a great danger of the reinforcement syndrome operating, whereby a palynologist uses archaeological evidence to interpret the pollen data and subsequently the archaeologist uses that interpretation as evidence for a particular interpretation of the original archaeological data! Some of the complications can be illustrated if we take three problems with the interpretation of so-called 'clearance events': clearance events can have many causes such as disease, windthrow, fire, felling and so on, which may occur in combination; it is difficult to distinguish between a large clearance at some distance and smaller clearances nearby; blurring of the pollen signal may be caused by several clearances overlapping in time, producing what looks like one long event (Buckland and Edwards 1984).

There has recently been a partial re-evaluation of the palynological evidence of some important ecological changes in north-west Europe such as the 'elm decline', now thought to be a combination of disease and human activity on the basis of both pollen and coleopteran data (Girling 1988). However, detailed pollen analysis combined with waterlogged archaeology can provide valuable insights into woodland management, as at the neolithic pile dwelling at Alvastra in Sweden, where both pollen and macrofossil evidence indicate intensive coppicing of the surrounding woodland (Goransson 1987). Some of the earliest palynological work was done on buried soils, where there are particular problems of preservation and bioturbation (Dimbleby 1985). However, the potential of palynology for sub-structure soils has long been recognized and formed the original data for Dimbleby's model of soil degradation and podzol formation associated with human activity being responsible for the creation of lowland heaths in Britain (Dimbleby 1974).

Until recently much of the non-pollen material on the laboratory slides was left unidentified and discounted – generally zygospores, ascospores and insect remains. Their identification and use in palaeoenvironmental reconstruction has been worked upon by van Geel (1986), and more recently by archaeologists (Coles 1989). Some types have very particular ecological requirements and so make excellent indicator types.

It is important to realize what pollen and spore analysis cannot do. Its prime role is the reconstruction of past vegetation cover, rather than dating: in the absence of documented marker species, the latter is hazardous and theoretically unsound due to the diachrony (time-transgressive nature) of vegetation change. Second, while pollen analysis can illustrate it can rarely explain, except when supplemented by another data type.

Diatoms

Diatoms are single-celled algae with internal valves (called frustules), which are made of opaline silica and thus can be preserved in a variety of sedimentary environments. They are found in all fluvial, lacustrine, estuarine, and marine environments and the death assemblage can directly reflect original floristic composition and productivity. For details of methodology and identification, see Batterbee (1986). Because many diatom species are extremely sensitive to salt content, nutrient status and pH, they are extremely useful in the reconstruction of past environmental change, including flooding by sea or freshwater (Brown and Barber 1985), lake history and changes in the surrounding environment (Haworth 1976; Bradbury *et al.* 1981) and the pollution of water bodies including acidification and eutrophication (Batterbee 1978; Flower and Batterbee 1983). Apart from inferences of catchment status such as soil conditions, diatoms have great potential for the reconstruction of local conditions in water bodies in or near archaeological sites and where local conditions have changed. An early example is Foged's (1978) analysis of the diatoms from the Danish medieval town of Svenborg.

RECONSTRUCTING THE FAUNA

Although derived from a less visible component of the natural landscape, faunal remains can provide detailed indirect evidence of climate and vegetation as well as direct evidence of the trophic structure of the ecosystem. There are close parallels here with the routine analysis of faunal remains on site (Chapter 14).

Invertebrate microfossils

Many faunal micro-organisms can be preserved and can be used as environmental indicators in geoarchaeological studies. These include foraminifera (protozoa with calcareous shells), ostracods (crustacea with calcareous shells) and coccolithophores (unicellular autotrophic marine algae); more details can be found in Lowe and Walker (1997). Three microfossils which may be of particular potential in archaeological studies are rhizopods, cladocera and chironomids.

Testate amoebae (rhizopods)

Testate amoebae or rhizopods are the shells (or tests) of freshwater amoeba (proto-zoa) found in lakes, peat bogs and soils. In wetland environments they can indicate local vegetation and nutrient status. In general they are most useful in the absence of plant macrofossils and in conjunction with other microfossil analyses, a specific example being the changes in raised bog surface conditions caused by climatic change (Frey 1964; Warner and Charman 1994). For an introduction to rhizopod analysis, see Tolonen (1986). The archaeological potential of rhizopods is greatest in wetland environments, although more work on soil rhizopods may broaden their use (Warner 1988).

Chironomids and cladocera

Chironomids are freshwater midges which can be identified from their larval head capsules. They have proved to be good indicators of ecological conditions (Amoros and van Urk 1989). Studies of Rhine sediments of medieval and post-medieval age have shown that much of the past river entomology can be reconstructed document-ing changing river and floodplain habitats associated with human settlement and exploitation (Klinke 1989). Similar results can be obtained from the analysis of cladoceran, water flees (Amoros and van Urk 1989; Roux *et al.* 1989). Both of these microfaunal techniques have considerable potential, not only in natural and semi-natural wetland habitats but also in anthropogenic habitats such as waterfronts, ditches, cisterns and ponds. Methods and further details can be found in Hoffman (1986) and Frey (1986).

Faunal invertebrate macrofossils

Coleoptera

The most common insect remains used in the reconstruction of natural environ-ments in archaeology are from beetles (coleoptera). Beetles are almost ideal environmental indicators because species distribution is closely related to tempera-ture, many are also host-specific, and they are highly mobile, thus reducing the lag effects so marked in vegetation response to climate change (Coope 1986).

Coleopteran analysis has provided a temperature curve for the last 15,000 years from Britain using the mutual climatic range method (Atkinson *et al.* 1986), although there is some debate as to the reliability of this method with past species distributions (Anderson 1993). In Europe the use of beetles as climatic indicators becomes more difficult from the Neolithic onwards, as their geographical ranges are affected by human landscape change, particularly deforestation, and the creation of internal climates. This response to human activity forms the basis of their use in environmental archaeology. They have been used to construct detailed pictures of local environmental changes associated with archaeological sites (Buckland 1979; Buckland and Kenward 1973). Coleoptera can be well preserved in alluvial contexts, if water levels have been maintained, and can give valuable evidence of changing river and floodplain conditions which in some cases are the result of human activities such as deforestation (Buckland and Dinnin 1992). The close association of some species with wood and woodland management makes them of great potential for the reconstruction of natural environments: an excellent example is the discovery of *Scolytus scolytus* (the Dutch elm bark beetle) at 'elm decline' levels in southern England (Girling 1988). Although this discovery is open to several interpretations, it does suggest a link between the human impact on the wildwood and pathogen spread. Coleopteran analysis undoubtedly has great potential for studies of both site conditions and changing landscapes (Ashworth *et al.* 1997; Osborne 1988).

Mollusca

The analysis of sub-fossil snail shells (mollusca excluding the cephalopoda) is one of the oldest and most practised methods of palaeoenvironmental reconstruction used in archaeology (Evans 1972; Sparks 1969). Snails are often preserved where pollen is not: in dry alkaline deposits and soils. It is not, however, a homologous technique, as molluscan analysis produces different evidence at different scales of past climate, soils and vegetation conditions. Also, molluscs are organisms which have become closely associated with humans through colonization of human habitats and through direct human exploitation as a resource. The two groups of mollusca of relevance here, the gastropods (snails) and bivalves (mussels and clams), have shells made of aragonite, a form of calcium carbonate. Identification of adults to species level is relatively easy with the aid of keys and a reference collection. They are generally restricted to lime-rich environments (required for shell construction), and many are calcicoles (lime-'lovers'), although there are a few which can be found in less-calcareous environments. A very few are even calcifuges (lime-'haters'), but they are small and poorly preserved. The shells are prone to dissolution by acidic water, a process which may be selective on those with the thinnest shells. Large soil or sediment samples are wet sieved and the sorted and counted snails expressed as a presence/absence table or a histogram of taxon percentages.

A substantial amount is known about the distribution and ecology of land snails, on the basis of which Sparks (1961) identified four fluvial habitat groups: (1) slum group – individuals tolerant of poor water conditions, ephemeral or stagnant pools, such as *Lymneae truncatula*; (2) catholic group – individuals that will tolerate a wide range of habitats except the worst slums, such as *Lymnaea peregra*; (3) ditch group – species found in ditches with clean slow water with abundant macrophytes (vegetation), such as *Planorbis planorbis*; (4) moving water group – species typical of larger water bodies such as lakes and streams, for example *Valvata piscinalis* and the larger freshwater bivalves such as the Swan mussel (*Anodonta cygnea*). Similarly, land snails can be divided into four groups: (1) marsh group – associated with fens and marshes, such as *Vallonia pulchella*; (2) dryland group, such as *Pupilla muscorum*; (3) open country group, such as *Vallonia* sp.; (4) woodland group – shade loving species such as *Discus rotundatus*. It is from the dryland and open country groups that the snails which adapted to agricultural land originally came. In addition, there are some species which adapted to other humanly created habitats (that is, they became 'synanthropic'), including carnivorous snails found in cemeteries.

The broad groupings above have been used to document land cover changes associated with prehistoric woodland clearance at many sites (Evans 1972). Some snails are sensitive to climate and this has been used in Quaternary palaeoenvironmental reconstruction and correlation. Along with lake sediments, pollen and diatoms, lacustrine mollusca have revealed how the early Holocene in the eastern Sahara was a far wetter and greener environment than the hyper-arid desert it is today (Petit-Maire and Riser 1983), a finding of great significance for the study of the predynastic cultures of the Nile valley. Similarly, the widespread presence throughout Britain between *c.* 6000 BC and *c.* 3000 BC of three land snails now absent from northern Britain (*Pomatia elegans*, *Lauria cylindracea* and *Ena montana*), along with the regional extinction of the European freshwater tortoise (*Emys orbicularis*), may reflect the warmer conditions of the European climatic optimum. Recent work on land snails has involved the use of numerical methods and ecological analogues in the reconstruction of what Evans calls past 'taxocenes' (Evans *et al.* 1992).

Marine mollusca come from a range of littoral habitats, from the rocks and pools of the intertidal zone to the edge of the continental shelf. They often make up a significant component of beach and marine sediments (such as crag deposits). Ecological groupings have been constructed based upon salinity, water depth and water temperature. Some species of whelk even vary in shape in response to the exposure of the coast and this has been used to map the gathering activity of mesolithic peoples in the Outer Hebrides and to indicate changes in storminess (Andrews *et al.* 1985). Because middens are rich sources of mollusca, considerable care is needed in the separation of any assemblage changes caused by local environmental change from those caused by social factors that might have effected procurement preferences and/or the location of procurement activity.

Vertebrates

Although their principal importance in archaeology is for palaeoeconomic studies (Chapter 14), animal bones do occur in natural contexts and their interpretation in part concerns the reconstruction of landscape. Whether for palaeoeconomic or environmental reconstruction, the use of vertebrate remains relies on knowledge of the biases of the samples. During the last thirty years vertebrate taphonomy has been the focus of considerable research, and this has allowed archaeologists to say far more about not only cause of death but also the sequence of events prior to and after death (Behrensmeyer and Hill 1980; Lyman 1994; Weigelt 1989).

Fish

Fish remains have generally been under-researched, and have until recently only been seen as of interest in relation to past diet (Brinkhuizen and Clason 1986; Casteel 1976). Casteel (1976) gives details of methodologies. There are serious problems of sampling and preservation involved: the surprising lack of fish bones from mesolithic sites in Britain as noted by Simmons *et al.* (1981) probably reflects both of these. Preservation is differential: the bones of salmonids and eels are less well preserved than those of the primary freshwater fish such as pike and perch (Simmons *et al.* 1981). Some progress has been made on the natural spread of fish across the northern continents after deglaciation. It is believed that all indigenous freshwater fish entered Britain via the continental land bridge severed by the English Channel *c.* 5500 BC, populating only the river catchments draining to the eastern English channel and the southern North Sea (Wheeler 1977). This means that in catchments outside this area, including all those further north than the Yorkshire Ouse, freshwater primary fish (but not eels and salmonids) were probably introduced. Unglaciated continental regions can probably be assumed to have had less variable fish ecologies, although there is some evidence that Holocene climate change has had some effect on the fish fauna of Russia (Casteel 1976).

Birds and small mammals

The sieving and/or flotation of sediments for small bones has now become routine practice, reducing the bias towards large herbivores and providing more informa-tion on the local natural and cultural landscape; details of methods, procedures, identification and report preparation can be found in Schmidt (1972), Grigson (1978) and Davis (1987). Bird remains are only commonly found in either human contexts or from cave deposits; as with other mammals, their recolonization of

250

Europe and North America in the Holocene occurred as their habitats moved north. One of the caves at Creswell Crags, in central/northern England, did not contain any evidence of human occupation and so could be regarded as a baseline for late glacial and early Holocene environmental data (Gilbertson and Jenkinson 1984). Seven species of falcon and five species of owl have been recovered from this cave, and these raptors are the main accumulating agency for small mammal remains.

Studies of bird bones show clearly how the range and diversity of wild birds have changed during the last 10,000 years. A few species known from archaeological sites have become extinct, a north-west European example being the great auk (*Pinguinus impennis*), which seems to have been a significant food source in the Neolithic in coastal areas (Smith *et al.* 1981). The hunting of birds in coastal high latitudes was a highly seasonal activity and integrated with the hunting of other mammals (Munzel 1983).

Nearly all the wild fauna that had reached Britain by the early Holocene survived into the mid and late Holocene (with the exception of the elk, *Alces alces*), and this seems also to hold true for southern Europe and North America. In the mammal record in Britain, we do, however, see a reduction in diversity after the Iron Age, clearly associated with the disappearance of natural habitats probably exacerbated by hunting. A critical threshold may have been reached, although at different times in different regions, when the landscape changed from a 'wildwood' with isolated, even if large, clearings, to a landscape of isolated woodland separated by open land as today – a change which would have isolated breeding groups of woodland mammals, making them more susceptible to local extinction. The same fragmentation occurred where tropical forests were replaced by prairies and savannahs, with or without human assistance.

Small mammals are particularly well preserved in cave sites due to a variety of accumulating agencies. In addition to the common native mammals, we see some which have now become rare in Britain. Bones of Bechstein's bat (*Selysius bechsteinii*) have been recovered from neolithic levels at Dowel Cave in Derbyshire (Smith *et al.* 1981) and the pine marten (*Martes martes*) is recorded from the neolithic barrow of Nutbane in Hampshire. Although nearly all small European mammals were associated with woodland conditions, most adapted to landscape and habitat change more easily than the large mammals. This was probably helped by the fact that they do not seem to have been significant food resources and did not provide obvious competition with domesticated animals for food. Those that died out were generally the larger species, valuable for their fur, such as the European beaver (*Castor fiber*) and/or those requiring large territories.

Larger mammals

Due to the importance of domesticates in later prehistoric archaeology, large wild animals have received most attention in palaeolithic studies in Europe and in the New World. Between about 14,000 and 10,000 years ago we see an acceleration of mammal extinctions in both the New and Old Worlds. Although the largest mammals (the 'megafauna') were most affected, so were some birds and small mammals. In northern Europe, late glacial/early Holocene extinctions included the woolly rhino (*Coleodonta antiquitatis*), the giant deer (*Megaloceras* sp.), the sabre-toothed tiger (*Smilodon*) and the mammoth (*Mammuthus primigenius*). In North America, the extinctions included the native American horse (*Equus occidentalis*), the mastodont (*Mammuth americanum*) and the American shasta ground-sloth (*Northrotheriops shastense*). The North American extinction event had more effect on the native fauna than anything during the preceding four million years (Martin and Klein 1984). This was a period of great environmental change and, especially in the New World, great cultural change as well. One explanation for the extinctions is the 'overkill' hypothesis: that new cultures massacred wild animals unused to human contact, in the same way that island extinctions in recent times were caused by the first arrival of humans. A second hypothesis is that the extinctions were related to climatic change. However, neither the climatic nor the overkill hypothesis seem adequate alone, as despite the cavalier approach to wildlife resources seemingly exhibited by cultures such as the Clovis in North America and evidence of similar 'game-drives' at this time in Europe, many abundant species did survive. It is most likely that it was the combination of climatic stress and the indirect effects of cultural change, such as habitat alterations, that marginalized and finally caused the extinction of these animals (Roberts 1998). The fact that the plentiful species that survived in North America, such as the bison, were important game species further weakens the overkill hypothesis.

Different regions obviously have very different Holocene faunal histories: even the history of large mammals in Ireland is different to that of mainland Britain, which is different again from that of continental Europe. Since large mammal bones are recovered from sites of human activity or rare natural traps, the records may only indicate presence in the region and tell us little about abundance. Although this limits their potential as records of landscape change, the large mammals are not simply important as indicators of human subsistence behaviour: for example, the effects on the environment of the introduction of domesticates, especially sheep and goats, have been devastating in the Mediterranean and in parts of the New World, whilst the history of recent introductions to Britain, such as the rabbit, mink and coypu, illustrate that environmental impacts can be dramatic and not always predictable.

RESOURCES AND THE NATURAL LANDSCAPE

Since practically every natural material is a potential resource, the history of resource use is the history of the transformation of nature through human labour. It is therefore possible to subdivide natural resources by use and labour input (processing) as well as by nature: that is, those related to subsistence (food, drink, medicines), agricultural resources, and settlement (space, soil fertility and water); and those related to industry (raw materials for the production of artefacts and new materials).

Until very recent times, wood has been by far the most important resource for the majority of structures. Wood was also the only fuel available in large quantities until relatively recently, and was also needed for tools or parts of tools (Taylor 1981). The archaeology of wood has been revolutionized by wetland archaeology, which has revealed that in some parts of Britain sophisticated wood technology and woodland management have existed certainly since neolithic times. Work in the wetlands of Florida has also revealed accomplished woodworking from the Archaic and other periods (Purdy 1992). Fuelwood was another fundamental locationally fixed resource for pre-industrial societies: in Europe, complex rights concerning the allocation of fuelwood had come into being by medieval times, in effect rationing the resource.

The relative importance of plants and animals in gatherer-hunter communities of the past has long been a matter of debate (Chapters 14 and 20). Ethnoarchaeological studies have shown how in some areas with low population densities, gathering-hunting lifestyles are both dependable and easier than agricultural lifestyles (Sahlins 1972) and that agriculturalists often revert, with ease, to gathering-hunting in times of poor harvest. When allowance is made for the bias in the record in favour of animal remains, it seems that many early farming communities were still partially dependent on wild food resources (Brothwell 1969; Dennell 1987; Zvelebil 1994). Ethnohistorical studies also provide examples of communities which span the continuum from vegetarian societies to those where the diet is predominantly meat. The taphonomic bias towards bones and agricultural plants in most environments places an extra premium on wetland sites, where wild plant foods may be preserved. Macrofossil databases (including some on the Internet: see Tomlinson and Hall 1996) illustrate how patchy the record is, both in time and space.

From the first use of stone tools, humans have sought rocks and minerals for industrial use. We can divide geological resources into those that occur in veins and bands (including gangue minerals), placer deposits and building materials which can be collected or quarried. How these resources were first located is virtually impossible to determine, but presumably natural outcrops in cliffs, stream beds, animal burrows and geobotanical knowledge all played a part. The large size of

253

many early industrial sites suggests that the exploitation of the resources involved considerable organization of labour. In many low-lying or soft rock areas stone had to be imported.

Because soils are viewed as a resource today there has been a tendency to look at soil development and change in the Holocene in terms of the increase and decrease of an agricultural resource. The problem here is that fertility, which is controlled by many factors including natural soil chemistry, organic cycling and human additions, is only one of the controls on crop yield – others include crop species/variety, cultivation practices, weather and harvesting techniques. At the local scale the main control on soil processes is land use, so soil history is intimately connected to vegetation history. The construction of large areas of *plaggen* or human-made soils in north-west Europe shows how fertility is closely related to farming activity.

Water increases in value as a resource as its supply decreases since, for any farming other than dry farming, demand is essentially non-elastic. Especially in climates with a pronounced dry season this has led to major environmental modifications in areas of moisture deficit in order to gather and store water, whilst in wet temperate environments many societies have invested considerable expenditure on water engineering projects such as fish ponds, weirs and mill ponds.

It is through the analysis of resources and potential resources that the reconstruction of natural landscapes enters fully into social and economic archaeology. Indeed environmental archaeology is in large part a history of the what and where: the identification, location and conversion of potential to realized resources through innovation (Chapter 14).

HAZARDS AND THE NATURAL LANDSCAPE

The influence of natural hazards on culture and settlement formed a popular theme in archaeology up to the 1960s – classic, if often flawed, examples include the possible impact of flooding on the Indus and other civilizations (Raikes 1965, 1967) and the indisputable effect on Pompeii of the eruption of Vesuvius. More recently, the role of natural events has been somewhat marginalized as freak and of little importance in relation to the normative models of processual and post-processual archaeology.

However, work in environmental archaeology has progressed alongside the development of quantitative palaeoecology, with an increased interest in the role of climate change. The effects of unusual natural phenomena on past human societies can be assumed to have been greater than on modern westernized society. Physically, economically, and psychologically, people in Antiquity were less insulated from extreme events than today, even if this insulation was counteracted to a degree by cultural incorporation and geoteleological beliefs. If we take the extreme case of

254

lightning-strikes, still today unpredictable and legally regarded as an act of God, many areas of the earth receive hundreds or thousands of strikes per year and death and injury are not as rare as might be expected. Before the invention of the lightning conductors, lightning-strikes would have been a common cause of settlement fires as well as the creation of forest clearings. While models of purposive forest clearance by the use of fire are well established, the opportunistic use of natural clearings has been neglected, despite ethnographic studies which show a range of fire-related behaviours from purposive and competent, through purposive and incompetent, to opportunistic (Pyne 1982).

Work is now underway on a wide range of environmental hazards, including storm surges (Bell 1992), earthquakes and floods (Brown 1996). This work is far more critical than previous 'catastrophe' studies and takes on board socio-economic work on human and institutional responses to hazards. It is in a sense ironic that one of the best ways to strengthen the current emphasis on models of socio-cultural causation for cultural change is to disprove any environmental causation, which can only be done through detailed environmental work.

RECONSTRUCTING NATURAL LANDSCAPES: FUTURE AGENDAS

The conceptualization of the landscape in archaeology has changed from a simplistic and determinist one in the early part of this century to the base of social, economic, and cognitive models. The increase in the variety of techniques available has led to a *gestalt*-like (sum – greater than its parts) gain in information, as these techniques not only complement each other but can generate completely new hypotheses. There have been significant advances in the power and use of environmental techniques to make useful statements about past landscapes. Whether these statements are archaeologically useful or not depends upon the purposes and paradigms of archaeology.

The use of ecological models has focused attention on the resource base and average conditions, but too often theories of adaptation have amounted to little more than descriptions of change (Shanks and Tilley 1987). They need not. One problem has been that anything more than this was tarred with the brush of environmental determinism.

Several areas of neo-deterministic work which seek to understand some of the complexities of the relationship between social processes and the natural environment and its perturbations are (re)emerging. This work seeks to avoid our predominantly western dichotomization of nature and culture and as such is neither atheoretical nor non-political. The agenda includes three areas of investigation. The first consists of studies of social and political response to natural events: a variety of perspectives can be taken, ranging from institutional, to the structural-Marxist, though all rest upon the processual linkage of event with response. Second are attempts to reconstruct aspects of cognitive processes important in the perception of nature (Renfrew and Zubrow 1990): one example is the 'meaning' of palaeolithic art and its relation to hunting and gathering activity and intentionality (Mithen 1991), along with the incorporation of uncertainty, risk and non-average behaviour (Allen 1989). Third are studies of the environmental effects of past social and political change, including migration, imperialism, and colonialism (MacKenzie 1990) – the biological expansion of Europe in the last thousand years can be regarded as only the latest chapter in a history of ecological imperialism (Crosby 1986). While these directions of research may, or may not, help to silence critics of environmental archaeology and environmental reconstruction (for example: Thomas 1990), there is no doubt that innovations in techniques and methodology will continue unabated, allowing more layers of the palimpsest that is the landscape to be revealed and related to history and contextualized social change.

REFERENCES

Allen, P. M. (1989) 'Modelling innovation and change', in S. E. van der Leeuw and R. Torrence (eds) *What's New: A Closer Look at the Process of Innovation*, London: Unwin Hymen: 258–80.

Amoros, C. and van Urk, G. (1989) 'Palaeoecological analysis of large rivers: some principles and methods', in G. E. Petts, H. Moller and A. R. Roux (eds) *Historical Change of Large Alluvial Rivers*, Chichester: Wiley: 143–66.

Anderson, J. (1993) 'Beetle remains as indicators of the climate in the Quaternary', *Journal of Biogeography* 20: 557–62.

Andrews, M. V., Gilbertson, D. D., Kent, M. and Mellars, P. A. (1985) 'Biometric studies of morphological variation in the intertidal gastropod *Nucella lapillus* (L): environmental and palaeoecological significance', *Journal of Biogeography* 12: 71–87.

Ashworth, A. C., Buckland, P. C. and Sadler, J. P. (1997) 'Studies in Quaternary entomology.' *Quaternary Proceedings* 5.

Atkinson, T. C., Briffa, K. A., Coope, G. R., Joachim, M. J. and Parzy, D. W. (1986) 'Climatic calibration of coleopteran data', in B. Berglund (ed.) *Handbook of Holocene Palaeoecology and Palaeohydrology*, Chichester: Wiley, 851–58.

Bagnold, R. A. and Barndorff-Nielsen, O. (1980) 'The pattern of natural size distributions', *Sedimentology* 27: 199–207.

Bailiff, I. (1992) 'Luminescence dating of alluvial deposits', in S. Needham and M. Macklin (eds) *Archaeology Under Alluvium*, Oxford: Oxbow Books: 27–36.

Baker, A., Smart, P. L., Edwards, R. L. and Richards, D. A. (1993) 'Annual banding in a cave stalagmite', *Nature* 364: 518–20.

Baker, V. R. (1974) 'Palaeohydraulic interpretation of Quaternary alluvium near Golden, Colorado', *Quaternary Research* 4: 94–112.

Baker, V. R. (1989) 'Magnitude and frequency of palaeofloods', in K. Bevan and P. Carling (eds) *Floods: Hydrological, Sedimentological and Geomorphological Implications*, Wiley: Chichester: 171–83.

Barber, K. E. (1981) *Peat Stratigraphy and Climate Change*, Rotterdam: Balkema.

Barber, K. E. (1986) 'Peat stratigraphy', in I. M. Stead, J. B. Bourke and D. Brothwell (eds) *Lindow Man: The Body in the Bog*, London: British Museum: 86–89.

Barber, K. E., Chambers, F. M., Maddy, D., Stoneman, R. and Brew, J. S. (1994) 'A sensitive high-resolution record of late Holocene climatic change from a raised bog in northern England', *The Holocene* 4: 198–205.

Barham, A. J. and Macphail, R. I. (1995) *Archaeological Sediments and Soils: Analysis, Interpretation and Management,* London: Institute of Archaeology, University College London.

Batt, C. M. and Noël, M. (1991). 'Magnetic studies of archaeological sediment', in P. Budd, B. Chapman, L. Jackson, R. C. Janaway and B. S. Ottaway (eds) *Archaeological Sciences. 1989: Proceedings of a Conference on the Application of Scientific Techniques and Archaeology*, Oxbow Monograph No. 9, Oxford: Oxbow: 234–41.

Batterbee, R. W. (1978) 'Observations on the recent history of Lough Neagh sediments II: Diatoms from the uppermost sediment', *Philosophical Transactions of the Royal Society B*, 281: 303–45.

Batterbee, R. W. (1986) 'Diatom analysis', in B. Berglund (ed.) *Handbook of Holocene Palaeohydrology and Palaeoecology*, Chichester: Wiley, 527–70.

Behrensmeyer, A. K. and Hill, A. P. (eds) (1980) *Fossils in the Making: Vertebrate Taphonomy and Palaeoecology*, Chicago: Chicago University Press.

Bell, M. (1992) 'Hazard frequency and response in coastal environments', Unpublished paper given to Theoretical Archaeology Conference, Leicester.

Bell, M. and Walker, M. J. C. (1992) *Late Quaternary Environmental Change*, Harlow: Longman.

Berglund, B. and Ralska-Jasiewiczowa, M. (1986) 'Pollen analysis and pollen diagrams', in B. Berglund (ed.) *Handbook of Holocene Palaeoecology and Palaeohydrology*, Chichester: Wiley: 455–84.

Berglund, B. E., Birks, H. J. B., Ralska-Jasiewiczowa, M. and Wright, H. E. (1996) *Palaeo-ecological Events During the Last 15,000 Years: Regional Synthesis of Palaeoecological Studies of Lakes and Mires in Europe*, London: J. Wiley.

Bintliff, J., Davis, B., Gaffney, C., Snodgrass, A. and Waters, A. (1992) 'Trace metal accumulations in soils on and around ancient settlements in Greece', in P. Spoerry (ed.) *Geoprospection in the Archaeological Landscape*, Oxbow Monograph 18, Oxford: Oxbow: 9–24.

Birks, H. J. B., Line, J. M., Juggins, S., Stevenson, A. C. and ter Braak, C. J. F. (1990) 'Diatoms and pH reconstruction', *Philosophical Transactions of the Royal Society, Series B*: 327: 263–78.

Boardman, J. and Bell, M. (1992) *Past and Present Soil Erosion*, Oxford: Oxbow Books.

Bowden, M. J., Kates, R. W., Kay, P. A., Riebsame, W. E., Warrick, R. A., Johnson, D. L., Gould, H. E. and Weiner, D. (1981) 'The effect of climatic fluctuations on human populations: two hypotheses', in T. M. L. Wigley, M. J. Ingram and G. Farmer (eds) *Climate and History*, Cambridge: Cambridge University Press: 479–513.

Brackenridge, G. R. (1984) 'Alluvial stratigraphy and radiocarbon dating along the Duck river, Tennessee. Implications regarding floodplain origin', *Bulletin of the American Geological Society* 95: 9–25.

Bradbury, J. P., Leyden, B., Salgado-Labouriav, M., Lewis, W. M., Scubert, C., Binford, M. W., Frey, D. G., Whitehead, D. R. and Weibezahn, F. H. (1981) 'Late-Quaternary environmental history of Lake Valencia, Venezuela', *Science* 214: 1299–1305.

Brewer, R. (1976) *Fabric and Mineral Analysis of Soils*, New York: Kriger.

Bridges, E. M. (1978) 'Interaction of soil and mankind', *Soil Science* 29: 125–39.

Briggs, D. J. (1977) *Sediments*, London: Butterworths.

Briggs, D. J. and Courtney, F. (1989) *Agriculture and Environment*, London: Longman.

Brinkhuizen, D. C. and Clason, A. T. (eds) (1986) *Fish and Archaeology: Studies in Osteo-metry, Taphonomy, Seasonality and Fishing Methods*, Oxford: British Archaeological Reports, International Series 294.

Brothwell, D. R. (1969) 'Dietary variation and the biology of human populations', in P. J. Ucko and G. W. Dimbleby (eds) *Domestication and Exploitation of Plants and Animals*, London: Duckworth: 531–46.

Brown, A. G. (1985) 'Traditional and multivariate techniques in the interpretation of flood-plain sediment grain size variations', *Earth Surface Processes and Landforms* 10: 281–91.

Brown, A. G. (1987) 'Long-term sediment storage in the Severn and Wye catchments', in K. J. Gregory, J. Lewin and J. B. Thornes (eds) *Palaeohydrology in Practice*, Chichester: Wiley: 307–22.

Brown, A. G. (1992) 'Slope erosion and colluviation on the floodplain edge', in M. Bell and J. Boardman (eds) *Past and Present Soil Erosion*, Oxford: Oxbow Books: 77–88.

Brown, A. G. (1996) 'Human dimensions of palaeohydrological change', in J. Branson, A. G. Brown and K. J. Gregory (eds) *Global Continental Changes: The Context of Palaeo-hydrology*, Geological Society Monograph, London: Geological Society: 57–72.

Brown, A. G. (1997) *Alluvial Environments: Geoarchaeology and Environmental Change*, Cambridge: Cambridge University Press.

Brown, A. G. (forthcoming) 'Characterising prehistoric lowland environments using local pollen assemblages', in K. J. Edwards and J. Sadler (eds) *Perspectives on the Holocene Environments of Prehistoric Britain* (*Quaternary Science Proceedings*).

Brown, A. G. and Barber, K. E. (1985) 'Late Holocene palaeoecology and sedimentary history of a small lowland catchment in Central England', *Quaternary Research* 10: 281–91.

Brown, A. G. and Keough, M. K. (1992a) 'Palaeochannels and palaeolandsurfaces: the geoarchaeological potential of some midland (U.K.) floodplains', in S. Needham and M. Macklin (eds) *Archaeology Under Alluvium*, Oxford: Oxbow Books: 185–96.

Brown, A. G. and Keough, M. K. (1992b) 'Holocene floodplain metamorphosis in the East Midlands, United Kingdom', *Geomorphology* 4: 433–45.

Brown, A. G., Keough, M. K. and Rice, R. J. (1994) 'Floodplain evolution in the East Midlands, United Kingdom: the Lateglacial and Flandrian alluvial record from the Soar and Nene valleys', *Philosophical Transactions of the Royal Society, Series A* 348: 261–93.

Brown, D. A. (1984) 'Prospects and limits of a phytolith key for grasses in the central US', *Journal of Archaeological Science* 11: 345–68.

Buckland, P. C. (1979) *Thorne Moors: A Palaeoecological Study of a Bronze Age Site*, Occasional Paper No. 8, Birmingham: Department of Geography.

Buckland, P. C. and Dinnin, M. H. (1992) 'Peatlands and floodplains: the loss of a major palaeontological resource', in *Conserving Our Landscape, Proceedings of a Conference at Crewe*, London: English Nature: 145–50.

Buckland, P. C. and Edwards, K. J. (1984) 'The longevity of pastoral episodes of clearance activity in pollen diagrams: the role of post-occupation grazing', *Journal of Biogeography* 11: 243–49.

Buckland, P. C. and Kenward, H. K. (1973) 'Thorne Moor: a palaeoecological study of a Bronze Age site', *Nature* 241: 405–6.

Bullock, P., Federoff, N., Jongerius, A., Stoops, G., Tursina, T. and Babel, V. (eds) (1985) *Handbook for Soil Thin Section Description*, Wolverhampton: Waine Publications, International Society of Soil Science.

Burrin, P. J. and Scaife, R. G. (1984) 'Aspects of Holocene valley sedimentation and floodplain development in southern England', *Proceedings of the Geologists Association* 95: 81–96.

Burrin, P. J. and Scaife, R. G. (1988) 'Environmental thresholds, catastrophe theory and landscape sensitivity: the relevance to the impact of man on valley alluviations', in J. L. Bintliff, D. A. Davidson and E. G. Grant (eds) *Conceptual Issues in Environmental Archaeology*, Edinburgh: Edinburgh University Press: 211–32.

Butzer, K. W. (1964) *Environment and Archaeology*, London: Methuen.

Butzer, K. W. (1982) *Archaeology as Human Ecology*, Cambridge: Cambridge University Press.

Casteel, R. W. (1976) *Fish Remains in Archaeology and Palaeo-environmental Studies*, New York: Academic Press.

Catt, J. (1986) *Soils and Quaternary Geology: A Handbook for Field Scientists*, Oxford: Clarendon Press.

Chambers, F. M. (ed.) (1993) *Climate Change and Human Impact on the Landscape*, London: Chapman and Hall.

Cheetham, G. H. (1976) 'Palaeohydraulic investigations of river terrace gravels', in D. A. Davidson and M. O. Shackley (eds) *Geoarchaeology*, London: Duckworth: 335–46.

Clarke, D. L. (1972) *Models in Archaeology*, London: Methuen.

Coles, B. (ed.) (1992) *The Wetland Revolution in Prehistory*, Exeter: Prehistoric Society and Wetland Archaeological Research Project.

Coles, B. and Coles, J. (1986) *Sweet Track to Glastonbury*, London: Thames and Hudson.

Coles, G. M. (1989) 'A note on the systematic recording of organic-walled microfossils (other than pollen and spores) found in archaeological and Quaternary palynological preparations', *Circaea* 7: 103–11.

Coope, G. R. (1986) 'Coleopteran analysis', in B. Berglund (ed.) *Handbook of Holocene Palaeoecology and Palaeohydrology*, Chichester: Wiley: 703–14.

Cornwall, I. W. (1956) *Bones for the Archaeologist*, London: Phoenix House.

Cornwall, I. W. (1958) *Soils for the Archaeologist*, London: Phoenix House.

Courty, M. A., Goldberg, P. and Macphail, R. (1989) *Soils and Micromorphology in Archaeology*, Cambridge: Cambridge University Press.

Cox, M., Straker, V. and Taylor, D. (1995) *Wetlands: Archaeology and Nature Conservation*, London: HMSO.

Crosby, A. W. (1986) *Ecological Imperialism: The Biological Expansion of Europe 900–1900*, Cambridge: Cambridge University Press.

Cutter, D. F., Rudall, P. J., Gasson, P. E. and Gale, R. M. O. (1987) *Root Identification Manual of Trees and Shrubs*, London: Chapman Hall.

Davis, S. J. M. (1987) *The Archaeology of Animals*, London: Batsford.

Dennell, R. W. (1987) 'Geography and Prehistoric subsistence', in J. M. Wagstaff (ed.) *Landscape and Culture*, Oxford: Blackwell: 56–76.

Dickson, C. A. (1970) 'The study of plant macrofossils in British Quaternary deposits', in D. Walker and R. G. West (eds) *Studies in the Vegetational History of the British Isles*, Cambridge: Cambridge University Press: 233–54.

Dimbleby, G. W. (1974) 'The legacy of prehistoric man', in A. Warren and F. B. Goldsmith (eds) *Conservation in Practice*, Chichester: Wiley: 279–90.

Dimbleby, G. W. (1985) *The Palynology of Archaeological Sites*, London: Academic Press.

Ellis, C. and Brown, A. G. (1998) 'The archaeomagnetic dating of palaeochannel sediments: data from the medieval channel fills at Hemington, Leicestershire', *Journal of Archaeological Science* 25: 149–63.

Evans, J. G. (1972) *Land Snails in Archaeology*, London: Seminar Press.

Evans, J. G., Davies, P., Mount, R. and Williams, D. (1992) 'Molluscan taxocenes from Holocene overbank alluvium in southern central England', in S. Needham and M. Macklin (eds) *Archaeology Under Alluvium*, Oxford: Oxbow Books: 65–74.

Faegri, K. and Iversen, J. (1991) *Textbook of Pollen Analysis*, Oxford: Blackwell.

Fieller, N. R. J., Flenley, E. C., Gilbertson, D. D. and Hunt, C. O. (1990) 'The description and classification of grain size data from ancient and modern shoreline sands at Lepcis Magna using log-skew Laplace distributions', *Libyan Studies* 21: 49–59.

Fieller, N. R. J., Gilbertson, D. D., Griffin, C. M., Briggs, D. J. and Jenkinson, R. D. S. (1992) 'The statistical modelling of grain size distributions of cave sediments using log-skew Laplace distributions: Creswell Crags near Sheffield, England', *Journal of Archaeological Science* 19: 129–50.

Fitzpatrick, E. A. (1984) *Micromorphology of Soil*, London: Chapman Hall.

Flower, R. J. and Batterbee, R. N. (1983) 'Diatom evidence for recent acidification of two Scottish lochs', *Nature* 305: 130–32.

Foged, N. (1978) *Diatom Analysis. The Archaeology of Svendborg, Denmark No. 1*, Odense: Odense University Press.

Foster, I. D. L., Grew, R. and Dearing, J. A. (1990) 'Magnitude and frequency of sediment transport in agricultural catchments: a paired lake catchment study in Midland England', in J. Boardman, I. D. L. Foster and J. A. Dearing (eds) *Soil Erosion on Agricultural Land*, Chichester: Wiley: 28–35.

French, C. A. I. (1990) 'Neolithic soils, middens and alluvium in the lower Welland valley', *Oxford Journal of Archaeology* 9: 305–11.

Frenzel, B. (ed.) (1991) *Evaluation of Climate Proxy Data in Relation to the European Holocene, Special Issue European Social Fund Project: European Palaeoclimate and Man*, Strasbourg: European Science Foundation.

Frey, D. G. (1964) 'Remains of animals in Quaternary lake and bog sediments', *Arch. Hydrobiol. Beih. Ergebn. Limnol.* 2: 1–114.

Frey, D. G. (1986) 'Cladoceran analysis', in B. Berglund (ed.) *Handbook of Holocene Palaeoecology and Palaeohydrology*, Chichester: Wiley: 667–92.

Fritts, H. C. (1976) *Tree Rings and Climate*, New York: Academic Press.

Gale, S. J., Gilbertson, D. D. and Hunt, C. O. (1986) 'ULVS XII: The infill sequence and water carrying capacity of an ancient irrigation channel, Wadi Gobbeen, Tripolitania', *Libyan Studies* 17: 1–5.

Gilbertson, D. D. and Jenkinson, R. D. S. (1984) *In The Shadow of Extinction: A Quaternary Archaeology and Palaeoecology of the Lake, Fissures and Smaller Caves at Creswell Crags SSSI*, Sheffield: Sheffield University, Department of Prehistory and Archaeology.

Girling, M. A. (1988) 'The bark beetle *Scolytus scolytus* (Fabricius) and the possible role of elm disease in the early Neolithic', in M. Jones (ed.) *Archaeology and the Flora of the British Isles*, Oxford: Oxford University Committee for Archaeology: 34–38.

Goransson, H. (1987) *Neolithic Man and the Forest Environment around Alvastra Pile Dwelling*, Monograph in North-European Archaeology No. 20, Lund: Laboratory of Quaternary Biology.

Greig, J. R. A. (1982) 'Past and present lime woods in Europe', in S. Limbrey and M. Bell (eds) *Archaeological Aspects of Woodland Ecology*, Oxford: British Archaeological Reports, International Series 146: 23–56.

Grigson, C. (1978) 'Towards a blueprint for animal bone reports in archaeology', in D. R. Brothwell, K. D. Thomas and J. Clutton-Brock (eds) *Research Problems in Zooarchaeology*, Occasional Paper No. 3, London: Institute of Archaeology: 38–46.

Grosse-Brauckmann, G. (1986) 'Analysis of vegetative plant macrofossils', in B. Berglund (ed.) *Handbook of Holocene Palaeoecology and Palaeohydrology*, Chichester: Wiley: 591–618.

GUESS version 1.1 (1986) *OPCN Wood Databases*, Raleigh: North Carolina State University, Department of Wood and Paper Science.

Haggett, P. (1965) *Locational Analysis in Human Geography*, London: Arnold.

Haworth, E. (1976) 'Two lateglacial (Late Devensian) diatom assemblages profiles from northern Scotland', *New Phytologist* 77: 227–56.

Hewitt, K. (1983) *Interpretations of Calamity*, London: Allen and Unwin.

Hodder, I. and Orton, C. (1976) *Spatial Analysis in Archaeology*, Cambridge: Cambridge University Press.

Hoffman, W. (1986) 'Chironomid analysis', in B. Berglund (ed.) *Handbook of Holocene Palaeoecology and Palaeohydrology*, Chichester: Wiley: 715–28.

Hunt, C. O., Mattingly, D. J., Gilbertson, D. D., Dore, J. W., Barker, G. W. W., Burns, J. R., Fleming, A. M. and van der Veen, M. (1986) 'ULVS XIII: Interdisciplinary approaches to ancient farming in the Wadi Mansur, Tripolitania', *Libyan Studies* 17: 7–47.

Ingold, T. (1986) *The Appropriation of Nature*, Manchester: Manchester University Press.

Jacobsen, G. L. and Bradshaw, R. W. H. (1981) 'The selection of sites for palaeovegetation studies', *Quaternary Research* 16: 80–96.

Jones, R. L. and Keen, D. H. (1993) *Pleistocene Environments in the British Isles*, London: Chapman and Hall.

Keeley, H. C. (1981) 'Recent work using soil phosphorous analysis in archaeological prospection', *Revue d'Archéometrie* 11: 89–95.

Kemp, R. A. (1985) *Soil Micromorphology and the Quaternary*, Technical Guide No. 2, Cambridge: Quaternary Research Association.

Klinke, A. (1989) 'The lower Rhine: palaeoecological analysis', in G. E. Petts, H. Moller and A. L. Roux (eds) *Historical Change of Large Alluvial Rivers*, Chichester: Wiley: 183–202.

Lageard, J. G. A., Chambers, F. M. and Thomas, P. A. (1995) 'Recording and reconstruction of wood macrofossils in three-dimensions', *Journal of Archaeological Science* 22: 561–68.

Lambrick, G. and Robinson, M. (1988) 'The development of floodplain grassland in the upper Thames valley', in M. Jones (ed.) *Archaeology and the Flora of the British Isles*, Oxford: Oxford Committee for Archaeology: 55–75.

Legge, A. J. and Rowley-Conwy, P. A. (1988) *Star Carr Revisited*, London: Birkbeck College, Centre for Extra-Mural Studies.

Lewin, J., Macklin, M. G. and Woodward, J. C. (1995) *Mediterranean Quaternary River Environments*, Rotterdam: Balkema.

Limbrey, S. (1975) *Soil Science and Archaeology*, London: Academic Press.

Lowe, M. J. and Walker, M. J. C. (1997) *Reconstructing Quaternary Environments*, second edition, London: Longman.

Lyman, R. L. (1994) *Vertebrate Taphonomy*, Cambridge: Cambridge University Press.

MacKenzie, J. M. (ed.) (1990) *Imperialism in the Natural World*, Manchester: Manchester University Press.

Macklin, G. M. and Lewin, J. (1994) 'Holocene river alluviation in Britain', *Zeitschrift für Geomorphologie* 88: 109–22.

Macphail, R. I. (1981) 'Soil and botanical studies of "dark earth"', in G. W. Dimbleby and M. Jones (eds) *The Environment of Man*, Oxford, British Archaeological Reports, British Series 87: 309–31.

Manchester, K. (1983) *The Archaeology of Disease*, Bradford: Bradford University Press.

Mansell, R. S., Selim, H. M. and Fiskell, J. G. A. (1977) 'Simulated transformation and transport of phosphorus in soil', *Social Science* 124: 102–9.

Martin, P. S. and Klein, R. G. (1984) *Quaternary Extinctions*, Tucson: University of Arizona Press.

Middleton, G. V. (1976) 'Hydraulic interpretation of sand size distributions', *Journal of Geology* 84: 405–26.

Mithen, S. J. (1991) 'Ecological interpretations of palaeolithic art', *Proceedings of the Prehistoric Society* 57: 103–14.

Moore, P. D., Webb, J. A. and Collinson, M. E. (1992) *An Illustrated Guide to Pollen Analysis*, London: Hodder and Stoughton.

Munzel, S. C. (1983) 'Seasonal activities at Umingmak a musk-ox hunting site on Banks island, North West Territories, Canada; with special reference to the bird remains', in J. Clutton-Brock and C. Grigson (eds) *Animals in Archaeology: Hunters and Their Prey*, Oxford: British Archaeological Reports, International Series 163: 249–58.

Needham, S. (1989) 'River valleys as wetlands: the archaeological prospects', in J. M. Coles and B. J. Coles (eds) *The Archaeology of Rural Wetlands*, Exeter: English Heritage and Wetlands Archaeology Research Project: 29–34.

Needham, S. and Macklin, G. M. (1992) *Alluvial Archaeology in Britain*, Oxford: Oxbow Monograph 27.

Osborne, P. J. (1988) 'A late Bronze Age fauna from the river Avon, Warwickshire, England: Its implications for the terrestrial and fluvial environment and for climate', *Journal of Archaeological Science* 15: 715–27.

Page, A. L., Miller, R. H. and Keeney, D. R. (eds) (1982) *Methods of Soil Analysis. Part 2 Chemical and Microbial Properties*, American Society of Agronomy.

Pals, J. P., Buurman, J. and van der Veen, M. (1992) *Festschrift for Van Zeist*, Review of Palynology and Palaeobotany 73.

Pearsall, D. M. (1989) *Palaeoethnobotany: A Handbook of Procedures*, New York: Academic Press.

Petit-Maire, N. and Riser, J. (eds) (1983) *Sahara ou Sahel? Quaternaire Récent du Basin de Taoudenni (Mali)*, Paris: Librairie du Museum.

Pettijohn, F. J. (1949) *Sedimentary Rocks*, New York: Harper and Row.

Pilcher, J. R. (1996) 'The past global (PAGES) project', in J. Branson, A. G. Brown and K. J. Gregory (eds) *Global Continental Changes: the Context of Palaeohydrology*, Special Publication No. 115, London: Geological Society: 251–56.

Piperno, D. R. (1988) *Phytolith Analysis*, San Diego: Academic Press.

Powers, A. H. and Gilbertson, D. D. (1987) 'A simple preparation technique for the study of opal phytoliths from archaeological and Quaternary sediments', *Journal of Archaeological Science* 14: 529–35.

Powers, A. H., Padmore, J. and Gilbertson, D. D. (1989) 'Studies of the late prehistoric and modern opal phytoliths from coastal sand dune and machair in northern Britain', *Journal of Archaeological Science* 16: 27–45.

Purdy, B. (1992) 'Florida's archaeological wet sites', in B. J. Coles (ed.) *The Wetland Revolution in Archaeology*, Exeter: Prehistoric Society and Wetlands Archaeological Research Project: 113–24.

Pyne, S. J. (1982) *Fire in America: A Cultural History of Wildland and Rural Fire*, Princeton, Princeton University Press.

Quine, T. A. (1995) 'Soil analysis and archaeological site formation studies', in A. J. Barham and R. I. Macphail (eds) *Archaeological Sediments and Soils: Analysis, Interpretation and Management*, London: University College London, Institute of Archaeology: 77–98.

Rackham, O. (1980) *Ancient Woodland: Its History, Vegetation and Uses in England*, London: Edward Arnold.

Raikes, R. (1965) 'The Mohenjo-Daro floods', *Antiquity* 39: 196–203.

Raikes, R. (1967) *Water, Weather and Prehistory*, London: Baker.

Reid, C. (1899) *The Origin of the British Flora*, London: Dulau.

Renfrew, C. and Zubrow, E. (eds) (1990) *Ancient Minds: Elements of a Cognitive Archaeology*, Cambridge: Cambridge University Press.

Richards, M. (1996) 'First farmers with no taste for grain', *British Archaeology* 12: 6–7.

Roberts, N. (1983) 'Age, palaeoenvironments and climatic significance of Pleistocene Konya lake, Turkey', *Quaternary Research* 19: 154–71.

Roberts, N. (1998) *The Holocene*, second edition, London: Blackwell.

Robinson, M. A. and Lambrick, G. H. (1984) 'Holocene alluviation and hydrology in the upper Thames basin', *Nature* 308: 809–14.

Rodwell, J. S. (1991–96) *British Plant Communities*, Volumes 1–3, Cambridge: Cambridge University Press.

Roux, A. L., Bravard, J.-P., Amoros, C. and Pautou, G. (1989) 'Ecological changes of the French upper Rhône since 1750', in G. E. Petts, H. Moller and A. L. Roux (eds) *Historical Change of Large Alluvial Rivers*, Chichester: Wiley: 323–50.

Rovner, I. (1971) 'Potential of opal phytoliths for use in palaeoecological reconstruction', *Quaternary Research* 1: 343–59.

Sahlins, M. (1972) *Stone Age Economics*, London: Tavistock Publications.

Salisbury, C. R. (1992) 'The archaeological evidence for palaeochannels in the Trent valley', in S. Needham and G. M. Macklin, *Alluvial Archaeology in Britain*, Oxford: Oxbow Monograph 27: 155–62.

Sangster, A. G. and Dale, H. M. (1964) 'Pollen preservation of under-represented species in fossil spectra', *Canadian Journal of Botany* 42: 437–49.

Schmidt, E. (1972) *Atlas of Animal Bones*, Amsterdam: Elsevier.

Schwartz, G. T. (1967) 'A simplified chemical test for archaeological field work', *Archaeometry* 10: 57–63.

Schweingruber, F. H. (1978) *Microscopic Wood Anatomy* (2nd edition), Teufen: Fluck-Wirth.

Shackleton, N. J. and Opdyke, N. D. (1977) 'Oxygen isotope and palaeomagnetic stratigraphy of Pacific core V28–239: late Pliocene to late Holocene', *Nature* 261: 547–50.

Shanks, M. and Tilley, C. (1987) *Re-constructing Archaeology*, Cambridge: Cambridge University Press.

Shotton, F. W. (1978) 'Archaeological inferences from the study of alluvium in the lower Severn–Avon valleys', in S. Limbrey and J. G. Evans (eds) *The Effects of Man on the Landscape: The Lowland Zone*, London: Council for British Archaeology Research Report 21: 27–32.

Simmons, I. G., Dimbleby, G. W. and Grigson, C. (1981) 'The Mesolithic', in I. G. Simmons and M. J. Tooley (eds) *The Environment in British Prehistory*, London: Duckworth: 82–123.

Smith, A. G., Grigson, C., Hillman, G. and Tooley, M. J. (1981) 'The Neolithic', in I. G. Simmons and M. J. Tooley (eds) *The Environment in British Prehistory*, London: Duckworth: 124–209.

Smithson, F. (1958) 'Grass opal in British soils', *Journal of Soil Science* 9: 148–54.

Sparks, B. W. (1961) 'The ecological interpretation of Quaternary non-marine mollusca', *Proceedings of the Linnean Society* 172: 71–80.

Sparks, B. W. (1969) 'Non-marine mollusca in archaeology', in D. Brothwell and E. Higgs (eds) *Science in Archaeology*, London: Thames and Hudson: 313–24.

Spaulding, W. G., Leopold, E. B. and van Devender, T. R. (1983) 'Late Wisconsin palaeo-ecology of the American South West', in S. C. Porter (ed.) *Late-Quaternary Environments of the United States: Volume 81: the Late Pleistocene*, London: Longman: 259–95.

Spindler, K. (1993) *The Man in the Ice*, London: Weidenfeld and Nicolson.

Starkel, L., Gregory, K. J. and Thornes, J. B. (eds) (1991) *Temperate Palaeohydrology*, Chichester: Wiley.

Stein, J. K. (1983) 'Earthworm activity: a source of potential disturbance of archaeological sites', *American Antiquity* 48: 277–89.

Street-Perrott, F. A., Marchand, D. S., Roberts, N. and Harrison, S. P. (1989) *Global Lake-level Variations from 18,000 to 0 Years Ago: A Palaeoclimatic Analysis*, Virginia: US Department of Energy Report TR046.

Sugita, S. (1994) 'Pollen representation of vegetation in Quaternary sediments: theory and methods in patchy vegetation', *Journal of Ecology* 82: 879–98.

Tauber, H. (1965) 'Differential pollen dispersal and the interpretation of pollen diagrams', *Danmarks Geologiske Undersogelse II*, 89: 1–69.

Taylor, M. (1981) *Wood in Archaeology*, Princes Risborough: Shire Archaeology.

Thomas, J. (1990) 'Silent running: the ills of environmental archaeology', *Scottish Archaeological Review* 7: 2–7.

Thompson, R. and Oldfield, F. (1986) *Environmental Magnetism*, London: Allen and Unwin.

Tolonen, K. (1986) 'Rhizopod analysis', in B. Berglund (ed.) *Handbook of Holocene Palaeoecology and Palaeohydrology*, Chichester: Wiley: 645–66.

Tomlinson, P. and Hall, A. R. (1996) 'A review of the archaeological evidence of food plants for the British Isles: an example of the use of the Archaeobotanical Computer Database (ABCD)', *Internet Archaeology* 1: 5.3 (http://intarch.ac.uk/).

Tubbs, C. (1968) *The New Forest: An Ecological History*, Newton Abbot: David and Charles.

Van der Veen, M., Grant, A. and Barker, G. (1996) 'Romano-Libyan agriculture: crops and animals', in G. Barker, D. Gilbertson, B. Jones and D. Mattingly (G. Barker ed.), *Farming the Desert: the UNESCO Libyan Valleys Archaeological Survey*, Paris: UNESCO, London: Society for Libyan Studies, and Tripoli: Department of Antiquities: 227–63.

Van Geel, B. (1986) 'Application of fungal and algal remains and other macrofossils in palynological analyses', in B. Berglund (ed.) *Handbook of Holocene Palaeoecology and Palaeohydrology*, Chichester: Wiley: 497–506.

Vita-Finzi, C. (1969) *The Mediterranean Valleys: Geological Changes in Historical Times*, Cambridge: Cambridge University Press.

Vita-Finzi, C. (1978) *Archaeological Sites in their Settings*, London: Thames and Hudson.

Walker, D. (1970) 'Direction and rate in some British post-glacial hydroseres', in D. Walker and R. G. West (eds) *Studies in the Vegetational History of the British Isles*, Cambridge: Cambridge University Press: 117–39.

Walker, R. G. (1984) *Facies Models* (2nd edition), Toronto: Geoscience Canada.

Warner, B. G. (1988) 'Methods in Quaternary ecology 5. Testate amoebae (Protozoa)', *Geosciences Canada* 15: 251–60.

Warner, B. G. and Charman, D. J. (1994) 'Holocene changes on a peatland in northwestern Ontario interpreted from testate amoebae (Protozoa) analysis', *Boreas* 23: 270–79.

Weigelt, J. (1989) *Recent Vertebrate Carcasses and their Paleobiological Implications*, translated from the original (1927) by J. Schafer, Chicago: University of Chicago Press.

West, R. G. (1977) *Pleistocene Geology and Biology*, London: Longman.

Wheeler, A. (1977) 'The origin and distribution of the freshwater fishes of the British Isles', *Journal of Biogeography* 4: 1–24.

Williams, M. A. J., Dunkley, D. L., De Deckker, P., Kershaw, A. P. and Stokes, T. (1993) *Quaternary Environments*, London: Edward Arnold.

Woodward, J., Lewin, J. and Macklin, M. G. (eds) (1995) *Mediterranean Quaternary River Environments*, Rotterdam: Balkema.

Zimmerman, E. W. (1951) *World Resources and Industries*, New York: Harper.

Zvelebil, M. (1994) 'Plant use in the Mesolithic and its role in the transition to farming', *Proceedings of the Prehistoric Society* 60: 35–74.

SELECT BIBLIOGRAPHY

There are a number of textbooks on environmental archaeology but they are all rather dated now, which is not surprising due to the fast-changing nature of the subject over the last two decades. The recent books divide into two groups, those on Quaternary Palaeoenvironments and specialist texts on selected techniques or groups of techniques. In the former category there are now some excellent books for the British Isles, including Bell and Walker (1992), Jones and Keen (1993) and Chambers (1993). An excellent global perspective is given by Williams *et al.* (1993). The techniques-oriented texts are cited in the main body of this chapter but reviews of techniques applicable to certain environments exist and can be helpful, examples being Brown (1997) for alluvial environments or Cox *et al.* (1995) for wetlands, and there are several manuals for different types of environmental data, good examples being Lyman (1994) for vertebrate taphonomy or Courty *et al.* (1989) for soils.

In addition there are now a number of regional syntheses which deal with palaeobotanical or general Quaternary and/or geoarchaeological studies, two obvious examples being a palynological review of Europe or Berglund *et al.* (1996) and Quaternary river studies in the Mediterranean by Lewin *et al.* (1995).

7

STUDYING PEOPLE

Simon Hillson

INTRODUCTION

This chapter is about the ways in which the physical remains of people can be studied and interpreted. Its aims are to outline the types of information that may be derived from the study of human remains; to show how they relate to the biology of the once-living people that they represent; to introduce enough of the methodology to allow a critical appraisal of reported results; and to assess the archaeological relevance of the results.

FORMS OF BURIAL

The archaeological record shows a variety of methods for disposing of the dead. Today's most common methods, *inhumation* and *cremation*, are also the most common in Antiquity, but many different rituals and processes can take place before bodies end up in the ground or the fire. In some cultures the dead are exposed before eventual disposal either on the ground or on a raised platform, the soft tissue allowed to decompose, and the bones and teeth then collected for burial: placed in a jar, in an earth grave, or a chamber which contains the remains of other individuals. Such exposure results in the loss of bones and may cause some weathering even before they are buried.

In inhumations, the body may have been buried straight in the ground, it may originally have been wrapped in fabric or skin, or it may have been encased in a coffin. Burials without a coffin may be extended (with trunk and legs straight out), flexed (somewhat bent at the hip), and contracted or tightly flexed (with the knees tightly tucked up to the chest). Extended inhumations are usually stretched out horizontal in a long grave, but may be vertical in a deep pit. Many burials contain only one individual, but others contain several and, where these have been disturbed, it can be a difficult job to distinguish them. Some cemeteries include burials of men, women and children, whilst others may be adults of one sex only. In some, there is little evidence of organization of burials, whereas others may be highly ordered. In most cemeteries, there is a preferred orientation of graves, but this is not always the case. In addition, human burials are not confined to cemeteries, and settlement sites frequently include them. Burial of children under the house floor is well known in a number of cultures, and isolated human bone or tooth fragments are common finds in the deposits of most archaeological sites.

Cremations are very variable in nature. A modern crematorium uses a high and constant furnace temperature, followed by mechanical crushing of the remaining burned bone to produce a consistent type and quantity of ash. An open pyre cannot be controlled in this way, and the efficiency of crushing by hand after the actual cremation varies greatly. It is therefore not surprising that both fire damage and size of fragments in ancient cremations vary a great deal. Some can yield almost as much information as an inhumation, whilst others contain almost nothing that is recognizable.

PRESERVATION CONDITIONS

Bones and teeth survive well under most conditions of burial – whilst the organic components that they contain are lost to a widely varying extent, the calcium phosphates that make up their mineral component are very stable. After all, teeth can survive in the hostile environment of the mouth for a century or more during life, and conditions in the soil are not so different – abrasive, wet and acidic! The main enemy is acid groundwater, with pH 4 being the critical point, but only peat bogs and the poor soils of moors and heaths become as acid as this and it is only in such situations that the mineral component is lost.

The larger and more robust bones such as the long bones of the legs and arms are usually the best preserved, with the least fragmentation. The small bones of the wrists and ankles are less commonly found, partly due to poorer survival but also poorer recovery during excavation, although the two larger ankle bones (talus and calcaneus) and some of the foot and finger bones do commonly survive. Vertebrae are usually recovered in a moderately complete state, whereas the innominate bones of the pelvis are often present but tend to be heavily fragmented and damaged. The sheet-like bones of the cranial vault survive well, as does the heavily constructed petrous temporal which encases the inner ear – the latter may be the only recognizable part of the skull to survive under severe conditions of burial. Jaws and teeth survive well, but the thin bones of the upper face are often crushed.

Cremation fires have clearly recognizable effects. For example, in teeth which were present in the mouth at the time of death, the enamel rapidly fractures away and almost never survives, but in children whose teeth were still developing inside the jaws there is a measure of protection which can allow the enamel to survive (McKinley 1989, 1994). In the dentine of the tooth roots and the bone of the skeleton, the collagen fibres that they both contain shrink, first producing a characteristic crazing of the surface and then twisting bones out of shape and causing them to fracture into characteristically shaped fragments. The mineral phase of bone and dentine also changes, especially at higher temperatures, and there are some colour changes, although these may be modified during burial in the soil (Shipman *et al.* 1984).

Soft tissues – skin, muscle, tendon, hair, nails, the tissues of the viscera and so on – survive only in archaeological contexts where the fungi and bacteria that would normally break them down are suppressed. Most mummies, for example, are preserved by drying, freezing, freeze-drying, or a combination of these processes. The most dramatic instances probably result from freeze-drying which preserved, for example, several Inuit women and infants who had been buried in a rock crevice at Qilakitsoq, West Greenland, in AD 1475 (Hart Hansen *et al.* 1991). The very cold, dry, conditions preserved not only skin but also internal organs with microscopic histological details intact, hair, and seal-skin clothing. One of the world's oldest mummified bodies, the late neolithic 'Ice Man' from Hauslabjoch in the Ötztal Alps bordering Austria and Italy, was also preserved in dry, cold, conditions, although it was discovered frozen into a glacier. The body was desiccated, hard and leathery, as were the skin clothes worn at the time of death (Spindler 1993). By contrast, the bodies of sixth- to fourth-century BC chieftains buried under mounds in the High Altai mountains of southern Siberia were frozen damp, although they had also been partially mummified before burial: the muscles had been removed through slits in the skin, the cavities stuffed with grass and the skin sewn up again (Rudenko 1970). The body of a young Inca girl, sacrificed and buried at the summit of the volcano Ampato in the Peruvian Andes, was also largely frozen in the intense cold above 20,000 feet, though the head was desiccated (Reinhard 1996).

Survival of soft tissues in Egypt and Nubia is instead due to drying alone, where natural mummies are common at all periods because the hot desert sand dried out the body rapidly. Deliberate mummification as practised in Egypt involved the removal of rapidly perishable organs, followed by drying achieved by covering the body with natron (sodium carbonate), which drew out the water by osmosis. The mummies were then coated with oils and resins, which would have helped to exclude water once the body had been dried. Mummification reached its height during the 21st Dynasty, with careful packing of body spaces, fitting of prostheses and elaborate wrapping (Spencer 1982). The Chinchorro people of Chile had their own unique system of mummification, dating from around 6500 BC. In its most developed form, the body was skinned, its soft tissues removed, and a clay model built up around the skeleton, re-covered with the skin to make a doll-like figure (Arriaza 1995).

Soft tissues are also preserved where waterlogging in the soil excludes oxygen to the extent that microbial activity is greatly reduced. Under these conditions, pre-servation of soft tissues is enhanced if the groundwater is acid or high in phenols. The tissues best preserved in these circumstances are those which contain large proportions of the proteins collagen (which occurs in tendon, bone, dentine and cement) or keratin (which occurs in the surface layers of the skin, in the hair and in the nails). In highly acid conditions, the bones and teeth are lost completely, whilst the soft tissues are well preserved. Still other conditions promote the survival of keratin rather than collagen and here all that remains may be the hair and nails. The peat bogs of north-west Europe have yielded large numbers of 'bog bodies'. In some, preserved in acid peats, the bones and teeth have been entirely lost, leaving the skin, connective tissue and internal organs compressed into a thin layer. Lindow Man, discovered in 1986 in Cheshire, England, was of this type (Stead *et al.* 1986; Turner and Scaife 1996). In other bog bodies, such as that of Tollund Man in Denmark, the bone survived under less acid conditions to give almost perfect preservation (Glob 1969).

The same special conditions that promote soft tissue survival also allow the preservation of clothing, body decoration, hair and so on. The dry conditions of Egypt have preserved the world's earliest linen dress, dating to the I Dynasty at around 3000 BC. In Pazyryk, the most famous of the High Altai barrows, one of the bodies was preserved complete with heavily tattooed skin – vigorous sweeping animal designs in black material introduced through deep pricks in the skin; there were also shirts made of hemp fabric, and various other items of clothing made of woollen felt and serge fabrics. Similar frozen ground conditions preserved the woollen clothes of the Norse inhabitants of Greenland buried in the churchyard of Herjolfsnes, including robes, stockings and hoods (Krogh 1967). Face tattoos, seal-skin parkas, boots and leggings were preserved in the women from Qilakitsoq, and the Ice Man had a leather shirt, loincloth and belt (complete with 'bumbag'), leggings and shoes, with a woven grass cloak, along with his weapons and tools. Clothes have also been preserved in the waterlogged conditions underneath the bronze age barrows of Jutland in Denmark; coffins made from split oak trunks also protected these burials and, whilst little remains of the bodies themselves, a whole variety of woollen cloaks, hats, dresses and footwear has been found (Glob 1974).

CONSERVATION

The conservation of soft tissues is a highly specialist job and a complete body represents a major problem but, fortunately in some ways, most remains are skeletonized. Where they are solid enough, bones and teeth are simply washed after excavation over a fine (1 mm) mesh to catch small fragments. They should be rinsed gently, never soaked, and should ideally be laid out to dry on trays lined with newspaper in an unheated but covered area. Particular care needs to be exercised around the ear region (to retain the tiny ear bones) and the jaws of children (to retain the developing teeth). For fine cleaning, an absolute alcohol or acetone soaked cotton wool bud is best (though both are highly flammable). At some sites, the bones are so fragmentary that conventional cleaning is impossible, and the remaining fragments have to be either lifted along with their supporting matrix, or gently excavated with wooden points before treatment by a conservator. When clean, the bones and teeth need careful storage and, in an ideal world, they would be maintained at the same level of humidity in which they were buried. This is rarely practicable, but the dry air of many heated stores is likely to cause some cracking. Normally, skeletons are packed into stout cardboard boxes with acid-free tissue paper.

COLLECTIONS AND POPULATIONS

Archaeological collections of human remains are often studied in a statistical way – that is, measurements and other observations of the individual remains in the surviving group are used to suggest the morphology, demography and health of the living human population from which they came (see pp. 281–5 below and Chapter 17). To do this it is necessary to assume that the process by which the individuals were selected from the living population was a random one. For this to be so, each person living in the population during a given time period would need to have had an equal chance of dying, then being buried in that cemetery and subsequently being excavated and joining the collection.

There are severe difficulties in this assumption. Reasoning backwards from the remains on the laboratory bench, these are unlikely to include all the remains of all the individuals contained in the cemetery from which they came. It is unusual for a whole site to be excavated and, even if this were the case, the skill of individual excavators varies widely and recovery could well be better in some parts of the site than others. It is not even safe to assume that the process of recovery was a random one: as described above, some elements have a distinctly poorer chance of recovery than others. Even if it were possible to recover all of the remains contained in the cemetery, it would still not include all the individuals buried there because sites become eroded, graves are disturbed (for example during periodic reorganizations or clearances of a cemetery) and the remains are weathered. Once again, many aspects of the process are likely to be non-random as adult remains generally survive better than juvenile remains because they are more robust, and some parts of the skeleton are more heavily constructed, and therefore more resistant, than others.

It is also difficult to determine the extent to which a cemetery really does represent any particular once-living population. The catchment area of a cemetery might well have included more than one distinct population and, if it were in use over some hundreds of years, then the characteristics of the population or populations included could well have changed. It is also not possible to say that the process of burial represents a random selection of individuals from the population/s, because there is ample archaeological evidence throughout the world of funerary segregation of the sexes, children and adults, and different classes (indeed, this is one of the interests in studying cemeteries). Furthermore, the individuals who die, and thus end up in the potential cemetery catchment, are a highly selected sub-set of a population – the very young, the elderly, the infirm and so on (see pp. 281–5).

Thus, it is almost never possible to say that a collection of human remains from a cemetery represents one population only. If, however, the collection is taken as representative of the general condition of populations within a broad area and time period, then this is an arguable position and supporting evidence can be gathered. Comparison with collections from other cemeteries nearby and in widely differing regions will make it possible to suggest the extent to which the collection under study fits into a regional trend. The homogeneity of skeleton size and shape within the collection may suggest the relatedness of the populations included, and the age and sex distributions of the individuals in the collection can yield evidence about their derivation (see p. 283). In all areas of work with human remains, however, a single collection from one cemetery can yield little reliable data on its own. It is when comparisons are made with other sites that more confident interpretations can be made and there is still insufficient attention given to comparative material. It should form part of project design at the planning stage.

SIZE, SHAPE, GENETICS AND POPULATION

There are about two hundred bones and thirty-two teeth in the average adult (Bass 1979; Brothwell 1981; Berkovitz and Moxham 1989; Hillson 1996). Young children have only twenty teeth but considerably more than two hundred separate bone elements, because many bones grow from separate centres. Even in adults, the total number of bones varies because there are many small additional bones that may be found in some people: someone with a really complicated set of these extra bones in their skull might add another thirty or so to the total. Similarly, although the normal number of teeth in the adult is thirty-two, the third molars (wisdom teeth) fail to develop in a large proportion of people, other teeth may be missing, and in some cases there are additional teeth.

All in all, the bones that make up the skeleton and the teeth that make up the dentition vary a great deal in size, shape and detailed features. In any one collection of material, this will partly be due to differences between males and females, or to the presence of both adults and children at different stages of the growth process. Adults of the same sex also, however, show considerable variation amongst themselves because people throughout the world look different and have differently shaped bodies, and this is reflected in their skeletons and dentition. Any one feature in an individual's bones or teeth is controlled by both the set of genes that they have inherited and the environment (in its widest sense) in which they grew up. Whilst physiological features such as blood groups can readily be related to individual genes, independent of environment, anatomical features in general are thought to be related to hundreds of genes and are quite strongly affected by the environment in which they developed. The exact balance between the two controlling factors is uncertain, and must vary for different features between individuals and between populations.

Metrical variation

For over one hundred years, the description and measurement of skull form have been a major area of research. Literally hundreds of measurements have been defined and a range of specialized equipment for taking them developed, including computer-controlled instruments that allow rapid measurement and reduce a skull to a set of three-dimensional coordinates. Until about 1945 many anthropologists believed that any skull could be classified into a 'racial type' on the basis of its form. Few would hold this view now, but most physical anthropologists would accept that there are general patterns in skeletal and dental form amongst the indigenous populations of the world. The largest studies of this kind are those of W. W. Howells (1973, 1989, 1995), who has shown that there are three main groupings of human skull shape: Africa south of the Sahara; Australasia; and Europe, Asia and the Americas combined. These groupings are paralleled quite closely by patterns of tooth crown morphology, and in the distribution of blood groups today. Dental and skeletal form are therefore routinely used to investigate the biological affinities of ancient populations.

One difficulty in analysing skull shape is its sheer complexity. The curved surface, with the variable joints between bones, makes it difficult to define measurements that can be repeated over and over again, and by different researchers, giving the same result. There is also the problem of what the measurements mean and what the most important aspects of skull shape are that need to be captured by them. Some measurements, for example, give general dimensions of major structures, like the cranium or brain box. Others just give the dimensions of individual bones within the main structures of the skull. Traditionally, linear measurements are taken between 'landmarks' defined on the skull surface, and most measurements are taken independent of one another – they literally are just single dimensions. It is possible to consider each one on its own, but to gain a record of overall shape it is clearly better to consider many together. This branch of statistics, termed multivariate analysis, in fact has many of its origins in the study of skull measurements (Marriott 1974).

Karl Pearson invented one of the first multivariate statistics, the coefficient of racial likeness, largely for use on skulls brought back to University College London from the excavations of Flinders Petrie at the end of the nineteenth century. Barnard similarly carried out one of the classical applications of discriminant analysis on four series of Egyptian skulls (Kendall 1975). Discriminant analysis is frequently used nowadays to demonstrate the extent to which groups of skulls can be distinguished solely on the basis of their measurements. The more reliably this can be done, the more divergent the groups as a whole are in skull form. The main difficulty in applying multivariate analysis to archaeological material is that the fragmentary nature of the skeleton often does not allow the same set of measurements to be taken for each individual. This is known as the problem of missing data or incomplete information and, whilst it is not confined to archaeology, causes particularly severe problems because none of the standard multivariate techniques will tolerate any missing data (Scott and Hillson 1988).

Non-metrical variation

Such measurements are known as continuous variants – that is, they vary continuously over a range, and any value of measurement within that range is possible. In addition to continuous variants, there is a large variety of small features in the skeleton and dentition which are not normally measured, termed non-metrical variants. These include anomalies in the sutures of the skull, or the presence of more than one foramen (a hole in a bone for the passage of nerve of blood vessels) where normally there is one, or an extra cusp on a tooth. They are recorded either as present or absent, or by some scale of scores expressing how strongly developed the feature is. Some of the features that are normally classified as non-metrical variants are really nothing more than continuous variants for which it is difficult to define a measurement. Other variants, however, behave in a different way. Whilst they do vary continuously when they are present, they can be absent completely.

The most extensively researched example of this is the presence and size of the third molar. This tooth is the most variable in the dentition, both in size and in form. It is also the tooth which is most often congenitally absent – up to one-third of the population may lack one third molar (or more) (Hillson 1996). This type of variation is called quasi-continuous. There is an underlying variation in third molar size which only becomes expressed when it reaches a certain threshold size. Above the threshold, the teeth vary continuously, whilst below the threshold they are not formed at all. Other dental variants such as presence and form of cusps or fissures in the crown probably function in a similar way, and have been carefully defined as a series of plaster models which form the Arizona State University system (Turner *et al.* 1991).

The interpretation of the frequencies of non-metrical variants is difficult. Dental variants have yielded consistent results, for example showing relationships between groups of Native Americans which are matched by other evidence for their affinities (Hillson 1996). Skeletal variants have so far tended to produce anomalous results, both when compared with skull measurements and other data (Berry and Berry 1967, 1972). It could well be that the systems for scoring them are simply recording the wrong aspect of them. Rather than their presence or absence, the continuous part of their variation might be the important thing.

Facial reconstruction

The underlying skull morphology does have an influence on the form of the face in living people, but the relationship is complex. First attempts to reconstruct facial appearance during the 1880s and 1890s included the skulls of Johann Sebastian Bach and Josef Haydn (Iscan and Helmer 1993) and used drawings based on skull profile, or clay modelling on a cast of the skull. With the addition of photographic superimposition and computer modelling techniques, these have remained the main methods. During the twentieth century, one centre for development of facial reconstruction for forensic purposes has been Russia, with the work of Gerasimov (1971) and colleagues. Their work included reconstructions based on archaeological skulls and, more recently, the British medical artist Neave (Prag and Neave 1997) has reconstructed heads from Egyptian mummies (David 1978; Neave 1979), Lindow Man (Stead *et al.* 1986) and Phillip of Macedon (Prag *et al.* 1984). Most reconstructions use figures for average thickness of soft tissue overlying particular landmarks on the skull, combined with a knowledge of the different muscles and other structures. Tests of reconstructions against photographs in forensic cases have yielded mixed results (Iscan and Helmer 1993) and, as might be expected, whereas the general form of the main features can be established in many cases, the important features of subcutaneous fat, hair, eyebrows, beard, ears, eyes and set of mouth are very difficult to determine. In a forensic case there may be other evidence to suggest these features, but in archaeology this is only possible when the reconstruction is of an identifiable historical figure, with associated portraits or statues.

MEN, WOMEN, AND DON'T KNOWS

All the primates, including humans, show sexual dimorphism, or a difference in form between males and females (Aiello and Dean 1990). It is more prominent amongst the Old World Monkeys, the Great Apes and ourselves, but amongst this group is greatest amongst the baboons and least in humans. Men are none the less noticeably larger and more bulky than women, and men's bones tend to be both bigger and more heavily built, with larger and more sharply demarcated areas for the attachment of bulkier muscles. Men also have larger and more heavily buttressed jaws, containing larger teeth – the canine, for example, is about 6 per cent larger in men than in women.

Length of long bones is highly correlated with stature, and for any long bone there is usually a statistically significant difference between men and women in one population (Brothwell 1981; Sjøvold 1988). There are similarly significant differences in the diameter of long bone shafts at their mid-point, and the major joints at the ends of long bones are also more robustly constructed in men. Measurements of the hip joint are amongst the more reliable discriminators, and the width of the knee joint is also strongly dimorphic, together with the size of the patella. Measurements of joint surfaces are more useful in archaeology than long-bone lengths or mid-shaft diameters, because bones often break along their length.

As well as differences in size and robustness that can be measured, some bones show differences that are evident with the naked eye. The best examples of this are the bones of the pelvis, the sacrum and the two innominate bones, which in humans form a bowl-like structure, broader and shallower in women than in men. The innominate bone in women is more 'stretched out', leading to differences in the shape of the pubis, the narrowness of the sciatic notch and the rotation of the auricular area (the joint surface for the sacrum). Similarly, the sacrum in women is broader and shorter, and its own auricular area is relatively short because of the rotation of the joint. Whilst these differences are easy to see when comparing two bones directly, they are much more difficult to assess objectively. Measurements have been developed but, lacking any well-defined landmarks, they are not very repeatable and measurements of long bones are more reliable.

The skull, including the lower jaw, is another traditional part of the skeleton for sex discrimination. The muscle groups that support the head on the neck are on average bulkier in men than in women and their areas for attachment on the base of the skull are larger and more prominently defined. The larger size of the jaws in men is shown in the greater robustness of the mandible and in measurable differences in the size of the palate. The teeth themselves are larger, if only by fractions of a millimetre, and tooth measurements can distinguish correctly between males and females in more than 80 per cent of cases. The buttressing of the upper jaw, which passes around the side of the eye sockets and up the front of the cranium, or brain box, is more pronounced in men than in women. In addition, the main muscles which operate the jaw, the temporalis and masseter, are bulkier in men than in women and their areas of attachment on the cranium and mandible are more extensive and more strongly defined.

In all of these features, however, there is considerable overlap between men and women, so that any study of human remains will inevitably have a group of individuals whose sex cannot be established. This may be due to damage which has removed the most diagnostic parts, but there are also always some individuals who are genuinely intermediate in form. Because of this, it is unwise to imagine that sex can be 'diagnosed' definitely one way or the other: it is always a balance of probabilities and, for this reason, it is generally better to carry out a statistical study of measurements. The usual technique is discriminant analysis, which makes it possible to assess the reliability of the measurements taken in a 'baseline group' of individuals from the collection under study whose apparent sex is particularly clear from the pelvis and skull. Where the measurements do seem to be reliable discriminators, the same techniques can be used to classify the remaining individuals from their measurements.

One remaining difficulty is in the distinction between skeletons of girls and boys, rather than adults. The main skeletal differences between men and women develop only after puberty and any discrimination developed from measurements on the skeletons of adults could not be applied to children. One answer is to use dental measurements (Hillson 1996) as teeth, once formed, do not change in size – their crowns are full-sized as soon as they are completed and can therefore properly be used to distinguish between males and females even amongst children. Another possibility for sex identification in the remains of children is to attempt to amplify DNA from the X and Y chromosomes, which has now been demonstrated in some archaeological infant remains (see pp. 299–301).

GROWTH AND AGEING

The process of growth in children and young adults leads to a whole range of changes in the skeleton and dentition, which can be seen clearly in archaeological material. A great deal is known, largely from X-ray studies of living children, about the pattern and timing of these changes, and they form the basis of a variety of methods for estimating age at death. On the whole, development of the dentition is thought to vary less from individual to individual than is skeletal growth, and the earlier stages vary less than the later stages of development, so that estimates for young children are more precise than those for older children, adolescents or young adults.

In most parts of the skeleton (the limbs, the vertebral column, the ribcage, and the base of the skull), the bones grow in the first place as cartilage, an organic tissue which is later replaced by bone – a process called endochondral ossification. A few weeks before birth, a small patch of bone starts to form in the 'primary centre' of ossification within the cartilage precursor of the bone and then, in the first year after birth, 'secondary centres' appear for the joint areas at the ends. Some years later, more secondary centres may appear at major bony extensions for the attachment of muscles. Eventually, the whole structure is replaced by bone, except for thin, convoluted plates of cartilage between the various centres of ossification. Growth still occurs in these plates until, at varying ages depending upon which part of the skeleton is involved, they are replaced by bone themselves (Fig. 7.1).

This process is gradual and varies between individuals, not only due to inherited characteristics but also to dietary differences, medical history and so on. It is, however, possible to gain an approximate idea of age at death by comparing the state of fusion of bones in a skeleton with standard tables derived from X-ray studies of living children (Bass 1979; Brothwell 1981). In very young children, where secondary centres are little developed, or so small that they are not easily recovered, it is possible to gain some idea of age at death from the dimensions of the primary centres of ossification of the main long bones. The various elements of growing bones look quite different to the adult form.

Between 1912 and 1938, T. Wingate Todd and colleagues assembled a large collection of skeletons dissected from cadavers from two hospitals in Cleveland, Ohio. This Hamann–Todd collection is most well known for the demonstration of a relationship between age and the form of the bony joint surfaces of the pubic symphysis (the joint at the front of the pelvis). In young individuals, these surfaces are crossed by a series of ridges and furrows (Todd 1920, 1921). With increasing age, the furrows are filled in until a relatively flat, smooth surface is produced, with well-defined edges. These edges then become more prominent, until a marked rim is produced, with a concave surface inside. In later adulthood the surface starts to break down into irregular pits and nodules. Todd's original work has been challenged and new age estimation schemes have been developed. The first of these arose from a study of the bodies of young men shipped home to the USA from the Korean War (McKern and Stewart 1957). Studies of women followed (Gilbert and McKern 1973), and still more studies were carried out by Judy Myers Suchey and colleagues using specimens collected from well-documented cadavers in the Los Angeles County Department of the Chief Medical Examiner-Coroner (Katz and

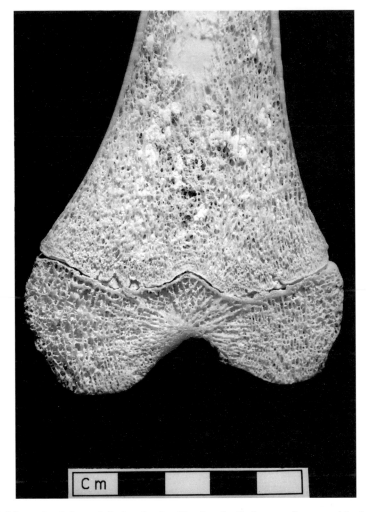

Figure 7.1 Line of epiphyseal fusion in the distal end of a human femur, with the surface of the knee joint downwards. The bone is from a modern anatomy collection, and has been sectioned to show the internal trabecular structure and thin outer jacket of compact bone. Source: S. Hillson.

Suchey 1986; Suchey 1979). A series of casts is available, showing different phases of development for males and females, with affiliated age ranges. These age ranges are still quite large and, as with most methods of ageing adults, only a broad estimate can be achieved.

Other age estimation methods are based on the auricular area of the innominate bone (Lovejoy *et al.* 1985), and the joints between the sternum and ribs (Iscan and Loth 1986a, 1986b), but one traditional method, fusion of the skull sutures, has had a chequered history. Sutures are the closely fitting joints between the flat bones that make up the skull vault. It used to be thought that, with increasing age, these joints were obliterated in a clear sequence. The reliability of this method was challenged by the work on the Korean War dead and, although recent research has taken sutures seriously again (Meindl and Lovejoy 1985), it does not seem possible to make precise estimates of age.

Whilst the formation of tooth crowns and roots takes place in clearly defined stages, eruption (their gradual movement through the jaws and gums into the mouth) is a continuous process, without clear stages, and carries on into adult life. It follows that tooth formation is the more reliable indicator of age at death. The timings of start of formation, completion of the crown, and completion of the root are known for different teeth from X-ray studies of living children, although these are difficult to apply to archaeological material. It is easy to see in archaeological jaws (Fig. 7.2) when the crown or the root have been completed, but these events are difficult to recognize on X-rays and have, in any case, to be interpolated between X-rays taken at intervals of months or years. Nevertheless, standard tables are available, and the development of the two dentitions is regarded as one of the best guides to age at death in children and young adults.

All the deciduous or milk teeth start to form before birth, and all their crowns are completed within the first year after birth. Their roots are completed by two or three years of age. The permanent teeth can be divided into three groups. The first molars start to form just before birth, and the incisors (except the upper second) and canines start early in the first year after birth, their crowns being completed

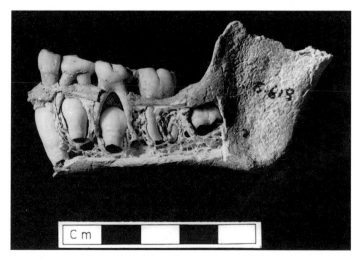

Figure 7.2 Developing teeth in the lower jaw of a child, around 7 years of age at death. The outer plate of bone has been dissected away to show the developing permanent canine, premolars and second molar still in their crypts. The deciduous canine and molars, and the permanent first molar, are erupted and worn. Source: S. Hillson.

279

between two and six years of age. Next come the second upper incisor, the pre-molars and second molars, which start to form from the end of the first year to the third year, their crowns being completed between four and eight years of age. Last are the third molars, or wisdom teeth, which only start to form between seven and fourteen years of age or so, and their growth is so variable that it is difficult to use for precise age estimates, but completion of the third molar roots during the twenties marks the last phase in dental growth.

The timing for dental growth becomes more variable with increasing age, so the earlier forming and erupting teeth show less variation between children than the later forming teeth. Similarly, for any one tooth type, the start of crown formation is less variable than the completion of the crown, which is in turn less variable than the completion of the roots and the timing of the appearance of the tooth crown in the mouth. It follows that age estimates based upon the growth of the crown, in particular, are better than those based upon root formation and eruption of the teeth. The eruption state of teeth in relation to each other, and to the bone of the jaw is, however, still less variable than skeletal growth changes and forms part of several standard age estimation tables (Smith 1991). In practice, the sequence of dental development varies from individual to individual, and some dentitions are difficult to place in one of the standard stages. Decisions of this kind can be made clearer by seriating the dentitions in a collection, from least to most developed.

It is important to realize that standard tables summarize developmental age, which is not the same thing as chronological age. It so happens that the dental development stages correspond with chronological ages more closely than do skeletal development stages, but diet, medical history, genetics and social factors all combine still to produce variation. The age standards have been developed largely from X-ray studies of healthy, well-nourished children from prosperous communities in the USA and Europe. They will not be representative of children in a death assemblage, who are much more likely to have suffered ill health and therefore to have had a more interrupted and slower development. The suggested ages are likely to be too young for them, even if the death assemblage is that of the population in which the growth studies were carried out. This will be doubly so if the archaeological material represents a population which did not have the health care and lavish diet of the middle class in the modern West.

Tooth wear is also an important method of age estimation (Hillson 1996). Molars are normally used, because the extent of 'occlusal attrition' (the wear produced by the upper and lower teeth rubbing together) can be monitored by the changing pattern of internal structure exposed in the facet. Most of the molars have four main cusps, and as the layer of enamel is penetrated, small dots of the yellower dentine show in the facet: first one, then two, three and four (Fig. 7.3). The dots increase in size until two of them coalesce, then three and then all four, so that a 'peninsula' of enamel is isolated in the middle of the facet. Finally, the enamel is

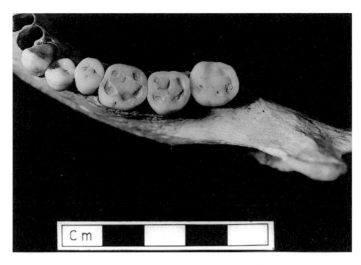

Figure 7.3 Occlusal attrition in lower teeth of an adult; the enamel surfaces of the molars have been worn down flat to expose areas of softer dentine. Source: S. Hillson.

confined to a rim around the circumference of the facet and the softer dentine forms a dished area in the middle. Wear may proceed until only remnants of the roots are left.

One of the most widely used methods for estimating dental attrition age is that of Brothwell (1981): a standard series of diagrams is used to assign molars to one of four stages, which have broad age ranges attached to them. The method was developed for pre-medieval British remains, but has been used throughout the world. Another method is that of Miles (1962), developed for an Anglo-Saxon cemetery in England, involving seriation of jaws in terms of severity of molar occlusal attrition. In the younger individuals, the development of roots, compared between first, second and third molars, can be used to calibrate the rate of attrition. If this rate is assumed to remain constant, then the remainder of individuals in the series can be assigned an age. In spite of this untestable assumption, the Miles method also seems to perform consistently (Kieser *et al.* 1983).

RECONSTRUCTING DEMOGRAPHY

In general biological terms, the course of our lives can thus be split into two phases – growth and maintenance. During the growth phase the skeleton and dentition gradually attain their mature form. During the ensuing maintenance phase the mature forms of the skeleton and dentition are actively maintained and there are progressive changes due to the processes of disease and ageing. In terms of modern populations, the dividing line between growth and maintenance occurs between twenty and thirty years of age. As we have seen, the age estimation methods available for the growth phase yield much more precise ages than those available for the maintenance phase. The difficulties posed by these contrasts are apparent if one compares the graph of age at death for a modern population with the graph estimated for ancient communities from their skeletal and dental remains (Waldron 1994).

Figure 7.4 shows the distribution of age at death for the people of rural Egypt who died during the year 1971–72. First, it must be remembered that, in any age at death graph, the individuals included cannot represent a cross-section of the ages of people in the living population concerned: they are a particular section of the population, and the diseases, accidents and conflict that they died from do not affect all sectors of the population in the same way, and some age groups are more likely to suffer than others. The most common age at death in the graph is between birth and five years – the 'early childhood peak'. This is followed by a period between five and fifty years, when death is much less common – the 'mid-life trough'. After fifty years of age there is a gradual rise to a peak at seventy-five or more years – the 'late adulthood rise'. This pattern is the same the world over. The early childhood peak may be much smaller, but it is always there. The mid-life trough may be deeper, shorter or longer, but it is always followed by a late adulthood rise. This arrangement is not only biological fact, but also makes common sense. Young children are

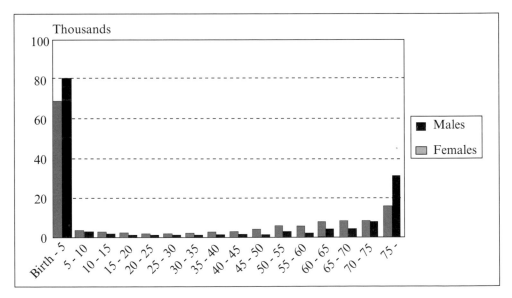

Figure 7.4 Age-at-death distribution for Egypt outside major cities, 1971–72. (Data from *Demographic Yearbook 1974*, 26th issue, New York: United Nations, 1975.) Source: S. Hillson.

vulnerable, especially where there are problems with nutrition and health care, and, similarly, the elderly become progressively more at risk with advancing age. It is apparent that the often-quoted average age at death of a population has little to do with the most likely age at death. For the graph in Figure 7.4 the average age at death is thirty-one years for both males and females – right in the middle of the mid-life trough when fewest people died.

Figure 7.5 compares the modern distribution with a graph of age at death estimated for 941 individuals collected from thirteen ancient Egyptian and Nubian cemeteries. It is an entirely different graph. There are very few children at all, let alone 0–5 year olds. The main peak is between thirty and forty years of age, and the estimated ages fall off rapidly after this. Most of the sites were excavated during the late nineteenth and early twentieth centuries, when recovery methods may not have been ideal, but many more recently excavated sites show a similar pattern, entirely contrary to what might be expected from any study of recent populations. Whilst it must be admitted that the difference could be due to a strongly contrasting biology in the ancient populations from which the cemetery collections were derived, this seems on the face of it to be very unlikely; a simpler explanation is that either the collection studied does not represent the original death assemblage, or that the methods for estimating age are faulty, or both.

Accepting that a death assemblage cannot be a cross-section of the living population, the human contents of a cemetery cannot represent a completely unbiased sample even of the death assemblage. In recent Egypt, it was common practice for young children to be buried under the house instead. This could partly explain the low frequencies of children in ancient cemeteries, but another factor may be the delicate nature of young skeletons and dentitions. They are less well preserved, are harder to recover and harder to study.

What of the paucity of older adult remains? The age standards for them are largely derived from post-mortem material and are thus likely to be applicable to a death assemblage, but the difficulty probably lies in their low precision. In dental attrition, joint surface changes or histological changes, the correlation with age is never very high and the variation between individuals becomes ever larger with increasing age. Age estimates for elderly individuals are therefore much less precise than for younger adults. There is only a limited number of broad age categories that individuals can be fitted into, and the oldest is likely to be very broad indeed – 'forty-five years or older' for example. It is not surprising, therefore, that age estimates for adults tend very much to be underestimates.

The balance between males and females seems to be affected less by archaeological processes. Roughly the same proportions of boys and girls are born in most populations, with a slight preponderance of boys to give ratios from 101:100 up to 113:100. The age at death graph in Figure 7.4 contains 148,463 boys and men, and 149,390 girls or women – a ratio of approximately 100:100. During the same year

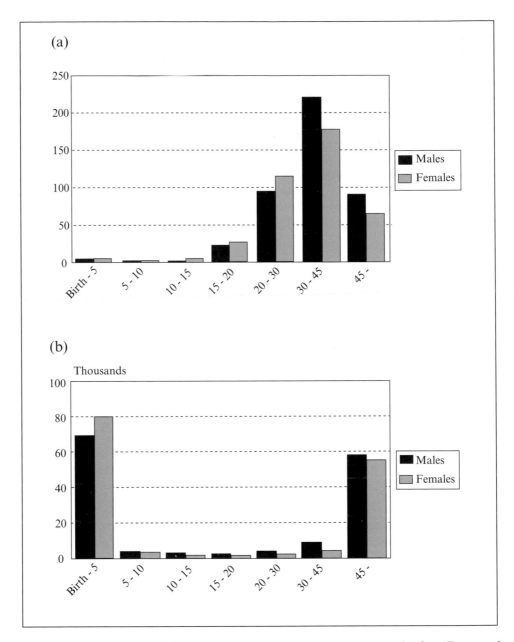

Figure 7.5 (a) Distribution of estimated age at death for thirteen cemeteries from Egypt and Nubia, ranging in context from Predynastic to Roman (data from author's Ph.D. dissertation, University of London). The age categories reflect the variable precision of age estimation methods in archaeology. (b) Data from Figure 7.4 arranged into the same age categories as Figure 7.5(a). Source: S. Hillson.

(1972), 614,159 boys and 573,127 girls were born, or a ratio of nearly 102:100. Girls and women, therefore, seem overall to have had a slightly increased chance of joining the death assemblage. This difference arises in childhood, when young girls tend to die at a slightly higher rate than young boys (the ratio is 100:108 for the under-twenty-year-olds in the graph). At every other stage, girls and women die at lower rates than men (the ratio is 106:100 for individuals twenty years of age or older). Accepting that children are not well represented in archaeological material and that it is difficult, in any case, to sex young individuals, the sex ratio would be expected to show slightly higher proportions of males. For adults in the graph derived from archaeological material in Figure 7.5, there are 436 males and 356 females, a ratio of 110:100. This is not far from the expected figure and, given the vagaries of archaeological recovery, is a close result. The slightly increased proportion of males could be due to the slightly more robust nature of the male skeleton which could lead to better preservation, and it is also possible that there is a bias towards males in the identification of sex from the skeleton.

HEALTH, NUTRITION AND SOCIAL CONDITIONS

Archaeological remains give a variety of information about health, but the most common features relate to injury, joint disease, dental disease and a limited range of infectious diseases.

Trauma

Injuries are amongst the most common conditions seen in ancient skeletons, although they still affect only a limited proportion of the individuals studied at most cemeteries. Of necessity all are injuries that have involved at least some fracturing or cutting of the bones. When this occurs and the individual survives, the break is first immobilized by a *callus* of rapidly formed bone, which is then gradually replaced by normal bone in the process of consolidation, and finally the bone contour is remodelled back to something approaching its original form. The extent to which the original appearance is restored depends largely upon the amount of displacement that occurred on either side of the break (Fig. 7.6). There are many archaeological examples of extensive and massively displaced fractures which have not only consolidated but also remodelled implying that, in spite of severe injuries, the individual has survived for many years afterwards. Similarly, there are many examples of fractures where no healing has taken place, where death presumably occurred soon after the injury was inflicted and, on occasion, it is possible to postulate the events leading up to death (Manchester 1983; Wells 1964).

285

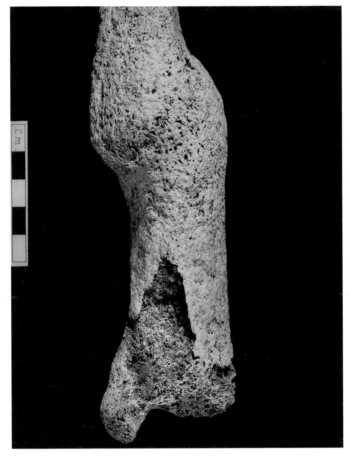

Figure 7.6 Healed fracture in the shaft of a tibia; the bone has been displaced to one side but has healed well. Source: S. Hillson.

Some types of fracture are commonly sustained when someone trips and falls. The end of the radius just above the wrist is frequently broken when the hands are stretched out to stop a fall. This is known as a Colles fracture, after a Dublin surgeon named Abraham Colles who reported it in 1814. A similar type of fall, onto the outstretched arm, is often the cause of a fractured collar bone or clavicle. A stumble may also cause injuries to the tibia, and especially the fibula, just above the hinge joint of the ankle. These are usually termed Pott's fractures, after Percival Pott of St Bartholomew's Hospital, London, who described them in 1769, and are related to strong twisting forces on the foot. They are especially common, for some reason, amongst Anglo-Saxon men in British cemeteries (Wells 1964). In recent times, skull fractures have most commonly been to the lower jaw, followed by upper jaw, cheekbone (zygomatic) and then nose, a pattern relating largely to car injuries

286

in which unsecured front seat occupants are thrown forward against the dashboard. Over the past few decades, cheekbone fractures have become more common and lower jaw fractures less common, and this is thought to represent a rise in violence at a time when seatbelts have become more commonly worn world-wide (Banks 1991). It is clear that interesting social interpretations could be made from the pattern of fractures.

Other injuries seem to be more clearly related to violence inflicted by people on one another. A break halfway down the forearm, involving both radius and ulna, is often caused when the arm is raised above the head to parry a blow. Such fractures are common in the skeletons of both men and women in Nubian cemeteries of a variety of dates (Wells 1964). There is evidence that the lower leg was a common site of injury in fighting with the long, broad sword of early medieval Europe, where the weight and length of the sword facilitated a rapid disabling blow to the leg below the shield. This is seen, for example, in the graves of warriors killed in AD 1361 at the battle of Visby on the island of Gotland (Wells 1964).

Skull fractures are common in some archaeological material, although they are most commonly fractures to the cranial vault rather than the face. In most cases these are well healed, but a proportion were either the fatal injury or occurred in association with other fatal injuries. Some must be due to falls directly onto the head, but most probably result from blows with a stick, club, mace, sword, spear and the like, and the varying outline of the lesion presumably reflects the type of weapon and mode of attack. Occasionally there is clear evidence of cuts from swords and axes, with secondary cracking around the main cut (Courville 1965a, 1965b; Manchester 1983). Where a projectile was the cause of the injury, it sometimes remains embedded in the bone as, for example, in a man buried outside the iron age British hill-fort of Maiden Castle with a Roman *ballista* bolt lodged in his spine (Wheeler 1943), or the tip of a flint arrowhead embedded in a sternum from Stonehenge (Manchester 1983).

One special case of skull injury is 'trephination', where a hole is deliberately cut in the cranial vault (Brothwell and Sandison 1967). This has been described in ancient skulls throughout the world and may have been carried out with a variety of intentions. In many cases it seems likely that some form of medical treatment was being attempted, but other rituals and beliefs may well be involved. Over one half of known trephinations show full healing of the bone, with a smooth remodelled edge to the hole. There may also be more than one – seven healed trephine holes are present in one South American skull.

At first sight, a study of the distribution of fractures amongst ancient people has great potential for elucidating some fundamental social changes, and there are some fascinating stories that can be developed around individual cases or cemeteries, but there are considerable difficulties at a population level. Although they are common relative to, for example, cases of infectious disease, fractures rarely involve more than a few per cent of individuals and, once a collection of skeletons has been broken down into comparable groupings of different sexes and age categories, there are not many cases left in each group. With all the vagaries of archaeological evidence, it is difficult to draw general conclusions from such data.

Joint disease

Joint disease (Rogers and Waldron 1995) is the most common type of pathology seen in archaeological skeletons – in many collections, almost all adults above middle age are affected. The changes can be grouped under two headings: bone proliferation, and erosion.

Bone often proliferates at the margin of the articular cartilage which forms the bearing surface of synovial joints such as the knee or hip, or where the edges of the intervertebral discs join the bodies of the vertebrae in the spine. In both situations, a frill of bone known as an 'osteophyte' runs around the edge of the joint. Osteophytes are very common in archaeological material and they are often found in association with other signs of joint disease, but they may also occur on their own. They increase generally with old age. Outgrowth of bone may also occur (but much less frequently), actually within the fibrous edge of the vertebral discs, to fuse vertebrae into the characteristic 'bamboo spine' of ankylosing spondylitis (AS for short). Such spines are spectacular, but rare finds. Slightly more common is fusion of vertebrae by ossification of the ligaments which run up and down the front of the spine, to give a 'dripping candlewax' appearance which is characteristic of the unrelated condition diffuse idiopathic skeletal hyperostosis (DISH). In this disease, it is also usual for bone to proliferate in the enthesis (the point at which a tendon joins the bone) of the knee and the Achilles tendon. Such 'enthesophytes' may also be found in skeletons where there is no evidence of DISH, and may be an indicator of injury to tendons due to heavy and repeated use of a particular part of the body, but they are little understood.

The word 'erosion' used in joint pathology implies a loss of the compact cortical bone layer which underlies the surface of synovial joints, to expose the underlying spongy trabecular bone. This is difficult to be sure about in archaeology because the ends of long bones, with their thinner layer of cortex, tend to suffer more post-mortem damage than the robust shafts. Erosion (without proliferation) in the hands and feet is typical of the inflammatory condition rheumatoid arthritis (RA), but very few cases have been seen in archaeological material. This may be because bone changes only appear at an advanced stage, or because hands and feet do not survive well archaeologically. Bone is much more commonly lost in a different process which involves the flat plates of bone forming the top and bottom of vertebral bodies, and to which the discs are attached. 'Degeneration of intervertebral discs' is marked by a pitting and roughening of the plates, usually accompanied by proliferation of osteophytes around their edge. This condition is very common in archaeology, especially in the base of the neck and in the lower back. Sometimes, a particular form of indentation in the bone plate, called a Schmorl's node, is caused by the pressure of material bulging out from the disc when it becomes herniated (a similar herniation which causes pain by pressing against a nerve is the injury called 'slipped disc').

The most common joint condition seen in archaeology, however, is the disease of synovial joints known as osteoarthritis (OA), caused by a degradation of the articular cartilage which coats the bony bearing surfaces of the joint. The underlying bone, which is what remains for archaeologists, may show pitting or an abnormality of contour or, when the cartilage has degraded completely, a shiny polished and grooved surface where bone has moved directly on bone. This defect is known as eburnation and is considered to be pathognomonic, or unambiguously diagnostic, of OA (Fig. 7.7). Changes to the joint surface are usually accompanied by osteophytes, but not always. Any of the body's synovial joints may be affected, but OA is particularly common in the hands, the accessory (non-disc) joints of the spine, the joint between clavicle and scapula which forms the point of the shoulder, the base of the big toe, the knee and the hip. The last three are clearly along an axis of heavy, lifelong, mechanical stress, and there is some association of OA in these joints with obesity. In addition, OA becomes progressively more common with increasing age, so it is often regarded as a condition related to progressive wear-and-tear of the joints through life. This has led to the idea that the distribution of OA can be indicative of activity and occupation in ancient people, but there is little clear evidence for a relationship between occupation and OA epidemiology in living populations. Similar claims for the distribution of enthesophytes are also difficult to support. With all the vagaries of derivation of archaeological material, a great deal of caution is needed before interpreting OA data. In addition, although the relationship of OA to age requires the rate of disease to be compared only between equivalent age groups, this relationship is not strong enough for it to be used in age–at–death estimation.

Dental disease

Dental diseases are probably the most common of all in archaeological collections (Hillson 1996). At some sites virtually all adults are to some extent affected, and a proportion of children may be involved as well. The main group of diseases is related to dental plaque, the deposits of bacteria and their products which build up on the surface of teeth. Even with effective brushing, plaque is impossible to remove entirely and, in the absence of any oral hygiene, the deposits grow until

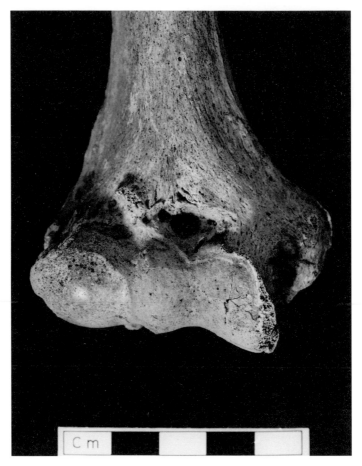

Figure 7.7 Osteoarthritis in an elbow joint; the joint surface to the distal end of the humerus is shown, with a clear area of eburnation and development of osteophytes. Source: S. Hillson.

checked by abrasion from lips, cheeks and tongue. Plaque deposits often become mineralized in life, to produce the hard material called dental calculus or tartar. Calculus deposits are extensive in most archaeological collections, suggesting that oral hygiene was of limited efficiency. The cell walls of the bacteria in plaque are mineralized during the formation of calculus so their outlines can be seen clearly in scanning electron microscope pictures of ancient calculus, and in effect they are fossil bacteria.

Another indicator of the presence of dental plaque is the loss of bone due to periodontal disease. The plaque bacteria provoke a reaction from the body's immune system, and long-standing plaque deposits produce periodic bouts of inflammation in the gums, so that even people with regularly brushed teeth have

290

some evidence of low-level inflammation somewhere in their gums. When these bouts of inflammation reach a certain level, the swelling of the gums allows plaque bacteria to enter the small groove in the gums around the base of the tooth crown. Once this has occurred, more severe bouts of inflammation ('periodontitis') may damage the joints that hold the roots of the teeth into their sockets. When this connection has been broken, the supporting bone around the sockets starts to resorb and, with repeated bouts of periodontitis, the whole jaw is remodelled and eventually the teeth are lost. Once this has happened, the bone heals over to produce a smooth, compact surface. Periodontal disease is the most common cause of tooth loss in living populations and seems to have been a major cause in the past as well – many adult archaeological jaw specimens show larger areas of exposed tooth roots than would normally be expected. When first fully erupted, a less than 1 mm wide band of root is exposed around the base of the crown above the bony socket but, with increasing age, this band increases in width ('growing long in the tooth'). Periodontal disease may in part be the cause of such root exposure, but there is another process involved. As the crowns of the teeth wear, constant adjustments need to be made to keep them in occlusion and all teeth continue to erupt slowly throughout life in order to compensate for the loss of crown height with wear. This also leads to root exposure. In jaws where the pattern of periodontal disease has been relatively even throughout, it can be difficult to distinguish between the effects of bone loss and continued eruption. Fortunately, in many jaws, the pattern of periodontal disease is irregular, affecting the molars more severely and earlier than the incisors, and the irregular bone loss that results can be detected with some confidence.

The most consistently recorded dental disease in archaeological material is dental caries, or tooth decay (Fig. 7.8). The bacteria in the dental plaque live by metabolizing organic components of the mouth fluids, but they also make use of the carbohydrates (sugar and starch) in the food which passes through the mouth. Sugars are small molecules and can diffuse immediately into the plaque, whereas starch is composed of long molecules that cannot enter directly, but it is broken down into sugars by amylase, an enzyme present in the saliva. When the plaque bacteria ferment sugars in order to produce the energy which they need for life, they also produce a by-product – lactic acid. A sugary drink causes a marked phase of plaque acidity, within two minutes, which takes half an hour or so to return to neutrality, whilst starches produce a less marked but longer-lasting acid phase. So, throughout the day, the acid levels in different areas of the plaque deposits fluctuate. During the acid phases, the calcium phosphate mineral of the enamel starts to dissolve, and during the neutral phases, mineral is redeposited in the enamel. This cycle of loss and repair can maintain the surface of the enamel in a steady state but, where the acid phases predominate, there is a net loss of mineral. To start off with, this produces only microscopic changes, but eventually a cavity forms. This cavity may

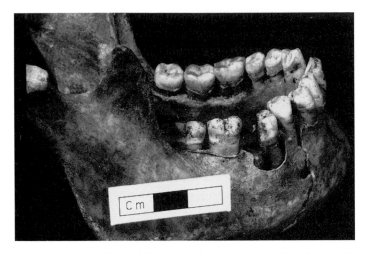

Figure 7.8 Dental caries causing widespread destruction in the first molar of a post-medieval lower jaw from London. Almost half the tooth has been destroyed by the cavity, penetrating to the pulp chamber and causing inflammation of the bone around the apex of the root – this is shown by the loss of bone around the tooth. The teeth also show a line of calculus deposits, following the original position of the gums. It is possible to see a groove-like defect of enamel hypoplasia in the teeth at the front of the jaw. Source: S. Hillson.

grow rapidly, cutting into the enamel, into the dentine and finally exposing the soft tissue of the pulp to infection, but it may also progress very slowly. Indeed, some cavities can be remineralized and stabilized without any surgical intervention.

The distribution of dental caries in a population is related strongly to the pattern of carbohydrate consumption. In most modern populations there is a high incidence of caries, particularly amongst children, which develops mainly within the deep fissures of the molars and in the difficult-to-clean 'contact area' just below the point at which neighbouring teeth meet. A different pattern is found in archaeological remains which date from before the nineteenth century, during which trade in cane sugar developed greatly. The most common form of dental caries in, for example, prehistoric European collections affects particularly the neck of the tooth, where the crown meets the root, and is mainly a disease of adults. This presumably reflects a diet which was high in starch, but low in sugar. Another interesting contrast may be made with adoption or intensification of agriculture – a clear cultural horizon, for example, in North America where the gradual change from fully hunter-gatherer Archaic contexts through to the increasingly maize-cultivating Woodland and Mississippian contexts apparently resulted in greatly increased carbohydrate consumption (see pp. 302–3). This change is marked by a progressive increase in dental caries, and an accompanying change in the pattern of dental attrition (Rose *et al.* 1991).

292

Inflammation of bone

Bone inflammation, or osteitis, is usually divided into 'periostitis' and 'osteo-myelitis' (Ortner and Putschar 1981; Roberts and Manchester 1995). Periostitis involves changes to only the outer, compact, part of a bone, whereas osteomyelitis involves the inner, spongy, part. Both types of inflammation may occur together. Evidence of a generalized, low-level periostitis is very common in some collections of material, with a thin layer of porous new bone on the surface. Its cause is complex and, although some researchers use it as an index of general infectious disease, such bone formation may occur for reasons other than inflammation.

The deeper seated forms of osteomyelitis are more clearly related to infections. Bacteria may enter the bone through a deep wound or a compound fracture (where a bone fragment pierces the skin from inside), or through the pulp chamber in a tooth with a deep carious cavity. In such cases, infection is usually by a broad spectrum of bacteria. In chronic osteomyelitis these are contained by a mass of granulation tissue, around which an area of bone is resorbed. Pus often forms within the mass and, eventually, bone is resorbed around a channel (*cloaca*) through which the pus drains. The area of bone may then heal. One common site of chronic osteomyelitis is in the bone of the jaw, where infection occurs through a pulp chamber exposed by dental caries and 'periapical abscesses' form around the apex of the tooth roots. Another common site is near the cartilage growth plate of bones near the knee in children, where blood-borne pathogens may settle.

Tuberculosis, leprosy and the treponemal diseases such as syphilis and yaws may also cause bone inflammation. Tuberculosis is normally due to infection through inhaled air by the tubercle bacillus *Mycobacterium tuberculosis*, although it may also be caused by eating meat or drinking milk from cattle infected with *Mycobacterium bovis*. The skeleton is only one of a number of parts of the body which may be affected and the osteitis caused progresses slowly, in particular foci. One common focus is the spine, where bone is replaced by fibrous tissue and the vertebrae collapse to produce the well-known hump-backed condition. Other parts of the skeleton may also be affected, such as the ends of long bones and the hip bones. Tuberculosis can be one of the more difficult diseases to diagnose in the skeleton because there are so many alternative possibilities to consider. In addition, spinal tuberculosis is predominantly a disease of children, and children's remains, as has been pointed out, are less well preserved than those of adults. Tuberculosis has been tentatively diagnosed in prehistoric European material and clear evidence of the disease has been found in the soft tissues of Egyptian mummies. It is thought that the Roman Empire was an important factor in the later spread of tuberculosis through the Old World.

Leprosy is caused by an infection of the similar bacterium *M. leprae*. It is primarily an infection of the skin and nervous system, but bones are involved due to paralysis of muscles (which causes bones to remodel in response to new stresses) and blood vessels that supply bones, and because the lack of sensitivity makes the extremities more prone to injury. Not all forms of leprosy produce bony changes. Where they do occur, the earliest involve loss of bone from the hard palate, the upper jaw and floor of the nose. Foot and finger bones may also be deformed, although these are harder to spot in fragmentary archaeological material. It seems likely that leprosy spread widely through Europe during the Roman period.

The treponematoses are a group of diseases due to infection by a genus (*Treponema*) of spirochaete bacteria. Today, the treponematoses include endemic syphilis, venereal syphilis, yaws and pinta. Similar diseases existed in ancient times, but it is not clear that they took exactly the same forms as today. The skeleton is only one part of the body to be involved. Small colonies of bacteria form, causing damage to any tissue with which they are in contact. The skull and the long bones are best for diagnosis and show a range of widespread pitting and cavities. Whilst a diagnosis of treponematosis may be quite clear, the distinction between the different types can be difficult. There are many different opinions upon the origins of the different forms.

By and large, good archaeological evidence of these major infectious diseases is much less common than either diffuse low-level periostitis or diseases of the joints, teeth and fractures. Certain sites may produce a great deal of evidence, such as the famous medieval leper hospital cemetery near Naestved in Denmark (Møller Christensen 1961), but a routine report will only rarely produce specimens of this kind.

THE MICROSCOPE AND HUMAN REMAINS

Bone

In life, bone is as alive as the rest of the body, with living cells, blood vessels and nerves (if a bone breaks, it hurts and bleeds), and as with most of the tissues of the body, bone is involved in a continuous process of tissue turnover. One type of specialist cell constantly cuts tunnels through the bone, whilst another group of cells follows behind and replaces it with new bone. A microscope section of bone shows rounded structures, made up of concentric layers, called osteones (also called osteons or Haversian systems), which represent this turnover process. Bone turn-over is involved in growth and is particularly important in the remodelling which takes place in, for example, the development of dimorphic features in the skull, pelvis and long bone shafts with sexual maturity. Bone turnover is also involved in the remodelling which takes place with disease. The pattern of osteones changes gradually with age and there have been several studies which suggest that the process may be used for estimating age at death.

The greatest difficulty for the microscopy of archaeological bone involves the changes that have taken place since death (Bell and Jones 1991). Under the microscope, damage is seen mostly as small zones of altered mineralization called diagenetic foci. Often these are scattered quite widely through a bone section, but they may be packed close together so that the whole section is altered. The foci are sometimes poorly mineralized, but may also be more heavily mineralized than the surrounding bone, and it is not clear what they represent. The surface appearance of archaeological bone varies a good deal from site to site, but is not a good guide to the internal preservation. Experimental evidence suggests that the foci start to form soon after death, and the degree of alteration is not related to the time spent in the ground. The two-thirds or so by weight of fresh bone which is mineral remains predominantly calcium phosphate, but the precise mineral phase may change. Cells and their contents are thought to decompose rapidly, although there is some evidence that fragments of cell wall may survive. Bone also contains a proportion of non-cellular organic material, in particular collagen, which is lost gradually, although the rate of loss is highly variable between sites (see pp. 302–3).

Dental tissues

Like bone, the teeth are made of mineralized tissues (Hillson 1996). They are more heavily mineralized than bone, particularly the dental enamel which coats the surface of tooth crowns and is almost entirely mineral. The main difference, however, is that the dental tissues – enamel, dentine and cement – do not turn over. Once formed, they may remain little changed throughout life. This means that the process of growth is preserved in their structure, giving rise to many different avenues of research.

Dental *enamel* is a dead tissue, even in living people. It has no cells and almost no organic content, and consists of microscopic bundles of tiny crystals, woven together into a strong structure. In life it is immensely resistant to the wear and tear, damp and widely varying acidity of the mouth. After death, it is the most resistant part of the body in all except highly acid conditions of burial and is therefore by far the most studied microscopically. *Dentine*, which makes up the main internal structure of the tooth and its roots, has a somewhat higher mineral content than bone, but similarly has a considerable proportion of collagen and other organic components. The cells of dentine do not, in fact, reside within the tissue, but line the pulp chamber and send long processes down microscopic tubules which run through almost to the boundary with the enamel or cement. *Cement*, which is much more similar to bone in composition, also has cells incorporated into its structure. The cement coats the surface of the roots and functions as an anchor for the collagen fibres of the ligament that binds the tooth into its socket. Collagen therefore dominates the structure of cement, which is built up from mats of fine fibres and includes large fibres from the ligament. Both dentine and cement are modified, after death, in a similar way to bone (Bell *et al.* 1991). They can show similarly large disruption, but the cap of enamel over the crown has a protective effect and the dentine underneath is often relatively well preserved even if the roots and bones are heavily damaged.

Dental enamel growth and enamel hypoplasia

A section through a tooth crown (Fig. 7.9) shows clearly the strongly layered structure of the enamel (Hillson 1996). The lines of the layering are regularly spaced and represent rhythms (twenty-four hourly and roughly weekly) in enamel deposition, so a count from the first layers under the cusp, down to the last layers at the base of the crown, gives an estimate of the time taken for the crown to form. The pattern of layers (which vary in prominence) can also be matched in all teeth which were being formed at the same time – somewhat like dendrochronology – and can be used to identify teeth belonging to one individual. It may even be possible to identify the point of birth as a particularly prominent layer under the first molar cusps and, when a child died before its crowns were complete, it is possible to produce a high precision age estimate by counting to the point at which formation was interrupted. Some anthropologists have defined a particularly prominent category of layers known as Wilson bands, which are believed to be caused by disturbances to growth such as disease or dietary deficiency.

It is possible to study part of the enamel layering without sectioning, because some of the internal growth layers outcrop on the crown surface to create a pattern of grooves (Fig. 7.10). These so-called 'perikyma grooves' can be seen clearly under low magnification (some even with the naked eye) in obliquely angled light. Wear destroys them, so specimens are best selected from young individuals, although the deeper grooves can be seen in protected areas of the crowns of quite worn teeth. Counts of perikyma grooves can be used for estimating age in children, in the same way as internal enamel layering can, as discussed previously. Disturbance to growth causes variation in groove spacing which can be seen clearly under low magnification. Larger variations of this kind produce a defect visible to the naked eye which is routinely diagnosed in archaeological dentitions as 'enamel hypoplasia'. Both clinical and experimental studies have linked hypoplasia to childhood fevers and dietary deficiencies and the distribution of hypoplasia in the teeth of different archaeological sites is used as an indicator of general health. It is suggested, for

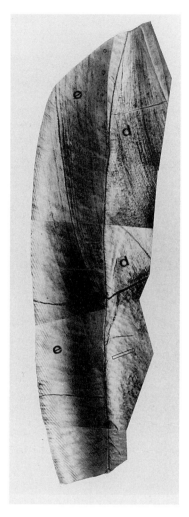

Figure 7.9 Section of part of a canine tooth crown from the site of Kerma, Nubia, built up from a mosaic of photomicrographs, taken in a polarizing microscope. The worn occlusal surface of the tooth is to the top, exposing some of the dentine (labelled 'd') which forms most of the right of the picture. The enamel (labelled 'e') coating the crown surface is on the left, with growth layers angling up towards the surface. Source: S. Hillson.

example, that the increasing rate of hypoplasia from Archaic to Woodland and Mississippian cultural contexts in North America represents the effect of larger settled communities (enhancing the spread of infectious disease) and the risk of reliance on one single agricultural food source (Goodman and Armelagos 1985; Goodman *et al.* 1984).

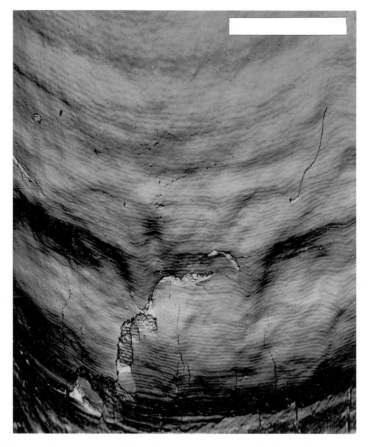

Figure 7.10 Enamel hypoplasia of the furrow type in a molar from Kerma (scanning electron micrograph of an epoxy resin replica of the crown surface). The fine grooves are the normal growth layering of the crown, but superimposed over it are large furrow-like defects formed by a combination of the finer grooves. The scale bar is 1 mm. Source: S. Hillson.

Histological age estimation in adults

Since the 1950s several age-at-death estimation techniques have been developed for forensic purposes, based on a number of age-related changes seen in tooth sections (Hillson 1996):

1 Secondary dentine deposition. After the root has been completed, dentine continues to be deposited at a slow rate to line the pulp chamber. In addition, patches of secondary dentine are laid down to seal the inner ends of dentinal tubules whose outer ends have been exposed by attrition and caries. Both processes lead to a gradual infilling of the pulp chamber with increasing age.

2 Root dentine sclerosis. The dentinal tubules are progressively filled in, starting

298

at the apex of the root, by heavily mineralized material. The area of infilled tubules appears transparent in a section of fresh dentine, and the size of this transparent area is correlated with the age of a patient when a tooth was extracted.

3 Cement deposition. As cement is deposited regularly throughout life, the thickness of the layer over the root becomes progressively greater. A number of studies have suggested that annual layers can be recognized in sections of human enamel, and that layer counts correspond closely to age at death. Other studies have yielded less encouraging results and a great deal must depend on the methodology used, because the cement layering in human teeth is very fine indeed.

It must be stressed that, although these changes do show correlations with age, the correlations are not very strong and vary from tooth to tooth and from study to study. They have, however, been developed into age estimation methods which do not perform much less well than the more traditional macroscopic techniques described earlier. These methods have been used widely for forensic purposes but, apart from a few experiments, have not been widely applied in archaeology because of the need for sectioning and, in particular, the highly variable preservation of dentine and cement.

'ANCIENT BIOMOLECULES'

Biological polymers

A polymer is a large molecule built up from sequences of small structural units joined together. Proteins are polymers whose structural units are the amino acids (over a hundred amino acids are known, but only twenty or so occur in mammal proteins). The most common protein in bone, at about 20 per cent by weight, is collagen. The nucleic acids (including DNA) are polymers with helical backbones to which are attached units called bases. DNA is responsible for defining the arrangement of amino acids in the proteins which are produced by living cells. Bases are arranged into sequences which encode the genes, each defining a particular protein.

Since 1980, DNA has become the centre of a great deal of attention (Brown and Brown 1994). DNA molecules are large polymers which reside in the nucleus and mitochondria of living cells (Strachan and Read 1996). Each strand of DNA has a 'backbone' to which is attached a sequence of 'bases'. These sequences are built up from an alphabet of different bases (adenine, guanine, cytosine and thymine), whose order defines the proteins for which different genes in each DNA molecule are

299

responsible. In living cells, DNA is usually found as a 'duplex' in which two complementary strands are twisted together, with each adenine on one strand matched by a thymine on the other and each cytosine similarly matched by a guanine. If the sequence of one strand in the duplex is known, then the sequence of the other strand can always be inferred. The length of DNA molecules is usually expressed as a count of base pairs in their sequence ('bp', not to be confused with years before present).

Each nucleus of a human cell contains forty-six very large DNA duplex molecules, made visible in stained preparations under the microscope as the twenty-three pairs of chromosomes (Strachan and Read 1996). These molecules vary from 55 million up to 250 million bp in length. In each one, it is thought that only around 30 per cent of the sequence defines genes, of which there may be 3,000 per chromosome – only a small fraction of genes have yet been mapped out (mostly those associated with inherited diseases), although the Human Genome Project aims eventually to produce a complete map. The length of the base sequence which codes for a particular gene is highly variable, but may be 10,000 to 15,000 bp and, in each, only about 10 per cent of this sequence actually codes a protein. Overall, the whole collection of genes, the nuclear genome, contains only one copy, or just a few copies, of each gene.

A living cell also contains many mitochondria, each of which also contains its own entirely separate DNA. Molecules of mitochondrial DNA are circular, with 16,569 bp sequences, known in their entirety and coding for thirty-seven genes (with only a very small proportion of non-coding sequence). Unlike the nuclear genome, there are thousands of copies per cell of these mitochondrial DNA molecules, although they make up only a tiny fraction of the total DNA in the cell as a whole because they are so much smaller. Another difference is that, whilst the nuclear genome is inherited from both mother and father, mitochondrial DNA is only inherited down the maternal line.

Research on DNA has developed on two fronts which are of relevance to human remains in archaeology. One is the invention of DNA-based methods for identifying, sexing and estimating relationships between people, as evidence in forensic cases (Strachan and Read 1996). These are routinely applied to DNA extracted from blood stains, soft tissues and so on. Sex is determined by demonstrating the presence of base sequences in genes specific to the X and Y chromosomes which determine sex, whereas relationships are usually determined by studying parts of the extragenic DNA (the part outside the genes) which have highly repetitive and highly variable sequences. The other major development is the demonstration of DNA survival in forensic bone specimens tens of years old, and in archaeological bones up to 10,000 years old (Hagelberg and Clegg 1991; Hagelberg *et al.* 1989, 1991). Currently, 2 g archaeological bone might yield 1–10 μg (0.000001–0.00001 g) DNA, of which only a few per cent is human and the bulk is bacterial. Most is in fragments of strands less than 300 bp long, and its duplex structure is likely to be much broken-down.

The study of DNA in archaeology has become possible through the invention, in 1986, of the Polymerase Chain Reaction (PCR) technique, which generates many copies of a defined part of the base sequence preserved in a tiny number of surviving DNA fragments. This allows routine laboratory methods to be used for sexing, establishing relationships and so on and, in theory, the technique will work even if only one fragment of a DNA strand containing the target sequence remains in the archaeological specimen. Most work in archaeology has however been carried out on mitochondrial DNA rather than nuclear, because the much greater number of copies makes it more likely that a particular target sequence has been preserved. There have been many problems in developing these methods for archaeology, including difficulties with extraction, with the presence of factors which inhibit PCR reactions and, particularly, with contamination by modern human DNA which is carried on the skin flakes, sweat, and droplets in exhaled air of excavators and laboratory technicians. It is, however, now established that 100 to 400 bp sequences of ancient human DNA can be amplified from bones up to 10,000 years old. This is not possible with all specimens and may even vary between neighbouring skeletons within one site, but generally there is a better chance of extracting DNA from well-preserved bone, rather than poorly preserved (Hagelberg *et al.* 1991). Paradoxically, bone and dentine seem to be better substrates than mummified soft tissues, which are readily contaminated by micro-organisms.

Since the first demonstration of DNA preservation in archaeological bone, it now seems possible to determine sex by distinguishing X and Y chromosomes in ancient DNA extracted from bones and teeth (Stone *et al.* 1996). DNA profiling techniques have been used to identify conclusively the bones of the last Tsar and his family, found in Ekaterinberg in 1991 (Gill *et al.* 1994). Still other work has involved a study of ancient migrations by examining mitochondrial DNA from archaeological bone specimens in North America (Merriwether *et al.* 1992; Stone and Stoneking 1993) and the Pacific (Hagelberg and Clegg 1993).

In addition to this work with human DNA, it now seems possible to extract and amplify the DNA of bacteria which is also preserved in ancient bones. Positive identifications of *M. tuberculosis* and *M. leprae* have been made for DNA extracted from bones showing the pathological changes (see pp. 293–4) expected for tuberculosis and leprosy respectively (Hummel and Herrmann 1995; Taylor *et al.* 1996; Waldron 1996). It is possible that viral DNA may eventually be detected in a similar way. These developments offer an important range of methods for confirming diagnosis in palaeopathology, or for diagnosing those conditions which leave no visible pathological sign in the bone.

Stable isotopes

The calcium phosphate mineral component of bone and dental tissues contains quantities of the element carbon, whilst the proteins present in bone, cement and dentine contain both carbon and nitrogen. The atoms of both elements can exist in a number of states (isotopes), the most famous of which is the radioactive form of carbon, ^{14}C. 'Normal' carbon (98.9 per cent of carbon) is the stable isotope ^{12}C, but there is also another stable isotope ^{13}C which is less abundant (1.1 per cent). For nitrogen, the 'normal' stable isotope is ^{15}N (99.6 per cent of nitrogen) and the other consistently occurring, but less common, stable isotope is ^{14}N (0.4 per cent). The abundance of the stable isotopes of carbon and nitrogen can be measured in collagen extracted from samples of archaeological bone using the technique of mass spectrometry (Ambrose 1993; De Niro 1987; Schwarcz and Schoeninger 1991), to produce the $^{13}C{:}^{12}C$ ratio ($\partial^{13}C$) and the $^{15}N{:}^{14}N$ ratio ($\partial^{15}N$).

Why would this be useful? The ratios of these isotopes in the bones of a particular animal are controlled by their position in the food chain. For example, $\partial^{15}N$ is affected partly by the proportion of nitrogen-fixing plants in the food chain. This could be related to the proportion of legumes in the diet, or the reliance upon marine resources which come from a food chain with blue-green algae at its base. It is also greatly affected by the proportion of protein in the diet – most of which comes from meat consumption. The values for $\partial^{15}N$ are therefore highest in the bones of people (and other animals) relying on marine resources and lower in those who rely mostly on terrestrial resources, and higher in both cases for carnivores than herbivores. In theory, the introduction of legumes into the diet should lower $\partial^{15}N$ values, but it has proved difficult to demonstrate this.

The carbon in collagen also comes mostly from the protein in the diet. $\partial^{13}C$ values are again slightly higher in people whose food is derived mostly from marine sources, but it is also affected by climate (it increases with higher average temperature and sunshine, and decreases with higher rainfall). The largest contrasts are between food chains based upon C4 plants as opposed to C3 plants. C3 plants include all trees and woody shrubs, the grasses from temperate environments and from shaded, woodland habitats; wheat, barley and rice are temperate grasses and so fit into the C3 group. C4 plants comprise the subtropical and tropical grasses, with the exception of those from shaded woodlands; the tropical/subtropical cereals maize, sorghum and millet are of C4 type.

One of the clearest contrasts which such methods can be used to investigate is the gradual adoption and intensification of agriculture in North America (Schwarcz and Schoeninger 1991). It is possible to monitor the greatly increased dependence on maize (a C4 plant) $c.$ AD 900–1000 as opposed to the indigenous gathered food plants (C3), through a clear change in $\partial^{13}C$ values of collagen extracted from human bones. This is paralleled by a simultaneous increase in dental caries and a change in

302

attrition pattern (Rose *et al.* 1991). The advent of beans into the diet at a similar date should have left its trace in the $\partial^{15}N$ values too, but this cannot be detected and it is not yet clear why not. Similar evidence for the adoption of maize has been found in Central and South America, and there is also evidence for the origins of millet cultivation in northern China at around 7000 BP. C4 plants did not form part of early agriculture in Europe and the pattern of carbon and nitrogen isotope values is instead interpreted in terms of the relative balance of marine and terrestrial resources, climate and, in particular, the reliance on meat. Some values for $\partial^{15}N$ in prehistoric European human remains are very high, perhaps indicating a much greater degree of carnivory and lesser reliance on cultivated plant foods than has hitherto been assumed.

It is also possible to determine $\partial^{13}C$ values for the carbon preserved in the mineral of dental enamel. The main difficulty with this is that there may be contamination by secondary carbonate deposition from groundwater, but the better preservation of enamel makes it possible to apply the technique to a wide range of material, for example early hominids from Africa (van der Merwe 1992). Further possibilities lie in comparisons between teeth (representing childhood) and skeleton (representing the condition at the time of death) which may show differences in stable isotope ratios implying a change in diet or movements of people (Sealy *et al.* 1995). Another possibility may be to monitor the effect of weaning, by detecting a decrease in $\partial^{15}N$ from the parts of teeth which were formed whilst a child was breast-feeding, to those parts formed after weaning.

CONCLUSION

Human remains are the closest approach that can be made to people from the past, and it could be argued that they lie at the centre of archaeology. Whenever a large cemetery is excavated, study of the human remains collection (which is, after all, the reason why the cemetery is there) should be fully integrated into the excavation, post-excavation work and report. The biological phenomena described in this chapter need to be interpreted in the light of other archaeological evidence relating to the way of life of the people buried in the cemetery. They also need to be compared between sites before they can tell a story: a few isolated bodies only rarely yield interesting interpretations on their own, so that the collection in any one cemetery must be put into context and the assembly of comparative data is an essential part of any project.

Today, most excavations of human remains take place under rescue conditions, where graves are to be destroyed by building or engineering works, but ideally, plans need to be made in advance for the study and subsequent disposition of the remains, including extensive consultation with concerned religious and cultural groups. Most countries in the world have legal requirements with which the excavators must comply but, in many cases, little distinction is made between the human remains themselves and other grave contents – they are all 'relics'. Many archaeologists feel that the ultimate aim should be to rebury human remains (or place them in a suitable ossuary) after they have been carefully studied, to a schedule agreed between all interested parties. It may sometimes be possible to agree a form of disposition which provides an appropriate resting place, whilst allowing occasional visits for further study in the future. One of the archaeologist's chief aims is to establish as closely as possible the cultural identity and affinities of the people buried at the site, and this may not be easy to accomplish, so that archaeological evidence becomes important when several modern cultural groups lay claim to a collection of material.

These ethical issues of reburial are discussed in Chapter 10 within the wider context of questions regarding the ownership of the past. Here it is sufficient to note how the issue of reburial places rigorous constraints on research. If there is only one chance to study the material before it is reburied, then the records must be right first time, standards (not only of recording, but of handling the material) must be as high as possible, the observations must also be as complete as they can be, and they must be compatible with the records of other researchers, working on other collections. There have been several attempts to define minimum standards for recording but the most widely used are the so-called Chicago Standards (Buikstra and Ubelaker 1994).

ACKNOWLEDGEMENTS

I would like to thank my colleague Dr Tony Waldron for commenting on a draft of this chapter. Stuart Laidlaw and his colleagues in the photographic studio of our department provided photographs in addition to my own.

REFERENCES

Aiello, L. and Dean, C. (1990) *An Introduction to Human Evolutionary Anatomy*, London: Academic Press.

Aitken, M. J. (1990) *Science-based Dating in Archaeology*, London: Longman.

Ajie, H. O., Kaplan, I. R., Slota, P. J. and Taylor, R. E. (1990) 'AMS radiocarbon dating bone osteocalcim', *Nuclear Instruments and Methods*, B52: 433–38.

Ambrose, S. H. (1993) 'Isotopic analysis of paleodiets: methodological and interpretive considerations', in M. K. Sandford (ed.) *Investigations of Ancient Human Tissue. Chemical Analyses in Anthropology*, Langhorne, Pa.: Gordon and Breach (Food and Nutrition in History and Anthropology, Volume 10): 59–130.

Angel, J. L., Suchey, J. M., Iscan, M. Y. and Zimmerman, M. R. (1986) 'Age at death estimated from the skeleton and viscera', in M. R. Zimmerman and J. L. Angel (eds) *Dating and the Age Determination of Biological Materials*, London: Croom Helm: 179–220.

Arriaza, B. T. (1995) *Beyond Death: the Chinchorro Mummies of Ancient Chile*, Washington, DC: Smithsonian Institution Press.

Banks, P. (1991) *Killey's Fractures of the Mandible* (4th edition), Oxford: Wright.

Bass, W. M. (1995) *Human Osteology, a Laboratory and Field Manual of the Human Skeleton* (4th edition), Columbia: Missouri Archaeological Society.

Bell, L. S. and Jones, S. J. (1991) 'Macroscopic and microscopic evaluation of archaeological pathological bone: backscattered electron imaging of putative Pagetic bone', *International Journal of Osteoarchaeology* 1: 179–84.

Bell, L. S., Boyde, A. and Jones, S. J. (1991) 'Diagenetic alteration to teeth *in situ* illustrated by backscattered electron imaging', *Scanning* 13: 173–83.

Berkovitz, B. K. B. and Moxham, B. J. (1989) *Color Atlas of the Skull*, London: Mosby-Wolfe.

Berry, A. C. and Berry, R. J. (1967) 'Epigenetical variation in the human cranium', *Journal of Anatomy* 101: 361–79.

Berry, A. C. and Berry, R. J. (1972) 'Origins and relationships of the ancient Egyptians. Based on a study of non-metrical variation in the skull', *Journal of Human Evolution* 1: 199–208.

Breathnach, A. S. (ed.) (1965) *Frazer's Anatomy of the Human Skeleton*, London: J. and A. Churchill Ltd.

Brothwell, D. R. (1981) *Digging Up Bones* (2nd edition), London and Oxford: British Museum and Oxford University Press.

Brothwell, D. R. and Sandison, A. T. (eds) (1967) *Diseases in Antiquity*, Springfield: Thomas.

Brown, T. A. and Brown, K. A. (1994) 'Ancient DNA: using molecular biology to explore the past', *BioEssays* 16: 719–26.

Buikstra, J. E. and Ubelaker, D. H. (eds) (1994) *Standards for Data Collection from Human Skeletal Remains*, Fayetteville: Arkansas Archaeological Survey (Arkansas Archaeological Survey Research Series No. 44).

Courville, C. B. (1965a) 'War wounds of the cranium in the Middle Ages; 1. As disclosed in the skeletal material from the Battle of Wisby (1361 AD)', *Bulletin of the Los Angeles Neurological Society* 30: 27–33.

Courville, C. B. (1965b) 'War wounds of the cranium in the Middle Ages; 2. As noted in the skulls of Sedlec Oxxuary near Kuttenberg, Czechoslovakia', *Bulletin of the Los Angeles Neurological Society* 30: 34–44.

David, R. (1978) *Mysteries of the Mummies*, London: Book Club Associates.

De Niro, M. J. (1987) 'Stable isotopy and archaeology', *American Scientist* 75: 182–91.

Gerasimov, M. M. (1971) *Face Finder*, New York: Lippincott.

Gilbert, B. M. and McKern, T. W. (1973) 'A method for aging the female Os pubis', *American Journal of Physical Anthropology* 38: 31–38.

Gill, P., Ivanov, P. L., Kimpton, C., Piercy, R., Benson, N., Tully, G., Evett, I., Hagelberg, E. and Sullivan, K. (1994) 'Identification of the remains of the Romanov family by DNA analysis', *Nature Genetics* 6: 130–35.

Glob, P. V. (1969) *The Bog People*, London: Faber and Faber.

Glob, P. V. (1974) *The Mound People*, London: Faber and Faber.

Goodman, A. H. and Armelagos, G. J. (1985) 'Disease and death at Dr Dickson's Mounds', *Natural History* 9/85: 12–19.

Goodman, A. H. and Rose, J. C. (1990) 'Assessment of systemic physiological perturbations from dental enamel hypoplasias and associated histological structures', *Yearbook of Physical Anthropology* 33: 59–110.

Goodman, A. H., Armelagos, G. J. and Rose, J. C. (1984) 'The chronological distribution of enamel hypoplasias from prehistoric Dickson Mounds populations', *American Journal of Physical Anthropology* 65: 259–66.

Hagelberg, E. and Clegg, J. B. (1991) 'Isolation and characterisation of DNA from archaeological bone', *Philosophical Transactions of the Royal Society of London*, Series B, 244: 45–50.

Hagelberg, E. and Clegg, J. B. (1993) 'Genetic polymorphisms in prehistoric Pacific islanders determined by analysis of ancient bone DNA', *Philosophical Transactions of the Royal Society of London*, Series B, 252: 163–70.

Hagelberg, E., Sykes, B. and Hedges, R. (1989) 'Ancient bone DNA amplified', *Nature* 342: 485.

Hagelberg, E., Bell, L. S., Allen, T., Boyde, A., Jones, S. J. and Clegg, J. B. (1991) 'Analysis of ancient bone DNA: techniques and applications', in G. Eglinton and G. B. Curry (eds) *Molecules through Time: Fossil Molecules and Biochemical Systematics*, London: The Royal Society: 399–408.

Hart Hansen, J. P., Mellgaard, J. and Nordquist, J. (eds) (1991) *The Greenland Mummies*, London: British Museum Press.

Hillson, S. W. (1992) *Mammal Bones and Teeth. An Introductory Guide to Methods of Identification*, London: Institute of Archaeology, University College London.

Hillson, S. W. (1996) *Dental Anthropology*, Cambridge: Cambridge University Press.

Howells, W. W. (1973) *Cranial Variation in Man. A Study by Multivariate Analysis of Patterns of Difference among Recent Human Populations*, Cambridge, Mass.: Harvard University (Papers of the Peabody Museum of Archaeology and Ethnology 67).

Howells, W. W. (1989) *Skull Shapes and the Map. Craniometric Analyses in the Dispersion of Modern Homo*, Cambridge, Mass.: Harvard University (Papers of the Peabody Museum of Archaeology and Ethnology 79).

Howells, W. W. (1995) *Ethnic Identification of Crania from Measurements*, Cambridge, Mass.: Harvard University (Papers of the Peabody Museum of Archaeology and Ethnology 82).

Hummel, S. and Herrmann, B. (1995) 'aDNA analysis in paleopathology: mini-review and prospects', *Paleopathology Newsletter* 91: 6–9.

Iscan, M. Y. and Helmer, R. P. (eds) (1993) *Forensic Analysis of the Skull. Craniofacial Analysis, Reconstruction and Identification*, New York: Wiley–Liss.

Iscan, M. Y. and Loth, S. R. (1986a) 'Determination of age from the sternal rib in White females: a test of the phase method', *Journal of Forensic Sciences* 31: 990–99.

Iscan, M. Y. and Loth, S. R. (1986b) 'Determination of age from the sternal rib in White males: a test of the phase method', *Journal of Forensic Sciences* 31: 122–32.

Katz, D. and Suchey, J. M. (1986) 'Age determination of the male Os pubis', *American Journal of Physical Anthropology* 69: 427–36.

Kelley, M. A. and Larsen, C. S. (eds) (1991) *Advances in Dental Anthropology*, New York: Wiley–Liss.

Kendall, M. (1975) *Multivariate Analysis*, London: Charles Griffin and Co. Ltd.

Kieser, J. A., Preston, C. B. and Evans, W. G. (1983) 'Skeletal age at death: an evaluation of the Miles method of ageing', *Journal of Archaeological Science* 10: 9–12.

Krogh, K. J. (1967) *Viking Greenland*, Copenhagen: The National Museum.

Lovejoy, C. O., Meindl, R. S., Pryzbeck, T. R. and Mensforth, R. P. (1985) 'Chronological metamorphosis of the auricular surface of the ilium: a new method for the determination of adult skeletal age at death', *American Journal of Physical Anthropology* 68: 15–28.

Lowenstein, J. L. (1985) 'Molecular approaches to the identification of species', *Science* 73: 541–47.

Lowenstein, J. M. and Scheuenstuhl, G. (1991) 'Immunological methods in molecular palaeontology', in G. Eglinton and G. B. Curry (eds) *Molecules through Time: Fossil Molecules and Biochemical Systematics*, London: The Royal Society: 375–80.

McKern, T. W. and Stewart, T. D. (1957) *Skeletal Age Changes in Young American Males, Analyzed from the Standpoint of Identification*, Natick, Mass.: Massachusetts Quartermaster Research and Development Command Report EP-45.

McKinley, J. I. (1989) 'Cremations: expectations, methodologies and realities', in C. A. Roberts, F. Lee and J. Bintliff (eds) *Burial Archaeology. Current Research, Methods and Developments*, Oxford: British Archaeological Reports, British Series 211: 65–76.

McKinley, J. I. (1994) *The Anglo-Saxon Cemetery at Spong Hill, North Elmham. Part VIII: the Cremations*, Dereham: Field Archaeology Division, Norfolk Museums Service (East Anglian Archaeology Report No. 69).

Marriott, F. H. C. (1974) *The Interpretation of Multiple Observations*, London: Academic Press.

Masters, P. M. (1986a) 'Age determination of living mammals using aspartic acid racemization in structural proteins', in M. R. Zimmerman and J. L. Angel (eds) *Dating and the Age Determination of Biological Materials*, London: Croom Helm: 270–83.

Masters, P. M. (1986b) 'Amino acid racemization dating – a review', in M. R. Zimmerman and J. L. Angel (eds) *Dating and the Age Determination of Biological Materials*, London: Croom Helm: 39–58.

Masters, P. M. (1987) 'Preferential preservation of noncollagenous protein during bone diagenesis: implications for chronometric and stable isotopic measurements', *Geochimica et Cosmochimica Acta* 51: 3209–14.

Meindl, R. S. and Lovejoy, C. O. (1985) 'Ectocranial suture closure: a revised method for the determination of skeletal age at death based on the lateral anterior sutures', *American Journal of Physical Anthropology* 68: 57–66.

Merriwether, D. A., Rothammer, F. and Ferell, R. E. (1992) 'Mitochondrial DNA variation in ancient and contemporary Amerindians using the tRNA[lys]-COII deletion and diagnostic restriction sites', *American Journal of Human Genetics* 51: A13.

Miles, A. E. W. (1962) 'Assessment of the ages of a population of Anglo-Saxons from their dentitions', *Proceedings of the Royal Society of Medicine* 55: 881–86.

Møller Christensen, V. (1961) *Bone Changes in Leprosy*, Copenhagen: Munksgaard.

Neave, R. A. H. (1979) 'Reconstruction of the heads of three ancient Egyptian mummies', *Journal of Audiovisual Media in Medicine* ii: 156–64.

Ortner, D. and Putschar, W. (1981) *Identification of Pathological Conditions in Human Skeletal Remains*, Washington, DC: Smithsonian Institution Press.

Prag, A. J. N. W. and Neave, R. A. H. (eds) (1997) *Making Faces. Reconstructing Ancient Heads*, London : British Museum Press.

Prag, A. J. N. W., Musgrave, J. H. and Neave, R. A. H. (1984) 'The skull from Tomb II at Vergina: King Phillip II of Macedon', *Journal of Hellenic Studies* 104: 60–78.

Reinhard, J. (1996) 'Peru's ice maidens. Unwrapping the secrets', *National Geographic* 189: 62–81.

Roberts, C. and Manchester, K. (1995) *The Archaeology of Disease*, Stroud: Alan Sutton Publishing Ltd.

Rogers, J. and Waldron, T. (1995) *A Field Guide to Joint Disease in Archaeology*, Chichester: Wiley.

Rose, J. C., Marks, M. K. and Tieszen, L. L. (1991) 'Bioarchaeology and subsistence in the central and lower portions of the Mississippi valley', in M. L. Powell, P. S. Bridges and A. M. W. Mires (eds) *What Mean These Bones? Studies in Southeastern Bioarchaeology*, Tuscaloosa and London: University of Alabama Press: 7–21.

Rudenko, S. I. (1970) *The Frozen Tombs of Siberia*, London: J. M. Dent and Sons.

Schwarcz, H. P. and Schoeninger, M. J. (1991) 'Stable isotope analyses in human nutritional ecology', *Yearbook of Physical Anthropology* 34: 283–321.

Scott, W. A. and Hillson, S. (1988) 'An application of the EM algorithm to archaeological data analysis', in S. Rahtz (ed.) *Computer and Quantitative Methods in Archaeology 1988*, Oxford: British Archaeological Reports, International Series 446 (ii): 43–52.

Sealy, J., Armstrong, R. and Schrire, C. (1995) 'Beyond lifetime averages: tracing life histories through isotopic analysis of different calcified tissues from archaeological human skeletons', *Antiquity* 69: 290–300.

Shipman, P., Foster, G. and Schoeninger, M. (1984) 'Burnt bones and teeth: an experimental study of color, morphology, crystal structure and shrinkage', *Journal of Archaeological Science* 11: 307–25.

Sjøvold, T. (1988) 'Geschlechtsdiagnose am Skelett', in R. Knußmann (ed.) *Anthropologie. Handbuch der vergleichenden Biologie des Menschen, Vol. Band I: Wesen und Methoden der Anthropologie*, Stuttgart: Gustav Fischer Verlag: 444–80.

Skinner, M. and Goodman, A. H. (1992) 'Anthropological uses of developmental defects of enamel', in S. R. Saunders and M. A. Katzenberg (eds) *Skeletal Biology of Past Peoples: Research Methods*, New York: Wiley–Liss: 153–75.

Smith, B. H. (1991) 'Standards of human tooth formation and dental age assessment', in M. A. Kelley and C. S. Larsen (eds) *Advances in Dental Anthropology*, New York: Wiley–Liss: 143–68.

Spencer, A. J. (1982) *Death in Ancient Egypt*, Harmondsworth: Penguin Books.

Spindler, K. (1993) *The Man in the Ice*, London: Weidenfeld and Nicolson.

Stead, I. M., Bourke, J. B. and Brothwell, D. R. (eds) (1986) *Lindow Man. The Body in the Bog*, London: British Museum Publications.

Stone, A. C. and Stoneking, M. (1993) 'Ancient DNA from a pre-Columbian Amerindian population', *American Journal of Physical Anthropology* 92: 463–71.

Stone, A. C., Milner, G. R., Pääbo, S. and Stoneking, M. (1996) 'Sex determination of ancient human skeletons using DNA', *American Journal of Physical Anthropology* 99: 221–28.

Strachan, T. and Read, A. P. (1996) *Human Molecular Genetics*, Oxford: BIOS Scientific Publishers.

Suchey, J. M. (1979) 'Problems in the aging of females using the Os pubis', *American Journal of Physical Anthropology* 51: 467–70.

Taylor, G. M., Crossey, M., Saldarnha, J. and Waldron, T. (1996) 'DNA from Mycobacterium tuberculosis identified in medieval human skeletal remains using polymerase chain reaction', *Journal of Archaeological Science* 23: 789–98.

Todd, T. W. (1920) 'Age changes in the pubic bone. I: The male white pubis', *American Journal of Physical Anthropology* 3: 285–334.

308

Todd, T. W. (1921) 'Age changes in the pubic bone. II–IV', *American Journal of Physical Anthropology* 4: 1–70.

Turner II, C. G., Nichol, C. R. and Scott, G. R. (1991) 'Scoring procedures for key morphological traits of the permanent dentition: the Arizona State University Dental Anthropology System', in M. A. Kelley and C. S. Larsen (eds) *Advances in Dental Anthropology*, New York: Wiley–Liss: 13–31.

Turner, R. C. and Scaife, R. G. (eds) (1996) *Bog Bodies. New Discoveries and New Perspectives*, London: British Museum Press.

Van der Merwe, N. J. (1992) 'Light stable isotopes and the reconstruction of prehistoric diets', in A. M. Pollard (ed.) *New Developments in Archaeological Science*, Oxford: Oxford University Press (Proceedings of the British Academy 77): 247–64.

Waldron, H. A. (1994) *Counting the Dead*, Chichester: John Wiley.

Waldron, T. (1996) 'Editorial: biomarkers of disease', *International Journal of Osteoarchaeology* 6: 324–25.

Wells, C. (1964) *Bones, Bodies and Diseases*, London: Thames and Hudson.

Wheeler, R. E. M. (1943) *Maiden Castle, Dorset*, London: The Society of Antiquaries of London, Reports of the Research Committee of the Society of Antiquaries.

SELECT BIBLIOGRAPHY

The main topics introduced in this chapter are expanded in the textbooks of Brothwell (1981), Bass (1995) and Hillson (1996), which also give access to the literature. The classic skeletal anatomy text is Frazer's (Breathnach 1965), and key differences between human and other mammal bones and teeth are described in Hillson (1992). Kelley and Larsen (1991) include a wide range of edited papers on dental matters. Methods for age estimation are surveyed in Angel *et al.* (1986), an important assessment of dental ageing methods is given by Smith (1991), and Sjøvold (1988) provides a comprehensive treatment of sex determination methods. Buikstra and Ubelaker (1994) define a wide range of techniques for studying human remains. Waldron (1994) provides a sharply focused discussion of the broader inferences that can be made from collections of archaeological human remains. Ortner and Putschar (1981) provide the standard textbook of bone palaeopathology, whilst Manchester (1983) gives a good introduction and Rogers and Waldron (1995) is a key source for joint disease. Brothwell and Sandison (1967) is now a rare book, but is one of the palaeopathology classics. Key reviews of enamel hypoplasia are given by Goodman and Rose (1990) and Skinner and Goodman (1992). The most comprehensive general text on molecular genetics is Strachan and Read (1996), whilst Brown and Brown (1994) provides a readily accessible introduction to ancient DNA. Stable isotope studies are surveyed by Ambrose (1993) and Schwarcz and Schoeninger (1991).

8

STUDYING STRUCTURES

Matthew Johnson

INTRODUCTION

When a foraging band of the !Kung San of the Kalahari Desert halt for an over-night stop, one of their number plants two sticks in the ground. These two sticks stand for the door-posts of the more substantial structures the !Kung build in other contexts. The planting of the sticks allows the !Kung to orient themselves in a ring around the central hearth, the men on one side, the women on the other. Outside the ring, as the sky darkens and the fire brightens, is a wilderness the !Kung consider as hostile, full of dangers and evil spirits. Thus, the placing of two sticks constitutes not just the dwelling, but the whole !Kung universe: it divides up the women and men, the families in the band, and the social and natural world beyond (Whitelaw 1994: 224). This story is one taken from the gallery of ethnographic examples habitually used by archaeologists to help interpret their findings. It illustrates in microcosm some of the common problems and possibilities raised by the archaeological study of structures.

These common themes are in part straightforward. First, all human groups need some physical form of shelter; all build in some form or another, however ephemeral that form might be. Lewis Binford and others have written of the emergence of 'home-base' behaviour as one of the criteria of the emergence of *Homo sapiens sapiens* (Binford 1983); and once such a home base is created, it naturally takes on a physical, archaeologically visible, form. Away from the Equator, shelter from the elements is as necessary as clothing and food to the physical basis of human existence.

Second, the shelter that is needed is symbolic as well as material in nature: that is, it is about cultural as well as physical needs. The size and shape of dwellings and other buildings are about family form and social sentiment, what a dwelling 'ought' to look like, as well as about environment. It follows that the form of structure used may tell archaeologists something about the social organization and cultural values of that group: the !Kung dwelling reflects !Kung values, how they see the world. Thus the size and organization of structures investigated archaeologically will reflect their former occupants' values and perceptions, though they may not do so in a direct or simple manner.

Third, however, the physical traces of that structure may be ephemeral and fragmentary in the extreme. This is particularly true when structures are not only ephemeral in form in the first place, but are subjected to the attrition and erosion of succeeding millennia. Wood rots; stone is systematically 'robbed' and reused by later builders; shallow foundations are truncated or removed completely by later ploughing. The practical and interpretive skills of the archaeologist may be stretched to the limit when dealing with patchy, imperfectly preserved, fragments of structures, just as those skills will be stretched to the limit with their interpretation. The pair of !Kung sticks may be impossible to find archaeologically after a few days, let alone centuries.

This complex set of problems, limitations, and opportunities is common to the archaeology of structures of all cultures and periods. Within this common set of problems and opportunities, however, lies a huge amount of variation in the type of structures built by ancient peoples, from the simple windbreaks and tents of nomads and hunter-gatherers to the huge monumental constructions of complex societies: the pyramids and ziggurats of the ancient civilizations, or the cathedrals, palaces, factories and tower-blocks of our own world. Each type of structure has particular potential and poses particular problems for the archaeologist, and there is corresponding variation in the ways in which different archaeologists choose to interpret excavated and standing remains. To illustrate these points, there follows a series of examples of structures from different contexts in space and time. In the following section I have selected four case studies to illustrate the huge differences in building traditions which archaeologists study, and I then turn to the technical and material basis for the building of structures, before examining the way these may be excavated, reconstructed and interpreted by the archaeologist.

STRUCTURES AROUND THE WORLD

The study of structures in pre-modern societies is not the preserve of archaeology alone: as the !Kung example makes clear, it impinges on the territory of the ethnographer and social and cultural anthropologist. Similarly, the study of structures built by more complex societies shares the academic territory of the architectural historian, whose aims and methods are somewhat different from the archaeologist's.

Within literate societies, the archaeologist will also have to intrude on the ground of the historian and historic conservationist, as I shall discuss later.

Hunter-gatherers at Molodova

The upper palaeolithic site at Molodova, in the Ukraine, was occupied by a small band of mobile peoples over thirty thousand years ago (Wymer 1982: 159). These people hunted mammoth, woolly rhinoceros, ox or bison, elk or moose, reindeer, and bear, in addition to foraging for plant foods. Molodova was an open site; that is, natural features such as caves or rock shelters were not used. There was also a lack of other forms of building material, given the harsh conditions of what was then the tundra. The people of Molodova chose to employ a highly unusual building material: mammoth bones. The bones were arranged in a rough circle about ten metres in diameter; within the circle archaeologists found a series of hearths, not all probably used at the same time. The bones were probably used to weigh down mammoth skin hides, as indicated in the reconstruction shown as Figure 8.1; the hides would be laid over a framework of branches (Wymer 1982).

Anasazi pueblos

The Anasazi culture of what is now the south-western United States flourished from the early tenth century AD onwards. The Anasazi lived in a distinctive form of structure, the 'pueblo' (Hill 1970). The pueblo form is still used by the Native American group most closely linked culturally to the prehistoric Anasazi, the Hopi, and insights into Anasazi architecture have been gained through the use of Hopi structures as analogies. The pueblo consisted of an agglomeration of sub-rectangular rooms, often arranged around one, two, three or four sides of a court-yard (Wetherill 1966; Fig. 8.2). The cells of this agglomeration could be added one to another to create a range of final forms. The overall shape of the whole pueblo could be sub-rectangular, circular or semi-circular, or end up simply as a row of rooms. The size of the pueblo could vary from the tiny to the monumental. External doors were rare or non-existent. Within these agglomerations, individual family units had a series of rooms, often reached from the roof above by a small step-ladder rather than through external doors. In the courtyard, or in other locations, circular structures called 'kivas' were partly sunk into the ground. The modern Hopi tribe use these kivas for ceremonial activities: their sunken position between the earth and the sky has symbolic resonance, as does the circular shape, which is seen as a microcosm of the world. It is reasonable to suppose that the Anasazi structures embodied a related set of beliefs.

312

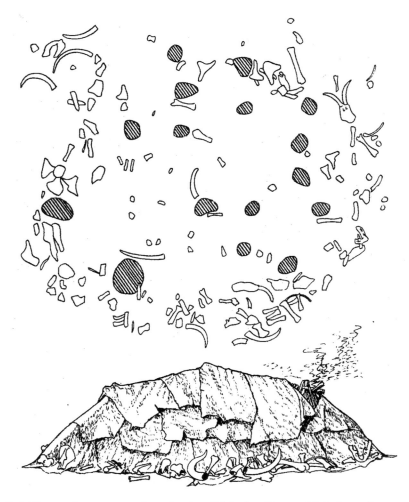

Figure 8.1 Plan and reconstruction of palaeolithic dwelling at Molodova. Source: Wymer 1982.

Many such structures were in spectacular positions, perched on cliff edges or, as at Mesa Verde in Colorado, below massive natural arches in the cliff walls. The usual method of building was through the use of sun-dried brick or clay walls. As the Anasazi culture reached its peak, however, around the time of the great Romanesque and Gothic cathedrals of Europe, many such pueblos became ever larger and were rebuilt in stone (Wetherill 1966). Such stone walls used a variety of techniques, but were of 'dry' construction: that is, they did not use mortar or other bonding between the stones. The outside walls could reach to a monumental height of over ten metres.

The reasons for the abandonment of these structures remains a mystery, though

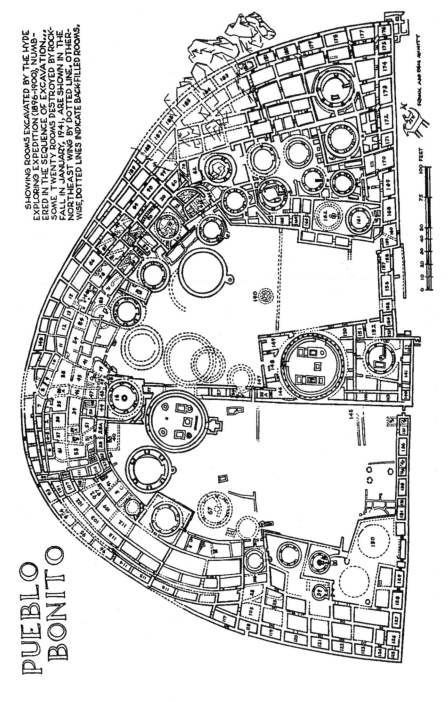

PUEBLO BONITO

SHOWING ROOMS EXCAVATED BY THE HYDE
EXPLORING EXPEDITION (1896-1900), NUMB-
ERED IN THE SEQUENCE OF EXCAVATION.
SOME TWENTY ROOMS DESTROYED BY ROCK-
FALL IN JANUARY, 1941, ARE SHOWN IN THE
NORTHEAST WING BY DOTTED LINE, OTHER-
WISE, DOTTED LINES INDICATE BACKFILLED ROOMS.

SMALL AND DEAD ROOMS ?

0 10 20 30 40 50   75   100 FEET

Figure 8.2 Plan of Pueblo Bonito, one of the greatest Anasazi pueblos at Chaco Canyon, New Mexico. Here, a cellular form of architecture usually executed in dried mud or adobe is recreated in stone. The circular areas are partly sunken structures called 'kivas', which have ritual function. Reproduced from R. Wetherill: *Anasazi* by Frank McNitt. © University of New Mexico Press.

increasing aridity of the climate is the preferred explanation of many archaeologists, as well as transformation of the environment brought about by stripping the landscape for timber (Betancourt and van Deveder 1981). The aridity of the region has in fact assisted in the interpretation of the pueblos: many timber floors have been preserved, with the result that dendrochronology (tree-ring dating) has been used to date many of the pueblos with great accuracy. The varying styles of stone walling have also been put into stratigraphic order, enabling very close dating of many structures by a combination of relative and absolute means (Wetherill 1966).

Great Zimbabwe

Great Zimbabwe is the only archaeological site in the world to give its name to a nation. It is in fact one of over 150 sites in modern Zimbabwe to exhibit signs of having broken from the African tradition of building in clay: these enclosures or *zimbabwes*, which date from the fourteenth to the eighteenth centuries AD, have monumental stone walls of varying heights. These walls appear to have surrounded clusters of clay-built dwellings, now vanished (Hall 1987, 103–16; Fig. 8.3). Great Zimbabwe itself is the largest of these sites, and was occupied from the tenth and eleventh centuries onwards, before it was transformed in the thirteenth and fourteenth centuries into a major regional centre for thousands of people (Huffman 1996). The site reached its height in the fifteenth century. The walls enclose the city as well as ritual areas; they were built with the simple technique of dry stone with few doorways or other features.

Who built these structures? They appear to be the products of cattle-raising chiefdoms who built their power on trade, particularly of gold (Huffman 1996: 176–8). Trade objects from as far away as China and the Islamic world have been found, indicating a complex social network indigenous to black Africa. Interpretations of the structures at Great Zimbabwe have varied, but in recent years it has been suggested that they must be interpreted in terms of ritual, with male/female oppositions repeated across the Great Enclosure (Huffman 1996; Fig. 8.3). In this interpretation, the enclosure may have acted as an initiation centre for girls.

Gothic cathedrals

The towns of medieval Europe often chose to express their wealth and confidence in the provision of ever larger and more elaborate structures for public worship, dominated by the great cathedrals. Such structures were distinctive in form, craftsmanship, and the sheer scale of their construction, dwarfing the wooden houses around them (Fone 1984). The building material was stone, though the roof

315

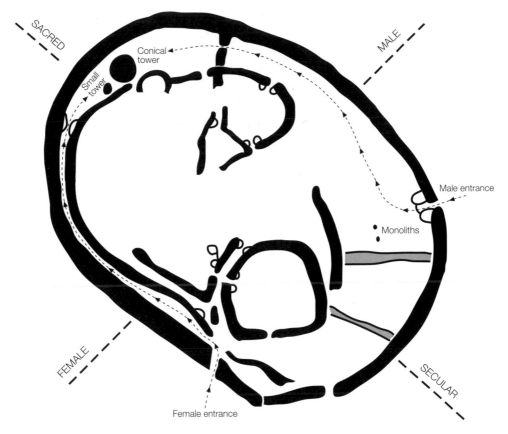

Figure 8.3 The Great Enclosure at Great Zimbabwe, showing Huffman's interpretation of the space in terms of sacred/secular and male/female space. Reproduced from M. Hall, *Farmers, Kings and Traders: The People of Southern Africa, 200–1860* with permission David Philip Publishers (Pty) Ltd, South Africa.

was of timber. Pointed stone arches were used, for structural as well as aesthetic reasons (Fig. 8.4): the keystone of the arch (the stone at the arch's summit) was more easily held in place, and the lateral stress of the arch was reduced in comparison with a round arch. Equally, however, the aesthetics became dynamic rather than static, the whole sequence of arches thrusting upwards towards the sky and to God.

Gothic cathedrals were built according to a fairly rigid set of rules. Arches set around a rectangle formed a bay, which could be vaulted over and supported on pillars; the form of the church was thus a series of stone bays. The whole structure being a skeletal one rather than based on thick stone walls, the space between the pillars could then be filled with coloured glass. The church as a whole thus became

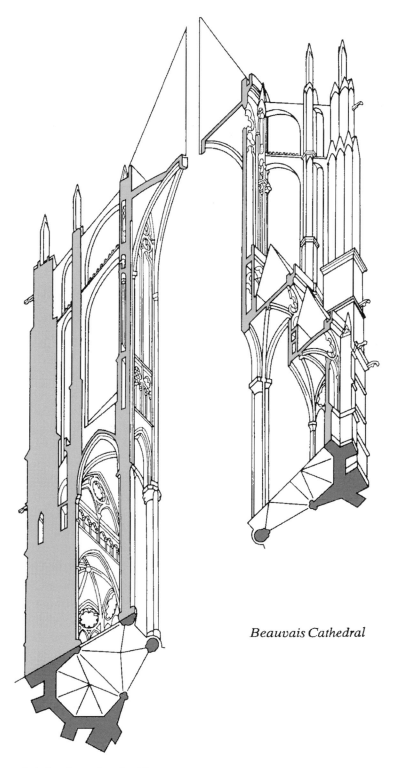

Beauvais Cathedral

Figure 8.4 Section of a Gothic cathedral: Beauvais. Source: *World Atlas of Archaeology*, Mitchell Beazley, 1988.

a forest of pillars, all thrusting upwards towards a stone vault, the whole being painted and filled with coloured light (Fletcher 1938: 326–29). As different and new as these aesthetics were, the form of Gothic cathedrals, with aisles or lower vaults running along either side of the main body of the church, reflected the Roman plan of early Christian basilicas a thousand years earlier (Fletcher 1938: 214–22). Moreover, however competitive and acquisitive were the communities who built them, these structures also reflected the values of medieval Catholicism. Thus the Gothic church reflected a complex series of structural, aesthetic, and symbolic requirements, as well as being reflective of the self-image and aspirations of the communities that built them. It has indeed been argued that their architectural complexity reflected the complexities of scholastic discourse of the age (Panofsky 1957).

TECHNICAL SYSTEMS

All human groups in the past were constrained by the materials to hand and the environment within which those materials occur – remains of prehistoric igloos have not been excavated in Egypt or India, nor have remains of sun-dried brick houses been found in the Arctic tundra! Prehistoric populations learnt to use the materials they found around them in ways that showed a deep understanding of the potentials and limitations of the natural environment, as we have seen in the Molodova example illustrated earlier. On the other hand, building materials can be used creatively in a variety of ways, and can be used to deceive or create a false impression. Such creative uses may offer the archaeologist a clue to the social status and function of a structure, and even its symbolic meaning. Thus Roman monumental structures were often built with a combination of brick and concrete, utilizing the potential of these materials to create arched, vaulted, and domed forms (Fig. 8.5). Nevertheless, they chose to mask these forms with façades of plaster or marble in order to create a more traditional Graeco-Roman exterior of pillars and lintels in the Classical Orders. This combination reflected both the Romans' engineering skills and their desire to retain the mental structures of the Hellenic past, rather as the architectural form of several Anasazi pueblos reflected their origins in clay-walled construction, although being built in stone.

This section will look at the properties, potential, and weaknesses of some of the more common building materials. It will stress through examples the very diverse ways in which materials were used by cultures before the great transformations of the Industrial Revolution. Such structural materials include timber, stone, and mud-brick or brick.

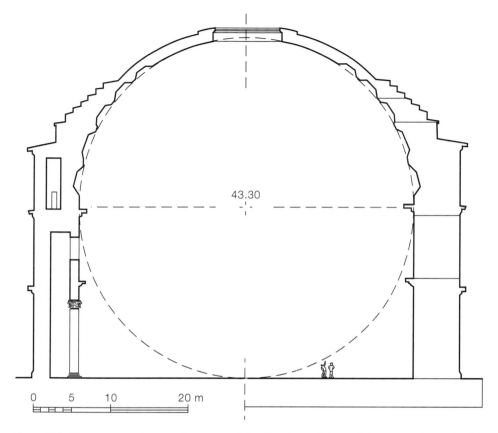

43.30

0   5   10   20 m

Figure 8.5 The construction of the dome of the Pantheon, Rome. The upper 'layers' of the dome were constructed using successively lighter building materials. The exterior, however, retained the traditional Hellenistic façade. Reproduced with permission of B. T. Batsford Ltd.

Timber

In many ways timber is the most versatile of all building materials. When used along the 'grain', or when trunks or branches of trees are used whole, timber has immense tensile strength, and may be used to create a skeletal framework support-ing the walls and roof of a structure. Planks and bark may be used to create the walls and roof themselves, or smaller branches and twigs used to create wattle walls and partitions. The timber posts supporting this skeletal structure may be buried in the ground at their base, or beams may be laid along the ground or in a trench as a foundation (known as sills or sill-beams).

So-called 'Celtic' huts in the Europe of the first millennium BC often consisted of a circular ring of posts, apparently linked together at their apex by a series of plates

319

or interlocking horizontal beams (Reynolds 1979). These supported a conical roof made by taking lighter poles, placing their bases on the tops of the walls, and lashing these together at the summit of the cone. Thatching, a thick covering of reeds lashed on to these poles, completed the roof. The walls would then be panelled with wattle lining, and this lining would be covered with dried mud or 'daub'. The 'wattle and daub' walls would be protected from the rain by having the thatched roof overhang the sides heavily. Such a circular building could only have a limited span governed by the height and weight of the roof. Sometimes larger structures could be created by widening the floor space inside and supporting the roof by an internal circle of posts. Similar structures have been recorded from some traditional African communities, and can be seen reconstructed in various open-air museums across Europe (Reynolds 1979) – as well as more famously if less accurately in Asterix cartoons!

The major problem with timber structures of any type that have earth-fast posts is that, when the posts are set in the ground, they rot relatively quickly; experimental reconstructions of post-built structures suggest this may happen in twenty to thirty years, or in other words a generation or so. Consequently, such structures must often have had a very limited life. That life may have been extended: for example, the bottoms of the posts were sometimes deliberately charred before burial in the ground, charring apparently inhibiting the decay of the post; in other contexts, as indicated for example by documentary records for medieval England, the rotten bases of timbers may have been cut off and the bases of the posts placed instead on stone 'pads' for support.

A more complex but durable method of timber framing can be seen in late and post-medieval northern Europe, and in areas of imperial European settlement around the world, in which 'sill-beams' or horizontal timbers at the foot of the structure are raised above the ground by being carried on small stone or brick walls. Posts are then linked by means of carpentered joints into the sill-beams, beams into the posts, and so on, creating a complex skeleton tied together by accurately carpentered joints and wooden pegs, rather like a structure made from 'Meccano' (Harris 1978; Johnson 1993; Fig. 8.6). In such a structure, the timber frame is rendered less susceptible to damp – many houses and farm buildings of this type have survived for over five or six hundred years.

The strengths of this particularly complex form of timber-framing are various. The structure may be prefabricated in its various parts before being assembled on site – there is archaeological evidence for this in the presence of Roman numerals scratched into the various beams, giving a guide to on-site assembly (Harris 1978). It is also stronger, and may even be taken apart, moved, and reassembled elsewhere, as can be seen at exhibits like Singleton in Sussex, England, and St Fagan's near Cardiff in Wales, where such structures have been reassembled as part of open-air museums (Moir 1997). However, this type of structure does require much better

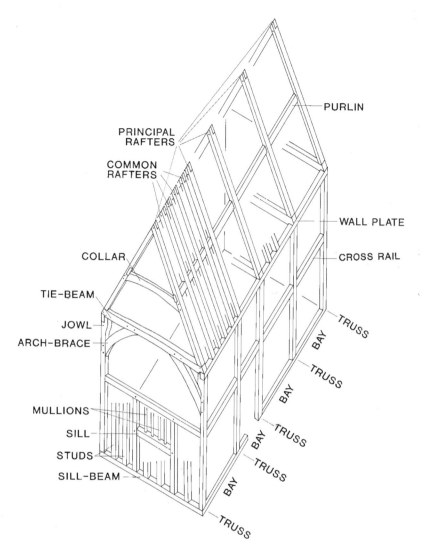

Figure 8.6 The timber 'skeleton' of a seventeenth-century East Anglian house. Source: Johnson 1993, fig. 3.1.

quality timber, and skilled carpentry. As massive and durable as many prehistoric houses may have been, the techniques for their construction were not as specialized; houses such as the 'Celtic' huts described may well have needed little specialist knowledge. Skilled carpenters with a knowledge of geometry, a deep understanding of the properties of timber, and an ability to prefabricate the timber skeleton in the builder's yard, are needed to build a timber-framed house.

321

The use of timber in such a way also requires quite complex systems of woodland management (Rackham 1986). To create this second kind of framing is not simply a matter of going out into woodland and cutting a tree down: timber for use as part of a structural frame has to be carefully grown, often over several generations; carpenters often show great skill in using timber that is curved or 'waney', masking or even making an advantage of its second-rate nature. Because of these requirements, substantial timber-framed buildings are thus symptomatic of quite complex, state-level, societies. Given the need for such management, such timber was often scarce, and poorer dwellings were either constructed in a cruder manner from sub-standard timber or from other materials.

Where wood was plentiful it was used to create solid walls, in the manner seen today in Canadian, Swiss or Scandinavian pine-built log cabins. Straight pines would be piled one on top of another with rough-hewn interlocking joints at the corners, with little or no foundation, the sheer weight of the walls giving stability. Native groups in what is now the north-west coast of North America used this technique (Oliver 1995).

Different kinds of wood have different tensile strengths and qualities. In the deciduous forests oak is the most popular wood for use as a building material; other kinds of timber have particular qualities, but oak has all-round strength. Nevertheless, elm and other woods are known.

Being perishable in the long run, wooden structures often have to be inferred indirectly by the archaeologist, as discussed in Chapter 4.

Stone

Like timber, there was a plentiful supply of raw stone in the landscape for prehistoric peoples to exploit; but again, like timber, the extraction and preparation of good quality stone for major building projects are lengthy and arduous processes.

The earliest stone structures known to archaeologists are the 'manuports' used to construct windbreaks in the Lower Palaeolithic of Africa (Binford 1983). These stones appear to have been carried a little distance and arranged to form some kind of shelter; as such, they form one of the first pieces of evidence for 'home-base' behaviour amongst the early hominids. Loose boulders or rubble of various kinds have been used in a variety of structures. Dry-stone walls have been created by many societies in many periods of the past in many different parts of the world, by the piling and simple coursing of such material. Again, stones can be piled up as 'rafts' to provide foundations for timber-framed or clay-walled structures. Piles of rubble of this kind can be used to provide a platform for the sorts of timber structures mentioned above. For a properly stone-walled structure, however, it is necessary to finish the stone to some degree, whether by facing it or extracting good quality stone from quarries if none is available on the surface.

It is not necessary to use mortar to build a stone structure. The Anasazi pueblos discussed earlier used high walls in 'dry' stone walling, as did the Incas (Fone 1984). Inca palaces often had walls of great height constructed with huge stones, each many hundreds of tons in weight; despite their size, these were crafted to fit tightly together. The great palaces of Mycenae and Tiryns in bronze age Greece were also constructed in this manner, with 'Cyclopean' walls (Fone 1984). Nevertheless, most stone walls of any size or pretension use some form of mortar for bonding. Roman and medieval walls had a distinctive method of construction, in which a wall was built by first raising the two faces a few courses in finished stone, filling the gap between with rubble, pouring mortar over that rubble, and continuing upwards in similar fashion when the first part of the structure had set (Adam 1994). As a result, the core of such walls was often quite weak.

Many stone buildings employ techniques apparently unsuited to their material. This is the case with Greek and Egyptian temples – monumental structures with tall pillars closely set and surmounted by stone lintels, even though post-and-lintel construction is a technique more suited to timber. Egyptian temples are clearly derived from wooden models (their capitals from acanthus leaves, for example) (Fletcher 1938: 41). Greek temples were often initially built in wood and replaced piecemeal in stone, and their design reflects these origins. The pillars stand for tree-trunks as posts, the lintel for the wall-plate, and so on (Fone 1984). A more primitive example of the same use of wooden techniques in stone is that of Stonehenge: the great lintels of the famous stone trilithons at Stonehenge have mortise-and-tenon joints, clearly derived from carpentry joints.

Different stones have different structural and aesthetic properties, and past cultures often employed a combination of stones within the same building. Sedimentary rocks such as limestone and sandstone tend to be workable, but are often soft and susceptible to erosion. Granite, conversely, is a hard rock that is durable but only worked with difficulty. Chalk is generally too soft to be used, though a hard variety known as 'clunch' is sometimes used, as at Ely Cathedral in England.

The use of flint in areas such as East Anglia in England is an interesting study in the way an intractable building material can be manipulated. Flint nodules can be laid in courses to form an undistinguished rubble-like wall. However, they are impossible to use for cornering, so poorer churches in East Anglia had circular bell-towers to avoid the need for corners, whereas richer communities used worked limestone (ashlar) or bricks for cornering. Two techniques could be used to create flint-walled structures in more ambitious ways. Large nodules could be 'faced' by chipping, and the chips then impressed into the mortar in the interstices, a technique known as 'galletting'; or the nodules could be squared into brick-like forms. All these methods can be seen on medieval and later buildings.

Stone walls vary greatly in their manner of construction. Random rubble walling is common, and need not be an indication of poverty – the 'Cyclopean' walls of Mycenae in Greece and of the Inca civilizations of Peru mentioned above are examples of this technique, where tightly jointed dry-stone walls of huge proportion represent immense effort. Walling is more commonly coursed or laid in rows, however, whether the blocks are shaped and finished or merely selected according to size. High walls would be built up in sections in the pre-modern period, each stage supporting the scaffold in its turn. Small holes for scaffolding can often be seen, and provide a clue to building technique: thus, the presence of holes in a 'spiral' pattern on circular towers and turrets of the Welsh castles of Edward I, indicating use of the French inclined scaffold rather than the horizontal English manner, suggests the presence of French masons during their construction.

Whatever the type of stone used, its use and quality will depend on local availability and the use of quarrying. Areas rich in stone may nevertheless be poor in terms of good-quality building material, either because the local stone is friable or otherwise unsuitable or because surface material has been shattered. High-quality stone therefore tends to come from quarries. These survive themselves as archaeological sites of importance, such as the Pentelic marble quarries from which the Parthenon and many other great Greek temples were constructed, the Egyptian granite quarries at Aswan, or the 'humps and bumps' that remain of stone quarries at Barnack in England (Alexander 1995). Quarries can be sourced, as can reused stone.

When a major stone building fell out of use, its materials were soon removed and reused in other, often more humble, buildings. Great medieval monasteries, the majority of Hadrian's Wall, and many other monuments, have all been completely or partly destroyed in this way, though sharp observation will usually reveal the reused stone in buildings in the vicinity. In other cases the outer 'skin' of finer faced stone has been removed, as most famously in the case of the Great Pyramids of Egypt.

Finally, one major advantage of stone structures for the archaeologist is their preservation though time. A stone wall can survive indefinitely, and far more damage has been done to ancient stone structures from deliberate destruction and removal of building materials than from natural erosion. Often good building stone will be taken away from a disused building for reuse elsewhere; archaeologists term this removal 'robbing'. In the case of limestone, modern farmers will destroy ancient building and process the stone in order to lime their fields. Apart from earthquake damage, the main natural threat to a stone wall is generally from frost cracking: if water can penetrate into a wall and then freeze, its expansion will crack the wall open. Fire can have an analogous effect – the Romans and later generations used knowledge of this to help in quarrying raw stone (Adam 1994). As a consequence of this relative durability, much of our knowledge of structures of all types

324

comes from stone structures. One example already mentioned is that of Stonehenge, where we may suppose that the stone trilithons are based on analogous
wooden structures (Richards 1991). Another is the site of Skara Brae in the Orkney
Islands of Scotland, where a series of neolithic houses in stone was excavated by
Gordon Childe (Parker-Pearson and Richards 1994a: 42–45; Fig. 8.7). Such was the
apparent scarcity of other materials at Skara Brae that even items of furniture such
as beds and cupboards were constructed using flat slabs of limestone, giving us
important clues as the appearance and internal organization of neolithic houses in
adjacent regions which survive simply as collections of post-holes.

Brick

Mud or earth has been used since at least the neolithic period in some form or
another. In hotter climates, walls of sun-dried mud were built, protected from rain
by some form of thatched roof. The great civilizations of Egypt and the Middle
East built great structures through the use of sun-dried bricks. Earth mixed with

Figure 8.7 Skara Brae, Orkney: a neolithic stone-built settlement. © Historic Scotland.

water and straw would be cast in a mould and left to dry in the sun. The 'tells', or hill-like build-up of such ancient sites, are principally made up of many millions of such bricks, each phase of the site being built on top of the collapsed mud-brick ruins of the previous one (Redman 1978).

In more temperate areas bricks needed to be fired in a kiln. This was a technique spread by the Romans in temperate Europe (Adam 1994): behind the stone or plaster façade of many Roman buildings is a core of brick and mortar. Early bricks tended to come out of the kiln in a variety of colours, and builders in medieval and later Europe exploited this to create patterns in brick walls. Bricks could be moulded in certain patterns, or carved or 'rubbed' more easily than stone to create mouldings and decorative features. Like stone, brick could be reused: the reuse of Roman brick in medieval or later structures is common across the former Roman empire (Wright 1972).

Concrete

Concrete was again a Roman innovation. Created from a mixture of stone and lime, liquid concrete will set into a solid, sturdy mass capable of withstanding great stresses and strains. The Romans used concrete to create a variety of architectural forms such as the great dome of the Pantheon (Adam 1994: 185; Fig. 8.5) that were not equalled in Europe until after the Middle Ages.

INVESTIGATING BELOW-GROUND STRUCTURES

So far, building materials have been discussed in terms of the uses to which they can be put and the limitations and possibilities which they offer. I now want to turn to the task that faces the archaeologist: that of working out the form and function of a structure in all its details from the often partial and fragmentary remains he or she may excavate or observe in other ways. How do we recreate the whole building from elusive and ephemeral remains in the ground?

Excavation

Of course, archaeology is more than excavation and we have already encountered archaeological examples of structures that are still standing, such as the major monuments of the ancient civilizations. Nevertheless most structures from the human past have left little or no trace above ground, and may have been built of inherently perishable materials such as wood. This is particularly true of dwellings of the mass of the population, as opposed to the palaces, mansions and ritual structures of the élite, though the latter have suffered disproportionately through their role as political symbols, most famously in the case of the Bastille.

A building that has been destroyed, or which has decayed, will leave traces in the ground of various kinds (see Chapter 5). More substantial structures need foundations of some kind dug into the subsoil and these are frequently preserved in the archaeological record. Sometimes, in addition, occupation debris or layers of material from destruction or decay will have built up around the lower part of a building, covering the lower walls, and this will mean that the lower parts of a structure remain preserved intact. On certain occasions more substantial remains even than this will have been preserved: for example, at least two Romano-British villas had gable walls that collapsed outwards in one piece, leaving the 'prone' wall and gable preserved in a horizontal position (King and Potter 1996; Fig. 8.8). Occasions such as this are very rare, however. More frequently, most of the former fabric of a building will have been 'robbed' or removed for other uses, or will have decayed leaving no trace. The excavator is therefore usually in the invidious position of having to reconstruct a building from what remains of the foundations alone. The difficulties of such an exercise are obvious, particularly since many plausible 'common-sense' rules of interpretation have to be questioned.

It would appear to be plausible, for example, that the grander or more 'permanent' a building in its lifetime, the more visible its remains will be to the excavator. This is not, however, necessarily the case. The size, pretensions and investment of labour in a building may have only an indirect relationship to its archaeological visibility. If we take the hypothetical example of a wooden structure with posts set in deep and substantial post-holes, such a structure will be highly visible archaeologically. It would nevertheless be vulnerable to relatively quick decay, as we have seen. If, on the other hand, the posts rested on stone pads rather than being set in the ground, or were tied together by a shallow sill-beam, the building might be much more permanent, but much more ephemeral in terms of its archaeological survival. Remains of such pads or sill-beams might easily be removed by ploughing, or be missed within the confines of a narrow trench.

In many cases quite substantial buildings have largely vanished and are revealed only by very slight traces of wear patterns on rubble or earth surfaces. The range of fifth-century AD buildings at Wroxeter are a classic example of this (Barker 1981). It is probable that similar structures have been missed on other sites of all areas and periods not dug with the appropriate techniques. In other cases, all physical traces of an earlier building will have been removed by builders of later periods taking the foundation stones for other purposes. Such later workers dug 'robber trenches' to remove the foundations; archaeologists can often use these trenches to their advantage, tracing their form to reveal the line of the original foundations (Barker 1986). In other cases floor levels inside a structure may also have been removed by ploughing or other surface disturbance, the excavator being left with the task of joining up post-holes like a row of dots to form a building. Sometimes the numbers of post- or stake-holes clearly form a line; in others, lines may remain unconvincing, particularly where several phases of building may be represented by a jumble of holes that are not clearly related one to another stratigraphically.

In an attempt to deal with these problems, archaeologists have refined their techniques of excavation and primary interpretation considerably over the last few years (Barker 1986). In terms of excavation, archaeologists are firstly much more sensitive to the information contained in the ground. Post-holes, in which a pit is dug, the post inserted, and the pit then backfilled, are differentiated from stake-holes, in which stakes are merely driven into the ground. Different types of post-hole may be seen: those in which the post is left to rot in its place, others where the post has been removed. Careful excavation will also reveal whether the post was a vertical one or set at an angle; this was done, for example, at Cowdery's Down, England (Millett 1983). This last detail may be important in ascertaining the form of the superstructure. Large-scale, open-area excavation is often crucial to the understanding of buildings that are not major monumental structures (Barker 1986). The often confused patterns of post-holes mentioned above are impossible to understand in a narrow trench or when covered with a grid of baulks. Similarly, differential wear on surfaces of rubble indicating the pressure of sill-beams can be missed outside a large open area or destroyed without being understood within a narrow trench. An important non-destructive source of information on vanished structures is that of geophysical prospection: as the technology behind geophysics has advanced, so the buried traces of structures can be revealed with more clarity (see Chapter 5).

Experiment and ethnography

In addition to refining their excavation techniques, archaeologists have sought to explore in more detail how structures in the past may have been built, used and decayed by constructing experimental structures in the present. Such experiments have been immensely valuable for the very simple reason that a clear knowledge of how a building 'stands up' in practice is needed in order to create a three-dimensional reconstruction from a two-dimensional plan. Such experimental reconstructions, based on the undeniable premiss that physical conditions were the same in the past as they were in the present, have been useful in filling the interpretive gap between the archaeological pattern and the appearance of the past structure as a whole (West 1985). This is particularly true of post-hole patterns, since the carpentry of timber buildings can be complex, as we have seen. Experimental, as well as paper, reconstructions of buildings are useful in this regard for isolating practical problems of construction. Ethnographic parallels are also useful here in providing a link between pattern on the ground and the standing structure(s).

Another problem is that, however unmistakeable the archaeological trace, the structure above may be open to a variety of interpretations. Many sites in first-millennium BC Europe have 'four-poster' structures, seen as four post-holes (Cunliffe 1991). What these structures looked like above ground, however, is a matter for speculation, as is their function. Paradoxically, structures with far less trace in the archaeological record may be reconstructed with far more confidence.

A good example of all these problems is the history of archaeological interpretation of Anglo-Saxon buildings. At first, early Anglo-Saxons were thought to live in small, partly subterranean structures called *Grubenhauser* after their German counterparts or sunken-floored buildings (SFBs) (Fig. 4.18). SFBs were characterized by a large, shallow pit dug into the ground, with post-holes and other features around the pit suggesting a timber superstructure; they were first noticed in section, in the sides of gravel pits in eastern and central England. However, it was subsequently shown by large-scale open-area excavations that SFBs were only one type of structure in Anglo-Saxon settlements; that they accompanied, and were probably ancillary to, larger rectangular halls, the latter being structures which, having no pit, would not be apparent in the sections of the gravel pits (Marshall and Marshall 1991). At the same time, the superstructure of the SFB was called into question: experimental reconstruction suggested that, if the pit really was used as a living-space, its sides would soon have been subjected to erosion in the absence of revetting. It seemed more plausible that the pit served a different function underneath a planked floor, and subsequent experimental reconstructions have suggested a loftier dwelling of less humble pretensions. The Anglo-Saxon 'sunken-floored building' has become, more cautiously, the 'sunken-featured building', and a combination of evidence from open-area excavation and experimental archaeology has led us to revise our view of its appearance and function.

INVESTIGATING AND INTERPRETING STANDING STRUCTURES

So far I have considered how archaeologists excavate and reconstruct past structures, but archaeology is as much concerned with standing as excavated structures, and the section below discusses the differences in method required to analyse such evidence. The greater knowledge of the upper parts of the building given by having a building more or less complete brings advantages but also complexities. Many more structural phases may be evident and these need to be recorded and interpreted. While rules of stratigraphy are still largely valid, structures may be propped up, undercut, or have fresh infilling. Ironically, a standing building may not be fully understood without careful piece-by-piece demolition, which is rarely possible given the conservation value of most such structures. Standing buildings are often still functioning structures, such as religious buildings, houses, and even industrial hardware, or high-status pieces of national or world heritage that cannot be dissected at will by the archaeologists.

In many ways, the division between buried and standing structures is an arbitrary one: the wider questions archaeologists want to ask will affect the way they dig up and record structures. A good example is the early history of excavation of medieval peasant houses. At Wharram Percy in England, peasant houses survived as upstanding earthworks (Fig. 26.3), and at first the archaeologists left baulks standing over the earthworks: this stress on vertical control was in concordance with the aim of establishing the date of desertion of the site. As excavation progressed, however, it became clear that the structures were much more ephemeral than first thought and that the baulks would have to be removed in order to understand the structures fully. Thus a change in excavation technique went hand in hand with a widening of the aims of the excavation, away from questions of dating towards those of the social and economic position of the peasant houses (Beresford and Hurst 1990).

Another example of the interaction between research themes and excavation techniques is the Romano-British town of Wroxeter (Barker 1986). For much of the last century, the major questions asked concerning this site were 'what was the chronology of the site and the appearance of the major public buildings?' More recently, large-scale open-area excavation has revealed a series of substantial buildings overlying the main early Roman structures, buildings that nevertheless left ephemeral traces. Again, this shift in technique has gone hand in hand with a shift in the focus of the questions asked, away from the identification of particular buildings towards the asking of wider social questions about the end of Roman Britain.

Hence excavation, primary interpretation, and wider research themes should not be unduly separated. A distinction should also not be overdrawn between archaeological forms of interpretation and those of other disciplines, most notably architectural history but also folk-life studies, anthropology, economic and cultural history, and conservation studies. Thus, many of the observations given above on structures and their interpretation derive strictly not from archaeology in its narrow sense but from other disciplines. Equally, however, in so far as such disciplines deal with physical remains of the past and their interpretation, they may be considered to overlap with archaeology. The greatest overlap is with architectural history. In many cases, the overlap is to the point where archaeology and architectural history are one and the same thing, as for example with the great palaces and temples of many of the ancient civilizations. The temples of the Maya civilization of Central America survive as great upstanding ruins, but knowledge of these structures was first gained by early archaeologists (Sabloff 1989). Again, archaeological excavation at the great temples of classical Greece was motivated in part by a desire to fill in the missing pieces of their architectural history (Ridley 1992).

Traditionally, architectural historians have tried to understand the aesthetic and engineering aspects of structures, and have tended to neglect the questions of social context and economic function that occupy the interest of the archaeologist. Questions such as 'when was it built?', 'who built it?' and 'what were the main stylistic influences of the structure?' have tended to delimit the scope and range of traditional architectural history (Porphyrios 1981). Many of the assumptions of this type of approach are also found in the techniques of typology in archaeology (see Chapter 5). More recently, however, architectural historians have broadened their approach, being more concerned with the social and economic functions of buildings. Mark Girouard, for example, has looked at the changing role of the English country house, tracing how great houses acted as symbols of power and as social centres for the local élite (Girouard 1978). He reviewed the different architectural developments of the sixteenth to nineteenth centuries so beloved of traditional historians – the introduction of the Classical Orders, Baroque, Palladianism, and so on – not just as a succession of styles, but in terms of what they can tell us about the social life of the owners and users of these houses.

Architectural historians have also expanded their field by looking beyond the great house: over the last forty years the study of traditional or vernacular buildings has been expanded into a major theme. Traditional or vernacular structures are those that are 'common, ordinary, regional and small' (Mercer 1975: 1). Their study has involved scholars in looking at the structures that housed the mass of the population rather than simply those of the élite, and at everyday life as well as the exceptional – concerns close to the heart of most archaeologists.

Parallel developments have led other disciplines also to develop a range of interests pertinent to the study of structures. Folk-life studies, developed from the late nineteenth century onwards, have always included an interest in traditional architecture (Ewart Evans 1966). Anthropologists have similarly become more sensitive to the material culture and technical systems of the peoples they have studied, while the so-called 'New Social History' and 'New Cultural History' have paid more attention to the evidence of the everyday structures of life such as dwellings and other buildings (Isaac 1983). When looking for models to interpret his or her evidence, therefore, the archaeologist is not short of complementary disciplines to turn to.

At the same time, archaeology has widened its interests beyond traditional questions of chronology and distribution. Archaeologists are now more willing to turn to contemporary ethnographic examples for models to interpret their evidence, and are more prepared to examine the social and symbolic aspects of structures. Archaeologists have therefore moved closer to the concerns of other disciplines also.

This interaction between different disciplines concerned with the study of structures can also be seen if we look at the early history of archaeological approaches to buildings. Early evolutionary approaches combined thinking on architecture and social evolution. Scholars such as Innocent (1916) and S. O. Addy (1898) asserted that there was a link between the house type characteristic of a human group and the position of that group on the evolutionary scale, between simple and complex. In particular, it was suggested by some nineteenth-century writers such as Addy that circular houses were symptomatic of matrilineal societies, whereas rectangular dwellings characterized patrilineal groups. Since in many areas of the globe rectangular houses appeared to succeed circular structures at some point in prehistory, this was interpreted as evidence for the end of matrilineal groups and their replacement by patrilineal cultures. Thus, the evolutionary schema fitted house type in with the evolutionary schemes of human society proposed by Morgan, Marx, Engels and others, of the kind discussed in Chapter 11. Such global evolutionary models were regarded with more and more scepticism as the nineteenth century progressed: scholars pointed out the difficulty of generalizing from present cultural groups to past ones and stressed the uniqueness of cultures (McNairn 1980). In terms of structures, then, archaeologists found evolutionary schema less appealing: rather, if each culture had its own form of dwelling, structures could be used as diagnostic of particular, unique cultural groups. Gordon Childe, for example, listed house form as one of the criteria for defining an archaeological culture (McNairn 1980).

The form of structures was thus used by the culture-historical school of archaeologists as one trait among others in the definition of archaeological cultures, though they accepted that it was less satisfactory than other stylistic traits such as ornamentation or burial practice, since house forms were far more obviously influenced by environment as well as cultural preference. The decoration of a pot is largely a matter of cultural choice. Not so, however, with the selection of materials and building techniques – an igloo would not be an appropriate cultural choice of dwelling in the Amazonian rain forest. However, distinctive forms of structure could be seen to 'get up and move' in Childe's terms (McNairn 1980), indicating the possibility either of the diffusion of cultural traits or of the migration of peoples.

A typical example of this type of approach to the significance of structures was the mapping of *Grubenhauser*, the sunken-featured buildings discussed earlier, typical structures in north-western Europe after the fall of the Roman Empire. These distinctive structures appear to be culturally diagnostic of 'Germanic' groups: they may be found in various contexts in the 'North Sea culture area' of early medieval Europe (West 1985). Again, distinctively long rectangular house forms moved with the *Linearbandkeramik* early neolithic culture across the loess soils of Europe in the fifth millennium BC (Hodder 1990). In both these cases, it is unclear whether the movement of forms of structure was a result of diffusion or migration; in other

332

words, whether a set of ideas including those on house forms was being transmitted between peoples, or whether peoples were moving across Europe taking their forms of dwelling with them.

In a more recent context of study, much interesting research has been done by post-medieval archaeologists and architectural historians on the movement of house forms from the Old World to the New (Fig. 8.9). Robert Blair St George has traced the movement of particular types of house plan from Puritan East Anglia in England to the seventeenth-century colonies of New England, whilst forms of house present in seventeenth-century western England have been excavated in Virginia (Blair St George 1987). These houses were built using very different techniques in the New World. Timber was more plentiful in the vast forests of Virginia and New England than in the old, deforested countryside of the mother country; and because Virginian planters did not intend to stay for more than a few years, posts were set in post-holes in Virginia long after the practice was abandoned in England. Despite these wide structural differences, the plans of dwellings in the two areas were strikingly similar. Virginia and New England shared the same similarities and differences in terms of plan that the West Country and East Anglia shared at 'home'.

West African forms of structure have also been shown to migrate in this way: forms derived from the Yoruba houses of West Africa appear to have been built by newly transported slaves in the West Indian plantations. Thereafter, through a process of 'Creolization' (the emergence of forms that were hybrid between the different ethnic groups in the Caribbean and North America), houses showing distinct West African influence were built on slave plantations in the Carolinas and other areas of the American colonies (Upton and Vlach 1987).

The New Archaeology of the 1960s and early 1970s (see Chapter 2) introduced a wide range of new techniques in the interpretation of structures. The origins of many of the scientific techniques mentioned above lie during this period. Perhaps more important, however, was the processual contribution to the interpretation of structures. The primary sentiment of the New Archaeology was one of optimism. In line with the general premises of processualism, it was argued that structures were not just unique creations of ancient peoples, opaque in their particularity: archaeologists were not just confined to talking about the technical aspects of dwell- ings – structures could tell us about the social dimensions of the past too. In particular, given the new stress on the ideas of adaptation and systems theory, structures were seen as settings for particular activities that were related one to another in a functional way. Lewis Binford himself concentrated on the more ephemeral evidence of hunter-gatherer sites, looking at the ways that stone tools and bones were distributed around different types of site. He argued that we could infer the size and composition of groups from aspects of their sites, and that ethnoarchaeology and archaeology of structures could be related. Thus, for example, he mapped the slight windbreaks and scatters of hunting debris associated with Nunamiut Eskimo hunting stands, which he felt offered a way to understand hunter–gatherer sites in the past (Binford 1983).

Work by processual archaeologists on more substantial structures included functional examination of palaces and other major structures in early state societies (Sabloff 1989). Palaces and temples were not simply regarded as élite buildings symptomatic of 'high culture' or 'civilization': their social role was also investigated. For example, it was argued that many of the great stone temples of the Maya civilization acted not simply as sites for the worship of the gods, but as centres for the redistribution of prestige items. Thus, the priesthood of the temples had economic and political power as well as religious significance. Archaeologists explained the rise of the Maya civilization in terms of the aggregation of this economic and political power. Thus, Maya temples were seen as more than just the mysterious relics of a lost and forgotten civilization: they were used to suggest why that civilization had developed and how it had functioned as a social network. Other élite structures were understood in similar ways. The great Minoan palaces such as Knossos and Phaistos were also seen as centres of redistribution, structures at the very top of an increasingly complex and stratified network of sites (Cherry 1986). So New Archaeology pushed the pendulum back from regarding structures as unique and particular towards looking at general stages in human evolution and the way in which types of structure reflected those stages.

New Archaeology also stressed the role that ethnographic analogy had to play in understanding structures. As we have seen, this stress on looking at non-western cultures in the present was not new, but the New Archaeologists were concerned to find out in more detail how contemporary structures were built, what their social and economic context was, and how they decayed and left archaeological traces. They then used this evidence as an aid to the understanding of prehistoric structures. New Archaeology also stressed the possibility of looking at the social nature of structures through the study of built space. One famous study was that of Hill (1970), who examined the pueblo architecture in the American Southwest and looked at the pottery found within these structures; using ethnographic analogy, Hill argued that pottery painting styles were passed down from mother to daughter. If this was the case, indication of localized pottery styles within different areas of the pueblo would point to a matrilocal society (one in which husbands moved to wives' residences rather than vice versa). Hill found that such concentrations existed; although the study was challenged, it remained an exciting example of the sort of social inferences that one could draw from the archaeology of structures.

One method of looking at the social role of rooms within a building is through the 'penetration analysis' of complex structures, a technique developed outside archaeology by Hillier and Hanson (1985). Hillier and Hanson's interest was in both modern and ancient architecture. Their method was to treat rooms as units, and map the links between rooms rather than their spatial proximity. This was important because, as with a maze, rooms can be physically close to one another but far apart in terms of access. This kind of topological analysis has led to a re-examination of the social roles of different rooms within, for example, medieval castles, Minoan palaces, Roman villas and many other such large structures (Locock 1994). Thus it has been shown how the layout of medieval nunneries differed from that of monasteries in very insignificant ways in superficial terms, but profoundly in terms of the arrangement of rooms (Gilchrist 1993).

More recently, archaeologists have expanded their scope of enquiry still more widely: they have looked beyond the social and economic functions of structures, and have turned to examine the symbolic meanings that structures might embody. Archaeologists have recognized that not only churches and temples carry symbolic meanings, but that everyday life and the space within which that life takes place is also meaningfully constructed. In other words, ordinary life is also organized around ideas: ideas of how to think and behave in a family, ideas about solidarity of community, ideas about time and work discipline. All these ideas will influence the way people choose to organize and arrange space within structures, however humble or ordinary the dwelling may have been.

In looking at the symbolic structures that lie behind physical ones, archaeologists have been encouraged by the work of anthropologists such as Pierre Bourdieu, who have shown how patterns of space within ordinary dwellings in non-western societies may represent very elaborate systems of symbolic meanings. Bourdieu showed for example how Berber houses in North Africa were split into men's and women's spaces, and how different activities such as cooking and sleeping were seen as 'male' and 'female' (Bourdieu 1973). This split was not one indicated by walls, but rather by the positioning of the hearth, the eating area, the bed, and so on, within the one large space of the house. At the same time the house as a whole was seen as a female domain, contrasted to the 'male' world outside. Bourdieu thus demonstrated that the Berber house is much more than just a machine for living in: it encodes and expresses different ideas about the sort of people Kabyle men and women are, and the way they should think and behave.

When archaeologists look at ancient and prehistoric structures it is more difficult to perform this kind of complex symbolic analysis since the inhabitants of ancient houses are long dead. They are therefore no longer available for the sort of observation and intensive questioning that Bourdieu and other anthropologists could indulge in. Nevertheless, the materials for such a kind of symbolic analysis are available if the archaeologist is sensitive enough to the evidence. He or she may look at the nature of physical boundaries between different areas of a dwelling, and interpret these as symbolic boundaries also. The relationship between the inside, social, world of the house and the outside, natural, world may also be examined in terms of the boundaries placed between the two areas. Inside the house, different areas of cooking, eating and sleeping may be discerned, and interpreted as activities taking place in different parts of the household. The provision of privacy, or the lack of it, may indicate the relative weight of community versus individual in that household and culture. Finally, the deposition of rubbish may be examined: as Lord Raglan pointed out, the house is kept clean not only for the sake of tidiness, but because it is sacred.

Ian Hodder has explored how the houses of early neolithic societies in the Near East and the Balkans expressed a series of ideas about nature and culture as well as about household relations. Hodder saw neolithic houses as expressive of an idea he calls the 'domus'. Through structural evidence Hodder sees the idea of the domus unfolding as neolithic culture spread across Europe; changes in house form playing a key role in this (Hodder 1990).

Work in pre- and protohistoric periods has linked changing architectural forms to changing perceptions of gender, status and ethnicity. Many of the iron age structures above have been seen in structuralist terms, linking left/right, front/back oppositions and orientation to cosmological and social ordering (Parker-Pearson and Richards 1994b). Studies of Roman villas have been the subject of much traditional work on art and architectural styles, and have been seen as fairly straightforward indices of 'Romanization'. Recent work has challenged such simplistic interpretations, and seen villa architecture in contexts across the Roman Empire as a far more complex expression of identity (Scott 1990; Scott 1994; Wallace-Hadrill 1988).

My own work on traditional architecture in Suffolk, England, has looked at how houses related to society in the late medieval and early modern periods (Johnson 1993; Fig. 8.10). The medieval house was dominated by a large central hall that was open to the roof. The hall was a symbolic expression of the relations between different parts of the household. Though it was not divided physically, the hall was divided into upper and lower ends, a divide that corresponded to master and servant. This divide was marked by architectural features such as the placing of windows and doors, and in some cases the raising of one end onto a 'dais' or low stage. Thus, the hall could symbolize community by being open to all while still demarcating wide difference in status within that community.

Changes in symbolic values can also be seen underlying the changes in houses at the end of the Middle Ages. The open hall was reduced in size and given a ceiling and chimney-stack. This reduced its importance as an expression of the household and its visual impact. At the same time other, more private, parts of the houses gained in importance. Increasing segregation between different parts of the house, a greater degree of privacy, and rising material comfort all added up to a 'process of closure'. This process went hand-in-hand with changes in the way houses were built, away from traditional systems of timber-framing towards more 'rational' and cost-effective methods, reflecting the rise of market capitalism. Closure and

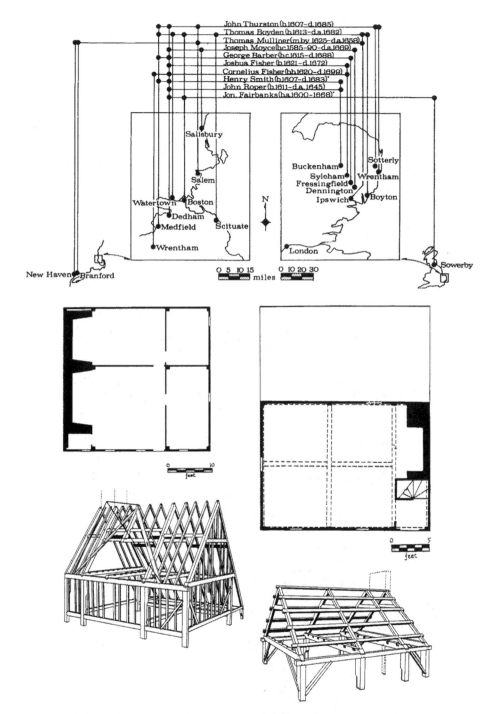

John Thurston (b.1607–d.1685)
Thomas Boyden (b.1613–d.a.1682)
Thomas Mulliner (m.by 1625–d.a.1658)
Joseph Moyce (bc.1585–90–d.a.1669)
George Barber (bc.1615–d.1688)
Joshua Fisher (b.1621–d.1672)
Cornelius Fisher (bh.1620–d.1699)
Henry Smith (b.1607–d.1683)'
John Roper (b.1611–d.a.1645)
Jon. Fairbanks (ba.1600–1668)'

Salisbury
Salem
Watertown • Boston
Dedham
Medfield
Scituate
Wrentham
New Haven • Branford

N

Buckenham
Syleham • Wrentham
Fressingfield
Dennington
Ipswich • Boyton
London

Sotterly

Sowerby

0 5 10 15 miles   0 10 20 30

0   10
feet

0   5
feet

Figure 8.8 Links in house plans between East Anglia and New England. The map above indicates the East Anglian origins of carpenters in seventeenth-century New England; below are the plan and roof frames of two seventeenth-century New England houses. Source: Museum of Fine Arts, Boston.

Figure 8.9 The collapsed gable wall of a Roman villa at Meonstoke, Britain: this wall collapsed forward at the end of the villa's life, leaving it substantially intact and prone on the ground. By kind permission of the Trustees of the British Museum. Drawn by S. Crummy.

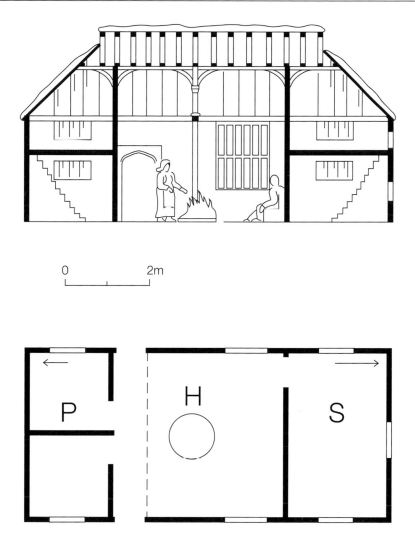

Figure 8.10 Traditional architecture in Suffolk, England: changes in symbolic values. Source: Johnson 1993.

technical changes reflected social changes, away from medieval towards modern patterns of family and household life.

There has been much work on similar lines in 'colonial archaeology', where scholars have looked at different architectural forms in terms of the archaeology of modernity. Much of this work has been done on the east coast of the USA (see Chapter 28), though other colonial contexts such as southern Africa have also produced exciting studies of both traditional and 'polite' architecture (Hall 1987).

CONCLUSION

All the examples of interpretation of structures given in the last section have their problems: all leave important factors out of their analyses, whether these are symbolic, cultural, economic, or environmental in nature. No single method of looking at structures has yet been seen as fully satisfactory. However, this is inevitable given the nature of archaeology: enquiry never stops, and our ideas and models are constantly being confronted with contrary evidence and being found wanting from the perspective of competing approaches. Nevertheless, this chapter must end with a paradox. We have seen that archaeologists are very good at recovering the fragmentary traces of structures through techniques that are constantly being refined, whether these are of remote sensing or of new excavation methods. Archaeologists have also spent much time learning to interpret better the traces which they find, having learnt the lessons of experimental archaeology and ethnoarchaeology. We have yet to develop the full potential of the archaeology of structures, however, in the field of our broader understanding of how past cultures used and thought about built space. We are very good at recording and interpreting the traces of structures at a primary level, but less good at understanding what they mean. We need more imagination and understanding of different cultural systems to make good this difference in the future.

REFERENCES

Adam, J. P. (1994) *Roman Building: Materials and Techniques*, London: Batsford.

Addy, S. O. (1898) *The Evolution of the English House*, London: Allen & Unwin.

Alcock, N., Barley, M. W., Dixon, P. W. and Meeson, R. A. (1996) *Recording Timber-Framed Buildings: An Illustrated Glossary*, CBA Practical Handbook in Archaeology 5, London: Council for British Archaeology.

Alexander, J. (1995) 'Building stone from the East Midlands quarries: transportation and usage', *Medieval Archaeology*: 107–35

Barker, P. (1981) *Wroxeter Roman City: Excavations 1966–1980*, London.

Barker, P. (1986) *Understanding Archaeological Excavation*, London: Batsford.

Beresford, M. and Hurst, J. G. (1990) *Wharram*, London: Batsford.

Betancourt, J. L. and van Deveder, T. R. (1981) 'Holocene vegetation in Chaco Canyon, New Mexico', *Science* 214: 656–58.

Binford, L. R. (1983) *In Pursuit of the Past*, London: Thames and Hudson.

Blair St George, R. (1987) ' "Set thine house in order": the domestication of the yeomanry in 17th century New England', in D. Upton and M. Vlach (eds), *Common Places: Readings in American Vernacular Architecture*, Athens: University of Georgia Press: 336–65.

Bourdieu, P. (1973) 'The Berber house', in M. Douglas (ed.) *Rules and Meanings*, Harmondsworth: Penguin: 98–110.

Cherry, J. (1986) 'Politics and palaces: some problems in Minoan state formation', in

C. Renfrew and J. Cherry (eds) *Peer Polity Interaction and Socio-political Change*, Cambridge: Cambridge University Press: 19–45.

Cunliffe, B. (1991) *Iron Age Communities in Britain* (3rd edition), London: Routledge.

Ewart Evans, G. (1996) *The Pattern Under the Plough*, London: Faber.

Fletcher, B. (1938) *A History of Architecture on the Comparative Method*, London: Batsford.

Fone, S. (ed.) (1984) *The World Atlas of Architecture*, London: Mitchell Beazley Publishers.

Gilchrist, R. (1993) *Gender and Material Culture: An Archaeology of Religious Women*, London: Routledge.

Girouard, M. (1978) *Life in the English Country House: A Social and Architectural History*, London: Yale University Press.

Glassie, H. (1975) *Folk Housing in Middle Virginia: A Structural Analysis of Historic Artifacts*, Knoxville: University of Tennessee Press.

Graves, C. P. (1989) 'Social space in the English medieval parish church', *Economy and Society* 18 (3): 297–322.

Hall, M. (1987) *Farmers, Kings, and Traders: The People of Southern Africa 200–1860*, Chicago: University of Chicago Press.

Harris, R. (1978) *Discovering Timber-Framed Buildings*, Aylesbury: Shire.

Hietala, H. J. (ed.) (1983) *Intrasite Spatial Analysis in Archaeology*, Cambridge: Cambridge University Press.

Hill, J. N. (1970) *Broken K Pueblo: Prehistoric Social Organisation in the American Southwest*, Anthropological Papers of the University of Arizona 18, Tucson: University of Arizona Press.

Hillier, W. and Hanson, J. (1985) *The Social Logic of Space*, Cambridge: Cambridge University Press.

Hodder, I. (1990) *The Domestication of Europe*, Oxford: Blackwell.

Howard, M. (1987) *The Early Tudor Country House: Architecture and Politics 1485–1550*, London: George Philip.

Huffman, T. (1996) *Snakes and Crocodiles: Power and Symbolism in Ancient Zimbabwe*, Johannesburg: Witwatersrand University Press.

Innocent, C. (1916) *The Development of English Building Construction*, Cambridge: Cambridge University Press.

Isaac, R. (1983) *The Transformation of Virginia 1760–1820*, Chapel Hill: University of North Carolina Press.

Johnson, M. H. (1989) 'Conceptions of agency in archaeological interpretation', *Journal of Anthropological Archaeology* 8: 189–211.

Johnson, M. H. (1993) *Housing Culture: Traditional Architecture in an English Landscape*, London: University College London Press.

Johnson, M. H. (1996) *An Archaeology of Capitalism*, Oxford: Blackwell.

Kent, S. (ed.) (1989) *Domestic Architecture and the Use of Space*, Cambridge: Cambridge University Press.

King, A. C. and Potter, T. W. (1996) 'A new domestic building-façade from Roman Britain', *Journal of Roman Studies* 2: 195–204.

Lefebvre, H. (1991) *The Production of Space*, Oxford: Blackwell.

Locock, M. (ed.) (1994) *Meaningful Architecture: Social Interpretations of Buildings*, Aldershot: Avebury.

Longacre, W. A. (1964) 'Archaeology as anthropology: a case study', *Science* 144: 1454–55.

McNairn, B. (1980) *The Method and Theory of V. Gordon Childe*, Edinburgh: Edinburgh University Press.

Marshall, A. and Marshall, G. (1991) 'Differentiation, change and continuity in Anglo-Saxon buildings', *Archaeological Journal* 150: 366–402.

Mercer, E. (1975) *English Vernacular Houses*, London: Her Majesty's Stationery Office.

Millett, M. (1983) 'Excavations at Cowdery's Down, Basingstoke, Hants, 1979–81', *Archaeological Journal* 140: 151–279.

Moir, J. (1997) 'Vernacular architecture: open air museums and the ecological framework', *Vernacular Architecture* 28: 20–24.

Moore, H. (1986) *Space, Text and Gender*, Cambridge: Cambridge University Press.

Oliver, J. (ed.) (1995) *Encyclopaedia of Vernacular Architecture*, Cambridge: Cambridge University Press.

Panofsky, N. (1957) *Gothic Architecture and Scholasticism*, London: Thames and Hudson.

Parker Pearson, M. and Richards, C. (eds) (1994a) *Architecture and Order*, London: Routledge.

Parker Pearson, M. and Richards, C. (1994b) 'Architecture and order: spatial representation and archaeology', in M. Parker-Pearson and C. Richards (eds) *Architecture and Order*, London: Routledge: 38–72.

Porphyrios, D. (ed.) (1981) *On the Methodology of Architectural History*, London: Architectural Design.

Rackham, O. (1986) *The History of the Countryside*, London: Dent.

Redman, C. L. (1978) *The Rise of Civilisation*, San Francisco: Freeman.

Reynolds, P. (1979) *Iron-Age Farm: The Butser Experiment*, London: British Museum.

Richards, J. (1991) *Stonehenge*, London: Batsford.

Ridley, R. I. (1992) *The Eagle and the Spade: Archaeology in Rome During the Napoleonic Era*, Cambridge: Cambridge University Press.

Ritchie, A. (1995) *Prehistoric Orkney*, London: Batsford.

Roberts, B. K. (1996) *Landscapes of Settlement: Prehistory to the Present*, London: Routledge.

Sabloff, J. A. (1989) *The Cities of Ancient Mexico*, London: Thames and Hudson.

Samson, R. (ed.) (1990) *The Social Archaeology of Houses*, Edinburgh: Edinburgh University Press.

Scott, E. (1990) 'Romano-British villas and the social construction of space', in R. Samson (ed.) *The Social Archaeology of Houses*, Edinburgh: Edinburgh University Press: 149–72.

Scott, S. (1994) 'Patterns of movement: architectural design and visual planning in the Romano-British villa', in M. Locock (ed.), *Meaningful Architecture: Social Interpretations of Buildings*, Aldershot: Avebury: 86–98.

Shackel, P. (1996) *Culture Change and the New Technology: An Archaeology of the Early American Industrial Era*, New York: Plenum.

Upton, D. and Vlach, M. (1987) *Common Places: Readings in American Vernacular Architecture*, Athens: University of Georgia Press.

Wallace-Hadrill, A. (1988) 'The social structure of the Roman house', *Proceedings of the British School at Rome* 56: 43–97.

West, S. (1985) *West Stow: The Anglo-Saxon Village*, East Anglian Archaeology 24, Ipswich: Suffolk County Planning Dept.

Wetherill, R. (1966) *Anasazi*, Albuquerque: University of New Mexico Press.

Whitelaw, T. M. (1994) 'Order without architecture: functional, social and symbolic dimensions in hunter–gatherer settlement organisation', in M. Parker Pearson and C. Richards (eds) *Architecture and Order*, London: Routledge: 217–42.

Wright, J. A. (1972) *Brick Building in England from the Middle Ages to 1550*, London: J. Baker.

Wymer, J. (1982) *The Palaeolithic Age*, Beckenham: Croom Helm.

SELECT BIBLIOGRAPHY

For archaeological methods generally, see Chapter 4, but Alcock *et al.* (1996) is an excellent practical guide to techniques of recording; other handbooks in the same series are useful for standing buildings. Harris (1978) is a clear, accessible and fascinating introduction to the complexities of timber framing. Shackel (1996) is an excellent study of industrial architecture in its context. In my own books (1993, 1996) I examine architecture – both traditional and polite – from a contextual perspective and try to relate it to wider cultural and social forces. Moore (1986) is a definitive ethnoarchaeological study. Kent (1989), Locock (1994), Samson (1990) and Parker-Pearson and Richards (1994a) provide collections of case studies from a variety of theoretical perspectives, and Graves (1989) and Gilchrist (1993) are useful interpretations of religious structures. For structural studies in other disciplines, see Porphyrios (1981) for a collection of readings that give a flavour of the methodology of architectural history, and Girouard (1978) and Howard (1987) for studies of the relationship between élite buildings and politics by architectural historians, whilst Bourdieu (1973) remains a classic study. Glassie (1975) is a classic structuralist text. Lefebvre (1991) and Roberts (1996) are examples of approaches derived from historical geography. The reader edited by Upton and Vlach (1987) gives a flavour of American architectural studies.

9

STUDYING ARTEFACTS

Elizabeth Slater

INTRODUCTION

For a discipline concerned with the study of human actions and human development through time, the central place accorded in archaeology to artefacts – objects
made and used by people – is not hard to understand. They are the direct products
of human intelligence and, however incomplete the archaeological record and
however selectively objects entered that record, they are actual items that were
deliberately made and utilized. The questions may be 'who?', 'where?', 'why?' or
'what?', and the artefacts may not be able the answer these directly, but they are one
of the most easily accessible and recognizable forms of evidence. Also it is the
collections of objects in museums, plus the standing monuments, that form much
of the public face of archaeology. Archaeologists may be ultimately concerned with
the broad issues of social, political and economic systems, and the individual objects
standing in serried ranks in museums may seem far removed from these, but it is
the objects that are a source of fundamental data: 'the things humankind makes and
uses at any particular time and place are probably the truest representation we have
of values and meaning within a society' (Kingery 1996: ix). How far, if at all, we can
approach any 'true' understanding or interpretation of the material record, or
whether any such record is even seen to exist, is a matter of much debate (Barrett
1994; Hodder 1991), but artefacts must still be worthy of study as one of the few
things to come to us directly from the past.

Each object currently known has its own history and participated in the
sequence: creation–use–deposition–recovery. It is these histories, often only
revealed through the study of the artefact itself, that form a major component of the
base data of archaeology. The problem is how to reach these because, when we are

344

confronted with an archaeological object, very little of its history is readily visible. Only two things are immediately apparent: the shape of the object, and the general type of material involved. With these two aspects readily accessible, and with (until the last few decades at least) a paucity of techniques available to extract more information, it is not surprising that the study of artefacts within archaeology has been dominated by consideration of form and material, augmented when possible with information on final context and association.

However, it was not just that form, material and context were visible, there was also an assumption that these aspects were normally sufficient to reveal the whole history of an object. As far as manufacture was concerned, identification of the material was thought to give information on how the object was made because only a few standard processes were postulated for the production of objects. Similarly, use could be determined via shape and context: shape because it was assumed that most objects had a utilitarian function and therefore the form of the object could say something about that use; context as a means of confirming final use. The main exceptions to this utilitarian approach were objects found in graves or other special deposits, and here context dominated, as they were ascribed a ritual or ceremonial function. As for the date of the object, for objects from historical periods this could come from historical dating and for those from prehistoric periods the shape and decoration of certain objects could be considered against chronological frameworks devised by various means in which objects had been placed by their form (their typology) into sequences of relative date. If scientific methods were employed at all, it was mainly to provide more detailed information on the material, such as whether an object of copper-coloured metal was made of pure copper or a mixture of copper and another metal, or whether objects were of a generally similar material and could therefore be classified into a group on the basis of a presumed common origin.

From this basis, the 1970s can be seen as a watershed in the study of artefacts because they heralded an expansion in the range of scientific techniques available and also reappraisal of the fundamental rationale of archaeology, its nature and theoretical frameworks. In this latter context there has been a continuous questioning of many of the basic assumptions of archaeological methodology, producing profound changes throughout archaeology not least on the study of artefacts; much of this volume is concerned with the resulting reinterpretations of artefactual material as, for example, elements of material culture (Chapter 11), a component of production and exchange (Chapters 15 and 16), and as social indicators (Chapters 12 and 22). Although this section is concerned with the narrower field of artefacts as material entities and, in particular, the insights to be gained from the scientific study of the physical and chemical aspects of artefactual materials, the impact has been no less profound. This is because approaches to the study of artefactual material – the areas deemed worthy of investigation as much as the interpretation of the artefacts themselves – have always been controlled by the prevailing orthodoxies on the nature of the past and the issues deemed significant at the specific time, as well as by the techniques available. What makes the last two decades appear, at present, to be a very significant period is that a re-evaluation of the questions to be asked of artefactual material came at the same time as the development of new techniques of examination, allowing new areas of research to be opened up. Thus, a pottery vessel might previously have been assessed solely in terms of its visual characteristics – its form, its colour, any decoration, type of clay used and where it was found – whereas it is now possible to try to investigate, via study of the artefact alone, the actual raw materials involved, their potential sources, place of manufacture, temperature and conditions of firing, date of firing, nature of any surface treatment, absorption of contents into the vessel walls, form of pigments or glaze, physical and chemical properties of the fabric and their possible influence on use. Therefore, many new opportunities have been opened up and many new questions can be addressed, just at the time when archaeology itself has been looking at the questions it should pose. However, whatever the last few years may have brought, archaeology as a discipline has a long history and many of the questions currently being asked are still rooted in past frameworks; thus it is not possible to approach the current study of artefacts without some appreciation of the historical picture.

HISTORICAL PERSPECTIVES

One of the most profound influences on the development of archaeology, and therefore on the study of artefacts, was the establishment of the Three Age System by C. J. Thomsen in the mid-nineteenth century (Chapter 1). In his observations of form within specific classes, Thomsen was seeing changes in shape as improvements through time. The overall tripartite sequence of worked stone followed by the products of technological processes, the metals of bronze and iron, was all well in keeping with the western European view of the primacy of technological development, an idea fostered by experience of the Industrial Revolution. These concepts of progress and progression were recurring elements in much archaeological work in the nineteenth century. Thus, in the 1870s General Pitt-Rivers used both archaeological and ethnographic material to argue that the forms of individual classes of object with a similar function must necessarily change and improve through time (Lane-Fox 1875), whilst Flinders Petrie, addressing the problem of the dating of prehistoric graves in Egypt, postulated that certain types of object or forms of decoration would appear, grow in importance and then decline, their relative abundance within grave assemblages thus being a guide to their position in a chronological sequence (Petrie 1899; see Chapter 5).

Whether considering the form, decoration or material of artefacts, these ideas of change and progress formed only a part of the overall evolutionist approach that dominated much of archaeological theory in Europe during the later nineteenth century. A further central tenet of this approach was the assumption that all human societies developed along a straight evolutionary line from 'barbarism' to 'civilization' (with occasional backsliding allowed), and that the artefacts produced by a society could serve as markers to identify the level reached by that society. The reliance on artefacts to provide the link through which other aspects of society could be established stemmed, in part, from the sheer quantities of material available compared with other archaeological evidence, but a further major impetus was increased European exploration and observation of the artefacts produced by contemporary non-western societies. Thus, the supposed early use of bronze and iron in Europe when compared with the scarcity of metal use by peoples of Australasia, North America and sub-Saharan Africa – areas deemed to have remained rooted in stone age technology – served only to reinforce the supposed primacy of artefacts as a guide to all aspects of society and the idea, in particular, that the production of metal artefacts was a mark of progress.

By the end of the nineteenth century, artefacts were still the main component of the archaeological record considered worthy of detailed study, with objects of stone and metal given particular significance. A broad chronological picture had been developed into which these objects could be placed. One major component was a long 'Age of Stone' that was thought still visible in many parts of the world. In favoured areas such as the Near East and the eastern Mediterranean, out of this barbaric Stone Age had come the early civilizations of Mesopotamia, Egypt and the Aegean. The great classical civilizations of Greece and Rome were viewed as the logical outcome of these moves towards civilization. Similarly, the appearance of new types of artefact and the use of new materials were seen as a part, almost an essential part, of the development of civilization. Ceramic and metal artefacts were necessarily attributed to more advanced societies, because pottery and metals had to be formed or manufactured via technical processes and were not as immediately available as stone, bone, wood and many other organic materials.

No real explanation for the appearance of ceramics and metals was thought necessary; all could be explained by the concepts of progress and evolution – after a certain amount of experience and experimentation, new materials would be introduced as society developed. Given the western European view of the primacy of technology, there was some interest in the actual processes involved, but it was generally assumed that the methods used, say, to fire pottery or to smelt ores to yield metal operated under basic scientific principles and thus would have been very similar to systems still operating in the nineteenth century AD (for example Gowland 1899). However, while there might still be no need to explain their appearance, that appearance was seen as important because the introduction and use of ceramics and metals were taken to mark or form the route to civilization (Rodden 1981). Therefore, with the beginnings of the latter part of the Stone Age (the Neolithic) and the Bronze Age then considered coincident, respectively, with the introduction of ceramics and non-ferrous metals, these transition points within the chronological framework came to be seen almost as important as the framework itself and as major milestones in human development.

By the early twentieth century, many aspects of the evolutionist approach had become untenable, not least because of the increasing recognition that societies with the same level of technology can have very different types of artefact, settlements, economies, social systems and so on. The idea of a single route from so-called barbarism to civilization dominated by theories of progress was not totally abandoned, but was allied to the concept of 'culture' (Chapter 11). There was much emphasis on the typology of small groups of objects deemed to be particularly diagnostic and which, in combination with common settlement types and burial rites, were held to represent particular groups: a prime example was the notion of a 'Bell Beaker culture group' within early bronze age Europe identified by the presence of a distinctive form of pottery and still considered in terms of this traditional terminology (for example Champion *et al.* 1984: 168). In essence, this culture-historical approach (typified by the writings of Gordon Childe) reinforced the importance attached to the shape of objects, to their typology. Collections of objects found on sites were considered in terms of their similarities or differences, and more detailed chronological frameworks based on very complex typological schemes were developed. This reflected the general concern at this time, described by Willey and Sabloff (1980) as the 'classificatory-historical' period in archaeology, to establish regional chronological systems that might eventually be tied into some historical structure. One of the key elements within the European system was comparison of artefact collections from different sites to try to determine the geographical distribution of certain 'culture traits'. This, in turn, introduced a spatial aspect into the study of artefacts. Objects found on sites spread over a large geographical area were being recognized as alike in form or carrying similar patterns of decoration and were being classified into cultural groups on the basis of appearance.

This inevitably prompted questions about how the objects reached the sites, and an interest in production and exchange on a regional basis. A necessary adjunct to this speculation was research into where a specific set of objects had been made: where had they come from? Was it feasible to assume, for example, that ceramics showing the same type of decoration were all made in the same place? Were particular raw materials or production centres under specific 'cultural' control? Indeed, for raw materials such as high quality cherts or metal ores that have specific geological associations and are not uniformly distributed, could the search for appropriate raw materials or the control of them have been a driving force that could explain patterns of settlement and economic trends? These questions, combined with improvements in analytical facilities, led to increased interest in the possibility of using chemical composition of artefacts as a further line of investigation (Peacock

1970). Thus began the systematic development of two aspects of the study of artefacts that remain paramount today: the use of a physical or chemical characteristic (be it colour, petrology, chemical composition, or isotopic composition) to classify objects into groups; and the use of that characteristic to try to link artefacts to the source of raw materials or to place of manufacture.

As early as 1796 Klaproth had analysed Roman glass and Greek and Roman coins, and by the mid-nineteenth century Wocel was already suggesting that chemical composition could be a guide to the source of archaeological materials (Pollard and Heron 1996). Others followed his lead, but the wet chemical techniques then available required large samples and analysis was mainly confined to determination of the type of material via the major elements, such as whether a metal coin was pure silver or a silver alloy; or a copper-based ear-ring of tin-bronze or brass (Davies 1934/35). From the 1940s, the development of more sensitive methods of chemical analysis, such as emission spectroscopy, that could operate with smaller samples at higher precision, meant that more elements could be analysed and that more objects were available for analysis. Analysis was still mainly for the major elements, thus little more than a further adjunct to description, but as more data were produced there was increased interest in the possible value of the minor and trace element content as a means of classifying or grouping objects (Caley 1964).

In the particular context of European prehistory, the main emphasis was on neolithic ceramics and copper-based artefacts of the Bronze Age (for example Brown and Blin-Stoyle 1959). In the culture-historical approach it was these types of object that had already been classified in terms of their typology and formed the basis of the typological and chronological frameworks. Thus chemical analysis was undertaken to test their validity and determine whether objects viewed as similar on typological, cultural or chronological grounds also showed similarities in composition that might suggest a common origin or tradition. However, as larger scale analytical programmes developed, there was a tendency to see the analytical data as more objective than qualities like decoration and style, and classification increasingly based on chemical composition alone, without the validity of the analytical groupings that emerged necessarily examined with sufficient rigour (Butler and van der Waals 1966; Junghans *et al.* 1968). If an object showed more or less than a specific concentration of an element, it went into one group or another and justification of the choice of the particular element or the concentration at which division was made was often lacking. In part through the emergence of multivariate computer systems that allow examination of the structure and stability of groupings, but mainly through an appreciation of the factors that can affect chemical composition from raw material to surviving object, the emphasis in chemical analysis has now moved towards a very rigorous appraisal of the interpretation of analytical data: objects may be apparently similar or different in chemical composition but what does this mean?; how valid are the groupings?; do they really reflect differences in raw materials and/or processes? Given analytical errors, how 'similar' is 'similar'? How much difference in composition can be allowed and the objects still put into the same group?

Amongst scientific techniques, new analytical and computer systems can therefore be seen to have had a very profound effect on the study of artefacts. The same can also be said of the increased use of scientific dating methods, because techniques such as radio-carbon and uranium-series have not only allowed direct dating of an individual object's creation or deposition but have also allowed the production of chronologies independent of historical and typological frameworks (Chapter 5). This has had three main effects on the study of artefacts: first, it allows assessment of whether objects really did change in form through time and thus whether date had any influence on artefact shape – the validity of complex typological dating sequences can be examined independently; second, where these sequences do collapse and date does not appear to be a controlling influence on artefact shape, consideration has to be given of other reasons for changes in form; and third, it releases objects from their role as chronological markers and promotes consideration of some of their other aspects.

The introduction of independent dating methods also allowed broader issues and assumptions about the material record to be examined including, as far as the Neolithic and Bronze Age of Europe are concerned, key questions relating to technical innovation and stagnation. In the early stages of the application of radio-carbon dating, for example, a major inference drawn from the dating of material from a few pertinent sites was the proposition that copper production began in south-east Europe without any external technical influences from Anatolia or western Asia (Renfrew 1969). Thus radio-carbon dating was suggesting that the production of metal from its ores, one of the key developments highlighted within the Three Age System, could have started independently in both western Asia and eastern Europe and, because of the apparently later appearance of metalworking in the intervening areas of Anatolia and the Levant, that the appearance of metalworking in Europe could no longer be explained by the simple diffusion of ideas from the Mesopotamia.

This particular example of the impact of the application of scientific dating methods has been taken not only because of its immediate significance but because the ideas were being presented in the late 1960s and early 1970s, a pivotal period for the study of artefacts and when new insights were still being grafted onto the existing concepts. Therefore, while the idea of independent development of metalworking questioned one of the major elements of the diffusionist approach it did not impact *per se* on the study of artefacts, because it was conducted within the pre-existing framework of artefact studies. The postulated early appearance of metal use in south-east Europe was still seen to require explanation and there was a lingering attachment to a concept that could be seen as 'technological determinism'; that is, that accumulated experience of one pyrotechnological process like pottery-firing could, with access to appropriate raw materials, lead to experimentation and the introduction of another pyrotechnological process such as metal ore smelting. In support of Renfrew's research a sherd of contemporary graphite ware was examined to determine its conditions of firing; the latter were initially assessed as firing at around 1050°C in a reducing atmosphere and, with the melting point of pure copper at 1083°C and the smelting of oxidized ores to yield metal requiring a reducing atmosphere, Renfrew concluded 'that refractory technology in the southeast European Chalcolithic had evolved sufficiently, in the firing of pottery, to provide the conditions required for the smelting and casting of copper' (Renfrew 1969: 38). Although more than one centre of innovation in metal use and production was being proposed, the casting of metals or the smelting of metal ores to yield metals were still seen as inherently 'difficult procedures', their first appearance as of great cultural significance for the area, and their roots lying within technological experience. Thus the application of radio-carbon dating in this area, and indeed scientific dating techniques in general, did not at that stage have any real effect on the way that the individual artefacts were actually considered.

What the results from scientific dating did do was contribute to the increasing dissatisfaction with the adequacies of the level of description sought within archaeology and growing recognition that a full re-assessment of the nature of the archaeological record was required (Chapter 2). Initially expressed via the Anglo-American perspective of the so-called New Archaeology (Binford 1972), these continuing debates on archaeological practice, principles, theory and philosophy have had a profound influence on the way that artefacts are viewed. Some of these major debates concerning artefacts have centred on the level of inference and the whole nature of the role of artefacts, much illuminated by insights from anthropology and ethnography (Hodder 1982). Various perspectives have emerged which see objects not as isolated items but as expressions of the whole society in which they were made and used. Why was an object produced? Why was it found in this particular context? What was its role? In place of descriptions of shape and material have come new questions: what does the form of an object indicate?; was shape dictated by use, material, period, culture, method of manufacture or combinations of these?; what is known of the function of an object?; can this be adequately assessed by consideration of context or is any direct method of examination possible?; what does the chemical analysis of a sample taken from an object actually mean? – is it a true reflection of the original composition of the object, and if so, can it be used to indicate the raw materials used to make it?; if objects have a similar composition, does this necessarily mean they were made in the same place?

How far these questions can be answered depends on the information that can be extracted. For an artefact considered as a material entity this can include its material, the types of raw materials and processes used to make it, the actual raw

351

materials, their source, the general location of production or actual manufacturing centre, why the object was made, its possible function, the detailed shape of the object and the degree to which its shape was dictated by its material or by function. However, before looking at some current examples of artefactual studies, it must be stressed that artefacts should not be looked at in isolation and one always has to bear in mind how they were produced and what effects that might have had on the final product. A piece of glass might be analysed to see if its composition can say anything about its place of manufacture, but how can that composition be considered unless something is known about the raw materials used? A chert object may show signs of deliberate heat treatment, but why might that have been done – was it to make the object easier to manufacture? Is the absence of a particular size of object of great significance or was it just impossible to produce objects of that size from the materials available? The person making the object may have been operating within a particular political, economic and social framework that dictated what was made, but at the point of production the direct involvement was with the object and the process. If it is considered in those terms, the analysis of an artefact should start with consideration of factors such as what raw materials were available, whether any differences in their composition could have been appreciated, and whether any choices could have been made, before we select out those analytical results that we think are significant. Similarly, if a piece of chert is showing some evidence of heat treatment but not enough to alter the properties sufficiently to have been appreciated by the person working the chert, is it reasonable to suggest that the heat treatment was deliberate? It is an obvious point, but one that becomes more pertinent as more levels of description are possible, that if we want to perceive artefacts as they were perceived in the past – if they are to be used as anything near 'a representation . . . of values and meaning within a society' (Kingery 1996: ix) – then we have to start by looking at them as they would have been seen in the past, while still asking the four basic questions of artefacts: what were they made of?; where were they made?; how were they made?; and why were they made?

WHAT IS THE OBJECT MADE OF? WHERE WAS IT MADE?

The level of description required rests, to some extent, on the reason why the question is being asked; but the nature of the material also has an influence. Thus for wood, bone, hides, leather and ivory, one can normally only reach the species of tree, the type of bone, the form of textile and the species or genera of the plant or animal from which the material derives. For pigments, dyes, resins, glues, many gemstones, ceramics, rocks and minerals, the question is still that of basic identification but at a more detailed level. Is it a piece of granite or limestone? Is it a garnet or ruby? Is this green pigment malachite or verdigris? Was the clay used for this

352

particular pottery vessel an earthenware or China clay? These questions are often answered via structural or physical analysis. For glasses, metals and ceramics, the questions may be more complicated: is this copper alloy a tin-bronze or a brass?; is this a lead glass?; what makes this glass blue? Such questions can only really be approached by chemical analysis. Overall, knowledge of what the object is made of usually comes by visual examination, microscopy, structural or chemical analysis.

Visual examination

Regardless of the current role of scientific techniques and the limitations of basic description, the most important technique in the study of artefacts is, and will remain, visual examination. Just by looking at the object (and this is probably all the study that 99 per cent of archaeological objects will ever receive), its form and shape can be seen, surface wear noted, evidence of manufacture and in most cases at least the basic material identified, although this is normally limited to the type of material – wood, leather, metal, bone, glass, and so on. Colour is another obvious, observable aspect, long used for identification, as noted in Agricola's *De Natura Fossilium* of 1546: 'colour, taste, odour and qualities of minerals that can be perceived by touch are the most widely known because they are more easily recognized by the physical senses than the qualities such as strength or weakness'. However, colour is not an infallible guide to identification even of minerals, although in archaeology it has often been thought that substances with strong colouration, such as pigments and gemstones, can be analysed solely by colour – not on the basis of any objective system, but just on the assumption that only a narrow range of materials would be involved. Thus, red transparent stones would be described as rubies (merely because red and transparent), and a yellow pigment as yellow ochre. As early as the 1930s, Lucas (1934: 339) was warning that many green stones within Egyptian archaeological collections had been wrongly described as emeralds and beryls, but once a positive identification enters the literature it is very hard to dislodge. The situation is not helped by the translations of early texts: for example, in Pliny the Elder's *Natural History* of the first century AD, the term 'adamas' is invariably translated as 'diamond' in English translations – leading to much discussion on the contemporary importance of these gems – even when there is nothing in the context to suggest that the term should be taken as anything more than 'colourless material'.

Colour, though, can be used for analysis in one area – that of precious metal alloys – because mixtures of gold and silver are likely to show different shades of colour depending on the proportions of the separate ingredients. Thus, from the prehistoric periods through to the present day, the colour of the streak left by a piece of gold drawn across a touchstone has been used to assess the purity of the gold, and this can be extended into quantitative assay if the mark is compared with those made by alloys of known composition. Comparisons with standards is necessary because colour assessment is very subjective, and there are many sets of universal standards that are used for descriptive purposes in other fields of materials analysis (Hunt 1989). The one most commonly used in archaeology is part of the Munsell system, primarily to give an objective record of the colours of soil and pottery.

The difficulties of using colour for identification have been noted but, given Agricola's comments on assessment based on colour, it may be tempting to classify artefacts in terms of colouration on the basis that this might have been significant originally. However, two points have to be borne in mind: the surface colour might have changed through time via processes such as weathering and corrosion and, particularly for manufactured materials, colour may not have been easy to control. The colouration of man-made glass is a very good example of this because strong and variable effects can be generated by low levels of elements, and it is often difficult to ascertain whether they entered the glass as deliberate additions or as impurities in the raw materials. To make a glass object the raw materials have to be melted together, the molten glass is worked to shape and then the solid object has to be reheated (annealed) to remove the stresses produced during working and make it less liable to break. Given the number of stages involved, and all the variations in melting and working conditions, it is very difficult to decide to what extent the final colour of many glass objects was actually under the control of the producers. Sellner and Camara (1979), for instance, found that differently coloured medieval glasses had ostensibly the same chemical composition, and that the final colour for glass containing 0.7 per cent iron and 1.7 per cent manganese could be anywhere within a range of bright blue through to amber and brownish purple, depending on the specific furnace conditions when it was melted. The basic conclusion must be that archaeological objects may often be divided into groups on the basis of their colour, on the grounds that colour is in some way significant, but if the assumption is that objects of similar appearance were made from the same raw materials or produced in the same place, then the degree of control over colour during production needs to be considered, as do the effects of burial and decay on surface appearance.

Microscopy

Despite the problems, visual examination by the naked eye or with a microscope remains the main method of identifying some of the natural materials. Standard optical microscopes can give a magnification range of ×10 to ×300, and can be used in reflection (where the light is reflected back from the surface of the material), or for transmission (where the light passes through the sample). There are numerous

Figure 9.1 SEM image showing the interior structure of a piece of bronze age pottery. Source: Maniatis and Tite 1981.

examples of the application of optical microscopy for the identification of natural materials, including the examination of the grain pattern on a piece of leather to determine the animal from which it was obtained (Haines 1981), the analysis of cell patterns in wood to establish the species, and observation of cross-sections of textile fibres not only to determine whether they are of wool, cotton, linen or silk but, in the case of animal fibres, even the breed of animal (Ryder 1983).

The level of identification has been much improved with the development of scanning electron microscopes, which use beams of electrons rather than light to give an image of the sample, offering both an increased range of magnification and, more importantly for identification, a greater depth of focus which allows a clear view of surface topography. The emergence of the SEM into a routine analysis technique in the 1970s is perhaps one of the most significant technical developments so far in the study of the material aspects of archaeological objects, not least because it can be used in different ways. In one mode, the image of the surface generated by the secondary electrons emerging from the sample gives both high magnification and good depth of focus, so that all the area of an uneven or rounded surface can be kept in focus at the same time (Fig. 9.1). This is used not only in the identification of seeds, textile fibres, woods, charcoal, pollen, and so on via their surface characteristics, but also to examine patterns of wear on objects, as in use–wear analysis of lithic objects (discussed on pp. 379–81). If the form or constituents of the object, rather than the surface, are of interest, the SEM can be used in another mode utilizing the image produced by back scattered electrons. In this case looking at, say, a section taken from the wall of a glazed ceramic, the image will show a 'picture' of the section with the clay body and glaze as distinct layers, because the brightness of various parts of the image are influenced by the chemical composition of the areas being scanned (Fig. 9.2). Chemical composition can be further investigated by utilizing a third component of the radiation emerging from the sample following interaction with the electron beam: X-rays. The energies of these X-rays are characteristic of the elements within the sample and, with an X-ray detector attached, these elements can be identified.

The ability to focus the electron beam down to about one micron and also to move it over the sample means that various forms of chemical analysis can be undertaken: the electron beam can be moved over the sample to give a point-to-point analysis for a particular element (useful to chart changes in composition from the surface to interior of an object); an area scan can yield the overall composition of the area scanned (useful for bulk analysis); or the distribution of a specific element within the area scanned can be displayed (useful to see if the composition shows any variation, or 'inhomogeneity', within the sample). A discussion of a broader range of applications of scanning electron microscopy in the study of artefacts is provided in Olsen (1988) and further examples are given below.

The visual examination by SEM or light microscope of many organic materials such as wood, leather and textiles can give useful information because the diagnostic characteristics are little changed from raw material to object. Another major group of materials used in their natural state are lithics, and for purposes of identification it is often useful to divide them into two large groupings: minerals and rocks. Minerals have a structure based essentially on a single component which

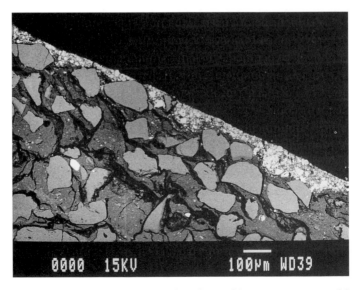

Figure 9.2 SEM image of a cross-section of a piece of iron age pottery with an iron-rich coating visible as a white layer against the grey of the interior. Source: Middleton 1987.

356

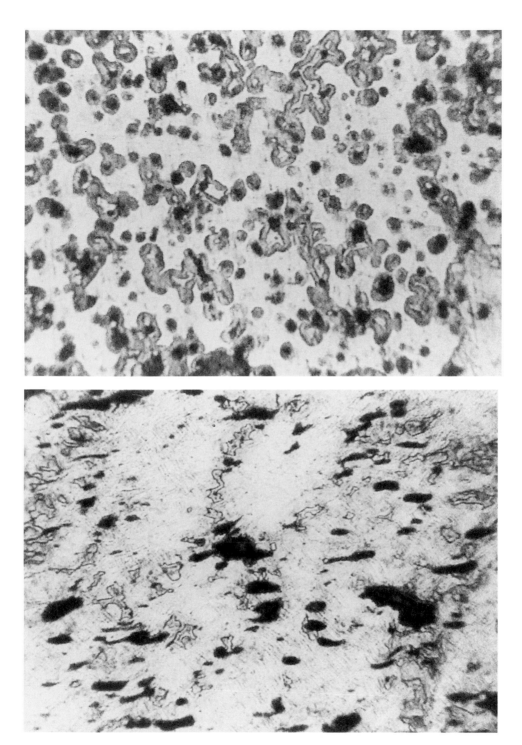

Figure 9.3 Sections of a copper–tin–lead alloy showing (a) the metallographic structure when cast, and (b) the structure after cold hammering; magnification ×400. © The British Museum.

comprises around 80–100 per cent of the weight of the material, with the rest made up of minor and trace components, but rocks are aggregates of separate minerals. Since a particular sample of rock may contain a very high proportion of one mineral, there is inevitably some shading between rocks and impure minerals, but this is a workable distinction that sees, say, a piece of the mineral ruby composed solely of grains of crystalline aluminium oxide (Al_2O_3) at one end of the spectrum and a granite rock made up of separate grains of quartz, albite feldspar, orthoclase, zircon, hornblende and biotite minerals at the other. The reason it is a useful distinction in this context is because different techniques need to be used to identify rocks and minerals.

Aside from the rare precious gems, amongst the most important minerals in archaeological terms are the natural glasses, usually seen archaeologically in the form of obsidian, and the cherts. Chemical analysis has shown that obsidians and cherts have very similar compositions, the major component in all cases being silicon dioxide (silica, SiO_2), and the main difference between them is their structure. Obsidians are glasses and have a typical, non-crystalline random structure, akin to man-made glasses, and it is this structure that gives them their vitreous characteristics. The cherts, in contrast, have a crystalline structure that consists of a very fine network of silica crystals, termed crypto-crystalline because the individual particles are so small. If they were made of pure silica, obsidians and cherts would be colourless. However, they often contain small quantities of impurities and the cherts, in particular, come in a vast range of colours because of differences in impurities. Long before their chemical and structural similarities were appreciated, these different forms acquired separate names – flint, jasper, carnelian, sard, onyx, bloodstone, basanite and so on – but they all have similar chemical and physical properties.

The uniformity in properties within the chert minerals, arising because of their uniformity in composition and structure, is in sharp contrast to the rocks which show major differences in properties both between rock types and within samples of rock classified as the same type. In geological terminology, it is mode of formation that is used in initial classification, into igneous, metamorphic or sedimentary, and thereafter the dominant minerals species that determine whether a rock is described as a granite, a marble, a calcareous sandstone and so on. Thus the several thousand varieties of rock have acquired their geological names, associated with particular physical and chemical properties, because of their specific genesis, geological associations, proportions and type of constituent minerals. Given that it is predominately the nature, quantity and the arrangement of the individual mineral grains within the rock (its petrology) that are used to classify and name rocks, it is hardly surprising that it is these characteristics that are used to identify samples of rock. The main technique employed for this is thin-section analysis using a microscope.

Thin-section microscopy is a very well-established technique in geology, being first developed around 130 years ago, and it has been used for the examination of archaeological material for almost as long (Shotton and Hendry 1979). It is a destructive technique: a thin sliver is taken from the object, mounted, polished down to a thickness of around thirty microns and examined under transmitted light. This light can be either normal white light or, more commonly, polarized light. The technique is used mainly on rocks and a petrologist uses a combination of the shape, colour, number and distribution of the individual grains within the lithic, plus their optical characteristics under polarized light, to determine the particular minerals present and, thereby, the type of rock or mineral. Thin-section analysis has been applied to many thousands of archaeological objects to establish the arte-factual material or, in the case of ceramics, the type of rock or mineral particles in the fabric. Detailed descriptions of the method and its archaeological applications are available in many texts, such as Kempe and Harvey (1983) on petrological analysis of rocks and mineral artefacts and Middleton and Freestone (1991) on the petrology of the rock or mineral fraction within ceramics.

While thin-section analysis is essentially a descriptive technique, indicating whether the rock is a gabbro, limestone, feldspar or whatever, the main aim with archaeological artefacts is usually to move beyond this and try, for instance, to classify objects into groups that seem to have been made from the same rock or to try to determine the actual geographical source of the raw materials by comparing the petrology of the artefacts with that of samples taken from various possible sources. Whether any discrimination is possible depends very much on the type of rock or mineral and the variations shown between and within different deposits, and thin-section analysis of the major components often has to be supplemented with chemical analysis of the trace and minor components to provide full character-ization. With rocks and minerals, these petrological and chemical characteristics are carried through unchanged from the raw materials to the object, and when there are sufficient diagnostic features to distinguish between potential sources, this petrological-chemical approach can be a very effective technique. It was used, for example, to link Egyptian limestone objects back to their source quarry (Harrell 1992), and to examine sea-borne trade in millstones within the eastern Mediterranean (Williams-Thorpe and Thorpe 1993).

Although pottery artefacts are composed mainly of clay, they often contain rock or mineral fragments embedded in the clay. These fragments can be visible to the naked eye and can also be seen if a small sample is taken from the object and examined under a microscope; in Figure 9.2, for example, the rock and mineral inclusions are clearly visible as white particles against the black background of the clay fabric. Not only can these lithic fragments be seen under the microscope, but if a thin-section is taken they can also be examined and identified via petrological analysis using the same procedures as for solid lithic artefacts. The classification of pottery into coarse or fine wares, or into groups on the basis of inclusions visible within the clay, has long been standard practice in archaeology (Darvill and Timby 1982), and thin-section analysis of ceramics containing rock or mineral particles is becoming increasingly common because it gives a further refinement in this classificatory system. In addition, as with lithic objects, thin-section analysis also offers the possibility of defining the area or region in which the pottery was made, although the interpretation of thin-sections from ceramics can be more complex than for those from lithic artefacts. This is because the mineral or rock inclusions in a ceramic fabric can derive from the clay or may have been deliberately added, wholly or in part, as temper (Rice 1987). However, in the context of classification and sourcing, this is a somewhat superfluous distinction because, regardless of whether the rock or mineral fraction came into the ceramic via the clay or the temper, it is still likely to reflect the local geology of the area where the object was made, and there are certainly many examples where petrological analysis has allowed the specific location or general area of production to be identified (see, for example, Middleton and Freestone 1991; Williams 1983).

As with all classification and provenancing work, there are some limitations to the technique. In particular, the mineral fraction in many ceramics is crystalline quartz, which is very common and undiagnostic as to origin, so any classification has to be based on the size and distribution of the quartz grains. There is also the possibility of transport in raw materials, well attested in the ethnographic record, but, as Williams *et al.* (1974) showed in the context of Roman coarseware, petrological analysis itself can sometimes be used to indicate long-distance transport of raw clay.

Structural analysis

Since, by definition, minerals are essentially composed of a single type of mineral, thin-section petrological analysis is not particularly helpful for their identification because it will simply show the presence of that mineral. Also, as indicated above, colour cannot be considered diagnostic. The other main general method of identification, chemical analysis, is of little value here either because it is not the elements present that are required but the actual chemical compounds: thus a chemical analysis of the copper ore malachite would just indicate that it contained copper, carbon and oxygen atoms and its identification as malachite would need to be confirmed by showing that those were combined into the particular variety of copper carbonate (chemical formula $CuCO_3.Cu(OH)_2$) that is termed malachite.

What is required is a determination of the actual compounds present, and the main technique historically used in archaeology for this is X-ray diffraction (XFD). This has proved extremely useful in certain circumstances but does have the limitation that it can only be used for the identification of crystalline solids and not for

organic substances or non-crystalline materials such as glasses. As with many techniques for identification, it can be difficult to interpret the results if the substance is
a very complex mixture of compounds. However, where fairly simple inorganic
compounds are involved, as in the identification of metallic ores, the corrosion
products on metals, decay products on lithic artefacts, or components of plasters,
XRD proves extremely useful. It is also ideal for the analysis of most inorganic
pigments: XRD studies of pigment samples from wall paintings (Filippakis *et al.*
1976) and ceramics (Noll and Hangst 1975) have shown what a wide range of
substances was used as pigments; far more than when identification was by visual
examination alone against an assumed, and limited, palette.

For the analysis of organic pigments, organic gemstones such as amber, resins,
glues, gums, and organic dyes, the main methods employed are infra-red analysis,
chromatography and mass spectrometry. Organic molecules are very complex, and
organic substances even more so because they can contain a whole range of different
forms of molecule, and identification is seldom based on a determination of the
actual molecules present but rather the data from examination of the sample compared with those for known substances. Thus, Beck *et al.* (1971) showed that amber
artefacts from Greece are likely to be of Baltic amber by conducting infra-red
analyses on samples from the objects and comparing them with the results from a
series of natural ambers of various origins. Similarly Wright and Wheals (1987)
were able to identify some samples of glues, gums and waxes taken from Egyptian
mummy cases via mass-spectrometry on these samples and comparison with the
data from seventy reference substances. The development of microanalytical techniques such as gas chromatography allied to mass spectrometry has opened up
many new possibilities in the analysis of organic substances, just as new biochemical
methods in the study of ancient biomolecules offer some of the most exciting
opportunities in other areas of archaeology. However, the detailed investigation of
organic substances to a level where the data would have a major impact on the
interpretation of artefactual material remains a very problematic area, not least
because of the changes produced in organic molecules by processes of decay and
attrition that cannot be reproduced in modern reference materials. Analytical data
need to be approached with caution, half the samples examined by Wright and
Wheals for instance had to remain unidentified, and many working in this
area stress the need for more fundamental research into the organic chemistry of
archaeological materials (Mills and White 1987).

Chemical and isotopic analysis

Microscopy may suffice for the classification of rock artefacts and the characterization of some ceramic fabrics, but for other major artefactual materials, particularly

metals and glass, visual examination just shows them to be metal or glass and to go beyond that into the type of metal or glass requires chemical analysis. There often seems to be a bewildering array of methods of chemical analysis, but most are based on very similar principles and the different techniques have mainly been developed to deal with particular materials, to allow the use of smaller samples, to improve handling procedures, or because they offer improvements in sensitivity or precision.

Some methods appear very complex because of the instrumentation involved. Others, including those based on specific gravity, look straightforward but are difficult in practice. The principle of specific gravity for identification or analysis is that all pure elements or compounds have their own characteristic specific gravity, akin to density and similarly calculated from measures of weight and volume, and that reference books provide tables of specific gravities of pure substances. Therefore, measurement of the specific gravity of an object thought to be made of a pure substance can, in theory, allow the identification of that substance. Obvious examples would be mineral gemstones, and specific gravity could also be used to distinguish between, for example, diamond, rock crystal and colourless glass. The only requirement is that the substance is known to be pure and, if used to distinguish between various possibilities, that the specific gravities are sufficiently different to make identification possible. As specific gravity of a mixture is the sum of those of the individual components, this method can also be used to look at the proportions of the constituents in simple mixtures if the types of material involved are known. This is all very simple, and would appear to offer an ideal method of analysing objects like coins where the basic constituents are presumed known and it would be too damaging to take samples for other forms of analysis. There are, however, problems with the technique, particularly in obtaining sufficiently accurate values for the volume and weight of the object, the two measures used to calculate specific gravity. The problems, but also the use of the method in the analysis of gold alloys where no other method is feasible, are discussed by Oddy and Blackshaw (1974).

Most of the other common techniques of chemical analysis involve some form of energy, normally described as a beam of radiation or a stream of particles, being directed onto the sample to be analysed. The changes produced by or to that beam or stream via interaction with the sample are then used to determine some of the elements present. This gives a qualitative analysis; for a full quantitative analysis of the actual concentrations the results for the sample normally have to be compared to those for a range of standards of known composition. All laboratories prepare their own standards but there are universal sets, such as those developed by the US National Bureau of Standards, used to check 'in-house' material and for inter-laboratory comparisons. Laboratories analysing archaeological material often arrange inter-laboratory checks on their results, and as techniques have improved and there is better understanding of the nature of materials, few report anywhere near the degree of discrepancy seen in Chase's oft-cited (1974) project when two bronze samples were sent to twenty-one laboratories and standard deviations of up to 200 per cent were observed for some elements! It is, though, still the case that analytical precision differs between techniques and it should never be assumed that data obtained using different methods on the same sample would be identical. This sometimes causes concern within archaeology, but any analytical limitations are normally far outweighed by the problems relating to the quality of samples and the interpretation of the analytical results. As Pollard and Heron (1996: 12) state in their excellent review of analysis techniques within archaeology, 'typically samples are far from ideal from the analytical point of view . . . archaeological chemistry [is] a challenging field and not one which can be regarded as just another routine application of analytical chemistry'.

The main methods used, so far, for the chemical analysis of archaeological artefacts are optical emission spectroscopy (OES), inductively coupled plasma emission spectroscopy (ICPS), X-ray fluorescence (XRF), atomic absorption spectrophotometry (AAS), neutron activation analysis (NAA), instrumental neutron activation analysis (INAA), proton-induced X-ray emission (PIXE) and proton-induced gamma-ray emission (PIGME). Several methods are employed because all have their own limitations and special requirements, and detailed descriptions can be found in several texts, such as Parkes (1986) and Pollard and Heron (1996).

One major factor governing their use in archaeology is the degree of damage they might cause the object. For analysis by OES, AAS and ICPS, a sample, albeit small, is required, which will be destroyed in the analysis. In NAA the material to be analysed is put into a nuclear reactor and bombarded with a stream of neutrons so that it becomes radioactive and, while a sample is not needed and the whole object could be irradiated, it is normally more practical to use small samples. With XRF and PIXE, a beam of X-rays or protons are directed at the surface of material to be analysed, and as the analysis is done directly on the surface, and this can be the surface of the object rather than a sample from it, these techniques are often described as non-destructive. Indeed, in the 1970s a form of X-ray fluorescence was termed the 'curator's dream instrument' because it was suggested that an X-ray source and detector could be wheeled into a museum and used to examine paint layers and artefact surfaces directly. However, whether useful results can be obtained in this way depends very much on the type of object and the reasons for the analysis. The incident beam penetrates to a depth of only 20–200 microns, and records the composition of this surface layer, and so is only useful if the composition of the surface layers is of particular interest or, if bulk analysis is needed, the composition of the surface can be assumed fully representative of the interior. This latter requirement is particularly problematic for archaeological material because there is the possibility not only of deliberate modification of the surface via processes such as gilding, but also of changes to the surface composition arising through burial, decay, corrosion and so on. Also, while it may be possible to obtain a form of qualitative analysis directly on the object, high-precision quantitative results require the surface analysed to be flat; sensitivity is much reduced if the incident and emitted radiation have to pass through air rather than a lighter gas or vacuum, and the size of the vacuum or gas chamber will therefore dictate whether the object can be examined without sampling.

It is not only the problems of sampling that restrict the use of analytical techniques in archaeology. Darkening produced by radiation, for instance, has to be considered for some types of transparent mineral gemstone and man-made glasses. However, the main constraints are often even more practical ones. Their influence on the choice of technique is well illustrated in the case of the analysis of the garnets in part of the seventh-century AD Sutton Hoo treasure (Bimson *et al.* 1982). The aim was to determine the types of garnet represented. The simplest way to do this would have been by specific gravity or optical properties, but the gems could not be removed from their mounts. X-ray diffraction would have been most appropriate to determine the actual mineral species, but the stones could not be sampled. XRF was finally chosen, but the objects were too large to fit into a vacuum system and the metal backings would have distorted under vacuum, so an in-air system was used with some of the important lighter elements having to go undetected. Some analytical data were obtained and possible sources for the stones given, but the research strategy was essentially a compromise between retaining the integrity of the artefacts and producing some useful information.

Regardless of the problems of selecting a suitable analytical method, many hundreds of thousands of archaeological objects, mainly metals, glass, lithics and ceramics, have been analysed over the last 150 years. It would therefore be impossible to consider all the applications of chemical analysis in the study of artefacts, but the interpretation of analytical data, and indeed the role of chemical analysis, is one of the areas that has seen the greatest changes and these can be illustrated in general terms by considering approaches to metals and glasses. These two materials cause particular difficulties in the interpretation of data because, unlike lithics and most objects of organic materials, there is a whole series of chemical processes – and thereby potential for alteration of the chemical composition – between extraction of the raw materials and the final sample taken from the finished object.

Metals

There are two main types of raw material for metal objects – metal ores and native metal. Native metals are found as metals and are immediately available for converting into an object. Native gold, either mined or collected from secondary deposits, has always been the main source of gold, and native coppers were exploited extensively by indigenous populations in North America and intermittently, often in the first stages of metal use, in many other parts of the world. There are also a few examples of the use of meteoric iron (iron deposited from the break up of meteors). However, despite the importance of native metal in certain contexts, all the evidence suggests that the majority of metal used throughout history has been derived from metal ores.

In the first half of the twentieth century, many hundreds of copper-based objects, mainly from the Bronze Age of Europe and the Near East, were analysed to determine the type of metal employed, to try to chart the sequence of metal use and the introduction of mixtures of metals in the form of alloys. General sequences were established which saw the earliest objects of pure copper, assumed to be native metal, followed by various impure coppers thought to represent smelted metal, then deliberate alloys of copper and tin (tin-bronzes), copper–tin–lead mixtures and then copper–zinc alloys (brasses). There was much discussion and interpretation of these sequences, with the use of impure copper and various forms of copper alloys attributed to improvements in the hardness or ease of working of these materials compared with pure copper (Wertime 1964). The chronological pattern of use of particular alloys also required explanation and has often been presented as the result of experimentation in mixing metals together or the availability of different ores allowing observation of the different metals that they would yield (Tylecote 1962).

With tin-bronzes typically containing 8–15 per cent tin and brasses with zinc to 20 per cent and more, charting composition in terms of the alloys only required analysis of the major components. However, the improvements in analytical methods by the 1960s started both to allow the determination of the minor and trace constituents and to suggest that these might have some potential value. The result was an expansion of analytical investigations of metals, well exemplified by the Stuttgart programmes that involved the analysis of over ten thousand gold and copper-based objects from the European Bronze Age (Junghans *et al.* 1968). With variations appearing in the composition of the objects, the final outcome of these programmes was the grouping of artefacts on the basis of similarities and differences in their minor constituents. This raised the questions of what the chemical analysis of archaeological artefacts was designed to achieve and whether, for example, the final chemical compositions of objects spanning thousands of years in time and drawn from locations thousands of kilometres apart could be discussed or explained against any single model, let alone whether the distribution or grouping of any type of object can be considered in terms of compositional data alone and without reference to the overall archaeological background and any social, cultural or economic influences. The other limitation was that, while there was some recognition that the processes of production of metal objects had an effect on their final composition, and therefore should be considered if objects were to be grouped on the basis of composition, this particular factor was not much considered.

This is no longer considered acceptable, and since the 1960s there has been much research on how the chemical composition of a sample drawn from a metal object should be interpreted (for example, Craddock 1980). The situation is complex because, for a metal derived from an ore, the ore has to be heated to a particular temperature in a specific atmosphere (that is, smelted) so that various chemical reactions can occur and metal produced. It is now appreciated that the minor and trace elements used in classification are not transferred unchanged ore to metal, and research is continuing into the compositional variability within ore bodies, the effect of smelting, any changes produced during melting and casting and so on. Most of this research has involved experimental smelting, comparing composition of the initial ore with the final metal (Tylecote *et al.* 1977), but for the Bronze Age in particular it has been hampered by the paucity of direct evidence of mines, smelting furnaces and working areas. However, the situation at least for Europe is now changing, with ore extraction dated to the Bronze Age recorded for mines in Italy, Austria, Ireland, Spain, England, Wales, Bulgaria and Rumania (Craddock 1995). Unfortunately, few of these sites show evidence of associated ore processing, smelting or direct metalworking and, as far as the elucidation of processes is concerned, what are needed are more complexes like those at Timna in the Sinai (Rothenberg 1990) where the original ore, furnaces, metal product, slag and other working debris could all be examined. This would both help understanding of compositional changes from ore to metal and provide more basic information on processes to aid identification. For example, from an analysis of crucibles, slags and other residues, Yener and Vandiver (1993) postulated the so-far rarely seen occurrence of tin ore smelting at a third-millennium BC site in Anatolia, but Muhly (1993) has argued that the mere presence of tin on the interior of the crucibles does not necessarily mean that they were used to smelt tin ores. Much of Muhly's argument rests on the highly contentious textual evidence for trade in tin and the archaeological feasibility of tin smelting in the Taurus at that date, but he also questions assumptions on the processes used to smelt tin oxide ores.

The difficulties of interpretation do not mean that chemical analysis of non-ferrous metal objects has been abandoned, rather that this is now done in full appreciation of limitations of this approach. For instance, analytical data continue to have a very useful role in the study of coinage (Bowman *et al.* 1989), in tracing the introduction of different forms of alloy like brass (Craddock 1978), in looking at the selection of particular metals for specific types of object (Northover and Gerloff 1988), and in the analysis of gold objects where, because of the use of native metal, some, but by no means all, of many of the problems introduced by intra-source variability and metal processing do not apply (Elùere 1987).

However, given the problems posed by chemical analysis, the introduction in the

1960s of the necessary instrumentation – high-precision heavy element mass spectrometers – prompted consideration of whether stable isotope analysis of lead could be an alternative means of establishing a basic 'fingerprint' that might be different between ore sources and also carry through into the metal product. In a simple exposition of a very complex phenomenon, the rationale behind this approach is that when the earth originally formed, deposits of lead/thorium and lead/uranium were laid down and as the radioactive ^{238}U, ^{235}U and ^{232}Th decayed through time to yield the lead isotopes ^{206}Pb, ^{207}Pb and ^{208}Pb respectively, the proportions, and therefore the ratios, of these isotopes became different between deposits. With the subsequent mineralization of this lead into lead ores, particularly galena (PbS), it separated from the uranium and thorium and the isotopic ratios were no longer subject to change but became fixed, and remained as a characteristic of the ore to be carried through into metal produced from it. Although based on lead, this form of characterization by stable isotope ratios is not restricted to objects of metallic lead: not only was lead a major component of leaded-glass and added to copper as an alloying agent, but most silver was derived from lead ores and contains a proportion of lead from those ores, and many copper ores are intimately associated with lead minerals and some of that lead can come though into the final copper. It is therefore a very versatile technique and since the 1960s many metallic ores and archaeological metal artefacts have been investigated using lead isotope analysis, most notably by teams at Oxford (Gale and Stos-Gale 1992) and Heidelberg (Wagner *et al.* 1989). However, as with many techniques, as the data accumulate problems emerge and the underlying tenets tend to be questioned, and there has been considerable debate on the basic significance of similarities and differences in lead isotope ratios and the validity of using them as a classificatory device (Budd *et al.* 1993), and these discussions may well continue.

Glass

Glass is another material where the current chemical, and for lead-based glasses isotopic, composition of the object comes at the end of a long series of processes, with the raw materials, processes of manufacture, weathering and decay all having an influence on final composition. However, when it comes to the interpretation of analysis, the difficulties come as much from the nature of the material itself as from the effects of processes. Three main uses of man-made glass can be seen amongst archaeological objects: free-standing glass in the form of glass objects; layers of glass (glazes) on ceramics and lithics; and vitreous coatings (enamels) applied to metals. Only a very few compounds can adopt the non-crystalline structure that both defines a glass and gives glass its particular properties, and most man-made glasses are based on silicon dioxide, silica. A glass can be produced just by heating pure silica until it fuses, but this fusion only occurs at a temperature of around 1700°C and until this century glasses could only be produced by mixing the silica with another compound (a flux) to lower the fusion point, allowing the flux and silica to melt together at around 900–1200°C to form a glass. Various elements can act as fluxes and one of the initial aims behind the chemical analysis of glass was to establish the form of flux used. From analysis, three basic types of glass are now recognized amongst archaeological material: soda glass with a high level of sodium from the use of a compound rich in sodium as a flux; potash glasses with a high level of potassium from potassium-rich compounds; and lead glass from lead fluxes. This correlates with the textual evidence: glass-making recipes, from the seventh-century BC tablets from the library at Nineveh (Oppenheim *et al.* 1988) through to medieval treatises, describe the main ingredients of glass as various mixtures of crushed quartz, rock, and sand (sources of silica), natron, other natural salts, plant ashes (sources of sodium and potassium) and lead compounds (Frank 1982; Henderson 1989).

However, there are limitations in the inferences that can be drawn from the chemical analysis of glass. Glasses differ from crystalline materials in that they contain no actual compounds but are just agglomerations of particles derived from the raw materials. Therefore analysis may show that a glass is high in sodium, and a sodium-rich flux was used, but it cannot readily indicate the form of that flux (Sanderson and Hunter 1980). Nor can it indicate what impurities might have entered the glass with the basic raw materials. Nowhere is this better illustrated than with the calcium and magnesium content of glasses. Most glass analyses reveal appreciable levels of these elements (*c.* 2–7 per cent) – their presence is very beneficial in soda and potash glasses because the fluxing elements make the glass susceptible to decay, which calcium and magnesium to some extent counteract. For a long time it was assumed that these elements had been added deliberately, using limestone, shells, dolomite rock and so on, but none of the texts mentions more than two ingredients and it is now considered that they entered glass as impurities in the silica or flux. Indeed, it may be that glasses made with purer ingredients without these stabilizing elements have simply not survived to be analysed. As the sixteenth-century English glass-maker Merrett said, 'in the finest glasses, wherein the salt is most purified, and in a greater proportion of salt to the sand, you shall find that such glasses standing long in subterraneous and moist places will fall to pieces, the union of the salt and sand decaying' (Frank 1982: 78), which suggests that Merrett was used to just the two ingredients, sand and salt, and did not recognize that purifying the raw materials had removed important constituents from the glass. The interpretation of chemical data on glass is therefore very challenging, but there is considerable interest in using chemical analysis to deter-mine the development of techniques for producing different kinds of glass (Bimson 1987; Henderson 1989; Kaczmarczyk and Hedges 1983).

HOW WAS IT MADE?

Information on processes can be obtained from documentary and pictorial sources, structures and residual debris at manufacturing and/or production centres, scientific data on the processes that must have been carried out, the artefacts themselves, and ethnographic and modern practices. Many of the descriptions of manufacturing processes used in archaeology come from these last two sources: practices such as the hand-moulding or wheel-throwing of ceramics, the spinning and weaving of fibres for textiles, and the cleaning, dressing and tanning of hides are universal. The main interest in these particular processes concerns the diversity in the methods and tools used.

The documentary record tends to be biased towards descriptions of production processes. Amongst the most interesting texts, if not always reliable or easy to translate, surviving from the classical Greek, Roman and medieval periods of Europe are Theophrastus' *De Lapidibus* (fourth–third centuries BC), Vitruvius' *De Architectura* (first century BC), Pliny the Elder's *Natural History* (first century AD), the *Stockholm and Leyden X* papyri (third century AD), the ninth-century AD *Mappae Clavicula*, Eraclius' *De coloribus et artibus Romanorum* (tenth century AD), Theophilus' *De Diversis Artibus* (twelfth century AD), Cennino Cennini's *Il Libro Coll'Arte* of the 1390s, the *Pirotechnicia* of Biringuccio of 1540 and Agricola's *De Re Metallica* of 1558. The direct information they provide on processes is very variable, as not only are many of these texts fragmentary, or copies of early texts and very difficult to translate, but they were seldom written as manuals on processes and the writers had very different levels of direct experience of the phenomena they seem to be describing. Thus sections of Pliny's *Natural History* are continually being re-translated in the light of current knowledge on first-century AD processes, and it is archaeological information that is being used to illuminate the text rather than the other way round. There is, though, potential in certain types of contemporary pictorial and textual information: nowhere to date is this better demonstrated than in the systematic research of Needham and colleagues into the documentary and archaeological data on science and civilization in China (Needham 1958).

Interest in the translation and interpretation of texts can itself prompt research in the study of artefacts. For instance, much of the interest in opaque glass, extensively researched by Bimson (1987) and others, stems from the so-called 'glass texts' amongst the seventh-century BC cuneiform tablets from the Nineveh library in Mesopotamia. These were long known to contain information on the production of coloured glasses, but this could only be fully elucidated through the study of contemporary artefactual material (Oppenheim *et al.* 1988), with more data on these opaque glasses appearing year by year. With opaque glasses it is not just a question of the form of object, where and when the glass was made, the colours produced and so on, but rather how the opacity was generated because, while opaque glazes appear very early in the history of glaze and glass production, opacity is technically difficult to generate, as glass only appears opaque because of the presence of small crystals within the glass matrix, and these crystals have to develop a crystalline structure while the basic glass remains non-crystalline. In a good example of research developing with the availability of techniques, it is only in recent years that the magnification offered by the scanning electron microscope has allowed the crystals causing opacity to be seen (Freestone 1987). With an X-ray analysis system attached to the SEM, or with the related instrument the electron microprobe, it is also possible both to view a high-magnification image of the sample and to obtain a chemical analysis of that area of the sample on a point by point basis and thereby determine the opacifier involved.

The new opportunities offered by the high magnification capabilities of electron microscopes are particularly well illustrated by Barber and Freestone's (1990) examination of the Lycurgus cup, a glass vessel of the Roman period in Europe dating to the fourth or fifth century AD. It is dichroic, that is it appears green if viewed in reflected light and purple if seen in transmitted light. Knowledge of how this effect was produced in modern glass led to the idea that the glass probably contained a very fine distribution of metallic particles, but also confirmed that it is extremely difficult to generate dichroism because the particles must fall within a very limited size range so that they both scatter and absorb light to give the two-colour effect. Chemical analysis of the cup in the 1960s showed that it was a soda-silica glass containing trace quantities of gold and silver, and it was assumed that the dichroic effect was produced by a dispersion of gold and silver particles, but it took until the 1980s before Barber and Freestone, using transmission electron microscopy, were able to see the minute particles and analyse them to confirm that they were of a gold/silver/copper alloy. With a particle size range of 50–100 nanometres (nanometre = 10^{-9} metre), they were working at the limits of the technique. This is an extreme example of the investigation of a very specialized manufacturing process (only around ten pieces of Roman glass showing dichroism still survive), but scanning electron microscopy and electron microprobe analysis have proved very potent techniques in the examination of a whole range of different types of artefact. They are particularly useful in the examination of artefacts composed of different layers (Fig. 9.2), where a chemical analysis of a sample would give the overall composition but not the composition of the individual components, nor information on how these related. Therefore the techniques have been used extensively in the study of glazes on ceramics (Middleton 1987; Maniatis et al. 1993), on lithics, including the particular lithic body termed faience (Tite and Bimson 1986) and for the characterization of vitreous and glassy material in general (Tite 1987).

Electron microprobe analysis is also much used in the study of layers on metal objects, to examine techniques of gilding and plating for example (Scott 1986), and to look more generally at how metal objects were made, their composition and how inhomogeneous that composition is. Establishing the degree of inhomogeneity is important if a sample is to be taken for chemical analysis, or if a surface analytical technique is to be used, because it is necessary to know how representative that sample or surface is of bulk composition. Inhomogeneity and methods of manufacture of metal objects can also be revealed using the technique of metallography under an optical microscope, the method most commonly used in the routine examination of metal objects. Metallography is very similar to other forms of microscopy, including thin-section analysis of lithics, in that it involves visual examination of the structure of a metal sample under a microscope. However, to appreciate fully its potential application in the study of archaeological objects it is necessary to understand the evolution of that structure. This can be explained relatively easily for pure metals, but is rather more complex for impure metals and alloys, though the basic principles are the same. In the case of the pure metals, if a piece of pure metal is melted and the liquid poured into a mould, as the temperature drops and the melting point of the metal is reached, small particles of solid start to form in the liquid. As time goes on, these particles grow in size until they eventually meet and the material is totally solid. Thus the solid consists of a number of blocks of metal (grains) that meet at grain boundaries; the size and form of these grains are significant because the patterning is very sensitive and can be readily altered by any subsequent stressing, working, or heating applied to the object.

In metallographic analysis, a sample is taken from the object, the surface is polished and then etched with a chemical. This etch attacks the surface preferentially at the grain boundaries and the net result is that, when the surface is examined under a microscope, the grain boundaries appear black and the individual grains can be seen (Fig. 9.3). The sizes, shapes and distribution of the grains can then to be used to elucidate the history of the manufacture of the object. If the object was simply cast, the structure will be in the 'as cast' state; if it was hammered to harden the metal or to finish shaping, the grains will be distorted; if it was a non-ferrous object heat-treated (annealed) to remove brittleness introduced by working, then evidence for this treatment should remain; if it is a piece of wrought iron worked solid from the smelting furnace it should contain particles of slag from the smelting process.

The evolution of the microstructure of impure metals and alloys, and their interpretations, are governed by the same basic principles, but the structures are more complex because they vary with the detailed composition of the metal. Space does not allow a full description here, but Thompson (1969) provides a well-illustrated guide to some of the types of microstructure seen in archaeological objects, both ferrous and non-ferrous. Ferrous objects, those of wrought iron, steel and cast iron, are all basically composed of iron, and the various materials owe their radically different properties and structures to very small variations in carbon content. Definitions differ, but material described as wrought iron in the archaeological literature generally means iron with less than 0.5 per cent carbon, steel has 0.5–2 per cent and cast irons 2–5 per cent carbon. The type of ferrous material that will be produced by smelting iron ores depends primarily on the ore and smelting process, and from the start of iron usage through to the medieval periods, wrought iron and steel were the main ferrous materials produced in the western hemisphere, with steels and cast irons predominating in China and other parts of the Far East (Needham 1958).

As wrought irons and steels have melting points around 1300 to 1500°C, objects of these materials were normally shaped by hammering the solid metal, rather than by casting, and to aid that working or change to their properties they were also subject to a whole range of heat treatments. Although they are essentially iron with very small variations in carbon content, wrought irons, steels, and cast irons show very different properties – wrought iron is malleable, steel tough, cast iron brittle – because their structures are altered by these small changes in composition. Their structures are also very sensitive to the effects of working and heat treatment. There are a few elements other than carbon in irons, and chemical analysis of ferrous materials is used, but it is neither particularly informative on the type of material, because few methods can give an accurate measure of carbon content, nor overly reliable because of the susceptibility of iron to corrosion, and so the study of ferrous objects usually concentrates on metallographic examination. Metallography can be used to determine the type of metal, act as a guide to composition, and also to elucidate the various working processes, including carburization to convert wrought iron into steel, used to manufacture anything from a wrought iron nail to a complex sword of steel (Lang 1988).

The production of ceramics, here defined as objects of fired clay, is theoretically much simpler – the clay fabric is moulded to form and the object fired. To go beyond that, to examine conditions or temperatures of firing, it is necessary to start at the beginning with the nature of clay itself. There are many different ways of classifying clays, but the most useful for archaeological purposes are those based on the formation of the deposits and those relating to the major minerals present. In terms of formation, clays are divided into primary (residual) clays that are still near the parent rocks from which they derived and secondary (transported) clays where the particles have been moved far from the parent rocks by the action of water, wind, earth movements and so on. This is a useful distinction if only because it is a clear reminder that clay deposits are likely to show variability in composition based on their genesis. Primary clays are generally high in a few specific minerals, whereas secondary clays can comprise aggregates of minerals derived from several sources, and during the course of transport and deposition they can incorporate high proportions of organic matter and impurity minerals. White china clays are typical examples of pure primary clays, and red earthenware clays with high levels of iron oxide contributing to their colour are common secondary clays.

The other aspect that influences the nature of the clay, and thus determines the appropriate firing conditions, behaviour during firing, appropriate uses for the clay and so on, is clay mineralogy. Since the major sources of clay minerals are felspathic rocks which contain appreciable levels of aluminium and silicon, the main clay-forming minerals have these two elements as their main constituents and are thus aluminium silicates in various forms, described overall as phyllosilicates and divided into the kaolin group, the smectite group, and the illite and chlorite groups on the basis of other components. Different proportions of the various mineral species give clays with specific properties: clays rich in illite minerals, for example, yield a very dense fabric with a glossy surface on firing (Maniatis *et al.* 1993). This gloss is the result of the development of a glassy, vitreous, phase, and the formation of this phase raises another basic distinction between clays – what happens when they are heated. When an object made of clay is fired, the main requirement is that the surfaces of the particles within the clay fuse together to produce a solid, water-resistant material. This fusion can be achieved by a solid–solid reaction where the particle surfaces sinter together or via the formation of a liquid phase which eventually solidifies around the particles and holds them together. Depending on the conditions and its composition, this liquid may solidify as crystals or as a glass, just as each individual clay mineral would eventually melt if the temperature was raised sufficiently high and would then solidify as a glass or a crystalline phase. However, as with the production of man-made glasses, the generation of the liquid phase can be promoted by the presence of other minerals, fluxes, that react with the clay particles to yield compounds with a lower melting point. Suitable fluxes include minerals containing sodium, potassium, calcium and various oxides of iron; if these are naturally present in the clay, or are added as a separate ingredient, they will have a major influence on the way the clay reacts during firing. Hence when, as in Table 9.1, optimum firing temperatures are quoted for types of clay, they have to be given as temperature ranges because each particular sample of clay will react slightly differently.

Clays, therefore, are extremely complex mixtures which show variations not only in their basic ingredients but also in other important aspects such as particle size and water content. This variability is often further compounded by the addition of a second component, temper. This is a possible second ingredient mixed with the clay – not in any fixed proportion but often in sufficient amounts to be visible with the naked eye. It could have been added, as it is today, for a range of practical reasons including improvement in the workability of the clay, to promote resistance to cracking during firing, or to reduce porosity in the final fabric and/or in response to cultural tradition. Various forms of temper addition have been recognized amongst archaeological ceramics, including blood, crushed pottery, shells, grass,

Table 9.1 Firing ranges for different types of clay and the temperatures at which certain changes occur on firing

Temperature (°C)	Changes in clay minerals
100–200	Clay begins to lose absorbed water
450–550	Kaolinite loses OH ions: metakaolin forms
500	Organic material oxidizes
550–650	Montmorillonite loses OH ions
573	Silica changes its mineralogical form
600–800	Micas lose OH ions
600–800	*Firing range for terracottas*
800	Iron chlorides volatalize
870	Calcium carbonate dissociates to calcium oxide
900–1200	*Firing range for earthenwares*
950	Calcium oxide reacts with clay minerals to form calcium silicates
960	Metakaolin recrystallizes on cooling
1000	Calcium ferrosilicates form
1100	Mullite forms
1100–1200	Vitrification range of ball clays
1100–1200	*Firing range for china clays*
1200–1350	*Firing range for stonewares*
1160	Potassium feldspar begins to melt
1170	Sodium feldspar begins to melt
1200	Calcium sulphate dissociates
1300–1450	*Firing range for porcelains*
1712	Silica melts

Source: Adapted from Rice 1987: 103.

rock fragments and minerals. As discussed previously in the context of thin-section analysis, pottery is often classified on the basis of its fabric, including the visual identification of a second component described as temper. It is not, though, always easy to distinguish between material deliberately added as temper and natural impurities already in the clay, but this only really becomes a problem following the chemical analysis of archaeological ceramics when it may be necessary to separate the contributions of the various components towards the overall composition. When looking at changes produced during firing, and thereby trying to establish the conditions of firing, it is behaviour of the fabric as a totality that is being examined.

As discussed above, when a clay body is fired it can undergo several possible alterations, and the different changes that occur, and the temperatures at which they theoretically take place, are used as the basis of many methods of thermal analysis (Table 9.1). Many techniques are used to try to assess the maximum firing temperature experienced by a sherd of pottery, but they are all based on the same principle: that the changes produced on firing are permanent and that if the sherd is reheated no further changes will occur until the original maximum temperature is exceeded. Most materials, including ceramics, expand when they are heated, but clays on firing can also suffer shrinkage as various minerals decompose or change their form, a liquid phase develops or the particles sinter together, and it is the combined effects of expansion and contraction that are investigated during thermal expansion tests. In this form of analysis the sherd is heated and its expansion or contraction measured as the temperature rises. The basic principle is that the material will show normal thermal expansion up to the original maximum firing temperature but, as that temperature is exceeded, the expansion continues but starts to be counter-balanced by the various contractions in the fabric until the point is reached where contraction exceeds expansion, with the net result that the sample starts to shrink. It is not quite as simple as this, because the duration of heating is also a factor and so the sherd has to be reheated, held for an hour at 50°C above the temperature when shrinkage was noted in the first experiment, and the final assessment of original firing temperature is calculated from the results of the two experiments. In thermo-gravimetric analysis, weight changes caused by water loss during heating are investigated, whereas in differential thermal analysis mineralogical changes above a certain temperature evidenced by the evolution or absorption of heat are used to estimate the original maximum temperature for the sherd.

A detailed discussion of these methods and their limitations is provided by Rice (1987: 432–35), but the main problem, as with several other methods of investigation of ceramic technologies (including the interpretation of results of experimental firings), is that the modifications produced during firing depend not only on the maximum temperature reached and the types and proportions of clay minerals originally present but also on the form and distribution of any temper, the rate of increase in temperature, the length of time the material was held at any tempera-ture, the cooling cycle and the atmospheric conditions. The other major difficulty is that these methods of thermal analysis examine an overall change of weight or size with temperature, and this may be merely external observation of the combined effect of several morphological alterations. For this reason there is increasing inter-est in the use of scanning electron microscopy in the study of ceramics, including assessment of firing temperatures and conditions (Maniatis and Tite 1981; Fig. 9.1). When dealing with this latter area it is often still necessary to examine the sample in the as-received state and then re-examine it after various sequences of heat treatment, but the SEM is thought to offer a particular advantage in that it allows the detailed examination of the actual structure of the fabric and any alteration in morphology related directly to the mineralogy can be identified, rather than relying on observation of effects that could be the result of several changes.

The general investigation of the effect of heat on materials, and the application

375

of techniques of thermal analysis in particular, has been mainly confined to the study of ceramics and clays, but there is now increasing interest in the possibility that lithic artefacts might show evidence of heat treatment and in the means by which this could be detected. During the early history of archaeology considerable significance was attached to the first appearance of pottery firing in any area because, apart from the natural effects of the sun and the use of heat in the preparation of food, this seemed to mark the first extensive application of heat to translate materials from one form into another. Once this concept had been grasped, it might have opened up the whole area of pyrotechnology. There are a few tentative suggestions that heat treatment of lithics might pre-date pottery firing in particular areas, but interest in this heat treatment lies less in this pyrotechnical aspect (in any case now largely abandoned as offering any form of explanation for technological innovation), and more in that it might have produced sufficient changes in the lithics to allow the date of heating to be determined by thermoluminescence or electron spin resonance. As the rationale behind heat treatment seems to have been to improve working properties, it would also give a clear sign that these properties were considered important in those particular instances.

Despite the variety of tools and techniques postulated for the working of lithics over the last two million years, the underlying processes, whether in quarrying, shaping, or finishing, can be reduced to three – flaking, pulverizing and abrasion. The basis of flaking is that a blow is delivered to the surface of the material, a small fissure forms and this crack then runs through the material so that a piece of material, a flake, is removed. All lithics are amenable to working by flaking because they are brittle, and therefore likely to break when struck; whether they are particularly suitable for this technique depends on the degree of control over the direction the crack takes. The actual material can have an influence because cracks will tend to follow pronounced lines of structural weakness, and lithics show great variations in these. At the one extreme, the amorphous glassy structure of a piece of obsidian, particularly one with no flaws, gives equal strength in all directions, and the material has little influence. The length and direction of the crack, and the shape of flake removed, are far more affected by the strength, angle and sharpness of the blows at the surface. They are therefore under the control of the worker. On the other hand, in contrast to the structure of obsidian, boundaries between mineral grains in rock are major lines of weakness and once a crack has been initiated it is likely to move along connecting boundaries, with the worker having far less influence. Hence in a very coarse-grained rock, where the boundaries are relatively few in number and very pronounced, the direction the crack will follow is difficult to control externally. Rocks classed as having good flaking properties tend to be fine-grained, reasonably homogeneous, brittle and hard; the majority are acid igneous rocks with a glassy silicate component. As with their structures, crypto-crystalline cherts lie somewhere between the rocks and obsidian. With the exception of novaculite which behaves like a coarse rock, cherts are akin to extremely fine-grained rocks. There are grain boundaries but the networks are very fine and the boundaries very numerous, and the net result is that the fracture surface could move in a multitude of directions, structure therefore exerting only a limited influence and the direction and angle of the blow from the knapper also being significant factors.

Trying to improve the flaking properties of cherts still further, and thus increase the degree of control offered to the worker, is the main explanation proposed for heat treatment. The idea that this treatment might have been carried out first came from nineteenth-century accounts of various procedures then used in several parts of the world (Hester 1972), prompting an interest in establishing whether it had been used in earlier periods. This has now been recognized by direct examination of archaeological objects. The early accounts describe various heating methods, including burying chert under a fire or pouring hot water over it, but they all suggest slow heating to relatively low temperatures. Various experiments have confirmed a limit of around a 50°C temperature rise per hour if the material is not to spall or crack, and they suggest that the optimum temperature to produce improvement in working properties depends on the particular sample, but normally lies between 300 and 500°C. There is general agreement from the various researchers that the flaking properties of poor quality material are definitely improved, though less consensus on the reasons for this. Some research has suggested that chert acquires a more amorphous glassy structure, but other work led to the idea that microcracks may form within the grains thus reducing their strength (Olausson and Larsson 1982). Whatever the mechanism, the historical accounts alone provide clear evidence that flaking properties were important in the situations described and that the subtle changes in properties produced by heat treatment must have been recognized and appreciated.

THE USE OF ARTEFACTS

This section is concerned with some types of direct evidence for the possible use of objects, coming mainly from the objects themselves. These forms of evidence include the shape of the object, context of final deposition, associations, textual and other historical data, the artefact's material and properties, traces of wear related to use and any diagnostic residues. The depth to which this evidence is explored depends to some extent on the reasons for trying to establish use, such as (for objects with an apparently utilitarian use): establishing specific activities represented on a site, particularly those such as food processing for which little other evidence may survive; determining the type of site – trading centre, kill site, workshop and so on; establishing whether the appearance of certain types of object seeming to have a particular use can be taken as an indication of an increase in that form of activity (for example, weapons being linked to warfare); assessing whether all objects classified as similar in use really did have the same use; determining whether variations in the form or typology of objects can be ascribed to differences in use; examining the significance of distribution patterns – for example, are objects containers and, if so, are they where they are because of their contents; and assessing possible reasons for making the objects from particular materials, whether these be local or non-local resources.

The properties of the materials

In terms of use, context and associations may be of assistance in assessing how the object entered its final deposition, but much archaeological material has no clear context or derives from waste deposits. Shape may in some circumstances be a guide to function, but there is such a long tradition of describing that shape in terms of modern artefact types and uses – a knife-shaped object is termed a knife, a hatchet-shaped object an axe – that it is difficult to escape the connotations and it is often the validity of these initial interpretations based on shape that needs to be tested; plus the idea that all objects of a similar form are likely to have had a common function. This is an area where material properties can come into play. They can seldom completely rule out a possible use, but common sense suggests that an axe-shaped object made of a very ductile material like gold is unlikely to have had much of a practical role. In contrast, the jadeite used for some axe-shaped objects of the European Neolithic has been deemed too hard because jadeites are very tough and difficult to work. Geochemical and petrological analysis (Woolley *et al.* 1979) of samples from some of the British axes has indicated that the jadeite itself derives from outside the British Isles, probably from a source in the Alpine area of Europe, and a combination of the source of the material, its resilience, the small number of such objects and their final contexts, plus the absence of any obvious wear from use, has led to the suggestion that these particular axes probably never had a strictly utilitarian function but might represent some form of currency, or be a product of gift exchange. Physical properties, including the suitability of different types of rock for tool use, were also considered by Bradley *et al.* (1992) in their analysis of other neolithic rock artefacts. They saw some correlation between the strength of the raw materials and the material extracted for axe manufacture but argued that all aspects of lithic resource exploitation could not be explained in strictly utilitarian terms.

Another example of the role of material properties in considerations of use follows from Coles's experiments with metal and leather shields (Coles 1962). Hundreds of shield-shaped objects of tin-bronze, wood and leather, plus metal swords and other possible weapons, have been recovered from later Bronze Age contexts in northern Europe. Coles made replica shields of copper and leather – not identical to any original but of comparable hardness – and tested them against slashing swords of tin-bronze. The leather shield survived, the copper one was cut in two by a single blow. This led Coles to suggest that the leather shields could have been protective devices, but this was an unlikely use for the metal ones.

Cooking vessels that are heated during use are subject to even more stringent conditions, and this is an area in which it is possible to theorize on the optimum properties for a material and then assess how nearly the fabric of particular vessels matches these criteria. Several requirements can be suggested, such as good thermal shock resistance so that the vessel does not crack on heating and cooling, high conductivity, minimum heat loss from the vessel's surface and low porosity if used with liquids. As scanning electron microscopy and other techniques now allow direct examination of pottery fabrics, there has been increased interest in looking at archaeological ceramics and ethnographic practices in terms of the physical properties of the materials. Thus Vandiver and Koehler (1986), for example, recognized two basic fabric types amongst Corinthian amphora and considered that calcium-rich, illite clays with potassium flux had been deliberately selected for vessels to be used with liquids because this particular combination of raw materials fires to give a dense, non-porous and glassy fabric. In contrast, Schiffer (1990), as have many others, has adopted an experimental approach and looked at the effect of various surface treatments – smoothing, polishing, resin coating and so on – seen amongst archaeological and ethnographic ceramics to see if they have any effect on the absorption and transfer of heat. However, just as there are many examples of postulated uses of ceramics being supported by an apparently deliberate selection of a fabric with appropriate properties, there are also many instances where there seem to be no deliberate modifications and the choice of raw materials cannot be explained by the presumed usage of the vessels (Woods 1986). Therefore, one cannot put too much emphasis on material properties as a guide to an object's function, particularly when dealing with complex materials such as ceramics. 'Because there may be a scarcity of clays suited to special purposes, other decisions [once the clay is selected from those available] – choices about temper, form, thickness and so forth – can be seen as accommodation strategies' (Rice 1987: 227). You make the most of what you have, and much depends on the first choice you make.

Use-wear

The most obvious sign that an object had a specific use is an alteration to the object that could only have been produced by that use. One of the most common forms of alteration is wear on the surface, normally the result of some action such as grinding or cutting that involves contact between materials. Observation of these wear patterns forms the basis of use-wear analysis in general – the thinning near a rivet hole in a metal dagger, abrasions on the interior of a pottery vessel (Hally 1983) – and some aspects of the functional microanalysis of lithics. Use-wear can be applied to any type of object, but much of the extensive research over the last thirty years has concentrated on lithics, and objects of chert and obsidian in particular. As it is based on effects that can often be seen with the naked eye, the history of use-wear analysis in archaeology extends back into the nineteenth century when comments were already being made on the changes produced on the surface of objects when they were used and the possible implications for the interpretation of archaeological material. As early as 1892 Spurrell, for instance, made a replica flint blade and used it to cut wood, bone, horn and straw, and he noted that the working of the straw, and only the straw, produced a noticeable shine on the tool edge. The generation of polishes on lithic objects during activities related to cereal processing was confirmed by others in the 1920s and 1930s, and the surface shine seen on many supposed harvesting implements came to be called 'corn gloss' or 'silica gloss'. The latter description was based on the idea that the polish might have been produced through contact between the tool and silica particles in plant stems but, despite a few attempts to try to understand the mechanisms of formation, interpretation of use-wear on lithic artefacts long remained based on empirical observation.

A major impetus towards more fundamental research, and the importance of observations under a microscope, came with the work of Semenov in Russia. He had examined the surfaces of bone and lithic objects at a range of magnifications, and postulated the idea that the use produced a number of modifications at the surface, in particular combinations of edge rounding, striations and polishes (Semenov 1964). Not all of his conclusions have been confirmed by later work, but they did provide a stimulus towards further research into the validity of use-wear and the factors that influence surface morphology. Much of the initial research on the validity of the technique continued the empirical, experimental, approach. Artefacts were made, mainly of flaked tools of cherts and in the form of known archaeological objects. The surface was examined and then, after the artefact had been used for a measured time in a particular way for a specific activity such as whittling dry oak or cutting fresh cowhide, it was re-examined to see if use had produced any observable changes, and whether these could be characterized in any way (Young and Bonnichsen 1984). Some of the main proponents of this approach then carried out blind tests where objects were made and used by one researcher and then passed to another who tried to assess area of the tool involved, type of use and material worked. It would appear essential that this form of test is carried out to give some guidance on the viability of use-wear, but there has been much discussion on the validity of such tests and the methodology employed (Bamforth *et al.* 1990).

Much of the debate centres on the differing views on what is being seen and it has been fostered because of the lack of a common theoretical framework. Also, what is visible depends very much on the magnification used: a chip from a blade edge can be seen with the naked eye, but small areas of sheen might only be revealed at a particular magnification. This has resulted in two somewhat divergent approaches to microwear analysis of lithics: the use of magnifications to around ×100 to look at edge damage; and the investigation of striations, micro-polishes and abrasions at ×100 to ×5000 or more. Advocates of the low-power approach (Odell and Odell-Vereecken 1981) suggest that experiments show that it has a role in use-wear analysis, and that the recurrence of similar patterns of damage on archaeological objects will allow the effects of burial etc. to be recognized more easily. Proponents of high magnification (Keeley 1980) postulate that all forms of damage can be caused by many factors, but that the changes that only become visible at high magnification are more likely to be directly attributable to use.

It has never been suggested that any simple equation could be used to relate surface morphology directly to the use of an object, and as time has gone on more and more variables in the generation of use-wear have emerged. The factors now seen as significant include the mechanical properties of the material of the object; the original form of the surface; the type and duration of any use; the material being worked; grit or other contamination coming between the object and workpiece; multiple use involving a single surface; trampling or other pre-depositional forms of wear; burial; recovery; and subsequent handling. In the last thirty years the influences of all of these factors, singly or in combination, have been investigated via experimental and theoretical approaches. Other issues have also been raised, such as the nature of polishes (Fullagar 1991) and whether the so-called 'corn gloss' is produced by abrasion or by deposition of siliceous material.

The greatest potential of use-wear analysis may eventually be seen to lie in its ability to distinguish objects that have had some form of usage from those that have not, but all these factors will still require consideration. Use-wear studies have so far related mainly to the apparently simple, single-phase, mineral lithics such as cherts and obsidian, as the need to understand the behaviour of the individual mineral phases in rocks would introduce a new level of complexity. However, microwear analysis of structurally diverse, composite materials such as bone and antler has now extended from detection of traces indicating working by lithic objects to wear generated when they might have been used as objects themselves. This introduces a whole new suite of non-use variables, from damage to antler *in vivo*, through butchery, taphonomy and extensive bone diagenesis during burial (Olsen 1989).

The development of microwear analysis of lithics has been looked at in some detail, not because it is a particularly important technique but rather because its history provides a prime example of some general principles relating to artefact analysis. A problem is identified, and a technique appears to offer a solution. Once the potential seems to have been established there is then a long, and often slow and ultimately unrewarding, period of research to confirm this potential. The main requirement is to establish a strong, theoretical basis, and a degree of fundamental understanding to uphold the validity of the approach. Any technique needs to be sufficiently robust to cope with variations in conditions and, particularly important when dealing with archaeological artefacts, not to require knowledge of the object's full history.

Surface residues

With the ability to look in detail at surface layers, there is growing interest in the absorption of material into surfaces, an understanding being necessary for research into decay, diagenesis, conservation, chemical analysis and dating as well as micro-wear. As this has coincided with the development of improved methods of bio-chemical assay, one line of research related to the function of objects has been investigations into the possibility that biological residues may remain on or within artefact surfaces. Several thousand lithic objects, for example, have been tested for the presence of blood protein, and traces of blood have been reported for around two thousand objects, with the oldest residues so far identified dating to about 100,000 years ago (Loy 1993). In a few cases it has been suggested that the species of animal involved could also be distinguished via DNA analysis, the form of crystallization of the protein or immunoassay techniques, although the validity of some of the results has been questioned (Hyland *et al.* 1990). This is inevitable at this stage in the development of a new area of research, particularly when dealing with biological material that is subject to decay, exposed on the surface of an object and therefore subject to contamination, and that survives in only trace quantities and can only be detected by very sensitive methods. Susceptibility to decay and degradation depends to some extent on the environment but, taking biomolecules as a whole, the best preserved are likely to be large-chain plant polymers (such as lignin in wood), followed by lipids, carbohydrates, then proteins and finally DNA (Evershed 1993), with blood protein therefore relatively unstable. Much fundamental research on modern blood samples is now in progress to determine the mechanisms of degradation and behaviour in different forms of environment. Whether blood residue analysis ever becomes a routine method in the study of artefacts depends on the outcome of this research and a better understanding of chemical and biochemical modifications through time.

As indicated above, lipids, defined as components of biological materials that are more soluble in organic liquids than in water (Evershed 1993: 75) and comprising a whole suite of compounds including cholesterol, fatty acids, and components of waxes, are reasonably stable. Also, by definition, they are little soluble in water and so once deposited onto or into a surface are likely to remain in place and not be distributed into the wider environment. Such transfer and deposition of plant and animal lipids onto artefact surfaces can occur during cooking or where porous vessels are used as containers. This is the basis of lipid analysis to determine artefact function, particularly in the case of the use of ceramic vessels. Traces of residues can be extracted using organic solvents and then analysed by infra-red or gas chromatography/mass spectrometry to determine the presence of any diagnostic components. This is one specific example of the use of these techniques in the general area of identification of organic substances and is subject to the same complexities, limitations and potential. Thus Gerhardt *et al.* (1990) showed via GC/MS analysis that extracts from three sixth-century BC vases contained plant and animal oils and fats suggestive of the presence of perfumed oil, but that a fourth vase, typologically distinct, only had plant residues diagnostic of cedar wood oil. They were thus able to demonstrate that the two forms of vase may have contained different types of substance and had different usages, but they were not able to detect the actual form of the perfumed oil, and whilst the extracts contained over one hundred substances, around half could not be identified.

There are several hundred similar examples of useful data emerging from lipid analysis in archaeology, and its application is in no way invalidated because only a portion of the compounds can be categorized and the level of identification achieved is variable. In this, and in other areas of archaeology, lipid analysis has opened up areas of investigation that could barely be envisaged ten years ago. It also offers a very good example of the way the scientific study of artefacts has altered over the years: samples are no longer packed into boxes, sent away for examination, and the results presented as a set of facts divorced from context and association. Instead, there is a continuous dialogue on what the artefacts represent, why they are being examined and what questions are being asked of them. In many respects the real study of artefacts in archaeology is only just beginning.

REFERENCES

Bamforth, D. B., Burns, G. R. and Woodman, C. (1990) 'Ambiguous use traces and blind test results: new data', *Journal of Archaeological Science* 17: 413–30.
Barber, D. J. and Freestone, I. (1990) 'An investigation of the origin of the colour of the Lycurgus Cup by analytical transmission electron microscopy', *Archaeometry* 32: 33–45.
Barrett, J. C. (1994) *Fragments from Antiquity*, Oxford: Blackwell.
Beck, C. W., Adams, A. B., Southard, G. C. and Fellows, C. (1971) 'Determination of the origin of Greek amber artifacts by computer-classification of infrared spectra', in R. H. Brill (ed.) *Science and Archaeology*, Cambridge, Mass.: MIT Press: 235–40.
Bimson, M. (1987) 'Opaque red glass: a review', in M. Bimson and I. C. Freestone (eds) *Early Vitreous Materials*, Occasional Paper 56, London: British Museum: 165–71.

Bimson, M., La Neice, S. and Leese, M. (1982) 'The characterization of mounted garnets', *Archaeometry* 24: 51–58.

Binford, L. R. (1972) *An Archaeological Perspective*, New York: Seminar Press.

Bowman, S. G. E., Cowell, M. R. and Cribb, J. (1989) '200 years of coinage in China: an analytical survey', *Journal of the Historical Metallurgy Society* 23: 25–30.

Bradley, R., Meredith, P., Smith, J. and Edmonds, M. (1992) 'Rock physics and the Neolithic axe trade in Great Britain', *Archaeometry* 34: 223–33.

Brown, M. A. and Blin-Stoyle, A. E. (1959) 'A sample analysis of British middle and late bronze age material using optical spectrometry', *Proceedings of the Prehistoric Society* 25: 188–208.

Budd, P., Gale, D., Pollard, A. M., Thomas, R. G. and Williams, P. A. (1993) 'Evaluating lead isotope data: further observations', *Archaeometry* 35: 241–47.

Butler, J. J. and van der Waals, J. D. (1966) 'Bell Beakers and early metal working in the Netherlands', *Palaeohistoria* 12: 41–140.

Caley, E. R. (1964) *Analysis of Ancient Metals*, Oxford: Pergamon Press.

Champion, T., Gamble, C., Shennan, S. and Whittle, A (1984) *Prehistoric Europe*, London: Academic Press.

Chase, W. T. (1974) 'Comparative analysis of archaeological bronzes', in C. W. Beck (ed.) *Archaeological Chemistry*, Advances in Chemistry series, 138, Washington, DC: American Chemical Society: 148–85.

Coles, J. (1962) 'European Bronze Age shields', *Proceedings of the Prehistoric Society* 28: 156–90.

Craddock, P. T. (1978) 'The composition of copper alloy used by the Greek, Etruscan and Roman civilisations. 3: The origins and early use of brass', *Journal of Archaeological Science* 5: 1–16.

Craddock, P. T. (ed.) (1980) *Scientific Studies in Early Mining and Extractive Metallurgy*, Occasional Paper 20, London: British Museum.

Craddock, P. T. (1995) *Early Mining and Metal Production*, Edinburgh: Edinburgh University Press.

Darvill, T. and Timby, J. (1982) 'Textural analysis: a review of potentials and limitations', in I. Freestone, C. Johns and T. Potter (eds) *Current Research in Ceramics: Thin-section Studies*, Occasional Paper 32, London: British Museum: 73–87.

Davies, O. (1934/35) 'The chemical composition of archaic Greek bronze', *Annual of the British School at Athens* 35: 131–37.

Elùere, C. (1987) 'Celtic gold torcs', *Gold Bulletin* 20: 22–37.

Evershed, R. P. (1993) 'Biomolecular archaeology and lipids', *World Archaeology* 25: 74–93.

Filippakis, S. E., Perdikatsis, B. and Paradellis, T. (1976) 'An analysis of the blue pigments from the Greek Bronze Age', *Studies in Conservation* 21: 143–53.

Frank, S. (1982) *Glass and Archaeology*, London: Academic Press.

Freestone, I. C. (1987) 'Composition and structure of early opaque red glass', in M. Bimson and I. C. Freestone (eds) *Early Vitreous Materials*, Occasional Paper 56, London: British Museum: 173–91.

Fullagar, R. L. K. (1991) 'The role of silica in polish formation', *Journal of Archaeological Science* 18: 1–24.

Gale, N. H. and Stos-Gale, Z. A. (1992) 'Lead isotope studies in the Aegean (The British Academy Project)', in A. M. Pollard (ed.) *New Developments in Archaeological Science*, Proceedings of the British Academy 77, Oxford: Oxford University Press: 63–108.

Gerhardt, H. O., Searles, S. and Biers, W. R. (1990) 'Corinthian figure vases; non-destructive extraction and gas chromatography-mass spectrometry', in W. R. Biers and P. E. McGovern (eds) *Organic Contents of Ancient Vessels: Materials Analysis and Archaeological Investigation*, Philadelphia: MASCA Research Papers in Science and Archaeology 7: 41–50.

Gowland, W. (1899) 'The early metallurgy of copper, tin and iron in Europe, as illustrated by ancient remains, and the primitive processes surviving in Japan', *Archaeologia* 56: 267–322.

Haines, B. M. (1981) *The Fibre Structure of Leather*, Nottingham: Leather Conservation Centre.

Hally, D. J. (1983) 'Use alteration of pottery vessel surfaces: an important source of evidence in the identification of vessel function', *North American Archaeologist* 4 (1): 3–26.

Harrell, J. A. (1992) 'Ancient Egyptian limestone quarries: a petrological study', *Archaeometry* 34: 195–211.

Henderson, J. (1989) 'Scientific analysis of ancient glass', in J. Henderson (ed.) *Scientific Analysis in Archaeology*, Oxford: Oxford Committee for Archaeology Monograph 19: 30–60.

Hester, T. R. (1972) 'Ethnographic evidence for the thermal alteration of siliceous stone', *Tebiwa* 15: 63–65.

Hodder, I. (1982) *The Present Past*, London: Batsford.

Hodder, I. (1991) *Reading the Past* (second edition), Cambridge: Cambridge University Press.

Hunt, R. W. G. (1989) *Measuring Color*, New York: Halsted Press.

Hyland, D. C., Tersak, J. M., Adovasio, J. M. and Siegel, M. I. (1990) 'Identification of the species of origin of residual blood on lithic materials', *American Antiquity* 55: 104–12.

Junghans, S. Sangmeister, E. and Schröder, M. (1968) *Kupfer und Bronze in der frühen Metallzeit Europas*, Stuttgart: Studien zu den Anfangen der Metallürgie Band 2 (SAM 2).

Kaczmarczyk, A. and Hedges, R. E. M. (1983) *Ancient Egyptian Faience*, Warminster: Aris and Phillips.

Keeley, L. H. (1980) *Experimental Determination of Stone Tool Uses: a Microwear Analysis*, Chicago: University of Chicago Press.

Kempe, D. R. C. (1983) 'Raw materials and miscellaneous uses of stone', in D. R. C. Kempe and A. P. Harvey (eds) *Petrology of Archaeological Artefacts*, Oxford: Clarendon Press: 53–79.

Kempe, D. R. C. and Harvey, A. P. (eds) (1983) *Petrology of Archaeological Artefacts*, Oxford: Clarendon Press.

Kingery, W. D. (ed.) (1996) *Learning from Things: Method and Theory in Material Culture Studies*, Washington, DC: Smithsonian Institution Press.

Lane-Fox, A. (1875) 'On the evolution of culture', *Notices and Proceedings of the Royal Institution of Great Britain* 7: 496–520.

Lang, J. (1988) 'Study of the metallography of some Roman swords', *Britannia* 19: 199–216.

Loy, T. H. (1993) 'The artifact as site: an example of the biomolecular analysis of organic residues on prehistoric tools', *World Archaeology* 25: 44–63.

Lucas, A. (1934) *Ancient Egyptian Materials and Industries*, London: Edward Arnold.

Maniatis, Y. and Tite, M. S. (1981) 'Technological examination of neolithic and bronze age pottery from central and southeast Europe and from the Near East', *Journal of Archaeological Science* 8: 59–76.

Maniatis, Y., Aloupi, E. and Stalios, A. D. (1993) 'New evidence for the nature of Attic black gloss', *Archaeometry* 35: 23–34.

Middleton, A. (1987) 'Technological investigation of the coatings on some "haematite-coated" pottery from southern England', *Archaeometry* 29: 250–61.

Middleton, A. and Freestone, I. (eds) (1991) *Recent Developments in Ceramic Petrology*, Occasional Paper 81, London: British Museum.

Mills, J. S. and White, R. (1987) *The Organic Chemistry of Museum Objects*, London: Butterworths.

Muhly, J. D. (1993) 'Early Bronze Age tin and the Taurus', *American Journal of Archaeology* 97: 239–53.

Needham, J. (1958) *The Development of Iron and Steel Technology in China*, London: The Newcomen Society.

Noll, W. and Hangst, K. (1975) 'Grun- und Blaupigmente der Antike', *Neues Jahrbuch fur Mineralogie Monatsheft* 12: 529–40.

Northover, J. P. and Gerloff, S. (1988) 'Bronze Age considerations in Atlantic Europe: materials selection and design', in E.V. Sayre, P. B. Vandiver, J. Druzik and C. Stevenson (eds) *Materials Issues in Art and Archaeology*, Pittsburgh: Materials Research Society: 199–204.

Oddy, W. A. and Blackshaw, S. M. (1974) 'The accuracy of the specific gravity method for the analysis of gold alloys', *Archaeometry* 16: 81–90.

Odell, G. H. and Odell-Vereecken, F. (1981) 'Verifying the reliability of lithic use-wear assessment by "blind tests": the low power approach', *Journal of Field Archaeology* 7: 87–120.

Olausson, D. and Larsson, L. (1982) 'Testing for the presence of thermal pretreatment of flint in the Mesolithic and Neolithic of Sweden', *Journal of Archaeological Science* 9: 275–85.

Olsen, S. L. (ed.) (1988) *Scanning Electron Microscopy in Archaeology*, Oxford: British Archaeological Reports, International Series 452.

Olsen, S. L. (1989) 'On distinguishing natural from cultural damage on archaeological antler', *Journal of Archaeological Science* 16: 125–35.

Oppenheim, A. L., Brill, R. H., Barag, D. and von Saldern, A. (1988) *Glass and Glassmaking in Ancient Mesopotamia*, Corning: The Corning Museum of Glass Press.

Parkes, P. A. (1986) *Current Scientific Techniques in Archaeology*, London: Croom Helm.

Peacock, D. P. S. (1970) 'The scientific analysis of ceramics: a review', *World Archaeology* 1: 375–89.

Petrie, W. M. F. (1899) 'Sequences in prehistoric remains', *Journal of the Royal Anthropological Institute* 29: 295–301.

Pollard, A. M. and Heron, C. (1996) *Archaeological Chemistry*, London: Royal Society of Chemistry.

Renfrew, C. (1969) 'The autonomy of the South East European Copper Age', *Proceedings of the Prehistoric Society* 35: 12–47.

Rice, P. M. (1987) *Pottery Analysis: a Sourcebook*, Chicago: University of Chicago Press.

Rodden, J. (1981) 'The development of the Three Age System: archaeology's first paradigm', in G. Daniel (ed.) *Towards a History of Archaeology*, London: Thames and Hudson: 51–68.

Rothenberg, B. (ed.) (1990) *The Ancient Metallurgy of Copper*, London: Thames and Hudson.

Ryder, M. L. (1983) 'A reassessment of Bronze Age wool', *Journal of Archaeological Science* 10: 327–31.

Sanderson, D. C. W. and Hunter, J. (1980) 'Major element glass type specification for Roman, post-Roman and medieval glasses', *Revue d'Archéometrie* 3: 255–64.

Schiffer, M. B. (1990) 'The influence of surface treatment on heating effectiveness of ceramic vessels', *Journal of Archaeological Science* 17: 373–81.

Scott, D. A. (1986) 'Gold and silver alloy coatings over copper: an examination of some artefacts from Ecuador and Colombia', *Archaeometry* 28: 33–50.

Sellner, C. and Camara, B. (1979) 'Undersuchung alter Glaser (waldglas) auf Zusammenhang von Zusammensetzung, Fabre und Schmeltzatmospare mit der Elektronen Spektroskopie und der Elektronspin Resonanz', *Glastechnie Berichte* 52: 255–64.

Semenov, S. A. (1964) *Prehistoric Technology*, London: Cory, Adams and Mackay.

Shotton, F. W. and Hendry, G. L. (1979) 'The developing field of petrology in archaeology', *Journal of Archaeological Science* 6: 75–84.

Spurrell, F. C. J. (1892) 'Notes on early sickles', *Archaeological Journal* 49: 53–69.

Thompson, F. C. (1969) 'Microscopic studies of ancient metals', in D. Brothwell and E. Higgs (eds) *Science and Archaeology* (second edition), London: Thames and Hudson: 555–63.

Tite, M. S. (1987) 'Characterisation of early vitreous materials', *Archaeometry* 29: 21–34.

Tite, M. S. and Bimson, M. (1986) 'Faience: an investigation of the microstructures associated with different methods of glazing', *Archaeometry* 28: 69–78.

Tylecote, R. F. (1962) *Metallurgy in Archaeology*, London: Edward Arnold.

Tylecote, R. F., Ghaznavi, H. A. and Boydell, P. J. (1977) 'Partitioning of trace elements between the ores, fluxes, slags and metal during the smelting of copper', *Journal of Archaeological Science* 4: 305–33.

Vandiver, P. B. and Koehler, C. G. (1986) 'Structure, processing, properties and style of Corinthian transport amphoras', in W. D. Kingery (ed.) *Ceramics and Civilisation: Ancient Technology to Modern Science: Volume 2*, Westerville: The American Ceramic Society: 173–215.

Wagner, G. A., Begemann, F., Eibner, E., Lutz, J., Oztunali, O., Pernicka, E. and Schmitt-Strecker, S. (1989) 'Archaometallurgische Untersuchungen an Rohstoffquellen des frühen Kupfers in Ostanatolien', *Jahrbuch des Römisch-Germanischen Zentralmuseums Mainz* 36: 637–86.

Wertime, T. A. (1964) 'Man's first encounters with metallurgy', *Science* 146 (3649): 1257–67.

Willey, G. R. and Sabloff, J. A. (1980) *A History of American Archaeology*, San Francisco: W. H. Freeman.

Williams, D. F. (1983) 'Petrology of ceramics', in D. R. C. Kempe and A. P. Harvey (eds) *Petrology of Archaeological Artefacts*, Oxford: Clarendon Press: 301–29.

Williams, J. L. W., Jenkins, D. A. and Livens, R. G. (1974) 'An analytical study of the composition of Roman coarse wares from the Fort of Bryn y Gefeiliau (Caer Llugwy) in Snowdonia', *Journal of Archaeological Science* 1: 47–67.

Williams-Thorpe, O. and Thorpe, R. S. (1993) 'Geochemistry and trade of Eastern Mediterranean millstones from the Neolithic to Roman periods', *Journal of Archaeological Science* 20: 263–320.

Woods, A. J. (1986) 'Form, fabric and function: some observations on the cooking pot in antiquity', in W. D. Kingery (ed.) *Ceramics and Civilisation: Ancient Technology to Modern Science: Volume 2*, Westerville: The American Ceramic Society: 157–72.

Woolley, A. R., Bishop, A. C., Harrison, R. J. and Kinnes, I. A. (1979) 'European Neolithic jade implements: a preliminary mineralogical and typological study', in T. H. McK. Clough and W. A. Cummins (eds) *Stone Axe Studies*, Research Reports 23, London: Council for British Archaeology: 90–96.

387

Wright, M. M. and Wheals, B. B (1987) 'Pyrolysis-mass spectrometry of natural gums, resins and waxes and its use for detecting such materials in ancient Egyptian mummy cases (cartonnages)', *Journal of Analytical and Applied Pyrolysis* 11: 195–211.

Yener, K. A. and Vandiver, P. B. (1993) 'Tin processing at Goltepe, an Early Bronze Age site in Anatolia', *American Journal of Archaeology* 97: 207–38.

Young, D. E. and Bonnichsen, R. (1984) *Understanding Stone Tools: a Cognitive Approach*, Orono: University of Maine at Orono.

SELECT BIBLIOGRAPHY

Within the vast range of publications detailing current attitudes toward artefacts within archaeology, several offer a particular scientific perspective of artefacts as elements of material culture. These include Brian Hayden's *Archaeology: the Science of Once and Future Things* (New York: W. H. Freeman 1993), Ian Hodder's *Symbols in Action: Ethnoarchaeological Studies of Material Culture* (Cambridge: Cambridge University Press 1982) and David Kingery's two edited volumes arising from conferences on material culture at the Smithsonian Institution, *History from Things: Essays on Material Culture* (1993) and *Learning from Things: Method and Theory of Material Culture Studies* (Washington DC: Smithsonian Institution 1996). As the range of materials is so large, there are few recent books that attempt to give a comprehensive overview of archaeological artefacts primarily as material entities, but for a very straightforward, practical introduction, there is Henry Hodges's *Artifacts* (London: John Baker 1964) and also John Delmonte's more eclectic and wide ranging *Origins of Materials and Processes* (Lancaster, Pa.: Technomic Publishing Co. 1984). Hodges's later volume (London: Allen Lane 1970) *Technology in the Ancient World* and K. D. White's (London: Thames and Hudson 1984) *Greek and Roman Technology* are very readable surveys of aspects of early technology and, while inevitably somewhat out of date in terms of archaeological interpretations, copiously illustrated with direct representations of technological processes drawn from contemporary documents and paintings. For more detailed descriptions of the nature of artefacts and examples of application of scientific techniques there are a large number of volumes on particular materials or techniques such as Olin and Franklin's edited volume (Washington, DC: Smithsonian Institution 1982) on *Archaeological Ceramics* or M. Hughes, M. Cowell and D. Hook's *Neutron Activation and Plasma Emission Spectrometric Analysis in Archaeology* (London: British Museum Press 1991) in the British Museum Occasional Papers Series, but one of the best and most comprehensive, with a title that belies its extensive coverage of ethnographic and functional interpretations, is Prudence Rice's *Pottery Analysis: a Sourcebook* (1987). More on processes of manufacture, but from the perspective of experimental archaeology and modern attempts at reconstruction, is provided in John Coles's *Experimental Archaeology* (London: Academic Press 1979), which sets out clear guidelines for the experimental work that is becoming such an integral part of artefact studies. Specific detail on the potential and limitations of many of the techniques now available for the scientific examination of artefacts and examples of their application can be found in Julian Henderson's *Scientific Analysis in Archaeology* (1989), Sheridan Bowman's *Science and the Past* (London: British Museum Press 1991), and in Mark Pollard and Carl Heron's comprehensive *Archaeological Chemistry* (1996).

10

PRESERVING AND PRESENTING THE EVIDENCE

Mike Parker Pearson

INTRODUCTION

Many people might think that the archaeologist's tasks are over once the fieldwork, analysis and publication have been completed. In fact two of the most important aspects of archaeology are the preservation of archaeological remains and the presentation of those remains, and of their interpretations, to a wider public. Preserving old ruins and presenting the past might not seem as exciting as making archaeological discoveries, but in recent years archaeologists around the world have been drawn into a number of important ethical, philosophical and political debates: who owns the past?, what should be preserved?, what should be presented?, whose history is it?

From beginnings in the last 500 years, nation-states developed legislation to protect their archaeological monuments. Today every nation has laws in some form or other that refer to archaeology. There is also a growing body of international laws and conventions to protect and present the archaeological heritage. The philosophy behind preservation is now widely accepted, though many cultures around the world may not share such concepts of antiquity and authenticity. From this philosophical position, principles for repair and restoration and for presentation and display can be set out. Archaeology has always had a political dimension, and the ways that the past is presented may bear on issues such as nationalism, ethnic identity and power in the local community, as well as education and tourism. Putting into practice the principles behind archaeological conservation and presentation requires particular knowledge and training. Finally, some of the most serious problems for archaeology are to do with looting and the art market. Many developing nations want their cultural treasures returned from the museums of Europe and

North America. All round the world sites are looted and artefacts illegally sold. Also many people in many different countries are coming into conflict with the authorities about their access to sites and to knowledge about the past.

A HISTORY OF PRESERVATION AND PRESENTATION

Every culture has a sense of history, whether constituted as a radical break with the past or as a long tradition of continuity and change. Prerequisites of the practice of archaeology are a sense of curiosity and a respect for the artefacts, monuments and landscapes which constitute the archaeological resource. The roots of European concern to preserve the physical vestiges of the ancient past can be found from the fifteenth century onwards (see Chapter 1). In China, antiquarian interest had developed by the tenth century.

The rise of archaeological preservation and the education of the populace that accompanied it, in western Europe and especially in Scandinavia, were aspects of the consolidation of state power which had been going on since the Renaissance. These European states, and the gentry who pursued antiquarian interests, were incorporating hitherto ignored 'prehistories' into the ideological fabric of society. The ancient past might be viewed as a vista of development towards civilization, within which national character and identity were gradually forged. At the same time, a spirit of scientific enquiry was also replacing rural superstitions surrounding the antiquities. Whereas the Scandinavian presentation of the past was aimed at the rural working classes, interest in Britain was largely confined to the upper and professional classes. By the 1870s in Britain there were many local archaeological societies whose members were nearly all men and were drawn from the clergy, from the aristocracy or from respected professions (Hudson 1981).

Within Europe, legislation concerning ancient monuments gradually gathered momentum after the Renaissance, though its application varied considerably between nations. In 1425 Pope Martin V ordered the demolition of new buildings which might cause damage to ancient monuments, whilst in 1462 a Papal Bull pronounced the protection of the ancient monuments of Rome. In 1624 in Rome an edict forbade excavation without prior authorization. In England in 1560 a proclamation by Elizabeth I forbade the 'defacing of Monuments of antiquity, being set up in the churches or other public places for memory, and not for superstition'. In Sweden a State Antiquary was appointed in 1630, whilst in 1666 the destruction of ancient monuments and relics, whether on private or public property, was prohibited. During the eighteenth and nineteenth centuries a number of European nations drafted protective legislation or set up organizations and individuals to preserve ancient monuments and relics. In 1721 the Secretary of the Society of Antiquaries of London paid ten shillings for erecting two oak posts to protect the Waltham Cross, a medieval monument, from damage by traffic.

Some nations were considerably ahead of others. In Denmark systematic protection began in 1807, when recommendations were issued for the preservation of monuments, the informing of the peasantry of their value and the establishment of a state archaeological museum. In 1847 the post of Inspector for the conservation of monuments was appointed. In later years more staff were taken on and in 1873 a fifty-year long project was begun to survey all visible monuments. In Britain the first Inspector of Ancient Monuments, General Augustus Pitt-Rivers, was not appointed until 1882. The first Ancient Monuments Act was also passed in that year, only after considerable opposition from Conservative politicians, like Sir Francis Hervey, ever suspicious of the interference of the state in the individual's rights, who demanded: 'are the absurd relics of our barbarian predecessors, who found time hanging heavily on their hands, and set about piling up great barrows and rings of stones, to be preserved at the cost of infringement to property rights?' (Wright 1985: 50).

Outside western Europe, legislative and organizational initiatives in monument preservation were generally later and varied even more in content, effectiveness and timing. In 1863 the British government in India assumed authority to preserve ancient monuments, well in advance of similar changes in Britain. In central America, Mexico recognized the importance of preservation from its independence in 1821, though it did not pass effective legislation until 1897. Guatemala and Honduras recognized similar concerns for their Maya sites in 1894 and 1889. Similarly important pre-Hispanic monuments in Peru were protected by decrees in 1822, 1837 and 1893. An Antiquities Act was not passed in the United States until 1906. In Africa, the then French colonies mostly adopted a 1956 French law; in English-speaking Africa, many states had heritage legislation in place by the time they gained independence.

In Asia, there had been an interest in preservation in Japan from the eighteenth century, made tangible by the 1897 Law for the Preservation of Ancient Temples and Shrines. In 1950 two subsequent laws, on national treasures and on historic sites, were combined in the Law for the Protection of Cultural Properties. In China, despite the early antiquarian interest, appropriate legislation was not passed until the twentieth century. In 1930 a Law on the Preservation of Ancient Objects was enacted, asserting state ownership of all ancient objects found underground. Among the South-East Asian states, legislation generally came late – for example 1966 in the Philippines and 1970 in Singapore. In Australia, legislation to protect Aboriginal relics and early colonial remains was also slow to arrive, with the Northern Territories the first area to be protected in 1955.

Today, throughout the world, the protection and preservation of archaeological remains are a significant component of archaeological practice. By 1975 American

New Archaeologists had coined the term 'Cultural Resource Management' (CRM) to refer to the ongoing process of archaeological conservation, embracing salvage archaeology as well as preservation strategies. Nineteen seventy-six was declared European Architectural Heritage Year and in subsequent years the notion of 'heritage' gained increasing significance in archaeological conservation, as well as being used in a multitude of contexts from building houses to selling cheese! In Britain, it became a statutory term in the 1983 National Heritage Act. Later on, UNESCO (the United Nations Educational, Scientific and Cultural Organization) created an International Committee on Archaeological Heritage Management (ICAHM) within its International Council on Monuments and Sites (ICOMOS). Today the term 'archaeological heritage management' (AHM) is used widely in the same sense as CRM, though perhaps more emphasis is laid on public presentation within the meaning of AHM.

Not all archaeological sites can be preserved for the immediate future because of unavoidable threats from construction or from longer-term agricultural practices. Of lesser magnitude are natural processes of erosion and decay. The recording of remains in advance of destruction, known as rescue archaeology in Europe and as salvage archaeology in North America, is a common response to endangered sites around the world. In many countries such work is funded by the state, as has been the case in Britain since the Second World War. In some countries, including Britain and Scandinavia, developers in the private sector also contribute to rescue work in advance of their construction projects. In Britain there was a state-funded boom in rescue archaeology between the 1960s and 1980s, when amateur and professional archaeologists effectively lobbied local and central government, as well as winning over a supportive public. With legislative changes, and the reassertion of a conservation ethic, there has been a change of emphasis to preservation *in situ*, with rescue excavation as a last solution. Nevertheless, rescue projects continue to thrive and there is increasing awareness of their need to address research issues. In the United States the story of salvage archaeology is similar. The 1974 Archaeological and Historic Preservation Act authorized federal agencies to fund salvage work on sites endangered by federal projects. In 1969 the National Environmental Policy Act had already required the involvement of archaeology in the preparation of Environmental Impact Statements in advance of developments. This requirement for prior archaeological evaluation in advance of planning permission for developments is also common practice in England.

NATIONAL LEGISLATIONS AROUND THE WORLD

The most effective protection for archaeological remains is in Denmark, where an enlightened public, a long tradition of archaeology, and an integration of archaeology and nature conservation, have been successfully combined. The 1937 Act protected all visible monuments (whether recorded or not) without compensation to landowners. A large number of monuments that were being ploughed away were also taken out of cultivation. In 1961 all monuments were given a 100-metre protection zone around them. In 1969 archaeological investigation of non-visible ploughed sites and monuments became obligatory prior to damaging construction works. Today, monument preservation is administered by the Agency for the Protection of Nature, Monuments and Sites, while rescue archaeology is coordinated by the National Museum.

Other nations of northern Europe have similarly effective legislation. In England, the 1979 Ancient Monuments and Archaeological Areas Act established the proper protection of Scheduled Ancient Monuments (SAMs). SAMs had been identified since 1882, but previously a landowner only had to give three months' notice to the government before destroying one. The number of SAMs in England is currently being increased to 45,000, but this figure is still less than 10 per cent of all known sites; with many others still undiscovered, only a small percentage of the total is therefore protected. In 1988 archaeologists funded by developers uncovered the remains of the Elizabethan Rose Theatre in London. The theatre was to be excavated archaeologically and 'preserved by record', but the general public, led by an on-site protest by groups of actors, was outraged that the theatre's remains would not be preserved. The developers changed their plans to accommodate the remains within the development, and English Heritage (the government agency created by the 1983 National Heritage Act to preserve ancient monuments and historic buildings) were subsequently asked to advise the government on a guidance note for unprotected sites (*Planning Policy Guidance Note 16: Archaeology and Planning* – known as PPG 16), which was issued by the Department of the Environment in 1990. Similar guidance notes have also been issued for Wales and Scotland. Although not legislation, this guidance advocates the prior evaluation of development proposals in archaeologically sensitive locations, encourages the preservation of sites which are not SAMs, and identifies the developer's responsibility for the preservation or recording of archaeological remains affected by the development.

The 1973 Protection of Wrecks Act attempts to protect such sites on the seabed, but is difficult to enforce, due to looting by scuba divers, and does not cover submerged settlement sites of the last glacial and postglacial periods. All around the world, in fact, the problem of protecting underwater sites, both inside and outside territorial waters, is far from solved and the legislation is generally inadequate (Chippindale and Gibbins 1990).

In France, archaeology is regulated by the Law of 27 September 1941 controlling Archaeological Excavations. All excavations for research into monuments or objects require approval and supervision. The state may carry out excavations on private land without the landowner's permission, though compensation is payable. Finds are divided between the landowner and the state, with the state having a right of pre-emption. All chance finds must be reported and protected, and development halted if finds are made during construction. The law was drafted by the wartime Vichy government of occupied France and has been identified with a cultural policy which exalted a chauvinistic and authoritarian politics. There has been an Antiquities Service since 1964 (after 1979 the Sub-Directorate for Archaeology), but the administrative and operational infrastructure is rather weakly developed in comparison with the rest of northern Europe. The French system is acknowledged by French archaeologists as inadequate, but its importance lies in its adoption by most of the other French-speaking countries of the world (O'Keefe and Prott 1984).

In the United States, legislation protects only sites on government land. The 1979 Archaeological Resources Protection Act improved the protection of sites on federal land and extended the protection to sites on American Indian reservations. Since the 1960s, the vast majority of states has also passed protective legislation, including laws to protect living traditions of Native Americans. The respect for living traditions has also become a key issue in New Zealand and Australia. In New Zealand, Maori and early colonial remains are protected by an Antiquities Act 1975 and a Historic Places Act 1980. In Australia many of the Aborigines' sacred places are natural features such as rocks, water-holes, trees and mountains, which are now protected by the 1975 Australian Heritage Commission Act.

As with western Europe, Russia developed its archaeological interests through collecting, including the nineteenth-century foundation of the Imperial Archaeological Museum. Within the old Soviet Union, sites were protected by the 1976 Law on the Protection and Use of Historic and Cultural Monuments. Each state within the CIS has separate legislation. A similar process of decentralization has occurred in China, though there is covering legislation provided by the 1982 Regulation on Preservation of Cultural Relics. All cultural objects are the property of the state and all excavations must be approved. An important feature is the emphasis on detailed consultation and planning of construction work. Archaeology has been directed at educating the people in patriotism and revolutionary fervour, and has become a major tourist attraction. In Japan, the 1950 Law for the Protection of Cultural Properties provides protection through historic site designation. The Agency for Cultural Affairs can require site investigations prior to construction and also request the developer's cooperation to preserve a site. In recent years, Japanese rescue archaeology has increased dramatically, employing thousands of excavators and involving huge rescue projects.

In Peru, a law from 1929 protects archaeological monuments in public and private ownership. Clandestine excavation and the export of relics are forbidden. Excavations require permits and are organized or monitored by the National Archaeological Service, which conserves pre-Hispanic monuments, relics and works of art. It is notable that such a strong legislative system was implemented so early, though implementing it effectively in the face of organized and large-scale looting has proved another matter.

In Africa, much of the protective legislation is the legacy of previous colonial powers: the Portuguese and Spanish colonists left none; the French imposed their own system; and the British colonial legacy varies from nation to nation. One of the greatest problems has been the removal of artefacts for sale in the Western art markets and many countries have legislation which protects ethnographic objects of recent date. In Nigeria, for example, antiquities regulations came into effect in 1957 to restrict exportation, while in 1974 the buying and selling of antiquities (defined as made before 1918) between unaccredited agents was banned.

INTER-STATE OR INTERNATIONAL PROTECTION

UNESCO was founded in 1946 as an intergovernmental organization made up of delegates of national governments. It is closely linked to ICOM (the International Council of Museums) and to ICOMOS, and has developed a major body of heritage law. UNESCO has also developed major preservation programmes, for example at the Aswan Dam in Egypt (Fig. 10.1), the Buddhist *stupa* (shrine) at Barabodur in Indonesia, and the ancient city of Mohenjo-Daro in Pakistan. UNESCO has also produced three conventions relevant to archaeological preservation and presentation: the Convention for the Protection of Cultural Property in the Event of Armed Conflict 1954; the Convention on the Means of Prohibiting and Preventing the Illicit Import, Export and Transfer of Ownership of Cultural Property 1970; and the Convention for the Protection of the World Cultural and Natural Heritage 1972 (also called the World Heritage Convention).

The World Heritage Convention includes major archaeological sites from all over the world such as Machu Picchu in Peru, Petra in Jordan, the Egyptian pyramids, Great Zimbabwe and Carthage (Fig. 10.2). Whilst UNESCO is funding repairs to the temple complex at Angkor in Cambodia, the site is not included due to past political instability. Israel is not a party to the Convention and thus only the Old City of Jerusalem (nominated by Jordan) is on the list. Iraq has only nominated Hatra, but not earlier Mesopotamian sites like Babylon and Ur. There is a World Heritage Fund which has a small budget for conservation, including emergency repair: it was used, for example, after earthquake damage in Quito, Ecuador, in 1987. There is also a list of World Heritage Sites in Danger, including Timbuktu (becoming engulfed by sand) and Chan Chan (which has suffered from looting and mudbrick erosion). UNESCO has also issued a series of recommendations, including international principles for excavation, safeguarding the beauty and character of landscapes and sites, protecting and preserving cultural heritage, protecting

Figure 10.1 The temple at Abu Simbel, Egypt. This enormous monument was moved in advance of flooding by the Aswan Dam. It now forms part of World Heritage Site 211. Photograph: P. Nicholson.

movable cultural property, and regulating the international exchange of cultural property.

The Council of Europe has also created rules of international law on the archaeological heritage. It has twenty-one member states and makes reports on archaeological issues such as the use of metal detectors. In 1992 it passed an updated European Convention on the Protection of the Archaeological Heritage and has prepared other conventions on offences against cultural property and on the underwater cultural heritage (Chippindale 1993). The European Community also issues directives which may have relevance to archaeology in its member states. The directive on Environmental Impact Statements has been relevant for the inclusion of archaeological considerations in evaluating the impact of proposed major development.

PHILOSOPHIES AND ETHICS OF PRESERVATION

It is again no question of expediency or feeling whether we shall preserve the buildings of past times or not. *We have no right whatever to touch them.* They are not ours. They belong partly to those who built them, and partly to all the generations of mankind who are to follow us. The dead still have their right in them . . . whatsoever it might be which in those buildings they intended to be permanent, we have no right to obliterate. What we have ourselves built, we are at liberty to throw down . . .

(Ruskin 1849: 201)

396

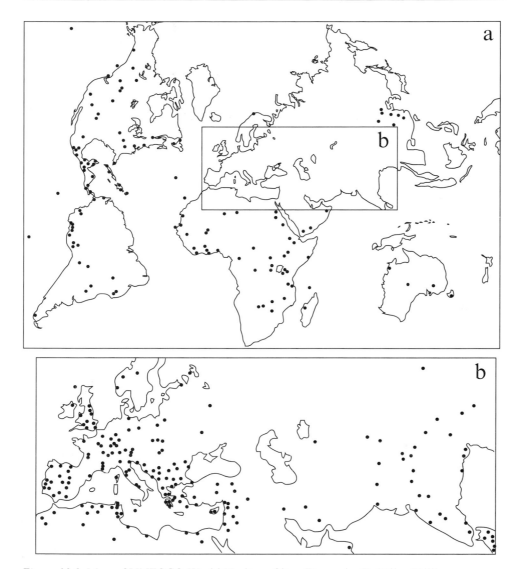

Figure 10.2 Map of UNESCO World Heritage Sites. Drawn by D. Miles-Williams.

Many people working to preserve historic buildings and archaeological sites would consider Ruskin's philosophy to have considerable relevance today. His values helped to change attitudes to demolition and restoration in the second half of the nineteenth century and have since guided generations of Inspectors of Ancient Monuments in the United Kingdom, as well as archaeologists in other countries. A more recent formulation of the theoretical, philosophical and ethical basis for conservation by an American archaeologist (Lipe 1974, 1984) highlights similar

397

concerns: the need for a set of values and attitudes about the continuity of life and culture (especially as the author saw them threatened by imminent nuclear holocaust); giving past lives and works the respect of our attention (and thereby respecting the rights of the future); and a concern with the long-term past, to remove our thoughts from the immediate concerns with the here and now, thus bridging the mortality of generations for us to reflect on the condition of humankind.

These concepts of value and meaning are very much bound up with Western philosophical notions of the importance of an objective materiality, where artefacts embody meaning in their own right and where temporality is reified and retained as knowledge. Amongst other cultures, however, the material vestiges of the past may count for little. Instead, the continuity and the permanence may reside in the living community and its continuous reproduction. In Japan, for example, individuals may be honoured as 'living national treasures' because of their artistic skill. In such instances the past is referenced as a living tradition, rather than as mute and sometimes incomprehensible relics. The Igbo of Nigeria stock their *mbari* houses with art objects but leave these to rot as soon as the process of collecting is completed (McBryde 1985). The Tandroy of southern Madagascar build massive tombs for their dead, but shun them on completion and leave them to crumble (Parker Pearson 1992).

European and American concepts of conservation have become widely accepted by archaeologists and legislators around the world (Cleere 1984, 1989; O'Keefe and Prott 1984). The material remains of the past are conceived as a non-renewable resource which is to be handed on intact to future generations for them to treasure and enjoy. There is no doubt that, in recent years, comparison and integration with the 'green movement' has influenced archaeologists' attitudes to the object of their study (Macinnes and Wickham-Jones 1992). As elements of the cultural environment, archaeological sites are treated in similar ways to the habitats of rare species or areas of outstanding natural beauty. In a number of nations, consideration for archaeological remains is one of many planning requirements for property developers. In these countries, the concept that 'the polluter pays' applies equally to archaeological sites unavoidably threatened by development as to chemical and other forms of pollution.

After the 'rescue' philosophy of the post-war period, archaeologists have become increasingly aware of the damaging effects of their own investigations: they destroy their evidence as they collect it. The concept of 'preservation by record' – creating an archive of finds and paper records – has been considered to be an acceptable substitute for an intact site, though it implies an objective and total retrieval which can never be achieved (Romer and Romer 1993). Archaeological investigation involves more and more non-destructive techniques, but excavation is a 'once only' intervention. The resource has to be carefully husbanded if it is to survive beyond the foreseeable future. In a world without the *in situ* and intact remains of the long-term past, we face something of an Orwellian future where there are no landmarks or physical presences of the ancient past in the landscape. In contrast, complete preservation restricts the very purpose for which we value the resource, as a means of finding out or of recovering the lost memory of humankind. In any case, how we decide what to preserve – and by implication what to let go – depends on the values and research aims of the present. These have changed through time and will continue to do so. There is thus an uneasy contradiction between a ravaged resource, plundered for short-term research goals, and a fossilizing knowledge based on limited interventions and ancient excavations of long ago.

PRINCIPLES OF RESTORATION AND CONSERVATION

Watch an old building with an anxious care; guard it as best you may, and at *any* cost, from every influence of dilapidation . . . Its evil day must come at last; but let it come declaredly and openly, and let no dishonesty and false substitute deprive it of the funeral offices of memory.

(Ruskin 1849: 200–1)

A distinction was made between preservation and restoration as long ago as 1849: Ruskin considered restoration to be 'a lie from beginning to end' (1849: 200); to restore was to mislead, to falsify and to destroy the authentic materials by manufacture of a copy. The Society for the Protection of Ancient Buildings (SPAB), formed in England in 1877, advised that all repairs should be honest and conspicuous, so that they might not be mistaken for the original fabric. To that end, many structures had their fabric repaired using mortared tiles instead of new stonework. The old conundrum of Alexander's axe illustrates the dilemma. As the wooden haft rotted so it needed a new handle. A while later the iron had rusted so badly that it needed a new blade. What was left of Alexander's axe? All of the original materials had been replaced: this was only Alexander's axe in that it was a copy. In Britain certain monuments have been restored so heavily that little remains of their original fabric – Nelson's warship HMS *Victory* and Westminster Abbey are two notable examples.

The aim of monument conservation is to arrest decay and preserve *in situ*. Ruskin and the SPAB abhorred any restorative work, realizing that all remains had a finite lifespan. In 1923, Frank Baines, HM Director of Works for ancient monuments and historic buildings in Britain, distinguished the concept of preservation from restoration, replacement, renovation and renewal. Instead, he defined preservation as 'a method involving the retention of the building or monument in a sound static condition, without any material addition thereto or subtraction therefrom, so that it can be handed down to futurity with all the evidences of its character and age unimpaired' (1923: 104).

399

Over time, however, the Office of Works was to alter its views on this theoretical divide. In 1931, Charles Peers outlined a more pragmatic approach: 'repair must neither deface nor obscure old work, but it is better to risk a deception by inconspicuous additions than to proclaim them by conspicuous and unsympathetic materials' (1931: 320). This approach guided much of their subsequent work. Restoration and renewal were employed when structurally necessary, for example on decayed roofs, windows and lintels. Techniques of restoration were used to conceal internal structural work such as concrete beams. The Office of Works never adopted the 'puritanical approach' of the SPAB, though aiming for unobtrusive yet unmistakeable substitution, particularly with modern materials. For example, at the late neolithic henge of Avebury, in Wiltshire, concrete markers were set up to indicate where standing stones had once been set, and at Stonehenge the eroded base of a stone was supported with concrete underpinning. Restoration was carried out only where a true replacement could be guaranteed and not where the original form was a matter of conjecture. At Stonehenge, fallen stones were set upright because there were records of their falling and their re-erection would aid the intelligibility of the monument.

During the course of the twentieth century conjectural restorations and reconstructions have become more acceptable. Mortimer Wheeler reconstructed the iron age defences of the hill-fort at Stanwick (Thompson 1981). More recently, South Shields District Council won a planning appeal to reconstruct a conjectural Roman stone gateway. Proposals for the Roman amphitheatre at Chester to be reconstructed were withdrawn in the face of strong opposition from conservation groups. Many other proposals on archaeological sites involve elements of conjectural reconstruction or representation in order to appeal to the public. There is undoubtedly a contradiction between an honest presentation of the evidence and intellectually accessible promotion. Such difficulties can be overcome by constructing replicas in the vicinity of the archaeological site, rather than attempting to reconstruct directly on the site itself, as in the case of the Eketorp fort in Sweden (Fig. 10.3).

The attempt to halt decay may also be considered in a philosophical sense as an attempt to end the history of particular monuments: they are thus suspended in time, set in the aspic of a dehistoricized present. But which physical aspects of their past should be preserved? In the early twentieth century the Office of Works in Britain shovelled out the moats, fishponds, refuse heaps, later rebuildings and destruction debris of medieval castles and monasteries in order to better preserve and display the medieval masonry remains. Today, however, we view the more ephemeral archaeological deposits and the post-medieval remains as having equal validity as the medieval stonework, although there are still problems with regard to where a cut-off point is made: should we so stringently deny or subdue our own impact on the remains of the past?

Figure 10.3 A reconstruction of the first-millennium AD fort at Eketorp, Sweden. The reconstruction has been built adjacent to the original site. Photograph: M. Parker Pearson.

UNESCO's recommendations, as exemplified in the 1966 Venice Charter, are clearly set out on these issues. Ancient monuments are a common heritage to safeguard for future generations in the full richness of their authenticity. They require permanent maintenance, the preservation of their settings, *in situ* preservation and the retention of component elements in context. Restoration should stop where conjecture starts and should be limited to reassembly. There should be respect for contributions of all periods of the monument's formation; there should be no additions if possible; and replacements must be harmonious but distinguishable. Additional recommendations were made in the 1987 Australia ICOMOS Charter for the Conservation of Places of Cultural Significance (known as the Burra Charter). Existing fabric should be respected. There should be the least possible intervention and the evidence of the fabric should not be distorted. Techniques of repair should be traditional, but tried and tested modern methods may be acceptable. Reconstruction should be used only where it is necessary for a monument's continued existence or to recover its cultural significance, and it should not constitute the majority of a monument's fabric. Adaptation of a monument to other uses must be limited to situations when conservation cannot be otherwise achieved, and it must not detract from the monument's significance.

The Burra Charter usefully summarizes definitions: *conservation* includes preservation, restoration, reconstruction, and adaptation; *preservation* is the maintenance of fabric and the retarding of deterioration; *restoration* is the removal of accretions, reassembly without new material, and returning to an earlier state;

reconstruction is the introduction of new materials but in a non-conjectural way; *adaptation* is modification to suit proposed compatible uses.

PRINCIPLES OF PRESENTATION AND DISPLAY

The chief aim of interpretation is not instruction but provocation.

(Tilden 1957: 9)

To display only what is authentic must surely on moral, logical or economic grounds be the proper aim.

(Thompson 1981: 96)

The promotion of archaeological sites and monuments has changed radically in the last twenty years. The previous philosophy is well summarized by Michael Thompson's book *Ruins – their Preservation and Display* (1981). He made a distinction between monuments – reminders of events, persons or activities, where moments of history might be revealed – and museums – repositories of objects out of context, places for study, self-instruction and education. The display of monuments required a series of steps. The site should be excavated to its last major phase of use, to reveal its formation and construction. Facilities for visitors should satisfy their physical needs (such as toilets and access points) as well as their intellectual needs (publications about the monument, on-site exhibitions, *son et lumière*). The scantier the remains, the more exhibits or on-site explanation were required. The appreciation of ruins required concentrated effort to understand their layout, their fragmentary survival and their multi-period additions. One of the standard characteristics of ancient monuments in Britain was the mown lawns surrounding stone masonry. These were considered an aesthetically satisfying contrast with the stone, a soft and dry surface and a means of exposing the lowest masonry walls and courses.

This was a purely 'archaeological' approach to appreciation. Within an ordered and controlled environment, the visitor had to work hard to understand why such sites were originally built and what they might have looked like. The evidence was stripped bare for investigation, guided by texts which were difficult to read and dry on interpretation. This approach was very different to eighteenth- and nineteenth-century concepts of the picturesque, the romantic (as championed by Walter Scott) and the Gothic revivalist movement, yet it was inherently elitist and increasingly out of touch with a society of mass cultural consumption. Archaeological excavations were similarly unfriendly to the general public, despite some notable exceptions such as Pitt-Rivers's excavations on Cranborne Chase at the turn of the century, or Mortimer Wheeler's excavations at Maiden Castle in the 1930s (Hudson 1981).

Despite Wheeler's overtures to the general public (in the form of postcards, finds

402

for sale, reports, public lectures, press conferences and newspaper reports), he maintained that two kinds of history were needed: one factual for scholars and the other fictional and mythical to keep the rank and file interested and in good heart (Hudson 1981: 67). Pitt-Rivers had also been a keen exponent of élitist notions, whilst emphasizing the need to educate the working classes so that they might be made 'cautious how they listen to scatter-brained revolutionary suggestions' (1891: 116). Doubtless such attitudes still exist in some quarters today, but many archaeologists would consider their relationship to the public as one of mutual dependence and respect. Archaeology is largely funded from public sources and the general public resents snobbish and patronizing attitudes by the experts.

World-wide there has been a growing professionalization within archaeology. Interested amateurs, or 'avocational archaeologists', have found that participation in field archaeology has become increasingly restricted. Results of recent surveys in Britain show that the general public, of all backgrounds, are more knowledgeable and receptive towards the work of archaeologists than before (Merriman 1990), but public access to archaeology is increasingly as passive consumers rather than active participants.

Today we can recognize several main strands to public involvement (Jameson 1997). These are archaeological tourism, political issues of national identity and ethnicity, applied archaeology, and the relationship of local communities to conservation/investigation projects.

Archaeological tourism

There has been an explosion in imaginative and informative presentations of archaeology and archaeological sites (Binks *et al.* 1988; Boniface and Fowler 1993). Many museums have abandoned the stuffy cases of artefacts in favour of more interpretive displays and accessible exhibitions which show how archaeologists make inferences about the past from material remains and depict vividly what life may have been like (Belcher 1991; Hooper-Greenhill 1990, 1992; Horne 1984; Pearce 1989, 1990, 1991; Southworth 1991; Stone and Molyneaux 1994; Walsh 1992). There are outdoor museums, such as the reconstructed iron age village at Lejre in Denmark, where visitors can also gain an idea of how people lived. Archaeological centres such as the Jorvik Viking Centre (Fig. 10.4) and the Archaeological Resource Centre (Fig. 10.5) at York have also helped to undermine the traditional distinction between museums and archaeological sites and to enliven public understanding. Many archaeological excavations make arrangements for the visiting public in the form of site guides, guided tours, audio and audio–visual devices and interpretation boards. Similar arrangements can be found on monuments open to the public and there are trails and itineraries for archaeological

Figure 10.4 A reconstruction of the past at the Jorvik Viking Centre, on the site of the Coppergate excavations in York, Britain: visitors are conveyed in 'timecars' around this presentation of life in the first millennium AD. © York Archaeological Trust.

visitors to landscapes as diverse as the Nile and its Egyptian monuments, the landmarks of an English medieval town, and the archaeological landscapes of an upland valley in the Derbyshire Peak District (Hodges 1991).

Two ethical dilemmas are apparent. First, visitors cause wear and tear – Stonehenge, for example, has been roped off to the public since 1979 because of erosion to the stones (Fig. 10.6). Second, many attractions are run by the private sector and in some cases there has been concern about the degree to which presentations are bogus or severely misleading. There are even major disagreements about museums, heritage centres and archaeological monuments in public ownership. Many charge admission fees, in addition to receiving state funds, discouraging the poorest sectors of society from visiting. The 'heritage industry' has received severe criticism in recent years (for example Ascherson 1987; Fowler 1992; Hewison 1987; Horne 1984; Walsh 1992) for its 'Disneyland' sensationalist promotion of bogus history for commercial gain.

Figure 10.5 Children and archaeology: at the Archaeological Resource Centre (ARC) in York, Britain, visitors are encouraged to handle archaeological finds. © York Archaeological Trust.

National identity

Archaeology has been for many years a tool of nation-building (Lowenthal 1985). Even attempts to transcend nationalism, such as the World Heritage Convention or the World Archaeological Congress, tend to highlight it as an intellectual version of the Olympic Games. National monuments like Great Zimbabwe or the Athenian Acropolis act as metonyms for the nation-state. National identities are nurtured and sustained by investment in the selection, preservation, and promotion of nationally important monuments. Excavations at Masada in the 1960s fostered Israeli beliefs in their historic rights to land, whilst Palestinians today claim that archaeological remains which record their ancestry in those lands are either ignored or bulldozed by Israeli archaeologists looking for Jewish remains, especially of the Roman period. In Mexico, the construction of a major national museum for pre-Columbian archaeology has been viewed in a similar vein (Trigger 1984). Nazi Germany promoted a particularly warped notion of Germanic supremacy, using the ideas of

405

Figure 10.6 Stonehenge in Britain. This monument has been the scene of violent confrontations between solstice-goers and police, and, since 1984, access has been carefully controlled by police and security guards. Photograph: M. Parker Pearson.

Gustav Kossinna to contend that all progress in prehistory had come from Indo-Aryan groups successively migrating out of what is now Germany (Arnold 1992). In addition, racist notions of blood and land were employed in defining 'Germanness'; the SS even included a section called the 'Ahnenerbe' (ancestral heritage). The small nation of Denmark has employed symbols and metaphors drawn from archaeological discoveries to promote national identity, particularly in the face of nineteenth- and twentieth-century German encroachment. The concept of the Vikings has a firm hold in the Danish consciousness, where one in eight of the population read *Skalk*, a popular archaeological magazine. In the United Kingdom, public concepts of the national heritage are dominated by stately homes and other historic buildings. The most symbolically resonant archaeological monument is Stonehenge (Fig. 10.6), the scene of a brutal attack in 1985 by police on 'New Age travellers' wishing to attend the midsummer solstice, from which they had been banned. Amidst considerable public resentment (they were reviled in the media as vagrant criminals), the travellers were targeted by the police as undesirables whose massed presence at Stonehenge solstices should no longer be tolerated because of their threat to public order.

Ethnicity

If we Aborigines cannot control our own heritage, what the hell can we control?

(Langford 1983)

The archaeology of colonialism has also caused political strife over rights to the archaeological past. Increasingly, minority indigenous groups in North America, Australasia, the Pacific and the Arctic have become politically concerned about the loss and desecration of their cultural heritage. The most intense controversy has been over the recovery and removal of human bones, raising a major ethical problem about the disturbance and display of human remains. Some scholars would maintain that all human remains should be re-buried. Others consider that their potential scientific value far outweighs any ethical concerns. As archaeology has become more accountable to its public, so archaeologists have had to enter into negotiations and compromises with ethnic groups (Layton 1989a, 1989b; Green 1984; Parker Pearson 1995; Rahtz 1985).

In the United States, Native Americans were appalled by racist treatment of burial evidence: Indian graves were excavated and curated by archaeologists, while contemporary remains of white settlers and soldiers were either exhumed by morticians or re-buried after analysis (such as the remains from the Little Big Horn battlefield of 1876). Political resistance to archaeologists' insensitive behaviour formed around pressure groups such as American Indians Against Desecration. The archaeologists initially refused to make any concessions, but in 1986 the Society for American Archaeology agreed to a set of guidelines recommending re-burial where some ancestral connection could be shown between excavated Indian burials and a present tribal group. Not all Native Americans have been happy with this compromise and problems still arise. The most far-reaching effects of the 're-burial' issue have been agreements to reinter often-extensive museum collections of Indian human remains, notably from the American Museum of Natural History, the Smithsonian Institution and Stanford University.

In Australia, there has been a similar history of confrontation and compromise. Palaeolithic bones have been returned and cremated. Other similarly ancient remains from Lake Mungo may well be kept by Australian Aboriginal groups in 'keeping places', sacred locked stores to which scholars may be admitted. Another scene of confrontation is the rock art of Australia. In 1985 Aborigines requested that they might paint over ancient rock paintings with new designs. A number of archaeologists were upset that this important prehistoric art was to be destroyed and considered that, as an asset to world heritage, it should be spared. Others viewed the Aboriginal case as more valid: for Aborigines, they pointed out, the value of the art resides in its practice rather than its age.

In New Zealand human bones have been removed from display. There have been conflicts over exhibitions of Maori culture, but these have been resolved through cooperation between museums and Maori groups. The *Te Maori* exhibition, which was taken to the United States, was accompanied by Maori elders and performers who conducted ceremonies at each city where the exhibition was set up. However, there were still misgivings that these treasures belonged more to the museum trustees than to the Maori. There were also clashes over interpretations given in the exhibition book. Whereas previous displays of Maori culture had been in the form of artefact typologies, the Hawkes Bay Museum set up a new kind of exhibition called *The Awakening: the Treasures of Ngati Kahungunu*. The design team included Maori advisers and attempted to instil a spiritual feel into the exhibition, abandoning the 'textbook on the wall' approach for a more shrine-like atmosphere.

Applied archaeology

In the 1970s Colonel Quadaffi of Libya agreed to a multinational archaeological project, on the grounds that the past must be used to serve the present. The project was funded by UNESCO to investigate why the productive farming areas of Roman Libya had turned to desert and what could be done to improve the suitability of the desert margins for agriculture. Archaeologists discovered that the climate was not so different in the Roman period and that Roman agriculture had been sustained by cleverly designed water catchment and irrigation systems built of stone in the dry river courses. After even a light rainfall, the wadis filled with water which could be trapped and diverted to small fields. With no great effort the Roman systems could be rebuilt and reused (Barker *et al.* 1996).

In Peru, an archaeological project along the Cusichaka river resulted in the discovery of ancient stone irrigation canals built by the Inca. The canals were abandoned at the time of the Spanish conquest and, after the canal system had been archaeologically recorded, a programme of repair and clearance has been started so that the canals may once more carry water from the mountains to irrigate arable fields (Erickson 1988).

Local communities and archaeology

Non-professional involvement in archaeology varies widely throughout the world, from active field projects by independent groups (as in Britain), to assistance of professionals (as in many European countries), to responsible clubs of metal detector users, to unlawful looting (or pot-hunting as it is called in North America) and collecting. Most national legislations and international agreements make some provision for the archaeological heritage as the public right of all citizens.

Nevertheless, the unrecorded looting of archaeological sites has become a major archaeological problem and ancient artefacts are more sought-after by collectors than ever before. In many parts of the world, illicit looting of sites forms a steady income for poor, rural communities who sell their 'mined' antiquities on to middlemen and international dealers. In other circumstances, local communities have reclaimed their history through such remains (as is the case among many Australian Aboriginal or North American Indian groups), actively preventing their destruction by illicit looters or even archaeologists.

In Europe, non-professional involvement in the conservation of the archaeological heritage includes not only the formation of local pressure groups but also the active management of archaeological sites, especially if they involve elements of nature conservation (Baker 1983; Hughes and Rowley 1986; Lambrick 1985). Pressure groups in recent years have been as diverse as the actors campaigning on site for preservation of the remains of the Shakespearean Rose Theatre in London (see p. 393), to local groups in Dorset, England, protesting at English Heritage's arrangements for excavations on the iron age hill-fort of Maiden Castle, which they claimed was being dug needlessly ('Don't rape the maiden' was one of their slogans).

In Britain and elsewhere in Europe, much active management of archaeological sites by local communities is carried out under the umbrella of wildlife conservation. Organizations such as the British Trust for Conservation Volunteers (BTCV) use volunteers to manage wildlife habitats, which occasionally will include archaeological sites. Other organizations such as the National Trust and the Prince's Trust tackle projects which are specifically archaeological in their conservation objectives, but these are relatively few in contrast to the upsurge in public participation in nature conservation. Worryingly, public participation in British archaeology has declined as volunteers in nature conservation have increased.

THE METHODOLOGY OF CONSERVATION MANAGEMENT

The stabilization of decay is a continuous activity which requires varying inputs of labour and funds depending on the nature of the remains and the circumstances of their setting. The concept of a management cycle has been proposed to outline the different stages of monument management and to highlight the need for continuous attention. For example, sites cannot simply be fenced and left: grass cover will regenerate to woodland; stonework and other upstanding remains will decay and collapse.

The management cycle can be characterized as:

1 *Identification:* archaeological remains in the landscape must be located, ideally by

systematic survey, though of course, many important sites are discovered by chance, often in the course of their destruction. Identified remains can be recorded on local or national Sites and Monuments Records (Larsen 1992).

2 *Assessment:* archaeological sites and landscapes must be assessed in terms of their importance or significance and their prospects for continued survival. Priorities for preservation have to be established and decisions taken about which sites can be saved and which must be excavated and recorded before destruction (English Heritage 1991b). These choices should be made in terms of local and wider research objectives, as well as the physical circumstances of survival. Survey and recording are particularly necessary at this stage.

3 *Stabilization:* a management plan should be drawn up to indicate the immediate and long-term steps that need to be taken to preserve the remains. The short-term stabilization may involve repair of masonry, burial of exposed deposits, or protection from artificial or natural forces. The most dramatic example is UNESCO's Egyptian project when temples and other structures were moved in advance of the floodwaters of the Aswan dam. Other examples include the provision of a protective roof over the remains, stabilization of river banks, immediate repairs to damaged masonry and clearance of damaging vegetation.

4 *Long-term management:* all archaeological remains require long-term attention, whether by incorporation into an agricultural regime (for example, regular grazing of buried sites), or by intensive monitoring and constant work involvement. Archaeological remains which require the most intensive looking after are waterlogged sites and standing monuments.

5 *Research:* without a research framework to promote interpretation and understanding, all archaeological conservation is pointless; research is required at all stages of the management cycle, both into suitable methods of conservation and into the sites themselves (Darvill *et al.* 1978; English Heritage 1991a).

Different conservation strategies are required for different archaeological environments. In many ways, a 'cook book' approach is not possible, since each particular site, monument, or landscape has its own unique combination of environmental, landholding, financial, and legal problems. The management plan drawn up for a particular site will have to be tailored for its specific circumstances. Nevertheless, we can group archaeological sites into six categories according to character and context.

In the case of wet sites, if organic remains are permitted to dry out, they will perish in a very short time. The bronze age wooden fort of Biskupin, in Poland, has seriously deteriorated due to de-watering (Fig. 10.7). In contrast, a large portion of the bronze age timber structure at Flag Fen, in England, has been preserved in a waterlogged condition by the construction of an artificial lake on the site. On the Somerset Levels, in England, large expanses of peat, containing prehistoric wooden

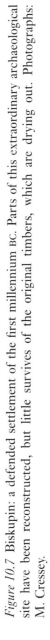

Figure 10.7 Biskupin: a defended settlement of the first millennium BC. Parts of this extraordinary archaeological site have been reconstructed, but little survives of the original timbers, which are drying out. Photographs: M. Cressey.

trackways, have been kept waterlogged by continuous pumping of water (Darvill 1987; Cox *et al.* 1995; Coles 1995).

Standing stone and brick monuments may suffer considerable problems of subsidence, stone damage, salt corrosion, weakening of the fabric and collapse. Regular repair and maintenance of stone structures require replacement of damaged or collapsed stonework, re-pointing of eroded masonry joints, gravity grouting (pouring liquid concrete into the top courses of the masonry core so that it percolates into all the crevices in the core), underpinning and shoring (incorporating concrete or steel beams into the fabric), rough racking (stabilizing exposed core surfaces) and protection of wall-tops (perhaps with a 'sacrificial layer' of stone or brick which must be regularly replaced as it erodes). Fired brick structures suffer similar problems to stone ones, but in addition are more vulnerable to corrosion by mineral salts. Plaster wall surfaces and floors are especially vulnerable to the elements (English Heritage 1994).

The third category consists of exposed stone, brick and mud-brick structures. The major problem of archaeological excavation is the long-term maintenance of newly exposed structures. In cold climates, freshly exposed stone and brickwork is likely to shatter and flake due to freeze–thaw action. Mosaic floors are similarly vulnerable. Occasionally, cob structures (walls built of mud and dung) may be excavated, for example at Banbury Castle, England. If these remain exposed they will crumble without an adequate cover. Mud-brick structures in warm climates are vulnerable not only to erosion by wind and rain but also to salt corrosion. For example, the prehistoric city of Mohenjo–Daro, in Pakistan, is the subject of a UNESCO project attempting to stem the damage caused by the joint action of salt corrosion and a rising water table. Sites exposed by archaeological excavation make good places for tourists to visit, but the maintenance costs and the problems caused by exposure to the elements can be severe. There is a case for the backfilling of excavations so that buried structures will be available for examination only when adequate resources have been found.

Sensitive closed environments form the fourth category. The palaeolithic cave of Lascaux in France has been closed to visitors for many years, though a replica has been constructed. Similar problems of condensation and bacterial attack have developed with other cave art at sites in France and Spain. The burial chambers in Egypt's Valley of the Kings are similarly at risk from moisture and salt penetration of the painted plaster (Romer and Romer 1993).

The most extensive damage to archaeological sites has occurred in the northern hemisphere due to mechanized agriculture within the last century. Wetlands have been systematically drained. Large expanses of heath, upland, pasture and woodland have been cleared and cultivated with a variety of ploughs, subsoilers and pan busters, which may penetrate between 20 and 50 centimetres below the surface. Large tracts of land have been mechanically planted for forestry and the timber trade, involving considerable damage to buried remains (Proudfoot 1989). Legislation varies between countries in its effectiveness to manage sites. Invariably, the sites are only discovered after the damage has been done, and only recently, in England's 'Monuments at Risk Survey', has anyone quantified the losses sustained.

Effective management here depends not only on legislation but also on the cooperation of farmers and landowners. Sites under pasture should be grazed but not over-stocked (which can lead to soil erosion). Sites in woodland may survive as earthworks but are vulnerable to damage from tree roots, and their improved management requires the designation of clearings through selective felling. Earthworks such as burial mounds will not survive more than twenty years of ploughing. Sites such as these and sites with intact cultural layers need to be taken out of cultivation and put down to pasture. Sometimes minimally destructive cultivation methods, such as direct drilling, are acceptable alternatives. Sites under cultivation are also particularly vulnerable to looting by metal detectors, a major problem in the arable landscapes of East Anglia, England, where organized gangs plunder sites under cover of dark. 'Seeding' of such sites with metal waste has been suggested but not implemented.

Finally, many towns and cities of the world are built on centuries or even millennia of development. Beneath the streets and buildings lie metres of complex archaeological stratigraphy (Carver 1987). The development of high-rise and other major architecture, especially in the last forty years, has posed a major threat to the survival of these deposits. In many European cities the archaeological response was too late and too little. In Britain and Scandinavia, particularly in the 1960s and 1970s, major urban excavation projects were initiated. Good examples are Winchester, London and York in England, Dublin waterfront in Ireland, and Trondheim and Bergen in Norway The management of above-ground industrial remains from recent centuries has also become a concern of archaeologists in both urban and rural settings (Palmer and Neaverson 1996).

There have been two recent developments in urban archaeological management which have ended the 'rescue' response approach. One is the provision of three-dimensional resource maps showing findspots, depths of deposits, areas destroyed and zones of differing significance. This approach was pioneered in Norway and has become a useful planning aid in Britain, Denmark and Sweden. The other is the capability of new legislation such as PPG 16 (see p. 393) to prohibit damaging development where there are deposits that justify continued preservation. In the same four countries there have been experiments to modify the development proposals so that archaeological deposits remain intact or relatively undamaged. After an archaeological evaluation to establish the character, depth and extent of archaeological deposits, it has been possible sometimes to change the layout of the development so that archaeologically sensitive areas remain unaffected. There have also been experiments with shallow, rafted foundations and with piled foundations to sit new buildings on top of archaeological remains without causing more than minimal damage.

The approach may have been successful in some instances, such as on the Roman forum site in London, but it requires considerable negotiation and control over site works and causes de-watering and disturbance (Biddle 1994). In many parts of the world the pressures for urban and industrial growth far outweigh any concerns for preservation within the urban setting. An international project into urban origins in East Africa is bringing to light new evidence beneath modern cities (Sinclair and Wandibba 1988). This may be a first step towards identifying and eventually preserving urban deposits in Zimbabwe, Somalia, Tanzania, Mozambique, Madagascar, Kenya, Zanzibar and the Comores.

METHODS OF PRESENTATION AND DISPLAY

In most parts of the world the display facilities for archaeological sites are limited or non-existent. In Cambodia, for example, the war-damaged temple complex at Angkor is still in need of emergency repairs. Many of the Egyptian temple sites have little on-site presentation material and visitors have to rely on idiosyncratic local guides or guidebooks brought by themselves. The wars in Iraq and the former Yugoslavia have damaged sites like Ur and Dubrovnik. A recent assessment of tourist needs at the Great Pyramids at Giza has identified inadequate parking, excessive harassment and insufficient information presentation as major drawbacks to be overcome. In war-torn Mozambique soon after the Frelimo revolution, an initial call for the people to visit their national museum, to reclaim their history, was immensely successful, but afterwards few ever bothered to come again. Presentational sophistication is most evident in North America and western Europe, among nations where the luxury of archaeology, and the facilities for its enjoyment, are most affordable.

On-site presentation

On-site presentation can take the form of written guidebooks, leaflets, brochures, booklets, catalogues, books and pamphlets, organized guided parties, interpretation centres or site museums, wayside exhibits, audio devices (both fixed and portable), and audio-visual interpretation (film, tape-slide, multiple projector tape-slide and dissolve units). The Carnac Archeoscope, in Brittany in France, is a new visitor centre for the prehistoric stone alignments there: it incorporates the latest audio-visual technology, with lasers, film, mirrors, artificial sunrise and scale models. At Stonehenge, in contrast, where the visitor facilities have been called 'a cheap

414

mess' (Chippindale *et al.* 1990), entry is via an underground concrete bunker and the stone circle is roped off from the public. Presentationally and politically, Stonehenge is deeply problematic: there are controversial plans to build a new centre half a mile away, and to raise awareness of the prehistoric landscape that surrounds the site. At most archaeological sites open to the public there are only rudimentary noticeboards and signs. Attractions such as the *son et lumière* shows in Egypt at the pyramids, the Sphinx at Giza and the temple at Karnak are rare outside Europe.

Archaeological landscapes

In many parts of the world there are concentrations of archaeological remains in relatively small areas which can be visited and explored. The Aboriginal rock art sites of Australia, the deserted neolithic and bronze age landscapes of England, and the Pueblo sites like Chaco Canyon in the United States, are all examples of areas where ancient landscapes can be appreciated.

Archaeological excavations

Visitor facilities have been installed at many excavations, either ongoing or long after excavations have ceased. At Olorgesaile, in Kenya, visitors can traverse a walkway above completed excavations that have revealed a lower palaeolithic occupation surface. At Kostienki, in Russia, a concrete visitor centre has been built over the remains of an upper palaeolithic mammoth-hunters' camp. Impressive Chinese sites, such as the imperial tomb at Xian, are also preserved *in situ* and receive millions of visitors. Excavations throughout Europe and North America have recently made considerably more effort to enlighten the public. One of the first sophisticated attempts was at Coppergate in York, where audio posts, a visitor centre and guided tours were arranged during the rescue excavation.

Reconstructional centres

One example of this approach is the West Stow Anglo-Saxon Village in East Anglia, England (Fig. 10.8), but the most developed is probably the Jorvik Viking Centre in York, on the site of the Coppergate excavations referred to above. This has proved extremely popular for its reconstructed people, smells and sounds within a realistic full-scale model of Viking York (Fig. 10.4). It also provides a mock-up of the dig and laboratory. This concept has been taken further at York's Archaeological

Figure 10.8 Combining experimental archaeology and tourism: a visitor to West Stow Anglo-Saxon Village in East Anglia, Britain, uses a reconstruction of a woodworking lathe. Photograph: M. Parker Pearson.

Resource Centre (the ARC), where the public can learn how archaeologists interpret from the raw evidence of excavated material (Fig. 10.5). The Archeodrome, in central France, is an outdoor theme park of reconstructed archaeological buildings conveniently sited at a motorway service station. The iron age village at Lejre in Denmark combines outdoor reconstructions with working displays and experiments in prehistoric agriculture and manufacture. Annapolis and Williamsburg, in the United States, are recreated colonial towns which combine archaeological investigation with detailed reconstructions, including costumed inhabitants.

Museum displays and exhibitions

The permanent collections of museums have, in many cases, yet to shake off the 'glass case' syndrome of rows of artefacts arranged in geometric patterns and illustrated with a minimum of information or with densely written labels which remain unread. By the 1970s a few museums developed less artefact-orientated and more interpretive exhibitions, such as the Museum of Man in Ottawa, or the Jorvik Viking Centre, which has labels for some exhibits saying 'please touch!' Reconstructions, attractive interpretive panels and imaginative displays of artefacts in context have become commonplace in Europe and North America.

Education in schools

Archaeology is not considered a proper subject of study for schoolchildren in most countries, but the work of a few dedicated teachers has ensured that it is incorporated into subjects such as history and geography (Corbishley 1992). School teachers can use teaching packs, experimental archaeology (such as making and firing pottery), role-play and a wide variety of introductory books and booklets. In England, English Heritage supports an education service which encourages the teaching of archaeology in schools and develops links between archaeological organizations and schools in their areas.

Literature

Mortimer Wheeler's distinction between academic facts and popular fiction is beginning to dissolve: accurate yet accessible publications are increasingly available. Professional archaeologists are increasingly interested in archaeological fiction, particularly its contextual and ideological aspects. The building block of archaeological publication is the project report, normally rather specialized for all but the keenest enthusiasts. Nevertheless, the scientific presentation of survey and excavation results is normally through publication, available in local libraries or in specialist national libraries. The inaccessibility and cost of these reports are also compounded by the long delays between excavation and publication. Some archaeologists consider that there has been a scandalous lack of publications in recent years, with more than half of excavations unpublished. In addition, results from new projects in Britain, the United States and Scandinavia are increasingly put into archives with only brief summaries published. There is an enormous literature on more general topics, directed both at specialists and the general public. Amongst archaeologists there is an increasing desire to draw the public into the subject, to guide rather than teach, in order to encourage and tap the undoubted enthusiasm and expertise of many non-professionals.

Other media

The popularity of archaeology in the 1990s may owe as much to fictional best sellers such as the Indiana Jones films or the Clan of the Cave Bear books than to a steady and sustained influence from more serious treatments. Archaeology has become the subject of theatrical plays, modern art and sculpture, television or radio dramas and documentaries, poetry and novels. Archaeological discoveries are reported on regional and national news, in documentaries and even in programmes devoted entirely to archaeology, such as *Down to Earth* and *Time Team*, two weekly series shown recently on British television.

ARCHAEOLOGICAL DEBATES AND PROBLEMS

The restitution of cultural property

[Between 1750 and 1830 English travellers] stole and purchased for trifling sums large quantities of items which formed part of the heritage of the countries they robbed in the name of science and scholarship, and with very rare exceptions this material has never been returned to its rightful owners.

(Hudson 1981: 70)

The British Museum and a large number of public and private collections in Britain and north-west Europe are crammed with the antiquities of Greece, Italy, Syria,

Figure 10.9 Advertising the past: a bus in Cambridge is festooned with advertising slogans for an archaeological museum. Photograph: M. Parker Pearson.

418

Palestine, Egypt, Africa, South America and the Pacific. Negotiations continue for the return of such cultural property, either between governments or directed by ethnic groups as in the requests for re-burial of human remains. The Egyptian government has recently requested the return of Cleopatra's Needle, an obelisk set up on the bank of the Thames in London. In Athens an empty museum has been constructed to house, one day, the marble sculptures which adorned the façade of the Parthenon until they were removed by Lord Elgin in 1801–3 and sold for £35,000 to the British Museum in 1816.

A number of arguments for and against cultural restitution have been rehearsed in the last fifteen years. The taking of cultural property in colonial times has been seen as unlawful in international law. It also deprives peoples and emergent nations of a cultural and national identity. Another argument is that antiquities and other works of art are best appreciated in the environment where they were made. Arguments for retention are as follows. Many of the items were collected legally according to the collectors' domestic law and their reading of international law. Certain museums, such as the British Museum, are regarded as world heritage in their own right and should be maintained for international culture (though all such 'international' museums are in fact on two continents, in the West). Another argument is that objects are best conserved in these museums until other nations' legislation and resources are satisfactory. The artefacts have also become part of the cultural history of the holding states. Finally, there is the fear that accession to one or two requests will 'open the floodgates' and these major museums will be emptied.

The various arguments for and against restitution have taken place within a postcolonial situation where some newly emergent nations complain that their heritage is ironically better represented in the museums of North America and Europe than in their own countries. Some Western curators are increasingly sympathetic (and there is a growing ethical concern amongst archaeologists world-wide), but others have not been prepared to make any concessions to restitution claims from countries of origin. Strong feelings have been aroused on both sides, but sometimes agreements have been successful, as in the case of the return of 1,200 objects to Zaïre by the Belgian Museum of the Congo. The British Museum has returned numerous objects since the last century, such as the beard of the Sphinx to Egypt in 1984. Some curators and archaeologists are concerned that the logical outcome of the restitution movement will be cultural isolation of many nations: for example, the only place to view Maori heritage would be New Zealand. As a result of this geographical restriction of access, they argue, we might encounter increased ethnic and nationalist chauvinism and racial intolerance, whereas we should be developing more tolerant attitudes to difference and diversity among the cultures of the world and exploring these differences with respect for peoples of other cultures. What is perhaps required is a true spirit of exchange amongst the nation-states and museums for the loaning of artefacts, the interchange of staff and skills, and the setting up of international travelling exhibitions.

The illicit collection and export of cultural property

The looting of archaeological sites has been going on for centuries (Prott and O'Keefe 1989). As the interest in antiquities developed in the Western world from the eighteenth century onwards, so the interest in public and private collecting has grown. As previously humble artefacts, such as pots or brooches, have become items of sometimes considerable financial value for collectors, the archaeological resource is under considerable threat. In Guatemala, for example, Maya tombs are looted by armed gangs who regularly outwit the insufficiently resourced government officials. In Peru in 1987, a staggeringly rich tomb at Sipán was looted of hundreds of gold and other grave-goods by local *huaqueros* (looters), though one archaeologist managed to document the tomb layout and its contents and to rescue some remains. This was just one incident among many in South America. In West Africa, archaeological sites have been almost completely destroyed in the search for terracotta figurines of the previous millennium. As is the case in the other developing nations of Africa, South and Central America and Asia, the culprits are often local impoverished peasants who earn small sums of money for their efforts. The winners in these situations are the middlemen and dealers who purchase the loot from the peasants for a pittance and then sell on for large sums in the international art markets.

In most cases the artefacts are taken illegally out of the country of origin, without an export licence. The Sipán treasures were exported initially to Britain and thence to the United States, since Britain does not have the kinds of legislation banning the import of unlicensed cultural treasures which are in place in the United States. Britain has also not signed the 1970 UNESCO Convention on the Means of Prohibiting and Preventing the Illicit Import, Export and Transfer of Ownership of Cultural Property. London is a major world art market and British politicians are more concerned to support that role than to eradicate the illegal trade. The problem is also shared by British archaeological institutions: until recently, for example, the Oxford Archaeological Laboratory carried out dating tests to authenticate collectors' objects without requiring to see an export licence from the country of origin.

It is not simply the developing nations that are continuing to be plundered of their archaeological heritage. The Mediterranean countries all have to contend with illicit excavation – in Italy, for example, the pickings from robbing Etruscan tombs are such that organized crime has been involved. In Britain, the 1970s craze for metal detectors has led to the widespread loss of coins, brooches, and other metal artefacts from archaeological sites, many of them protected by a law which is often difficult to enforce. In East Anglia, even on protected sites (Scheduled Ancient Monuments), many of the artefacts are loose in the ploughsoil and can be easily extracted, either clandestinely or with the landowner's connivance. In a recent case an East Anglian farmer attempted, unsuccessfully, to reclaim Roman bronze artefacts which had been stolen off his land and exported to America. Of course, many people who use metal detectors are aware of the protected sites and work with landowners' permission, often taking finds to local museums so that they may be identified and provenanced.

In North America there is a long tradition of 'pot-hunting', where amateur and professional looters have even employed bulldozers to dig out archaeological sites in search of artefacts to sell. Their work has been particularly devastating in the south-western United States, where they have looted sites of the Mimbres culture for their attractive pottery. Despite concerted preservation efforts by archaeologists (including purchase of intact sites), so many sites have been destroyed that our future knowledge of the Mimbres is now severely restricted. As in so many situations we may know much about the individual artefacts, which now adorn various collections, but we know nothing about their archaeological (and thus past social) context.

Who owns the past?

In England until 1966 there was a medieval law of Treasure Trove, recently updated, whereby newly discovered items of gold and silver belonged to the Crown providing that they had been hidden with an intention of subsequent recovery. This law was originally devised so that the king might lay claim to such treasures, but it has been wholly inadequate to protect archaeological discoveries in England (Palmer 1981; Sparrow 1982). Today in Britain, archaeological sites are owned by a multitude of largely private and some public concerns. Some are owned in the name of the British people, notably properties managed by English Heritage, Cadw, Historic Scotland and DoE Northern Ireland (the respective government agencies for England, Wales, Scotland and Northern Ireland), by the National Trust (a charity), or by local authorities (County and City Councils). Recent proposals by English Heritage to sell off 200 of the 400 monuments which they have statutory responsibility to care for on behalf of the nation, caused considerable concern. Their aim was to abandon the unprofitable monuments to local authorities and the National Trust, and to concentrate their efforts on the money-making attractions. The unsatisfactory access to one of these, Stonehenge (an English Heritage property surrounded by National Trust land), has prompted archaeologists and others to ask for whom and against whom the monument is being protected (Chippindale *et al.* 1990). The 1985 'Battle of the Beanfield' (see p. 406) and the memory of humankind. In doing so, we must constantly question and examine the myths that are created by archaeology's practitioners.

REFERENCES

Arnold, B. (1992) 'The past as propaganda', *Archaeology* 45 (4): 30–37.

Ascherson, N. (1987) 'Why "Heritage" is right wing', *The Observer*, 8 November: 9.

Baines, F. (1923) 'Preservation of ancient monuments and historic buildings', *RIBA Journal* 3rd Series 31 (4): 104–6.

Baker, D. (1983) *Living with the Past: the Historic Environment*, Bedford: Baker.

Barker, G. W., Gilbertson, D. D., Jones, G. D. B. and Mattingly, D. J. (1996) *Farming the Desert: the UNESCO Libyan Valleys Archaeological Survey*, Society for Libyan Studies, Paris: UNESCO, London and Tripoli: Department of Antiquities (two volumes).

Belcher, M. (1991) *Exhibitions in Museums*, London: Leicester University Press.

Biddle, M. (1994) *What Future for British Archaeology?*, Oxford: Oxbow Lecture 1.

Binks, G., Dyke, J. and Dagnell, P. (1988) *Visitors Welcome: a Manual on the Presentation and Interpretation of Archaeological Excavations*, London: HMSO.

Boniface, P. and Fowler, P. J. (1993) *Heritage and Tourism in 'the Global Village'*, London: Routledge.

Carmichael, D., Hubert, J., Reeves, B. and Schlanche, A. (eds) (1994) *Sacred Sites, Sacred Places*, London: Routledge.

Carver, M. O. H. (1987) *Underneath English Towns*, London: Batsford.

Chippindale, C. (ed.) (1993) 'Charter for the protection and management of the archaeological heritage', *Antiquity* 67: 402–15.

Chippindale, C. and Gibbins, D. (eds) (1990) 'Heritage at sea: proposals for the better protection of British archaeological sites underwater', *Antiquity* 64: 390–400.

Chippindale, C., Devereux, P., Fowler, P., Jones, R. and Sebastian, T. (1990) *Who Owns Stonehenge?*, London: Batsford.

Cleere, H. (ed.) (1984) *Approaches to the Archaeological Heritage*, Cambridge: Cambridge University Press.

Cleere, H. (ed.) (1989) *Archaeological Heritage Management in the Modern World*, London: Unwin Hyman.

Coles, B. J. (1995) *Wetland Management: a Survey for English Heritage*, Exeter: WARP.

Corbishley, M. (ed.) (1992) *Archaeology in the National Curriculum*, London: Council for British Archaeology and English Heritage.

Cox, M., Straker, V. and Taylor, D. (eds) (1995) *Wetlands: Archaeology and Nature Conservation*, London: HMSO.

Cracknell, S. and Corbishley, M. (eds) (1986) *Presenting Archaeology to Young People*, London: Council for British Archaeology.

Darvill, T. C. (1987) *Ancient Monuments in the Countryside: an Archaeological Management Review*, London: English Heritage.

Darvill, T. C., Parker Pearson, M., Smith, R. and Thomas, R. (eds) (1978) *New Approaches to Our Past*, Southampton: Southampton University Archaeology Society.

Department of the Environment (1990) *Planning Policy Guidance Note 16: Archaeology and Planning*, London: HMSO.

English Heritage (1991a) *Exploring Our Past: Strategies for the Archaeology of England*, London: English Heritage.

English Heritage (1991b) *The Management of Archaeological Projects (MAP 2)*, London: English Heritage.

English Heritage (1994) *Principles of Repair*, London: English Heritage.

Erickson, C. L. (1988) 'Raised field agriculture in the Lake Titicaca Basin: putting ancient agriculture back to work', *Expedition* 30 (3): 8–16.

Fowler, P. J. (1992) *The Past in Contemporary Society: Then, Now*, London: Routledge.

Gathercole, P. and Lowenthal, D. (eds) (1990) *The Politics of the Past*, London: Unwin Hyman.

Green, E. L. (ed.) (1984) *Ethics and Values in Archaeology*, New York: The Free Press.

Hewison, R. (1987) *The Heritage Industry: Britain in a Climate of Decline*, London: Methuen.

Hodges, R. A. (1991) *Wall-to-Wall History: the Story of Roystone Grange*, London: Duckworth.

Hooper-Greenhill, E. (1990) *Museum and Gallery Education*, London: Leicester University Press.

Hooper-Greenhill, E. (1992) *Museums and the Shaping of Knowledge*, London: Routledge.

Horne, D. (1984) *The Great Museum: the Re-presentation of History*, London: Pluto.

Hudson, K. (1981) *A Social History of Archaeology: the British Experience*, London: Macmillan.

Hughes, M. and Rowley, T. (eds) (1986) *The Management and Presentation of Field Monuments*, Oxford: Oxford University Press.

Hunter, J. and Ralston, I. (1993) *Archaeological Heritage Management in the UK*, London: Sutton.

ICOMOS (International Council on Monuments and Sites) (1966) *International Charter for the Conservation and Restoration of Monuments and Sites*, New York: UNESCO.

ICOMOS (International Council on Monuments and Sites) (1987) *The Australia ICOMOS Charter for the Conservation of Places of Cultural Significance*, New York: UNESCO.

Jameson, J. H. (ed.) (1997) *Presenting Archaeology to the Public: Digging for Truths*, Walnut Creek CA: Alta Mira Press.

Lambrick, G. (1985) *Archaeology and Nature Conservation*, Oxford: Oxford University Press.

Langford, R. K. (1983) 'Our heritage – your playground', *Australian Archaeology* 16: 1–6.

Larsen, C. U. (ed.) (1992) *Sites and Monuments: National Archaeological Records*, Copenhagen: National Museum of Denmark.

Layton, R. (ed.) (1989a) *Conflict in the Archaeology of Living Traditions*, London: Unwin Hyman.

Layton, R. (ed.) (1989b) *Who Needs the Past? Indigenous Values and Archaeology*, London: Unwin Hyman.

Lipe, W. D. (1974) 'A conservation model for American archaeology', *The Kiva* 39 (1–2): 213–43.

Lipe, W. D. (1984) 'Value and meaning in cultural resources', in H. Cleere (ed.) *Approaches to the Archaeological Heritage*, Cambridge: Cambridge University Press: 1–10.

Lowenthal, D. (1985) *The Past is a Foreign Country*, Cambridge: Cambridge University Press.

McBryde, I. (ed.) (1985) *Who Owns the Past? Papers from the Annual Symposium of the Australian Academy of the Humanities*, Melbourne: Oxford University Press.

Part II

THEMES AND APPROACHES

11

CULTURE AND IDENTITY

Julian Thomas

WHAT IS CULTURE?

Throughout its history, archaeology has concerned itself with the cultural lives of past peoples. Moreover, throughout the twentieth century, nationalist and ethnocentric interpretations of the past have been built upon the understanding that there was some direct relationship between assemblages of material culture preserved in the present and human groups which existed in the past (Champion and Diaz-Andreu 1995; Graves-Brown *et al.* 1995). However, precisely what archaeologists have considered themselves to be investigating has differed radically from one time to another. The word 'culture' has come to mean quite different things to different archaeologists, and in part this has been a consequence of the manifold interconnections between archaeology and other disciplines. A series of debates within those disciplines has penetrated into archaeological thought, which in turn has generated quite different traditions of inquiry of its own.

At base, many of these debates have centred upon opposed points of view adopted in relation to the problem of naturalism: that is to say, the question of whether and to what extent the philosophies and epistemology of the natural sciences can be applied to the study of the social and cultural lives of human beings (Bhaskar 1989: 67). Such a question is one which could not have arisen prior to a particular historical juncture, although one might argue over precisely when this occurred. It has been suggested that the specific notion of culture, conceived as a set of human products which can be transmitted from one person to another by non-biological mechanisms, did not exist before the nineteenth century (Kroeber and Kluckhohn 1952). It was at this point that Tylor came to define culture as those knowledges, arts, beliefs, customs and morals which human beings come to acquire as members of a society (Leach 1982: 38). For Tylor, culture was the equivalent of 'civilization', a set of traits which arise as the consequence of achieving a certain stage of evolutionary advance; 'culture' is thus a singular body rather than a plural set of entities. In medieval Europe, the word 'culture' was generally taken to refer to the nurture of living things. The notion that culture represents a mental phenomenon opposed to, and enabling, the manipulation of nature, seems to have developed with the emergence of western modernity (Jordanova 1989). This division paved the way for the separation of the human and the natural sciences, which would eventually be formalized by Dilthey (Foucault 1970). Yet the separation of culture and nature into separate spheres is not one which is recognized by many non-western communities (Strathern 1980), and its application to the distant past must consequently be regarded as suspect. In some circumstances, it may be more appropriate to think of culture as a means by which people engage with the material world (Thomas 1996).

The identification of culture as a distinct entity rests upon the understanding that there is something about human beings which makes them fundamentally different from other living systems. Culture is rooted in consciousness (Ingold 1983), and the character of human consciousness is given by the ability to consider one's own being as an issue (Heidegger 1962). Consciousness 'brings the selection of behavioural instructions under the control and direction of intentional agency. Human beings, in short, are selectors of their cultural attributes, not merely objects of selection' (Ingold 1986: 9). Thoroughly bound up with this capability is the question of complex language, and the ability to refer to one's self, and thereby to constitute oneself as a distinct social actor. So from the start, the issues of culture and identity are deeply connected, and it is through culture that both personal and group identity come to be constructed.

None the less, while it is generally accepted that culture, having emerged from a biological background, is transmitted by a quite separate mechanism, opinions vary as to the extent to which biological concepts can still be used in its understanding. At an extreme of naturalism, one position would hold that cultural instructions which result in particular behavioural patterns are genetically programmed, being reproduced according to the inclusive fitness which they impart to their 'carrier' (Cloak 1975). Thus in sociobiological terms, individual units of culture can be seen as the equivalent of genes, which survive or are eliminated by their ability to be copied into the heads of offspring. Under this rubric, culture is simply a much more efficient means for the transmission of selective advantage than heredity. A less extreme form of cultural evolutionism would merely suggest that particular forms of cultural behaviour tend to confer a greater survival chance upon a given population (Kirch 1980). Such a perspective often points to the 'speciation' effects of culture, the way that the adoption of culture makes particular groups more unlike one another, thereby introducing a model of group competition. Biological analogues for the process of cultural change thus have a tendency either to end up with a kind of genetic reductionism ('cultural traits confer selective advantage on the individual') or with functionalism ('cultural traits contribute to the adaptive potential of the group').

Within the forms of anthropology which have exerted a major influence upon the archaeological conception of culture, the aspect of the debate over naturalism which has been most prominent has been the contrast between organic and linguistic analogies. Thus culture may be compared to an organism which adapts to its environmental conditions, and whose attributes are explained in terms of their contribution towards the functioning of the whole; or it may be presented as the equivalent of a language, composed of rules and codes and held together by sense. Both of these models have a long history, yet their recent development in social thought takes the form of two traditions which both stem from the work of the sociologist Émile Durkheim (1858–1917). Thus in France, it has been Durkheim's interests in the way in which people classify the world, and collectively represent their societies (Durkheim 1915; Durkheim and Mauss 1963), which have proved most influential. These concerns, taken up by his students Robert Hertz (1916) and Marcel Mauss (1954), were the first steps towards a theory of culture as a symbolic cognitive structure, in which the significance of each element lies in its relation to the whole. It is thus quite legitimate to plot a line of development which leads from Durkheim to Lévi-Strauss (for example: 1966, 1969). Yet another side of Durkheim's work was deeply functionalist and concerned with the way in which the actions and predispositions of the subject formed a part of the organic social whole.

As Harris (1969: 473) points out, Durkheim's theories pre-empted the thinking of several American social anthropologists, notably Alfred Kroeber and Leslie White, while the influence upon the sociologist Talcott Parsons is well documented. His influence is generally connected with the re-emergence of evolutionary and nomothetic approaches in the mid-twentieth century. The convergence of thought between Durkheim and Kroeber is thus an intriguing circumstance. Kroeber's background lay in the historical particularist anthropology of Franz Boas, which dominated the American scene in the earlier part of the century. Rejecting the explicitly racist evolutionism of the nineteenth century, Boas maintained that each human society was unique, each had to be seen in its own terms, and that no value judgements could or should be made between them (Boas 1948). Boas, and his pupil Margaret Mead, followed this line of thought towards a consideration of the interaction between personality and culture, a trajectory which eventually led Mead into a turn towards Freudian psychoanalysis (Harris 1969: 422). Kroeber, by contrast, came to think of culture as a superorganic totality which dominated and determined the acts and preferences of the agent (Kroeber 1917).

It was with the return to evolutionism in American anthropology that the form of the organic analogy for culture which was to inform the New Archaeology came to be established. The two variants of cultural evolutionism concerned have been designated by Sahlins and Service (1960) as 'unilinear' and 'multilinear'. Thus the unilinear evolution promoted by Leslie White (1949, 1959) was concerned less with the specific cultural adaptations through which human groups move, and far more with supposedly universal evolutionary mechanisms which lie behind these changes, at the level of the living system. Julian Steward (1955), however, pursued an approach which insisted that cultural systems might progress along a series of parallel paths dependent upon the host ecology within which they developed. Steward's evolutionism was thus a 'cultural ecology', concerned with the interconnections between the cultural organism and its environment, and sensitive to the ways in which each affected the other. As such, it provides a very clear case of individual cultural units being seen as functional and adaptive units, although Steward expresses this more in the idiom of the machine than the organism.

American cultural anthropology, which maintained close ties with archaeology and which provided the context within which the New Archaeology emerged (see Chapter 2), was by the 1960s maintaining a functionalist view of culture derived to a greater or lesser extent from Durkheim. In Britain, a school of anthropology had developed which was functionalist without being evolutionary. In the period after the First World War, Malinowski's method of detailed field recording had contributed to a decline in an approach which compared cultural traits from different parts of the globe in the attempt to construct 'speculative histories' of culture areas (Leach 1982: 28). Studies like Malinowski's of the Kula exchange system (1922) or Firth's of the Tikopia (1936) emphasized that all aspects of culture had to be seen in context, as parts of an integrated whole. Both Malinowski and Radcliffe-Brown presented a picture of society which draws on the Durkheimian organicist view of culture. Malinowski's experiences drew him to an understanding that such an entity had the primary function of providing for the biological survival needs of the person. Radcliffe-Brown (1933), however, presented a variant which was closer to the spirit of Durkheim. His 'structural-functionalism' saw the significance of the cultural whole as the achievement of social solidarity and harmony, and strongly evoked a sense that this whole in some way transcended the objectives of the singular members of a society. British social anthropology, then, presented a model of culture which was strongly functionalist. However, the rejection of the use of anthropology in the construction of rather dubious schemes of global human development resulted in an almost total disregard for the issue of change through time. The societies presented by structural-functionalism strove to maintain their stability, and ideally remained unchanging and atemporal. This lack of a diachronic perspective is doubtless partially responsible for the greater academic distance between anthropology and archaeology in Britain than in America. Structural-functionalism may have provided the British archaeologist's notion of what anthropology was all about, and it may have been drawn upon at times for inspiration, but its evident shortcomings meant that archaeology in Britain never had the comfortable feeling of nestling within a parent discipline.

These factors may have contributed to the circumstance in which it was in Britain rather than in the United States that archaeology first came to criticize functionalism and experiment with linguistic notions of culture. Structuralism, as the movement which brought linguistic concepts into the study of culture, originated with Saussure's epochal *Course in General Linguistics* (Saussure 1959), which introduced the vision of language as a structured set of differences, coherent within itself but with no necessary connection to the world of things which it purports to describe. If language could represent such a deep structure, hidden but showing itself partially in the utterances of day-to-day speech, Lévi-Strauss (1968) argued that similar structures might lie behind all of the manifestations of human culture. His method of investigating this possibility was to analyse diverse phenomena such as kinship proscriptions, exchange transactions, myths, and masks in the search for rules and codes underlying cultural practice. In common with the functionalists, Lévi-Strauss thus saw culture as a 'thing', a totality; however, rather than an organic whole composed of those practices which could be observed articulated in the day-to-day struggle with nature, its unity lay at another level of reality, submerged within the human mind. This deep structure was drawn upon and engaged with the world through human practice, but not so much in the process of adaptation as in the ongoing project of 'putting things in their place', of making sense of the world by classifying it. The way in which people split their experience up, put phenomena into classes, and gave meaning to their exterior surroundings thus reflects in a real way the internal world of the human being. Ultimately, the fundamental structure which gives form to all human cultural experience is the structure of the human mind itself.

While structuralism was a stimulus for change within archaeological thought, there was no real point at which an exclusively 'structuralist' archaeology existed. The turn to linguistic and symbolic notions of culture in the 1980s was connected with the reassertion of the discipline's identity as a social science (Hodder 1981). The early 1980s represented a period in which British archaeologists began to widen the scope of their interests across the human sciences (Hodder 1985). In consequence, the adoption of a new set of ideas concerning culture was not restricted to anthropological sources, and was openly critical of the shortcomings of 'pure' structuralism. One source of inspiration to which a number of archaeologists have turned has been Anthony Giddens's 'theory of structuration'. This is an ambitious sociological project which seeks to integrate structuralist notions of deep structure (Giddens 1979) with Marxist perspectives on historicity and social relations (Giddens 1981) and a conception of the conscious

435

subject as a skilled social actor, the whole grounded in a quasi-Heideggerian critique of Cartesian views of time, space and Being (Giddens 1976, 1984).

Giddens emphasizes that the structures upon which people draw in social action are social and cultural in nature, rather than psychological. They are thus historical and contingent rather than written into the biological constitution of the person. Consequently, it becomes necessary to account for the processes by which people learn a set of cultural resources, yet are able to transform those resources through their practice (Bourdieu 1977). From Marxism, Giddens draws the insight that culture is a sphere of production, in which human beings labour to transform natural raw materials into something else, whether mental or material. Cultural production has the effect that products themselves (words, texts, material things) gain a degree of independence from their authors or creators (Giddens 1987). People thus live out their lives surrounded by a field of cultural products whose meanings they may or may not fully apprehend. It is not for the author to tie down the significance of a cultural product, and the 'reading' of symbols will vary according to context, enculturation and personal life history. Material products themselves construct the context in which utterances and the experience of other symbolic forms takes place (Barrett 1988).

It is evident, therefore, that in the human sciences as a whole, the concept of culture has little unity or integrity. Archaeology, in attempting to understand the diversity of past human experience, has managed to combine many perspectives to provide a singularly broad diversity of opinion. Since archaeologists have drawn upon the many meanings of culture in a somewhat profligate manner, the debates and directions of other disciplines have been rehearsed, rendered down and reconstituted to form a series of different configurations. Probably the best way in which to approach archaeological studies of culture and its relationship to the recognition or formation of identity is thus a chronological one, dealing with each of the major schools of thought in turn.

CULTURE AND ETHNIC IDENTITY: RATZEL AND KOSSINNA

The close connections which existed between geography and archaeology in the late nineteenth century and the early twentieth were underwritten by a changing political climate, in which the forces of nationalism, racism and imperialism jostled with each other. In this milieu, the establishment of past cultural and ethnic identities came to take on considerable importance. As Trigger (1989) suggests, the early stages of archaeological investigation were perhaps concerned more with time than with space. Prior to the final decades of the nineteenth century, archaeology was engaged in setting up universal evolutionary sequences rather than investigating the local variability of culture. Archaeological evidence was largely employed in the establishment of chronologies, and in gaining a general understanding of people's technological achievements at particular stages in the past (see Chapter 5). In the work of Lubbock (1865) or Sollas (1911), such conceptions of sequence were very explicitly linked with the notion of social evolution. Implicitly, these ideas suggest a unilinear evolutionary scheme, in which all races pass through Savagery and Barbarism on the way to Civilization, and in which presently existing hunting or farming societies can be regarded as the equivalent of our own ancestors.

Some forms of universal evolutionism were congruent with the ideal of the nation-state, in which each definable 'people' had the right to form a state, connected with a particular geographical space (Bassin 1987a: 474). As long as this notion dominated European political thought, western attitudes to the rest of the world tended to be benign, on the grounds that other peoples might, in time, graduate to the universal 'brotherhood' of nations. However, the period between 1870 and 1914 saw an unprecedented expansion of colonial empires centred on the principal European powers. Processes like the 'scramble for Africa' tended to produce their own legitimation, in the form of new political ideologies which stressed struggle and conflict as central to the health of societies. Germany was at this time in the throes of unification, yet the wide dispersal of ethnic Germans across Europe meant that it was unlikely that they could be brought within a single political entity under the rubric of 'natural justice' of the nation-state. Instead, pan-Germanism and notions of racial supremacy began to rise in popularity. In this climate, a search for the origins of particular races and peoples started to supplant the agenda of universal evolution.

It is important to point out that in different places the decline of universal evolutionism took very different forms. In America, the evolutionary anthropology of Tylor and Morgan was eclipsed in the early twentieth century by the particularism of Franz Boas. As we have seen, Boas argued that each society had to be seen in its own terms, as a unique manifestation of the human spirit which could not be measured against any other, and resulted from a unique sequence of historical events. Contingent factors were responsible for the gathering together of unique combinations of cultural traits, any of which might be equally significant in determining subsequent developments. Boas's relativism and particularism was thus anti-racist and humanitarian, in advocating respect for other peoples.

By contrast, in the late nineteenth century we can discern the emergence of the school of 'Anthropo-Geography' in Germany and Austria, in which the central figure was Friedrich Ratzel. Ratzel's work mixed the growing continental interest in maps and distributions with a strong environmental determinism. Human beings were seen as taking little part in their own destiny, being largely at the mercy of nature (Bassin 1987b: 117). While Ratzel's views shared with Social Darwinism a perspective that human societies were governed by natural laws, and that their behaviour was wholly analogous to that of individual organisms, he stopped short of any degree of racism. The identities of human groups had little to do with heredity or language, but were forged by a relationship between people and environment. Thus the basis for the integration of a state was the common occupation of a geographical location rather than race. Ratzel used new techniques of distribution mapping to demonstrate that artefacts like blowpipes and bows and arrows had only been invented once, and had then diffused around the world. As a result of environmental factors, the diffusion of cultural innovations into particular locations created 'culture areas', or geographical areas in which people tended to have similar ways of life and artefactual repertoires. For the most part, then, essentially passive human beings were moulded by the external influences of environmental conditions and the flow of incoming cultural innovations.

Ratzel's ideas were clearly an attempt to understand the ways in which regional identities are formed. His approach was by no means as extreme as that of two traditions which to a greater or lesser extent flow from his work. In Britain, one has the hyper-diffusionists like Perry, Raglan and Grafton Elliot Smith, whose ideas originated in more moderate work of the social anthropologist W. H. R. Rivers. Sceptical of the prevailing evolutionism of his time, Rivers argued that no universal law of culture could be held responsible for the diversity which he encountered in Melanesia (Slobodin 1978). Smith developed this emphasis on the uniqueness of cultural innovations into a theory that all human advances had followed from the emergence of sedentism in the Nile valley, and that all civilizations (including the Maya) were founded by the ancient Egyptians (Harris 1969: 382).

In Germany, Ratzel's legacy was to be the *Geopolitik* school of geography, which flourished in the period after the First World War. It is of key significance that maps demonstrating the distribution of persons of particular language groups were used by the allies at the Versailles peace negotiations, since the aim of the settlement was to allow self-determination for the peoples of central Europe after the break-up of the German and Austro-Hungarian empires. The lesson which was learned by nationalistic groups in Germany was that of the persuasive power of maps. Karl Haushoffer, who founded the *Zeitschrift für Geopolitik* in 1924, emphasized the potential of maps for propaganda purposes – in particular, the maps which were drawn of the 'true' geographical extent of the German people and their 'lost' domains in the east (Herb 1989). It was this sort of mapping which was to provide legitimacy for the Nazi expansion in the succeeding decades.

It is in the context of the *Geopolitik* that we can appreciate the eventual significance of the work of Gustav Kossinna, the archaeologist who took up Ratzel's techniques and applied them to the prehistoric material culture of central and northern Europe, at the start of the twentieth century. Kossinna was a strong German nationalist, and had moved from linguistics to archaeology in the hope of locating the original homeland of the Indo-Europeans, and hence of the Germans. His method was to trace historically documented peoples and tribes back as far as he could by conventional methods, and then to push back further using distribution maps of particular artefact types. It is really with Kossinna that we can first recognize the emergence of the concept of the archaeological 'culture', a set of material culture found repeatedly in association and assumed to relate in some way to the activities of a particular group of people (Veit 1989).

In his book *Die Herkunft der Germanen*, Kossinna (1911) presented a picture of how the Germans had started out as the Maglemosian mesolithic hunters of the Baltic area, and had gradually spread south and east through the prehistoric era, eventually creating the Greek and Roman civilizations, though unfortunately diluting their line by interbreeding with swarthy Mediterranean types in the process. Only in Germany itself did the race remain pure. Only the pure, active Germans were culturally creative, in distinction to the other, passive or retrogressive races. Kossinna describes the prehistoric Germans as 'a slim, tall, light-complexioned, blond race, calm and firm in character, constantly striving, intellectually brilliant, and with an almost ideal attitude towards the world and life in general' (quoted in Veit 1989: 38). Kossinna died in 1931, but not surprisingly his works were reprinted when the Nazis came to power and provided the basis for school textbooks on the early history of the Germans and propaganda posters showing the extent of their ancient territories.

NORMATIVE CULTURE HISTORY: CHILDE

Just as Kossinna originally came to archaeology through an interest in linguistics, so Vere Gordon Childe's earliest work was concerned with the identification of the Indo-Europeans or Aryans through the medium of prehistoric material culture (Childe 1915, 1926). In this sense Childe was initially involved with the use of the archaeological evidence as a means to substantiate preliterate ethnic entities which had been identified using written sources and to track them back into the past. Yet as Renfrew (1979: 15) has pointed out, this phase of his researches was one which he later came to all but disown, so that *The Aryans* barely merits a mention in his subsequent books.

As Sherratt (1989: 178) suggests, it is perhaps possible to distinguish between an 'earlier' and a 'later' Childe. The former was distinguished by an interest in philology, migration and Indo-European origins, the latter was more concerned with technology, evolution and a materialist interpretation of prehistory. However, while these extremes might isolate the starting and ending points of Childe's intellectual odyssey, there is no sharp break between the two, and each of his books appears to find him continuing to wrestle with the problem of material culture and its relationship to ethnic identity. His effort to bring together culture history and evolution, in particular, tends to lead him to contradict himself within any given theorization.

439

There is a further question regarding precisely how much of Childe's conceptual development stemmed from his professed Marxism and its irreconcilability with positions which he found himself adopting: it is probably an oversimplification to suggest that Childe 'became' a Marxist at a particular point, with an immediate transformation of his archaeology (Gathercole 1989).

Thus in *The Aryans*, Childe developed the notion that the character of particular groups derives from their use of a particular language, accepting an innate superiority of the Indo-Europeans arising from their having formulated a language which served as a superior medium for thought (Trigger 1980: 52). The consequences of this line of thinking doubtless became clear to him at a later stage (Trigger 1980: 91). Yet what is surprising is that Childe had already devised the central concept of the archaeological culture, which was to be his medium for resisting arguments of Kossinna's kind, in a work which was actually published earlier, *The Dawn of European Civilisation* (Childe 1925). Very much like Marx himself, Childe appears to have been capable of arguing rather different cases at one and the same time, in line with different arguments in which he found himself embroiled.

Childe's notion of the 'culture' certainly does draw upon Kossinna's method, especially in that he sees the integrity of individual cultures as being largely geographical (Childe 1942: 27). Yet his own methodology derives largely from Montelius, and he is emphatic that 'culture and race do not coincide' (Childe 1950: 1). As originally phrased, the archaeological culture was seen by Childe (1929: v) as 'certain types of remains – pots, implements, ornaments, burial rites, house forms – constantly recurring together'. Such an entity might reasonably be equated with an ethnic group, a 'people', yet a people was not the same thing as either a race or a linguistic group. What is remarkable about Childe's approach is that, rather than accept the existence of cultures on a purely empirical level, he went on to outline the mechanisms through which they came into being and 'hung together'. In coming to write his epochal summaries of Old World prehistory (Childe 1925, 1929, 1934), Childe condensed his knowledge of thousands of artefacts in hundreds of museums into defining cultural assemblages, made and used by particular groups of people at particular times. These cultures thus became the building blocks of the prehistory which still stands in place (in an elaborated form and with adjusted dating) today (Fig. 11.1).

Childe was willing to see the development of culture (in the generic sense) as a continuation of the evolutionary process. Much as Binford was later to maintain, culture involved means of adapting and coping which were extracorporeal and which could be discarded at will. However, one particular aspect of culture represented a quantum leap which separated human beings from other animals, and this was language: animals could and did learn behaviours from each other, but only human beings could express cultural concepts in the abstract. Thus 'the human parent can teach not only by example, but also by precept' (Childe 1936: 27).

440

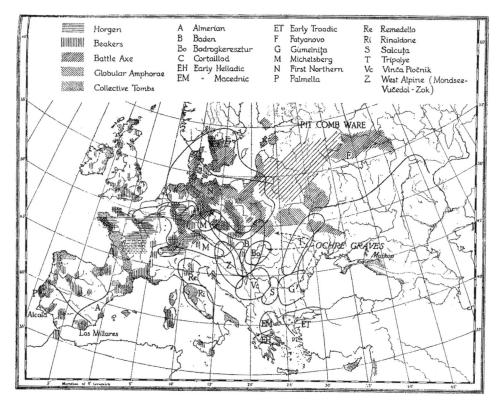

Legend:

Horgen
Beakers
Battle Axe
Globular Amphorae
Collective Tombs

A Almerian
B Baden
Bo Bodrogkeresztur
C Cortaillod
EH Early Helladic
EM " Macednic

ET Early Troadic
F Fatyanovo
G Gumelnița
M Michelsberg
N First Northern
P Palmella

Re Remedello
Ri Rinaldone
S Salcuța
T Tripolye
Vc Vinča Pločnik
Z West Alpine (Mondsee-Vucedol - Zok)

Figure 11.1 Culture history and cultural identity: V. Gordon Childe's map of Beaker and Battle Axe cultures in Europe. Source: Childe 1925.

Human young are frail, requiring a lengthy period of nurture, and it is in this period that cultural information can be learned. Yet the process of cultural inculcation requires a relatively stable social context, and hence more formal relations of immediate kinship tend to appear as human history progresses. Here, Childe's arguments draw quite explicitly on those of Engels (1968).

It follows from Childe's stress on language and learning that the acquisition of culture is a profoundly social process. Human beings are the heirs to a body of information and experience which has been gathered together by past generations (Childe 1942: 16). By accretion, then, human communities built up cultural traditions which had built into them a great weight of conservatism. New innovations might occasionally be made, but these were rare, and were unlikely to be thought of more than once by the human community at large. Thus the expected norm would be that 'men cling passionately to old traditions and display intense reluctance to modify customary modes of behaviour, as innovators at all times have found to their cost' (Childe 1936: 30). Consequently, a particular group of people would tend to make pots, tools and other artefacts in a standardized way, simply because a means of manufacture would be sedimented in social tradition. This much of Childe's argument seems relatively advanced to modern ears, such that aspects of Childe's 'cultural tradition' might be subsumed under Bourdieu's (1977) notion of the *habitus*, a culturally installed and conditioned structure of habitual actions and norms which tends to reproduce traditional practices and maintain social relationships.

However, the picture of prehistoric Europeans as uninventive dupes, waiting around for cultural innovations to be diffused from the Near East rather than as knowledgeable social actors, fits less easily into such a perspective. Childe's prehistory is one in which the iron grip of tradition weighs on the minds of the living, rather than one in which relations of power and dominance have to be invoked in order to explain the reproduction of cultural forms. Similarly, Childe's focus on language leads him into an advocacy of the 'normative' perspective which was to prove the Achilles' heel of culture historic archaeology. Since language was made up of conventional sounds which were taught to individuals as part of their enculturation, it was possible to use them to discuss objects which were not present at hand. Thus reasoning became a project which could be carried out 'in the head', rather than in the external world. By adopting this Cartesian dualism between an internal mind and an external world within which the lived body resided, Childe effectively set up the argument that (in the absence of written sources) a part of past humanity must always remain inaccessible to the archaeologist (for example, Hawkes 1954).

However, being able mentally to manipulate absent objects gave human beings the ability to hypothesize things which they had never seen: demons, spirits, men with wings. Language gave people the ability to transmit and culturally encode a metaphysical realm which had no basis in empirical reality. While in some cases such a metaphysics might atrophy into religion, which Childe saw as the essence of the despotism which stultified the Middle Eastern civilizations, an ideology might equally be favourable to the survival of the community. Abstract ideas might represent stimuli which might inspire people to actions over and above the needs of biological survival, and this in turn might affect the way in which their production of culture might develop. As human communities developed, a form of 'speciation' had taken place in which the material apparatus of particular groups became more and more distinctive and related to ethnic identity (Childe 1942: 25). But clearly, Childe saw the difference between this or that way of decorating a pot, this or that way of burying the dead, as essentially arbitrary. While the use of a particular artefact for a given purpose might be a decision which was functional, most of the information which separated equivalent artefacts of different cultures was of a kind which we would now call stylistic. As indicators of cultural or ethnic identity, each of these traits would be of equivalent importance. Each was simply a 'way of doing things', whose arbitrary morphology might be determined by mental and ideological norms whose genesis and significance were probably lost to us.

As we have already noted, a direct contrast and contradiction with this argument is found in Childe's insistence that a culture also represents an adaptation to a given environment: 'hence a culture evolved in the Mediterranean is not likely to be transferred bodily to say England, without undergoing very drastic modifications' (Childe 1950: 2). Why should this be so, if the differences between cultures were arbitrary and guided by random contingencies of social tradition and ideology? If cultural differentiation resided entirely 'in the head', why should not cultures in Greece and England be entirely similar? One move which could possibly have been taken would have been to follow that subdivision of the *Annales* school of historians who advocate a consideration of past mentalities (Le Goff 1985), and argue that environmental and climatic conditions are always mediated through mental processes and ideologies. The change of cultural form might thus be less as a means of adaptation to real circumstances than a means of expressing perceived conditions. Childe, however, is somewhat reticent in discussing the precise processes involved in the adaptation of culture to environment. Cultural change in his account is largely seen in terms of diffusion. Only where one entire repertoire replaces another outright might we legitimately talk of migration, while invasions where a ruling élite places itself above a local population might lead to no appreciable change in material culture whatsoever. Thus only the slow filtering of new ideas from one community to another gives a possible explanation for the introduction of cultural traits. At the same time, diffusion formed the central underlying assumption of the system of relative dating essential to Childe's prehistories (Chapter 5). What is intriguing to ask is whether Childe's legacy has suffered more from the empirical fact of the collapse of relative dating in the face of the radio-carbon revolution (Renfrew 1973) or from the theoretical assault on 'normative' culture history.

INVASION VERSUS ECOLOGY: CLARK

Childe's unease regarding invasions and migrations as sources of culture change was doubtless prompted by political concerns, and the parallels being drawn between the movements of past Aryan horsemen and their supposed modern counterparts. None the less, he found himself able to present a series of lectures in Norway in 1946 which dealt precisely with those cultural developments in prehistoric Europe which he could accept as attributable to folk movements (Childe 1950). It is interesting, then, to contrast this with one particular statement by one of Childe's contemporaries of a quite different political and theoretical persuasion, albeit one published some while after critiques of culture history had begun to emerge in the United States. In his classic 1966 paper, Grahame Clark complains of the way in which 'for much of the first half of the twentieth century, British archaeologists felt themselves under strong compulsion to ascribe every change, every development to overseas influences of one kind or another' (Clark 1966: 172). Thus, in classifying the iron age phases of the British Isles, Hawkes had chosen to attribute Iron Age A to Halstatt invaders, B to Marnian invaders, and C to Belgic invaders. Clark's sympathies being more with economic and ecological explanations of human behaviour (for example: Clark 1972), he was well placed to lead a critical reaction against the somewhat limited perspective offered by the 'invasion neurosis'. Giving an overview of cultural developments spanning the British Neolithic to Iron Age, Clark demonstrates effectively the monomania of the invasionists. In particular, the revelation that the similarities between the bronze age Hilversum urns of Holland and the Deverel-Rimbury pottery of southern Britain had been interpreted as evidence for an invasion of Holland from Britain by Dutch archaeologists, and the opposite by their British colleagues, demonstrated something of a lack of imagination (Fig. 11.2).

Yet, significantly, Clark had no qualms in asserting that the start of the neolithic period in Britain could be attributed to an invasion. Farming economy and 'the whole complex of technology, practices and ideas that make up our neolithic culture' (Clark 1966: 176) could only have come to Britain by way of actual population movement. What this seems to suggest about Clark's preconceptions is in itself

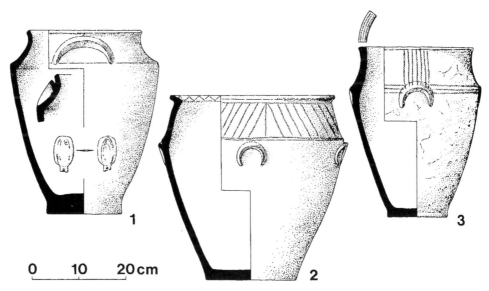

Figure 11.2 British biconical urns (1, 2) and a Dutch Hilversum urn (3): 1. Amesbury, Wiltshire; 2. Bulford barrow 47, Wiltshire; 3. Budel, North Brabant. Source: Megaw and Simpson 1984.

interesting. He appears to believe that the flotsam of pottery style or tool manufacture can easily be transferred from one community to another, but that a deeper and more important level of culture, 'base' rather than 'superstructure', required more fundamental changes to explain its transformation. In common with many of the archaeologists who were working in the 1960s and 1970s, Clark was beginning to see culture as something of a non-question. If radio-carbon dating had rendered relative dating unnecessary, archaeologists could confine their researches to the really important question of human development: how successive generations had provided themselves with subsistence. Such an exclusive focus on economic practice at the expense of cultural variability could certainly give an answer to the question which Childe had avoided: the primary explanation for all forms of human behaviour (at least as represented in the archaeological record) was given as the maintenance of a stable relationship between population levels and ecological conditions (Higgs and Jarman 1975).

ABSTRACT CULTURE SYSTEMS: CLARKE

By the time that Grahame Clark had committed his reservations to print, a quite different approach to culture was germinating in another quarter of Cambridge. While David Clarke had studied under Clark as a research student, his orientation was far more towards a vision of archaeology which was artefact-centred. Clarke's studies of British Beaker pottery had made use of classificatory techniques drawn from the natural sciences (for example, Sokal and Sneath 1963) in order to set up a more objective set of measures of artefact variability (Clarke 1962, 1967, 1970a). At the same time, he laid stress upon the ways in which a more scientific and disciplined approach might change the outlook of the discipline of archaeology, rather than merely the techniques which it made use of (Clarke 1973: 10). For Clarke, archaeology was a discipline which was disorganized and subjective, and which needed to reconsider and regularize its practices. Despite this, it was also a discipline with a recognizable identity, which could transform itself by making explicit its assumptions and procedures. Thus while archaeology had affinities with other disciplines, and could learn from contact with them, the character of its subject matter was such that it must develop a distinctively archaeological set of theories and methods. Archaeological data and historical data are not the same, and the narrative structure of written history is not appropriate to archaeology (Clarke 1978: 11); archaeology also has an affinity with anthropology and with geography, yet it has a more developed time dimension and a more distinct focus upon material culture than either.

As Shennan (1989a: 833) suggests, the consequence of this is that Clarke's archaeology is one which is centred upon the behaviour of groups of artefacts in time: he was concerned not with cultural ecology, but with cultural morphology (Chapman 1979: 111). In a way which owes something to Childe, Clarke's vision is one of material culture as a system which should be studied in its own right, which has affinities with ethnic or racial identity, political identity, and linguistic grouping, but which does not map directly onto any of these.

Clarke's approach to culture is most fully articulated in *Analytical Archaeology* (1968, 1978), a work which attempts to reformulate both the practice of archaeology and its perceived objects. As such, it sought to institute a series of models: of archaeological procedure as a systematic and explicit activity; of archaeological entities as composed of multiple, overlapping sub-units; and of archaeological processes as dynamic systems which could be described using general systems theory. Cultural systems, for Clarke, were integral whole units which exist in a state of dynamic equilibrium within an environment or context which is itself a system composed of sub-systems (1978: 42–45; Fig. 11.3). As such, the set of traits or elements which a culture historian might describe as a 'culture' might now be seen as a self-contained information system, continuously changing across time. Culture as a whole might be looked at as a system with sub-systems: social relationships, religion, psychological, economic and material culture, but it was only the last of these which was studied by archaeologists. Archaeological entities of this type might be bounded and defined at a number of different levels: artefact, type, assemblage, culture, culture group, and technocomplex. Each of the levels in this

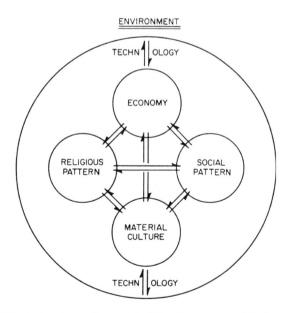

Figure 11.3 David Clarke's schematic model of the dynamic equilibrium existing between a single sociocultural system and its total environment system. Source: Clarke 1978.

446

hierarchy might be seen as an adaptive unit, operating within its environment (not merely in the ecological sense).

Clarke's expectation was that, in the normal state of affairs, an information system will oscillate around and towards a stable state, a state in which the cultural system maintains a steady relationship with its environment. Where some form of perturbation from outside disturbs this relationship, the adaptive response of a goal-seeking, self-regulating, system will allow it either to return to its stable state or to move to a new equilibrium basin. Clarke clearly imagined that culture, whether material or otherwise, operated 'as if' it were able to regulate its own behaviour, almost without reference to human agency (1978: 52). Clarke's culture systems are thus abstract – not merely in the sense that they are modelled on pro-cesses of information flow but also in that they represent a framework of analysis which only indirectly invokes a human presence in the past. Taken to extreme, this represents an ultimately pessimistic form of positivism: since the people are dead and gone, we can only study their artefacts, and any meaningful statements which we make can relate only to them.

Towards the end of *Analytical Archaeology*, Clarke began explicitly to address the relationship between the units of analysis which archaeologists might define and the entities with which other disciplines concern themselves. Using the example of the Bantu of southern Africa, Clarke pointed out that the term might be used to denote a racial, cultural, or political grouping, or a technocomplex (Fig. 11.4), none of which directly corresponded with each other (Clarke 1978: 372–73). Each of these units might share particular characteristics, yet they were basically different classifications established in different dimensions. Of course, this did not mean that the archaeological entity defined on the basis of material culture similarity and difference was any less real than the racial or political unit: it simply referred to a different order of reality.

Subsequently, Clarke worked through a more lengthy example of the implications

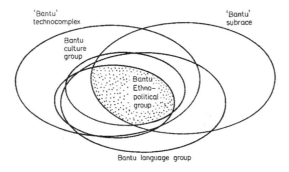

Figure 11.4 The relationship between different aspects of Bantu identity (cultural, techno-logical, racial and linguistic) as expressed by David Clarke. Source: Clarke 1978.

447

of the model for the archaeological past, by considering the character of cultural groupings in late bronze and early iron age Europe. Here, one has a lengthy sequence of cultural change, in which different entities have been established at different points, based upon different classes of evidence from burial furniture to written testimony. According to Clarke, the consequence was that archaeologists had effectively been committing what Wittgenstein would call a 'category error', seeking to characterize 'Celtic material culture', and thus conflating terms drawn from two quite different systems of classification. The relationship between material culture, language and ethnicity was bound to be a more complex one than this allowed: 'what might be said with a fair degree of probability is that the majority of tribes showing the full La Tène assemblage were Celtic speaking and that, even so, some would belong to other language groups and some Celtic-speakers would possess other material culture' (Clarke 1978: 379).

Clarke has a real and important point to make here regarding the complexity of the different ways in which human societies can be bounded and defined. However, we could argue that the outcome is somewhat equivocal, and this may explain the relatively limited impact of the substantive elements of Clarke's approach (Shennan 1989a: 831). Clarke was prepared to distinguish different dimensions of the identity of human groups, yet he seemed unwilling to spell out the ways in which these dimensions articulate with each other. Each appears to be equally real, and the limitation which Clarke places upon archaeology is that it must apprehend the past in the single dimension which is open to it: material culture. Consequently, the entities which it will define will be the rather abstracted traits, the 'culture groups' and 'technocomplexes' of his hierarchy – he seems to admit no closer access to past human social life. Similarly, the ways in which the variability within the archaeological evidence was generated appear to emerge from the formal structure of culture itself and its relationship with its environment, rather than being connected with the playing out of human purposes. Inevitably, this approach led him into a retreat from social reality, to a position in which he found himself arguing that culture consisted of a series of quasi-autonomous levels or spheres which are difficult to relate to each other. It may well have been the recognition of this difficulty which later led him to an abrupt change of direction and to the declaration that *Analytical Archaeology* had been 'an old-fashioned book' (Clarke 1970b).

CULTURE AS ADAPTIVE STRATEGY: BINFORD

While Clarke attempted to salvage what he could of the culture concept, in the United States a still more radical reassessment was under way. In the 1960s, the so-called New Archaeology built upon the ideas of the likes of J. W. Bennett, W. W. Taylor and A. C. Spaulding, calling for a rigorous, scientific, anthropological archaeology. A central element of the agenda of the New Archaeology was the replacement of the notion of cultures as the shared ideational framework of groups of people, with one of culture (singular) as a strategy in which people participated. Culture should thus not be thought of as a set of ideas held commonly in the minds of definable groups, so much as a pool of available responses with which to cope with changing environmental circumstances.

The opening salvo of the debate, and the classic exposition of the new perspective, was Lewis Binford's article 'Archaeology as anthropology' (Binford 1962). Here Binford argued that, while archaeologists had long paid lip-service to the goal of contributing to broader anthropological debates relating to the explanation of cultural diversity, in practice little had been contributed at this level. Archaeologists had done much to demonstrate the range of variability of human culture, but had not advanced beyond the descriptive. The reason which Binford gives for this is a failure to think of archaeological data in a systemic framework. Following White, Binford held that culture was 'man's extrasomatic means of adaptation' (Binford 1965: 205). It followed that culture could not be localized in any one element of the overall system of relationships between persons and their surroundings but was to be found at the junction between several sub-systems. Culture should be studied precisely through a concern with the interactions of different sub-systems – demography, climate, vegetation, technology and so on.

Binford was quick to stress that he was not proposing a form of environmental determinism. Human beings exist within a world composed of ecological systems, and culture is an intervening variable between the organism and its environment (Binford 1962: 219). Thus, while other animals must adapt biologically to changing circumstances, human beings have the option of adopting cultural innovations as a means of coping. Clearly, Binford conceived of the process of cultural change in Darwinian terms. Culture is not limited to the range of behaviours evidenced in the archaeological record (Binford 1973: 229); culture represents a 'pool' of variability which is acted upon by selective pressures, the equivalent of the genetic variability which forms the raw material of biological evolution. This variability represents the content rather than the form of cultural systems, and is subject to more or less stochastic variation through time, a phenomenon which Binford labels as 'cultural drift' (Binford 1963: 91). Binford's use of this term, as an analogue with biological process, is to be distinguished from any similar usage in culture historic archaeology.

Interestingly enough, in seeking to avoid determinism, Binford's first attempts to define what culture is and how it works allowed a surprising range of phenomena to be studied by the archaeologist. Claiming that material culture and technology should not be conflated, Binford argued that three types of material culture can be defined, and that these function in quite different areas of human enterprise (1962: 220). Thus *technomic* artefacts are those which are directly engaged with adaptation to environmental conditions, *sociotechnic* artefacts operate in the social sub-system, expressing social relationships, and *ideotechnic* artefacts are essentially ideological devices, which secure acceptance of and enculturation into the prevailing socio-cultural milieu. Such a conception is clearly functionalist in the extreme, in proposing that each element of culture has its part to play in securing the overall adaptive fitness of the cultural system. However, the immediate upshot of this functionalism was the perception that archaeologists were now able to study and explain a wider range of more interesting phenomena. Far from being limited to those aspects of human practice which could be directly inferred from the material evidence alone (Hawkes 1954), a range of seemingly 'irrational' behaviours could be explained in terms of their contribution to the functioning and integration of the cultural system as a whole.

The particular example which was chosen to demonstrate this greater explanatory range was one which was characteristic of a new mood of optimism. At the start of the 1970s a series of studies appeared which purported to explain prehistoric mortuary practices in adaptive and systemic terms (Binford 1971; Saxe 1970). In these studies, mortuary practice was presented as a communication system which served to express the precise social role at death of particular persons. Its adaptive significance thus lay in communicating to the community as a whole the loss of one of its members, and to facilitate the rebuilding or reallocation of the relationships and functions of the deceased. Binford's prescription for the archaeological study of culture was thus one which allowed a far greater range of phenomena to be studied, even if in a very restrictive way. By definition, culture is important when it is engaged in the adaptation and maintenance of internal homeostasis of the group. Beyond this, cultural manifestations which cannot be directly tied to adaptive strategy are considered to be aspects of a pool of variability, which enables flexible responses to be made to changing conditions. However, the content, as opposed to the mere existence, of this variability was given little consideration, and its involvement in in-group strategies was not addressed.

The contrast between 'normative' culture history and Binford's systemic evolutionism is nowhere demonstrated with such clarity as in the celebrated debate over 'Mousterian variability' (see also Chapter 12). In a meticulous series of analyses of measurements and indices relating to lithic assemblages of the middle palaeolithic Mousterian in south-west France, François Bordes had demonstrated the existence of a series of distinctive assemblages, which he explained in culture-historic terms as diagnostic of the coexistence of a number of tribes or peoples (Bordes 1973; Bordes and de Sonneville-Bordes 1970). Binford's reconsideration of these materials was to question whether a series of different assemblages need necessarily represent a series of different cultures, or whether it might simply be the case that the same group of people were using a slightly different technology under different conditions (Binford and Binford 1966, 1969). His argument was not that a given assemblage is a type fossil which is produced as a determined response to a given climatic stimulus. The archaeological record represents the use of a set of cultural materials in a strategic adaptive behaviour, and what is evidenced at each particular site is the technology required to carry out a particular set of activities under a given set of conditions:

> I do not wish to imply that there is a causal relationship between the form of the environment and the form of the assemblage, only that the utility of a given location for particular forms of human use is modified with changes in the environment.

(Binford 1973: 232)

'CERAMIC SOCIOLOGY': DEETZ, HILL, LONGACRE

The same optimism which characterized studies of prehistoric social structure based on mortuary analysis can be seen in a group of papers published in the 1960s which made use of stylistic variation in ceramics as a means of addressing patterns of residence and descent (Deetz 1968; Hill 1970, 1972; Longacre 1964). All were concerned with pueblo settlements (large, conglomerate residential structures in the American Southwest: Fig. 11.5), and all were attempting to substantiate whether currently extant patterns of social structure had prehistoric antecedents. The arguments began with the observation that, in modern-day pueblo society, the skills of pottery manufacture and decoration are passed from mother to daughter (Hill 1970: 37). These communities are matrilocal; that is, husbands at marriage go to live in the family home of their new wife. It follows, then, that microtraditions of potting style build up in the individual matrilineages (Deetz 1968: 45). Using data from the excavated pueblo at the Carter Ranch Site, Longacre set out to test the hypothesis that a similar pattern of residence and descent existed during the life of the site, in the period AD 1100–1250. If it were the case that matrilocality and matrilineality existed in the past, it might be expected that particular stylistic elements on pots would be localized in specific areas of the site. For the prediction to hold true, it would be necessary that then, as now, potting had been an exclusively female activity. Moreover, the pottery analysis would have to be compared with a series of non-female associated artefacts, which should not demonstrate the same localized patterning of stylistic traits (Hill 1970: 38). If spatial variation was demonstrable over the site, it would still have to be shown that the spatial units so defined were functionally equivalent, rather than representing different activity areas, in which characteristic forms of pottery might easily be employed.

At the Carter Ranch, 175 design elements of pottery were found to have a non-random distribution across the site. Moreover, particular design elements appeared to cluster in contiguous groups of rooms. The results of the investigation of design

451

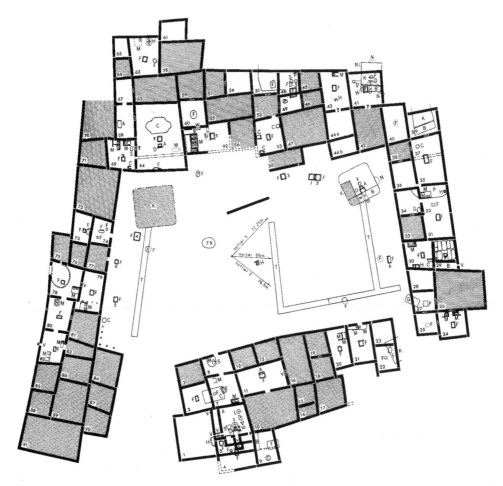

Figure 11.5 Plan of Broken K Pueblo, east-central Arizona. Reproduced with permission of The Field Museum of Natural History, Neg#A99799, Chicago.

structure were then subjected to a multiple regression analysis, which in turn suggested that three major groupings of rooms could be distinguished on stylistic criteria. Each of these groups was associated with a particular *kiva*, or ritual structure, and ceramics recovered in the cemetery associated with the settlement could be linked with the individual groups (Longacre 1964: 1455). The results thus appeared to be consistent with the model of developing microtraditions of style in potting, each associated with a particular matrilineage. While the Deetz/Longacre/Hill model was originally developed at the microspatial scale, later applications considered its implications at the inter-community level: using very much the same kinds of decorative and other stylistic traits, the attempt was made to measure the degree of similarity between different sites, based upon the supposition that the degree of similarity is a direct product of the intensity of interaction between communities (Plog 1978).

On more sober reflection, some of the enthusiasm for 'ceramic sociology' in the 1960s came to be thought of as misplaced. While the analyses were framed as testable hypotheses in true positivist style, many of the law-like statements thereby generated rested upon a complex series of assumptions. In consequence, while the outcome of the empirical test on the evidence might be favourable, an enormous problem of 'equifinality' remained: that is to say, so much had to be assumed before the analysis could proceed that the results might be generated by a number of different processes which were not accounted for in the hypothesis. Some of the complexities of these processes began to emerge as time went on. For instance, it was evident that across the present-day Southwest neither kinship systems nor the mechanisms by which the skills of potting were passed on were as standardized as had been assumed (Stanislawski 1973). Similarly, there was considerable evidence that pottery had been exchanged over large distances, and while this might constitute interaction it certainly would not result in the clear-cut stylistic consequences of intermarriage between communities. Finally, as Plog (1978) points out, the whole approach was somewhat innocent of the processes by which the archaeological record is formed. There is no guarantee, for instance, that pots will enter the archaeological context in the same spatial location in which they were either made or used, and a distinction needs to be made between those vessels recovered in circumstances which suggest use within a particular room and more generalized demolition spreads. But beyond these procedural and empirical concerns it can also be objected that such an approach to artefact style neglected both the social processes which lay behind the production of material culture and the specificity of the cultural context, in the desire to erect global generalizations concerning stylistic behaviour (Shanks and Tilley 1987: 89).

STYLE, INFORMATION AND IDENTITY: SACKETT AND WIESSNER

Binford's original discussion of a systemic approach to material culture had left the issue of style somewhat open. Technomic, ideotechnic and sociotechnic artefacts all had primary attributes which distinctively engaged them in a particular sphere of practice. However, there were particular formal characteristics of artefacts which existed over and beyond that which could be related directly to variability in the technological or social sub-systems, or in the nature of raw materials (Binford 1962: 219).

> These formal qualities are believed to have their primary functional context in providing a symbolically diverse yet pervasive artefactual environment promoting group solidarity

and serving as a basis for group awareness and identity. This pansystemic set of symbols is the milieu of enculturation and a basis for the recognition of social distinctiveness.

(Binford 1962: 219)

Binford's conception of style at this stage was one which presented it as that element of culture which is left over as a residue, once its prime adaptive significance has been exhausted. As the Deetz/Hill/Longacre argument demonstrates, this leaves some degree of uncertainty regarding the mechanisms through which style operates. At what level does style guarantee group affiliation?

One answer to this problem is provided by Wobst (1977), who suggests that style, rather than being a necessarily integrative mechanism, functions as a means of transmitting information. The character of the message transmitted, and the medium through which it is expressed, will depend upon the social distance between the sender and their target population. Thus any or all items of material culture may contain coded messages in the form of stylistic variation, yet different aspects of the total cultural repertoire will be active in different forms and levels of social interaction. Moreover, it will generally be the case that, within any definable social unit, common encoding and decoding strategies will exist, and that common responses will be elicited by given stylistic elements (Conkey 1978: 64). Wobst's and Conkey's arguments open the way for a broader discussion of the ways in which style can operate at different levels and in different contexts. Such a discussion can be found in the ongoing exchange between James Sackett and Polly Wiessner.

Interestingly, the debate has its origins with the question of Mousterian variability. Reviewing the issues which had been drawn out of the Binford/Bordes dialogue, Sackett (1973: 320) sought to clarify issues by drawing a distinction between the *functional mode* and the *stylistic mode* of a given artefact. These refer to the respective roles of the artefact in technical operation and as an indicator of cultural tradition. The stylistic mode will potentially be present in all archaeologically recovered artefacts, since it is highly likely that something which could fulfil the same function could be made in a different way. Stylistic variation thus exists between artefacts which are 'equal in use', or as he later termed it, 'isochrestic' (Sackett 1986: 268). The particular stylistic variation which the artefact will assume is determined by a given historical and cultural setting, such that objects will tend to fit into traditions of manufacture. 'Thus any statement which concerns the manner in which artefact variability is symptomatic of tradition is by definition a stylistic statement' (Sackett 1973: 321). These traditions of isochrestic variation are not generated in any conscious way, but are the consequence of picking up the techniques of manufacture for an artefact in a particular context. While people may be perfectly able to identify the workmanship of another community, this may not be through distinct features which they could easily verbalize. On the contrary, the bulk of the information which we can potentially use to detect ethnic groups in the archaeological record is not so much actively encoded as inculcated (Sackett

454

1986: 268). The element of stylistic variability which Sackett calls 'iconic', which knowingly symbolizes and asserts group identity, he considers to be extremely rare.

It is with this last part of Sackett's argument that Wiessner takes issue. In a way which is closer to the arguments of Wobst and Conkey, she argues that agents can actively manipulate the signifying capacity of material culture in such a way as to elicit a desired response from a defined audience (Wiessner 1984: 193). In particular, style is seen as a means by which the relationship between the person and society may be mediated (Wiessner 1989: 59). Stylistic variability is thus taken to be representative of a universal human cognitive process – that of social identification through comparison: 'style is one of several means of communication through which people negotiate their personal identity *vis-à-vis* others' (Wiessner 1989: 57). Accordingly, archaeologists might conceivably make use of style as a means of monitoring changes in the relationship between individual and society across time. Using her ethnoarchaeological studies of the Kalahari San, Wiessner argued further that different forms of stylistic behaviour could be defined, which have different aims. Where stylistic attributes refer primarily to the self, and are used by the individual as a means of articulating personal identity within the community, style is being used 'assertively'. This, claims Wiessner, is the case with the bead headbands worn by San women (1984: 193). On the other hand, where stylistic variation is used as a means of signalling group or ethnic affiliation, one is dealing with 'emblemic' style. Wiessner's example of emblemic style is the projectile points of the San which, while small, are widely exchanged, such that persons will be very aware of the origin of a projectile within a particular community (Wiessner 1983).

While Sackett and Wiessner appear on the surface to be arguing from irreconcilable points of view, at another level of generality their positions are not so far different. Both appear to accept a distinction between stylistic traits which are invested in material items in an unconsidered manner, simply because this is 'the way of doing things', and a more active encoding of messages. Their argument is really one concerning human nature, and the extent to which people routinely conceptualize and account for their actions.

FROM FUNCTIONALISM TO STRUCTURALISM: HODDER

Suppose we have a virilocal residence situation in which the women who are 'marrying in' alter their pottery-making and other styles to conform to those of their mothers-in-law and sisters-in-law! The question is, will a woman in this situation abandon the kinds of style elements she learned in her natal household and adopt new ones to conform to those of her new household?

(Hill 1970: 41)

So, whatever a woman may feel she really is, she can outwardly express different identities, and there is rarely any ambiguity about which identity she is overtly expressing at any one time.

(Hodder 1982a: 21)

In Britain, the decisive move away from organic and functionalist models of culture arose from the vacuum left behind by the demise of the 'culture concept'. Neither Clarke's purely 'archaeological' reformulation of culture systems, nor the agenda concerned with stylistic interaction and information exchange, appeared able to account satisfactorily for the entities which formed the backbone of European prehistory. The rootedness of archaeological thought in a notion of geographical areas characterized by co-variant material culture traits rebelled against these formalizations, yet a return to a normative conception of culture was impossible. The sense of unease which this situation produced is well captured in Ian Hodder's 1978 collection of essays, *The Spatial Organisation of Culture* (Hodder 1978a). The volume contained articles qualifying or expressing grave doubts concerning both the traditional archaeological culture (Shennan 1978) and the Deetz/Hill/Longacre model of stylistic learning mechanisms (Stanislawski and Stanislawski 1978). Perhaps most interesting of all are Hodder's own contributions, which review 'simple correlations between material culture and society', concluding that some material traits form bounded spatial entities equivalent to the Childean culture, but that others do not. Compounding this uncertainty was the observation by Hodder and Orton (1976) that 'random association groups' of traits might produce entirely arbitrary 'cultures' of no empirical validity whatsoever. Hodder's initial response to this state of affairs was to invoke a closer scrutiny of the social processes which lie behind the distribution and mutual association of artefact types. The first results were speculative rather than conclusive (Hodder 1978b).

It was this concern for the status of the material culture as a heuristic entity which led Hodder to undertake a series of ethnoarchaeological studies in East Africa, eventually reported as *Symbols in Action* (Hodder 1982a). The most sustained example within the book concerns the Pokot, Njemps and Tugen tribes of the Lake Baringo area of Kenya. Questionnaire survey and itineraries of artefacts within hut compounds demonstrated both that the three groups were very aware of their separate identities (Fig. 11.6), and that various types of item showed quite abrupt breaks of distribution at tribal borders (Fig. 11.7). Identification with the tribe was clearly demonstrated in dress, and in particular in the wearing of pendant ear decoration by the women. Particular kinds of pottery, wooden stools, and even the positions of hearths within huts, were also specific to particular tribes. Moreover, verbal testimony made it clear that these preferences were not merely the consequence of unconsidered action, but that these items were perceived as bound up with tribal identity.

The recognition that the maintenance of these boundaries was most marked in

456

Figure 11.6 Artefacts from a Tugen compound, as recorded in Hodder's survey of material culture in the Lake Baringo area. Source: Hodder 1982.

locations where there was a particular stress on material resources led Hodder to formulate an initial interpretation of these phenomena in processual and adaptive terms (Hodder 1979). Thus boundary maintenance through material expression might be linked in a lawlike manner to the severity of resource competition. The rejection of this relatively formal and generalized explanation appears to have emerged from a combination of attention to the detail of the study material and a developing critique of functionalist models of culture. This latter Hodder (1981, 1982b) clearly saw as the prerequisite for the emergence of a mature social archaeology. Hodder advocated the adoption of a quasi-structuralist notion of deep structure, covering the rules and codes which underlie the surface phenomena of social life or of archaeological evidence (Hodder 1982b: 7). None the less, he recognized the lack of a concern with agency within structuralism, and derived from Giddens (1979) the understanding that active human agents transform generative cultural structures through their social practice (Hodder 1982b: 8).

In the light of these considerations, a more complex and context-specific account of boundary maintenance was possible. One significant factor was the comparative ease with which persons could move from one tribal area to another, adopting the dress and material culture of the local group and thereby becoming affiliated to that identity. Clearly, what was taking place was quite distinct from the culture-historic view that material culture passively reflected the accepted norms of a

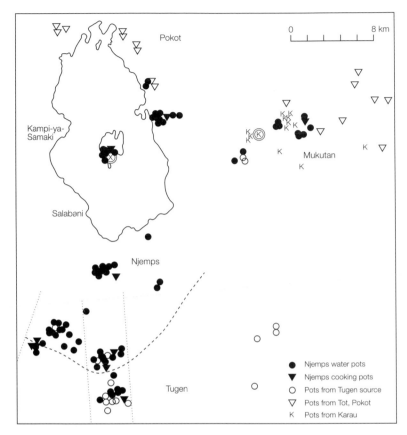

Figure 11.7 Distribution of pottery types in the Lake Baringo area; double circles enclose the potters at Karau (K) and Kokwa (X). Source: Hodder 1982.

society. In the Baringo area, people were quite aware of the potential of things outwardly to express particular identities, irrespective of whatever ethnic group they might feel themselves to belong to (Hodder 1982a: 21). The explanation offered for these phenomena still concerned conflict and competition for resources, but the particular mechanisms involved were contingent ones. The positive adoption of the material trappings of an ethnic identity allowed people to be recognized as eligible for the support and protection of the *moran*, or young spear-carrying men, of a particular tribe. This support was at more of a premium in areas where disputes over property were most likely to occur, and hence it would be in these areas that group identity would be most unambiguous (Hodder 1982a: 31). That this process was not limited to the unconsidered action of making particular objects in particular ways is evident from the marked preferences which particular tribal groups showed for types of items acquired from a distance. Stools and pots of particular patterns, although made by persons from different ethnic groups, were none the less held to symbolize particular attributes of affiliation to a given identity (Hodder 1982a: 54).

Another point at which the Baringo material challenged both normative and functionalist models of culture was found in the way that not all traits conformed to tribal boundaries in their distribution: these were not simply neutral or null traits without symbolic significance; on the contrary, they demonstrated that cultural entities could not be considered as undivided totalities. Two particular cases are of note. First, the *moran* in each tribe use spears which are quite similar in general style (Hodder 1982a: 65). The spear is not necessarily the most effective weapon either for hunting or for warfare, and at marriage it is replaced as a ubiquitous male item by a carved stick. Spears and sticks respectively are symbols of young and elder male status or identity, carrying connotations of sexual prowess or of the prerogative to speak in public. Since the spear symbolism works at a tangent to group affiliation, its variability is not distributed spatially in the same way. Indeed, the way in which the *moran* of the Tugen and the Njemps carry similar spears refers in an implicit and non-verbal way to a degree of solidarity between all young men, who consider themselves collectively to be exploited by the elders. The symbolism of spears is thus a means of expressing a degree of resistance against this state of affairs. In the same way, the calabashes which women use as containers for milk provide 'a medium for silent discourse between women' (Hodder 1982a: 69). In areas like the decoration of pottery and their own dress, Njemps and Tugen women conform closely to norms which have been set for them by a male-dominated society. Calabashes, however, represent a field for decorative traits controlled and executed entirely by women: they both comment on and express covert resistance against that society by referencing ties of birth and marriage which extend beyond ethnic borders.

Symbols in Action provided the stimulus for a rethinking of the archaeological understanding of culture, since its evidence would not accord with the precepts of either traditional culture history or the Binfordian model of culture as adaptive strategy. Most significantly, it killed off any lingering impression that a fixed relationship could obtain between social form and material expression. Rather, people knowledgeably constructed identities for themselves using material culture as a medium. Culture was not a superorganic intelligence, working 'behind the backs' of people to enable the adaptation of the group, but a set of affordances passed down by past generations with which people worked. Since these affordances were at any given point the result of a particular trajectory of development, and since they provided the context for human actions which could change the cultural heritage to be passed on to the next generation, the approach came to stress historicity. From a generalizing and law-seeking functionalism, archaeology had moved at a stroke to a (broadly) post-structuralist historical particularism.

POST-STRUCTURALIST AND HERMENEUTIC VIEWS OF CULTURE

What had effectively emerged by the middle of the 1980s was a conflict over the way in which the archaeological record was to be conceptualized. As Patrik (1985) indicates, processual archaeology had represented archaeological materials as being the equivalent of a fossil record, a physical imprint of past patterns of behaviour. By contrast, the emerging tradition of symbolic and structural archaeologies had come to think of material traces as encoded with meaning, and as part of the symbolic construction of personal and group identity. In consequence, the archaeological record was conceived of as being something like a text. Increasingly, the implications of this point of view began to be worked through, and a series of sources within the literary humanities started to be drawn upon in order to enrich the study of material culture. It is important to point out that these approaches were by no means homogeneous, and could lead in very different directions. In particular, we might point to the distinct influences which were exerted by post-structuralism and hermeneutics, and the resulting rather different ways in which the use of culture by human beings was considered.

Hermeneutic approaches stress the way in which meaning is unfolded out of a text through a gradual process of interpretation, and have a lineage which stretches back through German historiography and biblical exegesis. It is central to the hermeneutic standpoint that symbols require interpretation: the reader actively produces a meaning from a text by engaging with it in an act of reading (Moore 1990; Warnke 1987). It is not the case that one simply extracts a meaning which is locked within a text: the reader actively constructs an interpretation for himself/ herself (Outhwaite 1985). There is consequently no guarantee that the reader's meaning will correspond with that which was intended by the author. The text escapes the author, and things can be read into it which he or she never intended. The attempt to understand what the author intended in writing cannot come from the text alone, but from a 'fusion of horizons', a recognition of the author's context and attitude (Gadamer 1975). Even then, the interpretation can scarcely correspond entirely with the author's meaning, and interpretation comes to be seen as an endless work of refinement and checking: the 'hermeneutic circle'. Ricoeur (1981) has suggested that the distinguishing feature of a text is that it takes discourse and fixes it, giving it a stable form which can be interrogated in the absence of the author. None the less, he also indicates that the methodology of text-interpretation can be applied in a wider variety of contexts within the human sciences, where purposeful human action is regarded as the equivalent of a text. The potential of this proposition was perhaps demonstrated most strikingly by Moore in her study of the contemporary Marakwet of Kenya (1986). Moore presents a picture in which human existence can be compared to a continuous process of reading and writing, where bodily movement through culturally encoded spaces both draws on and recreates their meaning, a meaning which is nevertheless created by the agent and which as a result may vary from person to person.

It was a not dissimilar notion of culture as text which Hodder adopted in the mid-1980s and combined with a stress on the active human subject in order to develop a post-processual, contextual archaeology (Hodder 1985, 1986). If the meaning of material culture was not fixed, and was open to interpretation, then in order for communication to take place at all the significance of symbols would have to be negotiated between persons (Hodder 1988). By 'reading' the meaning of artefacts and at the same time 'rewriting' their significance, human beings were depicted as constantly redefining their position in the world. Cultural meaning is therefore based in interpretation, although Hodder was at pains to stress that the significance of objects is not entirely arbitrary. Material things always have a context of use and an everyday significance, upon which secondary and connotative meanings may be built up (Hodder 1989). Moreover, the attribution of significance to a symbol was held to be contextual, so that how an object was interpreted might depend upon the other items with which it was associated: Hodder gives the example of a safety pin, which 'means' different things when attached to a baby's nappy or a punk's leather jacket (Hodder 1985).

This emphasis on the role of agents as building culture through interpretation is one which fits with a growing awareness of ethnicity as not so much an objective fact as a subjective attribution (Shennan 1989b). The implications of a more fluid conception of ethnicity are brought out by the plight of the Mashpee Wampanoag, a Native American group whose status of an identifiable bounded community had evidently waxed and waned historically (Clifford 1988: 336). Yet in order to claim ancestral lands in court, the Wampanoag had been required to demonstrate an authentic and constant identity since pre-colonial times. But beyond this, a concern with the ways in which human subjects are differentially positioned culturally articulates with a growing archaeological interest in gender issues (Gero and Conkey 1991). This is an area too vast and important to be done justice here, but we might mention Judith Butler's (1993) discussion of the way in which sexed identities are created and continually reinforced through bodily performance, a process in which material culture might be expected to be implicated (and see also the discussion of gender in Chapter 12). On the basis of Hodder's arguments, the task of the archaeologist now came to be redefined as one of 'reading the past', building up patterns of association and contextual location which to an extent parallel the process of reading on the part of the native. Here again there is a parallel with Gadamer's hermeneutics, in the attempt to work towards an interpretation which approximates to that of people in the past.

It is perhaps more difficult adequately to express the content of post-structuralist theories of culture, so diverse are the approaches which might be grouped under that rubric. If we confine ourselves to the notion of text, quite a different way of

461

thinking about material culture can be derived from the approaches to signs taken by the likes of Jacques Derrida and Roland Barthes. Derrida, for instance, elaborated upon Saussure's argument that a language or sign-system is structured not by relationships between things and signifiers (words, symbols) but by relationships internal to language itself, to argue that the circulation of signs endlessly delays any direct encounter with the signified concept or object (Derrida 1986). Language is slippery and impossible to pin down, so each signifier does not lead us to a full grasp of what is being said, but to other signifiers which explode out endlessly. Language is therefore not a set of labels which relate to things in a straightforward, one-to-one way, but is composed of limitless chains of signification. Similarly, Barthes points out that endless meanings can be drawn out of a single text, since any set of words is networked in innumerable ways to other texts, concepts and events. A text is a site of production where a reader labours to produce a meaning for him or herself, *working* the language in order to bring about signification (Barthes 1981). These perspectives would deny the existence of any founding meaning hovering in the shadows behind any text, which one has to uncover through analysis. While an author may have assembled a set of signifiers in a particular way, there is no reason to suspect that he or she had a more perfect understanding of what (s)he was trying to say (but failing) than does the reader. No deeper truth is locked inside the text, and no empathy with the author will lead us to a 'correct' reading.

Applied to material culture, these ideas produce a strikingly different understanding. Material things are seen as having a symbolic content which signifies, which can be worked like language to produce meaning. Like language, material symbols are networked to each other, by connotation and metaphor. As Hodder suggests, context is of central importance, but juxtaposition does not so much tie down the meaning of an object as allow new meanings to be elicited from it. Meaning is potentially limitless, and culture as a whole can be conceived as a vast web of interconnected signifiers (Shanks and Tilley 1987). Moreover, it is not merely the case that human beings make use of material things to negotiate their social position. Neither persons nor things spring into the world fully formed and without precedent. Rather, both people and material culture are the products of the continuous process by which society renews itself (Barrett 1987; Shanks and Tilley 1987). Society is reproduced by people carrying forward the order and values of past generations, and the production, maintenance, and persistence of objects is central to this: a society exists *through* material culture (Miller 1987). Moreover, human beings do not simply take up culture in order strategically to alter or maintain their position within society. It is impossible for any human subject to gain a sense of identity without first inserting himself/herself into culture and language (Lacan 1977).

In several respects, a perspective informed by both hermeneutics *and* poststructuralism requires a radical rethinking of the practice of archaeology. First, the degree to which society, personal identity, and material culture are inextricably bound up makes the whole notion of an 'archaeological record' difficult to sustain. It is not the case that societies or people move through time spewing out material culture like a trail behind them. Rather, the whole material world, natural and cultural, represents a set of resources which are constantly encountered, interpreted, encoded and transformed by human beings. Thus, as Barrett (1988) suggests, archaeological traces are not so much a 'record', a blueprint of past social relations, as *evidence for* past processes of social reproduction. The web of signification and meaning was one within which people gained their identities as human subjects and struggled through their existence. Second, if we come to recognize that our reading of these traces is most unlikely to map directly onto a past understanding of the world, and that it represents a labour in itself, the emphasis shifts from *reading* to *writing* the past. This is not a case of passively allowing the remains to 'speak' to us of the past: it is an active production which is of and for the present.

REFERENCES

Barrett, J. C. (1987) 'Contextual archaeology', *Antiquity* 61: 468–73.

Barrett, J. C. (1988) 'Fields of discourse: reconstituting a social archaeology', *Critique of Anthropology* 7 (3): 5–16.

Barthes, R. (1981) 'Theory of the text', in R. Young (ed.) *Untying the Text*, London: Routledge and Kegan Paul: 31–47.

Bassin, M. (1987a) 'Imperialism and the nation-state in Friedrich Ratzel's political geography', *Progress in Human Geography* 11: 473–95.

Bassin, M. (1987b) 'Race contra space: the conflict between German *Geopolitik* and National Socialism', *Political Geography Quarterly* 6: 115–34.

Bhaskar, R. (1989) *Reclaiming Reality: A Critical Introduction to Contemporary Philosophy*, London: Verso.

Binford, L. R. (1962) 'Archaeology as anthropology', *American Antiquity* 28: 217–25.

Binford, L. R. (1963) '"Red ochre" caches from the Michigan area: a possible case of cultural drift', *Southwestern Journal of Anthropology* 19: 89–108.

Binford, L. R. (1965) 'Archaeological systematics and the study of culture process', *American Antiquity* 31: 203–10.

Binford, L. R. (1971) 'Mortuary practices: their study and potential', in J. A. Brown (ed.) *Approaches to the Social Dimensions of Mortuary Practices*, New York: Memoirs of the Society for American Archaeology 25: 6–29.

Binford, L. R. (1972a) 'Comments on evolution', in L. R. Binford, *An Archaeological Perspective*, New York: Seminar Press: 105–13.

Binford, L. R. (1972b) 'Archaeological perspectives', in L. R. Binford, *An Archaeological Perspective*, New York: Seminar Press: 78–104.

Binford, L. R. (1973) 'Interassemblage variability – the Mousterian and the "functional" argument', in A. C. Renfrew (ed.) *The Explanation of Culture Change*, London: Duckworth: 227–54.

Binford, L. R. (1983) *In Pursuit of the Past: Decoding the Archaeological Record*, London: Thames and Hudson.

Binford, L. R. and Binford, S. (1966) 'A preliminary analysis of functional variability in the Mousterian of Levallois facies', *American Anthropologist* 68: 238–95.

Binford, L. R. and Binford, S. (1969) 'Stone tools and human behaviour', *Scientific American* 220 (4): 70–84.

Binford, L. R. and Sabloff, J. A. (1982) 'Paradigms, systematics and archaeology', *Journal of Anthropological Research* 38: 137–53.

Boas, F. (1948) *Race, Language and Culture*, London: Macmillan.

Bordes, F. (1973) 'On the chronology and contemporaneity of different palaeolithic cultures in France', in A.C. Renfrew (ed.) *The Explanation of Culture Change*, London: Duckworth: 217–26.

Bordes, F. and de Sonneville-Bordes, D. (1970) 'The significance of variability in Palaeolithic assemblages', *World Archaeology* 2: 61–73.

Bourdieu, P. (1977) *Outline of a Theory of Practice*, Cambridge: Cambridge University Press.

Bradley, R. J. (1983) 'Archaeology, evolution and the public good: the intellectual development of General Pitt-Rivers', *Archaeological Journal* 140: 1–9.

Butler, J. (1993) *Bodies That Matter*, London: Routledge.

Champion, T. C. and Diaz-Andreu, M. (1995) *Nationalism and Archaeology in Europe*, London: University College London Press.

Chapman, R. (1979) '*Analytical archaeology* and after – introduction', in *D. L. Clarke, Analytical Archaeologist*, London: Academic: 109–43.

Childe, V. G. (1915) 'On the date and origin of Minyan Ware', *Journal of the Hellenic Society* 35: 196–207.

Childe, V. G. (1925) *The Dawn of European Civilisation*, London: Kegan Paul.

Childe, V. G. (1926) *The Aryans: A Study of Indo-European Origins*, London: Kegan Paul.

Childe, V. G. (1929) *The Danube in Prehistory*, Oxford: Oxford University Press.

Childe, V. G. (1934) *New Light on the Most Ancient East: The Oriental Prelude to European Prehistory*, London: Kegan Paul.

Childe, V. G. (1936) *Man Makes Himself*, London: Watts.

Childe, V. G. (1942) *What Happened in History*, Harmondsworth: Penguin.

Childe, V. G. (1950) *Prehistoric Migrations in Europe*, Oslo: Aschehaug.

Clark, J. G. (1966) 'The invasion hypothesis in British archaeology', *Antiquity* 40: 172–89.

Clark, J. G. (1972) *Star Carr: A Case Study in Bioarchaeology*, Modules in Anthropology 10, Reading, Mass.: Addison-Wesley.

Clarke, D. L. (1962) 'Matrix analysis and archaeology with particular reference to British Beaker pottery', *Proceedings of the Prehistoric Society* 28: 371–83.

Clarke, D. L. (1967) 'A tentative reclassification of British beaker pottery in the light of recent research', *Palaeohistoria* 12: 179–98.

Clarke, D. L. (1968) *Analytical Archaeology*, London: Methuen.

Clarke, D. L. (1970a) *Beaker Pottery of Great Britain and Ireland*, Cambridge: Cambridge University Press.

Clarke, D. L. (1970b) 'Analytical archaeology: epilogue', *Norwegian Archaeological Review* 3: 25–33.

Clarke, D. L. (1973) 'Archaeology: the loss of innocence', *Antiquity* 47: 6–18.

Clarke, D. L. (1978) *Analytical Archaeology* (2nd edition, edited by R. Chapman), London: Methuen.

Clifford, J. (1988) *The Predicament of Culture: Twentieth-Century Ethnography, Literature and Art*, Cambridge, Mass.: Harvard University Press.

Cloak, F. T. (1975) 'Is a cultural ethology possible?', *Human Ecology* 3 (3): 161–82.

Conkey, M. W. (1978) 'Style and information in cultural evolution: toward a predictive model for the Palaeolithic', in C. Redman, M. Berman, G. Curtin, W. Langhorne, N. Versaggi and J. Wanser (eds) *Social Archaeology: Beyond Subsistence and Dating*, London: Academic: 61–85.

Culler, J. (1975) *Structuralist Poetics*, London: Routledge and Kegan Paul.

Deetz, J. (1968) 'The inference of residence and descent rules from archaeological data', in L. Binford and S. Binford (eds) *New Perspectives in Archaeology*, Aldine: New Mexico University: 41–48.

Derrida, J. (1986) 'Différance', in M. C. Taylor (ed.) *Deconstruction in Context: Literature and Philosophy*, Chicago: University of Chicago: 396–420.

Diener, P., Nonni, D. and Robkin, E. E. (1980) 'Ecology and evolution in cultural evolution', *Man* 15: 1–31.

Durkheim, E. (1915) *The Elementary Forms of the Religious Life: A Study in Religious Sociology*, London: Allen and Unwin.

Durkheim, E. and Mauss, M. (1963) *Primitive Classification*, London: Cohen and West.

Edmonds, M. R. and Thomas, J. S. (1987) 'The Archers: an everyday story of country folk', in A. G. Brown and M. R. Edmonds (eds) *Lithic Analysis and Later British Prehistory*, Oxford: British Archaeological Reports, British Series 162: 187–99.

Engels, F. (1968) 'The origin of the family, private property and the state', in *Karl Marx and Frederick Engels: Selected Works in One Volume*, London: Lawrence and Wishart: 461–585.

Firth, R. (1936) *We, the Tikopia: A Sociological Study of Kinship in Primitive Polynesia*, London: Allen and Unwin.

Flannery, K. V. (1973) 'Archaeology with a capital S', in C. Redman (ed.) *Research and Theory in Contemporary Archaeology*, London: John Wiley: 47–53.

Flannery, K. V. (1983) *The Cloud People*, London: Academic.

Foucault, M. (1970) *The Order of Things*, London: Tavistock.

Friedman, J. (1979) 'Hegelian ecology: between Rousseau and the World Spirit', in P. Burnham and R. Ellen (eds) *Social and Ecological Systems*, London: Academic: 253–70.

Gadamer, H. G. (1975) *Truth and Method*, London: Sheed and Ward.

Gathercole, P. (1989) 'Childe's early Marxism', in V. Pinsky and A. Wylie (eds) *Critical Traditions in Contemporary Archaeology*, Cambridge: Cambridge University Press: 80–87.

Gero, J. and Conkey, M. (eds) (1991) *Engendering Archaeology: Women and Prehistory*, Oxford: Blackwell: 31–54.

Giddens, A. (1976) *New Rules of Sociological Method*, London: Hutchinson.

Giddens, A. (1978) *Durkheim*, London: Fontana.

Giddens, A. (1979) *Central Problems in Social Theory*, London: Macmillan.

Giddens, A. (1981) *A Contemporary Critique of Historical Materialism*, London: Macmillan.

Giddens, A. (1984) *The Constitution of Society*, Cambridge: Polity Press.

Giddens, A. (1987) 'Structuralism, post-structuralism and the production of culture', in A. Giddens, *Social Theory and Modern Sociology*, Cambridge: Polity: 73–108.

Graves-Brown, P., Jones, S. and Gamble, C. S. (eds) (1995) *Cultural Identity and Archaeology*, London: Routledge.

465

Harris, M. (1969) *The Rise of Anthropological Theory*, London: Routledge and Kegan Paul.

Hawkes, C. (1954) 'Archaeological theory and method: some suggestions from the Old World', *American Anthropologist* 56: 155–68.

Heidegger, M. (1962) *Being and Time*, Oxford: Blackwell.

Herb, H. (1989) 'Persuasive cartography in *Geopolitik* and National Socialism', *Political Geography Quarterly* 8: 289–303.

Hertz, R. (1916) *Death and the Right Hand*, Aberdeen: Cohen and West.

Higgs, E. S. and Jarman, M. R. (1975) 'Palaeoeconomy', in E. S. Higgs (ed.) *Palaeoeconomy*, Cambridge: Cambridge University Press: 1–8.

Hill, J. N. (1970) 'Prehistoric social organisation in the American southwest: theory and method', in W. A. Longacre (ed.) *Reconstructing Prehistoric Pueblo Societies*, Albuquerque: New Mexico University: 11–58.

Hill, J. N. (1972) 'A prehistoric community in Eastern Arizona', in M. P. Leone (ed.) *Contemporary Archaeology: A Guide to Theory and Contributions*, Carbondale and Edwardsville: Southern Illinois University Press: 320–32.

Hill, J. N. and Gunn, J. (eds) (1977) *The Individual in Prehistory*, London: Academic.

Hodder, I. R. (ed.) (1978a) *The Spatial Organisation of Culture*, London: Duckworth.

Hodder, I. R. (1978b) 'Social organisation and human interaction: the development of some tentative hypotheses in terms of material culture', in I. R. Hodder (ed.) *The Spatial Organisation of Culture*, London: Duckworth: 199–269.

Hodder, I. R. (1979) 'Social and economic stress and material culture patterning', *American Antiquity* 44: 446–54.

Hodder, I. R. (1981) 'Introduction: towards a mature archaeology', in I. R. Hodder, G. Isaac and N. Hammond (eds) *Pattern of the Past*, Cambridge: Cambridge University Press: 1–13.

Hodder, I. R. (1982a) *Symbols in Action*, Cambridge: Cambridge University Press.

Hodder, I. R. (1982b) 'Theoretical archaeology: a reactionary view', in I. R. Hodder (ed.) *Symbolic and Structural Archaeology*, Cambridge: Cambridge University Press: 1–16.

Hodder, I. R. (1985) 'Post-processual archaeology', in M. B. Schiffer (ed.) *Advances in Archaeological Method and Theory 8*, London: Academic Press: 1–26.

Hodder, I. R. (1986) *Reading the Past: Current Approaches to Interpretation in Archaeology*, Cambridge: Cambridge University Press.

Hodder, I. R. (1988) 'Material culture texts and social change: a theoretical discussion and some archaeological examples', *Proceedings of the Prehistoric Society* 54: 67–76.

Hodder, I. R. (1989) 'This is not an article about material culture as text', *Journal of Anthropological Archaeology* 8: 250–69.

Hodder, I. R. and Orton, C. (1976) *Spatial Analysis in Archaeology*, Cambridge: Cambridge University Press.

Ingold, T. (1983) 'The architect and the bee: reflections on the work of animals and men', *Man* 18: 1–20.

Ingold, T. (1986) *The Appropriation of Nature: Essays on Human Ecology and Social Relations*, Manchester: Manchester University Press.

Jordanova, L. (1989) *Sexual Visions: Images of Gender in Science and Medicine Between the Eighteenth and Twentieth Centuries*, London: Harvester Wheatsheaf.

Kirch, P. V. (1980) 'The archaeological study of adaptation: theoretical and methodological issues', in M. B. Schiffer (ed.) *Advances in Archaeological Method and Theory 3*, New York: Academic Press: 101–56.

Klindt-Jensen, O. (1975) *A History of Scandinavian Archaeology*, London: Thames and Hudson.

Kossinna, G. (1911) *Die Herkunft der Germanen. Zur Methode Siedlungsarchäologie*, Würzburg: Kabitzsch.

Kroeber, A. (1917) 'The Superorganic', *American Anthropologist* 17: 283–89.

Kroeber, A. and Kluckhohn, C. (1952) *Culture: A Critical Review of Concepts and Definitions*, Papers of the Peabody Museum of American Archaeology and Ethnology 47, Cambridge, Mass.: Harvard University Press.

Lacan, J. (1977) 'The mirror stage as formative of the I', in J. Lacan, *Écrits: A Selection*, London: Tavistock: 1–7.

Leach, E. (1982) *Social Anthropology*, London: Fontana.

Le Goff, J. (1985) 'Mentalities: a history of ambiguities', in J. Le Goff and P. Nora (eds) *Constructing the Past*, Cambridge: Cambridge University Press: 166–80.

Lévi-Strauss, C. (1966) *The Savage Mind*, London: Weidenfeld and Nicolson.

Lévi-Strauss, C. (1968) *Structural Anthropology*, Harmondsworth: Allen Lane.

Lévi-Strauss, C. (1969) *The Raw and the Cooked*, London: Jonathan Cape.

Longacre, W. A. (1964) 'Archaeology as anthropology: a case study', *Science* 144: 1454–55.

Lubbock, J. (1865) *Pre-Historic Times*, London: Williams and Norgate.

Malinowski, B. (1922) *Argonauts of the Western Pacific*, London: Routledge.

Mauss, M. (1954) *The Gift*, London: Routledge and Kegan Paul.

Megaw, J. V. S. and Simpson, D. D. A. (1984) *Introduction to British Prehistory*, Leicester: Leicester University Press.

Miller, D. (1987) *Material Culture and Mass Consumption*, Oxford: Blackwell.

Moore, H. (1986) *Space, Text and Gender*, Cambridge: Cambridge University Press.

Moore, H. (1990) 'Paul Ricoeur: action, meaning and text', in C. Y. Tilley (ed.) *Reading Material Culture*, Oxford: Blackwell: 85–120.

Outhwaite, W. (1985) 'Hans-Georg Gadamer', in Q. Skinner (ed.) *The Return of Grand Theory in the Human Sciences*, Cambridge: Cambridge University Press: 21–40.

Patrik, L. (1985) 'Is there an archaeological record?', in M. B. Schiffer (ed.) *Advances in Archaeological Method and Theory 8*, London: Academic: 27–62.

Patterson, T. C. (1995) *Toward a Social History of Archaeology in the United States*, Fort Worth: Harcourt Brace.

Plog, S. (1978) 'Social interaction and stylistic similarity: a reanalysis', in M. B. Schiffer (ed.) *Advances in Archaeological Method and Theory 1*, London: Academic: 143–82.

Radcliffe-Brown, A. R. (1933) *The Andaman Islanders*, Cambridge: Cambridge University Press.

Renfrew, A. C. (1973) *Before Civilization: The Radio-carbon Revolution and Prehistoric Europe*, Harmondsworth: Penguin.

Renfrew, A. C. (1979) 'Introduction: problems in European prehistory', in A. C. Renfrew, *Problems in European Prehistory*, Edinburgh: Edinburgh University Press: 1–21.

Ricoeur, P. (1981) *Hermeneutics and the Human Sciences*, Cambridge: Cambridge University Press.

Sackett, J. R. (1973) 'Style, function and artefact variability in palaeolithic assemblages', in A. C. Renfrew (ed.) *The Explanation of Culture Change*, London: Duckworth: 317–25.

Sackett, J. R. (1985) 'Style and ethnicity in the Kalahari: a reply to Wiessner', *American Antiquity* 50: 154–59.

Sackett, J. R. (1986) 'Isochrestism and style: a clarification', *Journal of Anthropological Archaeology* 5: 266–77.

Sahlins, M. D. and Service, E. R. (1960) *Evolution and Culture*, Ann Arbor: University of Michigan.

Saussure, F. (1959) *Course in General Linguistics*, London: Peter Owen.

Saxe, A. A. (1970) 'Social Dimensions of Mortuary Practice', Ann Arbor: University Microfilms, unpublished Ph.D. thesis.

Shanks, M. and Tilley, C. (1987) *Social Theory and Archaeology*, Cambridge: Polity.

Shennan, S. J. (1978) 'Archaeological "cultures": an empirical investigation', in I. R. Hodder (ed.) *The Spatial Organisation of Culture*, London: Duckworth: 113–40.

Shennan, S. J. (1989a) 'Archaeology as archaeology or as anthropology? Clarke's *Analytical Archaeology* and the Binfords' *New Perspectives in Archaeology* twenty years on', *Antiquity* 63: 831–35.

Shennan, S. J. (1989b) 'Introduction: archaeological approaches to cultural identity', in S. J. Shennan (ed.) *Archaeological Approaches to Cultural Identity*, London: Unwin Hyman: 1–32.

Sherratt, A. (1989) 'V. Gordon Childe: archaeology and intellectual history', *Past and Present* 125: 151–85.

Slobodin, R. (1978) *W. H. R. Rivers*, New York: Columbia University Press.

Sokal, R. R. and Sneath, P. H. A. (1963) *Principles of Numerical Taxonomy*, London: Freeman.

Sollas, W. J. (1911) *Ancient Hunters and Their Modern Representatives*, London: Macmillan.

Spaulding, A. C. (1968) 'Explanation in archaeology', in L. Binford and S. Binford (eds) *New Perspectives in Archaeology*, New York: Seminar Press: 33–39.

Stanislawski, M. B. (1973) 'Review of "Archaeology as anthropology: a case study" by W. A. Longacre', *American Antiquity* 38: 117–22.

Stanislawski, M. B. and Stanislawski, B. B. (1978) 'Hopi and Hopi–Tewa ceramic tradition networks', in I. R. Hodder (ed.) *The Spatial Organisation of Culture*, London: Duckworth: 61–76.

Steward, J. (1955) *Theory of Culture Change*, Urbana: University of Illinois.

Strathern, M. (1980) 'No nature, no culture: the Hagen case', in C. P. MacCormack and M. Strathern (eds) *Nature, Culture and Gender*, Cambridge: Cambridge University Press: 174–222.

Thomas, J. S. (1996) *Time, Culture and Identity*, London: Routledge.

Thompson, M. (1977) *General Pitt-Rivers: Evolution and Archaeology in the Nineteenth Century*, Bradford-on-Avon: Moonraker.

Trigger, B. G. (1980) *Gordon Childe: Revolutions in Archaeology*, London: Thames and Hudson.

Trigger, B. G. (1989) *A History of Archaeological Thought*, Cambridge: Cambridge University Press.

Veit, U. (1989) 'Ethnic concepts in prehistory: a case study on the relationship between cultural identity and archaeological objectivity', in S. J. Shennan (ed.) *Archaeological Approaches to Cultural Identity*, London: Unwin Hyman: 33–56.

Warnke, G. (1987) *Gadamer: Hermeneutics, Truth and Reason*, Cambridge: Polity.

White, L. (1949) *The Science of Culture: A Study of Man and Civilisation*, New York: Grove.

White, L. (1959) *The Evolution of Culture*, New York: McGraw-Hill.

Wiessner, P. (1983) 'Style and social information in Kalahari San projectile points', *American Antiquity* 48: 253–76.

Wiessner, P. (1984) 'Reconsidering the behavioral basis for style: a case study among the Kalahari San', *Journal of Anthropological Archaeology* 3: 190–234.

Wiessner, P. (1989) 'Style and changing relations between the individual and society', in I. R. Hodder (ed.) *The Meanings of Things*, London: Unwin Hyman: 56–63.

Willey, G. and Sabloff, J. (1980) *A History of American Archaeology*, New York: Academic Press.

Wobst, H. M. (1977) 'Stylistic behaviour and information exchange', in C. E. Cleland (ed.) *Research Essays in Honour of James B. Griffin*, Research Papers of the University of Michigan 61, Ann Arbor: University of Michigan Press: 317–42.

SELECT BIBLIOGRAPHY

As this chapter has hoped to demonstrate, archaeological understandings of culture have been varied and contradictory, so that some breadth of reading is needed to gain a sense of the diversity. Trigger (1989) can be recommended as an overview of the issues concerned, while Harris (1969) provides a wide-ranging if partisan introduction to the anthropological background. Childe (1950), Binford (1962, 1965), Hodder (1978a, 1986) and Barrett (1988) can be taken as statements characteristic of different stages in the development of the debate. The contemporary political significance of ethnic interpretations of past identities is well covered by papers in Shennan (1989b), Graves-Brown *et al.* (1995) and Champion and Diaz-Andreu (1995). The implications of the arguments for gender identities have barely been touched on here, and the reader is referred to Gero and Conkey (1991) as a first step in this direction.

12

THE ORGANIZATION OF SOCIETY

Chris Gosden

INTRODUCTION

The notion of social organization refers to the form, structure and pattern of relationships of people within society, which can include the interweaving of institutions, economic structures, familial or kin organization and position of a local group within the world system existing at the time. One of the most contentious questions asked by archaeologists has been 'what sorts of social forms existed in the past?' This question has been linked to the more pessimistic query 'can we understand past societies on the basis of archaeological evidence?' The fact that no convincing answers exist for either of these questions provides this chapter with a structure. My aim here is to provide an outline of the debates that are taking place at present within archaeology as to our understanding of past social forms and to sketch their historical genesis. I shall divide approaches into four: culture history; functionalist/evolutionary approaches (also known as processual archaeology); Marxist views; and the post-processual/hermeneutic stance (hermeneutics being the study of meaning or interpretation). This division necessitates an exaggeration of the differences between views which overlap on some points, but it will serve to give the flavour of present disagreements.

The term 'social organization' is questionable. Culture historians have often had little use for a general concept such as social organization, preferring to concentrate on the specifics of local cultural form and sequence as they arise from ethnic affinities or diffusion from neighbouring groups. Functionalists spend much time attempting to define sub-systems within society and to measure the nature of their interrelations; such an analytical stance splits the social world in order to see how it fits together, facing the obvious objection that it is the analyst who does the splitting. Marxists employ the idea of social organization, whilst being wary of its mechanistic overtones: power is central, and many positions of power are defined in relation to people's access to the means of production, whether this access is structured through class or kinship networks. Hermeneutic approaches see social forms as symbolic structures which cannot be split into well-defined parts, reacting to the attempts of the analytical method to divide the world and to the feeling that terms like organization make us see society as a mechanism with certain ends or functions, rather than a symbolic structure which creates meanings by which people can live. They highlight the ways in which power relations derive from and make use of differences of gender, age and class in the field of social conflict.

Running parallel with the different views on the nature of society are varying views on social change. Functionalism, Marxism and culture history have a tendency to see change as directional, moving from simple to complex forms of organization. This may be framed in progressive terms, where it is said that complexity is in some ways superior to simplicity: complex societies have greater capacity to process energy or more efficient structures of administration. Or change may simply be seen as teleological: history has of necessity to move from clan- to class-based systems. The notion of prehistory as charting the nature of growth and complexity has come under fire, often by those with hermeneutic interests. Complexity is often judged by our standards, focusing on a greater technological capacity, a greater number of divisions and ranks of society and a greater specialization of tasks. Durkheim's use of an organic analogy underlies much of this thought (Giddens 1978): this compares biological evolution from single-celled organisms to creatures like ourselves with multiple organs with particular functions, to the movement from hunter-gatherer to state systems. The use of the organic analogy, however, ignores the fact that societies may be complex in different ways. Australian aboriginal groups have extremely restricted forms of material culture, but a huge profiferation of kinship and ritual knowledge. If modern–day Sydney were compared to Arnhem Land groups on the basis of complexity of ritual knowledge or kin links there is no doubt which society would look simple and which complex!

Criticism of the teleological structure of much of the argument about past social change (teleological in the sense of history being drawn towards a particular end state) has been extremely useful in opening up the parameters by which we try to understand past societies. But it must also be said that the 'onwards and upwards' view of human prehistory did provide a coherent narrative structure through which to tell the story of the past. In its absence, there is considerable experiment in our approach to past social forms, but no new coherent directions have emerged to replace the old framework.

In addition to the model of society they employ and the view of social change, each approach to past social structure must also look at the nature of the analogies they use between present and past social forms. Here the relationship between archaeology and anthropology is crucial. Over the last 150 years archaeology has drawn upon the findings and approaches within social anthropology and this still continues today. Thus culture history is closely allied to an ethnology which collated information on cultural differences and probed local sequences of change. Functionalism drew on both British social anthropology of the 1920s and 1930s, where Malinowski and Radcliffe-Brown hammered out much of the intellectual apparatus of functionalism, as well as on the evolutionary writings of Leslie White in America (Kuper 1996; Stocking 1987). Hermeneutic views of society are closely modelled on a recent turn to symbolic anthropology. Marxism obviously takes a framework from Marx and Engels but blends this with the work of Morgan, who himself influenced Marx, and French Marxist anthropologists such as Meillassoux, Terray and Godelier (Seddon 1978).

Criticism is necessary not just of the biases of these anthropological sources of inspiration, but also of the special problems with the nature of the archaeological data. The first and foremost of these is the chronological grain of archaeological evidence. For much of prehistory, our minimum unit of analysis is a century, or four human generations, given the imprecision of the radio-carbon method. For the Palaeolithic, we may not be able to define periods of less than one or several millennia (see Chapter 5). Such broad spans of time bring the whole notion of society into question and make it certain that we cannot tackle social structure and change in the same manner as an anthropologist can. Thus we must include in any discussion of past society the differences between anthropological and archaeological data and the re-ordering of our conceptual apparatus that these differences necessitate. Bearing this in mind I shall first present a more detailed discussion of each of the four approaches to past societies, before going on to consider the problems of analogies between past and present and the differences in the nature of archaeological and anthropological data. This general discussion will be followed by examples of particular approaches to past societies which will be used to discuss the larger issues in a more detailed context.

CULTURE HISTORY

In many ways the approach which emphasizes culture history has the least explicit theoretical structure and the least well-defined discussion of the nature of society and social change. The lack of self-consciousness of culture historians derives partly from the fact that this stance was seen to derive out of commonsense views of the world and the division of human diversity into groups and areas. Culture history as found in archaeology is closely connected with ethnology, which from the nineteenth century onwards was concerned with the classification of different groups, customs and material culture known from travellers' tales and the accounts of missionaries and colonial officers. Culture history was both an attempt at classifying cultural and ethnic groups and an emphasis on local historical circumstances in the generation of social forms. Although linked with diffusion as an agent of social change, much change was seen to be generated locally and to have given life a regional flavour overwhelming broader similarities of social groups over space and time. Culture history was thus opposed to comparative studies stressing similarities in the social process over broad areas and time periods.

Gordon Childe was responsible for the most sensitive and directed handling of culture history. In the absence of absolute dating methods, Childe built on the typological schemes of Montelius in order to bring out and order spatial and temporal differences in the archaeological evidence from Europe. These spatial and temporal differences were indications of archaeological cultures, which Childe defined as 'certain types of remains – pots, implements, ornaments, burial rites, house forms – constantly recurring together' (Childe 1929: v–vi). The geographical extent and duration of these cultures had to be established empirically by means of stratigraphy, seriation and controlled comparison (Fig. 12.1). Furthermore, Childe argued that only a small range of artefacts was suitably sensitive to change to be useful in these comparisons. Locally made pots, ornaments and burial rites derived from local tastes were resistant to change. They were consequently useful for defining local cultural groups. Utilitarian items such as tools and weapons diffused rapidly from one group to another if they represented an improvement on previous technologies. The widespread diffusion of utilitarian items provided the means for broad chronological comparisons which created cultural chronologies prior to the invention of radio-carbon dating.

As his career progressed, Childe moved away from the cataloguing of material culture and became more interested in the distinctive features of local sequences and the historical reasons underlying local differences. In particular, he attempted to account for the different destinies of Europe and the Near East (Childe 1928, 1930). Whereas the Near Eastern centres in Mesopotamia and Egypt had enjoyed a head start on their European counterparts in that they had developed farming, pottery, and metallurgy first, along with a political organization based around the state, it was Europe that had been first to the Industrial Revolution. Others, such as Kossinna, working with the concept of archaeological cultures, had ascribed these different histories to properties of blood or spirit: it was the natural energy of the European Aryans that led them to build on the initial advances of the Semites (Trigger 1989: 163–67). Explanations with such racist overtones were abhorrent to Childe, who looked for the answer in the social structure of the respective areas.

Childe saw the development of agriculture in the Fertile Crescent as a crucial turning point in human history. On the basis of the Neolithic Revolution here, he argued, surplus production increased faster than the population and led to a concentration of political power, the rise of city life and progress in industry.

473

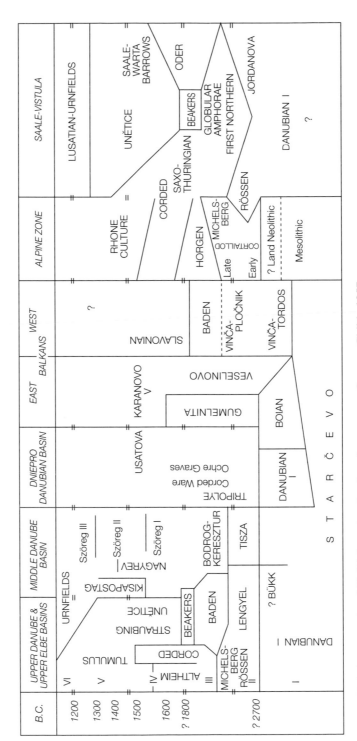

Figure 12.1 An example of Childe's regional cultural sequences. Source: Childe 1957.

Technological knowledge, such as metallurgy, then spread to outlying regions such as Europe as the result of trading surplus food and finished artefacts for raw materials (Childe 1928). Once in Europe, bronze technologies were seen to be undertaken by full-time craftsmen, operating outside the bounds of kinship groups. The smiths, as relatively free agents, broke down previous forms of self-sufficiency and set up long-distance trading networks of raw materials and finished products across Europe. This led to the growth of societies in Europe which were structurally different from those in the Near East. In the latter region the industrial process was directly controlled by the upper classes and much of the product was wasted in conspicuous consumption or military conflict; also, demand for raw materials in surrounding areas reduced the amounts reaching the higher centres. By contrast, in Europe industrial crafts were operated outside the bounds of kinship and individual groups and this encouraged inventiveness and an individual spirit. The looser structure of Europe, not dominated by a theocratic élite, led to continual change and the sturdy individualism in which the Industrial Revolution was eventually grounded (Childe 1930).

I have outlined Childe's ideas in some detail as they are crucial to our understanding of the topic of social organization. Although I have included Childe's work under the heading of culture history, his ideas span pretty well all the approaches I have outlined above. The following features of Childe's scheme are of particular note: although he started off trying to account for the peculiarities of societies localized in time and space, Childe soon moved to broader explanatory frameworks. Basic to these are the three revolutions in productive capacity and social form: the agricultural, the urban and the industrial. Each was predicated on the former, such that city life could only come about once agricultural surpluses enabled some people to live without farming and industrial production developed through the spur to invention provided by city life.

Although Childe felt it necessary to recognize these broad processes at work in the world, he was also sensitive to local time and place, teasing out what was special about Europe. This sensitivity to local conditions and developments derived from Childe's early interest in culture history and is seen by many today as the strongest feature of the cultural historical approach (see Hodder 1986). In his recognition of broad social processes, Childe comes close to more recent processualist and Marxist views on the movement from kin-based to class-based societies, whilst his emphasis on local change and meanings bears comparison with some aspects of the post-processualist approach. The wide span of interests and subsequent influences exercised by Childe makes him a central figure (even *the* central figure, perhaps) in approaches to past society.

Culture history is still the most common mode of archaeology world-wide, concentrating as it does on local social features, whether these be of Slavic groups (Sklenář 1983) or the Polynesians (Bellwood 1980). This popularity is likely to increase with the rise of micro-nationalism in various parts of the world. Although out of favour with elements of archaeology more orientated towards theory, the interest in local distinctiveness and sequence found in culture history may well marry together with recent interests in the links between material culture and ethnicity and the so-called 'contextual archaeology' as developed by Hodder (1986).

FUNCTIONALIST AND EVOLUTIONARY APPROACHES TO SOCIETY

Functionalism and an interest in evolution are not necessarily connected, although over the last forty years in archaeology they have tended to be. Of the two, the evolutionary view is the older approach, going back to the middle of the nineteenth century. Indeed, Childe saw his initial moves towards culture history as a reaction against an older evolutionary view; the development of the notion of culture was closely connected with a view of change based around evolution. The nineteenth-century background needs to be taken into account before we can understand more recent developments.

By the 1860s and 1870s, two sets of influences were developing which helped shape travellers' tales into a nascent ethnography and which from there influenced archaeology. The first was a concept of culture, given one of its clearest expressions by Edward Tylor. The notion of culture was used to tease out general features of all societies which could then be used for comparison between various times and places. 'Culture, or Civilization, taken in its widest ethnographic sense, is that complex whole which includes knowledge, belief, art, morals, law, custom and any other capabilities and habits acquired by man as a member of society' (Tylor 1871: 1). Culture could be investigated on general principles which would reveal laws of human habit and thought. What is most notable about Tylor's use of the term 'culture' is that he always used it in the singular, never in its plural form. Culture was something that all human groups had, although they did not all have it in equal measure: this becomes more obvious when we realize that 'culture' and 'civilization' were equivalent terms for Tylor, some peoples being more civilized than others. The degree of culture could be measured along a scale that ran from savage to civilized:

> the educated world of Europe and America practically settles a standard by simply placing its own nations at one end of the social series and savage tribes at the other, arranging the rest of mankind between these limits according to how they correspond more closely to savage or to cultured life.
>
> (Tylor 1871: 23)

The classification as to high or low development depended first of all on technology and practical knowledge, as well as on the firmness of moral principles and the degree of social organization. It was thus possible to arrive at a ranking of types of society – Australian, Tahitian, Aztec, Chinese, Italian, to use examples Tylor cited – that no one could dispute. Such classifications were not simply of present utility, but could also be used to order the past. By assuming an unchangeable human nature, all social forms from all times and places could be placed in their rank – and judged as to how far they fell short of the Anglo–Saxon pinnacle!

The general notion of social progression evidenced in the work of Tylor was combined by the anthropologist Morgan with more specific ideas on social evolution which took their overall inspiration from Darwin. In his most general work, *Ancient Society* (1877), he presented a historical scheme for social change which ran from savagery to civilization. He divided this history into two lines: that of inventions and discoveries, which was a cumulative history, each age building on the last; and that of institutions, in which change unfolded rather than accumulated. These two lines of history were linked and mutually supporting. As far as institutions were concerned, Morgan made another twofold division between the *gens*, in which personal ties of blood and marriage predominated, and political society, which was founded on territory and property rather than on personal relations. This division between kinship and civil society still provides a framework for understanding change to this day and much recent discussion of the growth of the state focuses on the breakdown of kin-based society.

Morgan combined information from ethnography and historical sources to come up with a global scheme of human change, based on the notion that so-called savage groups around the world preserved in their social forms previous stages in the progressive history of humanity. The very earliest stages of people's spread across the globe were not thought to be preserved today, but there were many examples of a savage way of life. Savages lacked pottery and, by implication, the settled village life which brought progress in the simple arts. Australian aborigines and the Athabascan tribes around Hudson's Bay formed examples of this stage of life and were people who also lacked sophisticated forms of marriage, brothers and sisters often marrying each other. Three stages of barbarism spanned the invention of pottery, the domestication of animals and development of metal working. The upper barbarians were known from the earliest historical sources, which gave details of the Greek tribes at the time of Homer or the Italians before the founding of Rome. These groups mark the boundary of kinship society which had been transcended by the 'Semitic' civilizations of the Near East and subsequently the Aryan city-states and empires of Greece and Rome. These ancient civilizations still contained survivals of kinship life, particularly in the form of the *gens*, which could be discerned even within the city of Imperial Rome.

The fact that all the peoples of the earth exemplify these stages, he argued, demonstrated the unity of origins of humanity. Progression up these stages was powered by technical inventions. Here the barbarian ages were the most important for subsequent progress, with their development of the domestication of plants and animals, which secured the food supply, and the eventual mastery of metals. 'Furnished with iron tools . . . mankind were certain of attaining to civilization' (Morgan 1877: 43). This in turn powered the eventual move from kin to civil society and the parallel changes in family type from the consanguine to the monogamous family. Central to all these moves was the developing notion of private property: once this concept had become a 'controlling passion', civilization had begun.

The comprehensive nature of Morgan's scheme, which tied in technical change with familial and group forms of organization, made it impressive to contemporaries such as Marx and Engels, as well as to people like Leslie White in the subsequent century. Not only was Morgan's scheme of influence, but he also mentioned an extra problem which confronted all subsequent investigators into social change: what sort of evidence can we expect to find of different forms of society? Here his concentration on technical change provided part of the answer. Archaeologists like Lubbock (1912) had taken the classification of artefacts produced by Thomsen, Montelius and Worsaae into Stone, Bronze and Iron Ages and used it as evidence of progressive stages in human history. What Lubbock did not provide was a systematic historical scheme in the same manner as Morgan had done. However, the combination of the classification and implied dating of artefacts which had been carried out in Europe and Morgan's scheme made possible the empirical investigation of social forms through archaeological evidence, which set a direction and standard for all subsequent investigations.

To oversimplify somewhat, it is probably true to say that the early years of this century were more concerned with debates about whether change occurred in human society due to diffusion or local development than with the exact nature of society. The broad schemes of progress in which all human groups past and present could be compared were replaced by local particular histories, emphasizing the rootedness of social life in particular environments and the distinctiveness of individual cultures. The lack of large comparisons meant that less effort was expended on outlining the general features of social organization and social change. Instead, culture history became the fashion, which attempted to explain the coming into being of distinctive local ways of life. Whereas Tylor and Morgan had tended to talk of culture in the singular, a plural view of culture was central to culture history and cultural differences were often seen to parallel ethnic differences. Because cultures were seen as self-generating, little attention was placed on how society was organized and the forces for change. However, in the middle of this century the ideas put forward by Morgan were to emerge to have a considerable influence on archaeology.

This re-emergence was due to the influence of writers such as Leslie White, who opposed the historical particularism of Boas, then dominant in American anthropology (Trigger 1989: 290). White saw himself as establishing a science of 'culturology' aimed to investigate the laws and principles guiding culture. The central element to any culture was its technical means and the form of interaction with the environment. 'Culture advances as the amount of energy harnessed per capita per year increases, or as the efficiency or economy of the means of controlling energy is increased, or both' (White 1959: 56). Due to this stress on energy, social structure was not paid much attention. Culture was seen to have four components: the ideological, sociological, sentimental/attitudinal, and technological (White 1959: 6). These factors were related but by no means equal: 'in the system that is culture, technology is the independent variable, the other sectors the dependent variables' (White 1959: 26). Social evolution was a function of technological development, and the main point to focus on in understanding this development was the organization of society around its technical means.

Many of White's views seem outlandish today and we could ignore them completely were it not for the fact that two of the predominant strands of thought in archaeology which characterized the 1960s and 1970s came into being through his work. The first was the flowering of the idea of society as organization, a notion with definitely mechanistic overtones, many of which derive directly from White. The study of social organization concentrates on how different elements of society (subsistence, craft production, ideology) functioned in order to maintain a society in harmony with its environment. The increased differentiation of the individual sub-systems led to greater specialization of functions by people within society, a more efficient processing of matter and information which was the motor for progress up the ladder from simple forms of organization to complex ones. The second element of White's influence was his stress on broad regularities in human history, which could be summed up in generalizations about how culture worked. These in turn could form a firm basis for the study of society in all times and places, including those of interest to archaeologists.

Processual archaeology

Whilst it is overly simplistic to put the development of processual archaeology down to the influence of one man, White's views coloured the approach taken by many processual archaeologists, especially in America. Such influence did not only stem from White directly, but also came through his students. Sahlins and Service (1960) took White's general scheme of unilinear human evolution, modified it somewhat to take into account slightly different local developments, and gave it more specificity by generalizing from detailed anthropological work carried out since the 1920s. They developed the scheme of social evolution which is still most commonly in use amongst archaeologists today. This began with bands of hunters and gatherers, who existed in small groups with few social inequalities and a simple material culture, and ended with large nation–states whose intensive farming and

479

industry produced a massive material culture, internal differentiation and special-ization of tasks, plus structures of law enforcement to contain the stresses set up by marked social inequalities. Holocene history for many areas of the globe was thus seen as a move from independent, internally undifferentiated bands extracting little energy from the environment, to interdependent, internally differentiated nation-states, with massive energy budgets (Fig. 12.2).

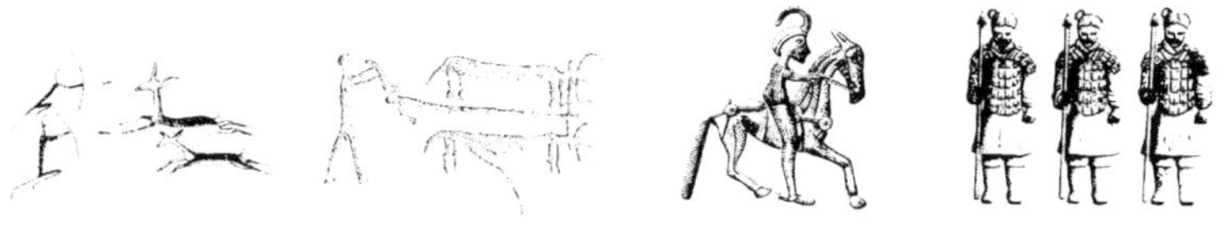

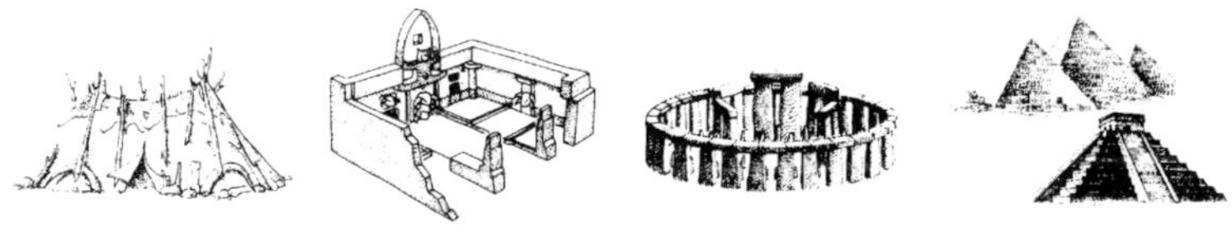

	BAND	SEGMENTARY SOCIETY	CHIEFDOM	STATE
TOTAL NUMBERS	Less than 100	Up to few 1,000	5.000–20,000 +	Generally 20,000 +
SOCIAL ORGANIZATION	Egalitarian Informal leadership	Segmentary society Pan-tribal associations Raids by small groups	Kinship-based ranking under hereditary leader High-ranking warriors	Class-based hierarchy under king or emperor Armies
ECONOMIC ORGANIZATION	Mobile hunter-gatherers	Settled farmers Pastoralist herders	Central accumulation and redistribution Some craft specialization	Centralized bureaucracy Tribute-based Taxation Laws
SETTLEMENT PATTERN	Temporary camps	Permanent villages	Fortified centers Ritual centers	Urban: cities, towns Frontier defences Roads
RELIGIOUS ORGANIZATION	Shamans	Religious elders Calendrical rituals	Hereditary chief with religious duties	Priestly class Pantheistic or monotheistic religion
ARCHITECTURE	Temporary shelters	Permanent huts Burial mounds Shrines	Large-scale monuments	Palaces, temples, and other public buildings
ARCHAEOLOGICAL EXAMPLES	All Paleolithic societies, including Paleo-Indians	All early farmers (Neolithic/ Archaic)	Many early metalworking and Formative societies Mississippian, USA Smaller African-kingdoms	All ancient civilizations e.g. in Mesoamerica, Peru Near East, India and China; Greece and Rome
MODERN EXAMPLES	Eskimo Kalahari Bushmen Australian Aborigines	Pueblos, Southwest USA New Guinea Highlanders Nuer & Dinka in E. Africa	Northwest Coast Indians, USA 18th-century Polynesian chiefdoms in Tonga, Tahiti, Hawaii	All modern states

Figure 12.2 The social typology band to state. Drawn by Simon S. S. Driver, from *Archaeology: Theories, Methods and Practice* by Colin Renfrew and Paul Bahn, published by Thames and Hudson Ltd, London, 2nd edn, 1996.

Building on this scheme, processual archaeology attempted to identify broad processes whereby societies became more complex. Local sequences were often seen not to be important in their own right but as instances of global processes. As a generalization, we can say that whereas culture history was interested in the forces that make societies different, processual archaeology focused on what makes them the same. Living societies could be studied in order to throw light on the past, not for any specific parallels they might offer, 'but rather that the more general *processes* at work today in these small, living societies may serve as viable models for such processes in the past' (Renfrew 1976: 278). Prime amongst these concerns for processual archaeologists has been the spatial structure of past communities, as expressed both in terms of settlement patterns and forms of interaction between groups (Clarke 1977). Exchange and settlement pattern have often been linked together as indicators of the nature of the social structure (Earle and Ericson 1976). Spatial interests have often focused on the growth of élites, living in large central settlements and regulating the flows of material through trade and exchange, such that more of the products pass through the central places than smaller more peripheral settlements (Renfrew and Cherry 1986). The stress on generalizations about the processes at work in human societies also led to changes in archaeological method, in particular an emphasis on field survey (Foley 1981): as human groups live in areas rather than in single sites and it is the structure of habitation in an area that is important, geographically more widespread sets of data were necessary than those offered by excavation.

The functionalist/evolutionary approach seeks out regularities in society through the implementation of reliable and repeatable methodologies. The strengths and weaknesses of the approach both derive from the broad comparative method. The idea that all of human history can be contained in the movement from simple to complex social forms provides a narrative structure within which global comparisons are possible; this in turn provides some means of looking at stable features of human life and the nature of variability between social forms. However, the very terms 'simple' and 'complex', and the cluster of technological and institutional features on which they are based, provide a limited view of human life and its variations. Critics of the processual approach have argued that it dehumanizes the past, relegating most of the characteristics that make us human to what White referred to as 'ideological, sentimental and attitudinal' and giving ancient societies the look of large modern corporations, struggling to minimize the use of material and energy and to maximize outputs (Shanks and Tilley 1987).

Despite the criticisms that have been levelled at processual archaeology, it continues to be a major strand of archaeological thought and research. This is partly because of the large narrative structure composed around the band to state theme, which many still see to have global utility. Despite the criticism that has been made of this theme, no large alternatives have come along to replace it. Indeed, much of the recent history of archaeology has seen a move away from big narrative structures towards a plurality of small schemes. One exception to such a move is Marxism, a growing force in European and North American archaeology over the last twenty years, as well as in countries of the southern hemisphere.

MARXIST APPROACHES TO SOCIETY

Much of the explanation for the causes of social change within the functionalist/evolutionary approach was based around biological pressures, either those deriving from changes in the natural environment or from growth in human populations. Marxism, by contrast, seeks mainly social causes for change, chief amongst which are power struggles between different elements of society be these clan, class or gender. As is well known, Marx himself took a historical view of human society, holding that no point in time could be understood without looking at the social forces which have led up to that point (Marx 1963). He developed a generalized history of modes of production from primitive communism to present-day capitalism. Marx's view of a mode of production was that it was made up of the forces of production, which were the technological means by which society produced the goods it wanted, and the relations of production, which specified the relations between people pertaining to both the division of labour and the division of the items produced. With the exception of the influences from Morgan, Marx paid little attention to modes of production outside those known from the history of Europe. This has left Marxist anthropologists and archaeologists with a series of basic principles pertaining to the process of labour and the social and ideological relations resulting from that process, but little in the way of specific models to apply to non-capitalist societies. Also over the century since Marx died there have been subtle currents within Marxist thought which have subjected principles drawn from Marx to constant criticism and revision.

Out of this multitude of arguments we can isolate two strands of thought which have been influential in anthropology and archaeology. The first debate concerns the relationship of economic forms to other areas of life. As a generalization, it is possible to say that early in this century there was a tendency to economic and technological determinism on the part of Marxist thinkers. Here the division between base and superstructure in society has been vital. The base is seen to be composed of the economic forces of society: the forces and relations of production. These influence the superstructure of society, made up of the social divisions into kin groups or classes and the ideological apparatus or world-view of the group. Those holding to a strict division between base and superstructure see cause flowing in one direction from the forces of production, such that once one can understand these forces all other elements of society become clear.

It is possible to see in the later writings of Childe a form of economic determinism. In his view it was the relatively flexible position that bronze age tinkers held in Europe which led to their inventiveness and the growth of the individual spirit characterizing Europe. Similarly, the economic revolution brought about by the Neolithic sowed the seeds for the eventual birth of the Industrial Revolution. Criticisms of this view reassert the balance between the economy and the rest of society, such that the superstructure is seen to influence the economic structure. Thus the economy can be seen as first amongst equal sets of causes, rather than as a prime mover (Fig. 12.3). In broad terms the move away from economic determinism was instituted by people like the critical theorists of the Frankfurt school, who saw twentieth-century capitalism as moved by ideological forces ranging from Nazi propaganda to advertising campaigns designed to foster mass consumption (Held 1980). Through these influences, Marxism has come to be interested in structures of power, class and gender as well as the symbolic systems maintaining social forms and inequalities.

More recently the work of Althusser, amongst others, has been concerned to provide theory for understanding the links between economic forces and other aspects of society (Althusser 1969). Structural Marxism, as this trend is known, has been influential on the other main area of Marxist thought influencing archaeology. This is contained in the works of anthropologists inspired by Althusser, who gathered empirical evidence of a variety of non-capitalist social forms. Writers such as Meillassoux (1981), Terray (1973) and Godelier (1977) tackled a particular aspect

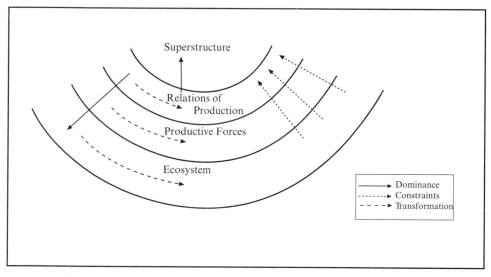

Figure 12.3 Friedman and Rowlands's view of base–superstructure relations. Source: Friedman and Rowlands 1978.

of the base–superstructure problem: what sorts of relations of production are exercised in the absence of classes and how is the control over production translated into social power and standing? One answer given to this problem was that direct control was not exercised over production at all, but that power derived from the control of the flow of high-ranking items of exchange. These in turn were used to control the flow of people in marriage, which had important consequences for the demographic strength of a group. In societies dominated by kinship, the conclusion consequently was that it was the relations of reproduction which were central to the social process, rather than the relations of production.

These ideas had a direct impact on archaeology in the form of the prestige goods model put forward by Frankenstein and Rowlands (1978) and given more general features by Friedman and Rowlands (1978). The former paper looks at the development of chiefdom structures in Europe north of the Alps under the influence of trade from the Mediterranean. Greek and Etruscan items were incorporated into the exchange networks to the north such that the flow of artefacts could be used to control both the movement of locally produced items and of marriage partners. Here again, direct control over agricultural or craft production is seen to be less important than the flow of people in marriage. The Frankenstein and Rowlands paper also fits in with a further strand of Marxist thought: the spatial structure of economic units within a larger whole or 'world system'. This influence derives from the work of Wallerstein (1974, 1980), whose interest was in the growth of capitalism. Wallerstein's main point was that it is impossible to understand the development of capitalism by focusing just on Europe, as many historians had done, and ignoring the rest of the world which contributed raw materials, labour and precious metals to the industrial process. In his view, Europe and the rest of the world were involved in one set of relations which could not be analysed piecemeal, but had to be seen as a global whole, with Europe forming the centre of the world economy and the rest of the world a periphery.

Through the 1970s, archaeologists struggled to reconcile an interest in local development, which had arisen to replace diffusionism, with an interest in trade and exchange as both an indicator and cause of particular social structures. Wallerstein's ideas are attractive in that they allow us to set local sequences of change in a broader social perspective, which includes links between regions through the movement of materials and people. His influence has thus spurred a number of studies of various archaeological periods and places (Rowlands *et al.* 1987). It is instructive to note in passing the difference between the spatial analyses carried out by processual archaeologists and those with Marxist leanings. Whereas the former tend to fix upon the increased efficiencies brought about by centralized coordination, the latter look at the structures of power and the benefits accruing from being in the centre of a world system rather than on the periphery.

There is no obvious dividing line between Marxist and post-processual approaches, the point of contrast lying in the fact that the Marxists tend to concentrate on the notion of society as a whole held together and torn apart by economic and ideological forces, whereas the post-processualists eschew any totalizing models, concentrating instead on the development of smaller narrative structures to examine finer-grained aspects of social life. Both hold in common, however, a growing interest in practical aspects of consciousness. For the Marxist, the concentration on practice derives from a general materialist orientation, whereby it is felt that action shapes the world and creates human beings at the same time. For those with a more hermeneutic viewpoint, practical consciousness intersects with discursive consciousness through which the group makes sense of the world, discursive knowledge being made effective through practice in and on the world. Both Marxists and post-processualists share an interest in the interaction of discursive and practical consciousness, which they see as providing an escape from the social pigeon-holing brought about by the band to state typology. However, the former would tend to stress the practical as the place to start in generating understanding, whereas the latter stress the idea that the world must be conceived of symbolically before it can be acted upon.

Over the past fifteen years, Marxism has opened up archaeological debate to theory and data from outside the discipline, particularly that within Marxist anthropology (see Spriggs 1984). In doing so it has countered the implication underlying much of the work in processual archaeology, that social formations are benign, operating for the general good and able to supply society's wants with increased efficiency and on a larger scale as time goes by. Marxism in both anthropology and archaeology has had to struggle to re-apply theory developed mainly to understand class-based societies to kin-ordered groups. Such a re-application has focused on the reproduction of people as an issue as crucial as the production of things. The application of Marxist theories to archaeology has not always been successful and this is in part because of the relatively limited range of anthropological models drawn upon. Many of these stem from African anthropological case studies concerned with the nature of lineages and closed spheres of exchange. Such cases provide a rather slender basis for global models applicable to kin-based societies everywhere. Nevertheless, Marxist theory continues to be the centre of energetic debate, which often cross-cuts the issues tackled by the last approach to society I have distinguished: post-processualism.

POST-PROCESSUALIST APPROACHES TO SOCIETY

As the name implies, post-processualism originally defined itself through criticizing the processualist approach (Hodder 1982; Shanks and Tilley 1987). The main emphases of the initial critique were on the functionalist and evolutionary orientations of processualism. As I have mentioned above, the post-processualists dislike the mechanistic and totalistic view of society; that is, the view that society could be seen as a whole made of individual parts which functioned together like the engine of a car. Not only was this mechanistic view bad enough, but it was also contained within a scheme which said that social engines became more efficient through time, leading to the latest superior model: the states of modern Europe and the USA.

In attempting to develop a new view of society, post-processualism, like Marxism, drew on areas of theory outside the discipline. The first of these was an intellectual trend which had come and gone: structuralism. Based upon Saussure's methods for analysing language as a structured set of differences (Saussure 1959), anthropologists such as Lévi-Strauss developed structuralist approaches to all human products (Lévi-Strauss 1968). Just as meaning in language derived from the structured differences between words, human culture as a whole – whether systems of myth, habits of dress, building styles or forms of ritual – could be seen as a series of structures for producing meaning. The meeting of nutritional requirements was a necessary, but not a sufficient, condition for life. In order to live and thrive, people need structures of meaning within which they can create a world for themselves.

Several implications flow from such an emphasis on the centrality of meaning to human life. The first is that society is not a series of physical mechanisms for processing matter and information, but a structure of contested meanings through which life is made worth living. The second is that the external world is not straightforwardly and objectively perceived, but rather constructed and reworked in imagination before it is encountered in practical action. People do not adapt to external physical circumstances in a predictable manner, but can conceive of the same set of environmental conditions in quite a different manner depending upon their culturally created views of the world.

Structuralism as such passed away as a force within anthropology before archaeologists became interested in these matters. Nevertheless, the emphasis on meaning and the construction of the world stayed on as lasting effects. Social forms were not simply seen as the creators of meaning beneficial to everyone. Meaning and power were closely connected; here, the work of Foucault was influential (Miller and Tilley 1984). Foucault (1980) held that power is the ether in which the social world exists; it encompasses everything. Individuals and groups are constantly striving to maintain and enhance their position within the world in a struggle of each against each. Power is not simply repressive, in this view, but the creative spring from which derives all movement. Our position within the world determines how we see and explain the world. It also influences how we try and convince others of our views. Those in positions of dominance have greater scope to develop a wide ranging view, to hem in the meanings of others and to arbitrate as to which meanings are socially permissible and which not. Power and discourse are intimately linked in a to-and-fro motion of dominance and resistance.

Ritual is a point of concentration for many post-processual studies, as it is felt that ritual is a crucial vehicle for creating meaning, but also an area where active contests of power take place. Ritual may mask social inequalities rather than highlight them. For instance, Shanks and Tilley's (1982) study of neolithic tombs in Britain and Sweden looks at how disarticulated human bones are grouped in tombs in a manner which shows distinctions between the left and right sides of the body, the upper versus the lower limbs and the trunk as against the limbs. Although there may have been conflicting groups in life, for instance the lineage heads versus the bulk of people doing the work, these contradictions are hidden in death where all bodies are treated in the same manner according to complex sets of oppositions between body parts. A sophisticated symbolic scheme acted to hide quite simple inequalities.

The hidden nature of much social practice is a recurring theme of post-processual attempts to understand society. One of the major areas which has remained hidden is that of gender relations. Recently explicit attempts have been made to uncover gender relations in the past (Gero and Conkey 1991). The investigation of gender challenges a number of assumptions, prime amongst which is the idea that we have an ahistorical human nature which provides the same well-spring of action in all periods. Countering this is the view that all elements of the human personality are the product of history: we are part of a changing network of relations which shape us. Gender, in this view, is not based in biological differences between the sexes but is rather a changing product of the manner in which men and women relate to each other. Gender is not a static innate quality, but is historically engendered. Furthermore, as Conkey and Gero (1991: 3) point out, archaeology has worked with implicit notions of gender which have highlighted activities associated with men, such as hunting and stone tool knapping. Conkey and Gero state three major aims of their book: to expose gender bias in all phases of archaeological enquiry from its assumptions and concepts to the nature of the acceptable evidence; to find women in archaeological contexts and to identify their role in gender relations; and to criticize underlying assumptions about gender and difference (Conkey and Gero 1991: 5). A central feature of the detailed investigations of the book is a concentration on the division of labour in past societies and how far this was structured by relations of gender. The discussion on gender links in with more generalized discussions of agency and how far individuals and groups can be discerned as the agents through which social structures are reproduced (Shanks and Tilley 1987: ch. 3).

Recent trends within post-processual thought have brought archaeology into line with current discussions within other disciplines. Radical questioning of all our premises is the aim here. The very categories of society – social structure, the individual and the author of archaeological works – have been called into question (Bapty and Yates 1990), following streams of thought deriving from Nietzsche and Derrida. A radical questioning of all current assumptions opens the field to many possible ways of approaching the past. Where, how and whether these will crystallize into new directions is unclear at present.

Post-processual views have, of course, not escaped criticism, chief amongst them being the extent to which we can understand meaning, ritual, gender and individual agency on the basis of the archaeological record. There are a number of issues here which take us to the heart of the archaeological endeavour. The first is that question that I have not so far raised: is a social archaeology of any sort possible? There are those who believe it is not. Higgs and Jarman (1975) put forward the view that, over the long term, social and cultural forces are irrelevant: what matters is people's adaptation to the environment over periods of millennia, which is based on etho-logical forces shaping us as a species. A similar view is put forward by Bailey (1981), who feels that long-term processes, which are mainly to do with the relationship between people and the environment, will show up well in the archaeological record, whereas shorter-term processes, which are mainly social in nature, will be much more difficult to perceive. A counter view has been advanced by Bradley (1991), who notes that many elements of social and cultural forms change extremely slowly, emphasizing continuity, rather than rapid change. Long-lasting elements of social life such as style and ritual may well show up in the archaeological record: in some instances, in fact, social forces may be more visible than short-term fluc-tuations in the environment which may structure people's forms of subsistence. The attempts by both Bradley (1991) and Hodder (1990) to identify and explicate long-term social trends in the archaeological record from Europe go a considerable way to meeting the objections of those who say that social forces only operate on the short term.

PROBLEMS WITH USING THE PRESENT TO UNDERSTAND THE PAST

One feature that all attempts to understand prehistoric societies share is that they draw on our knowledge of the present to interpret the past. Since the nineteenth century, Europeans have been fascinated by social forms unlike their own. Ameri-can, African, Asian or Australian societies were of interest, not simply due to their strangeness but rather for the light that strange customs could throw on 'modern' European ways of life. As anthropology crystallized into a discipline in the late nineteenth century, the search was initiated for pristine forms of society which could best exemplify states and stages of human development. Once understood, these groups could say something about us and our origins: the morals, customs, institutional and technical forms of the western world could be thrown into sharp relief by the things that they were not. Observations of other societies were not made at random or left unsynthesized, they were incorporated into narrative structures through which tales were told about the world. As Fabian (1991) has noted, these structures generally had a moral purpose: anthropology's practice was one of

> incorporating strange, disquieting cultures and, indeed, our traumatic confrontations with these cultures (such as discovery, conquest, colonization) into *narratives of cultural evolution*, that is, narratives of fulfillment ... these topics were selected and treated such that they served to explain, and often legitimize, the modern state of affairs. The important thing in tales of evolution remains their ending.
>
> (Fabian 1991: 193)

As we have seen, the categorization of society into band, tribe, chiefdom and state, which derives from the last century, has been used to structure prehistory and the social changes which took place from the Palaeolithic to the present. Ironically, although various social forms could be lined up to form a global history, individually most social groups were seen not to have a history of their own. The 'simpler' societies in particular were seen to represent pristine examples of their type and thus to exemplify general features of such social forms everywhere: Tongan chiefdoms could then be used as templates for the groups that built Stonehenge. Although recent moves in archaeology have attempted to discard evolutionary schemes, the use of parallels between past and present goes on, such that neolithic groups in southern Britain now often look more like Madagascans than Tongans, as parallels are drawn from more theoretically informed anthropology.

There are two points which are objectionable here. The first is the aspect Fabian alluded to, whereby Europeans fit the societies of the world into a comfortable structure culminating in their present ways of life. The second is the notion that some social forms do not have a history and are thus ripe for comparative purposes, where a moment's thought will show that all societies studied by anthropologists have had a recent calamitous history due to their contact with colonial powers and that the latter forms the latest chapter in each group's local history (Wolf 1982). The encroachment of the modern world system has led to depopulation, enslavement and ecological disaster, as well as forms of resistance to these processes which have had their own social effects. Thus although Europeans have been fascinated by survivals from past times, no group has ever lived outside a web of historical connections which were undergoing a process of constant change.

The groups seen least likely to have histories are hunter-gatherers, with their low levels of technology and lack of pronounced social inequalities, two of the main motors of history. During the nineteenth century, many Europeans viewed hunter-gatherer groups in places like Malaya, Borneo and the Philippines as relict populations displaying ways of life which had vanished elsewhere due to the incursions of farming groups. Modern ethnographers tend to take a different view. Rather than seeing forest-dwelling groups as being living fossils keeping palaeolithic traditions alive into the modern era, these groups are seen as having a particular position within a 'world system' that came into being some 1,500 years ago.

Hoffman (1984) provides the most explicit presentation of this view and argues that the Punan of Borneo were once farmers who now live in the upper forested reaches of river valleys in a close symbiotic relationship with their farming Dayak neighbours who live at the coastal ends of the valleys. The Punan supply forest products (resin, birds' nests, camphor, rattan, rhinoceros horns and so on) to the Dayaks, and more especially into trading networks which transport these items to China. The Punan have positioned themselves in the rain forest for historically specific reasons, Hoffman argues, responding to Chinese demands for forest products by specializing in their supply, a form of trade which may go back to the middle of the first millennium AD when the first trading empires were set up. Hoffman (1984: 144–45) feels that many, if not all, the nomadic groups of south-east Asia may be designated as secondary hunters and gatherers, people who gave up farming to exploit a new set of social and economic opportunities. This example could be multiplied endlessly, showing for instance that the 'Big Men' societies of Papua New Guinea may well have altered in fundamental ways in the last century or less.

There are different reactions to the realization that all groups in the world have a recent history and a prehistory of their own. Marxist thinkers accept the fact of history, but try to pick out well-documented instances of recent history to illuminate the prehistoric past. Thus much of the Frankenstein and Rowlands model of the contact between Mediterranean city-states and groups north of the Alps is based on contacts between the Portuguese and West African groups from the fifteenth century onwards. Post-processualists also acknowledge history, but see past and present as radically different. No parallels can be drawn between groups known from recent history and those evidenced by archaeology. This relativist stance is modified in practice by the use of general ideas to do with the legitimating functions of ritual, or even more generalized notions such as 'habitus' (a set of bodily dispositions to action – Bourdieu 1990) and practice drawn from anthropological writings.

In many ways the major problem facing anthropology and archaeology concerns notions of history and generalization. Since the debates between evolutionists and culture historians, the question has been posed: how far can we pick out general features of society which can be used for widespread comparisons and how far can each society only be understood in its own terms? Neither of the extreme reactions of unthinking comparison or total relativism is a viable option. And we are still faced with the problem as to which aspects of society we can discuss in generalized terms and which not. There is no end in sight to this debate, nor will it go away. All I have been able to do here is to highlight the problem without proposing even the glimpse of a solution.

In the rest of this chapter I offer some brief case studies to illuminate in a more concrete manner the general debates that I have outlined above.

PALAEOLITHIC STUDIES

The Palaeolithic poses some of the 'big questions' that have fascinated the European mind: what were our ultimate origins, what features make us human, how are we related to the rest of the biological world and what sort of history do relations of sex, gender and inequality have in the deep past? I cannot possibly attempt to tackle all these topics here, but will pick out contrasting approaches to the same material which exemplify the four stances on social archaeology I have identified (see also Chapters 18 and 20).

One of the most famous debates concerns the meaning of Mousterian assemblages. Here two approaches, the culture-historical and the processual, can be clearly contrasted as represented respectively by the opinions of Bordes and Binford (Fig. 12.4). Cave sites in south-west France such as Combe Grenal and Peche de l'Aze yielded layers with a series of tool types dating to the Middle Palaeolithic. Bordes (1973) divided these tools into five variants based on a complex classification and analysis of the tool morphologies, interpreting them not as an evolutionary sequence but as evidence of distinct cultural groups moving in and out of the area at various times. This movement explained why the tool types were found interleaved with each other, not in a succession from one type to another. Binford, whilst accepting Bordes' typology of tools, argued that the variation in the Mousterian assemblages is a reflection of different tasks carried out by the same group at different sites or at the same site at different times of the year (Binford 1973). He supplemented his archaeological analysis by looking at the structure of life of mobile people existing in the present, such as Australian Aboriginal groups and Alaskan Inuit. Because the energy and materials necessary for life were differentially distributed across the environment, people would have to move in order to exploit these. Patterns of movement were basically structured by the form of the environment, so what was needed to understand the archaeological record was, first of all, a series of principles specifying how people used the landscape, which could be derived from the present-day models, and second, a further series of principles laying out the processes by which the archaeological record was created.

The idea that the structure of energy and matter within the environment is the main shaper of hunter-gatherer life has been generalized over recent years into what is known as the global hunter-gatherer model (Gamble 1986: 34–39). The basis for this model is that there is a differential distribution of energy through the world's ecosystems, with a decrease in productivity away from the equator. As the ways of life of hunters and gatherers are thought to be patterned around the

491

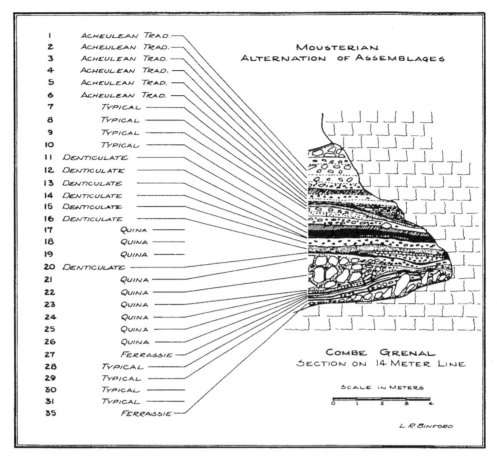

Figure 12.4 Archaeological section from the Mousterian site of Combe Grenal in France, illustrating alternating assemblages. Source: Binford 1983. With permission of Thames and Hudson.

availability and distribution of resources, the decrease in productivity with increased latitude is seen to be of considerable significance: in general terms, groups nearest the equator are most dependent on plant foods, those furthest away on animals or fish. Storage of the relevant foods is also dependent to a degree on latitude. As the length of the growing season shortens and the hunting of large mammals and fish (which may only be available for a short season) becomes more important, then storage of the resulting produce is given greater emphasis. Storage is linked with mobility, in that high mobility is found in equatorial environments with abundant but dispersed resources. Sedentary strategies are most common in boreal and temperate forest areas. Finally, technology is at its most complex in highly seasonal environments, where resources only come on stream for short

492

periods of the year. Technology has to be of sufficient complexity to ensure success. This imperative influences both the sophistication of the equipment used and the thought and planning that goes into its use.

These generalizations were arrived at by looking at known cases of hunter-gatherer groups around the world today and ignore the fact that these people have a particular set of recent histories, which may not make them good exemplars of the groups found in the Palaeolithic. Such a model emphasizing responses to the environment also plays down the nature of cultural and social perceptions of the physical world, which may in turn structure the strategies used to gain a living and the social uses to which food is put (Chapter 18). On the positive side, the global hunter-gatherer model has provided the basis for understanding the fluctuations in response to the changing environments of the Pleistocene.

A significant milestone in the study of the nature of palaeolithic society was Isaac's attempts to probe the origins of human behaviour in some of the earliest fossil records (Isaac 1978). Looking at the early evidence from East Africa, he argued that central foci on the landscape would have formed an essential component of foraging patterns. He envisaged a division of labour by gender, with the males foraging for meat and the females for plant food, the groups combining at a 'home base' for the sharing of food, places which would also have provided the locus for the care of young and other maintenance activities. The model has been widely discussed and criticized, the main point of much criticism being that the combination of bones and stone tools may be evidence not of central foci of activity but simply of the points on the landscape at which carcasses were butchered (Potts 1984). Potts has argued that an efficient way of exploiting carcasses would be to cache stone tools and move the animals to the tools, the accumulations of stone and bone soon resembling the Plio-Pleistocene archaeological sites. Caching of stones has been observed amongst chimps and these sites demonstrate patterns of behaviour linking hominids to other animals, in contrast to Isaac's view of them as evidence of the elements that make us distinctively human. While by no means conclusive, these arguments demonstrate the power that the palaeolithic evidence has to stimulate thought on the bases of human life and society.

No better demonstration of this can be found than in the recent explorations of gender relations in the Palaeolithic. Many have made the general point that, on the basis of ethnographic analogies, the plant food gathered by women contributes more to the diet of the group than the meat hunted by men: the term 'gatherer-hunter' ought to be employed and the nature of models of the Palaeolithic, which are often based around male activities, should be reviewed (Bender 1978). Also, the nature of gender as a category is being held up to question and its historical transformations probed.

Conkey (1991), for example, has attempted to identify the contexts of life in the Magdalenian phase of the Upper Palaeolithic in which gender may have been at work. Her main focus is large aggregation sites which contain a record of groups larger than the household, and she notes that a feature of attempts to create an order beyond the household are that age and sex differences are played upon. Gender relations are thus a prime structuring principle in the network of social relations. These relations also use material culture as an active and constituting medium and not as a passive vehicle for attaining utilitarian ends. Gender relations can then be sought in material culture. She gives the example of the site of Cueto de la Mina, a rockshelter and a small cave excavated in 1904 situated 1.8 km inland from the Bay of Biscay. It contains evidence of a multitude of activities including engraving bone and antler tools, working sea shells, processing vegetation, working hides, the butchering and processing of animals. The resources collected in the cave came from the coast, woodlands and the plains; a journey of several days would have been necessary to obtain some of these items.

Conkey does not offer specific gender attributions in analysing tasks, but instead attempts to provoke thought in two directions. The first is to question the gender attributions that have been made for artefacts found at Cueto de la Mina. Some 200 pieces of worked bone and antler were recovered from the site, some of which have been seen as harpoons used for male hunting practices, but she raises the possibility that the holes and barbs on these objects could have been used for cordage, producing sets of lines for nets and ropes (Conkey 1991: 76). As well as the critique of the unconscious bias towards identifying male activities, Conkey looks at the chains of activities that may have been carried out at the site and the forms of organization lying behind them. She points out that, at any point in time, dozens of people may have been coming and going at Cueto de la Mina engaged in a range of tasks, which would have necessitated a partitioning of people, labour, and space. In addition, tasks would have interlocked, such that the products of one set of activities would have supplied raw materials for another. Technologies are not merely means to exploit the environment, but derive from culturally embedded conceptual frameworks. Artefacts are not simply raw material for classification or evidence of production, but can show us how streams of activity are embedded socially and the relations set up during these activity streams.

The weakness of her study is that she offers no concrete analysis of the abundant archaeological materials, but – like many post-processual archaeologists – she is trying to provoke questions rather than provide answers. This is such a new strategy of thought in archaeology that it will take some time for it to be accepted, but as a means of getting to grips with intractable problems it has obvious attractions. We can say that gender is not rooted in biology and that any assumptions we make about gender roles 17,000 years ago will simply reflect our own society and its world-view, such as that men engage in technical tasks such as tool making and dangerous tasks such as hunting. Once these views have been questioned, there is nothing immediately to replace them with. One reaction is to say that gender relations in the Palaeolithic are not amenable to archaeological analysis. Another is to follow Conkey's strategy of opening up the area to thought without necessarily providing answers or methods for finding answers. This is a courageous move and in line with general attempts within feminist thought to eschew easy answers and linear trains of thought. Gender provides an area of questioning that is likely to destabilize many areas of archaeological thought. It is easy to predict that gender as a topic will provide an arena for heated controversy in years to come.

PACIFIC PREHISTORY

Pacific prehistory forms one of the strongholds of culture-historical thought within archaeology. This may well be because the ethnological impulse to classify cultural differences still has considerable influence on attempts to understand divisions that are often made in the present. When the Dutch established themselves in the Spice Islands of Indonesia during the sixteenth century, they placed an embargo on trade voyages entering the area from the east. As a consequence, the boats of other nations, such as the Spanish, French and British, who carried out the majority of the European exploration of the Pacific, entered that ocean from the east. The peoples they first encountered there became known as the Polynesians, whom the European explorers tried to fit into their view of the world. The Polynesians were often seen as a 'nation' of one ethnic group and from the first there was speculation as to their origins. In 1831 the French explorer Dumont d'Urville divided the Pacific into four ethnic blocks (Fig. 12.5): Polynesia (many islands), Micronesia (small islands), Malaysia (island south-east Asia) and Melanesia (black islands). This emphasis on the Polynesians was reinforced by the fact that much of the early archaeology of the Pacific was carried out in Polynesia, primarily in New Zealand and Hawaii.

Kirch and Green (1987) demonstrate the modern approach to culture history in this region. They begin by noting that Polynesian groups in the present share a physical type, systemic cultural patterns and historically related languages, allowing them to be grouped as a 'substantive segment of culture history'. As these traits are traced back in time they are seen to converge, until they can be localized in a small group in a restricted area: Tonga, Samoa, Uvea and Futuna. Archaeologically speaking, this early group is manifest through the Lapita culture, which can be glossed as 'ancestral Polynesian society'. Lapita sites span the period between 3,500 and 2,000 years ago, and are found from the Bismarck Archipelago to Tonga and Samoa. The Lapita sites display a range of material culture, most striking of which is fine dentate-stamped pottery (pottery with decorations made with a toothed stamp), but which also includes the first well-developed shell industries so characteristic of Pacific life, chipped and polished stone, evidence of marine exploitation

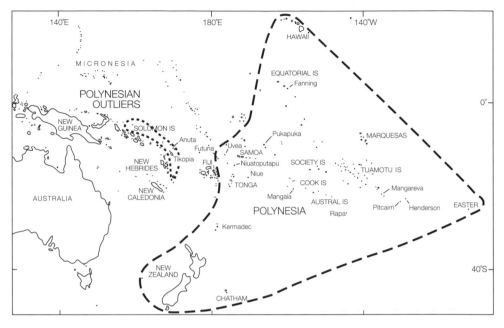

Figure 12.5 Polynesian societies within Oceania. Source: Kirch and Green 1987.

and a horticultural subsistence base. It was an eastern sub-group of the Lapita culture as a whole which is seen to be the foundation for Polynesian life. The ultimate origin of the Lapita cultural complex is seen in this model to lie in south-east Asia, the homeland of the Austronesian languages spoken by the Polynesians. The Lapita group thus migrated out of south-east Asia about 3,500 years ago, settled for a while in Melanesia on which it had no ultimate cultural effect, before moving on to meet its destiny in Polynesia. Moving forward in time from this founding movement, culture history linked to an evolutionary framework can look at how individual Pacific islands have diverged from the founder culture through environmental influence, differential demographic pressure and the social processes of colonization (Kirch and Green 1987).

Such a developmental sequence has a teleological structure which attempts to catch the Polynesians in the process of becoming. It ignores the fact that many of the features associated with the Polynesians today may be of relatively recent origin. For instance, the Tongan kingdom, one of the exemplars of chiefly society used in the band to state model, appears only to have come into existence in the last few hundred years. Before that, life may well have been radically different in terms of cultural forms and social hierarchy. A Pacific prehistory centred around the Polynesians also places Melanesia firmly on a lower evolutionary rung, the conduit of the

Lapita culture between its south-east Asian origin and its Polynesian flowering. It also reinforces a distinction reminiscent of Lévi-Strauss's division between 'cold' and 'hot' societies, with the 'Big Man' societies of the Melanesians possessed of less dynamism than the chiefdom societies of the Polynesians.

Studies of contact history in the Pacific have opened up the possibility that many of the social forms witnessed today may have been radically altered through the process of colonization and the nature of indigenous resistance (Sahlins 1985; Thomas 1991). To seek their origins in the deeper prehistoric past is to pursue something that was never there. An approach such as Sahlins's, which focuses on the cultural logics underlying Pacific social action and history, opens up the possibility of more sensitive forms of culture history, able to examine local sequences in terms of patterns of praxis and the cultural foundations of such practice. Archaeology has yet to make use of such a scheme for understanding the rich sets of material culture available from the recent and prehistoric periods in the Pacific.

HISTORICAL ARCHAEOLOGY

The most pressing social questions are those closest to us in time. Historical archaeology sets out to understand the unfolding of the world economy over the last few centuries on the basis of material culture. The process of colonization is tackled in a critical manner by those in former colonies such as the USA, Canada, Australia and New Zealand, whilst in Europe the centre of interest is the industrial process which derived raw materials and labour from Europe's world connections (see Chapters 28 and 29). Wallerstein's scheme of core and periphery commonly provides a general framework for such investigations, although no syntheses on the scale of Wallerstein's original work have as yet derived from historical archaeology (Paynter 1982; Wallerstein 1974, 1980). The process of European expansion brought with it considerable cultural mixing and contact, both between Caucasians and aboriginal inhabitants of the continents colonized and also with other groups, such as Asians, who moved in complex patterns of their own through the colonial world. It is no surprise, then, that issues of ethnicity, class and inequality are common themes in historical studies. As the effects of colonial history still shape the world in which we live, the issues debated within historical archaeology flow into broader streams of political debate over the rights of indigenous peoples and the exact and often bloody nature of the colonial encounter. Much could obviously be said on such topics, but space precludes detailed discussion here (see McGuire and Paynter 1992 for a recent survey of such issues). Instead, I have chosen a single example which will bring out some of the quirkiness of the colonial process and display in miniature a number of the issues tackled within historical archaeology.

Port Essington was a short-lived settlement in tropical northern Australia, close

497

to the present-day city of Darwin. Port Essington was not occupied for long (1838–49) and represents the best known of the aborted European colonies in nineteenth-century Australia. However, the excavator has argued that Port Essington should be regarded not as a failed settlement but as a strategic manoeuvre within a wider political game (Allen 1973). Halfway between its two nearest British neighbours in Singapore and Sydney, some 4,000 km from each (Fig. 12.6), Port Essington represented the only white settlement of the time on the northern coast of Australia. Its position and military nature demonstrate the role the site played in maintaining British sovereignty in a region of strategic importance, which might otherwise have been challenged by the French, Dutch or even the Americans.

The settlement was inhabited almost entirely by marines, there being few convicts or free settlers. The site was on a headland which had defensive advantages and was protected by a gun emplacement and small defensive earthwork. Excavation and historical documents revealed that the settlement was composed of a series of living quarters for officers and men, including a government house for the commander, as well as a kitchen, hospital, a smithy, store, bakehouse and a number of other facilities intended to make the settlement as self-sufficient as possible. Allen sees the colony not just in global strategic terms, but as a microcosm of frontier colonial society. The archaeology and the documentary evidence reveal a small, predominantly male, society living in extreme isolation in inhospitable conditions. As such, Port Essington forms an exemplar of the situations which gave rise to Australian legends of sport, mateship and drinking. The evidence also tells of social division and severe hardship, which receive less emphasis in later legends: nearly a quarter of the inhabitants of Port Essington died of malaria during the life of the settlement, but no estimate can be made of the deaths in nearby aboriginal groups from introduced diseases. There is archaeological evidence, in the form of middens close to the settlement with flaked glass in them, that personal relations between the white colonists and aboriginal groups may have been quite good by the standards of the time. However, even in the absence of much premeditated violence, white presence in the area brought disruption and death to the original inhabitants to an unknown degree.

The archaeology contains evidence of internal divisions and original links to far distant homelands. The men lived in huts with reed walls and thatched roofs with earth floors, while the officers occupied more substantial quarters built on piles which saved them from termite damage. After 1839, when a typhoon destroyed the settlement, building was started in brick, using the products of a brickmaker whose ship had been wrecked in the typhoon. At this time, brick cottages were built for the enlisted men with families by Cornish masons, who included chimneys constructed in typical Cornish style using techniques that can be traced back to the medieval period. The artefacts used on the colony were almost all of British manufacture, travelling from London to Sydney and then to north Australia. The artefactual

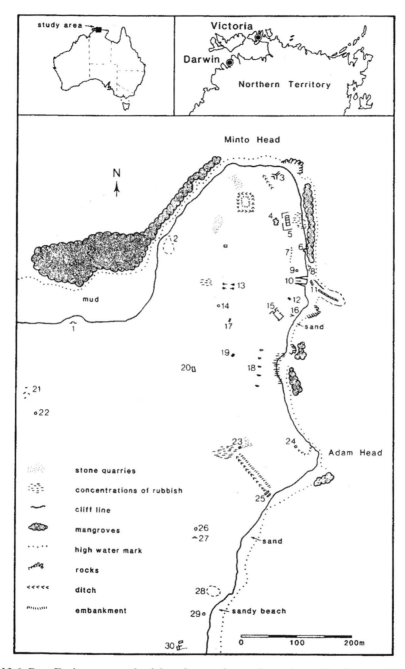

Figure 12.6 Port Essington, a colonial settlement in northern Australia. Source: Allen 1973, Fig. 1.

499

suite gives an insight into the productiveness of British industry at this time, supplying colonial outposts large and small all over the world. Datable artefacts from the excavation also show the speed at which new styles reached the settlement, there being little lag between the introduction of new types in Britain and their appearance in Port Essington, one of the most isolated points of the Empire.

This example illustrates how archaeology provides a grain and quality of evidence that contemporary documents do not. Study of material culture can show people trying to create a world for themselves with known dimensions, either through importing the latest materials or by drawing on folk traditions of construction and manufacture. Similar forms of accommodation were necessary for aboriginal groups, who found their familiar environment drastically altered by the entry of whites and the social fabric of the group under threat. The tensions created by new relations between black and white were played out all over the Australian continent from 1788 onwards, leaving a legacy that contemporary Australia is still attempting to come to terms with. Part of the process of understanding relations between black and white in the present derives from a comprehension and recognition of the nature of the history of those relations. Here, a socially oriented historical archaeology has a vital part to play.

CONCLUSION

In general terms, attempts to understand society on the basis of the archaeological record have oscillated between an emphasis on broad processes and a concentration on fine details. Such a to-and-fro motion has played itself out since the evolutionary schemes of the nineteenth century were replaced by culture histories, being repeated again in the last fifteen years as post-processual archaeology has staged a critique of the global history of processes created by the New Archaeology from the 1960s onwards (see Chapter 2). At present it seems unlikely that such oppositions will either disappear or cease, although the exact directions in which social archaeology is heading are difficult to discern.

A second ongoing argument in which there may be more sign of resolution is over whether social archaeology is possible. As we have seen, a common criticism of attempts to understand past societies has been that social processes are by their nature short term and thus are obscured by the coarseness of the archaeological record. Recent emphases on the long-term nature of social processes by Bradley (1991) and Hodder (1990) have stressed the idea that archaeologists may be able to pick up long-term continuities in human societies beyond the ken of other social sciences. We are not, therefore, condemned to practising 'ethnography with a shovel', but can attempt to define and discern levels of social history unfolding over centuries and millennia. Such attempts at long-term history involve not only empirical investigation but also a criticism of the categories we bring to the understanding of society. Notions such as gender, species and ethnicity are mainly derived from our life in the here and now, and may not be appropriate to understanding the long term. For instance, we are used to thinking of gender relations as being worked out in the home or the workplace, and find it hard to conceive of how gendered social structures may unfold over hundreds and thousands of years. We may well question attempts to use the idea of gender in this way, arguing that to see long-term continuities in gender structures may be a means of justifying and naturalizing present inequalities by highlighting the fact that they have a long history resistant to change.

The nature of past society will remain the most controversial area of archaeology as it connects so closely with present-day controversies. In a century which has seen our broad cosmologies break down, archaeology has often been used to orientate our world-views, as evidenced by the proliferation of films and novels set in the prehistoric past. There is much at stake when a discipline can contribute to a society's sense of itself. This is especially true when social divisions lead to different and conflicting interpretations of the past, as they do in each and every area of the world (see Chapter 10). Many of the ideas presented in this chapter derive from white, male, academics living in wealthy areas of wealthy nations. These facts could not help but colour the views of society which have been put forward. With an ever larger number of professional archaeologists drawn from different backgrounds of race, class and political attitude, it is inevitable that differing views of society will proliferate. The challenge of the next few years will be to find a language within which to present and debate competing pictures of society which does not prejudge the issues in advance of the debate. How far the narrative structures through which we presently discuss past societies make such an open debate possible remains to be seen.

REFERENCES

Allen. J. (1973). 'The archaeology of nineteenth century British imperialism: an Australian case study', *World Archaeology* 5 (1): 44–51.

Althusser, L. (1969) *For Marx*, London: Verso.

Bailey, G. (1981) 'Concepts, timescales and explanations in economic prehistory', in A. Sheridan and G. Bailey (eds) *Economic Archaeology*, Oxford: British Archaeological Reports (International Series) 96: 97–117.

Bapty, I. and Yates, T. (eds) (1990) *Archaeology after Structuralism*, London: Routledge.

Bellwood, P. S. (1980) 'The peopling of the Pacific', *Scientific American* 243 (5): 138–47.

Bender, B. (1978) 'Gatherer-hunter to farmer: a social perspective', *World Archaeology* 10: 204–22.

Binford, L. (1973) 'Interassemblage variability – the Mousterian and the "functional argument", in A. C. Renfrew (ed.) *The Explanation of Culture Change*, London: Duckworth: 227–54.

Binford, L. (1983) *In Pursuit of the Past*, London: Thames and Hudson.

Bordes, F. (1973) 'On the chronology and contemporaneity of different palaeolithic cultures in France' in A. C. Renfrew (ed.) *The Explanation of Culture Change*, London: Duckworth: 217–26.

Bourdieu, P. (1990) *The Logic of Practice* (translated by R. Nice), Cambridge: Polity Press.

Bradley, R. (1991) 'Ritual, time and history', *World Archaeology* 23: 209–19.

Childe, V. G. (1928) *The Most Ancient East: the Oriental Prelude to European Prehistory*, London: Kegan Paul.

Childe, V. G. (1929) *The Danube in Prehistory*, Oxford: Oxford University Press.

Childe, V. G. (1930) *The Bronze Age*, Cambridge: Cambridge University Press.

Childe, V. G. (1957) *The Dawn of European Civilisation* (6th edition), London: Routledge.

Clarke, D. (1977) *Spatial Archaeology*, New York: Academic Press.

Conkey, M. W. (1991) 'Contexts of action, contexts of power: material culture and gender in the Magdalenian', in J. M. Gero and M. W. Conkey (eds) *Engendering Archaeology*, Oxford: Basil Blackwell: 57–92.

Conkey, M. W. and Gero, J. M. (1991) 'Tensions, pluralities and engendering archaeology: an introduction to women in prehistory', in J. M. Gero and M. W. Conkey (eds) *Engendering Archaeology*, Oxford: Basil Blackwell: 3–30.

Connah, G. (1988) *Of the Hut I Builded: The Archaeology of Australia's History*, Cambridge: Cambridge University Press.

Earle, T. and Ericson, J. (1976) *Exchange Systems in Prehistory*, New York: Academic Press.

Fabian, J. (1991) 'Of dogs alive, birds dead, and time to tell a story', in J. Bender and D. E. Wellbery (eds) *Chronotypes: the Construction of Time*, Stanford: Stanford University Press: 185–204.

Foley, R. (1981) 'Off-site archaeology: an alternative approach for the short sited', in I. Hodder, G. Isaac and N. Hammond (eds) *Pattern of the Past: Studies in Honour of David Clarke*, Cambridge: Cambridge University Press: 157–85.

Foucault, M. (1980) *Power/Knowledge* (edited by C. Gordon, translated by C. Gordon, L. Marshall, J. Mepham and K. Soper), New York: Harvester Wheatsheaf.

Frankenstein, S. and Rowlands, M. (1978) 'The internal structure and regional context of early Iron Age society in south-western Germany', *Bulletin of the Institute of Archaeology* 15: 73–112.

Friedman, J. and Rowlands, M. (1978) 'Notes towards an epigenetic model of the evolution of "civilization"', in J. Friedman and M. Rowlands (eds) *The Evolution of Social Systems*, London: Duckworth: 201–76.

Gamble, C. (1986) *The Palaeolithic Settlement of Europe*, Cambridge: Cambridge University Press.

Gero, J. M. and Conkey, M. W. (eds) (1991) *Engendering Archaeology*, Oxford: Basil Blackwell.

Giddens, A. (1978) *Durkheim*, London: Fontana/Collins.

Godelier, M. (1977) *Perspectives in Marxist Anthropology*, Cambridge: Cambridge University Press.

Held, D. (1980) *Introduction to Critical Theory: Horkheimer to Habermas*, London: Hutchinson.

Higgs, E. S. and Jarman, M. (1975) 'Palaeoeconomy', in E. S. Higgs (ed.) *Palaeoeconomy*, Cambridge: Cambridge University Press: 1–7.

502

Hodder, I. (ed.) (1982) *Symbolic and Structural Archaeology*, Cambridge: Cambridge University Press.

Hodder, I. (1986) *Reading the Past*, Cambridge: Cambridge University Press.

Hodder, I. (1990) *The Domestication of Europe*, Oxford: Basil Blackwell.

Hoffman, C. L. (1984) 'Punan foragers in the trading networks of southeast Asia', in C. Schrire (ed.), *Past and Present in Hunter Gatherer Studies*, Orlando: Academic Press: 123–49.

Isaac, G. (1978) 'The food-sharing behavior of protohuman hominids', *Scientific American* 238: 90–108.

Kirch, P. V. and Green, R. C. (1987) 'History, phylogeny and evolution in Polynesia', *Current Anthropology* 28: 431–56.

Kuper, A. (1996) *Anthropology and Anthropologists*, London: Routledge.

Lévi-Strauss, C. (1968) *Structural Anthropology*, Harmondsworth: Penguin.

Lubbock, J. (1912) *Pre-historic Times* (6th edition), London: Williams and Norgate.

McGuire, R. H. and Paynter, R. (1992) *The Archaeology of Inequality*, Oxford: Basil Blackwell.

Marx, K. (1963) *Economic and Philosophical Manuscripts* (translated by T. Bottomore), New York: F. Ungar.

Meillassoux, C. (1981) *Maidens, Meal and Money: Capitalism and the Domestic Economy*, Cambridge: Cambridge University Press.

Miller, D. and Tilley, C. (eds) (1984) *Ideology, Power and Prehistory*, Cambridge: Cambridge University Press.

Morgan, L. H. (1877) *Ancient Society*, Tucson: University of Arizona Press (1985 edition).

Paynter, R. (1982) *Models of Spatial Inequality*, New York: Academic Press.

Potts, R. (1984) 'Home bases and early hominids', *American Scientist* 72 : 338–47.

Renfrew, C. (1976) *Before Civilization*, Harmondsworth: Penguin.

Renfrew, C. and Bahn, P. (1996) *Archaeology: Theories, Methods and Practice* (2nd edition), London: Thames and Hudson.

Renfrew, C. and Cherry, J. (eds) (1986) *Peer Polity Interaction and Sociopolitical Change*, Cambridge: Cambridge University Press.

Rowlands, M., Larsen, M. and Kristiansen, K. (eds) (1987) *Centre and Periphery in the Ancient World*, Cambridge: Cambridge University Press.

Sahlins, M. D. (1985) *Islands of History*, Chicago: University of Chicago Press.

Sahlins, M. D. and Service, E. R. (eds) (1960) *Evolution and Culture*, Ann Arbor: University of Michigan Press.

Saussure, F. de (1959) *A Course in General Linguistics*, New York: Philosophical Society.

Seddon, D. (1978) *Relations of Production*, London: Frank Cass.

Shanks, M. and Tilley, C. (1982) 'Ideology, symbolic power and ritual communication: a reinterpretation of neolithic mortuary practices', in I. Hodder (ed.) *Symbolic and Structural Archaeology*, Cambridge: Cambridge University Press.

Shanks, M. and Tilley, C. (1987) *Social Theory and Archaeology*, Oxford: Polity Press.

Sklenář, K. (1983) *Archaeology in Central Europe*, Leicester: Leicester University Press.

Spriggs, M. (1984) *Marxist Perspectives in Archaeology*, Cambridge: Cambridge University Press.

Stocking, G. (1984) *Functionalism Historicized*, Madison: University of Wisconsin Press.

Stocking, G. (1987) *Victorian Anthropology*, New York: The Free Press.

Terray, E. (1973) 'Classes and class consciousness in the Abron Kingdom of Gyaman', in

503

M. Bloch (ed.) *Marxist Analyses and Social Anthropology*, London: Malaby Press: 85–135.

Thomas, N. (1991) *Entangled Objects*, Cambridge, Mass.: Harvard University Press.

Trigger, B. G. (1989) *A History of Archaeological Thought*, Cambridge: Cambridge University Press.

Tylor, E. B. (1871) *Primitive Culture*, New York: Gordon Press (1974 edition).

Wallerstein, I. (1974) *The Modern World System, I*, New York: Academic Press.

Wallerstein, I. (1980) *The Modern World System, II*, New York: Academic Press.

White, L. (1959) *The Concept of Cultural Systems*, New York: McGraw-Hill.

Wolf, E. R. (1982) *Europe and the People Without History*, Berkeley: University of California Press.

SELECT BIBLIOGRAPHY

There is no one book which adequately surveys approaches to prehistoric society. An extremely important general account of trends within archaeology is contained in Trigger (1989). Between them, Stocking (1987) and Kuper (1996) provide a good overview of the history of anthropology. Clear programmatic statements of the various positions distinguished here are given by V. G. Childe (1957) *The Dawn of European Civilisation* for the culture historical approach, by C. Renfrew (1984) *Approaches to Social Archaeology* (Edinburgh: Edinburgh University Press) for the processualist stance and by I. Hodder (1986) for some elements of post-processualism. The essays gathered together in Spriggs (1984) give the best single volume overview of the themes tackled by Marxist archaeologists. An enlightening debate on processual and post-processual archaeology by many of the major participants is contained in *Norwegian Archaeological Review* 1989, volume 22 (1). The most recent and varied reading derives from the post-processual school. Notable titles include the first concerted attempt to develop a feminist approach to archaeological data by Gero and Conkey (1991) and efforts to include Nietzsche and Derrida within archaeological discussions by Bapty and Yates (1990), plus a range of mainly historical archaeological studies in McGuire and Paynter (1992). Major case studies include Hodder (1990), who tries to identify long-term symbolic structures in Europe from the Palaeolithic to the end of the Neolithic, and R. Bradley (1990) in his *The Passage of Arms* (Cambridge: Cambridge University Press), where he examines the deposition of hoards over a number of millennia from the Neolithic to the Iron Age. J. Barrett (1994), in *Fragments from Antiquity* (Oxford: Blackwell), also provides an influential case study within a post-processual framework.

13

SETTLEMENT AND TERRITORY

John Bintliff

INTRODUCTION

In 1970 Vita-Finzi and Higgs published a challenging and entirely novel proposition for the archaeological community; namely, that human communities
throughout history and prehistory practised territorial behaviour in regard to their
exploitation of landscapes. We were thereby offered an exciting new methodology
for research in the delineation and analysis of such territories – Catchment Analysis
(Vita-Finzi and Higgs 1970). Throughout the 1970s, many scholars adopted the
technique in widely separated countries around the world, not least a generation
of researchers based in the home of this 'palaeoeconomy' approach, Cambridge
University. However, during the 1980s and into the early 1990s only limited
publications have appeared in which territorial theory has been employed by
archaeologists, despite a continual growth in interest amongst cultural anthropologists. The reasons for the limited success of the approach are varied, but can
broadly be ascribed to philosophical and technical difficulties.

During the late 1960s and the early 1970s, archaeology in the West was revital-
ized in both practice and theory by the impact of New or Processual Archaeology,
associated with a proliferation of new ideas and methods. Challenging approaches
from ecology were just one strand in this burgeoning of new concepts (Clarke 1972:
6–7, 46–47). By the early 1980s, however, there had occurred a critical redirection
of archaeological theory away from processualism into structuralism (Hodder
1982b) and later forms of post-processualism (Hodder 1986). In contrast to the
development of theory in related disciplines with a far larger research community
such as geography, history and social anthropology, new directions in archaeological
theory during this century appear to be associated with the displacement and

rejection of earlier theoretical systems, rather than with the cumulative growth of a spectrum of complementary or alternative approaches (Bintliff 1986).

Central to post-processualism is philosophical idealism, which diverts research attention from forms of human behaviour shared with the rest of the animal kingdom towards a supposedly unique capacity for humans to create the world around them. This, some critics say, takes the study of human communities in the direction of an anthropocentrism which is pre-Freud, pre-Darwin and even pre-Galileo. Effectively it has certainly taken human ecology as a variant of general ecology out of the attention of most archaeologists, although contemporary concern about the Earth's resources and our future as an element in world ecology are at a high level of public awareness. In fact this shift towards idealism in archaeological theory and that of all other human-centred disciplines has far more to do with contemporary economics than world ecology (Bintliff 1991, 1993, 1995).

If it can be argued that ecological approaches, especially Catchment Analysis, have been neglected in archaeology for a priori reasons since the later 1970s, we can also identify intrinsic, technical, problems which have prevented a wider recognition of the major potential of such a methodology and hindered its general acceptance as a tool of settlement archaeology. Fundamentally, it must be admitted that after the pioneer paper by Vita-Finzi and Higgs, only limited modifications were made to the theory of human territoriality in archaeology, leaving a growing number of weaknesses and criticisms unresolved and even unanswered by its practitioners.

It is not the purpose of this chapter to seek to restore human ecology to its proper role as a major focus of archaeological interest, but it *is* intended that it should resolve outstanding problems with territorial analysis and thereby provide a firm foundation for the latter's general application to ancient settlement systems.

HUMAN TERRITORIES: THE DEVELOPMENT OF A METHODOLOGY AND CRITIQUES

In the initial publications of Site Catchment theory, Vita-Finzi and Higgs and colleagues were able to cite a limited body of observations from ethnography and human geography (such as Chisholm 1962: 73, 142ff.) in support of 'quanta' in human territorial size which could provide the basis for the operation of territorial research in the field. Thus it was suggested that hunter-gatherer settlements might be associated with territories of up to a 10-kilometre radius from the home base, pastoral herder sites with some 7.5-kilometre radius of territory, and farming communities with a 5-kilometre territorial radius. The fundamental explanation for such regularities lay in the related principles of least effort and land rent: as members of a human community travel out into the landscape surrounding their residential base, the work they can accomplish in food procurement declines with increasing distance due to time lost in return travel. With the increased productivity per square kilometre of landscape made possible through the adoption of domestic animals, and even more so through the discovery of cereal cultivation, the large size of hunter-gatherer territories was reduced in societies with a predominantly pastoral and agricultural economy, since smaller areas closer to the settlement both offered equivalent quantities of food and required more intensive labour that could not be diluted through time-consuming travel.

From an admittedly slim number of empirical observations, the Cambridge palaeoeconomy group suggested that a global average of human walking-time of some 5 kilometres an hour would allow archaeologists to set territorial radii for sites in each of the three main economies (hunter-gatherer, pastoral and cereal farmer) at a 2-hour, 1.5-hour and 1-hour distance respectively from the settlement. In practice (Jarman *et al.* 1972), practitioners of catchment analysis had soon realized that map distance for walking-times of 2, 1.5 and 1 hour varied according to physical relief: thus on a completely flat plain without a major river crossing, one might walk as much as 7 kilometres in an hour, whereas in very rugged hill country the same time would find one as little as 2 to 3 kilometres as the crow flies away from the settlement. In most cases the deviation between map distance and walking time is not great, and many case studies have continued to use compass-drawn radii for boundary definition. For detailed work, however, it is clearly advisable that walking-time provides the more exact measure of catchment radii.

Proceeding from the delimitation on a map of these circular boundaries, the catchment analyst would plot the distribution of varying land classes, topographic details, vegetation and water resources within the territory so defined, so as to 'read the mind' of those past settlers who located their residences in order to exploit these particular resources. Not only would one expect to discover that the overall bounded territory was especially favourable for the needs of that past community, but a further consideration of the underlying principle of the friction of distance would suggest that, even within the territory, those resources to be given most attention or demanding most labour would be found closest to the home base. Thus it was predicted that the evaluated contents of the bounded territory would be found to be unusually rich in those resources exploited by the past community, compared with their distribution in the region as a whole (for example, conditions favouring the proliferation of wild plants and animals, grazing opportunities for domestic animals, fertile soil for cultivated crops). Furthermore, following the model of von Thünen, the ancient settlement might have been surrounded by a series of land use zones, up to the territorial boundary, all concentric around the residential focus, with those subsistence activities demanding most labour being practised in the innermost zones, and the least demanding economic activities being carried out in the outermost zones.

507

A fundamental criticism of territorial analysis takes issue with the central assumption that past human communities have adapted their behaviour to ecological principles, either intuitively or consciously. Confronted with the apparent ethnographic evidence for territoriality, the response has been to cite alternative case studies where human settlements appear irrationally sited for economical use of the landscape, and where 'uniquely human' needs are dominant over ecological pressures (social factors, ritual factors, and so on).

It is certainly the case that territorial analysis deliberately confines its sphere of operation to those past settlements where it is believed that the majority of the inhabitants were concerned with food production from local resources, and excepts sites of an essentially military, cult, industrial, or commercial character. None the less, in the pre-industrial world only a tiny fraction of settlements will not have been predominantly located for exploiting the food resources of their immediate environment, still leaving vast scope for catchment analysis. This criticism is only valid if it can justify the claim that essentially food-producing settlements could be located *without primary concern* for access to areas in the landscape vital for their economy.

Examination of supposedly ecologically irrational settlement systems tends to reveal sound ecological principles. Two examples will suffice. Ian Hodder (Hodder 1982a; Hodder and Orton 1976) cited Jackson's survey of studies on African cultivators, where quite often the village site is surrounded by an extensive zone of the poorest agricultural land, beyond which lies far better soil. In fact a close study of the relevant case studies (Bintliff 1981) revealed that the reason for this situation was prolonged, intense, cultivation of the area closest to these villages in a landscape with naturally poorly developed soils, resulting in soil impoverishment. This society practised a cyclical relocation of villages onto fresh soils when land exhaustion reached a critical level, in a pattern of shifting agriculture. In other words, this example serves rather to reinforce the principles underlying catchment analysis.

A second example concerns the Nuba of the Sudan, whose farming villages lie along very poorly resourced ridges, avoiding fertile valley land below (Hodder 1982c: 127ff.). Essential to our full understanding of this settlement 'preference' is the fact that the valley land has become occupied by a different ethnic group which has driven the indigenous people into marginal hill locations for their livelihood. The ecological archaeologist, provided that his or her dating methods allow the inference that these two settlement systems are contemporary and complementary, will be less concerned with the question of why the hill culture does not occupy the plains, than with understanding how and why the marginal lands sustained settlement by a different cultural group. There is, none the less, a genuine point to learn from here, in that a given community may find itself forced to make a livelihood in a particular environment, rather than having the luxury of an empty landscape and total choice. Military pressure from more powerful cultures is one factor in history;

another, perhaps commoner, factor is the cyclical occupation of marginal lands resultant from pressurized population overspill out of more fertile heartland environments.

The lesson for catchment analysis is, however, a minor caveat: the researcher must extend the range of questions asked of a particular settlement location beyond the usual one of 'why did people choose this spot?', to include 'if this spot was a settlement focus, what are the advantages and limitations of its territory?' In a sense, both these questions are directed to the unchanged central aim of catchment analysis, which is to evaluate the way that – intentionally or otherwise – a given site location will be intimately related to the economic practices of that settlement's inhabitants. The way that microclimate, topography, soil types, and grazing potential are distributed within the territory, and how these factors vary with distance from the settlement, are critical considerations for the demographic history of the community and the economic options taken, regardless of whether the settlers chose to locate here or were forced to make a living from that spot.

A FLEXIBLE MODEL OF TERRITORY

Hunter-gatherer societies that survive today, or which survived until recently, exploit on average larger territories and have lower-density populations than either predominantly pastoral or predominantly arable communities. Yet there is a striking range of behaviours consistently associated with the density and predictability of hunter-gatherer resources, although recent research modifies environmental determinism by showing how communities culturally select their range of resources before adapting to the latter's parameters. A minority of hunter-gatherer groups lives in particularly prolific resource zones (for example, the north-west Pacific coast) where food is especially abundant, predictable, and spatially very concentrated: such unusual circumstances overlap with the resource potential available to communities practising herding and farming of small landscapes.

Dyson-Hudson and Smith (1978) argue from a wide range of such examples that the nature, scale, and importance of territory to a human group vary systematically with the properties of key resources available to and/or selected by the group as central to its economy (Fig. 13.1). Where resources are neither concentrated nor very predictable (Mode B), the human group will exhibit little or no systematic territorial behaviour. The group will be very mobile and exploit a very wide and annually or seasonally variable range of landscapes, heading opportunistically for the most favourable resource zones each season. Since the latter will shift across the countryside, characteristic relations with other human groups will be open and unaggressive. There are no 'hot spots' of high resource potential worth laying preferential claim to as a territorial focus, and shared access between groups to a

509

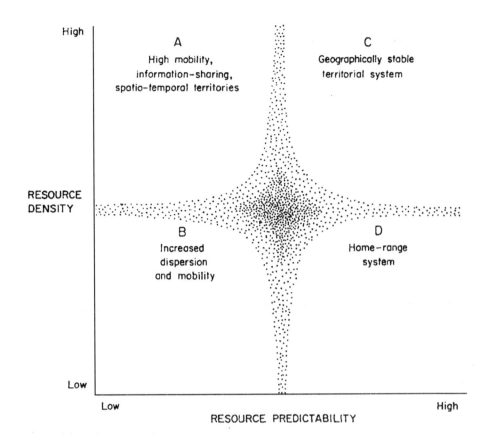

RELATIONSHIP BETWEEN RESOURCE DISTRIBUTION AND FORAGING STRATEGY.			
Resource Distribution	*Economic Defendability*	*Resource Utilization*	*Degree of Nomadism*
A. Unpredictable and Dense	Low	Info-sharing	High
B. Unpredictable and Scarce	Low	Dispersion	Very high
C. Predictable and Dense	High	Territoriality	Low
D. Predictable and Scarce	Fairly low	Home ranges	Low-medium

Figure 13.1 Model for the creation of human territoriality. Reproduced by permission of the American Anthropological Association from *American Anthropologist* 80: 1, March 1978. Not for further reproduction.

wide area of low-density resources is a policy of most benefit to the individual group. Families may shift residence between groups to increase adaptiveness.

In Mode A, the predictability of resources remains low but their occurrence is now localized into 'hot spots'. For the human groups concerned, this still requires a wide-ranging annual territory, and the precise location of key localized resources remains uncertain from season to season. It therefore continues to be infeasible to try and appropriate blocks of landscape as a preferential group territorial focus. On the other hand, key resources are focused into small areas, even though their position cannot be predicted. The required behaviour will be high mobility around a large landscape, and information-sharing between groups enabling a general concentration on 'hot spots' at certain times of the year.

Mode A already contains the seeds of a more sedentary and localized behaviour within the landscape. In Mode D, resources are found in low-density form but now with great predictability across the landscape. This still means that a human group needs potential access to a wide territory each year, but the requirement of inter-group shared access is obviated by the assurance that many distinct areas of each region have a reliable productivity. Under such circumstances, it is argued that each human group assumes preferential access to a particular district, its 'home-range', whilst foraging wider alongside other groups to complement and buffer over-dependence on the home-range. In the Australian Aborigine system, even the home-range can be used by other groups with the permission of the 'owners'; that is, if extremely severe years do not cause a critical reliance on the home-range.

Finally, Mode C represents the behaviour of human groups where resources are both highly predictable and very dense. Here cooperation and open access to the wider landscape are replaced by a systematic close tie between each group and a specific area; here resources are adequate for that group's flourishing and are sufficiently localized to sustain a behaviourally limited form of exploitation, perhaps from a single point of sedentary life central to the territory. Outsiders have little or no access to this narrow territory.

The sequence B–A–D–C is a trend of increasing behavioural focusing and territoriality. At one end of the spectrum, human groups can have fluid membership and no specific attachment to particular areas of landscape; at the other, the human group can become largely endogamous, with a fixed membership and economic behaviour highly localized on a territory largely or wholly claimed by the group for itself. In essence, we may expect the sequence broadly to mirror the behavioural implications of the increase in productivity achieved by the adoption of domestic plants and animals, and later by increases in economic productivity per acre occasioned by innovations such as the Secondary Products Revolution, animal traction and the plough (for both, see Sherratt 1981), developed bronze metallurgy and the spread of iron-working (Bintliff 1984, 1997). In the case of prehistoric Europe, from Palaeolithic to Mesolithic, then to Neolithic, Copper and Bronze Ages into the consecutive phases of the Iron Age, we would expect human behaviour on average to have become more territorial and more localized.

A second figure from anthropological case studies (Fig. 13.2) demonstrates how

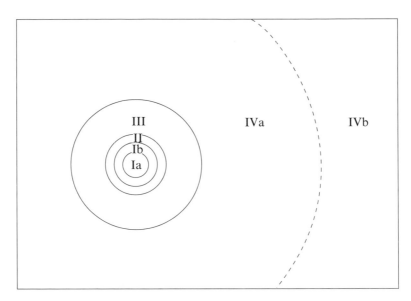

Figure 13.2 Concepts of radial territoriality in south-east Arabia. Ia: permanent cultivation (tree crops); Ib: permanent cultivation from less reliable base flow (alfalfa); II: seasonal crops; III: village grazing and sown land; IVa: mixed-herding nomads; IVb: camel-herding nomads. Source: Wilkinson 1983.

the entire range of minimal to maximal territorial behaviour may be found in a single historic landscape, in this case the traditional Middle East (Wilkinson 1983). In the centre of this district of south-east Arabia is a fertile oasis with perennial, abundant, irrigation water and highly intensive garden agriculture (Ia); its fields are privately owned and jealously guarded from outside access, whilst residence remains close to the resource and movement to subsistence activity minimal within the small zone concerned. Immediately concentric are other zones used by the sedentary village, but where water availability is less secure: in turn, permanent fodder crops, then seasonal crops (Ib and II) yield to village grazing (III). Formally delimited holdings and restricted family access are transformed into more communal, shared, access along this axis. Beyond this block of highly productive land use, significantly characterized by its exploiters as the 'sown' lands, lie the 'desert' lands, where water availability and average productivity drop to a low level and where extensive forms of land use are the rule, with flexible area use by year, season and month. Even here there is a distinction between the less arid and more vegetated sheep–goat zone (IVa) and the extremely arid camel-grazing zones (IVb), accompanied by a difference in the concept of grazing rights.

In summary, the total spectrum of land use here, conditioned primarily by the remarkable contrast within small distances in productive natural resources, creates a parallel spectrum of territorial behaviour, in which strictly private and spatially well-defined territory is modified by the other end of the behavioural spectrum to almost non-existent territorial behaviour as regards use of camel-grazing in the inner deserts. Notably, however, critical wells within the desert zone form miniature replicas of the oasis effect, as their rareness and predictability cause 'islands' of extreme territoriality to emerge in and immediately around them. We might consider the Arabian case to exemplify the broad trend from least-intensive forms of hunter-gatherer land use to most-intensive forms of commercial agriculture, and to represent to us the main lines of the development of territorial behaviour in world economic prehistory and the history of rural life.

HUMAN TERRITORIES: FROM STATIC TO DYNAMIC MODELS

A more consciously constructive critique of catchment analysis to that of Hodder, which will offer us a springboard for a thorough reworking of the approach, can be found in that masterly textbook of mature New/Processual Archaeology – Kent Flannery's (1976) *The Early Mesoamerican Village*. Central to Flannery's contribution to territorial analysis is his case study of the early maize-farming communities along the Atoyac Valley in the north-eastern district of the Oaxaca Valley (Fig. 13.3).

The first thing to note is that the settlement system along the valley can be understood dynamically, providing us with invaluable insights into changing attitudes to inter-site spacing and hence catchment boundaries. The earliest settlement is that of San José Mogote in the valley centre, significantly in one of the most fertile locations where the valley bottomlands are unusually broad. We cannot estimate its original catchment by internal evidence, in the absence of neighbours, but we might reasonably speculate that most of its subsistence activities will have lain within a classic 5-kilometre or 1-hour radius (T1). Some confirmation for this stems from the second phase of farming settlement in the valley, when two new hamlets (Sta. Marta Etla and T. Largas) are established upstream and downstream of Mogote, plausibly by colonization from the founder village. As Flannery shows, the three farming hamlets of this stage are so regularly spaced as to imply a 5-kilometre radius territory for each (T2).

In a third stage of settlement evolution, a further two hamlets are established in the valley, but this time they are positioned exactly intermediate to the existing three hamlets. Once again Flannery suggests that these represent population overflow from the existing hamlets, and illustrates how the implied territorial network has been transformed into a rather exact series of 2.5-kilometre radius catchments (approximately half-hour territories) (T3). There is in fact one final stage of new foundations, where very small foci appear within some of these territories,

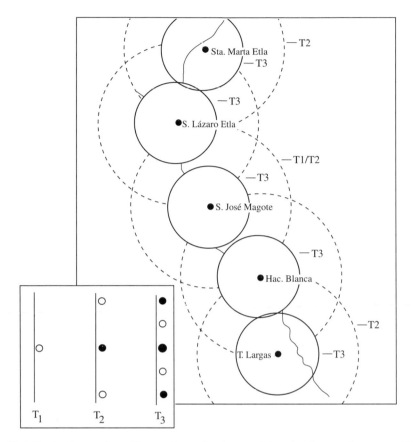

Figure 13.3 Early Formative villages along the Atoyac River in the north-eastern Valley of Oaxaca (Mexico); catchment circles with radii of 2.5 kilometres (solid line), 5 kilometres (dashed line). Inset: idealized model of settlement evolution along the Atoyac River during three temporal phases. Source: Flannery 1976.

apparently close satellites of the main settlements. It is also significant that, whereas Mogote exhibits a continual population rise until it represents the 'central place' for the valley, the other four main settlements remain as small hamlets for upwards of a thousand years, suggesting that their half-hour interval network approximates to a kind of long-term stability.

Flannery's thoughtful discussion demonstrates a dynamic development of territory size, so that we may conclude that the 5-kilometre farming radius may operate in certain settlement scenarios, such as pioneer farming 'infill' situations, but not others, with mature 'filled' farming landscapes stabilizing into 2.5-kilometre radius catchments. It also raises an unexpected but crucial difficulty: given that the Atoyac valley settlements are located to give prime access to the most important local

514

resource – the fertile valley bottomland, for maize agriculture – how much territory is required to feed the estimated population of the five major settlements?

All but Mogote are argued to have been quite small hamlets of less than a hundred people, and their chief needs would have been met by a very small area of alluvial land indeed. Even Mogote at its peak was probably not straining the alluvial land's productivity within its 2.5-kilometre radius territory. It is therefore undeniable that the initial 5-kilometre radius and even the later stable 2.5-kilometre radius cannot arise from an area of land required by these settlements for intensive land use: they appear to have far more territory than they really need.

Flannery's solution is to shift discussion away from resource control towards social factors. When Mogote colonizes the valley with daughter settlements, the intervening distance is not economic but 'social'; the same must hold for the subsequent division of territory to provide discrete territories for the next group of daughter hamlets. Groups leaving older hamlets settle near their relatives, but maintain a greater separation in space than simple land use economics require, for reasons to do with their evolving social organization. Flannery does not offer any additional information about how these social factors operate, and it rather appears that this is a tentative suggestion to replace the seeming inadequacy of simple environmentalism. As we shall see later, social factors do indeed have a fundamental role to play in the establishment of village networks like that in the Atoyac valley, but there are more plausible ways to account for regularities in settlement spacing and associated territory size which remain within the realm of functional economic behaviour.

It is important to remind ourselves that case studies of settlement networks in many different parts of the world reveal a similar propensity for evolving community patterns to settle into regular spacings. In what follows, I shall narrow our focus onto pre-industrial mixed farming societies. Do we find that such systems repeat the ideal maxima of catchment analysis, or dynamic 'nested' patterns as in the Atoyac valley?

Dennell and Webley's (1975) neolithic Bulgarian *tell* villages show a tendency to crystallize into territories of some 3–4 kilometre radius, relatively stable over more than a millennium (inter-site distance is 5–6 kilometres, but the territories are asymmetric to the *tells*). In a very different area and time period – ninth-century AD Brittany – plentiful historic sources show an established village pattern (*plebes*) with a consistent inter-site distance indicating territorial radii of 3–4 kilometres (Davies 1988; Fig. 13.4); however, during high medieval and early modern times, parish numbers almost doubled, giving average radii of 2–3 kilometres. In early medieval Holland, settlement territories have been inferred with a 2.5-kilometre average radius (Heidinga 1987). In high medieval northern France, a typical village territory was 2.5 kilometres in radius (Pounds 1974: 188), whilst contemporary English village parishes cluster into two groups: early 'heartland'/secondary

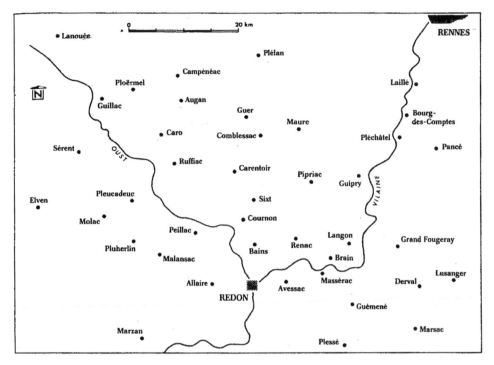

Figure 13.4 Ninth-century AD 'plebes' and 'plebiculae' (villages and hamlets) in Brittany. Source: Davies 1988.

pioneer woodland larger territories of 2–3 kilometre radius; and secondary infill/ upland smaller territories of 1–2 kilometre radius (Beresford and St Joseph 1979; Everitt 1986). Brian Roberts's detailed study of Warwickshire medieval village territories (1977) found a median of 2.5 kilometres to their boundaries.

In fact, settlement systems with radii of 2–3 kilometres, comparable with Flannery's inferred stable Mexican pattern, are hitherto the most frequently represented. Ellison and Harriss (1972), in their territorial analysis of southern English settlement systems from bronze age to early medieval times, found a radius of 2 kilometres most appropriate from empirical indications. In Classical Greece (Bintliff 1994), mature systems of villages and small towns in central Greece gravitate around a territory of 2.5-kilometre radius (Fig. 13.5), as does the remoter countryside of the hinterland of ancient Athens (Fig. 13.6); however, in the immediate environs of Athens, much smaller village territories of 1–2 kilometre radii appear.

It is clear from these archaeological and historical case studies that a number of what we might tentatively call 'settlement quanta' are becoming recognizable in farming territory dimensions – recurrent values, or better: ranges of values. When

516

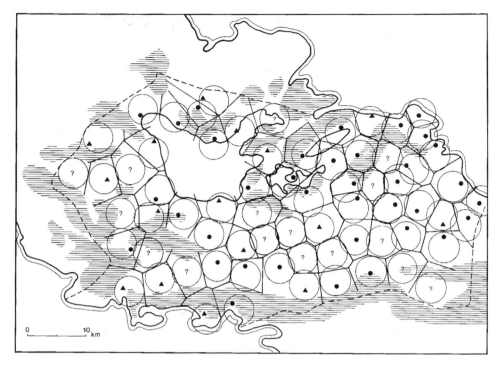

Figure 13.5 Known (solid symbols) and hypothesized (question-marks) nucleated settlement system in the classical era for the region of Boeotia, central Greece; cities are indicated by triangles, villages by circles. Best-fit circles of 2.5-kilometre radius have been fitted within village–city subsistence territories first defined through Thiessen polygons (the solid line cells). Shading represents infertile uplands. Source: J. Bintliff 1994.

information is detailed enough to allow us to follow the evolutionary dynamics of a settlement system, we sometimes observe the metamorphosis of a network from one set of values to another, usually smaller, set. It is not problematic to detect the underlying mechanisms at work, which are the same that we have observed in the Atoyac valley: as a landscape is populated by villages, large territories are established first, but over time the further multiplication of settlements occurs through infill between pioneer communities, an accommodation achieved through the progressive subdivision of land at the expense of existing territorial units.

This transformational series may be hypothesized to include quanta from a 5-kilometre radius, through 3–4 kilometres, to 2–3 kilometres, and finally to 1–2 kilometres, rarely to less than 1 kilometre. Flannery's Atoyac valley seems to move directly from 5 to 2.5 kilometres without an intervening stage, and finally gives rise to occasional tiny satellite hamlets nested within the 2.5-kilometre territory and with arguably less than 1-kilometre radius catchments. It is likely, however, that

517

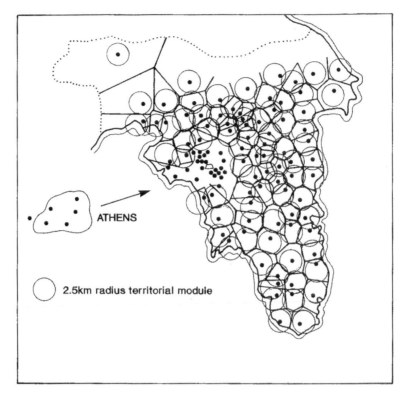

Figure 13.6 Known village communities in classical Attica (the territory of ancient Athens): territorial analysis through Thiessen polygons (the solid line cells) within which a best-fit module of 2.5-kilometre radius has been fitted, with the exception of the dense cluster of villages around Athens city itself. Source: J. Bintliff 1994.

Flannery has omitted to take account of the rather special characteristics of riverine settlement networks; to investigate this, we need to consider the geometry of territory.

THE GEOMETRY OF TERRITORY

The evolution of Atoyac valley settlement was constrained by the linear character of the river, since the prime locational attraction for its early farming villages was river alluvium for highly productive maize agriculture. As villages multiplied they expanded in axial, one-dimensional mode upstream and downstream. None the less, as Flannery reminds us, villagers in the valley were also regularly exploiting a wider range of resources in the adjacent piedmont zones and remoter upland areas on either side of the river. If the initial hamlet of Mogote and its first wave of two

518

daughter settlements suggest a territory of 5-kilometre radius, this is largely taken up with such non-riverine landscape (cf. Fig. 13.3, stages T1 and T2). The restriction of settlement expansion to a riverine, one-dimensional, axis produces clear boundary restrictions along the river, with inter-site distances being reduced from 10 to 5 kilometres with the second wave of settlement infill (T2 to T3). Significantly, however, there continue to be no restrictions on the lateral extent of village territories (Fig. 13.7a), which will doubtless have remained at their full extent. In other words, approximately circular territories of 5-kilometre radius were converted into more narrow, rectangular, territories with a 2.5-kilometre radius upstream and downstream, and a 5-kilometre radius on either side of the river. Although Flannery represented the evolution of settlement as a process of halving the territorial radius, in fact this only operates on the one-dimensional river axis. On his interpretation, the actual subdivision of territory from a 5-kilometre catchment to one of 2.5 kilometres would be not a halving but a quartering of territory. In actuality, as can be seen through Thiessen-polygon analysis, when the three early hamlets increase to five, territories of approximately 5-kilometre radius decrease to oblong catchments some 2.5-kilometre radius on the one river axis and 5 kilometres on the other, resulting in a halving of territorial area, in predictable conformity to the regular interstitial location of one new hamlet between each pair of existing hamlets. If the Atoyac T3 territories had been exactly concentric rather than asymmetric, their radius would be around 3–4 kilometres.

It is generally advantageous to combine the overall concept of radial territories with empirical outlining of likely boundaries between neighbouring sites utilizing a technique such as Thiessen polygon analysis, so that asymmetrical territories can be identified at an early stage. Thiessen analysis is a simple method for suggesting plausible boundaries between territories of settlements considered originally to have been of comparable status, and operates as follows: connecting lines are drawn faintly between each contiguous settlement, then bisected, with strongly emphasized lines being drawn at right angles to the bisection points; these lines at right-angles to connecting lines are then extended until they bisect each other, thus creating polygonal cell walls around each settlement – the Thiessen Polygons. On the reasonable principle that a boundary between two communities of comparable status is more likely to be at a midpoint between these settlements than close to one particular community, these midpoint cell walls are taken as approximations to actual territorial divisions.

What axial settlement networks emphasize is the path of the priority resource zone and its properties, so that continued village colonization produces skewed territory shapes. This process was shown very clearly by Ellison and Harriss (1972) in their analysis of the well-known 'strip-parishes' of the southern English chalk downlands (Figs 13.7b and 13.7c), where early medieval settlements multiply along valley systems through continuous subdivision of valley land (early settlements

(a)

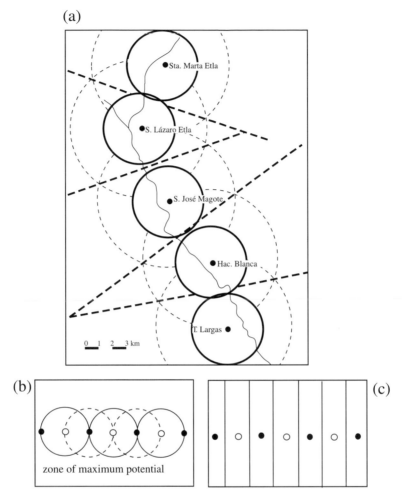

Figure 13.7 (a) Formative villages in the Atoyac valley, Mexico, with 2.5-kilometre radius territories modified by Theissen polygon analysis, (b) and (c) creation of strip territories through linear infill along a preferred resource band. (a) Source: Flannery 1976; (b) and (c) Source: Ellison and Harriss 1972.

white, secondary black), whilst retaining similar lengths of elongated territory stretching up onto plateau country to either side.

The other examples of territorial quanta for farming systems that we cited earlier do not belong to axial systems like the Atoyac valley, but to a much commoner form of settlement evolution in which desirable resources extend in all directions. These two-dimensional systems are typified by villages which multiply across the landscape in all compass directions from primary colonies (Fig. 13.8a). If we rerun

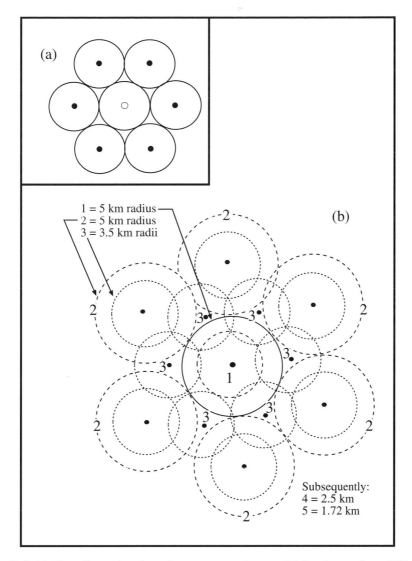

Figure 13.8 (a) Two-dimensional settlement expansion model (re-drawn from Ellison and Harriss 1972: fig. 24.16); (b) model of secondary expansion 2 from primary settlement 1 followed by tertiary interstitial infill 3. Source: J. Bintliff.

the dynamic spread of farming villages, this time allowing daughter colonies to spread in all directions from a single pioneer community before interstitial infill, the sequence might run as follows (Fig. 13.8b): pioneer village colonizes its surroundings (Phase 1); in an ideal scenario a single, 5-kilometre radius, origin community would eventually be surrounded by a complement of six secondary hamlets each with a 5-kilometre radius catchment (Phase 2); if a tertiary series of daughter villages was founded between all the existing six villages, the new radius for all hamlets becomes 3.5 kilometres (Phase 3); if a further series of daughter settlements infilled between the tertiary network, average catchment size for all settlements decreases to a 2.5-kilometre radius (Phase 4); a final subdivision of existing territories accommodates yet one more series of daughter settlements appearing between all previous hamlets, producing average catchment radii of 1.72 kilometres (Phase 5).

Three points are worth making in connection with this geometrical series of colonizing and infilling villages. First, although it might seem overly mathematical and 'inhuman' to reduce human settlement history to a game of landscape geometry, as if ancient farmers went out each time marking boundaries in fractions of modern kilometres, actually we are merely reducing to quantitative form a very simple operation: the equal division of an existing territory between an old village and new neighbours appearing between it and its former nearest neighbours. In effect, the territories of each stage of settlement are being subdivided by half to give land to interstitial colonies. This basic series of equal subdivision produces the observed series of decreasing catchment radii with each new generation of settlements, from 5 to 3.5 to 2.5 to 1.72 kilometre radii. Of course there is no reason to suppose that these exact figures were duplicated in the real process of dividing lands equally with daughter settlements, rather one might look for settlement networks peaking in the following ranges of quanta: c. 5, 3–4, 2–3 and 2–1 kilometres as plausible evidence for different stages in the maturity of agricultural settlement infill in particular landscapes.

Second, our discussion of settlement geometry dynamics underlines the importance of delineating the overall shape and symmetry, or asymmetry, of empirical territories, through a simple technique such as Thiessen polygon analysis, rather than taking a measure such as inter-site distance as a reliable guide to the average radius or radius-equivalent of a settlement's catchment. Villages may appear to cluster closely when they locate on a restricted resource which is clustered, but their individual territories may extend asymmetrically to greater distances as in the Atoyac valley, or the strip parishes of Saxon England. In contrast, in a landscape where resources vary little two-dimensionally or are found widely if discretely, settlement locations may be found to approximate closer to the geometric focus of circular territories, as in Classical Greece, ninth-century AD Brittany and neolithic Bulgaria.

Third, our proposed colonization model is strikingly comparable with that developed by Bylund from theoretical and empirical evidence for the early modern colonization process in northern Sweden (Bylund, 1960: fig. 4, Model F).

A final variation can be noted: if resources are 'isotropic' (equal in all directions), settlement territories will not only tend to recurrent size/radius/quanta and be evenly packed across the landscape, but the village or hamlet will tend to be exactly central to its territory. If, however, resources are distributed patchily across the landscape, and/or the settlement focus requires localized factors such as spring-water or a defensive position, the village may occupy a position asymmetric to its modular territory. Thus in Figures 13.5 and 13.6 the modular territories have been defined by Thiessen polygons and the module size detected through placing best-fit standard-radius circles within them. Providing that distances are limited to the furthest boundary (usually less than one hour), the friction of distance will allow such asymmetries as a trade-off against other locational considerations.

FLANNERY'S CARRYING CAPACITY CRITIQUE

Through our examination of Dynamic Catchments we have developed a new, flexible model of farming catchments 'nested' over time as the settlement system matures, population rises and existing territories have to be equably subdivided. In fact we can suggest that only two additional explanatory elements are needed to supplement the 'territory halving' process, in order to account for our entire sequence of nested catchments from 5 to 2–1 kilometre radii networks.

The first factor operates at the very beginning of farming settlement sequences, and relates to a putative outer, limiting, parameter of a 5-kilometre or 1-hour radius catchment. In Vita-Finzi and Higgs's first statement of Site Catchment Analysis this radius was considered as a recurrent constraint for farming sites. The figure originates essentially from observations in recent rural societies in various parts of the world where traditional technologies dominated, being indirectly derived from Chisholm's (1962) generalization that distance constraints become significant in a 2–4 kilometre radius from the farm and lead to little intensive agriculture beyond 5 kilometres. Interesting and promising though this statement is, it is perhaps surprising that empirical evidence *can* be found in archaeological and historical settlement systems for the effective operation of such a quantum in conditioning pioneer catchment boundaries. The initial infill of the Atoyac valley is such a case in point. It is also possible to simulate the creation of later systems with 3–4, 2–3 and 1–2 kilometre radius catchments through the simple operation of a settlement doubling/territory halving principle. According to whether resources are isotropic-ally (relatively widely and equally) distributed, or clustered, these quanta of matur-ing settlement catchments may be recognized in a 'pure' form as symmetrical territories, sites in geometric focus, approximately circular shape, or 'skewed' form as asymmetric territories, sites decentred, territory shapes irregular. We can further characterize these two modes as 'quantum-radius' and 'quantum-radius equivalent' territories.

We noted earlier that both the first wave of 5-kilometre radius farming hamlets in the Atoyac valley, and the second wave of 3.5-kilometre radius-equivalent settle-ments, created catchments far in excess of their subsistence needs, with the possible single exception of the prime central-place village of Mogote, based on calculations of population derived from the surface area of these sites. On the face of it, this seems to undermine the initial thesis of Vita-Finzi and Higgs and their sources in human ecology, that catchment sizes are the product of the resource needs of a community and the least effort principle active in obtaining those resources. On this basis Flannery moved to consider 'social' explanations for catchment size.

The natural question to put is why, at a certain stage, offspring settlements begin to appear between existing communities and take territory from them? In the Atoyac case, for example, it is reasonable to consider most of the valley as barely exploited from the pioneer hamlet of Mogote, so that its initial pair of daughter settlements were free to append full 1-hour territories to the borders of their catchment. When the following pair of daughter hamlets was given off, however, it appears that remoter upstream and downstream locations were not available, so that these surplus populations had to be accommodated within the existing territories of older settlements. The same can be claimed for the addition of tiny satellite hamlets at an even later stage, located close to some members of the stable hamlet network.

Here Flannery's observations on carrying capacity of the landscape come into their own: we can now see that such a process of territorial subdivision was not actually problematic, as the 1-hour catchments were something of a luxury for the early hamlets, enclosing more resources than were essential to their comfortable survival. The primary 1-hour radius might be hypothesized to be a maximal resource zone easily buffering the community against shortages, yet compatible with the friction of distance. Indeed, we might suggest that the sequence from 1-hour radius through the other quanta to a 2–3 kilometre radius may proceed quite frequently without undue stress on the communities involved. What was at first obtained at least in part extensively could be produced intensively later, but within a smaller radius. At this point, however, further territorial subdivision could leave a nucleated village community with inadequate 'buffering' against bad harvests, crop pests, and other threats that often strike such societies. Hypothetically, we might see something of the order of a 1-kilometre radius territory as a critical radius, enclosing the necessary resources for farming communities to ensure survival in the long term. This lower limit constitutes our second factor in territorial dynamics.

The most frequently observed empirical quantum is a 2–3 kilometre radius settlement network. It is likely that this favoured range of catchment represents the ideal compromise between the need to move from the ideal 1-hour radius (essentially set by time–labour constraints) to allow for settlement infill within a landscape, and the need to avoid extreme diminution of territory and the threat of disaster from over-reliance on limited resources. A corollary of this train of thought is that settlement systems in the 3–4 and 2–3 kilometre quanta are probably reasonably stable, whilst those in the 1–2 kilometre range may be symptomatic of societies under resource and/or overpopulation stress.

In the above reflections I may have seemed to generalize rather grandly, on a world scale, and without regard to culture or period variations. It is of course necessary to avoid claiming 'laws' of settlement behaviour valid for any time or society, based on a relatively small series of case studies, even if they do surprisingly derive from contrasted cultural contexts and physical environments. So we should set out the scope and applicability of a revised, flexible territorial analysis, for which we have laid the foundations above.

I have tried to demonstrate that empirical research on pre-industrial farming settlements supports the existence of several quanta of territorial size. In some individual examples, settlement networks appear to gravitate from one quantum to the next, smaller, quantum. It can be suggested on theoretical grounds that such sequences are the result of a simple process of subdivision of landscape between parent and daughter communities. The value of these quanta might be set from two enclosing parameters – the 1-hour/5-kilometre radius walking-time constraint, and a critical radius of some 1 kilometre enclosing a survival resource zone, together with the dynamic process of geometric halving. Mature, stable, systems in the 2–3 kilometre range might occur with predictable frequency as a result of population growth, landscape infill, and catchment subdivision, constrained by the desire to control a territory with buffering capacity beyond the quanta of stress and bare survival.

Although it might be expected that in many regions and cultures the first development of farming villages, or subsequent recolonization phases following decline or abandonment, would follow an infill sequence beginning with individual sites adopting the time-conditioned 1-hour radius, it is quite conceivable that settlers spreading outwards from a mature settlement network which had already reached a 'stable' half-hour radius norm might carry that quantum with them. If settlement was large scale under conditions of considerable population pressure, it is also possible that even smaller territories might be established, unless the newly colonized area was reasonably extensive. Only with the painstaking reconstruction of stage-by-stage settlement dynamics shall we be able to identify which of these processes operated in a particular district. The averages quoted above for the size of different types of English medieval parishes may reflect the latter two models at work.

But could farming societies adopt very different forms of settlement, ignoring the pathways that these examples illustrate? We cannot deny this, and it would be against the spirit of the present exercise to claim universal laws. All that we can argue for is an understanding of how particular empirical networks may have arisen. A characteristic of our dynamic modelling is its 'ideal' form. We have tended to speculate in general terms about axial or two-dimensional landscapes, allowing those two to be uniform. In reality, all landscapes are more varied than this, and the precise point chosen for a village may be the result of a combination of locational factors, as already noted in connection with ancient Greek village/city-state territories. Thus the catchment could have been selected both in terms of the overall availability of preferred resources and the position of older settlements, yet within that catchment village location might be influenced by a prominent spring, a defensive hill, favourable winds, a river crossing, as well of course – as we have seen – by the shape of a critical resource. It may be helpful to see locational strategies as a kind of game played out in time and space, in which several factors, some competing, were demanding the attention of settlers at one and the same time. And let us not forget an earlier caveat, that in some societies the rules of that game were largely set to the disadvantage of settlers, when dominant groups displaced or marginalized subordinate communities into restricted environments. In extreme cases of the latter kind, locational decisions may have been made by others, imposing catchment constraints on communities; even so, the study of such territories will be highly revealing both of the pressures such landscapes could impose on village development, and the various ways marginal groups sought to adapt to their particular circumstances such as through the development of special economies, investment in resource enhancement through terracing, water control and so on.

SETTLEMENT SIZE AND SOCIAL SPACE

Two fundamental questions we now need to turn to are: why do farming people live so frequently in agglomerated settlements, typically 'the village'?, and why do villages and hamlets produce daughter settlements which infill the landscape around them?

No family can survive without frequent association with a wider human society: apart from the search for non-incestuous mates to perpetuate the population, human groups require in the longer term the mutual support of a number of families, to provide help in time of sickness, danger, or premature death, to assist in work tasks where several adults are advantageous if not essential, and also to provide a pool of practical lore about resources, technology, and life-skills. One oft-quoted figure suggests that a human group of some twenty-five individuals or more might be the scale of such a minimal support-group required as near-neighbours for a successful human community (Dodgshon 1987). In practice, observable villages are usually a good deal larger than this lower limit, though characteristically with populations typically in the hundreds rather than thousands.

Of course such a district-society need not live in a single camp or hamlet, but could occupy individual homes or clusters of homes in a dispersed network stretching across a small landscape. This kind of dispersed community is especially associated with landscapes where resources are patchy or land use is very extensive, and is common in predominantly pastoral economies. Space precludes a discussion of territoriality in dispersed agro-pastoral communities, where interesting modifications to catchments occur, although still within a definable 'village territory'. On the other hand, it is more common for village–hamlet communities to live predominantly or essentially at a single nucleated location, at which point our nucleated community catchment quanta might be expected. However, whether the self-defining 'community' of hamlet or village is nucleated or dispersed, the extraordinary prevalence of this mode of society in mixed-farming societies around the world, with average membership well above the twenty-five or so minimum, requires explanation.

In 1972 the social anthropologist Anthony Forge published an analysis of community size in traditional rural Indonesia. Using a very large database, he proposed the following principles underlying regularities in the size and social organization of Melanesian settlements: (1) in communities up to some 150 members (or some thirty-five adult men), face-to-face relationships and direct close kinship were sufficient for coherent social structure; (2) communities larger than 150 and up to 300/400 members (35–85 adult men) consistently adopted sub-group organization such as clans, subclans and lineages to facilitate social cohesion, these sub-groups being manifested by hamlet strings or clusters making up the overall settlement (the latter sometimes stockaded); and (3) if communities developed beyond 300/400, they split into totally separate residential blocks with their own landholding zones and often stockades. By far the commonest settlement size was Type 2, with Type 3 argued to be a specific response to regular warfare (two or three Type 2 communities linked politically for mutual defence). Although these societies are described as 'egalitarian', they are actually characterized by typical 'Big Man' dominance structures – the dominance of a few males without hereditary power.

Forge suggested that Big Man systems favoured the emphasis on Type 2 villages: with less than thirty-five adult males (Type 1 settlements), individual Big Men could achieve prolonged influence, whilst with more than eighty-five men the number of players for dominance would be too large for any control over 'the power game' to be exercised. The optimum community of 150–350 had the right range of Big Men to sustain their existence in a stable structure without risk of individual tyranny. Since communities over 150 members require subdivision to place people into manageable categories, village structure had to be modified into distinct social, religious, and often residential groups. When communities reached numbers over 400 or so, they had to be composed of village pairings or triads. Archaeologically, we might view this series of social and political communities of increasing size using different terms from Forge: on the ground we would see Type 1 as small hamlets, Type 2 as a hamlet cluster or village, and Type 3 as separate but contiguous villages, each composed of hamlet clusters.

The physical anthropologist Robin Dunbar has also addressed the same question of quanta in the social groupings of traditional societies (Dunbar 1992, 1996). His approach has been radically different, focusing on an hypothesized connection between the complexity of the brain in primates and the size of their social groups, and in particular on the size of the neocortex area believed to be linked to socialization. Finding a demonstrable trend in primates, he extrapolated the ratio to predict from neocortex proportions the natural size of social groups whose interrelations were suited to the relative brain complexity of humans: the number was approximately 150. Put in very simple terms, Dunbar argued that human and primate social groups that operate on the primary principle of individual members memorizing each other's personal attributes and relations, are limited in size by the filing and sorting capacities of the relevant part of the brain. Assembling together a set of statistics for stable groupings of mobile or settled hunter-gatherers, and non-hierarchical traditional agricultural societies (localized clans and hamlets respectively), he found their average size to be 153. The simple explanation for recurrent limits on these human social groups that are not internally stratified is our inability to memorize upwards of 200 or so individuals in face-to-face contact, as well as updating their interrelations over time.

Dunbar's thesis is strikingly consistent with that of Forge, with the latter demonstrating that village communities that do manage to pass beyond the 200 or so population threshold achieve this through the creation of formal social subdivisions as well as residential segregation. The operation of social stress on communities rising beyond the 150–200 person level provides a very plausible explanation for the widely observed phenomenon of village fission in traditional farming societies studied by ethnographers. It can even be demonstrated that, in some societies, recognition of this process has become formalized into a cultural norm: amongst the ultra-traditionalist, primitive-Christian Hutterite communities of North America, for example, it is a fixed principle that when a village grows beyond 125 members it must split in two, on the explicit grounds that the social cohesion of the community is threatened above that level (Holzach 1979).

Thus there is a natural tendency for human residential groups to stabilize between twenty-five and 150–200 members, in the absence of strong mechanisms to counteract social division. We can group such strong mechanisms, allowing communities to grow to many hundreds or even thousands in size, into two basic types: horizontal mechanisms, where the society is subdivided into complementary social units such as clans, lineages, moieties; and vertical mechanisms, where the society is stratified in a hierarchy of authority.

Another parameter that is of central relevance to pre-industrial settlement systems is that of mating networks. Wobst (1974, 1976) has claimed that human groups need to operate marriage networks of at least 400–500 individuals to avoid the negative effects of an inbred gene pool on human health and fitness. The implication for the work of Forge and Dunbar is that, although the most natural social group for human cognition is below 150 members, other, equally natural, forces will require such groups to maintain exogamous relations with their neighbours.

In Melanesia, Forge showed that the village population norm of 150–350 or so individuals per community only found social coherence through the existence of internal subdivision into social and physical sub-groupings. Interestingly, he commented that these sub-groups have important social relations, not just with the other sub-groups constituting the immediate village community, but with groups of a similar order in other villages. Since the community will not be large enough for a Wobstian gene pool, clan/subclan networks of this kind would be essential to allow adequate mates to be found beyond the Type 2 village. With Forge's Type 3 communities, combining two or three Type 2 communities, total population will be above the mating network parameter, and one could consider whether the advantages of such political groups go beyond the considerations of defence paramount in Forge's analysis. Significantly though, the increasing separation in space that we see in Melanesia when crossing from Type 1 to 2 and then to Type 3 communities indicates the difficulty of sustaining a genuinely physically cohesive nucleated settlement of more than some 150 members.

SETTLEMENT FISSION AND THE EVOLUTION OF NETWORKS

This preceding discussion provides insights into the processes of settlement fission and landscape infill that we have already observed empirically in Formative Mesoamerica and Anglo-Saxon England. The fact that fission seems to occur well before population presses against available territory, at hamlet level, can be given a social explanation (just as Flannery had surmised), and we may expect to find the relevant hamlets to be characteristically less than two hundred inhabitants, but rarely smaller than twenty-five people (Dunbar's average is 150, but the range of empirical examples is 100–230). The corollary is that settlements which push well above the Forge/Dunbar face-to-face threshold can be expected to have adopted sub-groupings, whether through lineages, clans, or dominance hierarchies; possibly such categories may be spatially discrete within such larger settlements.

Before taking our discussion of these latter, larger, villages any further, it is worth testing the proposition of social group quanta on other empirical databases. One of the largest settlement inventories in pre-industrial times is the Domesday Book, in which William the Conqueror sought to tabulate the human, animal, and land resources available to him in recently conquered Anglo-Saxon England (Hill 1981; Fig. 13.9). A commonly accepted estimate gives 2–3 million people for Domesday England, a figure which doubled or trebled by the early thirteenth century. Current opinion would consider this AD 1086 record as that of a countryside composed of 'naturally arising' village communities whose population was typically well below the maximum capacity of the land to support.

Rather surprisingly, although innumerable analyses have been made of the

Figure 13.9 Settlements in Domesday Book. Source: D. Hill.

statistics available in Domesday Book, only one source to my knowledge interests itself in the size of listed 'vills' (Hallam 1981), despite the fact that there are some 13,400 villages inventoried. Although these 'vills' include both nucleated and dispersed communities, for our purposes the significant fact is that they exist as social groups within a defined territory, that is, they are 'village communities'. Hallam's comments on average village size are general but significant: eastern England – 150 people; south-east England – 150; east Midlands – 115; south England – 120; the Welsh Borderlands – 54; Devon – 88; Cornwall – 82; Yorkshire – 21. The most reasonable hypothesis to account for these data is that the consistent range of average village size, remarkably within that predicted theoretically above, is the product of the preferred maintenance of face-to-face communities at this stage in settlement growth and landscape infill. It is probable that surplus growth above 150 has been exported via fission to adjacent, underdeveloped or undeveloped sectors of the regional landscape. Intriguingly, this would suggest that the wider political context of later Anglo-Saxon society, strongly hierarchical and nascent-feudal *above* the level of the village community, is not the central factor in the colonization of the landscape and the mode of rural settlement. Early medieval settlement units in Holland have also been postulated to have held around a hundred individuals (Heidinga 1987: 164).

From this basis we may search for additional settlement systems conforming to these norms. It may be expected that communities fissioning below the 150–200 person range will be especially typical for rural societies in which both internal social stratification and horizontal social segmentation are insignificant. It is most appropriate to approach cultural contexts believed likely to be characterized by relatively simple internal social structure, such as early farming communities. One example is the Neolithic of the Middle East, where farming villages appear on average to be composed of populations of 50–200 people (Redman 1978: 143, 181, 188). For the neolithic *tell* societies of the Balkans, John Chapman (1989) has indicated village populations averaging 60–90 and rarely more than 120 people. Flannery's farming hamlet network in the Atoyac valley stabilizes at under a hundred people per hamlet, except for the original settlement of San José which predictably develops into a central place with putative social hierarchy. The Domesday example shows that even within Anglo-Saxon England, a society with a highly developed state structure and class divisions, the dominant form of settlement, the rural village (whether nucleated or dispersed around its defined territory), has a population dynamic appropriate to a relatively undifferentiated community. For more recent times, a well-documented study of the Greek Peloponnese around AD 1700 shows that the average population in a sample of over 1,400 villages is consistently under a hundred people (Sauerwein 1969).

Following Wobst's principle of the extended mating-network, such 'basic' village systems can be expected to practise exogamy or out-marriage in order to participate in a genetic pool removed from the obvious dangers of close-kin inbreeding. In fact a creative tension has now been created between the operation of the Forge/ Dunbar social fission model and the Wobst demographic pool model. Should we not consider the likelihood that one of the principal reasons why pioneer settlements grow to fission size and populate their *immediate* neighbourhoods is to provide an immediate reservoir of marriage partners? Does this requirement not also provide a motor for landscape colonization and infill, preventing pioneer settlements from stabilizing below the Forge/Dunbar threshold? Such considerations may help to explain some of the more paradoxical features of recorded village colonization processes, such as the early neolithic Linear Pottery culture of central Europe, where typically small communities of pioneer farmers spread the entire breadth of Europe at a rate inconsistent with land exhaustion.

FROM VILLAGE TO CITY-STATE: THE 'DORFSTAAT' MODEL

When the inhabitants of a village exchange marriage partners with neighbouring communities, such exchanges are frequently associated in the ethno-historic record with accompanying dowries of land, stock or other property. Let us envisage a scenario at a very advanced stage of landscape infill, when large, original, village territories have become subdivided into smaller units, and the inhabitants are using the entire bounded catchment to its full extent. A new form of demographic tension could arise, where villages compete over boundary lands and yet need to obtain marriage partners from the same adjacent settlements. Having to give arable land or pasture away to another village might seem to be compensated for through reciprocal land dowries being gained by a village, yet the usufruct or more usually rights over the products from land in another village territory, remote from one's home, are an inadequate substitute for family lands near the village that have now passed partly or wholly into the economy of non-villagers.

In real life, the tension between maintaining the integrity of village lands when population is high and the need to marry out if communities are below the gene-pool threshold, has resulted in a cross-cultural form of 'joking relationship' recorded by ethnographers working in traditional farming societies (for example, Tak 1990). Boys from other villages seeking to court and marry village girls risk ducking in the village fountain and other forms of rough-handling. Villages denigrate their neighbours through nicknames and stereotyping, exaggerating their own community's virtues and importance, in what has been dubbed in the Italian context *campanilismo* (after the symbolic competition between villages to erect bell-towers that put their neighbours to shame). Such recent behaviour represents a milder version of more aggressive competition for resources in earlier periods when state power was less all-embracing in rural areas of Europe. Thus in the Italian

Apennines up until the eighteenth century, villages disputing valuable borderlands practised armed raids against each other.

It might be asked how far the tension between exogamy and territorial integrity is a conscious problem for traditional village societies living at high density in a totally infilled landscape. Susan Freeman, in her remarkable ethnography of the village of Valdemora in northern Spain (Freeman 1968, 1970), provides major insights into this question by contextualizing her small community within the wider cultural anthropology of traditional Spanish villages. The people of Valdemora occupy a small territory in the upland Sierra Morena, squeezed by neighbouring villages on all sides. With a population that historically never seems to have surpassed 200, it has always needed to practise exogamy. Yet the villagers explicitly point this out, bewailing the fact that Valdemora can never grow to become a true *pueblo* – the large village type which Freeman considers to have been dominant in wide swathes of Spain in recent centuries – where populations of 500 to 1,000 or more are largely endogamous and can keep village lands essentially within the community.

Clearly the achievement of a community size of 500 or more offers very special advantages to a village using its traditional territory to the full. Not only does the potential for a predominance of endogamy act to keep the village resources within the control of village members, but this centripetal force gives the village greater scope to manage the village territory as a communal asset, something which is very necessary when land use is intensive. If land is scarce, the community needs to have the power to reassign it to reflect the fluctuating size and needs of individual families, to systematize communal grazing, and other forms of benevolent inter-ference in the economic life of the village. As we have seen, the growth of population to such a size puts village society well beyond the Forge/Dunbar range of face-to-face social relations, and predicates a transformation of political structure within the rural community.

Such a dramatic transformation in socio-economic structure can be documented in the historic development of European villages, and its outcome forms a central consideration in the ethnography of rural Western Europe. The 'corporate community' is a specific form of village organization in which wide-ranging powers over the disposal of land, animals, and labour are centralized in a village council. Membership of this council is customarily confined to adult male landowners, who often must possess a certain property qualification (a landholding in itself adequate for supporting a family). If we consider that, in many historic village communities, one half or more of the families had less than this scale of holding, and had to supplement their income through sharecropping, labouring, cottage industry and other means, and that in any case women and subadults are automatically excluded from the institution, then we can easily calculate how the numerical constraints required for a face-to-face society may be adapted to allow total community size to break through the 150–200 population limit. If the effective community of power, the village council, stays within the face-to-face range of 150 but represents, for example, only one half of the adult men, and each adult man represents a family of five (to take common averages for historic villages in Europe), the total village community can be as large as 1,500–2,000 people, and can easily solve most of its marriage-partner needs internally. The Forge/Dunbar threshold has been overcome through vertical stratification of power, but in itself the élite group of the corporate community is especially effective if it can remain on the scale of the face-to-face community. The rural anthropology of the west European countryside teaches us that such large, introspective, communities have a changed ethos from their small, relatively undifferentiated, ancestors: in Italy and Spain, for example, inhabitants of the characteristic medium-to-large villages or pueblos talk of themselves as 'villagers by day' when they are out in the fields, and 'townsfolk by night' when the inhabitants participate in the intense social and political life of their nucleated communities.

The famous historical geographer of the early decades of this century, Alfred Philippson, once wrote a seemingly innocuous and esoteric sentence for posterity to solve: why were there so many *poleis* (ancient city-states) in Thessaly, a region of north-central Greece (Philippson 1951: 224)? The significance of this question stems from traditional conceptions about the origins of the ancient Greek city-state. It has usually been assumed that mountainous Greece, with its innumerable small plains separated by rocky massifs and the Aegean sea, gave rise by natural geography to isolated communities of a town-like character, emerging to statehood within their separate micro-environments. That thesis fails completely to explain the abundance of ancient poleis in the vast, open plains of Thessaly. In 1956 a pupil of Philippson, the equally renowned geographer of the Graeco–Roman world Ernst Kirsten, published a lengthy monograph on the history and geography of the Greek city-state, the underlying purpose of which was to provide the answer to Philippson's query. Kirsten's solution was simple, pragmatic, and even today the most convincing one. Rather than focus on the famous and unique historical properties of the Greek city-state, we should seek to understand it as a geographer would, as a form of settlement on a certain size scale and positioned in an associated landscape also of a certain scale. If we take this radical approach we see that the typical Greek polis is small, characteristically no more than a few thousand people, and its bounded territory or 'chora' is typically from 2–3 to 5–6 kilometres in radius. Clearly it is a special kind of village, a large village, and a politically very complex village, but none the less it is essentially a metamorphosis or politicization of the village, which Kirsten therefore termed the *Dorfstaat* or village-state model.

The ancient historian Eberhard Ruschenbusch (1985) has subsequently quantified the proposition: collating all the available information regarding the 700–800 city-states of the classical Aegean world, he found that 80 per cent have territories of a 5–6 kilometre radius or less, and 69 per cent have citizen male populations of 400 on average (perhaps 2,000–3,000 or so people in total). If the territory is as much as 5–6 kilometres in radius, and this is not a consequence of the inclusion of much uncultivable land, it will usually be because, during the transformation of the village to city-state, it has often given rise to, or absorbed, one or two small satellite hamlets. In central Greece and Attica, I have suggested that during the iron age recolonization of the landscape, interstitial settlement crystallized into a network of 2–3 kilometre and locally even 1–2 kilometre radius territories, creating what I have termed 'proto-poleis' or potential village-states (Bintliff 1994; Figs 13.5 and 13.6). In the Aegean as a whole, these were mostly absorbed over time into larger village-states.

Kirsten went on to distinguish a second kind of city-state, which either develops out of the Dorfstaat or is different in origin. These towns are much larger, with populations in the tens of thousands, and territories tens of kilometres in radius. On a scale comparable to medieval European towns, and supported by a network of lesser nucleated settlements within their territory (some of which were formerly autonomous Dorfstaat cities), such city-states are true towns for the geographer, and fit what Kirsten dubbed the *Stadtstaat* or town-state model. Obvious examples are Athens, Corinth, Argos, and Thebes.

What German scholars term the 'Normalpolis' of some two thousand or so inhabitants is generally associated in Archaic to classical Greece with a form of moderate democracy called the hoplite constitution. In this political structure, the dominant share of power in the 'village-state' belongs to a well-defined class of landholders, those of the 'hoplite' status or above (the aristocrats). In general, between a third and a half of the free farming population might possess sufficient land to achieve hoplite rank, the equivalent of an independent farmer with adequate resources for his family and the purchase and maintenance of the armour and weaponry for service in the citizen heavy-armed division (the essential defence force of the city-state).

The comparison between the Greek polis and the 'corporate community' of recent traditional rural Europe is striking, when we consider the village origin and character of the Greek city-state, the hoplite constitution, and the typical size range of the population and its territory. But it goes further, since the Greek polis jealously guarded its territory. Normally land could only be owned by citizens, citizen status was conditional on both land ownership and usually a certain size of estate, whilst Greek cities were totally male-orientated in inheritance rights. Thus it was possible and not unusual for females from other states to marry into the polis, but normally impossible for males to do so. The polis was also usually large enough to have in any case a high rate of endogamy. These widespread mechanisms ensured the territorial integrity of the hereditary male landowning community which constituted the essential core of the Greek city-state.

535

If Kirsten provided the central explanation of the high frequency and small scale of the typical ancient Greek city-state, we can now provide a mechanism to account for the 'politicization' of the village into the form of the miniature state: the 'corporate community' arises amongst a dense, mature, network of villages as a solution to social and gene-pool constraints in circumstances where communal land management is essential.

We are beginning to document the stages of development of this process of village-state formation in Greece, and the subsequent transformation of a small minority of these into town-states. In the Early Iron Age or Geometric period, population density is low, and the characteristic form of settlement is that of village or hamlet communities with a large territory, dispersed widely across the landscape. By the classical period, village fission has infilled the entire cultivable landscape with more closely packed and modular village territories, the average catchment being a 2–3 kilometre radius (Fig. 13.5). Many of these villages have been transformed into tiny states or poleis between Geometric and classical times, but increasingly the larger communities are absorbing surrounding smaller neighbours – villages or small poleis – into larger territories dominated by a medium-sized polis. During the fourth century BC in Boeotia, finally, the largest regional settlement, Thebes, which may have remained a small town throughout the Early Iron Age, achieves total dominance over all other poleis in the region as a Stadtstaat.

In the neighbouring Greek province of Attica (Fig. 13.6), this cumulative process must have occurred much earlier. By the time we get our first full picture of rural life in the region, the final Archaic era, as a result of the very detailed village distribution revealed to us through the political reforms of Kleisthenes in the late sixth century BC, the 139 listed village communities all belong to a single state – that of the city of Athens, already a true town of over 10,000 inhabitants. In the outer rural areas, however, the villages still retain a 'stable' territory of around 2.5-kilometre radius, whilst in the countryside around the precociously large true town of Athens the average territory has a 1.7-kilometre radius (strikingly similar to our ideal subdivision of 2.5-kilometre radius territories). The estimated populations of these small urban hinterland villages are surprisingly large, often nine hundred or so people, further indication of high demographic pressure, and it is unsurprising that from this time onwards Athens requires regular food imports to feed its population, as well as sending out frequent colonies ('cleruchies') and developing a far-flung empire.

The transformation from small, relatively egalitarian, hamlets into large villages with corporate community organization and a bias towards endogamy and a highly territorial approach to resources, may be a tendency which is latent in many evolving settlement systems of agriculturalists. I suspect this model could be helpful in explaining the rise and nature of the numerous, small city-states of the Levant in the Early to Middle Bronze Age, as well as the extraordinary profusion of hill-fort focused communities found throughout Europe in the Iron Age, whose distribution in space is comparable to early modern village-hamlet networks. Possibly it may help account for the rise in the Near East and Balkans, even in pre-pottery and early neolithic times, of unusually large and seemingly complex villages, such as Çatal Hüyük, Ain Ghazel or Knossos.

THE ORIGINS AND DEVELOPMENT OF THE MEDIEVAL VILLAGE COMMUNITY IN WESTERN EUROPE

It is widely agreed that the typical early medieval rural community in western Europe was very small, with plentiful resources. Population rise throughout the period AD 500–1000 occurred through settlement growth, fission and landscape infill. In more detailed regional databases, such as those we illustrated earlier for ninth-century Brittany or eleventh-century England, the countryside is already heavily settled, but there is still room for further, internal community growth. The on-average 3–4 kilometre radius territories of the Breton 'plebes' (Fig. 13.4) will be subdivided in medieval and post-medieval times to accommodate almost as many new parishes. Provisional calculations of ninth-century village populations suggest, though, that already the average community was well above the Forge/Dunbar face-to-face society and probably large enough for a predominance of endogamy. Predictably, there exists already at this date a highly organized village council (Davies 1988). In contrast in England some two centuries later, the Domesday Book reveals the dominance of villages and hamlets that lie within the parameters of a 'face-to-face' society. Instead of the doubling of village numbers, the English trajectory in the twelfth and thirteenth centuries is the doubling or trebling of average village populations, thus taking the typical village into the model already achieved in ninth-century Brittany. The eleventh-century population of England may have been in the order of 2.5 million, but according to Brian Roberts (pers. comm.) a figure of 7 million by 1300 is not unreasonable. On the ground, the ultimate product of these two different settlement transformations will end up looking very similar: large rural communities, usually well above the 100–200 person range and not infrequently at or above the 500 range, existing within catchments tending to two of our spatial geometry modes, the 'stable' 2–3 kilometre or 'pressurized' 1–2 kilometre radius.

Brittany is thus precocious in terms of village size, and the English pattern of slower growth beyond the 'face-to-face' scale seems to be more typical of western Europe as a whole, where the five centuries from c. AD 800 to 1300 have been broadly summarized as a fundamental *moyenne durée*, or an era of 'medium-term historical process', characterized by the transformation of the small rural settlement into a larger and more complex form – the Corporate Community. The reasons for political change are already familiar from our preceding discussion, but the activity of medieval village councils in adapting to a very high pressure of population on land manifested itself in a unique and very striking fashion, through a complete refashioning of the landscape over vast areas of western Europe (Fox 1981, 1992).

For centuries after the collapse of Roman rule, farming families in the typical hamlet or small village were able to open up holdings in any convenient part of its territory and graze their stock over the broad uncultivated zones. As village populations rose beyond the Forge/Dunbar threshold, fission allowed surplus population to infill neighbouring zones or more distant woodland and waste. Yet population growth continued, doubling or trebling average rural community size between early and late medieval times. Just as the social community had to adjust towards an internally stratified political management, so also the economic basis of the village could no longer exist on the basis of each family farming where it wanted and grazing at will; land and pasture were now too precious. The most obvious difficulty was to control grazing land so that animals were kept away from the key arable fields. The animals themselves were essential to the village economy for complementary products, fertilizing manure, and as a vital source of traction for ploughing and transport of rural production.

Pressure for radical restructuring of the village landscape came from parallel and related changes in levels of power above the individual village community. In the early medieval period in many regions of western Europe, clusters of hamlets or villages, often contiguous, were linked into a network of estates belonging to lords, royalty or the Church (Aston 1985; Blair and Sharpe 1992; Everitt 1986; Hooke 1988; Fig. 13.10). The estate centre tended to be one of the earliest villages, and predictably occupied one of the most fertile districts in each region. Subsequent colonization produced a group of smaller communities in less developed landscapes. Although these satellite hamlets might be expected to produce much of their own food, the estate owner stimulated their surplus production of complementary products for export to the estate centre; this might be barley, wood, animal products, and indeed the multiple estate might be run so that animals were moved around between different village territories to make optimal use of the abundant uncultivated lands.

In the later Middle Ages, however, this kind of economy gave way to a much more intensive and individual village-based approach. In a high proportion of cases in predominantly arable landscapes, each village became an individual estate of a particular landowner, and he or his bailiff resided within its catchment. Even where landowners retained many villages in their estate, they were now managed with greater emphasis on self-sufficiency in a broad range of crops and stock. The reasons for these general shifts in the medieval economy lie in a nexus of changes: growing populations were sustained by taking into cultivation an ever greater sector

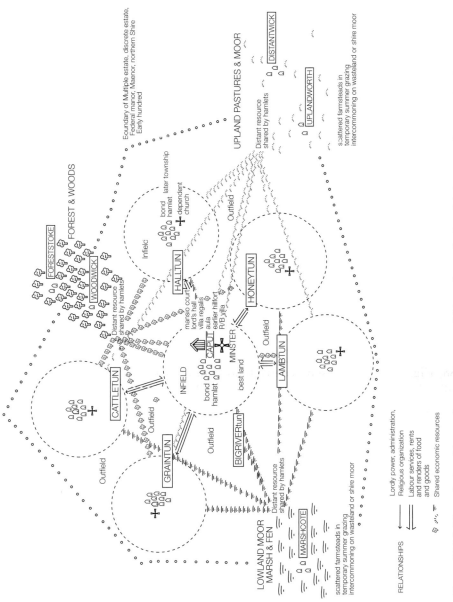

Figure 13.10 The relationships and arrangements within a theoretical multiple estate. Source: M. Aston.

of the village catchment, reducing land which could be devoted to specialist production such as woodland or pasture; social changes broke up large estates in which the Church and the king were often the original landowners, and a new class of local lords was required to pay higher taxes to the state.

These changes were mutually reinforcing and meant that the maximal production of local foodstuffs was required from a typical mixed farming community. With more and more village land converted into arable fields, the vital management of stock had to be reorganized to be as efficient as possible. Throughout western Europe, village councils imitated each other in carrying through a dramatic restructuring of the landscape (Fox 1981, 1992; Harvey 1989; Hooke 1988): in place of the patchwork of individual arable fields, fallow fields, private and communal grazing land, two and more commonly three giant land blocks were laid out across the parish, devoted respectively to cereals, fallow and pasture each year (Fig. 13.11: models B and C). All villagers were now obliged to conform to splitting their land and stock into these blocks, which rotated function each year or every few years. This was a revolutionary solution to the problems of keeping stock from the crops, of access for stock, and ensuring all the land was worked, and was certainly a central factor in the overall rise in productivity underpinning the remarkable population boom of the later medieval centuries.

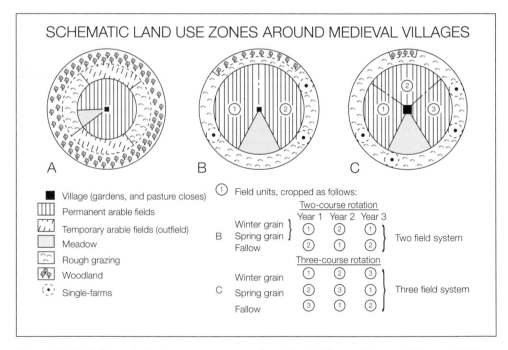

Figure 13.11 Schematic land use zones around medieval villages. Source: Roberts 1977.

540

Opinion is divided over the feasibility of sustaining such high rural populations, and it is certainly the case that from the late thirteenth century onwards, the trend was reversed, with widespread village abandonments and the conversion of large sectors of arable landscape into less intensive pasture economies. It was a central proposition of M. M. Postan that overexploitation of the land led to the breakdown of the medieval rural economy in western Europe (Postan 1975), to which can be added climatic deterioration in more westerly, northerly, and upland environments (Lamb 1977: 449ff.). The Postan thesis still has strong adherents bringing new evidence to bear (Clark 1992). Less controversially, it might be claimed that the sheer density and size of villages, and the intensity of land use, taken with the partition of land that placed a very high proportion of village territories in the non-buffered 1–2 kilometre radius range, betray a rural economy that could not be sustained in the medium term.

The interdependence and mutual feedback between social and economic process have been strongly emphasized by Harold Fox in his theory of medieval village development in England (see also Bois 1992 for parallels in France). Population growth creates pressure on village resources as territories grow smaller. Larger villages require political reorganization, and this is also necessary to reorganize the village's internal resources more efficiently. Hence the rise of the corporate medieval village community is the product of social pressure and at the same time a response to land management pressure. The respective role of village communities or their feudal lords in encouraging village nucleation and radical land reorganization is disputed. Probably both encouraged a natural adaptive process with cross-cultural resonances. In the absence of powerful feudal lords and strong overarching state structures, these repetitive processes might otherwise have led to innumerable small, competing, polities such as in ancient Greece. Indeed I would suggest that the rise of hundreds of small city-states claiming variable degrees of autonomy in early medieval north-central Italy represents exactly such a contemporary outcome, achieved predictably in regions of weak feudal power and remote and relatively ineffective state power (Waley 1988).

CONCLUSION

In this chapter I have suggested that, behind the enormous variety of habitats settled by human communities past and present, and in the context of widely divergent social and political systems, it has been proved possible to isolate a limited set of factors and processes which have had an extraordinary influence on the size, spacing, and socio-economic organization of rural communities. I have argued that none of these factors is unavoidable in settlement history, and in none the less seeking to account for their remarkable prevalence I would prefer to banish any trace of determinism through an appeal to the new science of complexity (Lewin 1993). Within this grouping of theories, semi-autonomous variables clustered into interactive ensembles are probabilistically likely to be drawn into stable configurations of complex behaviour. In the terminology of chaos–complexity theory, our recurrent factors are the so-called 'strange attractors' or gravity-forces that continually pull the development paths of human settlement history into their sphere of operation.

ACKNOWLEDGEMENTS

This chapter has benefited from the advice and criticism of Geoff Bailey, Bob Layton, and Brian Roberts.

REFERENCES

Aston, M. (1985) *Interpreting the Landscape. Landscape Archaeology in Local Studies*, London: Batsford.

Beresford, M. W. and St Joseph, J. K. S. (1979) *Medieval England. An Aerial Survey*, Cambridge: Cambridge University Press.

Bintliff, J. L. (1981). 'Theory and reality in palaeoeconomy: some words of encouragement to the archaeologist', in A. Sheridan and G. Bailey (eds) *Economic Archaeology*, Oxford: British Archaeological Reports, International Series 96: 35–50.

Bintliff, J. L. (ed.) (1984) *European Social Evolution: Archaeological Perspectives*, Bradford: University of Bradford Press.

Bintliff, J. L. (1986) 'Archaeology at the interface: an historical perspective', in J. L. Bintliff and C. F. Gaffney (eds) *Archaeology at the Interface: Studies in Archaeology's Relationships with History, Geography, Biology and Physical Science*, Oxford: British Archaeological Reports: 4–31.

Bintliff, J. L. (1991) 'Post-modernism, rhetoric and scholasticism at TAG: the current state of British archaeological theory', *Antiquity* 65: 274–78.

Bintliff, J. L. (1993) 'Why Indiana Jones is smarter than the post-processualists', *Norwegian Archaeological Review* 26: 91–100.

Bintliff, J. L. (1994) 'Territorial behaviour and the natural history of the Greek polis', in E. Olshausen and H. Sonnabend (eds) *Stuttgarter Kolloquium zur Historischen Geographie des Altertums*, 4, Amsterdam: Hakkert Verlag: 207–49, Plates 19–73.

Bintliff, J. L. (1995) ' "Whither Archaeology?" revisited', in M. Kuna and N. Venclova (eds) *Whither Archaeology? Papers in Honour of Evzen Neustupny*, Praha: Institute of Archaeology: 24–35.

Bintliff, J. L. (1997) 'Regional survey, demography, and the rise of complex societies in the ancient Aegean. Core-periphery, neo-Malthusian, and other interpretive models', *Journal of Field Archaeology* 24: 1–38.

Blair, J. and Sharpe, R. (1992) 'Introduction', in J. Blair and R. Sharpe (eds) *Pastoral Care before the Parish*, Leicester: Leicester University Press: 1–10.

542

Bois, G. (1992) *The Transformation of the Year One Thousand*, Manchester: Manchester University Press.

Bylund, E. (1960) 'Theoretical considerations regarding the distribution of settlements in inner North Sweden', *Geografiska Annaler* 42: 225–31.

Chapman, J. C. (1989) 'The early Balkan village', *Varia Archaeologica Hungarica* 2: 33–53.

Chisholm, M. (1962) *Rural Settlement and Land Use*, London: Hutchinson.

Clark, G. (1992) 'The economics of exhaustion, the Postan theory, and the agricultural revolution', *Journal of Economic History* 52: 61–84.

Clarke, D. L. (1972) 'Models and paradigms in contemporary archaeology', in D. L. Clarke (ed.) *Models in Archaeology*, London: Methuen: 1–60.

Davies, W. (1988) *Small Worlds: the Village Community in Early Medieval Brittany*, Berkeley: University of California Press.

Dennell, R. W. and Webley, D. (1975) 'Prehistoric settlement and land use in southern Bulgaria', in E. S. Higgs (ed.) *Palaeoeconomy*, Cambridge: Cambridge University Press: 97–109.

Dodgshon, R. A. (1987) *The European Past: Social Evolution and Spatial Order*, London: Macmillan.

Dunbar, R. (1992) 'Why gossip is good for you', *New Scientist*, 21 November: 28–31.

Dunbar, R. (1996) *Grooming, Gossip and the Evolution of Language*, London: Faber and Faber.

Dyson-Hudson, R. and Smith, E. A. (1978) 'Human territoriality: an ecological reassessment', *American Anthropologist* 80: 21–41.

Ellison, A. and Harriss, J. (1972) 'Settlement and land use in the prehistory and early history of southern England: a study based on locational models', in D. L. Clarke (ed.) *Models in Archaeology*, London: Methuen: 911–62.

Everitt, A. (1986) *Continuity and Colonisation*, Leicester: Leicester University Press.

Flannery, K. V. (ed.) (1976) *The Early Mesoamerican Village*, New York: Academic Press.

Forge, A. (1972) 'Normative factors in the settlement size of Neolithic cultivators (New Guinea)', in P. J. Ucko, R. Tringham, and G. W. Dimbleby (eds) *Man, Settlement and Urbanism*, London: Duckworth: 363–76.

Fox, H. S. A. (1981) 'Approaches to the adoption of the Midland system', in T. Rowley (ed.) *The Origins of Open-Field Agriculture*, London: Croom Helm: 64–111.

Fox, H. S. A. (1992) 'The agrarian context', in H. S. A. Fox (ed.) 'The Origins of the Midland Village', Leicester (Papers prepared for a discussion session at the Economic History Society's annual conference, unpublished).

Freeman, S. T. (1968) 'Corporate village organisation in the Sierra Ministra', *Man* 3: 477–84.

Freeman, S. T. (1970) *Neighbors. The Social Contract in a Castilian Hamlet*, Chicago: University of Chicago Press.

Hallam, H. E. (1981) *Rural England 1066–1348*, Sussex: The Harvester Press.

Harvey, P. (1989) 'Initiative and authority in settlement change', in M. Aston, D. Austin and C. Dyer (eds) *The Rural Settlements of Medieval England*, Oxford: Blackwell: 31–43.

Heidinga, H. A. (1987) *Medieval Settlement and Economy North of the Lower Rhine*, Assen/Maastricht: Van Gorcum.

Hill, D. (1981) *An Atlas of Anglo-Saxon England*, Oxford: Blackwell.

Hodder, I. (1982a) *The Present Past*, London: Batsford.

Hodder, I. (ed.) (1982b) *Symbolic and Structural Archaeology*, Cambridge: Cambridge University Press.

Hodder, I. (1982c) *Symbols in Action*, Cambridge: Cambridge University Press.

Hodder, I. (1986) *Reading the Past*, Cambridge: Cambridge University Press.

Hodder, I. and Orton, C. (1976) *Spatial Analysis in Archaeology*, Cambridge: Cambridge University Press.

Holzach, M. (1979) *Das Vergessene Volk*, Deutscher Taschenbuch Verlag.

Hooke, D. (1988) 'Introduction: later Anglo-Saxon England', in D. Hooke (ed.) *Anglo-Saxon Settlements*, Oxford: Blackwell: 1–8.

Jarman, M. R., Vita-Finzi, C. and Higgs, E. S. (1972) 'Site catchment analysis in archaeology', in P. J. Ucko, R. Tringham and G. W. Dimbleby (eds) *Man, Settlement and Urbanism*, London: Duckworth: 61–66.

Kirsten, E. (1956) *Die Griechische Polis als historisch-geographisches Problem des Mittelmeerraumes*, Colloquium Geographicum Band 5, Bonn: Ferd. Dümmlers Verlag.

Lamb, H. H. (1977) *Climate. Past Present and Future. Vol. 2. Climate History and the Future*, London: Methuen.

Lewin, R. (1993) *Complexity. Life at the Edge of Chaos*, London: J. M. Dent.

Philippson, A. (1951) *Die Griechischen Landschaften* (Edited by H. Lehmann and E. Kirsten), Bd I.1, Frankfurt: V. Klostermann.

Postan, M. M. (1975) *The Medieval Economy and Society*, London: Penguin Books.

Pounds, N. J. G. (1974) *An Economic History of Medieval Europe*, London: Longman.

Redman, C. L. (1978) *The Rise of Civilization*, San Francisco: W. H. Freeman and Co.

Roberts, B. K. (1977) *Rural Settlement in Britain*, London: Hutchinson.

Ruschenbusch, E. (1985) 'Die Zahl der griechischen Staaten und Arealgrösse und Bürgerzahl der "Normalpolis"', *Zeitschrift für Papyrologie und Epigraphik* 59: 253–63.

Sauerwein, F. (1969) 'Das Siedlungsbild der Peloponnes um das Jahr 1700', *Die Erdkunde* 23: 237–44, Beilagen VI u. VIa.

Sherratt, A. (1981) 'Plough and pastoralism: aspects of the secondary products revolution', in I. Hodder, G. Isaac and N. Hammond (eds) *Pattern of the Past. Studies in Honour of David Clarke*, Cambridge: Cambridge University Press: 261–305.

Tak, H. (1990) 'Longing for local identity: intervillage relations in an Italian town', *Anthropological Quarterly* 63: 90–100.

Vita-Finzi, C. and Higgs, E. S. (1970) 'Prehistoric economy in the Mt. Carmel area of Palestine: site catchment analysis', *Proceedings of the Prehistoric Society* 36: 1–37.

Waley, D. (1988) *The Italian City-Republics*, London: Longman.

Wilkinson, J. C. (1983) 'Traditional concepts of territory in southeast Arabia', *Geographical Journal* 149: 301–15.

Wobst, H. M. (1974) 'Boundary conditions for paleolithic social systems', *American Antiquity* 39: 147–78.

Wobst, H. M. (1976) 'Locational relationships in palaeolithic society', *Journal of Human Evolution* 5: 49–58.

SELECT BIBLIOGRAPHY

Susan Tax Freeman's wonderful Spanish village study (1970) from the ethnographic present is admirably complemented by Wendy Davies's remarkably rich portrayal of early

544

medieval villages in Brittany (1988). Harold Fox's exciting model for the evolution of English medieval villages into corporate communities as human ecology (1992), sadly remains unpublished, but the groundwork can be found in an earlier publication (1981). Robin Dunbar has recently produced a volume on his stimulating theories for human social evolution (1996). I have tried to bring together the concept of the corporate community, human ecology, and rural settlement geography in my extended paper on the ancient Greek city-state (Bintliff 1994), which was initially inspired by the neglected and obscurely published masterpiece of Kirsten (1956).

14

FOOD AND FARMING

Graeme Barker and Annie Grant

INTRODUCTION

The purpose of this chapter is to review the evidence of archaeology for the prehistory and history of food, and for the changing relationship between food (and the associated products of food production) and human culture. The *Shorter Oxford English Dictionary* defines food as 'what one takes into the system to maintain life and growth, and to produce waste' (*SOED* 1973: 782), the latter part of the definition nicely presaging the necessary relationship between inputs and outputs in the acquisition of food that is an important theme for this chapter. Humans share their need for food with the rest of the animal kingdom, but the techniques we have evolved to obtain our food set us completely apart, in sustaining extraordinary densities of population and threatening the sustainability of the environment in ways unmatched by other species. Furthermore, animals eat food to stay alive, but for all humans, even in the most demanding environments, eating is inextricably related to culture, and is the primary context of most social relations (Goody 1982).

We must also remember that humans – farmers especially – do not exploit plants and animals simply for their food and drink. A critical aspect of agriculture is the production of food for livestock – hay and fodder crops – to maintain stock through the seasons when grazing is poor, to improve stock health for breeding, and so on; and many hunter-gatherers in the past have also sought to improve grazing conditions for the game they exploited. Plants, terrestrial mammals, sea mammals, birds and fish produce a wide variety of oils for lighting and fuel. Straw and dung are both important sources of fuel for many societies. Humans have clothed themselves entirely with plant and animal products until the advent of artificial fibres. Plant products, bone, antler, horn and leather, augmented with stone and metal, have had

546

much the same role in tool and ornament making before plastics. Plants have always been the main source of medicines, potions and drugs until the development of the modern pharmaceutical industry.

Humans have occupied the globe for several million years, and for most of that time they have obtained their food by various combinations of gathering, collecting, scavenging and hunting (Chapters 19 and 20). The production of food on a systematic basis has a much shorter history (Chapter 21), its beginnings generally equated in time with the transition to the modern climatic era, the Holocene, some 12,000 years ago, though in many parts of the world the transition to food production was thousands of years later, and a very few societies have remained hunter-gatherers to the present day. For the *SOED*, farming is 'the business of cultivating land and raising stock' (1973: 727), and is equated with agriculture: 'the science and art of cultivating the soil, including the gathering in of the crops and the rearing of live stock' (1973: 39–40). The mixture of art, science and business in these definitions is a useful introduction to an important distinction used in this chapter. In discussing the acquisition of food in the past we are sometimes dealing with 'subsistence', in the sense of what people lived on, but often also with 'economy', in the sense of the management and mobilization of resources – the creation of food and related products surplus to the immediate requirements of the human group, and the use of that surplus for non-subsistence purposes such as feeding non-producers in a community, or for barter, payment of tax or tribute, or sale in a market (Barker and Gamble 1985).

Like all the thematic discussions in this section of the *Encyclopedia*, therefore, this chapter has an impossibly wide remit in time and space, and we have only been able to select what seem to us key themes, and illustrate them with case studies from a wide variety of regions, periods and societies. The acquisition of food may seem one of the most mundane activities that we can study in the archaeological record, relatively amenable to archaeological investigation. The exploitation of plants and animals for food by past humans, however, whilst certainly reflecting adaptations to the constraints and opportunities of particular environments, was also associated in intimate and complex ways with human culture – with technological skill, demographic pressures, economic structures, the aspirations of particular social groups, perceptions of risk and opportunity, and ritual life.

SOURCES AND METHODS

Documents

We are concerned in this book first and foremost with archaeological evidence, but of course archaeologists interested in food and farming can, for the historic periods of the past, learn a great deal from a wide variety of written sources. From the earliest civilizations of Mesopotamia, Egypt and the Aegean to the modern era, states have created huge archives of official records documenting their involvement in the management of food production and distribution, in trade of agricultural products, in market prices, and taxation systems. At the other extreme are what we can glean from individuals' life experiences as shown in personal diaries and the like, such as the jottings by serving Roman soldiers on wooden writing tables at the Vindolanda fort on Hadrian's Wall. In between is a huge mass of written material of potential use – official inscriptions on public monuments, private inscriptions on buildings and tombs, agricultural treatises, poems and so on.

Of course there are many instances where documentary evidence gives us a mine of information about aspects of food and farming that we could never glean from archaeology. A good example is the wealth of written records left by the ancient Egyptians on the use of plants in medicine (Reeves 1992). We learn that fir resin was used as an antiseptic and for embalming, aloe for catarrh, cinnamon for ulcerated gums, incense for sweetening air and as a fumigator, fleabane for driving fleas out of a house, henna to treat hair loss, root of pomegranate to dislodge roundworm, beer for boils (rubbed on, not drunk!) and, as a remedy for crying children, a paste of *spn* seeds (probably poppy) mixed with fly dung from the walls, strained and drunk for four days.

Like archaeological data, the references to food and farming in the huge variety of written material left by past societies cannot be taken simplistically as 'telling us how it was'. Literacy has rarely been widespread, so the majority of people within the historic period did not create history in the sense of writing it. Then there is the mix of fact and fiction in so many ancient sources that makes reading somebody like the fifth-century BC Greek historian Herodotus such a delight. To this we must add the agenda of the writer: the Celts living on the fringe of the Roman world, for example, were variously portrayed by Roman authors as bloodthirsty barbarians deserving to be conquered, or Noble Savages living in peace and harmony as models for the innocence Rome had lost – descriptions that tell us more about Roman politics than iron age societies. There are numerous other examples of descriptions of the lifeways of peoples beyond the frontier, whether Arabs through the eyes of Crusaders, indigenous Americans in the nineteenth century through the eyes of contemporary white politicians and soldiers, or the Indian peoples of the Amazonian rain forest in the modern era. The Roman agronomists such as Cato, Pliny and Varro are invaluable sources for learning about Roman farming in Italy, so long as we remember that much of their writing consists of exhortations on 'best practice' rather than literal descriptions of what most Roman farmers might actually have done (White 1970).

Iconography

One of the defining features of our species is the making of art, and the representation of experience through iconography (Mithen 1996). Most of the great art systems of prehistoric Europe – upper palaeolithic cave art, the Levantine mesolithic rock shelter paintings of the Iberian peninsula, the Scandinavian and alpine rock carvings of later prehistory, the artefact decoration of the Celtic Iron Age – include representations of activities associated with subsistence, whilst from societies such as ancient Egypt there are enchanting models of agricultural and domestic scenes (Stead 1994). The designs pecked into the surfaces of glacial boulders in the Val Camonica in northern Italy, for example, generally regarded as mainly bronze age (second millennium BC) in date, include scenes of people hunting deer with dogs, of ploughing with a crook ard pulled by a pair of what are assumed to be cattle or oxen, and villages of small wooden houses surrounded by small rectangular fields (Anati 1976). Potentially such material is an exceptionally rich source of information, as long as we do not try to divide it into things we think we can recognize as scenes of everyday life, on the one hand, and evidence of 'ritual' on the other. Of course prehistoric artists drew on their experiences in the world they inhabited, but we cannot select out what we think we can understand, as mirror images of everyday life: everything that we know of art systems produced by people such as Kalahari San and Australian Aborigines today, for example, emphasizes the powerful and complex links between the production of motifs and ritual behaviour, with designs often being made after dreams and trances, sometimes drug-induced (Lewis-Williams 1983). Even in the case of art systems produced by 'more accessible' peoples such as the Romans, modern scholarship emphasizes the complexity of meanings and messages encoded in apparently straightforward images of, say, agricultural or hunting scenes in the mosaic floor of a villa (Scott 1997).

Artefacts

For most historic periods of archaeology the function of many artefacts associated with hunting, farming, food preparation and eating can usually be discerned given the other sources of information on technology available, such as written records and the variety of iconographic material, like the carvings in some English churches of different craftsmen, or illustrations in illuminated manuscripts and early books showing hunting, pastoral and agricultural scenes (Langdon 1988; White 1984). Prehistorians can learn from the same sources, and also from the ethnographic record of contemporary or recent non-industrial societies, and it is from typological comparisons with the latter sources in particular that most of the common functional descriptions used by archaeologists for prehistoric artefacts – axe, knife, scraper, strainer, sickle, harpoon, mortar, and so on – are derived.

However, in most instances we can only infer the function of an artefact, not know it, and there are good reasons to emphasize the need for considerable caution in the straightforward interpretation of function on the basis of typological similarities, and even more so when artefact types are being used to identify systems of subsistence. Artefacts of similar shape and size can be used for entirely different purposes. Grinders and sickles have sometimes been regarded as useful indicators of early farming, yet grinders can be used for grinding cultivated seeds, or wild seeds, or substances such as ochre for body painting, and sickles can be used for harvesting cultivated plants, or wild plants, or fodder for animals, or thatch for housing. The geometric flint microliths of the European Mesolithic are assumed to have been armatures for arrows, and most of them presumably were, given the discovery of wooden arrowshafts with microliths attached in resin as points and barbs, but in a famous discussion of mesolithic subsistence David Clarke (1976) pointed to one ethnographic example of identical microliths being mounted upright in a wooden board and used for shredding vegetable foods. An added complication is that the same artefacts might well be used for different purposes during their lifetime, and ethnographic studies suggest that many an artefact in prehistory passed between functional and ceremonial uses – several times, perhaps – through its 'biography', with different meanings to different people at different times (Hodder 1982).

Despite these problems, there is much we can learn from the artefactual record about food and farming. When preservation conditions are good, the material that survives can be so specific that it is difficult to deny reasonable interpretations of function. The prehistoric 'lake villages' of the alpine region in Europe are a good example of a waterlogged archaeological context which has yielded a remarkable array of artefacts where functions associated with a wide range of hunting, fishing, and agricultural activities can be postulated with reasonable confidence (Fig. 14.1). A rich variety of wooden, or wooden-based, agricultural, gathering and food-processing equipment has survived from waterlogged prehistoric, Roman, and medieval sites in Europe, as have desiccated artefacts from the arid regions of the world, from the Peruvian desert to Tutankhamun's tomb in Egypt. Artefacts of organic materials associated with food and farming found in the excavations of the waterlogged deposits of Viking Dublin included: wooden churns, shovels and spades; ropes and tethers of tree roots and withies; hurdles of coppiced wattles; wooden spindles, bone whorls, weavers' swords of wood, weaving tablets of antler, horn and bone, a wide variety of bone needles, and hundreds of examples of cloth and spools of thread; a huge variety of leather goods; and even mosses collected as lavatory paper (Wallace and O'Floinn 1988).

Also, some artefacts are so specific that their general purpose seems not in doubt.

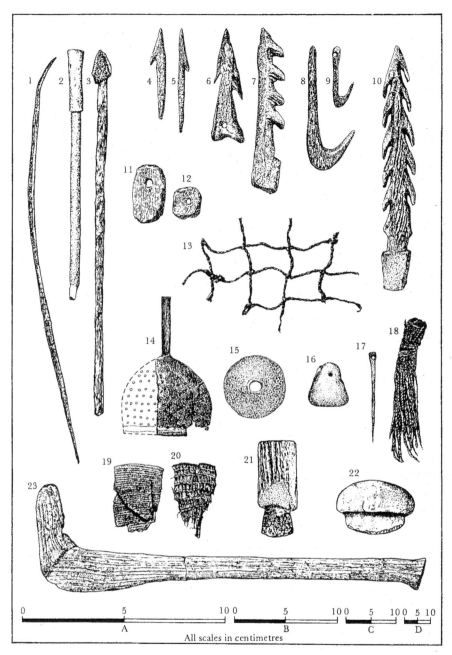

Figure 14.1 Artefacts associated with hunting, fishing, and farming activities from water-logged prehistoric sites in Switzerland. 1. wooden bow; 2. wooden fowling arrow; 3. wooden arrow with flint point; 4, 5. bone harpoons; 6, 7. antler harpoons; 8, 9. bone fish hooks; 10. antler harpoon; 11, 12. wooden floats; 13. fish net; 14. wooden carving board for flax; 15. bone spindle whorl; 16. clay loom weight; 17. bone needle; 18. skein of thread; 19, 20. textile fragments; 21. stone axe in antler sleeve; 22. flint knife or scraper in wooden sleeve; 23. wooden handle for axe or adze. All at scale B except 13 (A), 14 and 23 (C) and 1 (D). Source: G. Barker 1985.

In this category we can include hand cultivation tools such as shovels, spades, and hoes, wooden ards (primitive ploughs that cut a furrow but did not turn the sod) and ploughs, metal ploughshares, metal sickles and scythes, horse-riding equipment such as saddles, bits, bridles and horseshoes, and transport items such as sledges, carts, carriages, and chariots, skis and snow-shoes (Clark 1952). Bronze age 'Canaanite jars' from the Ulu Burun wreck off southern Turkey contained pistacia resin, the essential ingredient of incense, and had dockets attached to some of them identifying their contents with the Egyptian word for incense, *sntr* (Mills and White 1989).

Archaeological science can also aid us considerably in the interpretation of artefacts (Chapter 9). In one common approach, microscopic traces of use-wear damage on the cutting edges of prehistoric flint artefacts are compared with use-wear patterns on the edges of replicated tools used separately for, say, chopping bone, cutting meat, scraping leather, and cutting up plant foods (Donahue 1988; Keeley 1980). Microscopic traces of the food or other organic materials with which the artefact has been in contact may also sometimes be identifiable by chemical analysis: in the case of Palaeoindian stone tools, for example, it has indicated their use for plant collection and processing (Briuer 1976). Gas chromatography and mass spectometry have been used to identify the presence of oil and wine in classical amphorae (Condanin *et al.* 1976; Rottländer and Hartke 1982). Potsherd residues are one of the main indicators of plant domestication and use in tropical areas where macroscopic plant remains survive very poorly (Hill and Evans 1989). Residue analysis of earthenware bottles in the frozen tombs of Pazyryk on the Russian steppes indicates that they were probably filled with a version of the traditional drink of the steppe nomads, koumiss (Rudenko 1970). Isotopic analysis of organic matter encrusted on potsherds from sites in the Peruvian Andes showed that the pots had contained tubers such as potatoes, and even indicated that the potatoes had been boiled and mashed (Hastorf and DeNiro 1985).

Settlements, structures and fields

The earlier archaeological literature was full of inferences about people being either hunters or farmers, or at least either nomads or settled people, on the basis of the settlement traces found, on the assumption that hunters always move around the landscape leaving few traces, whereas agriculturalists always stay in one place and build permanent dwellings. Inevitably, better understanding of the ethnographic record has demonstrated that archaeologists need to assume that most settlement forms *per se* cannot be taken as simple indicators of subsistence behaviour, or even of degrees of mobility or sedentism.

As with artefacts, individual structures revealed by excavation may well be open to alternative interpretations as to function. The classic examples are 'four-posters', the square settings of four post-holes cut into the subsoil on many British iron age sites – what structure was built on top of four posts? The most reasonable interpretation is that the four post-holes are all that is left of above-ground granaries, but ethnographic analogies have been cited of 'four-posters' variously supporting dwellings, hayricks, chicken coops, pigsties, racks for smoking and drying meat, lookout towers, and scaffolds for exposing corpses. However, much can be learned from the structural evidence of some settlements when the evidence is very specific. In many past societies, farmers lived under the same roof as their livestock, and from a variety of prehistoric and early historic settlements excavated in temperate Europe, from the first *Linearbandkeramik* farmers to the Vikings, we can see from floor plans how the dwellings were divided into space for people and space for cattle, the latter further divided into stalls for individual beasts (Hvass 1993; Whittle 1993; Fig. 14.2). In English deserted medieval villages, we can recognize distinct types of accommodation for humans, livestock and equipment in the 'toft' or farmyard, though sometimes the livestock and equipment were housed separately and sometimes incorporated within the main residential building depending on factors such as status, topography and regional custom (Astill 1988a).

We can also learn much about the function of structures from archaeological science. A detailed analysis of food refuse in and around two late neolithic water-logged sites in the Jura mountains in France has revealed a great deal about the function of the different buildings (Arbogast *et al.* 1995). Similar survival of organic remains at waterlogged bronze age farms in the Netherlands has enabled the recognition of houses, barns, byres, and hayricks – the latter consisting of a single post-hole at the centre of a circular gully, with numerous remains of the house mice and field voles that made their homes at the bottom of the haystacks (Ijzereef 1981). There are comparable examples of Roman-period, Viking and later medieval farms in Scandinavia and northern Germany. At the other extreme, good survival conditions in the Libyan desert allowed the recognition of many aspects of Roman-period farms: the dwellings, storage buildings, press buildings for producing olive oil, water storage cisterns, and even the stalling areas for the flocks, as the sheep and goat dung survived in the arid climate (Barker *et al.* 1996).

In many regions there is also a rich archaeology for the agricultural landscape beyond the farm or village. Throughout north-west Europe, for example, there are extensive traces of fossil 'field systems' of prehistoric, Roman and medieval date, surviving especially in upland and pasture areas as the low banks of earth or stones that formed the field boundaries. Dartmoor in south-west England is a good example of an upland region where the study of such evidence has given us excellent information about agricultural organization from prehistoric to medieval times, in terms of both the functioning of agricultural systems and the social

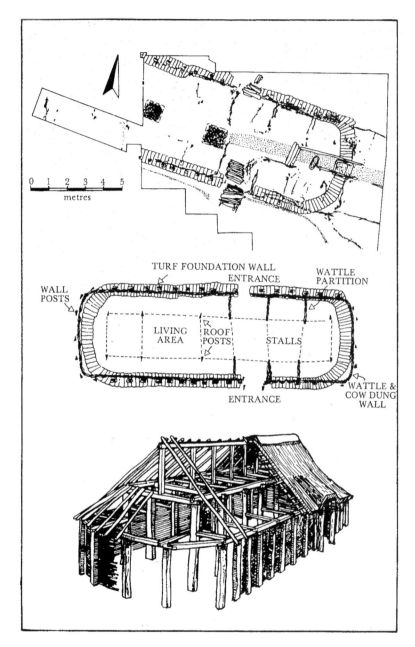

TURF FOUNDATION WALL
ENTRANCE
WATTLE PARTITION
WALL POSTS
LIVING AREA
ROOF POSTS
STALLS
ENTRANCE
WATTLE & COW DUNG WALL

Figure 14.2 A reconstruction of the Tofting farmhouse in northern Germany. Source: G. Barker.

context in which they operated, from individual farms to community landscapes (Fleming 1988; Fleming and Ralph 1982).

In addition to field boundaries, traces of ancient ploughing within them survive in many parts of Britain and Ireland now used for pasture or rough grazing; they take the form of long narrow banks separated by shallow depressions, variously termed 'ridge and furrow', 'rig (or rigg) and furrow' or 'lazy beds' (Astill 1988b). Rather comparable field systems were created by Palaeoindian farmers in the American Midwest using hoes made of large mammal scapulas (Gallagher *et al.* 1987). In the Mediterranean region, air photography has revealed extensive systems of Roman land division in the lowland zone, the 'centuriation' well known from the classical authors, where square fields of standard size were laid out on a single axis across the landscape (Chouquier *et al.* 1987). Studies have also begun of the chronology and functioning of ancient terrace systems in the Mediterranean uplands (Moody and Grove 1990; Wagstaff 1992), as in the semi-arid regions of North America (Sandor *et al.* 1990). By contrast, field-system archaeology in arid regions such as North Africa, the Middle East and the American Southwest is extremely well developed, the focus here generally being on the functioning of such systems in terms of capturing and diverting seasonal floodwaters, as is discussed later (see pp. 576–8).

Palaeoecological indicators

Many of the indicators of past environments discussed in Chapter 6 are also important for the information they can provide about the effect of human activities on past landscapes.

Soil science, for example, can be an important indicator of human settlement and agricultural activities such as grazing and manuring, because such activities can affect the physical and chemical properties of sediments (Courty *et al.* 1990; Limbrey 1975). These techniques can be invaluable at a variety of scales, from providing insights into the function of individual buildings and fields, and the agricultural activities implied by the creation of buried soils or palaeosols (Fieller *et al.* 1985), to regional geomorphological studies of Holocene valley alluviation, a phenomenon which is variously explained in terms of either climatic change, or activities such as cultivation and pastoralism, or combinations of the two (van Andel *et al.* 1985; Bell and Boardman 1992; Lewin *et al.* 1995).

Pollen analysis, or palynology, has been of critical importance once the possibilities were realized of interpreting pollen diagrams as signatures not only of ecological change in response to climatic change but also of human activities affecting vegetation, though there is the need to refine techniques for distinguishing such 'human impacts' from clearings caused by natural events such as forest fires and freak storms (Edwards 1989).

Many pollen-bearing deposits also contain phytoliths, minute particles of silica from plant cells, and they have also been found surviving within potsherds and on the surfaces of artefacts and teeth. Like pollen, phytolith assemblages can be invaluable indicators of both plant assemblages in the past and of human activities affecting those assemblages (Pearsall 1989; Piperno 1985). Moreover, being specific to different parts of the plant, phytoliths can also be useful for differentiating between wild and domestic plants, and in some instances may provide evidence of the conditions in which plants were grown (Rosen 1994). Land molluscs have also been used like pollen and phytoliths as indicators of agricultural activities. Snails are adapted to different ecologies, such as wet and dry soils, grassland and woodland, so changes in snail populations through time can be used like changes in pollen spectra, as in the classic study of snail assemblages underneath the neolithic barrow of South Street near Avebury in southern England, interpreted as evidence for woodland clearance by neolithic farmers prior to the construction of the barrow (Evans 1971).

Human remains

Simon Hillson in Chapter 7 describes the rich variety of information about diet, health and disease that can be gleaned from the application of archaeological science to human skeletal remains. When survival conditions are good, as in many water-logged and desiccated environments, the evidence may even include the stomach contents of bodies (Brothwell 1986; Glob 1971) and faecal material (Callen 1969; Hillman 1986; Holden 1994; Reinhardt and Bryant 1992; Sobolik 1990), providing us with extraordinary snapshots of single meals, with information on condiments, nutrition, pharmacology, and food processing and preparation, as well as insights into health and disease from parasite levels (A. K. G. Jones 1992). Coprolites can be a remarkable mine of information – they may contain macrobotanical, microbotanical, macrofaunal and microfaunal remains (bone, hair, shell, undigested plant remains, pollen, phytoliths, fungal spores, parasite eggs and so on) – but their study is not for the faint-hearted: techniques include not only visual identification and chemical studies but even odour analysis (Moore *et al.* 1984) and experimental studies on modern material (Osborne 1983)!

More commonly we have to glean insights into diet from skeletal remains: from tooth wear and decay, and from the changes to bone chemistry caused by long-term reliance on plants, meat and/or fish that may be revealed by isotopic analyses of bone collagen. In Portugal, for example, isotopic analyses document a change from a predominantly meat diet amongst mesolithic people to a neolithic agricultural diet higher in plant foods, coinciding with evidence for a decrease in tooth wear and in the incidence of caries as a result of the dietary shift (Lubell *et al.* 1994). There are comparable studies of dietary shifts accompanying agriculture in North America, in many cases associated with health decline (Cohen and Armelagos 1984; Katzenberg 1992). In ancient Egypt, plaque-related diseases and tooth wear both increased with urbanization as the amount of meat decreased in the average diet, and enamel hypoplasia increased in children's teeth because of vitamin deficiencies at weaning (Hillson 1979).

Plant remains

Macrobotanical plant remains survive on archaeological sites in a number of ways: as impressions in fired clay, such as pots, ovens, and hearths; as waterlogged, desiccated, or mineralized remains, preserved respectively by anaerobic conditions, aridity, and by calcium phosphate replacement (commonly in latrine deposits); and – especially – as carbonized or charred remains, burnt either in a major conflagration or accidentally during processing (some cereal crops in antiquity had to be roasted to remove their husks). Occasionally large samples of plant remains are found in storage pits, pottery vessels, ovens and the like, but more commonly they are extracted from bulk soil samples by one of a series of painstaking processes: dry sieving in the case of desiccated remains, wet sieving for mineralized seeds, and water flotation for carbonized seeds.

Macrobotanical remains are often informative about past environments, and they may also provide indications of seasonal activities by the communities which harvested them; they also of course inform on diet. However, beginning with pioneering work by Robin Dennell (1972) on samples of carbonized plant remains from neolithic *tell* villages in Bulgaria, the focus of much research in archaeobotany has been on refining our understanding of the formation processes that create different kinds of plant samples, and their significance in terms of cultivation and processing systems (Greig 1989; Hastorf and Popper 1989; G. E. M. Jones 1992; Jones 1985; van der Veen 1992a). In support of this there has been a great deal of ethnoarchaeological research amongst traditional farming communities in countries such as Greece and Turkey to try to define the 'archaeobotanical signatures' (such as different mixes of seeds, chaff, and weeds) created by different cropping regimes and processing systems (Hillman 1981; Jones 1984; Fig. 14.3).

A key focus of much archaeobotanical research has been and remains on the origins and spread of crop farming in different regions of the world (Harris 1996; Harris and Hillman 1989; Ucko and Dimbleby 1969; see Chapter 21), but the increasing sophistication of archaeobotanical methodologies in terms of contextual analysis has also enabled archaeobotanists studying the cereal-based agricultural systems of Europe and the Near East to reconstruct not only diet and subsistence but also cultivation regimes, scales of agricultural production, and economic

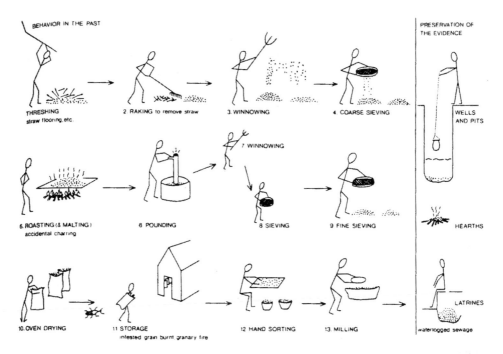

Figure 14.3 Cereal crop processing: ethnoarchaeologicial studies of these activities in traditional farming communities help archaeobotanists to recognize such acitivities in archaeological samples. Drawn by Annick Boothe, from *Archaeology: Theories, Methods and Practice* by Colin Renfrew and Paul Bahn, published by Thames and Hudson Ltd, London, 2nd edn, 1996. After Greig 1983.

processes such as specialization in production, the exchange of foodstuffs, and intensification (Jones *et al.* 1995; Jones 1985; Murphy 1983; van der Veen 1992a).

Animal bones

The study of animal bones from archaeological excavations began in the nineteenth century – for example, with identifications of the bone fragments found in palaeolithic caves in France and in the 'lake villages' of the alpine countries. These early studies tended to be by veterinarians, who were primarily interested in the morphology of the species represented and, in the case of bones from Pleistocene sites, on the information they provided about the contemporary glacial or interglacial environment. This information remains of interest, but in recent decades the focus of this branch of study, archaeozoology, has shifted to what animal bones can tell us about the people who exploited the animals.

As in the case of human remains, unusually wet or dry survival conditions may yield entire bodies with their stomach contents, skin, faecal matter and so on, but on most archaeological sites the evidence consists of bones: either articulated skeletons (or parts of skeletons) of animals that had died of disease or been buried for ritual purposes, or fragments of butchered bone discarded as food refuse (Davis 1986). The latter may include fish and birds as well as mammals. Microfauna (rodents, frogs, and so on) are generally analysed, like insect remains, primarily for their information on local environments (of which they can be sensitive indicators), though coprolite studies (for example from Palaeoindian sites in the south-west United States) show that some past societies subsisting in hostile environments had to include bugs and beetles in their diet as well as larger animals.

The information commonly recorded in an archaeozoological analysis includes the identification of the species represented and their relative frequency, the parts of the skeleton present, the age of the animals at death (calculated from long bone fusion and tooth eruption and wear: Wilson *et al.* 1982), evidence for sex (either morphological, or from measurements), for butchery techniques in the form of cut, chop or saw marks, and for disease and injuries, whether healed or fatal (Davis 1986; Grayson 1984; Klein and Cruz-Uribe 1984; Payne 1972). Measurements of groups of bones are also used variously as indicators of domestication, environmental change, and changes in husbandry techniques.

As in the case of archaeobotany, there has been a great deal of research by archaeozoologists on developing methodologies for recognizing the many 'taphonomic' biases that have affected the material under study in its long journey from being part of a living herd of animals to becoming a pile of fragments in the laboratory (Lyman 1994). Whilst these biasing factors are still imperfectly understood, archaeozoologists have been increasingly successful in demonstrating that their materials can provide a remarkable range of information about ancient societies: on the exploitation of animals for subsistence purposes, whether by scavenging, hunting, or herding, or combinations of these activities; on stock-keeping for different husbandry goals, whether for meat and/or for the 'secondary products' of live animals such as milk, wool, and traction; on stock management for the purposes of producing a surplus of animals on the hoof or of animal products, for gifts, exchange, trade, or tribute; and on the role of animals in human ritual. Animal remains may also be indicative of the season of occupation of a site, on the evidence of migratory fish and birds, deer antler, and jaw bones of young animals if the season of birth can be judged (for example: Brinkhuizen and Clason 1986; Grigson and Clutton-Brock 1983; Legge and Rowley-Conwy 1988).

Molluscs

Molluscs provided a useful, sometimes critical, source of meat for past societies, and the chemical composition and robustness of their shells mean that the latter often survive on archaeological sites. Many hunter-gatherer societies in the recent past, for example in South America, Australia and southern Africa, have collected shellfish, many food-producing societies have used shellfish as a welcome addition to the diet, and shellfish have often been a critical resource for many coastal communities (Bailey and Parkington 1988; Grigson and Clutton-Brock 1983). Techniques have been developed for using the species ecology, shell shape and shell chemistry of marine shellfish for reconstructing the environment of the midden in terms of coastal ecology and levels of salinity, whilst the season of collection may also be adduced from species demography, growth lines, and oxygen isotope analysis (Bailey *et al.* 1983; Claessen 1993; Killingley 1981).

Attempts have also been made to calculate the dietary value of a shell midden for the community that created it, usually by estimating the quantity of shells, converting that figure into meat weights, and then trying to compare this information with similar calculations for the other sources of plant and animal food used by the community (Koike 1986). Such studies face enormous problems, given the difficulties of estimating the total population of a midden, the heavily seasonal use often made of shellfish, the numerous uses of shellfish in addition to that of human food (for fishbait, for example, or for items for tool manufacture and trade), the common practice of drying shellfish for later eating, and unknown cooking practices. In general, archaeologists have tended to downplay the value of shellfish as a food source given the amount of time and effort needed to collect them – you need to collect over 50,000 oysters or over 150,000 cockles, for example, to get the calorific value of one red deer (Bailey 1978) – but for many communities shellfish may have been a critical starvation food. Also, ethnographic studies of some Australian aboriginal communities indicate that shellfish collecting was valued by the women as 'quality time' to enjoy each other's company and that of their children.

Ancient DNA

The principles of ancient DNA studies described in Chapter 7 in respect of human remains apply equally to studies of plants and animals. This is a new area of research of great potential, though with formidable methodological difficulties. At the time of writing, for example, there are a number of research projects on ancient DNA underway in Britain funded by the Natural Environment Research Council, grouped within what is termed the Ancient Biomolecules Initiative. Many of these projects are addressing themes relevant to this chapter and to Chapter 21, such as the domestication and early breeding history of cattle in Europe and Africa, horse in Siberia and eastern Europe, llama and alpaca in South America, sorghum in Africa and wheat in Greece (Eglington 1996). In virtually all cases the recovery of ancient DNA is proving so piecemeal that, whilst the occurrences are providing intriguing hints about domestication and husbandry history, most of the useful information from these projects has been coming from studies of DNA in modern populations – but the situation is likely to change in the near future as we move from the present experimental phase of laboratory techniques.

Experimental archaeology and ethnoarchaeology

Archaeologists can only explain the past in terms of observations of the present, particularly for the periods before writing, but we obviously cannot make the same one-to-one linkage between, say, modern hunter-gatherers and prehistoric hunter-gatherers that the geographer can make between the behaviour of modern and ancient rivers. Hence experimental archaeology and ethnoarchaeology both play vital roles in helping us move from observations of systematic patterning in archaeological data to more robust explanations of such patterning.

Experimental work has already been mentioned in the context of artefact analysis, and in terms of farming prehistory sites such as the Butser Iron Age Farm in Hampshire, southern England, have also been useful for understanding the possible efficiency of prehistoric farming methods, and storage pits, and the kinds of structures built where only ground plans have survived from excavations (Reynolds 1979). These kind of experiments sometimes tell us how things could not possibly have been done, rather than the opposite, but they still give salutary lessons. One important proviso is that we cannot recreate ancient animals and people: thus modern Dexter cattle are as small as iron age cattle were in Britain, but putting a twentieth-century English academic, two Dexter cattle, and a replica of a prehistoric plough together (as was done in a famous experiment at Butser) clearly does not give us an exact guide to the efficiency or otherwise of iron age ploughing techniques and iron age farmers!

Ethnoarchaeology is the study of contemporary communities with the specific purpose of understanding the relationship between their behaviour and the kind of archaeological signatures created by it (Gould 1980). The work by archaeobotanists on crop processing activities has already been mentioned, and ethnoarchaeological research has been just as fundamental for archaeozoologists in understanding the taphonomic processes that affect faunal samples (for example: Binford 1978, 1984; Brain 1981). Beyond these studies, however, ethnoarchaeology has also helped promote an awareness of how the creation of archaeological residues such as bone and seed samples can be structured by social relations as much as by subsistence needs and economic goals (Hodder 1982).

SCALES OF PRODUCTION

As mentioned at the beginning of this chapter, the acquisition of food and of associated animal and plant products can operate at a variety of scales. First and foremost are the most basic requirements of subsistence, to obtain sufficient food to maintain human life. If the system can be intensified in some way so as to obtain a surplus, whether of live animals, or of plant and animal foods, or of plant and animal non-food products, then it has the capacity to support one or more of a variety of economic goals. More food means that more people within the community can be fed, including non-food-producers such as craft specialists, priests, and élite groups. Within communities and between communities, people can compete for resources, with the winners taxing the losers. Social obligations can be met with gifts. There are the means for trading with neighbouring communities for scarce resources. The ability to intensify subsistence systems to create surplus food and food products that sustain new social and economic relations has been a cornerstone of human prehistory and history.

Yet at the same time, the other theme running through agricultural history is the difficulty most subsistence farmers face in intensifying production. In medieval Europe, for example, cereal yields were invariably low, animals small and unproductive compared with today, and technologies primitive, resulting in a vicious circle of low-input/low-output farming: 'the evil of small harvests due to insufficient manuring, the lack of manure being in turn the result of small agricultural production, making it impossible to keep more cattle . . . How narrow were the boundaries that restricted the practice of farming. The opportunities in ancient farming were very limited' (Slicher van Bath 1963: 10, 23). The same was true of the peasant farmer in Roman times: without proper fodder, the problems of maintaining a team of plough cattle through the summer drought could leave the oxen so weak that one of the Roman agronomists recommended the Italian farmer to feed grain to his oxen before the ploughing season to build their strength up, starving his own family in the process (White 1970). Even in today's global market, much of the developing world is still characterized by agricultural communities operating at the most marginal levels of subsistence.

So how and why have many human communities managed to intensify their food-production systems so successfully and so spectacularly from the earliest agriculture 10,000 years ago to the agro-businesses of the modern industrialized nations? In the case of European agricultural history, Grigg (1982) discusses the contrasting evidence for the influence of four major stimuli in the intensification of agricultural systems: changes in climate and environment; the invention and adoption of new technologies, such as more efficient ploughs and harvesting tools; the pressure of rising populations; and social change. There is the same theorizing regarding agricultural intensification in prehistory too (Barker 1985). Most of these theories have also characterized the debate over how and why agriculture was invented in the first place, and in time adopted by most of the world's population (see Chapter 21).

In recent years one important theme in the debate on the social context of intensification has been the emphasis on how farmers, like hunters, need to deal with risks, hazards and uncertainties in their decision-making (Halstead and Jones 1989). Strategies need to be in place for dealing with the expected unpredictabilities of fluctuating harvests. These may include practical mechanisms such as storing food, diversifying the food supply, or subdividing fields, but they can also include social mechanisms of mutual obligation as in the case with many subsistence farmers today, where a family can help out its neighbour one year in the knowledge that it might need the same thing the next; in many societies, too, valuable equipment is owned communally and shared. Thus few subsistence farmers in fact operate as independent economic units, and systems of 'social storage' amongst past subsistence farmers, whilst developed as a mutual self-help system, must have had the potential to allow particular individuals or communities to gain advantage over others through the acquisition and control, rather than sharing, of resources (Halstead and O'Shea 1989).

Although we can discern many instances of significant agricultural intensification in the archaeological record, it is extremely difficult to identify causation with much confidence. In prehistoric Europe, for example, there are many examples of agricultural intensification, but in virtually all cases these are associated with significant changes in other aspects of the cultural system: new technologies for tillage or harvesting, for example; or more complex societies than hitherto; or larger populations than hitherto; extensions in the settled area; or combinations of any of the above. Did the adoption of the new technology allow more land to be cultivated, or the same land more productively, with more food allowing populations to rise? Did the rise in population force the adoption of a new, more productive, but more labour-intensive, technology or agricultural system? Did technological change and agricultural intensification facilitate social stratification? Was the rise of élites in pre-state and state societies the context in which new technologies were adopted – and controlled by them – to create more surpluses? Add to this the undoubted effects of significant climatic change, which we can generally discern, and the unknown but probably significant effects of the small-scale fluctuations in sequences of good and bad harvests which we generally cannot, and we are invariably faced with sequences of agricultural intensification where the chickens and eggs of causation are impossible to separate.

It is also important to emphasize that agricultural change, like the transition to farming that preceded it, need not be, and certainly was not in the past, unilinear, an inexorable process of increasing intensification. It must be expected that archaeology will increasingly reveal examples of subsistence 'de-tensification' as well as of intensification as its database grows more detailed, though such fluctuations are only gradually being detected (e.g. van der Veen 1992a).

The following sections sketch in the variety of hunting, agricultural and pastoral systems we can discern in the archaeological record, before we turn to the social archaeology of food and farming.

HUNTING SYSTEMS

There has been an enormous amount of debate regarding the subsistence behaviour of the early hominids, but microscopic studies of their teeth and isotopic analyses of their bones suggest that they had a predominantly vegetarian diet. It is now thought that they probably foraged in sexually discrete groups, eating as they went – no home bases, no hunting, no food-sharing as once thought (Chapters 19 and 20). They probably scavenged, though, taking meat from carcasses killed by lions, leopards and hyenas, activities in time greatly aided by primitive hand-tools. The critical factor in the effective colonization of the northern latitudes was the ability to use hunting as a means of coping effectively with the shorter days and harsher winters than further south (Dennell and Roebroeks 1996). It is quite likely that these early humans practised 'confrontational scavenging', allowing other carnivores to kill large animals and then chasing them away to get at the meat themselves, but the nature and location of the butchery marks on bones of rhinoceros, horse, bison and giant deer at Boxgrove indicate that the carcasses were more or less intact when butchery started, making it likely that the people were hunting these large animals (Roberts 1996). Another technique seems to have been to stampede animals into swamps or over cliffs (Scott 1980).

Most middle palaeolithic sites in Europe consist of caves containing evidence for flint knapping and carcass butchery associated with fire, but true hearths or camp-sites are very rare (Stringer and Gamble 1993). In a detailed case study of two caves in central Italy, Mary Stiner (1991, 1994) found that one of these caves, Grotta Guattari, had mainly heads and hooves of animals such as red deer and fallow deer, whereas the other cave a few kilometres away, Grotta Sant' Agostino, had most parts of their bodies represented. The Grotta Guattari was also used by hyenas, whose scavenging activities left very similar faunal samples to those left by the Neanderthals. The implication is that Neanderthal bands roamed the landscape practising a mixture of hunting and scavenging, one possibility being that they divided these activities between males and females. They then transported the meat back to convenient locations such as caves for defrosting by fire and (as far as we can tell) immediate consumption. Skeletal studies show how hard life was for them, with hunting as likely to end in a bruising close-quarter wrestling match as in a clean kill at a distance (Stringer and Gamble 1993). All was not mayhem, however: some Neanderthal faunal samples suggest 'controlled, focussed, and selective hunting strategies' (Gaudzinski 1996: 37) like those of the Upper Palaeolithic (see also, for example, Patou-Mathis 1994).

The last 40,000 years of the Pleistocene were characterized in the northern latitudes by some of the most hostile glacial conditions ever endured by humans, yet this was the period when fully modern humans were able to spread from Eurasia to North America and Australia. The period also witnessed extraordinary transformations in technology and subsistence, and probably also in cognitive skills (Dennell 1983; Mithen 1996; and see Chapters 18 and 20). In Europe, there is consistent evidence that upper palaeolithic hunters specialized in hunting migratory herbivores such as reindeer and horse in the north and red deer and steppe ass in the south. It used to be argued that the reindeer hunters followed the herds over hundreds of kilometres throughout the annual migrations, more or less to the exclusion of other game (Sturdy 1975), but the consensus now is that most of the hunting bands were probably more like the Nunamiut caribou hunters of Alaska who specialize in intercepting the deer at key ambush locations during their seasonal migrations, augmenting this meat with other food sources at other times of the year (Binford 1978; Weniger 1987). In France, detailed studies of cave faunas indicate that different bands of upper palaeolithic hunters camped at different points along the migration routes, killing the deer at different seasons (Boyle 1996; Fontana 1995). At Canecaude in the Aude basin, reindeer made up almost 90 per cent of the animals killed, though the wide variety of other species (cattle, horse, chamois, red deer, ibex, pig and small game such as hare) implies a range of hunting skills from spearing at a distance (using spear-throwers) to trapping (Fontana 1995). Red deer and steppe horse hunting in the Mediterranean seems to have been as strongly seasonal as reindeer hunting north of the alps (Donahue 1988). Such specialized hunters would have had to have developed effective strategies for dealing with fluctuations in prey numbers, and Mithen (1990) argues that palaeolithic cave art probably had such a function: images not just of different species of animals and birds (and of different types such as old, young, male, female, healthy, sick) but also of their tracks, hoofprints and dung, and of the terrain where they were most likely to be found, suggest that the caves must have acted in part as invaluable repositories of hunting lore, for example when hunters needed to vary between cooperative game drives and individual stalking.

In some parts of the world highly specialized systems of hunting remained effective methods of subsistence after the end of glacial conditions – the bison hunters of the North American plains are a good example (Speth 1983) – but more commonly diversified systems of hunting, fishing and gathering developed. In Europe the postglacial climatic warming created a landscape of forests, lakes and rivers teeming with wild life, and mesolithic subsistence systems adapted accordingly. The classic site remains Star Carr in northern England excavated in the late 1940s and early 1950s by Grahame Clark, where *c.* 7500 BC a platform of birch branches and brushwood was constructed at the edge of a lake; bones of a variety of animals were dumped around it such as elk, cattle, pig and roe deer, but especially red deer (Clark 1954). The site has been interpreted variously as a winter base camp (Clark 1972), an all-year-round ambush location (Andresen *et al.* 1981) and most recently (on the basis of a taphonomic study of red deer body parts and roe deer tooth eruption) as a summer hunting camp (Legge and Rowley-Conwy 1988). Presumably Star Carr represents one, possible brief, moment for a community that practised a cycle of hunting, fishing and gathering within an annual territory that probably extended from the coast to inland hills. The shell middens of the tiny island of Oronsay off the Scottish mainland are another example of a 'seasonal snapshot' – in this case of a community who probably moved between the mainland and the adjacent islands (Mellars 1988). In southern Scandinavia, in contrast, we are fortunate in having a series of well-excavated sites with excellent conditions of organic survival both on the coast and inland, and elegant models of seasonal cycles of hunting, fishing, and gathering have been proposed as a result (Bang-Andersen 1996; Larsson 1978, 1983; Zvelebil and Rowley-Conwy 1986; Fig. 14.4).

In general we know far less about mesolithic plant gathering than hunting, fishing, fowling and shellfish collection (Clarke 1976), but Zvelebil (1994) argues convincingly that a wide variety of berries, nuts, leaves and roots was collected, involving not only the use of a number of hand-tools but also perhaps even protective tending and weeding – a form of horticulture, in effect. These findings also accord with the growing palynological evidence that mesolithic hunters were burning and clearing forest to encourage secondary growth, thus improving feeding conditions for animals such as red deer (Caseldine and Hatton 1993; Simmons and Innes 1987; Simmons *et al.* 1989). By *c.* 5000 BC integrated systems of hunting, fishing and gathering (and horticulture?) sustained highly complex and more-or-less sedentary mesolithic communities in a number of regions of Europe, particularly coastal regions with plentiful terrestrial and marine foods (Rowley-Conwy 1983; Zvelebil and Rowley-Conwy 1986).

Comparable systems of hunting, fishing and gathering developed during the Holocene in many regions of the world, especially where marine and terrestrial resources were abundant (Bailey and Parkington 1988). In Japan, as in Europe, these systems proved resilient enough to sustain highly complex societies much like the Ainu of more recent times, who were stratified into nobles, commoners and slaves, the nobles undertaking the prestige hunting of dangerous game, and lower class groups specializing more in fishing (Akawaza and Aikens 1986; Watanabe

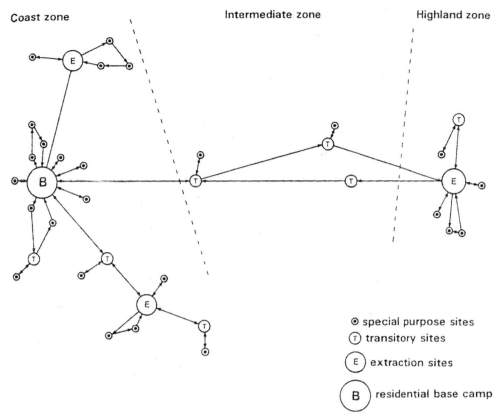

Figure 14.4 A model of mesolithic seasonality and territoriality in southern Norway. Source: Bang-Andersen 1996.

1972). The Ganges valley in India and the eastern seaboard of North America are other examples of regions where rich resources sustained more-or-less sedentary and stratified societies (Chattopadhyaya 1996; Sanger 1996). Similar arguments to those put forward in Europe for forest management by postglacial hunter-gatherers have been proposed for the tropical forests of South America (Linares 1976) and Asia (Groube 1989).

Wild foods have remained a critical resource for many farmers from the earliest history of agriculture, and remain so for most agricultural societies outside the industrial world. In prehistoric Europe, many societies relied more on foraging than farming for hundreds and in some cases thousands of years after they first began to use domestic plants and animals (Barker 1985), and the same is true of many other regions of the world (Hall 1987; Harris and Hillman 1989 *passim*; Stark and Vorhies 1978; Tankersley and Isaac 1990; Zvelebil 1986). In the case of complex societies relying on agriculture for their sustenance, the pursuit of wild foods has commonly taken two forms: to provide a supplement for people subsisting on a monotonous diet of plant staples; and as a leisure pursuit for the wealthy, one of the ways of demonstrating their 'otherness' from the rest of the population: the iconography of all the ancient civilizations is invariably full of images of the chase. In medieval England, considerable investments were put into creating and protecting suitable habitats for game – deer-parks, dovecotes, 'pillow-mounds' (warrens constructed for rabbits), fishponds and so on – and in legislating to circumscribe ordinary people's access to wild resources (Grant 1988).

AGRICULTURAL SYSTEMS

Temperate

It is not the purpose of this chapter to debate the arguments surrounding the change from hunting to farming, but certainly in most of temperate Europe given the kind of evidence described above it seems increasingly difficult to maintain the thesis of a simple dichotomy between mesolithic hunting and neolithic farming that has been one of the central tenets of prehistoric archaeology for well over a century (Barker 1985; Zvelebil 1986, 1996). In many parts of temperate Europe, early neolithic subsistence is now seen as having more in common with late mesolithic subsistence than with the agricultural systems that developed later in the Neolithic (Thomas 1996). In Britain, for example, stable isotope studies of skeletons indicate an early neolithic diet dominated by meat and leafy vegetables, with cereal foods of little importance – grain may have been grown on a very limited scale largely for ritual purposes (Evershed *et al.* 1991; Richards 1996); one recent suggestion (based on pot residues) is that much of it may in fact have been for brewing rather than eating (Dineley 1996).

What is clear is that the agricultural systems that developed in temperate Europe using the exotic domesticates from the Mediterranean and the Near East were, from the outset, well adapted to the cooler, wetter and more forested environments (Bogucki 1988): thus cattle were generally more important than sheep; the ceramic sieves of the first *Linearbandkeramik* farmers (Bogucki 1984) suggest that milk may have been extracted for human use from a very early stage in cattle and sheep husbandry; and spring sowing may also have been developed. Some of the most remarkable insights into the nature of early temperate farming come from the alpine 'lake villages' (mostly in fact small farmsteads) because of the extraordinary survival of organic materials. At Thayngen Weier in Switzerland, for example, cattle byres were recognized from the presence not only of cattle dung and bedding straw but also insect remains including the puparia of the common house fly, which liked to overwinter in warm cow houses; structures with deposits rich in macrobotanical remains of ivy, ash, twigs, clematis, and elm shoots, and with very high frequencies of pollen of fodder plants such as ivy, were identified as the barns containing the winter leaf fodder for the cattle (Guyan 1966). As noted earlier, the tradition of humans sharing their houses with their cattle has endured in many parts of temperate Europe for most of the prehistory and history of farming (Hvass 1993; Whittle 1993; Fig. 14.2).

Although many elements of the 'Secondary Products Revolution' (Sherratt 1981, 1983) were probably a feature of temperate European farming from the beginning (Chapman 1982), the exploitation of animal secondary products (the products of the live animal such as milk, wool, and traction power) probably did not develop on a systematic basis until the third and second millennia BC, coinciding with increasing social complexity (Chapter 22). Bogucki (1993) argues that there may have been a causal relationship: in providing meat, milk and wool, sheep and goats were ideal as 'insurance', as a 'walking larder', whereas cattle would have been an expensive luxury for meat given their slower growth rates – they needed some four years to get to optimum body weight – so the development of dairying made them more useful, but it was traction that really made them come into their own. Traction enabled farmers to raise production by cultivating more land (though switching from hand-tools to ploughs probably meant that yields per hectare fell) and transporting bulk goods (crops, fodder, fuel wood) from remote locations to the residential base. Cattle would have increased in value as assets worth accumulating through barter, bridewealth, gift exchange and raiding, facilitating the development of social stratification as winners (whether families or individuals) moved upwards and losers moved downwards into dependency relationships.

Associated with these social developments were transformations in the agricultural landscape. In the earlier neolithic systems of subsistence, land ownership seems often to have been communally based, with ancestral rights reinforced and legitimated through the siting of burial monuments. By the second millennium BC, however, there is increasing evidence for people demarcating their land with formalized boundaries – banks, fences, hedges, and ditches (Fleming 1988; Taylor 1996). Much has been learnt of the organization and functioning of the farms at the centre of such landscapes from modern extensive excavations of waterlogged settlements and their surrounding pens, paddocks and drove-roads (Ijzereef 1981; Pryor *et al.* 1985).

By the first millennium BC we can discern complex agricultural economies operating at the regional scale in the highly stratified competitive world of the pre-Roman Iron Age. In central-southern England, for example, contextual studies of large samples of botanical and faunal remains from different kinds of settlement indicate that grain and animals on the hoof were bartered between communities and exchanged within client relationships (Grant 1984; Jones 1985). Rising populations coincide with widespread evidence for agricultural intensification in the centuries preceding the Roman conquest: both field systems and pollen diagrams indicate an expansion of the agricultural area, improved ploughs allowed the cultivation of heavier soils, and different crop mixes were developed to take advantage of these (Jones 1986; van der Veen 1992a). In Holland there is the first clear evidence for sod manuring of sandy soils (*plaggen* culture) at this time, though it may have begun earlier (Groenman-van Waateringe 1978). With Romanization there is increasing evidence for specialization in agricultural production for urban markets, but the core of the system remained cereal farming on the lowlands to feed the urban population, with cattle-keeping critical for ploughing and manuring the arable land (Grant 1989; King 1989). One interesting result of Romanization, though, was the development of viticulture in north-west Europe, remarkable evidence for which has been found recently in the excavation of a Roman farm in Northamptonshire in the English Midlands, where the vineyard survived as a series of parallel ditches containing post-holes, depressions made by the root balls of plants, and plentiful vine pollen found in the trench fills – the excavator calculated that the 6 kilometres of trenches represented 4,000 vines, or 15,000 bottles of wine (Meadows 1996).

In northern Europe outside the Empire, agricultural systems remained much like those of the pre-Roman Iron Age, though there is some evidence for the production of grain and animals (and even furs in the far north) for the Roman markets (Randsborg 1985; Zvelebil 1985). Gennep, a migration period (fourth/fifth century AD) centre in the Dutch Meuse area, is a good example of a well-preserved settlement with farmhouses, barns, granaries, ovens and wells, an élite stronghold whose inhabitants controlled local trade routes, received cereals, cattle and pigs as tribute, and spent most of their time raising horses, hunting, and drinking (Heidinga 1994). In Scandinavia at this time the number of cattle byres on farms and the size of their surrounding fields suggest similar landscapes of inequality, with cattle a standard of value and a means of payment (Nasman 1996). Soil analyses indicate that the fields were cultivated in single course rotations without fallow, so requiring much manure, but excavations of key sites such as Vorbasse (Hvass 1993) and of well-preserved field systems (Widgren 1983, 1990) indicate that, during the course of the first millennium AD, there were developments in efficiency: infield land was fenced off as manured arable fields and meadows for winter fodder, and separated from summer pasture on the surrounding outland.

One of the most elegant studies of the long-term development of an agricultural landscape in the temperate zone, in many ways typical in its trends, has been the investigation of the Ystad region in southern Sweden by an interdisciplinary team of ecologists, archaeologists, and human geographers (Berglund 1991; Fig. 14.5). Agricultural settlement began in the Neolithic, when crops such as emmer, einkorn and naked barley were introduced, though there were many similarities with preceding mesolithic subsistence in terms of forest management and seasonal territoriality. Phase 2 marked the development of permanent agriculture in the Bronze Age,

570

TOOLS AND TECHNIQUES

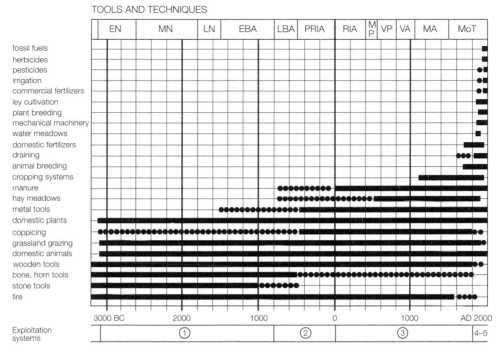

Figure 14.5 The development of agricultural systems in the Ystad area, southern Sweden. For explanation of the five exploitation systems, see text. EN – early neolithic; MN – middle neolithic; LN – late neolithic; EBA – early bronze age; LBA – late bronze age; PRIA – pre-Roman iron age; RIA – Roman iron age; MP – migration period; VP – Vendel period; VA – Viking age; MA – Middle Ages; MoT – modern time. Source: Berglund 1991.

characterized by cattle longhouses, fodder collection, and the manuring of fixed fields. Phase 3, beginning in the first millennium AD, was characterized by the development of infield–outfield systems, with one-course tillage (of hulled barley and rye especially) of manured fields, and coppice–pastures beyond. Feudal landscapes were in place by the tenth century, becoming increasingly segregated in the ensuing centuries, but the agricultural system remained essentially unchanged until the early eighteenth century (Phase 4), when the permanent arable was improved by external nutrients and yields increased by three-field tillage. The late nineteenth and twentieth centuries (Phase 5) have been marked by the extraordinary transformations to the landscape caused by the development of capitalistic industrial farming, with its crop rotation systems, the use of under-draining and marling, and mechanization.

Mediterranean

Until the introduction of modern mechanized systems, farming in the semi-arid landscapes of the Mediterranean was characterized by extensive cereal farming, the fields being prepared for sowing by light ploughs pulled by oxen, cattle or horses; by a reliance on the small stock best adapted to coping with the paucity of summer feed, sheep and goats, with much use made also of the donkey for transport; and by the integration of cereal and animal husbandry with the cultivation of vines, olives and other tree crops such as figs. Until recently it was common in many regions to see the intermingling of these crops in systems of 'polyculture' – alternate rows of olive trees and vines, with small patches of cereals and legumes grown in between, especially on terraced hillslopes. The other feature of traditional Mediterranean land use has been transhumant systems of grazing, in which large numbers of livestock (especially sheep and goats) were driven on the hoof each year between widely separated winter upland and summer lowland pastures. Archaeology now shows that many aspects of this 'traditional' Mediterranean farming have in fact only developed very slowly (Barker 1995; Halstead 1987a, 1987b).

Agriculture seems to begin rather suddenly in the eastern Mediterranean about 7000 BC, the settlement of Knossos on the island of Crete remaining the single most convincing example of the traditional colonization model. In the central and western Mediterranean, however, there now seems to have been a very long period of several thousand years during which mesolithic populations made some use of domesticates but relied predominantly on hunting, fishing, and gathering, the latter including the harvesting of morphologically wild cereals and legumes (Barker 1985; Rowley-Conwy 1995). Lewthwaite (1986) suggests that the domesticates may have spread westwards as part of exchange systems of prestige goods between indigenous hunting populations, agriculture only finally becoming established throughout the Mediterranean basin as the mainstay of subsistence by about the fourth millennium BC.

Early farming here was practised in a predominantly forested landscape, often by springs and in other areas of natural moistness. The diet of these societies was probably dominated by plant foods, both gathered and cultivated (the latter with simple hand-tools), the livestock being kept on only a small scale, quite possibly for social as much as for subsistence reasons (Halstead 1981, 1987b, 1996a). By the fourth millennium BC, as agriculture spread throughout the region, there are indications of the beginnings of traditional dryland cereal farming, integrated with systems of sheep/goat husbandry in which the animals were kept both for their meat and their milk. Halstead (1992a) suggests that livestock exchange amongst these societies, in exchange for surplus arable produce, is likely to have been an important element in the process of wealth differentiation and social ranking that is increasingly visible at this time. In the third millennium BC the evidence for social

572

stratification is even clearer, and it coincides with the first clear evidence for the development of viticulture, presumably for the production of wine as an élite drink – the evidence is strongest in the Aegean Early Bronze Age, where it was also associated with olive cultivation and terrace cultivation (Renfrew 1972), but there are indications of viticulture amongst the contemporary societies of the central and western Mediterranean too (Barker 1995; Chapman 1990).

The second millennium BC in the Aegean was the period of the Minoan–Mycenaean civilization. The remarkable tablet archives suggest that palaces such as Knossos and Pylos owned huge estates in their territories and extracted surplus foodstuffs and other agricultural products such as wool from their subservient populations, giving food rations back in return – mainly bread and oil, the traditional poverty diet of the Mediterranean peasant. One of the more striking features of the tablets is that a palace such as Pylos owned flocks of sheep in the tens of thousands, but probably only a dozen plough oxen – they are named individually in fact. Halstead (1992b) suggests that the palace élites farmed their estates extensively, the land being ploughed by their oxen and their flocks probably being managed in systems of transhumance, whereas the peasants were farming small plots intensively and keeping small flocks of sheep and goats, the entire system being meshed together in flows of goods and services to and from the palaces – the system of surplus banking termed 'social storage' by Halstead. In Spain at this time the control of the plough teams may also have been a key feature of élite power (Gilman 1981). In the Italian peninsula, pollen evidence shows that the mountain forests were now being opened up (whether by climate change or human action or both is not clear), and there is also good archaeological evidence for the expansion of settlement into the highest mountains, presumably for summer shepherding (Barker 1995) (one bronze age settlement on the Maiella mountain is on the site of a modern ski resort, for example).

Many aspects of Mediterranean farming, therefore, were in place by the end of the second millennium BC, but it was not until classical times that the Mediterranean landscape as we know it today really took shape. In the images on painted Greek vases and Etruscan tombs, as well as from the surviving artefacts and models, we can see virtually the full range of agricultural equipment and activities of the present-day Mediterranean farmer prior to mechanization. Archaeobotanical evidence indicates that the development of the Etruscan city-states in central Italy was accompanied by an expansion in the number of cereal and legume species cultivated alongside olives, vines and figs, a frieze in one of the Etruscan tombs at Tarquinia showing mixed crops in rows suggesting that the advantages of polyculture were now deliberately sought. *Cuniculi*, underground channels, were cut to divert water through hillsides onto irrigated fields. A recently excavated Etruscan farmstead (Fig. 14.6) had evidence in its structures and artefacts for wine-making and cheese-making, and the excavators calculated that, if ancient Etruscans drank more or less

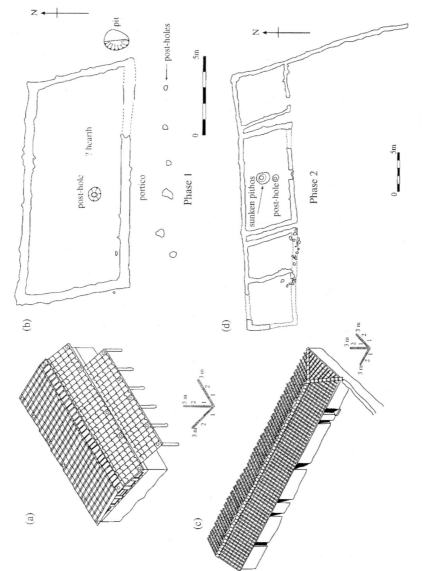

(b)

post-hole
? hearth

portico

Phase 1

pit

post-holes

N

0 5m

(d)

sunken pithos
post-hole

Phase 2

N

0 5m

(a)

3 m
2
1
3 m
2
1
3 m
2
1

(c)

3 m
2
1
3 m
2
1
3 m
2
1

Figure 14.6 Podere Tartuchino, an Etruscan farm. Source: Barker and Rasmussen 1997.

the same as modern Italian farmers (a total unquantifiable it has to be admitted!), the family would have been producing a surplus of wine more than three times their own needs (Perkins and Attolini 1992). The faunal samples from Etruscan towns indicate the intensification of animal husbandry in the countryside to supply the growing urban populations with meat and secondary products, and specialized butchery systems can be identified; but trace element and dentition studies of Etruscan skeletons reveal a steady decrease in animal and vegetable products in the diet, and the dominance of cereal foods (Barker and Rasmussen 1998). Similar trends in farming and diet accompanied urbanization in Greece (Foxhall 1997; Garnsey 1988, 1992). For most ordinary people in these early Mediterranean states, the main opportunities to taste fresh meat were probably the religious festivals, a situation in many respects unchanged until recent times.

Although one of the most striking features of the Roman landscape is the evidence of land allotment or centuriation as revealed by air photography (Chouquier *et al.* 1987), probably the most important development was the growth of the large estate at the expense of the small farm. The trend had begun in classical Greece – half of Attica, the territory of Athens (so often portrayed as a democracy of peasant citizens) may have been owned by less than 10 per cent of the population (Foxhall 1992) – but it accelerated dramatically with the expansion of Rome, as the wealthy élites of first Italy and then the provinces invested their ever-increasing riches in slave-staffed estates specializing in production for the marketplace. The trend is clear not only in the written sources but also in the ploughsoil evidence of numerous archaeological surveys (Alcock 1994; Barker and Lloyd 1991; Carreté *et al.* 1995; van Andel and Runnels 1987). Large-scale excavations of the villas at the centre of these estates such as Settefinestre in Italy have revealed in extraordinary detail how close was the organization of such establishments to the ideal described by the Roman agronomist Varro: the *pars urbana* or living space for the noble family, and the *pars rustica*, with its facilities for processing and storing agricultural products, together with the accommodation for the slaves (Carandini 1985). The piles of broken wine amphorae outside Rome's port of Ostia and the cargoes of numerous shipwrecks around the Mediterranean are further eloquent testimony to the success of such estates in supplying the burgeoning urban markets of the Empire. Large-scale long-distance transhumance was another component of estate farming (Whittaker 1988). The evidence for high rural populations and large-scale agricultural practices coincides in many regions with geomorphological evidence for significantly accelerated rates of erosion (Lewin *et al.* 1995).

With the collapse of the western Roman empire there was generally a considerable decline in population, and it was not until the tenth century or so that the pattern was established of nucleated village settlement so typical of the Mediterranean landscape today. In the Biferno valley in central-southern Italy a programme of archaeological survey and excavation documented a series of cycles of expansion and contraction in village settlement over the past thousand years, the expansion phases generally coinciding with geomorphological evidence for accelerated erosion as land was taken back into cultivation or used more intensively (Barker 1995). There is similar evidence from Greece (van Andel and Runnels 1987) and Spain (Fédéroff 1998). The most striking feature of all these studies, however, is that the damage pales into insignificance compared with the effects of mechanization and agri-business in the past few decades.

Arid

Deserts are the most hostile environments for human subsistence, particularly so for farmers, because of the scarcity of perennial water supplies, the paucity, irregularity and geographically localized nature of rainfall, and the effects of these factors on plant growth. The !Kung San of the Kalahari desert and the Australian Aborigines are well-known examples of peoples who have developed effective ways of living in deserts by combining the hunting of small mammals with collecting a very wide range of edible plants, tubers, snails and grubs within carefully organized systems of seasonal scheduling and mobility (Gould 1980; Lee 1979). The other way of living in arid environments is pastoralism (discussed on pp. 584–7), whereby people rely on the animals they herd to convert the desert vegetation into humanly accessible protein, systems which invariably require seasonal mobility in search of pasture. However, archaeology also provides evidence for human societies which have succeeded in living in arid environments as more-or-less sedentary farmers, practising forms of subsistence that involved a significant element of crop cultivation, invariably based on the careful management of water. Techniques included digging canals to divert water from river valleys onto adjacent arid lands; cutting underground conduits to reach aquifers; and, especially, 'floodwater farming', the construction of diversion walls and checkdams to capture the floodwaters that flow down hillslopes after rainstorms. The term 'floodwater farming' was first used by Bryan (1929) to describe the traditional systems of farming practised by the indigenous peoples of Arizona, and archaeological evidence for floodwater farming proves the antiquity of such systems, not only in this region (Fish and Fish 1994) but also in North Africa, the Middle East and Arabia (Gilbertson 1986; Gilbertson and Hunt 1996). One of the best-known studies of the archaeology of floodwater farming was in the Negev desert of Israel, where the systems were reconstructed by the investigators and shown to function efficiently (Evenari *et al.* 1971).

It is important to remember that today's deserts have not always been so. In the Sahara region, for example, the transition to the Holocene 12,000 years ago brought sufficient rainfall to create a lush vegetation of woodland, shrubs, and grasses around rivers and lakes, and grassland on the intervening plateaux, allowing populations of hunter-fisher-gatherers to expand westwards right across the interior of North Africa from the Nile valley (Barich 1987; Wendorf and Schild 1980). These people then changed to pastoralism as the present-day climate and environment of the Sahara gradually developed from the sixth millennium BC onwards (Muzzolini 1993). Although these pastoralists probably grew cereals on a small scale, the first evidence for systematic cultivation in the Saharan oases is only in the late second and early first millennia BC (van der Veen 1992b). In the Fezzan region of southern Libya, it was based on the construction of *foggaras*: subterranean channels connected by vertical shafts, cut into the hillsides to collect water from underground aquifers and channel it down to the fields on the oases floors – similar structures, termed *qanats*, have also been a feature of arid-zone farming in parts of the Middle East. Significantly, this dramatic intensification in investment was in the context of the development of sedentary stratified societies in fortified settlements, who emerge a few centuries later into history (in the writings of the Greek historian Herodotus) as the Garamantes tribe.

As Wittfogel (1957) originally argued, many early states were situated in semi-arid lands and were supported by irrigation agriculture, and certainly in the Middle East, air photography has been used with remarkable effect to document the development of canal-building and irrigation farming between the Tigris and Euphrates rivers that formed the basis of successive civilizations from the Sumerians onwards (Adams 1981), and the diversion canals and floodwater catchments that sustained substantial settlements on the arid steppes further north (Wilkinson 1993). Field survey here suggests that fallowing and manuring were well understood as moisture conservation measures (Wilkinson 1990). There have been comparable studies of the irrigation systems of the early states of Peru and Mesoamerica (Blanton *et al.* 1981; Coe 1974; Farrington 1980). However, in the arid zone proper, perhaps the most striking feature of land use history in many regions has been the alternation between periods of intensive high-input/high-output sedentary agriculture sustaining high populations and phases of low-input/low-output subsistence pastoralism with lower-density populations. The former, moreover, have invariably been associated with social intensification, and often also with political change in the adjacent core regions of primary settlement. Two examples illustrate this.

In the Wadi Faynan in southern Jordan, for example (Barker *et al.* 1997), the agricultural sequence begins with an early neolithic (eighth millennium BC) village, situated at the head of the wadi by a perennial spring – the location is typical of many early farming settlements in the region such as Jericho and Beidha, presumably selected so that crops could be grown without irrigation in the damp soil by the spring (Sherratt 1980). By the fifth millennium BC, when the environment was significantly wetter than today, people were growing crops on soils that were naturally irrigated by floodwaters, but the first evidence for floodwater farming in the form of simple drystone diversion walls and terraces coincides with the emergence of stratified societies in the Bronze Age. This is also the case in the Negev nearby (Levy 1995a), where similar structural evidence for floodwater farming is further supported by phytolith evidence (Rosen 1994). The development of the iron age states in the first millennium BC was the context for the construction of an extensive and elaborate field system in the Wadi Faynan: floodwaters issuing from side wadis were trapped by drystone barrages, and diverted through sluices and baffles down onto terraced fields. The system was further expanded at the time of the Nabataean kingdom, and reached its climax during the centuries of Roman occupation, when it was used to feed a large population of slaves working in neighbouring copper mines. Erosion and wadi-downcutting gradually rendered the system unworkable by the end of the Roman period, and the region has been used since then for pastoralism.

The second example comes from Tripolitania in north-west Libya, from the pre-desert region between the well-watered coastal zone and the Sahara (Barker *et al.* 1996). The region was occupied by transhumant pastoralist populations until the Romans took control in the first century AD, at which point the local Libyan élites organized their followers (quite possibly by coercion) into sedentary farms producing foodstuffs for the markets provided by the coastal towns and the oases forts – potsherds with graffiti scratched on them (*ostraca*) at the Bu Njem fort, for example, describe the arrival at the fort of farmers from the surrounding area bringing fresh food and olive oil (Marichal 1992). Hundreds of villa farms were built in the pre-desert, their facilities including elaborate olive presses capable of producing a surplus of oil substantially beyond the needs of the community, surrounded by field systems where the floodwaters from the surrounding hills were concentrated (Fig. 14.7). Animal husbandry was reduced in importance because the main grazing areas for the stock were now enclosed for cultivating what seems, on the archaeobotanical evidence, to have been a remarkable range of crops: cereals (barley, wheat), pulses (lentil, pea), oil plants (olive, safflower, linseed, castor), Mediterranean fruits (grape, fig, pomegranate, almond, peach), African fruits (date, water melon) and herbs (van der Veen *et al.* 1996). In the southern parts of the pre-desert the communities seem to have reverted back to pastoralism after a couple of centuries, but in the better-watered northern wadis sedentary farming outlasted the collapse of the Roman markets and survives in places today.

Tropical

Though often envisaged as a kind of Garden of Eden, tropical rain forests are difficult to exploit by foraging alone (Bailey and Headland 1991), and the archaeological evidence in fact indicates that, from their earliest occupation, they were exploited by well-adapted foraging technologies that presaged horticulture. One

578

feature of many tropical rain forests are toxic plants that, if treated, are very valuable – they are often abundant, available for long periods, and storable – and a variety of tools had to be developed to deal with these: stone knives to crack nuts, stone grinders to crush kernels, baskets to leach out toxicity. Burnt endocarps of the toxic fruit *Pangium edule* have been found in the Niah cave in Borneo in levels probably as early as 40,000 BP (Bellwood 1990) and Groube (1989) suggests that waisted axes in New Guinea indicate that strategies were developed to change rain forest plant ecosystems from the earliest periods of occupation as early as 40,000 years ago, creating disturbed patches of forest to encourage economically important plants to thrive. Rain forest organic residues have now been identified on the edges of stone tools from Yombon, New Britain, *c.* 35,000 years ago (Pavlides and Gosden 1994). In South America, well-developed foraging technologies were practised by 11,200 years ago at Caverna da Pedra Pintada, Brazil (Roosevelt *et al.* 1996). In Australia, the tropical rain forests of the north-east were exploited for foraging by about 5,000 years ago, and by about 2,500 years ago this had developed to include the intensive exploitation of toxic nuts, using a distinctive technology (Cosgrove 1996).

The conventional wisdom has been that neolithic farmers colonized south-east Asia, spreading southwards from the Chinese mainland to Indonesia between about 6,000 and 4,000 years ago (Farrington 1990; Spriggs 1989). The process has been linked with the appearance of particular pottery styles such as Lapita ware, and with theories of language spread based on linguistic studies of the present-day languages of the region, rather like Renfrew's model of the colonization of Europe by neolithic farmers speaking an original Indo-European language (Renfrew 1987). As with the latter case, the situation now appears to be much more complicated. The most remarkable evidence remains the discovery of swamp drainage systems in the highlands of Papua New Guinea at the Pleistocene/Holocene boundary, probably for taro cultivation (Bayliss-Smith and Golson 1992; Golson 1990). Gosden (1992) documents the evidence for two-way transfers across the region as a whole, of Melanesian plants for south-east Asian animals. Developing from the 'forest management' mentioned earlier, there seems to have been a long process of experimentation from the late Pleistocene through the Holocene which involved extending the natural range of plants and animals and altering the ecologies in which they could be husbanded. The simple spread southeastwards of taro and yam, the basis of Pacific agriculture, is now doubted, and some food plants and animals certainly spread the other way; the cuscus *Phalanger orientalis* may have been taken to Timor by early foragers, and the wallaby *Thylogale brunii* may have been moved by people through the islands of the Bismark archipelago; and wild and tame pigs may have been exploited in extensive systems of management long before domestic pigs were husbanded intensively.

The study of farming systems in tropical environments is greatly hampered by

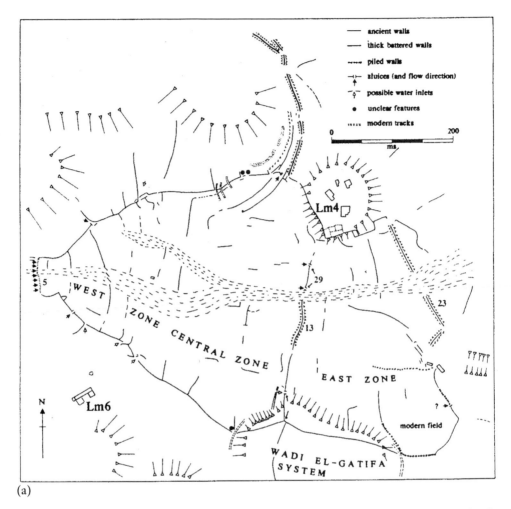

(a)

Figure 14.7 (a) A Roman-period farm and its system of floodwater farming in the Tripoli-
tanian pre-desert, Libya, and (b – opposite) plan and reconstruction of a Roman-period
olive press in the same region. Source: Barker *et al.* 1996.

the poor survival conditions of organic remains, especially of the root and tuber
crops that are the major staples of these regions (Hather 1992). In the islands north
of New Guinea pollen and charcoal have both been used successfully to document
the development first of small-scale swidden agriculture and then its replacement
by an 'agroforest' of breadfruits, taro, coconuts and yams (Athens *et al.* 1996). The
critical source of information has been phytoliths recovered from sediments, artefact surfaces and pottery fillers (Pearsall 1989; Pearsall and Trimble 1984), and the
combination of pollen and phytolith analysis has been used successfully in the New
World tropics to document the gradual development of swidden farming after

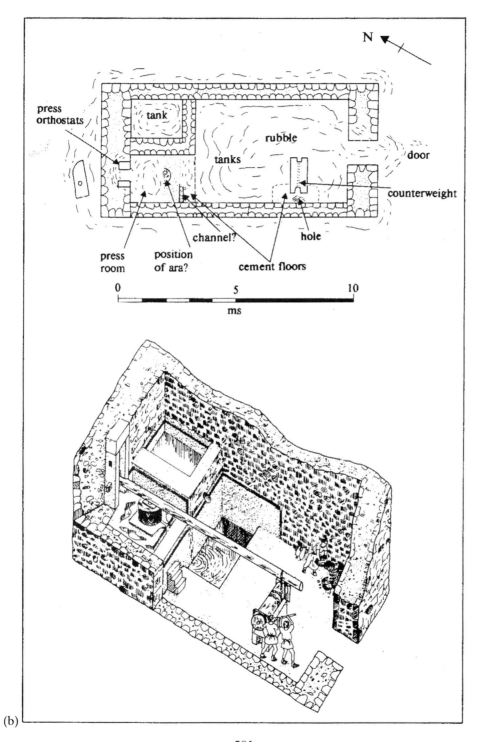

(b)

millennia of forest disturbance and manipulation, augmented in some regions by systems of intensive farming in the last 2–3,000 years (Pearsall 1996; Voorhies 1996). In recent years, too, these methodologies have been greatly strengthened by the realization that the soft tissues (parenchymatous) of root and tuber crops can be recognized in carbonized form by scanning electron microscopes – presumably they were overlooked or misidentified in the past as wood charcoal: remains of sweet potato, for example, have been found in Mangaia, one of the Cook Islands, from contexts dating to around AD 1000, clear evidence for its transferral from South America to Polynesia by this time (Hather and Kirch 1991).

In addition to botanical and faunal remains, the archaeological record of tropical farming includes field evidence for agricultural practice, beginning with the water disposal channels (over 750 metres long) cut in the Kuk Swamp of New Guinea 6,000 years ago (Hope and Golson 1995). A variety of irrigation systems sustained significant populations and complex social structures in central and South America, such as the Maya in Belize (Kirke 1980), and prehispanic chiefdoms in Colombia (Parsons and Denevan 1974) and Venezuela (Spencer and Redmond 1992). Some of the most remarkable relict landscapes are the buried paddy fields of Japan, where more than two hundred sites have now been excavated, their principal use for wet rice cultivation (for crops like taro and millet can also be grown in irrigated fields) confirmed by phytolith analysis (Barnes 1990) and even the discovery of the root holes of rice seedlings (Imamura 1996; Fig. 14.8).

Rice seems to have been cultivated first in the Yangtze valley of central China, between 9,000 and 6,000 years ago. Wild rice grew naturally in the coastal swamps and inland marshes of east and south-east Asia, and, for reasons that are not yet clear, by about 3,000 years ago many sedentary coastal and lacustrine communities were incorporating rice cultivation within their existing systems of hunting, fishing and gathering (Higham 1996). Rice grains, husks and phytoliths recovered from sediments and pottery fillers document the rapid spread of rice throughout the islands of south-east Asia (Glover and Higham 1996). Though the spread of rice has traditionally been correlated with the spread of farmers, in fact often it does not seem to have been an important crop until a few centuries ago, many people living by a combination of foraging and forest cultivation and taking their carbohydrates from plants such as the sago trees that grow wild in the forest – in Borneo, for example, rice cultivation sustained the coastal trading states of the medieval period, but most people in the interior have only turned to rice cultivation in living memory. Whilst the evidence for the history of tropical agriculture remains very fragmentary, the clear impression provided by the data is that there was no simple transition from hunting/gathering to farming, that systems of forest management were developed from very early in the history of their occupation and that the 'agroforest' has provided the principal means of sustenance for many people until the most recent past.

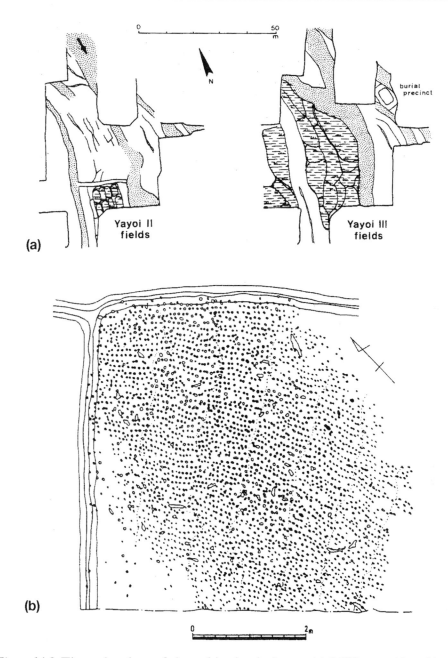

Figure 14.8 The archaeology of rice cultivation in Japan: (a) 2,000-year-old paddy fields excavated at Tamazu Tanaka and (b) traces of the root holes of rice seedlings on the surface of an excavated field at Hyakkengawa-Haroajima. (a) Source: Barnes 1992; (b) Source: Imamura 1996.

PASTORALISM

There are many definitions of pastoralism, as with the related concepts of nomad-
ism and transhumance, but for the purposes of this discussion we mean simply
forms of subsistence based predominantly on the management of animals. Pastoralism was regarded by Victorian archaeologists as a primitive form of husbandry, an
intermediate step in the ladder of progress between hunting and farming
(Westropp 1872), but anthropological studies of present-day pastoralists demonstrate both the complexity of pastoralism and also how pastoralist societies invariably operate in symbiotic relationships with agricultural societies (Dahl and
Hjort 1976; Khazanov 1984; Spooner 1973). The latter point is certainly confirmed by historical studies of pastoralist societies (Braudel 1972; Whittaker 1988;
Zeder 1994).

The study of pastoralism in antiquity presents archaeologists with considerable
methodological problems. Pastoralists today are invariably characterized by mobility, moving on foot or mounted (at least until the advent of trucks) as they shift their
animals between areas of grazing from season to season, so commonly they use
rather ephemeral shelters for themselves and their animals, and do not carry round
with them large quantities of material culture with later archaeologists in mind.
One result has been that archaeologists have too often had to have recourse to
postulating the presence of pastoralists on the basis of negative evidence: in the arid
regions of the Near East, for example, periods without settlements but with burial
cairns have been interpreted as periods of pastoralism, in this case part-supported
by biblical references to desert nomads (Bar-Yosef and Khazanov 1992; Finkelstein
1995), and rather similar arguments used to be put forward to explain periods of
European prehistory where burial monuments were the most visible component of
the archaeological record (Fleming 1971; Gimbutas 1965). In the context of these
debates, pastoralist societies have been studied by ethnoarchaeologists in terms of
the kind of 'archaeological signatures' created by their use of territory, structures,
artefacts, animals and plants (Barker and Grant 1991; Bar-Yosef and Khazanov
1992; Chang and Koster 1986; Cribb 1991; Gifford-Gonzalez 1984). Whilst our
understanding remains limited, there are now increasing examples of archaeological
studies where pastoralist societies can be recognized with some confidence.

There has been much debate amongst archaeologists about the antiquity of
Mediterranean pastoralism, particularly of the specialized forms of long-distance
transhumance still practised today (though fast disappearing) and recorded by
Roman and medieval writers, whereby huge numbers of livestock, especially sheep
and goats, were driven between lowland winter and summer upland pastures
(Maggi *et al.* 1991). Arguments used to be presented for the existence of long-
distance transhumance in various periods of Greek, Italian, southern French, and
Iberian prehistory, but the consensus now is that, whilst it may have been a

584

component of Minoan–Mycenaean estate farming, it was otherwise not a feature of Mediterranean prehistory, developing only with the emergence of the classical states (Barker 1989; Forbes 1995; Halstead 1996b).

The archaeological record of the arid zones on the fringe of the Tigris–Euphrates states of Mesopotamia has commonly been interpreted as cycles of land use oscillating between sedentary agriculture (the systems of floodwater farming discussed earlier) and pastoralism. In the Negev desert of Israel, for example, the Chalcolithic and Early Bronze II/III periods are usually characterized as socially complex and sedentary, and the Early Bronze I and IV periods as phases of 'reversal' or 'decline' to pastoralism explained variously in terms of climatic shifts, humanly adduced degradation, internal social change and external political influence (Levy 1995b). The models are certainly over-simplified: the presence of pigs in some of the 'pastoral' periods suggests that we are looking at shifts in a balance between mixed farming and semi-sedentary pastoralism or 'agro-pastoralism' (Grigson 1995), and specialized pastoralist communities may in fact have been a feature of Chalcolithic, Nabataean and Roman/Byzantine societies (Levy 1992). In the latter period, detailed fieldwork is beginning to identify at least three categories of pastoral sites in the Negev: large camps with numerous living structures; small camps with fewer structures; and ephemeral or tent sites consisting of stone lines, cleared areas, fire pits and ceramic scatters (Rosen 1992; Fig. 14.9). Bedouin-style camel pastoralism seems to have begun in the Arabian desert in the second millennium BC in the context of developing trade systems linking New Kingdom Egypt, the Levantine city-states and the Babylonian empire (Zarins 1989).

In North Africa, Saharan rock art is thought to reflect the changing ideologies of Saharan societies during the transition from hunting to herding between *c.* 6000 and 2000 BC, as well as acting as mechanisms for the exchange of information about the landscape they inhabited. In the Libyan study referred to earlier (Barker *et al.* 1996), tent footings and hut foundations with Roman pottery suggest that transhumant pastoralists continued to inhabit the pre-desert even though the main wadis were taken into cultivation by the kind of estates mapped in Figure 14.7. Camels were used by the pre-desert farmers for ploughing and as pack animals, and camel pastoralism in the desert seems also to have developed in the Roman period, perhaps partly in response to the opportunities provided by trans-Saharan trade (though the late Roman authors concentrate more on the considerable threat posed by these nomads to the coastal cities and farms).

Early agriculture in subequatorial Africa was a mixture of crop cultivation and small-scale stock-keeping, settlement concentrating in general on forested waterside locations (Sutton 1996), but as agriculture expanded to more open environments during the first millennium AD, animal husbandry increased in importance. Cattle-keeping in particular was a critical component of the *zimbabwe* state societies that developed in the early second millennium AD (Barker 1988). The élites

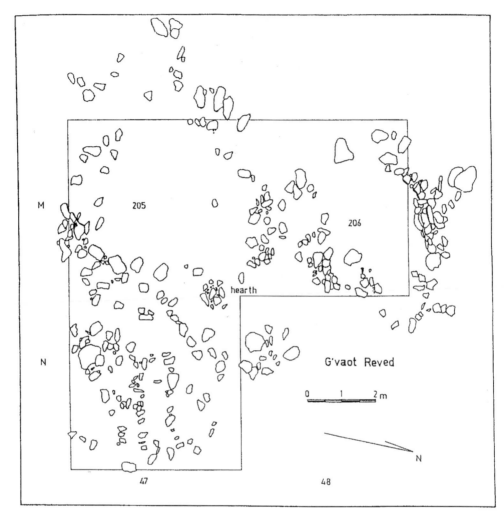

Figure 14.9 Plan of a first-millennium AD tent camp from Giv'ot Reved in the Negev desert, Israel. Source: Rosen 1992. © University Museum Publications.

controlled large herds of cattle which were probably moved on a seasonal basis between the high veld in summer and the low veld in winter to keep them free of tsetse fly (Garlake 1978). These states were linked in trading relationships not only with the Arab and Portuguese trading settlements on the coast but also with complex pastoralist societies to the west on the fringe of the Kalahari desert, where élite groups living in regional centres were supported by tribute from subordinate cattle-herders – the camps of the latter have been plotted by air photography because their

586

dung deposits are covered now by grasses tolerant of high levels of phosphates and nitrates (Denbow 1984).

The horse, hunted in late glacial times, is thought to have died out in most of Europe in the Holocene, surviving on the Russian steppes and being eventually domesticated there. On the evidence of microwear on premolar teeth, horses at Dereivka in the Ukraine were being bridled by *c*. 4000 BC (Anthony *et al.* 1991), though the faunal analysis suggests they were the critical meat source for the community (Levine 1990; Olsen 1996). Although the horse was probably first domesticated on the steppes as a meat source, its critical role elsewhere was for riding and pulling carts, its widespread adoption invariably associated with the emergence of élites and other indicators of social intensification (Sherratt 1981). The first historically known horse-riding nomads of the Eurasian steppes are the Cimmerians and Scythians, recorded from the early first millennium BC, but the hundreds of high-status graves dating to the third millennium BC containing wagons or carts and horses are commonly taken as evidence for the emergence of similar pastoralist societies at this time. From western Europe to China, the wagon was replaced by the chariot during the first millennium BC, and then abandoned in favour of cavalry warfare (Piggott 1992).

As with the horse on the Eurasian steppes, it seems likely that the camelids of South America were initially domesticated as a meat source but were then valued more as they are today – the llama principally as a beast of burden, though also important for wool, dung (as fuel and fertilizer) and in ritual, and the alpaca as a wool-producer (Browman 1989). Specialized camelid pastoralism is practised today in locations largely unsuited to agriculture such as the high grasslands of Peru, whereas in most regions their husbandry is complementary to agriculture. The latter situation seems also to have been the case in antiquity (McGreevy 1989).

FOOD AND CULTURE

In a famous analysis of the meaning of cooking for human societies, the structural anthropologist Lévi-Strauss (1965) defined what he termed an underlying 'culinary triangle' of opposing relationships between raw, cooked and rotten food, cooked food being transformed by culture and rotted food being transformed by nature. He went on to argue that the principal modes of cooking form another structured set, transforming raw food (in his terms, meat) by the addition or subtraction of air, water and culture (the cooking apparatus). Thus roasting was a process by which meat was brought into direct contact with fire without the mediation of any cultural apparatus, air, or water, and the process was only partial – roast meat is only partly cooked (at least when properly cooked in France!). By contrast, boiling was a process which reduced raw food to a decomposed state similar to natural rotting, but through the mediation of both water and culture (the pot). Smoking was a process of slow but complete cooking mediated by air but not by culture. The scheme became evermore complicated as he tried to place grilling, steaming and frying into the triangle, and as Edmund Leach commented in his analysis of Lévi-Strauss's arguments, 'at this point some English readers might begin to suspect that the whole argument was an elaborate academic joke' (Leach 1970: 31). However, his principal point was that, whereas animals just eat food, what is and is not food for humans, and what food is eaten by humans on what occasion, is largely determined by their social conventions (Goody 1982).

From his fieldwork amongst the Nuba of Sudan, for example, Ian Hodder (1982) argued that two neighbouring tribes, the Moro and the Mesakin, whilst practising similar systems of subsistence, in fact created rather different faunal samples in and around their settlements because of contrasting social relations, gender roles and ideological systems. In the compounds of the Moro, for example, were found only the jaws and skulls of pigs, whereas in those of the Mesakin there were jaws and skulls of pigs, goats, and cattle. The Moro hid the bones in the roofs of granaries, the Mesakin displayed them openly in front of the granaries. Pigs were critical for Moro marriage dues, cattle feasting was important for Mesakin burial ceremonies. There were strict concepts of purity and cleanliness, and complex social behaviours associated with a fear of ritual pollution of cattle and cattle milk, interpreted by Hodder as a symbolic expression of the fear felt by men of pollution by women. The implications for archaeozoologists, he concluded, were very clear:

> archaeologists studying the economy through bones appear to assume that their evidence of relative proportions of animals, butchering practices, age distributions, herd control and so on are somehow free of all symbolic content: theirs is supposed to be a practical, rational, scientific world. But meat-eating, the division of the carcass and the dispersal of the bones must always have had a symbolic content behind which there is a conceptual order. Beyond the functioning of 'the economy' is a conceptual scheme and meaning.
>
> (Hodder 1982: 116)

It is debatable whether the implications of the Nuba study are quite so icono-clastic for archaeological studies of food and farming as Hodder argues: the fact that the subsistence systems of the two societies are fundamentally the same, and would appear so to archaeologists if they had access to the full suite of subsistence data from the two societies, is rather encouraging for archaeologists attempting to reconstruct long-term patterns of hunting and farming from such data. Neverthe-less, the Nuba study is an important reminder of the central role that plants and especially animals play in human social relations as well as in subsistence, and it is clear that environmental archaeology has enormous potential to contribute to studies of past societies through investigations of the cultural values of food (e.g.

Chaix *et al.* 1995; Manning and Serpell 1994; Meniel 1988; Ryan and Crabtree 1995).

Although fire is commonly found in the caves occupied by Neanderthals, micro-scopic studies of tooth wear and damage suggest that Neanderthals, like their predecessors, ate their food more or less raw, gripping a lump of meat between their teeth and then either tearing and yanking bite-sized chunks from the bone, or hacking them off by sawing away in front of their faces with a flint flake (Stringer and Gamble 1993). The same marks on children's teeth conjure up a nice image of Neanderthals teaching their toddlers their table manners: 'use your Stanley knife properly, dear'! In contrast, upper palaeolithic societies were certainly practising meat drying, smoking and storage, and stone-lined hearths also indicate that cook-ing was now the norm. Given the increasing evidence in their material culture for status differentiation amongst many late glacial and early Holocene hunter-gatherers, it is quite possible that food was another indicator of status (Bender 1979). Hayden (1992) has in fact argued that, if competitive feasting began to supplant food-sharing amongst such societies living in resource-rich areas, the need for food to meet increasing social demands might have been a factor in persuading them to commit to agriculture.

Clear evidence for the links between food and culture can be discerned amongst later agricultural societies. In later neolithic Britain, for example, the analysis of faunal samples in henge monuments such as Durrington Walls suggests 'a highly organized system of animal management in which pigs were specifically bred for feasting purposes and were slaughtered in large numbers', probably in ritual activities involving the entire community (Thomas 1984: 206). With the emergence of élite groups, the link between food and status seems inherent in the production of alcoholic drinks such as wine, mead and beer; both the Sumerians and Egyptians associated brewing and wine-making with particular deities, and the occurrence of beer residues in beakers in ritual contexts in Britain suggests that here too these activities also had a strongly magical aspect (Dineley 1996; Vencl 1994). Wine was a critical indicator of status in Greece and Rome, where the élites of both societies indulged in the long eating and drinking bouts of the *symposion* (Murray and Tecusan 1995). Another indicator of status has often been sugar: in ancient Egypt, for example, the lifestyles of the élite are differentiated from the poor in the amount of tooth decay caused by their sugar-rich diet (Hillson 1979).

There are many examples of societies for whom animals on the hoof, cattle in particular, were a critical resource for exchange and alliance formation, for bridewealth and other social obligations within the community, and for distribution for status – and thus the primary target for inter-communal warfare. Examples include the 'hillfort societies' of the British Iron Age (Grant 1984) and the Ger-man tribes on the fringe of the Roman empire (Roymans 1996). The early medieval communities of Ireland recorded by the Early Christian sagas were very similar, as were those of Scandinavia, where the Old Nordic word for goods and property was *fae*, 'horned animal' (Nasman 1996). In the case of the *zimbabwes* states of central-southern Africa, too, faunal analysis indicates that prime young cattle were brought to the chiefly enclosures for consumption, the provision of their meat for the court or capital being an important aspect of élite power (Reid 1996). At the Manekweni *zimbabwe*, the middens by the chief's hut and by those of the court were dominated by the bones of prime young beef, whereas the middens on the edge of the enclosure where the lower-status people lived had poorer cuts from older animals, and a variety of game (Barker 1978).

King (1984) argues that eating beef was also an important indicator of status (in this case the acquisition of Roman culture) in the towns and villas of Roman Britain, a habit he suggests was imported by soldiers who had previously served on the German *limes*. In Roman Italy, on the other hand, pork was generally the highest status meat, the subject of innumerable recipes in the Roman literature, and pigs dominate the faunal samples of towns like Capua, Naples, Pompeii, Ostia and Rome. At the Settefinestre villa the faunal sample indicates a clear separation in the quality of food eaten by the senatorial family and the slaves who worked the estate, the food refuse of the former consisting of prime cuts of young animals including many burnt fragments, presumably from roasting, whereas the latter consisted of poorer cuts, from older animals, probably boiled as a broth (King 1985).

Another indicator of status in food is the consumption of exotic items not available to the general populace. The aristocratic diet at Settefinestre typically included venison and game birds, and the faunal samples from medieval castles in England commonly include substantial frequencies of deer, game birds and waterfowl (Grant 1988).

The archaeology of gender has scarcely been investigated by environmental archaeology, but one of the most exciting examples of the potential of the archaeology of food to inform on gender relations is Hastorf's study of Andean chiefdoms (Hastorf 1991), described in Chapter 22. The integration of archaeozoology, archaeobotany and isotopic analyses of skeletons indicates that male and female diet was at first very similar, but gender relations then changed significantly with the incorporation of these societies into the Inca state: the women worked harder, producing maize for male beer-drinking at public and political occasions, men also ate more meat within the same political arena, and women were increasingly restricted to domestic activities.

The symbolic association of modern humans with the animals they hunted is evident from palaeolithic art (Mithen 1996), and probably from the famous red deer head-dress at Star Carr (Clark 1954). The dog seems to have been the animal first tamed by humans, and it is significant that from the beginnings of this companionship there are examples in both European and American hunter-gatherer societies of dogs being buried in graves with humans, as well as sharing in their daily life and food (Clutton-Brock and Noe-Nygaard 1990). Later dog burials presumably symbolize the social and ideological role of hunting for the élites of many agricultural societies (Hamilakis 1996). The powerful symbolism of cattle for agricultural societies is evident from the 'bull shrines' at the neolithic settlement of Çatal Hüyûk and the 'heads and hooves' graves in English neolithic tombs to the 'pastoral ideologies' in which were embedded the social relations of the German tribes beyond the *limes* (Roymans 1996: 55) and those of the Great Zimbabwe élites (Reid 1996). There is as long a tradition of animal sacrifices amongst the pastoralists of the Eurasian steppes, from the Bronze Age even to the nineteenth century, when a European traveller witnessed the sacrifice of 100 horses and 1,000 sheep at the burial of a Kirghiz prince – a first-millennium AD grave at Lake Baikal has recently been reported in which a prince lay side by side with his horse, the latter having been sacrificed and part-eaten at the funeral meal and the animal then recreated around its skeleton by stuffing the hide (Crubézy *et al.* 1996).

Faced with the evidence of 'ritual deposits' such as this, and 'normal' settlement evidence, it is all too easy for archaeologists to do as Hodder warned, separating the evidence into domestic and ideological spheres. This may be a feature of our own largely secular world, but cannot have been so in the past – the medieval peasant lived with Christianity in field and farm as well as in church, and activities as mundane as breeding rabbits are now seen as imbued with symbolic meaning (Stocker and Stocker 1996). Ideology and domestic life were inextricably enmeshed in neolithic and bronze age societies in Europe (Garwood *et al.* 1991), and comfortable assumptions about the nature of British iron age society are also having to be discarded (Grant 1984; Hill 1995). The study of pit-fills at sites such as Danebury and Winklebury has revealed 'special deposits' amidst the rubbish such as complete animal and human carcasses, and parts of carcasses, both probably the result of sacrifice (Fig. 14.10), along with what seem to be ritual settings of mundane rubbish such as potsherds and broken quern-stones. Wild animals and plants seem to have played an insignificant part of the diet of these people, yet wild animals are frequently found in ritual deposits. The structuring of the evidence suggests linkages and taboos in human–animal relationships every bit as complicated as those of the Moro and the Mesakin today. There are increasing indications of similar ideologies underpinning Romano-British society (Grant 1991; Scott 1991), in striking contrast with the traditional models emphasizing the modernity of that world. Such studies make it very clear that archaeologists will only be able to understand the history of food in human societies, and the complexity of the hunting and agricultural systems developed for its acquisition, if we learn to bridge the disciplinary gaps and integrate the goals and methodologies of archaeological science with those of social archaeology.

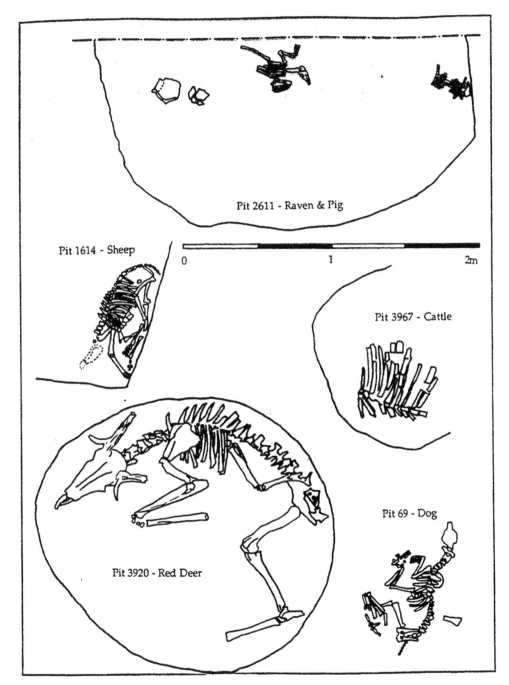

Figure 14.10 Deposits of articulated animal bones – 'special deposits' – in pits at the iron age settlement of Winklebury in southern England. Source: J. D. Hill.

REFERENCES

Adams, R. McC. (1981) *Heartland of Cities*, Chicago: University of Chicago Press.

Akazawa, T. and Aikens, C. M. (eds) (1986) *Prehistoric Hunter-Gatherers in Japan: New Research Methods*, Tokyo: University of Tokyo, University Museum.

Alcock, S. (1994) *Graecia Capta*, Cambridge: Cambridge University Press.

Amick, D. S. (1996) 'Regional patterns of Folsom mobility and land use in the American Southwest', *World Archaeology* 27: 411–26.

Anati, E. (1976) *Evolution and Style in Camunian Rock Art*, Capo di Ponte: Centro Camuno di Studi Preistorici.

Anderson, P. (1980) 'A testimony to prehistoric tasks: diagnostic residues on stone tool working edges', *World Archaeology* 12: 181–94.

Andresen, J. M., Byrd, B. F., Elson, M. D., McGuire, R. H., Mendoza, R. G., Staski, E. and White, J. P. (1981) 'The deer hunters: Star Carr reconsidered', *World Archaeology* 13 (1): 31–46.

Anthony, D. W., Dimitri, Y. and Dorcas, B. (1991) 'The origin of horseback riding', *Scientific American* 12: 44–48.

Arbogast, R.-M., Petrequin, A.-M. and Petrequin, P. (1995) 'Le fonctionnement de la cellule domestique d'après l'étude des restes osseux d'animaux: le cas d'un village néolitique du lac de Chalin (Jura, France)', *Anthropozoologica* 21: 131–46.

Astill, G. (1988a) 'Rural settlement – the toft and the croft', in G. Astill and A. Grant (eds) *The Countryside of Medieval England*, Oxford: Basil Blackwell: 36–61.

Astill, G. (1988b) 'Fields', in G. Astill and A. Grant (eds) *The Countryside of Medieval England*, Oxford: Basil Blackwell: 62–85.

Athens, J. S., Ward, J. V. and Murakami, G. M. (1996) 'Development of an agroforest on a Micronesian high island: prehistoric Kosraean agriculture', *Antiquity* 70: 834–46.

Bailey, G. N. (1978) 'Shell middens as indicators of postglacial economies: a territorial approach', in P. Mellars (ed.) *The Early Postglacial Settlement of Northern Europe*, London: Duckworth: 37–63.

Bailey, G. N. and Parkington, J. (1988) *The Archaeology of Prehistoric Coastlines*, Cambridge: Cambridge University Press.

Bailey, G. N., Deith, M. and Shackleton, N. J. (1983) 'Oxygen isotope analysis and seasonality determinations: limits and potential of a new technique', *American Antiquity* 48: 390–98.

Bailey, R. C. and Headland, T. N. (1991) 'The tropical rain forest: is it a productive environment for human foragers?', *Human Ecology* 19 (2): 261–85.

Bang-Andersen, S. (1996) 'Coast/inland relations in the Mesolithic of southern Norway', *World Archaeology* 27: 427–43.

Barich, B. (1987) *Archaeology and Environment in the Libyan Sahara*, Oxford: British Archaeological Reports, International Series 368.

Barker, G. (1978) 'Economic models for the Manekweni zimbabwe', *Azania* 13: 71–100.

Barker, G. (1981) *Landscape and Society: Prehistoric Central Italy*, London: Academic Press.

Barker, G. (1985) *Prehistoric Farming in Europe*, Cambridge: Cambridge University Press.

Barker, G. (1988) 'Cows and kings: models for *zimbabwes*', *Proceedings of the Prehistoric Society* 54: 223–39.

Barker, G. (1989) 'The archaeology of the Italian shepherd', *Proceedings of the Cambridge Philological Society* 215: 1–19.

Barker, G. (1995) *A Mediterranean Valley. Landscape Archaeology and* Annales *History in the Biferno Valley*, London: Leicester University Press.

Barker, G. and Gamble, C. (1985) 'Beyond domestication: a strategy for investigating the process and consequence of social complexity', in G. Barker and C. Gamble (eds) *Beyond Domestication in Prehistoric Europe: Investigations in Subsistence Archaeology and Social Complexity*, London: Academic Press: 1–31.

Barker, G. and Grant, A. (1991) 'Ancient and modern pastoralism in central Italy: an interdisciplinary study in the Cicolano mountains', *Papers of the British School at Rome* 59: 15–88.

Barker, G. and Lloyd, J. A. (eds) (1991) *Roman Landscapes: Archaeological Survey in the Mediterranean Region*, Archaeological Monographs 2, London: British School at Rome.

Barker, G. and Rasmussen, T. (1998) *The Etruscans*, Oxford: Blackwell.

Barker, G., Gilbertson, D., Jones, B. and Mattingly, D. (1996) *Farming the Desert: the UNESCO Libyan Valleys Archaeological Survey*, Paris: UNESCO, London: Society for Libyan Studies, Tripoli: Department of Antiquities (two volumes).

Barker, G., Creighton, O. H., Gilbertson, D., Hunt, C. O., Mattingly, D. J., McLaren, S. and Thomas, D. L. (1997) 'The Wadi Faynan project, southern Jordan: a preliminary report on geomorphology and landscape archaeology', *Levant* 19: 17–40.

Barnes, G. L. (1990) 'Paddy soils now and then', *World Archaeology* 22: 1–17.

Bar-Yosef, O. and Khazanov, A. (eds) (1992) *Pastoralism in the Levant: Archaeological Materials in Anthropological Perspectives*, Monographs in World Archaeology 10, Madison, Wis.: Prehistory Press.

Bayliss-Smith, T. and Golson, J. (1992) 'Wetland agriculture in New Guinea highlands prehistory', in B. Coles (ed.) *The Wetland Revolution in Prehistory*, Exeter: WARP/Prehistoric Society: 15–27.

Bell, M. and Boardman, J. (eds) (1992) *Past and Present Soil Erosion: Archaeological and Geomorphological Perspectives*, Oxford: Oxbow.

Bellwood, P. (1990) 'Foraging towards farming: a decisive transition or a millennial blur?', *Review of Archaeology* 11 (2): 14–24.

Bender, B. (1979) 'Gatherer-hunter to farmer: a social perspective', *World Archaeology* 10 (2): 204–22.

Berglund, B. (ed.) (1991) *The Cultural Landscape During 6000 Years in Southern Sweden – the Ystad Project*, Ecological Bulletins No. 41, Lund: Munksgaard.

Binford, L. R. (1978) *Nunamiut Ethnoarchaeology*, New York: Academic Press.

Binford, L. R. (1984) *Faunal Remains from Klasies River Mouth*, New York: Academic Press.

Blanton, R. E., Kowalewski, S. A., Feinman, G. and Appel, J. (1981) *Ancient Mesoamerica*, Cambridge: Cambridge University Press.

Bogucki, P. (1984) 'Ceramic sieves of the Linear Pottery Culture and their economic implications', *Oxford Journal of Archaeology* 3: 15–30.

Bogucki, P. (1986) 'The antiquity of dairying in temperate Europe', *Expedition* 28 (2): 51–58.

Bogucki, P. (1988) *Forest Farmers and Stockherders: Early Agriculture and its Consequences in North-Central Europe*, Cambridge: Cambridge University Press.

Bogucki, P. (1993) 'Animal traction and households in neolithic Europe', *Antiquity* 67: 492–503.

Boyle, K. (1996) 'From Laugerie Basse to Jolivet: the organization of Final Magdalenian settlement in the Vézère valley', *World Archaeology* 27: 477–91.

Brain, C. K. (1981) *The Hunters or the Hunted? An Introduction to African Cave Taphonomy*, Chicago: University of Chicago Press.

Braudel, F. (1972) *The Mediterranean and the Mediterranean World in the Age of Philip II*, London: Fontana.

Brinkhuizen, D. C. and Clason, A. T. (1986) *Fish and Archaeology: Studies in Osteometry, Taphonomy, Seasonality and Fishing Methods*, Oxford: British Archaeological Reports, International Series 294.

Briuer, F. L. (1976) 'New clues to stone tool function: plant and animal residues', *American Antiquity* 41: 478–84.

Brotherston, G. (1989) 'Andean pastoralism and Inca ideology', in J. Clutton-Brock (ed.) *The Walking Larder*, London: Unwin Hyman: 240–55.

Brothwell, D. (1986) *The Bog Man and the Archaeology of People*, London: British Museum Publications.

Browman, D. L. (1989) 'Origins and development of Andean pastoralism: an overview of the past 6000 years', in J. Clutton-Brock (ed.) *The Walking Larder*, London: Unwin Hyman: 256–68.

Bryan, K. (1929) 'Floodwater farming', *Geographical Review* 19 (3): 444–56.

Callen, E. O. (1969) 'Diet as revealed by coprolites', in D. Brothwell and E. S. Higgs (eds) *Science in Archaeology*, London: Thames and Hudson: 235–43.

Carandini, A. (1985) *Settefinestre. Una Villa Schiavistica nell'Etruria Romana*, Modena: Panini.

Carreté, J.-M., Keay, S. J. and Millett, M. (1995) *A Roman Provincial Capital and its Hinterland: the Survey of the Territory of Tarragona, Spain, 1985–90*, Michigan: Journal of Roman Archaeology Supplement 15.

Caseldine, C. and Hatton, J. (1993) 'The development of high moorland on Dartmoor: fire and the influence of mesolithic activity on vegetational change', in F. Chambers (ed.) *Climatic Change and Human Impact on the Landscape: Studies in Palaeoecology and Environmental Archaeology*, London: Chapman and Hall: 119–31.

Chaix, L., Olive, C., de Roguin, L., Sidi Maamar, H. and Studer, J. (eds) (1995) *L'Animal dans l'Espace Humain, l'Homme dans l'Espace Animal*, Paris: Anthropozoologica 21.

Chang, C. and Koster, H. A. (1986) 'Beyond bones: towards an ethnoarchaeology of pastoralism', in M. B. Schiffer (ed.) *Advances in Archaeological Method and Theory 9*, New York: Academic Press: 97–146.

Chapman, J. C. (1982) 'The Secondary Products Revolution and the limitations of the Neolithic', *Bulletin of the Institute of Archaeology* 19: 107–22.

Chapman, R. (1990) *Emerging Complexity: the Later Prehistory of South-East Spain, Iberia and the West Mediterranean*, Cambridge: Cambridge University Press.

Chattopadhyaya, U. C. (1996) 'Settlement pattern and the spatial organization of subsistence and mortuary practices in the mesolithic Ganges valley, north-central India', *World Archaeology* 27 (3): 461–76.

Chouquier, G., Clavel-Lévêque, M., Favory, F. and Vallat, J.-P. (1987) *Structures Agraires en Italie Centro-Meridionale: Cadastres et Paysages Ruraux*, Rome: Ecole Française de Rome.

Claessen, C. (1993) 'Choices and problems in shell seasonality', *Archaeozoologica* 5: 55–76.

Clark, J. G. D. (1952) *Prehistoric Europe: the Economic Basis*, London: Methuen.

Clark, J. G. D. (1954) *Excavations at Star Carr, an Early Mesolithic Site at Seamer, near Scarborough, Yorkshire*, Cambridge: Cambridge University Press.

Clark, J. G. D. (1972) *Star Carr: a Case Study in Bioarchaeology*, McCaleb Module in Anthropology 10, Reading, Mass.: Addison-Wesley Publishing Company.

Clarke, D. L. (1976) 'Mesolithic Europe – the economic basis', in G. de G. Sieveking, I. H. Longworth and K. E. Wilson (eds) *Problems in Economic and Social Archaeology*, London: Duckworth: 449–81.

Clutton-Brock, J. and Noe-Nygaard, N. (1990) 'New osteological and C-isotope evidence on mesolithic dogs: companions to humans and fishers at Star Carr, Seamer Carr and Kongemose', *Journal of Archaeological Science* 17: 643–53.

Coe, M. (1974) 'The chinampas of Mexico', in E. Zubrow, M. C. Frotiz and J. M. Fritz (eds) *New World Archaeology. Theoretical and Cultural Transformations*, San Francisco: Freeman: 231–39.

Cohen, M. and Armelagos, G. (eds) (1984) *Palaeopathology at the Origins of Agriculture*, Orlando, Fla.: Academic Press.

Condanin, J., Formenti, F., Metais, M. O., Michel, M. and Blond, P. (1976) 'The application of gas chromatography to the tracing of oil in ancient amphorae', *Archaeometry* 18: 195–201.

Cosgrove, R. (1996) 'Origin and development of Australian aboriginal tropical rainforest culture: a reconsideration', *Antiquity* 70: 900–12.

Courty, M.-A., Goldberg, P. and Macphail, R. I. (1990) *Soils and Micromorphology in Archaeology*, Cambridge: Cambridge University Press.

Crabtree, P. and Ryan, K. (eds) (1991) *Animal Use and Culture Change*, Philadelphia: MASCA, University Museum of Archaeology and Anthropology.

Cribb, R. (1991) *Nomads in Archaeology*, Cambridge: Cambridge University Press.

Crubézy, E., Martin, H., Giscard, P.-H., Batsaikhan, Z., Erdenebaatar, S., Verdier, J. P. and Maureille, B. (1996) 'Funeral practices and animal sacrifices in Mongolia at the Ugur period: archaeological and ethno-historical study of a *kurgan* in the Egyin Gol valley (Baikal region)', *Antiquity* 70: 891–96.

Dahl, G. and Hjort, A. (1976) *Having Herds: Pastoral Herd Growth and Household Economy*, Stockholm: Stockholm University.

Davis, S. (1986) *The Archaeology of Animals*, London: Batsford.

Denbow, J. R. (1984) 'Cows and kings: a spatial and economic analysis of a hierarchical early iron age settlement system in eastern Botswana', in M. Hall, G. Avery, M. L. Wilson and A. J. B. Humphreys (eds) *Frontiers: Southern African Archaeology Today*, Oxford: British Archaeological Reports, International Series 207: 24–39.

Dennell, R. (1972) 'The interpretation of plant remains', in E. S. Higgs (ed.) *Papers in Economic Prehistory*, Cambridge: Cambridge University Press: 149–60.

Dennell, R. W. (1983) *European Economic Prehistory*, London: Academic Press.

Dennell, R. and Roebroeks, W. (1996) 'The earliest colonization of Europe: the short chronology revisited', *Antiquity* 70 (269): 535–42.

Dineley, M. (1996) 'Finding magic in stone age real ale', *British Archaeology* 19: 6.

Donahue, R. E. (1988) 'Microwear analysis and site function of Paglicci Cave level 4a', *World Archaeology* 19: 357–75.

Edwards, K. (1989) 'Meso-neolithic vegetational impacts in Scotland and beyond: palynological considerations', in C. Bonsall (ed.) *The Mesolithic in Europe*, Edinburgh: J. Donald: 143–56.

Eglington, G. (ed.) (1996) *ABI Newsletter* (November 1996 Issue No. 3), Swindon: Natural Environment Research Council.

Evans, J. G. (1971) 'Habitat changes on the calcareous soils of Britain: the impact of neolithic man', in D. D. A. Simpson (ed.) *Economy and Settlement in Neolithic and Bronze Age Britain and Europe*, Leicester: Leicester University Press: 11–26.

Evenari, M., Shanan, L. and Tadmor, N. (1971) *The Negev: the Challenge of a Desert*, Cambridge, Mass.: Harvard University Press.

Evershed, R. P., Heron, C. and Goad, L. J. (1991) 'Epicuticular wax components preserved in potsherds as chemical indicators of leafy vegetables in ancient diets', *Antiquity* 65: 540–44.

Farrington, I. S. (1980) 'The archaeology of irrigation canals, with special reference to Peru', *World Archaeology* 11 (3): 287–305.

Farrington, I. S. (ed.) (1990) *Prehistoric Intensive Agriculture in the Tropics*, Oxford: British Archaeological Reports, International Series 232.

Fédéroff, N. (1998) 'L'apport de la micromorphologie des sols à la reconstitution des paléo-paysages (application au bassin Méditerranéen pour la période 3000 av. J.C./1800 ap.J.C.)', in P. Leveau, F. Trément, K. Walsh and G. Barker (eds) *Mediterranean Landscape Archaeology 2: Environmental Reconstruction*, Oxford: Oxbow: 55–66.

Fieller, N., Gilbertson, D. D. and Ralph, N. G. (eds) (1985) *Palaeoenvironmental Investigations: Research Design, Methods and Data Analysis*, Oxford: British Archaeological Reports, International Series 258.

Finkelstein, I. (1995) *Living on the Fringe: the Archaeology and History of the Negev, Sinai and Neighbouring Regions in the Bronze and Iron Ages*, Monographs in Mediterranean Archaeology 6, Sheffield: Sheffield Academic Press.

Fish, S. and Fish, P. (1994) 'Prehistoric desert farmers of the Southwest', *Annual Review of Anthropology* 23: 83–108.

Fleming, A. M. (1971) 'Territorial patterns in bronze age Wessex', *Proceedings of the Prehistoric Society* 37: 138–66.

Fleming, A. M. (1988) *The Dartmoor Reaves*, London: Batsford.

Fleming, A. M. and Ralph, N. (1982) 'Medieval settlement and land use on Holne Moor, Dartmoor: the landscape evidence', *Medieval Archaeology* 26: 101–37.

Fontana, L. (1995) 'Chasseurs magdaléniens et rennes en Bassin de l'Aude: analyse préliminaire', *Anthropozoologica* 21: 147–56.

Forbes, H. (1995) 'The identification of pastoralist sites within the context of estate-based agriculture in ancient Greece – beyond the "transhumance versus agro-pastoralism" debate', *Annual of the British School at Athens* 90: 325–38.

Foxhall, L. (1992) 'The control of the Attic landscape', in B. Wells (ed.) *Agriculture in Ancient Greece*, Stockholm: Skrifter Utgivna av Svenska Institutet i Athen 4, 42: 155–59.

Foxhall, L. (1997) *Olive Cultivation in Ancient Greece: Seeking the Ancient Economy*, London: Institute of Classical Studies.

Gallagher, J. P., Boszhardt, F. R., Sasso, R. F. and Stevenson, K. (1987) 'Oneota ridged field agriculture in southwestern Wisconsin', *American Antiquity* 50: 605–12.

Garlake, P. S. (1978) 'Pastoralism and *Zimbabwe*', *Journal of African History* 194: 479–93.

Garnsey, P. (1988) *Famine and Food Supply in the Graeco-Roman World*, Cambridge: Cambridge University Press.

Garnsey, P. (1992) 'Yield of the land', in B. Wells (ed.) *Agriculture in Ancient Greece*, Stockholm: Skrifter Utgivna av Svenska Institutet i Athen 4, 42: 147–54.

Garwood, P., Jennings, D., Skeates, R. and Toms, J. (eds) (1991) *Sacred and Profane*, Oxford: Oxford University Committee for Archaeology Monograph 32.

Gaudzinski, S. (1996) 'On bovid assemblages and their consequences for the knowledge of subsistence patterns in the Middle Palaeolithic', *Proceedings of the Prehistoric Society* 62: 19–39.

Gifford-Gonzalez, D. P. (1984) 'Implications of a faunal assemblage from a pastoral neolithic site in Kenya: findings and perspectives on research', in J. D. Clark and S. A. Brandt (eds) *From Hunters to Farmers: the Causes and Consequences of Food Production in Africa*, Berkeley: University of California Press: 240–51.

Gilbertson, D. (ed.) (1986) *Runoff Farming in Rural Arid Lands*, *Applied Geology* theme volume 6 (1).

Gilbertson, D. and Hunt, C. O. (1996) 'Romano-Libyan agriculture: walls and floodwater farming', in G. Barker, D. Gilbertson, B. Jones and D. Mattingly, *Farming the Desert: the UNESCO Libyan Valleys Archaeological Survey. Volume One: Synthesis*, Paris: UNESCO, London: Society for Libyan Studies, Tripoli: Department of Antiquities: 191–225.

Gilman, A. (1981) 'The development of social stratification in bronze age Europe', *Current Anthropology* 22 (1): 1–8.

Gimbutas, M. (1965) *Bronze Age Cultures in Central and Eastern Europe*, The Hague: Mouton.

Glob, P. V. (1971) *The Bog People*, London: Paladin.

Glover, I. and Higham, C. (1996) 'New evidence for early rice cultivation in south, southeast and east Asia', in D. Harris (ed.) *The Origins and Spread of Agriculture and Pastoralism in Eurasia*, London: UCL Press: 413–41.

Golson, J. (1990) 'Kuk and the development of agriculture in New Guinea: retrospection and introspection', in D. E. Yen and J. M. J. Mummery (eds) *Pacific Production Systems*, Canberra: ANU, Occasional Papers in Prehistory 18: 139–47.

Goody, J. (1982) *Cooking, Cuisine and Class*, Cambridge: Cambridge University Press.

Gosden, C. (1992) 'Production systems and the colonization of the western Pacific', *World Archaeology* 24 (1): 55–69.

Gould, R. A. (1980) *Living Archaeology*, Cambridge: Cambridge University Press.

Grant, A. (1984) 'The animal husbandry', in B. Cunliffe, *Danebury: an Iron Age Hill-fort in Hampshire, Volume II The Finds*, London: Council for British Archaeology, Research Report: 496–548.

Grant, A. (1988) 'Animal resources', in G. Astill and A. Grant (eds) *The Countryside of Medieval England*, Oxford: Blackwell: 149–87.

Grant, A. (1989) 'Animals in Roman Britain', in M. Todd (ed.) *Research in Roman Britain 1960–1989*, London: Britannia Monograph 11: 136–46.

Grant, A. (1991) 'Economic or symbolic? Animals and ritual behaviour', in P. Garwood, D. Jennings, R. Skeates and J. Toms (eds) *Sacred and Profane*, Oxford: Oxford University Committee for Archaeology Monograph 32: 109–14.

Grayson, D. K. (1984) *Quantitative Zooarchaeology*, New York: Academic Press.

Greig, J. (1983) 'Plant foods in the past: a review of the evidence from northern Europe', *Journal of Plant Foods* 5: 179–214.

Greig, J. (1989) *Archaeobotany*, Handbooks for Archaeologists 4, Strasbourg: European Science Foundation.

Grigg, D. B. (1982) *The Dynamics of Agricultural Change*, London: Hutchinson.

Grigson, C. (1995) 'Plough and pasture in the Early Bronze Age of the southern Levant', in T. Levy (ed.) *The Archaeology of Society in the Holy Land*, London: Leicester University Press: 245–68.

Grigson, C. and Clutton-Brock, J. (1983) (eds) *Animals and Archaeology: 2. Shell Middens, Fishes and Birds*, Oxford: British Archaeological Reports: International Series 183.

Groenman-van Waateringe, W. (1978) *'Are we too loud?' Third Beatrice de Cardi Lecture*, London: Council for British Archaeology.

Groube, L. (1989) 'The taming of the rainforest: a model for Late Pleistocene forest exploitation in New Guinea', in D. Harris and G. C. Hillman (eds) *Foraging and Farming: the Evolution of Plant Exploitation*, London: Allen and Unwin: 292–317.

Guyan, W. H. (1966) 'Zur Herstellung und Funktion einiger jungsteinzeitlicher Holzgeräte von Thayngen-Weier', in R. Deger, W. Drack and R. Wyss (eds) *Helvetia Antiqua*, Zurich: Schweizerisches Landesmuseum: 21–32.

Hall, M. (1987) *The Changing Past: Farmers, Kings and Traders in Southern Africa, AD 200–1860*, Cape Town: David Philip.

Halstead, P. (1981) 'Counting sheep in neolithic and bronze age Greece', in I. Hodder, G. Isaac and N. Hammonds (eds) *Pattern of the Past: Studies in Memory of David Clarke*, Cambridge: Cambridge University Press: 307–39.

Halstead, P. (1987a) 'Man and other animals in later Greek prehistory', *Annual of the British School at Athens* 82: 71–83.

Halstead, P. (1987b) 'Traditional and ancient rural economy in Mediterranean Europe: plus ça change?', *Journal of Hellenic Studies* 107: 77–87.

Halstead, P. (1992a) 'Dimini and the "DMP": faunal remains and animal exploitation in late neolithic Thessaly', *Annual of the British School at Athens* 87: 29–59.

Halstead, P. (1992b) 'Agriculture in the bronze age Aegean', in B. Wells (ed.) *Agriculture in Ancient Greece*, Stockholm: Skrifter Utgivna av Svenska Institutet i Athen 4, 42: 105–17.

Halstead, P. (1996a) 'The development of agriculture and pastoralism in Greece: when, how, who and what?', in D. Harris (ed.) *The Origins and Spread of Agriculture and Pastoralism in Eurasia*, London: UCL Press: 296–309.

Halstead, P. (1996b) 'Pastoralism or household herding? Problems of scale and specialization in early Greek animal husbandry', *World Archaeology* 28 (1): 20–42.

Halstead, P. and Jones, G. (1989) 'Agrarian ecology in the Greek islands: time stress, scale and risk', *Journal of Hellenic Studies* 109: 41–55.

Halstead, P. and O'Shea, J. (eds) (1989) *Bad Year Economics: Cultural Responses to Risk and Uncertainty*, Cambridge: Cambridge University Press.

Hamilakis, Y. (1996) 'A footnote on the archaeology of power: animal bones from a Mycenaean chamber tomb at Galatas, NE Peloponnese', *Annual of the British School at Athens* 91: 153–66.

Harris, D. R. (ed.) (1996) *The Origins and Spread of Agriculture and Pastoralism in Eurasia*, London: University College London Press.

Harris, D. R. and Hillman, G. C. (eds) (1989) *Foraging and Farming: the Evolution of Plant Exploitation*, London: Unwin Hyman.

Hastorf, C. (1991) 'Gender, space and food in prehistory', in J. Gero and M. Conkey (eds) *Engendering Archaeology: Woman and Prehistory*, Oxford: Basil Blackwell: 132–59.

Hastorf, C. and DeNiro, M. J. (1985) 'Reconstruction of prehistoric plant production and cooking practices by a new isotopic method', *Nature* 315: 489–91.

Hastorf, C. A. and Popper, V. S. (eds) (1989) *Current Palaeoethnobotany: Analytical Methods and Cultural Interpretations of Archaeological Plant Remains*, Chicago: University of Chicago Press.

Hather, J. (1992) 'The archaeobotany of subsistence in the Pacific', *World Archaeology* 24 (1): 70–81.

Hather, J. and Kirch, P. V. (1991) 'Prehistoric sweet potato (*Ipomoea batatas*) from Mangaia island, central Polynesia', *Antiquity* 65: 887–93.

Hayden, B. (1992) 'Models of domestication', in A. B. Gebauer and T. D. Price (eds) *Transitions to Agriculture in Prehistory*, Madison, Wis.: Prehistory Press: 11–19.

Heidinga, H. A. (1994) 'Frankish settlement at Gennep: a Migration Period centre in the

Dutch Meuse area', in P. O. Nielsen, K. Randsborg and H. Thrane (eds) *The Archaeology of Gudme and Lundeborg*, Copenhagen: University of Copenhagen: 202–7.

Higham, C. (1996) 'The transition to rice cultivation in south-east Asia', in T. D. Price and A. B. Gebauer (eds) *Last Hunters – First Farmers*, Santa Fe: School of American Research: 127–55.

Hill, J. D. (1995) *Ritual and Rubbish in the Iron Age of Wessex: a Study in the Formation of a Specific Archaeological Record*, Oxford: British Archaeological Reports, British Series 242.

Hill, II. E. and Evans, J. (1989) 'Crops of the Pacific: new evidence from the chemical analysis of organic residues', in D. R. Harris and G. C. Hillman (eds) *Foraging and Farming: the Evolution of Plant Exploitation*, London: Unwin Hyman: 418–25.

Hillman, G. C. (1981) 'Reconstructing crop husbandry practices from charred remains of crops', in R. Mercer (ed.) *Farming Practice in British Prehistory*, Edinburgh: Edinburgh University Press: 123–62.

Hillman, G. C. (1986) 'Plant foods in ancient diet: the archaeological role of palaeofaeces in general and Lindow Man's gut contents in particular', in I. Stead, J. B. Bourke and D. Brothwell (eds) *Lindow Man: the Body in the Bog*, Ithaca: Cornell University Press: 99–115.

Hillson, S. (1979) ' Diet and dental disease', *World Archaeology* 11 (2): 147–62.

Hodder, I. (1982) *Symbols in Action*, Cambridge: Cambridge University Press.

Holden, T. (1994) 'Dietary evidence from the intestinal contents of ancient humans with particular reference to desiccated remains from northern Chile', in J. G. Hather (ed.) *Tropical Archaeobotany. Applications and New Developments*, London: Routledge: 65–85.

Hope, G. and Golson, J. (1995) 'Late Quaternary change in the mountains of New Guinea', *Antiquity* 69: 818–30.

Hvass, S. (1993) 'Settlement', in S. Hvass and B. Storgaard (eds) *Digging into the Past: 25 Years of Archaeology in Denmark*, Aarhus: Royal Society of Northern Antiquaries and Jutland Archaeological Society: 187–94.

Ijzereef, G. F. (1981) *Bronze Age Animal Bones from Bovenkarspel*, Amersfoort: Rijksdienst voor het Oudheidkundig Bodemonderzoek.

Imamura, K. (1996) 'Jomon and Yayoi: the transition to agriculture in Japanese prehistory', in D. Harris (ed.) *The Origins and Spread of Agriculture and Pastoralism in Eurasia*, London: UCL Press: 442–64.

Jones, A. K. G. (1992) 'Coprolites and faecal material in archaeological deposits: a methodological approach', in M. Bernardi (ed.) *Archeologia del Paesaggio*, Florence: Insegna del Giglio: 287–304.

Jones, G. E. M. (1984) 'Interpretation of archaeological plant remains', in W. van Zeist and W. A. Casparie (eds) *Plants and Man*, Rotterdam: Balkema: 43–61.

Jones, G. E. M. (1992) 'Weed phytosociology and crop husbandry: identifying a contrast between ancient and modern practice', in J. P. Pals, J. Buurman and M. van der Veen (eds) *Festschrift for Professor van Zeist. Review of Palaeobotany and Palynology* 73: 133–43.

Jones, G. E. M., Charles, M., Colledge, S. and Halstead, P. (1995) 'Towards an archaeobotanical recognition of winter cereal irrigation: an investigation of modern weed ecology in northern Spain', in H. Kroll and R. Pasternak (eds) *Res Archaeobotanicae*, Kiel: Oetker-Voges Verlag: 49–68.

Jones, M. (1985) 'Archaeobotany beyond subsistence reconstruction', in G. Barker and M. Jones (eds) *Beyond Domestication in Prehistoric Europe: Investigations in Subsistence Archaeology and Social Complexity*, London: Academic Press: 107–28.

Jones, M. (1986) *England before Domesday*, London: Batsford.

Katzenberg, M. A. (1992) 'Changing diet and health in pre- and protohistoric Ontario', in R. Huss-Ashmore, J. Schall and M. Hediger (eds) *Health and Lifestyle Change*, Philadelphia: MASCA Research Papers in Science and Archaeology 9: 23–31.

Keeley, L. (1980) *Experimental Determination of Stone Tool Uses. A Microwear Analysis*, Chicago: Chicago University Press.

Khazanov, M. (1984) *Nomads and the Outside World*, Cambridge: Cambridge University Press.

Killingley, J. S. (1981) 'Seasonality of mollusk collecting determined from O-18 profiles of midden shells', *American Antiquity* 46: 152–58.

King, A. (1984) 'Animal bones and the dietary identity of military and civilian groups in Roman Britain', in T. F. C. Blagg and A. King (eds) *Military and Civilian in Roman Britain*, Oxford: British Archaeological Reports, British series: 187–217.

King, A. (1985) 'I resti animali', in A. Ricci (ed.) *Settefinestre. Una Villa Schiavistica nell' Etruria Romana 2: La Villa e Suoi Reperti*, Modena: Panini: 278 99.

King, A. (1989) 'Villas and animal bones', in K. Branigan and D. Miles (eds) *The Economies of Romano-British Villas*, Sheffield: Sheffield University, Department of Archaeology and Prehistory: 51–59.

Kirke, C. M. St. (1980) 'Prehistoric agriculture in the Belize River valley', *World Archaeology* 11 (3): 281–86.

Klein, R. G. and Cruz-Uribe, K. (1984) *The Analysis of Animal Bones from Archaeological Sites*, Chicago: University of Chicago Press.

Koike, H. (1986) 'Prehistoric hunting pressure and paleobiomass: an environmental reconstruction and archaeozoological analysis of a Jomon shellmound area', in T. Akazawa and C. M. Aikens (eds) *Prehistoric Hunter-Gatherers in Japan – New Research Methods*, University Museum Bulletin 27, Tokyo: University of Tokyo: 27–53.

Langdon, J. (1988) 'Agricultural equipment', in G. Astill and A. Grant (eds) *The Countryside of Medieval England*, Oxford: Basil Blackwell: 86–107.

Larsson, L. (1978) *Agerød I:B – Agerød I:D, A Study of Early Atlantic Settlement in Scania*, Lund: CWK Gleerup.

Larsson, L. (1983) *Agerød V: An Atlantic Bog Site in Central Scania*, Lund: Acta Archaeologica Lundensia 12.

Larsson, L., Callmer, J. and Stjernquist, B. (eds) (1992) *The Archaeology of the Cultural Landscape: Fieldwork and Research in a South Swedish Rural Region*, Acta Archaeologica Lundensia Series 4, no. 19, Stockholm: Almquist and Wiksell International.

Leach, E. (1970) *Lévi-Strauss*, London: Fontana.

Lee, R. B. (1979) *The !Kung San: Men, Women and Work in a Foraging Society*, Cambridge: Cambridge University Press.

Legge, A. J. and Rowley-Conwy, P. A. (1988) *Star Carr Revisited: a Re-Analysis of the Large Mammals*, Oxford: Alden Press.

Levine, M. (1990) 'Dereivka and the problem of horse domestication', *Antiquity* 64: 727–40.

Lévi-Strauss, C. (1965) 'Le triangle culinaire', *L'Arc* 26: 19–29.

Levy, T. (1992) 'Transhumance, subsistence, and social evolution in the northern Negev desert', in O. Bar-Yosef and A. Khazanov (eds) *Pastoralism in the Levant: Archaeological Materials in Anthropological Perspectives*, Monographs in World Archaeology 10, Madison, Wis.: Prehistory Press: 65–82.

Levy, T. (1995a) 'Cult, metallurgy and rank societies – chalcolithic period (ca.4500–3500 BCE)', in T. Levy (ed.) *The Archaeology of Society in the Holy Land*, London: Leicester University Press: 226–43.

Levy, T. (ed.) (1995b) *The Archaeology of Society in the Holy Land*, London: Leicester University Press.

Lewin, J., Macklin, M. and Woodward, J. (eds) (1995) *Mediterranean Quaternary River Environments*, Rotterdam: Balkema.

Lewis-Williams, J. D. (1983) *The Rock Art of Southern Africa*, Cambridge: Cambridge University Press.

Lewthwaite, J. (1986) 'The transition to food production: a Mediterranean perspective', in M. Zvelebil (ed.) *Hunters in Transition*, Cambridge: Cambridge University Press: 53–66.

Limbrey, S. (1975) *Soil Science and Archaeology*, London: Academic Press.

Linares, O. F. (1976) 'Garden-hunting in the American tropics', *Human Ecology* 4: 331–49.

Lubell, D., Jackes, M., Schwarcz, H., Knyf, M. and Meiklejohn, C. (1994) 'The mesolithic–neolithic transition in Portugal: isotopic and dental evidence of diet', *Journal of Archaeological Science* 21: 201–16.

Lund, J. and Thomsen, V. (1981) 'On the reconstruction of an iron age house', *Kuml*: 187–205.

Lyman, R. L. (1994) *Vertebrate Taphonomy*, Cambridge: Cambridge University Press.

McGreevy, T. (1989) 'Prehispanic pastoralism in northern Peru', in J. Clutton-Brock (ed.) *The Walking Larder*, London: Unwin Hyman: 231–39.

Maggi, R., Nisbet, R. and Barker, G. (eds) (1991) *Archeologia della Pastorizia nell'Europa Meridionale*, Bordighera: Istituto Internazionale di Studi Liguri (two volumes).

Manning, A. and Serpell, J. (eds) (1994) *Animals and Human Society*, London: Routledge.

Marichal, R. (1992) *Les Ostraca du Bu Njem*, Rome: Libya Antiqua Supplement 7.

Meadows, I. (1996) 'Wollaston: the Nene Valley – a British Moselle?', *Current Archaeology* 150: 212–15.

Mellars, P. A. (ed.) (1988) *Excavations at Oronsay*, Edinburgh: Edinburgh University Press.

Meniel, P. (ed.) (1988) *L'Animal dans les Pratiques Religieuses: les Manifestations Materielles*, Paris, Anthropozoologica (troisième numero special).

Mills, J. S. and White, R. (1989) 'The identity of resins from the late bronze age shipwreck at Ulu Burun (Kas)', *Archaeometry* 31 (1): 37–44.

Mithen, S. J. (1990) *Thoughtful Foragers: A Study of Prehistoric Decision-making*, Cambridge: Cambridge University Press.

Mithen, S. J. (1996) *The Prehistory of Mind*, London: Thames and Hudson.

Moody, J. and Grove, A. T. (1990) 'Terraces and enclosure walls in the Cretan landscape', in S. Bottema, G. Entjes-Nieborg, and W. van Zeist (eds) *Man's Role in the Shaping of the Eastern Mediterranean*, Rotterdam: Balkema: 83–191.

Moore, J. G., Krotoszynski and O'Neill, H. J. (1984) 'Fecal odorgrams: a method for the partial reconstruction of ancient and modern diets', *Digestive Diseases and Sciences* 29 (10): 907–11.

Murphy, P. (1983) 'Iron age to late Saxon land use in the Breckland', in M. Jones (ed.) *Integrating the Subsistence Economy*, Oxford: British Archaeological Reports, International Series 181: 177–210.

Murray, O. and Tecusan, M. (eds) (1995) *In Vino Veritas*, London: British School at Rome.

Muzzolini, A. (1993) 'The emergence of a food-producing economy in the Sahara', in T. Shaw, P. Sinclair, B. Andah and A. Okpopo (eds) *The Archaeology of Agriculture: Food, Metals and Towns*, London: Routledge: 227–39.

Nasman, U. (1996) 'Scandinavian society', in K. Randsborg (ed.) *Roman Reflections in Scandinavia*, Rome: L'Erma di Bretschneider: 145–49.

Olsen, S. (1996) 'Prehistoric adaptations to the Kazak steppes', in G. Afanas'ev, S. Cleuziou,

J. R. Lukacs, and M. Tosi (eds) *The Prehistory of Asia and Oceania*, Forli: Colloquia of the XIII International Congress of Prehistoric and Protohistoric Sciences, volume 16: 49–60.

Osborne, P. J. (1983) 'An insect fauna from a modern cesspit and its comparisons with probable cesspit assemblages from archaeological sites', *Journal of Archaeological Science* 10: 453–63.

Parsons, J. J. and Denevan, W. M. (1974) 'Pre-Columbian ridged fields', in E. Zubrow, M. C. Frotiz and J. M. Fritz (eds) *New World Archaeology. Theoretical and Cultural Transformations*, San Francisco: Freeman: 241–48.

Patou-Mathis, M. (1994) 'Archéozoologie des niveaux Moustériens et Aurignaciens de la Grotte Tournal à Bize (Aude)', *Gallia Préhistoire* 36: 1–64.

Pavlides, C. and Gosden, C. (1994) '35,000-year-old sites in the rainforests of West New Britain, Papua New Guinea', *Antiquity* 68: 604–10.

Payne, S. (1972) 'On the interpretation of bone samples from archaeological sites', in E. S. Higgs (ed.) *Papers in Economic Prehistory*, Cambridge: Cambridge University Press: 65–91.

Pearsall, D. M. (1989) *Palaeoethnobotany. A Handbook for Procedures*, San Diego, Calif.: Academic Press.

Pearsall, D. M. (1996) 'Domestication and agriculture in the New World tropics', in T. D. Price and A. B. Gebauer (eds) *Last Hunters – First Farmers*, Santa Fe: School of American Research: 157–92.

Pearsall, D. M. and Trimble, M. K. (1984) 'Identifying past agricultural activity through soil phytolith analysis: a case study from the Hawaian islands', *Journal of Archaeological Science* 11: 119–33.

Perkins, P. and Attolini, I. (1992) 'An Etruscan farm at Podere Tartuchino', *Papers of the British School at Rome* 60: 71–134.

Piggott, S. (1992) *Wagon, Chariot, and Carriage*, London: Thames and Hudson.

Piperno, D. R. (1985) 'Phytolith analysis of geological sediments from Panama', *Antiquity* 59: 13–19.

Pryor, F., French, C., Crowther, D., Gurney, D., Simpson, G. and Taylor, M. (1985) *The Fenland Project No. 1. Archaeology and Environment in the Lower Welland Valley*, Norwich: East Anglian Archaeology 27.

Randsborg, K. (1985) 'Subsistence and settlement in northern temperate Europe in the first millennium AD', in G. Barker and M. Jones (eds) *Beyond Domestication in Prehistoric Europe: Investigations in Subsistence Archaeology and Social Complexity*, London: Academic Press: 233–65.

Reeves, C. (1992) *Egyptian Medicine*, Princes Risborough: Shire Publications.

Reid, A. (1996) 'Cattle herds and the redistribution of cattle resources', *World Archaeology* 28 (1): 43–57.

Reinhardt, K. J. and Bryant, V. M. (1992) 'Coprolite analysis: a biological perspective on archaeology', in M. B. Schiffer (ed.) *Archaeological Method and Theory 4*, Tucson: University of Arizona Press: 245–88.

Renfrew, C. (1972) *The Emergence of Civilization*, London: Methuen.

Renfrew, C. (1987) *Archaeology and Language: the Puzzle of Indo-European Origins*, London: Thames and Hudson.

Reynolds, P. J. (1979) *Iron Age Farm. The Butser Experiment*, London: British Museum Publications.

Richards, M. (1996) 'First farmers with no taste for grain', *British Archaeology* 18: 6.

Roberts, M. (1996) ' "Man the Hunter" returns at Boxgrove', *British Archaeology* 18: 8–9.

Roosevelt, C., Lima da Costa, M., Lopez Machado, C., Michab, M. *et al.* (1996) 'Palaeo-indian cave dwellers in the Amazon: the peopling of the Americas', *Science* 272: 373–84.

Rosen, A. M. (1994) 'Identifying ancient irrigation: a new method using opaline phytoliths from emmer wheat', *Journal of Archaeological Science* 21: 125–32.

Rosen, S. A. (1992) 'The case for seasonal movement of pastoral nomads in the late Byzantine/early Arabic period in the south central Negev', in O. Bar-Yosef and A. Khazanov (eds) *Pastoralism in the Levant: Archaeological Materials in Anthropological Perspectives*, Monographs in World Archaeology 10, Madison, Wis.: Prehistory Press: 153–64.

Rottländer, R. C. A. and Hartke, I. (1982) 'New results of food identification by fat analysis', in A. Aspinall and S. E. Warren (eds) *Proceedings of the 22nd Symposium on Archaeometry*, Bradford: University of Bradford: 218–23.

Rowley-Conwy, P. C. (1983) 'Sedentary hunters: the Ertebolle example', in G. N. Bailey (ed.) *Hunter-Gatherer Economy in Prehistory: a European Perspective*, Cambridge: Cambridge University Press: 111–26.

Rowley-Conwy, P. (1995) 'Wild or domestic? On the evidence for the earliest domestic cattle and pigs in South Scandinavia and Iberia', *International Journal of Osteology* 5: 115–26.

Roymans, N. (1996) 'The integration of Lower Rhine populations in the Roman empire', in J. Metzler, M. Millett, N. Roymans and J. Slofstra (eds) *Integration in the Early Roman West*, Luxembourg: 47–64.

Rudenko, S. (1970) *Frozen Tombs of Siberia: the Pazyryk Burials of Iron Age Horsemen*, London: Dent.

Ryan, K. and Crabtree, P. (eds) (1995) *The Symbolic Role of Animals in Archaeology*, Philadelphia: MASCA, University of Pennsylvania, Museum of Archaeology and Anthropology.

Sandor, J. A., Gersper, P. L. and Hawley, J. W. (1990) 'Prehistoric agricultural terraces and soils in the Mimbres area, New Mexico', *World Archaeology* 22: 70–86.

Sanger, D. (1996) 'Testing the models: hunter-gatherer use of space in the Gulf of Maine, USA', *World Archaeology* 27: 512–26.

Scott, E. (1991) 'Animal and infant burials in Romano-British villas: a revitalization movement', in P. Garwood, D. Jennings, R. Skeates and J. Toms (eds) *Sacred and Profane*, Monograph 32, Oxford: Oxford University Committee for Archaeology: 115–21.

Scott, K. (1980) 'Two hunting episodes of middle palaeolithic age at La Cotte de la St Brelade, Jersey', *World Archaeology* 12 (2): 137–52.

Scott, S. (1997) 'The power of images in the late Roman house', in R. Laurence and A. Wallace-Hadrill (eds) *Domestic Space in the Roman World: Pompeii and Beyond*, Ann Arbor: Journal of Roman Archaeology Supplement 22: 53–68.

Sherratt, A. (1980) 'Water, soil and seasonality in early cereal cultivation', *World Archaeology* 11 (3): 313–30.

Sherratt, A. (1981) 'Plough and pastoralism: aspects of the Secondary Products Revolution', in N. Hammond, I. Hodder and G. Isaac (eds) *Patterns of the Past: Studies in Memory of David Clarke*, Cambridge, Cambridge University Press: 261–305.

Sherratt, A. (1983) 'The secondary exploitation of animals in the Old World', *World Archaeology* 15: 90–104.

Simmons, I. and Innes, J. (1987) 'Mid-Holocene adaptations and later mesolithic forest disturbance in northern England', *Journal of Archaeological Science* 14: 385–403.

Simmons, I., Turner, T. and Innes, I. (1989) 'An application of fine-resolution pollen analysis to later mesolithic peats of an English upland', in C. Bonsall (ed.) *The Mesolithic in Europe*, Edinburgh: Edinburgh University Press: 206–18.

Slicher van Bath, B. H. (1963) *The Agrarian History of Western Europe AD 500–1850*, London: Arnold.

Sobolik, K. D. (1990) 'A nutritional analysis of diet as revealed in prehistoric human coprolites', *Texas Journal of Science* 42 (1): 23–36.

SOED (1973) *Shorter Oxford English Dictionary*, Oxford: Oxford University Press.

Spencer, C. S. and Redmond, E. M. (1992) 'Prehispanic chiefdoms of the western Venezuelan *llanos*', *World Archaeology* 24 (1): 134–57.

Speth, J. D. (1983) *Bison Kills and Bone Counts: Decision Making by Ancient Hunters*, Chicago: University of Chicago Press.

Spooner, B. (1973) *The Cultural Ecology of Pastoral Nomads*, Modules in Anthropology 5, Reading, Mass.: Addison-Wesley.

Spriggs, M. (1989) 'Dating the island southeast Asian Neolithic', *Antiquity* 63: 587–613.

Stark, B. L. and Vorhies, B. (1978) *Prehistoric Coastal Adaptations*, New York: Academic Press.

Stead, M. (1994) *Egyptian Life*, London: British Museum Press.

Stiner, M. (1991) 'The faunal remains at Grotta Guattari: a taphonomic perspective', *Current Anthropology* 32 (2): 103–17.

Stiner, M. (1994) *Honor among Thieves: a Zooarchaeological Study of Neanderthal Ecology*, Princeton: Princeton University Press.

Stocker, D. and Stocker, M. (1996) 'Sacred profanity: the theology of rabbit breeding and the symbolic landscape of the warren', *World Archaeology* 28: 265–72.

Stringer, C. and Gamble, C. (1993) *In Search of the Neanderthals*, London: Thames and Hudson.

Sturdy, D. (1975) 'Some reindeer economies in prehistoric Europe', in E. S. Higgs (ed.) *Palaeoeconomy*, London: Cambridge University Press: 55–95.

Sutton, J. E. G. (ed.) (1996) *The Growth of Farming Communities in Africa from the Equator Southwards*, Nairobi: British Institute in Eastern Africa (*Azania* special volume 29–30).

Tankersley, K. and Isaac, B. (eds) (1990) *Early Palaeoindian Economies of Eastern North America*, Research in Economic Anthropology Supplement 5, Greenwich, Conn.: JAI Press.

Taylor, J. (1996) 'Iron Age and Roman Landscapes in the East Midlands: a Case Study in Integrated Survey', Durham: University of Durham, unpublished Ph.D. thesis.

Thomas, J. (1984) 'Ritual activity and structured deposition in later neolithic Wessex', in R. Bradley and J. Gardiner (eds) *Neolithic Studies: a Review of Some Current Research*, Oxford: British Archaeological Reports, British Series 133: 189–218.

Thomas, J. (1996) 'The cultural context of the first use of domesticates in continental central and northwest Europe', in D. Harris (ed.) *The Origins and Spread of Agriculture and Pastoralism in Eurasia*, London: UCL Press: 310–22.

Ucko, P. J. and Dimbleby, G. W. (eds) (1969) *The Domestication and Exploitation of Plants and Animals*, London: Duckworth.

van Andel, Tj. and Runnels, C. (1987) *Beyond the Acropolis: the Archaeology of the Greek Countryside*, Stanford: Stanford University Press.

van Andel, Tj., Runnels, C. and Pope, K. (1985) 'Five thousand years of land use and abuse in the southern Argolid', *Hesperia* 55: 103–28.

van der Veen, M. (1992a) *Crop Husbandry Regimes*, Sheffield: University of Sheffield, Department of Archaeology and Prehistory.

van der Veen, M. (1992b) 'Garamantian agriculture: the plant remains from Zinchecra', *Libyan Studies* 23: 7–39.

van der Veen, M., Grant, A. and Barker, G. (1996) 'Romano-Libyan agriculture: crops and animals', in G. Barker, D. Gilbertson, B. Jones and D. Mattingly, *Farming the Desert: the UNESCO Libyan Valleys Archaeological Survey. Volume One: Synthesis*, Paris: UNESCO, London: Society for Libyan Studies, Tripoli: Department of Antiquities: 227–63.

Vencl, S. (1994) 'The archaeology of thirst', *Journal of European Archaeology* 2.2: 299–326.

Voorhies, B. (1996) 'Subsistence strategies on the eve of complexity: the late archaic period in south coastal Chiapas, Mexico', in T. R. Hester, L. Laurencich-Minelli and S. Salvatori (eds) *The Prehistory of the Americas*, XIII International Congress of Prehistoric and Protohistoric Sciences, volume 17, Forli: 19–25.

Wagstaff, M. (1992) 'Agricultural terraces: the Vasilikos valley, Cyprus', in M. Bell and J. Boardman (eds) *Past and Present Soil Erosion: Archaeological and Geographical Perspectives*, Oxford: Oxbow Monographs 22: 155–61.

Wallace, P. and O'Floinn, R. (1988) *Dublin 1000: Discovery and Excavation in Dublin 1842–1981*, Dublin: National Museum of Ireland.

Watanabe, H. (1972) *Ainu Ecosystem: Environment and Group Structure*, Tokyo: University of Tokyo Press.

Wendorf, F. and Schildt, R. (eds) (1980) *The Prehistory of the Eastern Sahara*, New York: Academic Press.

Weniger, G. C. (1987) 'Magdalenian settlement and subsistence in southwest Germany', *Proceedings of the Prehistoric Society* 53: 293–307.

Westropp, H. (1872) *Prehistoric Phases*, London: Bell and Daldy.

Wheeler, A. and Jones, A. K. G. (1989) *Fishes*, Cambridge: Cambridge University Press.

White, K. D. (1970) *Roman Farming*, London: Thames and Hudson.

White, K. D. (1984) *Greek and Roman Technology*, London: Thames and Hudson.

Whittaker, C. R. (ed.) (1988) *Pastoral Economies in Classical Antiquity*, Cambridge: Cambridge Philological Society, supplementary volume 14.

Whittle, A. (1993) *Problems in Neolithic Europe*, Cambridge: Cambridge University Press.

Widgren, M. (1983) *Settlement and Farming Systems in the Early Iron Age. A Study of Fossil Agrarian Landscapes in Ostergotland, Sweden*, Stockholm Studies in Human Geography 3, Stockholm: University of Stockholm.

Widgren, M. (1990) 'Strip fields in an iron age context: a case study from Vastergotland, Sweden', *Landscape History* 12: 5–24.

Wilkinson, T. J. (1990) 'Soil development and early land use in the Jazira region, Upper Mesopotamia', *World Archaeology* 22 (1): 87–103.

Wilkinson, T. J. (1993) 'Linear hollows in the Jazira, Upper Mesopotamia', *Antiquity* 67: 548–62.

Wilson, B., Grigson, C. and Payne, S. (1982) *Ageing and Sexing Animal Bones from Archaeological Sites*, Oxford: British Archaeological Reports, British Series 109.

Wittfogel, K. A. (1957) *Oriental Despotism*, New Haven: Yale University Press.

Zarins, J. (1989) 'Pastoralism in southwest Asia: the second millennium BC', in J. Clutton-Brock (ed.) *The Walking Larder*, London: Unwin Hyman: 127–55.

Zeder, M. (1994) 'Of kings and shepherds: specialised animal economy in Ur III Mesopotamia', in G. Stein and M. S. Rothman (eds) *Chiefdoms and Early States in the Near East*, Madison, Wis.: Prehistory Press: 175–91.

Zvelebil, M. (1985) 'Iron age transformations in northern Russia and the northeast Baltic', in G. Barker and M. Jones (eds) *Beyond Domestication in Prehistoric Europe: Investigations in Subsistence Archaeology and Social Complexity*, London: Academic Press: 147–80.

Zvelebil, M. (ed.) (1986) *Hunters in Transition*, Cambridge: Cambridge University Press: 67–93.

Zvelebil, M. (1994) 'Plant use in the Mesolithic and its role in the transition to farming', *Proceedings of the Prehistoric Society* 60: 35–74.

Zvelebil, M. (1996) 'The agricultural frontier and the transition to farming in the circum-Baltic region', in D. Harris (ed.) *The Origins and Spread of Agriculture and Pastoralism in Eurasia*, London: UCL Press: 323–45.

Zvelebil, M. and Rowley-Conwy, R. C. (1986) 'Foragers and farmers in Atlantic Europe', in M. Zvelebil (ed.) *Hunters in Transition*, Cambridge: Cambridge University Press: 67–93.

SELECT BIBLIOGRAPHY

The methodologies of subsistence reconstruction are well summarized by C. Renfrew and P. Bahn in their *Archaeology – an Introduction* (London: Thames and Hudson 1995). For artefact studies, see the Select Bibliography in Chapter 9. An excellent example of field system analysis is provided by Fleming (1988). The techniques of archaeobotany are discussed by Greig (1989), Hastorf and Popper (1989) and Pearsall (1989), there are many case studies in Harris and Hillman (1989) and a good detailed regional study is provided by van der Veen (1992a). The numerous books on the methodologies of archaeozoology include Davis (1986), Grayson (1984) and Wilson *et al.* (1982); there are relevant case studies in J. Clutton-Brock, *The Walking Larder* (London: Unwin Hyman 1989), and a good site-based study is Ijzereef (1981). There are useful examples of the contribution of geoarchaeology and palynology to agricultural studies in Bell and Boardman (1992), Fieller *et al.* (1985) and Lewin *et al.* (1995). Ethnoarchaeology is introduced by Gould (1980), relevant fieldwork is described by Hodder (1982), and the role of experimental archaeology is implicit in Reynolds's description of the Butzer Iron Age Farm (Reynolds 1979).

The conflicting evidence for Neanderthal hunting and scavenging is summarized well by Stringer and Gamble (1993), whilst studies of later prehistoric hunting and gathering include Bailey and Parkington (1988), the excellent re-analysis of the Star Carr fauna by Legge and Rowley-Conwy (1988), and (for upper palaeolithic hunting and its relations with ideology) Mithen (1990). Prehistoric farming in Europe is synthesized by Barker (1985), Bogucki (1988) and Whittle (1993), and there are useful papers in Barker and Gamble (1985). M. Jones (1986) provides an attractive synthesis of long-term landscape change in Britain; there is a much more detailed study of landscape change at the regional scale in southern Sweden given by Berglund (1991); the archaeology of Roman farming is summarized by K. Greene, *The Archaeology of the Roman Economy* (London: Batsford 1986); and for medieval England there are many relevant papers in G. Astill and A. Grant, *The Countryside of Medieval England* (Oxford: Blackwell 1988). Barker (1995) provides a useful case study of interdisciplinary landscape archaeology in the Mediterranean, and Barker *et al.* (1996) in the Saharan desert; tropical work is described in Farrington (1990), in several papers in Harris and Hillman (1989) and in J. Hather *Tropical Archaeobotany. Applications and New Developments* (London: Routledge 1994). For the archaeology of pastoralism see Bar-Yosef and Khazanov (1992). For issues of food and culture, and animals and ideology, see the papers in Garwood *et al.* (1991), Crabtree and Ryan (1991) and Ryan and Crabtree (1995), and the excellent case study by Hill (1995). Decision-making by farmers is addressed by Halstead and O'Shea (1989).

15

PRODUCTION AND EXCHANGE IN PREHISTORY

Timothy Earle

INTRODUCTION

The economic basis of human society is undeniably important. To understand the operation and evolution of past societies, investigations of production and exchange have become a central concern to archaeologists. This chapter summarizes the ways that production and exchange are studied by prehistorians and the theoretical significance of economies for understanding past human societies.

Our understanding of social process emphasizes three perspectives on production and exchange. The first perspective views the ways a human society extracts, processes, and distributes the necessities for human existence. An ecological approach, which studies a society's subsistence economy, has been the research agenda for the processual archaeologists of North America (Binford 1964; Flannery 1968a) and Europe (Bailey 1983; Higgs 1972). Local specialization and exchange have been viewed as means of adaptation. The second perspective studies how the political economy functions to finance the institutions of chiefdoms and states and to support the stratification on which these societies rest. Means of finance include the mobilization and distribution of staples and wealth (D'Altroy and Earle 1985). Approaches within social archaeology have looked at prestige goods exchange (Earle 1982b; Friedman and Rowlands 1977), peer–polity interaction (Renfrew and Cherry 1986), and centre–periphery relations (Algaze 1989; Rowlands *et al.* 1987). The third perspective studies how a society's relationships and categories become objectified ('real' if you will) through the economic process. As seen in the writings of the post-processualists (Bradley and Edmonds 1993; Hodder 1982a, 1984), the production and distribution of material goods are part of a broad social process in which individuals actively construct systems of meaning and relationships. From each of these perspectives, production and exchange are basic to the function and operation of human societies. These three approaches are in no sense mutually exclusive; rather, they express complementary uses of the economy in everyday life, political manoeuvring, and rituals of past societies.

RESEARCH TRENDS

Studies of production and exchange mirror the broader history of the discipline of archaeology (Chapter 2). Key intellectual and methodological themes of economic anthropology and geography show their strong influences within our investigations of past societies (Earle 1985a; Earle and Preucel 1987; Torrence 1986; Willey and Sabloff 1974). Although a full discussion of this history could form a separate chapter, I shall summarize some of the trends as a background.

Traditional archaeology frequently explains cultures as collections of traits deriving from migration, diffusion, and 'influence'. Exchange is a vehicle for cultural interchange. Attempts to look at these relationships systematically include such work as Stjernquist (1967) and Curtin (1984). A critical juncture for archaeology was the substantivist critique within economic anthropology and the subsequent formalist–substantivist debate (LeClair and Schneider 1968; Polanyi *et al.* 1957; for archaeology, see Earle 1985a). In his analysis of the ancient economies of the Middle East and Africa, Polanyi (*et al.* 1957, Polanyi 1968) noted that economies were embedded in the broader socio-political organization, such that economic forms varied greatly cross-culturally. Substantivism suggested that, through the study of economy for which archaeology has ample methods, researchers can investigate the social organization of extinct societies. Polanyi's typology of economic relationships (reciprocity, redistribution, and market exchange) became connected to specific stages of cultural evolution: band, tribe, chiefdom, state (Service 1962). Therefore, in the checklists of traits indicative of different social forms, economic organization was taken as distinctive of social evolution. Renfrew (1973), for example, identified as chiefdoms the bronze age societies of Wessex, southern England, on the basis of archaeological evidence for redistribution.

Substantivist investigations of exchange and social organization expanded in the early 1970s (Sabloff and Lamberg-Karlovsky 1975; Wilmsen 1972). Sabloff and Freidel (1975) investigated the island of Cozumel as a way to understand how ports-of-trade function in long-distance trade between archaic states (see also Chapman 1957). As a broader study of state formation in south-east Asia, Wheatley (1975) investigated changes from reciprocity to redistribution as means of economic institutionalization.

Especially influential were Renfrew's (1975) models of the different types of exchange that could be anticipated archaeologically (Fig. 15.4). His article focused

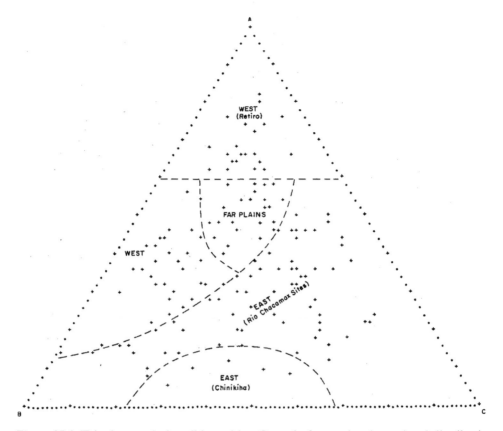

Figure 15.1 Tripolar graph describing with a Q-mode factor plot the regional distribution of plain ware Mayan ceramics; analysis shows different local production locales. Source: Fry 1980.

region, Mexico and Guatemala. Initial use of obsidian focused on the nearer Guatemalan sources, and the Mexican sources became dominant only during Late Post-Classic, presumably as a result of the economic incorporation of the coastal region within the Aztec empire. Importantly, no comparable shift towards Mexican sources was documented for the Middle Classic Period, when Teotihuacan was at its height. This contrast in obsidian procurement suggests that these two great Mesoamerican empires had distinct economic relationships with the Guatemalan coast, at least as far as obsidian exchange was concern.

The focus on obsidian, at the exclusion of other materials that are technically more difficult to source, has probably given an unrealistically narrow view of early exchange. Obsidian is usually a fairly minor, utilitarian industry, and the nature of its production and exchange most probably did not accurately reflect economic

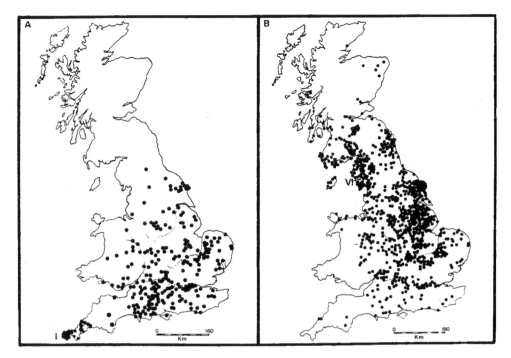

Figure 15.2 Distribution of British neolithic stone axes from source Group I (left) and Group IV (right). Source: Bradley and Edmonds 1993.

activities involving bulkier craft industries such as potting, and wealth industries such as metalworking. These latter industries, however, involve synthetic materials highly altered from their original state and thus difficult to source. Promising characterization work is now available, as for Mesoamerican ceramics (Bishop 1980; D'Altroy and Bishop 1990; Fry 1979, 1980; Neff 1989), European bronzes (Liversage and Liversage 1989), Polynesian basalts (Weisler 1993), and other materials.

Accompanying the technical advances in chemical characterization, economic studies in archaeology have been greatly aided by improvements in computer technology. Harbottle (1982), for example, demonstrates the necessity of computer-aided clustering procedures in characterization studies. More generally though, computer analysis of large datasets is now the backbone of economic studies in archaeology.

An early breakthrough in 'archaeo-economics' was the application of mathematical, descriptive, procedures adapted from the quantitative geography of the 1960s (especially Haggett 1965) and introduced broadly to archaeology by David Clarke's (1972) *Models in Archaeology* and by Hodder and Orton's (1976) *Spatial Analysis in Archaeology*. These works, although largely descriptive, have proved extremely

613

helpful in exchange studies. Hodder (1974), for example, used a two-dimensional analysis of fall-off in the frequency of materials from their sources to study different kinds of exchange. In such studies, the abundance of a material from a known source is expected to 'decay' (become less common) at sites of greater distances from the source. This fall-off in abundance reflects the increasing costs of transportation and other difficulties of exchange. Figure 15.3 illustrates how the fall-off curves for different goods contrast with each other, reflecting such things as value of the goods and their mechanisms of exchange.

Colin Renfrew (1975) developed a typology of exchange, based heavily on Polanyi's earlier work, and showed graphically how these would look in terms of the fall-off curves of commodities (Fig. 15.4). Thus with reciprocity, outside of the

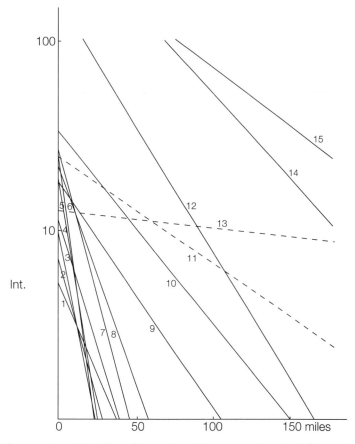

Figure 15.3 Contrasting fall-off gradients for different archaeological materials from the Old World. Regression lines 1 and 3–7 represent the rapid decline in most ceramic objects away from source; in contrast, lines 13 and 14 represent distributions of two neolithic axe groups, and line 12 represents Anatolian obsidian. Source: Hodder 1974.

'supply zone' where access to the resource was direct, the abundance of materials decays monotonically or uniformly with distance. In contrast, with redistribution, peaks in the frequency of goods would be observed at distribution centres. Originally it was hoped that different models of exchange would be represented by different regression formulae (Findlow and Bolognese 1982), such that specific fall-off models would identify specific mechanisms of exchange, but problems exist with simple correspondences (Renfrew 1977), and this exercise has been largely abandoned.

Three-dimensional analysis, as an alternative, involves surface trend studies such as SYMAP (Ericson 1977; Hodder and Orton 1976). SYMAP represents the frequency of traded materials by contour intervals on a map. In his description of California exchange, Ericson (1977) shows how the frequency of obsidian decays in concentric rings away from a source, distorted by such factors as the availability of high quality chert, a good substitute for obsidian among the chipped stones. Computer analysis permitted the use of large-scale, regional, databases and the fitting of data to various mathematical models.

Statistical analysis of large datasets has proved essential for increasingly sophisticated studies of production. For studies of lithic production, computer-aided analysis allows the routine study of chipping debris into the various steps of manufacture ('stages of reduction'). Production is broken down into stages such as core preparation, core reduction, blade requisition, and so on. Analysing manufacturing debris, Ammerman and Andrefsky (1982), for example, suggest how the composition of débitage may be matched to the appropriate stage in the reduction sequence, thus allowing the recognition of the different steps in the manufacturing process at different locations across the landscape.

Torrence (1986) argues for the need to develop middle-range theories that link specific social and economic behaviours with patterns of production and consumption debris. She develops these models from ethnographic description of lithic tools, in such diverse contexts as the generalized stone-age gatherers of Australia and the highly specialized gun-flint makers of Europe, and then uses descriptive statistics of archaeological obsidian debris from Melos, in the Aegean, to look at the degree of standardization and specialization in the blade industry there. Counter to earlier assumptions, she argues that, because of the lack of standardization in the artefactual classes, the obsidian was apparently produced opportunistically by many craftsmen with a low degree of standardization in the products, indicating little control in the production process. John Clark and William Perry (1986) have studied a large sample of ethnographic cases of specialization to develop the kind of middle-range theory envisaged by Torrence, and these models are being investigated now for materials other than obsidian.

For ceramics, similar systematic analyses of metric measurements for large datasets permit investigation of standardization and specialization. Using a large

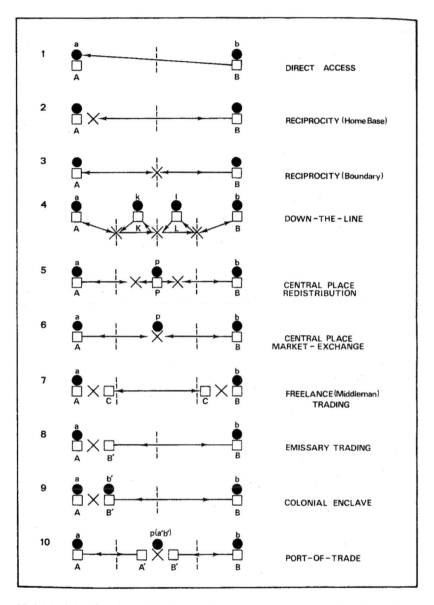

Figure 15.4 Models of different institutional forms of exchange and their spatial implications for archaeology. Circles a and b represent the points of origin and distribution for a commodity, with A and B representing the producer and recipient respectively. P indicates a central place with a central person who distributes objects. X represents exchange events. Source: Renfrew 1975.

sample of Mayan sherds, Rice (1981) argues that particular variation in technological characteristics such as paste, temper and firing, indicate the relative number
of hands at work (Hagstrum 1985). Using ethnographic studies to understand the
social context of ceramic production, Hagstrum (1986) and Costin (1991) investigate the changing nature of production and exchange in ceramics following Inca
imperial conquest of the Andean central highlands.

Because it is impossible to give an accurate and full description of the many
techniques available and used in archaeological studies of production and exchange,
I refer the reader to some of the synthetic treatments, including Harbottle (1982) on
characterization, Renfrew (1975, 1977) on exchange, and Tosi (1984), Torrence
(1986) and Costin (1991) on specialized production. What I want to concentrate on
here is the theoretical significance for economic studies by giving examples of work
in prehistoric archaeology.

PRODUCTION AND EXCHANGE: SIGNIFICANCE TO ARCHAEOLOGY

The material and economic foundation of human society is broadly recognized. A
population must be fed, its institutions financed, and its culture fashioned. Past the
obvious necessity, I shall argue that the details of production and exchange provide
a critical means to understand how human society works. The goals of archaeology
are many, but a central challenge is to explicate the processes resulting in the
evolution of complex societies (see Chapters 22 and 23). In this regard, studies of
economy play a particularly important role. It will be my argument here that the
economy provides the foundations of power and symbolism upon which complex
social institutions are constructed. Archaeology, with its temporal perspective and
its rich material record, provides the suitable venue to investigate these evolutionary
issues. In fact, I believe that these issues can best be investigated by archaeology,
and that archaeo-economics should be a centre-piece for archaeology's contribution
to knowledge of human societies. The three significant scenes of economic action
that I discuss are the subsistence economy, the political economy, and symbolic
materialization.

The subsistence economy

The first and most basic problem for any human society is material provisioning.
Although humans do not live on bread alone, without bread they do not live at all.
Making a living is so basic that it is often taken for granted, but the subsistence
process suffuses social life and provides details of political control in complex

617

societies (see Chapter 14). Intensification in the subsistence economy creates specific problems that require group coordination and thus offers opportunities for control by leaders (Johnson and Earle 1987: fig. 1). The legitimacy of a social order, its system of stratification and patterns of control, ultimately rest on the reliability of its subsistence system.

The most basic consideration in the subsistence economy is the actual provisioning of food. In pre-industrial society, provisioning seems to have been largely the responsibility of the householding group or extended family. The Domestic Mode of Production, in which households provided for their own subsistence, was at least an ideal in most societies down to recent times (Johnson and Earle 1987). In the Domestic Mode of Production, since production is for use by the household, exchange is non-existent. If this is ideal for most societies, why then should inter-household exchange develop? This is a central question for archaeology.

An answer that was generally accepted by the cultural ecologists of the 1950s and 1960s was that, as population grew and people settled down, local, sedentary households and groups became specialized in the most efficient and reliable local foods and then exchanged their local specializations regionally. Service (1962) saw this as the justification for the development of redistribution in chiefdoms, and Sanders (1956) saw it as the justification for the development of markets in early states. In both circumstances, the development of a regional political organization was interpreted as caused by a need for central management. Chiefs were thought to coordinate the regional distribution of foods, and the state provided the superstructure for the market.

Although logically sound, archaeological evidence has not supported this adaptationalist argument (Brumfiel and Earle 1987). First, it must be acknowledged that some level of exchange existed in all societies. Thus quite extensive food exchange was common in several hunter-gatherer cases such as the coastal Chumash (Arnold 1992) or the Eskimo (Johnson and Earle 1987). Correspondingly, it is surprising how little subsistence exchange has actually been documented archaeologically in complex societies. This negative evidence may in part be a result of inadequate data recovery procedures on excavations: where such procedures as flotation for botanical remains and screening for bones are used, as for example in the Mantaro Valley and at Pacatnamu in Peru, the evidence suggested that virtually all food was obtained from the immediate catchment of the excavated settlements (Earle 1985b; Gumerman 1991; Hastorf 1993). In Hawaii (Earle 1977), Europe (Friedman and Rowlands 1977; Kristiansen 1984), and the Valley of Mexico (Brumfiel 1976), archaeological evidence was used to question the adaptationalist logic of developing subsistence exchange linked to population growth and political integration. Rather, it is now thought that subsistence exchange became elaborated in many situations as a result of development in the political economy, as described in the next section.

Alternatively, exchange may be tied to a need to reduce subsistence risk. Using ethnographic evidence from the !Kung San hunter-gatherers of the Kalahari, Polly Wiessner (1982) has argued that social relationships maintained by continual inter-personal exchange solve the problem of high risk in subsistence. For the American Southwest (Minnis 1985) and the Midwest (Braun and Plog 1982; Halstead and O'Shea 1989), social relations and exchange are seen as solving problems of risk. On the Marquesan Islands of Polynesia, large subterranean pits used to store fermented breadfruit buffered the local community against devastating droughts (Kirch 1991b).

Less problematic has been the archaeological evidence for exchange in utilitarian craft products, whose raw materials are localized in their distribution or whose manufacture requires unusual skill (Andrefski 1994). In terms of localized distribution of raw material, the most important factor appears to be the mobility of the population. In the Archaic and Woodland periods of the American Midwest, for example, Morrow and Jefferies (1989) argue that, by picking up stone resources during the seasonal round (that is, by 'embedded procurement'), there was no need for inter-group exchange. For the Melos obsidian, Torrence (1986) envisages that a maritime population would simply have exploited this island source as part of their broader subsistence strategies. Under these circumstances, localized resource use would only require exchange if the annual movement of a group did not encompass the distribution of the required resource.

The localized distribution of raw materials used for formal tools resulted in exchange in working tools and utensils in situations where local groups defended territories. This would explain, for example, the fairly extensive exchange in obsidian among the hunter-gathering populations of California (Ericson 1977, 1981). Close by the obsidian sources, within a local group's territory, obsidian was used generally for all lithic implements; at greater distances, where territorial boundaries must be passed, it became used for special tools such as arrow points, for which obsidian is particularly well suited (Bettinger 1982; Ericson 1982).

An excellent example of trade in pottery is described for the simply organized island populations off the northern coast of New Guinea (Allen 1985; Irwin 1978, 1985; Yoffee 1985). In this island environment, clay suitable for pottery was not generally available, and a specialized industry of ceramic manufacture was developed on the island of Mailu, from whence it was distributed by traders along the coast of New Guinea and to the off-shore islands. This trade existed in the absence of a complex regionally organized society.

As another example of exchange in utilitarian goods, late in the prehistory of the Peruvian highlands, most stone tools were produced from immediately available stone, but sickle blades were manufactured by a few villages positioned close to a high quality chert source and then exchanged to other communities in the vicinity (Russell 1988). In the same region, production of utilitarian pots for local exchange took place at a few communities, presumably because of localized clay resources or the skill required in potting (Costin 1986; Hagstrum 1989). Considering the size and complexity of the Inca empire, the archaeology showed that the overall extent and volume of specialization and exchange were, however, unexpectedly limited.

These three case studies raise the intriguing question of how exchange in utilitarian products relates to the evolution of complex societies (see also Chapter 23). Minimally, increasing population density and decreasing mobility require either increasing exchange or the shift to more local (and often inferior) materials. Both Sanders (1956) and Service (1962) see the increase in population density resulting in an initial settling in and intensification of production that necessitates exchange and the development of regional polities with central managers to regulate exchange. Since these provocative early statements, however, archaeological and historic evidence on specialization and exchange seems to contradict these adaptational propositions (see, for example, Hughes 1994).

The first thing to note is that there is not a simple relationship between the amount of exchange and social complexity. Therefore, in New Guinea, opportunities for exchange did not result in the development of chiefdoms or states. In fact, although the early hierarchical society of Lapita may have been based to some measure on broad-scale exchange (Kirch and Hunt 1988), extensive exchange has been documented in the absence of strong leadership and regional organization (Allen 1985). In contrast, among the Mississippian chiefdoms, the extensive production and exchange of localized salt lay outside chiefly control (Muller 1987), and in Hawaii the complex chiefdoms of late prehistory existed with a low volume of exchange in food and utilitarian products; the exchange that did exist seems largely unregulated by the chiefly hierarchy (Earle 1977; Lass 1994). In other words, the chiefly redistribution on Hawaii did not involve staples or working tools, thus making Service's argument invalid. In terms of more complex societies, the highland Andean Inca state existed without a market, and exchange in utilitarian products was limited and highly specific; it was not controlled by the state apparatus (Earle 1985b; LaLone 1982). Where markets did exist, as in the Aztec state, the justification for their development seems to be more political than subsistence-based. In simple terms, exchange does not uniformly increase through prehistory, as might be expected in simpler evolutionary models; rather, the amount of exchange documented archaeologically is highly variable through both time and space (Earle 1994).

What we are seeing is that the development of exchange in subsistence goods was tied in large measure to the development of the political economy. I shall now consider the nature of the political economy in non-industrial societies to see the political causes for the development of systems of specialized production and exchange.

The political economy

The evolution of social complexity involves two related processes: (1) increasing social stratification, as wealth becomes concentrated in socially distinguished segments of society; and (2) increasing political integration as institutional mechanisms of control are elaborated. The political economy provides the organizational mechanism to mobilize the resources that enrich the élites and finance their institutions of control. Evidently, the evolution of social complexity depends on the development of the political economy, and these developments involve radical transformations in systems of production and exchange. Essentially I am arguing that economic transformation was largely a result not of a gradual process of adaptation but of a revolutionary process of political transformation.

D'Altroy and Earle (1985) have distinguished staple finance and wealth finance as two means to mobilize the materials required for the support of the ostentatious lifestyles and governing institutions of the ruling élite. For some purposes it is desirable to consider these types of finance as alternative opportunities representing different advantages and limitations to an emerging élite. The use of a particular system of finance is seen as creating specific properties of stability and growth that have profound ramifications for the long-term maintenance and expansion of the related polities. In fact, any political system depends on hybrid systems that seek to overcome limitations in the ideal forms. I shall first consider how the two systems can be considered separately and then consider how they must be combined.

Staple finance (Polanyi 1968) involves the mobilization of staple goods, especially food and rough cloth, from a commoner population, as rent for access to land owned by the élite class or specific institutions. A good example of how this works is the political economy of the complex chiefdoms of Hawaii in the late prehistoric period (Earle 1977, 1978; compare Stein 1994 for 'Ubaid chiefdoms). The chiefdoms depended on systems of 'redistribution' – not for commodity exchange but for finance. In these systems, chiefs, as owners of the land through conquest and allocation by the ruling paramount, offered subsistence land plots to commoners in return for their labour on lands producing for the chiefs. The food grown on the chiefly lands provided for the chiefs' subsistence, for periodic feasts which they hosted, and for support of specialists working for the chiefs. These specialists included warriors to protect the chief and to seize new lands, managers to guarantee the production on the chiefs' lands, craft specialists manufacturing weapons and wealth, and a cadre of other personnel. Essentially the development of a non-producing sector to the society simply involved an expropriation of staples from the commoners who produced them so as to support the élite sector of society. Staple finance is a simple form of rent or taxation, in which the products needed by the élites are demanded from the commoners in return for guarantees of access to needed productive resources.

621

The best known example of staple finance is the famous redistribution system of the Inca empire. Although state redistribution was originally thought by the substantivist John Murra ([1956] 1980) to be a system of commodity exchange, archaeological investigations have shown that it served primarily as a system of state finance. In his excavations of the massive Inca storage facilities at Huanuco Viejo, Morris (1967) showed that the contents of the store houses were produced within the administrative region of the state centre and did not involve transfer of specialized goods across the diverse environmental zones dominated by the Inca state. In other words, although the state was spread over areas where local specialization could have been appropriate, the state was not involved in the exchange of specialized subsistence products.

Rather, the mobilization and local massive storage of staple products involved maize, tubers, quinoa, sandals, and cloth that were used by the military and others working for the state (D'Altroy 1992; D'Altroy and Earle 1985; Earle and D'Altroy 1982, 1989; LeVine 1992). The land was the property of the state through conquest. In return for access to community lands used for subsistence, the community had to provide labour to cultivate the state's lands and for special state projects related to construction, wealth manufacture, and warfare. As in the Hawaiian case, no market system developed. A complex political system, with a wide range of non-producing personnel (warriors, priests, managers, builders, and craftsmen), was supported directly by the mobilized staples. The best evidence of the staple finance is the massive storage complexes constructed by the Inca through their empire (LeVine 1992).

The alternative ideal type of finance involves the production and circulation of wealth. Wealth is concentrated value which, in contrast to staples, is relatively easy to move and which is used as a political currency to compensate those working for a ruling institution (D'Altroy and Earle 1985).

How does wealth work in the political economy? First, wealth must be rare and valued. The simplest form of wealth, perhaps, is domesticated animals (see Chapter 14): rich in fat and protein, animals are highly desired both for subsistence and for the special meals of feasts. Animals are rare because of the labour needed in husbandry. For example, the raising of pigs is the base for the political economy of highland New Guinea, but the problems of raising pigs are extraordinary. In fact, when pig density exceeds what can be supported by simple foraging, it takes as much human labour to support one pig as it does to support one person (Johnson and Earle 1987)! Interestingly, the growth and elaboration of chiefdoms in late neolithic/early bronze age England and Denmark seem to be related to the elaboration of an economy conditioned by animal production (Earle 1991; Randsborg 1989). Such a system represents certainly an intermediate case between wealth and staple finance.

The development of wealth finance typically involves the local manufacture of special goods by gifted craftsmen and/or the long-distance exchange of wealth from foreign lands. For Formative Mesoamerica (roughly 1500–500 BC), Flannery (1968b) describes how wealth was exchanged over great distances during the development of the Olmec and other chiefdoms of Mesoamerica. He sees this exchange as being part of alliances linking chiefdoms that had developed autarkically: the separate chiefdoms of Oaxaca, producing magnetite mirrors used by the Olmec, came to share elements of a common élite culture. For the chiefdoms of Panama, Mary Helms (1979) argues that long-distance exchange of wealth, such as the gold from Colombia, was not a trivial exchange for foreign trinkets: rather, foreign objects were fundamentally linked to esoteric knowledge external to daily, mundane existence. This knowledge represented power to chiefs vying for access to the esoteric objects and their related knowledge. The symbols, represented frequently on items of personal adornment such as jewellery and clothing, identified the ruling chiefs closely with divine forces. The feather cloaks of the Hawaii chiefs, as an example, were quite literally clothing of the gods (Earle 1990). Chiefs controlled, or at least sought to control, access to foreign wealth and associated esoteric knowledge by negotiating personal networks of exchange and in some cases monopolizing the technology of transport – boats.

Wealth could of course also involve the local manufacture of special objects. To be especially valued, the supply of this wealth needs to be limited. Locally produced wealth characteristically included highly crafted ceramics and metal goods, both requiring sophisticated manufacturing procedures, and cloth, able to absorb unlimited amounts of labour in its manufacture. The control over production of such wealth was exercised through patronizing highly gifted specialists attached directly to the chiefly households. Thus, in the pre-contact Hawaiian chiefdom, the craftsmen who manufactured the elaborate cloaks of the chiefs were part of the paramount chief's personal household (Earle 1987). Alternatively, control over the technology of transport may be a source of chiefly power, as in the chiefly Chumash planked canoes (Arnold 1992). The development of such attached specialization as manufactured fine craft items can be seen as part of the broader political process to control the production and circulation of wealth.

Europe in the Late Neolithic and Early Bronze Ages provides excellent examples of the dynamic role of wealth in political manoeuvring among chiefdoms interlocked by exchange over vast areas. Friedman and Rowlands (1977) constructed a model of 'prestige goods systems', in which they showed how the development of ranking results from political manipulation of exchanges in wealth and wives, building the prestige of individual lineages in a positive feedback system – their model is a sophisticated representation of what Renfrew and Cherry (1986) called 'peer polity interaction'. The application of the Friedman–Rowlands model to Europe has been developed especially by Kristiansen (1984, 1987, 1991). Starting in the neolithic period, production and circulation of wealth involved polished stone axes

(Bradley and Edmonds 1993; Hodder and Lane 1982), stone daggers and battle axes (Kristiansen 1984), and cattle (Earle 1991; Kristiansen 1991). Shennan (1986) describes how the dramatic social transformation associated with the Bell Beaker complex stretched across much of Europe and involved exchange in amber, copper daggers, and their local flint copies. Objects of exchanged wealth became the medium for political rivalry and status definition. Their production and circulation, however, were difficult to control, and the degree of stratification and political centralization was modest.

With the increasing role of metal used for both personal adornment and weaponry, a new source of wealth was created that was easier to control and thus could better form the basis for increasing social differentiation. In particular, the metal came from a greater distance and was manufactured only by craftsmen possessing the remarkable (and occult?) knowledge of metallurgy. Kristiansen (1987) argues that the technical sophistication of metallurgy meant that the few gifted and knowledgeable craftsmen could be easily controlled by their attachment to the highly ranked chiefs. He also shows how the symbols represented by the wealth of the Bronze Age identified chiefs in a very broad cultural system that stretched from Scandinavia to the Aegean.

A related set of theories that investigate broad-scale systems of production and trade with social evolution is the literature on World Systems Theory (see also Chapter 16). Originally formulated by Wallerstein (1974), the development of European capitalism is seen as based on the creation of a world-wide economy in which the industrializing core (Europe) dominated the periphery (the Third World). Schneider (1977) argued that Wallerstein's original conception could be applied successfully to pre-capitalist economies by focusing on the production and circulation of wealth. Attempts to apply World Systems Theory to the evolution of society in pre-industrial contexts are now widespread. Frankenstein and Rowlands's (1978) pioneering study showed how the development of stratification in the European Iron Age could be understood by its articulation with the state societies of the Mediterranean. Rowlands et al. (1987) bring together case studies from archaeology which investigate core–periphery economic relationships. The Uruk empire of early Mesopotamia is a well-studied case of how an imperial core, rich in irrigated agricultural lands, ultimately depended on establishing external trade and tribute relationships with a periphery that was rich in raw materials such as obsidian, metal, wood, and the like (Algaze 1989). The most important point of these works is to show that the social dynamics of any region can only be understood in the context of broad patterns of interaction and dependency. Kristiansen (1991) argues that social evolution must be conceived of as a spatial (as well as a temporal) process; therefore, the chiefdoms of northern Europe must be understood as they articulated with the Mediterranean states in a continuing, active system of commodity exchange and ideological interchange.

624

A good example of this large-scale, economic dynamic can be seen during the Roman Iron Age in Scandinavia. Located four to six hundred kilometres north of the imperial border zone (the *limes*), a rich and select inventory of Roman glass, silver, gold, and other metalwork goods was distributed widely through Scandinavia, but concentrated on the Danish islands such as at Gudme (Thrane 1988), Hoby, and Himlingoje (Hansen 1987). Why is all this wealth found so distant from the civilized Roman world? Minimally, it seems that the concentration of finds along the coasts and islands of the Baltic suggests that the goods were moved by ship (Thrane 1988: 194). Hedeager argues that the careful selection of goods and their distribution 'can only be explained as being the result of a very deliberate and well-organized trade, whose business it was to obtain these sought-after Roman goods in fairly large consignments for the North' (1988: 149). Later, during the Viking period, the economy of northern Europe was transformed from a prestige goods exchange system into (more or less: see Chapter 16) a mercantile market economy (Hedeager 1994). Early on, Viking warriors raided the south for metal wealth that was reworked into decorative objects of status worn especially by women, but then, as regional market towns developed through the Viking world, wealth became minted instead into currencies to finance emerging international markets.

When considering the role of wealth and related ideology, it is essential to see how these economic systems are grounded in the more mundane world of the subsistence economy. For example, the control over production by attached specialization may be exercised simply through control over a system of staple finance in which the mobilized goods are used in part to support the specialists who produce the wealth (D'Altroy and Earle 1985; Earle 1978).

In his analysis of the grinding querns from the Aegean from the Neolithic into the Bronze Age, Runnels (1985) describes a marked increase in the size of the grinding equipment correlated with increasing exchange for the stone needed for the grinding equipment. Why should the grinding querns have increased in size? What we know is that, during the Bronze Age, the development of complex society and the palace economy of Knossos and Mycenae financed itself through an export economy involving such items as wine and olive oil (Gilman 1991; Runnels 1985). To support the labour required in this economy, it was probably necessary to develop a local market to supply the labourers with their daily bread. At the same time, local markets also expanded in ceramics (Davis and Lewis 1985).

Using archaeological data, Brumfiel (1980) described how the development of marketing in the Valley of Mexico was an outcome of an expanding Aztec political economy. She begins by arguing against the idea presented originally by Sanders (1956) that markets developed to feed an expanding population specializing in local products. Rather, she shows how the markets of the Aztecs provided a means by which objects of wealth received in payment for state services could be converted into staple goods. The development of an integrated wealth finance system depends on means for the emerging specialized sector, paid in wealth goods, to obtain staple goods. Here the market acted to channel the flow of staples from the commoners to support the new class of administrators and officials. Polanyi (1968) has argued that currency developed not as a medium of exchange, but as a means of political payment by which a state superstructure operated.

The important point is that complex societies rely on a political economy as a means to obtain and retain dominance. Systems of finance develop as part of emerging institutional complexity, and these can involve a variety of means to move goods in a systematic way. Most importantly, two problems must be solved: (1) support of a non-producing sector of society; and (2) central control over the economy. The solution was tailored to particular local conditions reflecting economic opportunities as external demand for local goods and foreign wealth, but in all situations a mechanism to link subsistence mobilization and wealth integration was sought.

Symbolic materialization

A critical problem in all human society is of course the continual maintenance ('reproduction') of social order and social relationships. Much of the literature in sociology, social anthropology, and structural Marxism has described how social relationships are created. Such work stems from the functionalist traditions of the French sociologist Durkheim and has been elaborated especially by British social anthropologists such as Radcliffe-Brown and Evans-Pritchard. The substantivist economists pick up on this theme. For them, the economy is a process institutionalized in the established social order (see Polanyi *et al.* 1957). This structural functionalism has been reborn and reconstructed in the popular sociological and anthropological literature of structural Marxism (Friedman 1974; Giddens 1979; Godelier 1977; Gregory 1982). For example, in the historically documented exchange involving spouses and prestige goods between the islands of Tonga, Fiji, and Samoa, objects can be seen as 'material manifestations of social relations' (Kaeppler 1978: 246). The essence of the economy was the social and political relationships that it materialized. The important point from this perspective is that social structure and political process are the main determinants of economic organization and operation. Individuals act within this system to position themselves advantageously, and in these individual acts transform the system.

In archaeology, structuralism and structural Marxism have been significant threads of the radical critique of the New Archaeology (Friedman and Rowlands 1977; Hodder 1982a; Kristiansen 1984). This critique, often referred to as 'post-processual' archaeology, raises important questions about the adequacy of popular adaptationalist theories (cf. Earle and Preucel 1987). In terms of archaeological

626

views of the economy, the main thrust has been to focus on the social determinants of economic behaviour in ways not dissimilar to the earlier substantivists.

Hodder argues for a 'contextual approach to prehistoric exchange':

> An exchange act involves an appropriate choice of gift within a social and ideological context. The thing exchanged is not arbitrary, and its associations and symbolism play an active part in the construction of social strategies. As archaeologists, we need to examine the symbolic and ideological dimensions of exchange.
>
> (Hodder 1982a: 199)

This focus on meaning develops the substantivists' notion of values which were relative to an individual society and existed because of their appropriateness for maintaining the existing social order. Hodder, however, stresses the meaning itself rather than the function of it in social process.

The find contexts, for example, of neolithic polished flint axes away from their sources demonstrate varying ritual and utilitarian uses (Hodder and Lane 1982). For axe production (especially at the Great Langdale source) and subsequent exchange, Bradley and Edmonds (1993) argue that the expansion and collapse of the axe trade must be viewed in terms of the changing nature of socio–political relationships within and between regions through Britain. To understand pre-historic economies thus leads researchers towards an understanding of human organization and cultural meaning in the past.

In a provocative essay, Appadurai (1986) argues that commodities have 'social lives'. Commodities are objects of material culture intended for exchange; the exchange life of the object is imbued with meaning that it takes on in actual inter-personal transactions. The prime example is of course the Kula objects, the exchange history of which is known and which creates increased value for the objects. In order to understand the development of specialization and complex economies with such commodities, Renfrew (1986) discusses the wealth objects from the famous chalcolithic cemetery at Varna in the Balkans. He argues that the creation of this wealth was part of a broader social process of display and personal differentiation and identification. Value, or so he postulates, was created by social exchange and not from the inherent properties of the object.

As described earlier, Helms (1979) describes how the exchange of special objects like gold ornaments from Colombia or the magnetite mirrors from Oaxaca was linked to obtaining esoteric knowledge used by chiefs as a source of power and legitimacy. To understand exchange is to understand how the objects carried meaning and how possession or gifting of such objects created specific social relationships of alliance and dependency.

The analysis of the meaning of objects is essential to determine the reasons for their production and exchange and the significance of that exchange in social life. Sørensen (1987), for example, analyses how female decorative objects of bronze were used in Denmark to define styles with local referents, in direct contrast to male

627

weaponry that was used to establish strong external referents to warrior élite styles across Europe. For many, material culture has become a useful window into cultural meaning. I suggest that it is more than this.

Culture must be materialized, given physical form in speech, ceremony, and object (DeMarrais *et al.* 1996). If you conceive of culture as shared rules of behaviour passed on through socialized learning, all culture must be held within an individual's head, and likelihood for coherence would be low. Rather, social groups and cultural meaning can be seen as created in ceremony and at least partially recorded in the material culture. It is common for post-processualists to talk of reading the past. In fact that may be apt if one considers that material culture is the means to encode, represent, and transfer social meaning. Thus material culture becomes the very essence of culture and not simply a window into its form.

CONCLUSION

Production and exchange are very basic to social life. Because of recent scientific breakthroughs involving everything from chemical characterization to computer modelling, the archaeologist's ability to study exchange has increased dramatically. Sustained investigations of production and exchange have illustrated how archaeological evidence of these economic events permits insights into the social organization of past human societies. Theoretically, attention has focused on production and exchange as critical causes of social evolution and as the very medium in which social life becomes realized. Of all archaeological work, investigations of production and exchange will continue to play a central role as we derive new knowledge of and meaning about the past.

REFERENCES

Algaze, G. (1989) 'Cross-cultural exchange in early Mesopotamian civilization', *Current Anthropology* 30: 571–608.

Allen, J. (1985) 'Comments on complexity and trade: a view from Melanesia', *Archaeology in Oceania* 20: 49–57.

Ammerman, A. J. and Andrefsky, J. W. (1982) 'Reduction sequences and the exchange of obsidian in neolithic Calabria', in J. E. Ericson and T. K. Earle (eds) *Contexts for Prehistoric Exchange*, New York: Academic Press: 149–72.

Andrefsky, W. (1994) 'Raw-material availability and the organization of technology', *American Antiquity* 59: 21–34.

Appadurai, A. (1986) 'Introduction: commodities and the politics of value', in A. Appadurai (ed.) *The Social Life of Things: Commodities in Cultural Perspective*, Cambridge: Cambridge University Press: 3–63.

Arnold, J. (1992) 'Complex hunter-gatherer-fishers of prehistoric California: chiefs, specialists, and maritime adaptations of the Channel Islands', *American Antiquity* 57: 60–84.

Bailey, G. (ed.) (1983) *Hunter-Gatherer Economy in Prehistory*, Cambridge: Cambridge University Press.

Baugh, T. and Ericson, J. (eds) (1994) *Prehistoric Exchange Systems in North America*, New York: Plenum Press.

Bettinger, R. (1982) 'Aboriginal exchange and territoriality in Owens Valley, California', in J. Ericson and T. Earle (eds) *Contexts for Prehistoric Exchange*, New York: Academic Press: 103–27.

Binford, L. (1964) 'A consideration of archaeological research design', *American Antiquity* 29: 425–41.

Bishop, R. (1980) 'Aspects of ceramic compositional modeling', in R. Fry (ed.) *Models and Methods in Regional Exchange*, Washington, DC: Society of American Archaeology: 47–65.

Bradley, R. and Edmonds, M. (1993) *Interpreting the Axe Trade: Production and Exchange in Neolithic Britain*, Cambridge: Cambridge University Press.

Braun, D. (1986) 'Midwestern Hopewellian exchange and supralocal interaction', in C. Renfrew and J. Cherry (eds) *Peer Polity Interaction and Socio-Political Change*, Cambridge: Cambridge University Press: 117–26.

Braun, D. and Plog, S. (1982) 'Evolution of "tribal" social networks: theory and prehistoric North American evidence', *American Antiquity* 47: 504–25.

Brumfiel, E. (1976) 'A regional growth in the eastern Valley of Mexico: a test of the "population pressure" hypothesis', in K. Flannery (ed.) *The Early Mesoamerican Village*, New York: Academic Press: 234–49.

Brumfiel, E. (1980) 'Specialization, market exchange, and the Aztec state: a view from Huexotla', *Current Anthropology* 21: 459–78.

Brumfiel, E. and Earle, T. (1987) 'Introduction', in E. Brumfiel and T. Earle (eds) *Specialization, Exchange, and Complex Societies*, Cambridge: Cambridge University Press: 1–21.

Burger, R. and Asaro, F. (1977) 'Análisis de rasgos significativos en la obsidiana de los Andes central', *Revista del Museo Nacional* 43: 281–325.

Chapman, A. (1957) 'Port of trade enclaves in Aztec and Maya civilizations', in K. Polanyi, A. M. Arensberg and H. W. Pearson (eds) *Trade and Market in the Early Empires*, Glencoe, Ill.: Free Press: 114–53.

Clark, J. and Parry, W. (1986) 'Craft specialization and cultural complexity', *Research in Economic Anthropology* 12: 289–346.

Clark, J., Lee, T. and Salcedo, T. (1989) 'The distribution of obsidian', in B. Voorhies (ed.) *Ancient Trade and Tribute: Economies of the Soconusco Region of Mesoamerica*, Salt Lake City: University of Utah Press: 268–84.

Clarke, D. (ed.) (1972) *Models in Archaeology*, London: Methuen.

Costin, C. (1986) 'From Chiefdom to Empire State: Ceramic Economy among the Prehispanic Wanka of Highland Peru', Los Angeles: UCLA, Department of Anthropology, Ph.D. dissertation.

Costin, C. (1991) 'Craft specialization: issues in defining, documenting, and explaining the organization of production', *Archaeological Method and Theory* 3: 1–56.

Curtin, P. (1984) *Cross-Cultural Trade in World History*, Cambridge: Cambridge University Press.

D'Altroy, T. (1992) *Provincial Power in the Inka Empire*, Washington, DC: Smithsonian Institution Press.

D'Altroy, T. and Bishop, R. (1990) 'The provincial organization of Inka ceramic production', *American Antiquity* 55: 120–38.

D'Altroy, T. and Earle, T. (1985) 'Staple finance, wealth finance, and storage in the Inca political economy', *Current Anthropology* 26: 187–206.

Davis, J. and Lewis, H. (1985) 'Mechanization of pottery production: a case study from the Cycladic Islands', in B. Knapp and T. Stech (eds) *Prehistoric Production and Exchange: the Aegean and Eastern Mediterranean*, Los Angeles: UCLA, Institute of Archaeology: 79–92.

DeMarrais, E., Castillo, L. J. and Earle, T. (1996) 'Ideology, materialization, and power strategies', *Current Anthropology* 37: 15–31.

Dixon, J. E. (1976) 'Obsidian characterization studies in the Mediterranean and Near East', in R. Taylor (ed.) *Advances in Obsidian Glass Studies*: Park Ridge, N.Y.: Noyes Press: 288–333.

Drennan, R. (1976) 'Religion and social evolution in Formative Mesoamerica', in K. Flannery (ed.) *The Early Mesoamerican Village*, New York: Academic Press: 345–68.

Earle, T. (1977) 'A reappraisal of redistribution: complex Hawaiian chiefdoms', in T. Earle and J. Ericson (eds) *Exchange Systems in Prehistory*, New York: Academic Press: 213–29.

Earle, T. (1978) *Economic and Social Organization of a Complex Chiefdom: the Halelea District, Kaua'i, Hawaii*, Anthropological Papers 63, Ann Arbor: University of Michigan.

Earle, T. (1982a) 'Prehistoric economics and the archaeology of exchange', in J. Ericson and T. Earle (eds) *Contexts for Prehistoric Exchange*, New York: Academic Press: 1–12.

Earle, T. (1982b) 'The ecology and politics of primitive valuables', in J. Kennedy and E. Edgerton (eds) *Culture and Ecology: Eclectic Perspectives*, Washington, DC: American Anthropological Association, Special Publications 15: 65–83.

Earle, T. (1985a) 'Prehistoric economics and the evolution of social complexity', in B. Knapp and T. Stech (eds) *Prehistoric Production and Exchange: the Aegean and Eastern Mediterranean*, Los Angeles: UCLA, Institute of Archaeology Monograph 25: 106–11.

Earle, T. (1985b) 'Commodity exchange and markets in the Inca state: recent archaeological evidence', in S. Plattner (ed.) *Markets and Marketing*, Lanham, Md.: University Press of America: 368–97.

Earle, T. (1987) 'Specialization and the production of wealth: Hawaiian chiefdoms and the Inka empire', in E. Brumfiel and T. Earle (eds) *Specialization, Exchange, and Complex Societies*, Cambridge: Cambridge University Press: 64–75.

Earle, T. (1990) 'Style and iconography as legitimation in complex chiefdoms', in M. Conkey and C. Hastorf (eds) *The Uses of Style in Archaeology*, Cambridge: Cambridge University Press: 73–81.

Earle, T. (1991) 'Property rights and the evolution of chiefdoms', in T. Earle (ed.) *Chiefdoms: Power, Economy, and Ideology*, Cambridge: Cambridge University Press: 71–99.

Earle, T. (1994) 'Positioning exchange in the evolution of human society', in T. Baugh and J. Ericson (eds) *Prehistoric Exchange Systems in North America*, New York: Plenum Press: 419–37.

Earle, T. and Christenson, A. (eds) (1980) *Modeling Change in Prehistoric Subsistence Economies*, New York: Academic Press.

Earle, T. and D'Altroy, T. (1982) 'Storage facilities and state finance in the upper Mantaro Valley, Peru', in J. Ericson and T. Earle (eds) *Contexts for Prehistoric Exchange*, New York: Academic Press: 265–90.

630

Earle, T. and D'Altroy, T. (1989) 'The political economy of the Inka Empire: the archaeology of power and finance', in C. C. Lamberg-Karlovsky (ed.) *Archaeological Thought in America*, Cambridge: Cambridge University Press: 183–204.

Earle, T. and Ericson, J. (1977) 'Exchange systems in archaeological perspective', in T. Earle and J. Ericson (eds) *Exchange Systems in Prehistory*, New York: Academic Press: 3–12.

Earle, T. and Preucel, R. (1987) 'Processual archaeology and the radical critique', *Current Anthropology* 28: 501–38.

Ericson, J. (1977) 'Egalitarian exchange systems in California: a preliminary view', in T. Earle and J. Ericson (eds) *Exchange Systems in Prehistory*, New York: Academic Press: 109–26.

Ericson, J. (1981) *Exchange and Production Systems in Californian Prehistory*, Oxford: British Archaeological Reports, International Series 110.

Ericson, J. (1982) 'Production for obsidian exchange in California', in J. Ericson and T. Earle (eds) *Contexts for Prehistoric Exchange*, New York: Academic Press: 129–48.

Ericson, J. and Baugh, T. (eds) (1993) *The American Southwest and Mesoamerica: Systems of Prehistoric Exchange*, New York: Plenum Press.

Ericson, J. and Earle, T. (eds) (1982) *Contexts for Prehistoric Exchange*, New York: Academic Press.

Ericson, J. and Purdy, B. (eds) (1984) *Prehistoric Quarries and Lithic Production*, Cambridge: Cambridge University Press.

Findlow, F. and Bolognese, M. (1982) 'Regional modeling of obsidian procurement in the American Southwest', in J. Ericson and T. Earle (eds) *Contexts for Prehistoric Exchange*, New York: Academic Press: 53–81.

Flannery, K. (1968a) 'Archaeological systems theory and early Mesoamerica', in B. J. Meggers (ed.) *Anthropological Archaeology in the Americas*, Washington, DC: Anthropological Society of Washington: 67–87.

Flannery, K. (1968b) 'Olmec and the Valley of Oaxaca: a model of inter-regional interaction in Formative times', in E. Benson (ed.) *Dumbarton Oaks Conference on the Olmec*, Washington, DC: Dumbarton Oaks: 79–117.

Flannery, K. (1972) 'The cultural evolution of civilizations', *Annual Reviews in Ecology and Systematics* 3: 399–425.

Flannery, K. (ed.) (1976) *The Early Mesoamerican Village*, New York: Academic Press.

Frankenstein, S. and Rowlands, M. (1978) 'The internal structure and regional context of early iron age society in southwestern Germany', *University of London Institute of Archaeology Bulletin* 15: 73–112.

Friedman, J. (1974) 'Marxism, structuralism and vulgar materialism', *Man* (N.S.) 9: 444–69.

Friedman, J. and Rowlands, M. (1977) 'Notes towards an epigenetic model of the evolution of "civilization"', in J. Friedman and M. Rowlands (eds) *The Evolution of Social Systems*, London: Duckworth: 201–76.

Fry, R. (1979) 'The economics of pottery at Tikal, Guatemala: models of exchange for serving vessels', *American Antiquity* 44: 494–512.

Fry, R. (ed.) (1980) *Models and Methods in Regional Exchange*, Washington, DC: Society of American Archaeology, Paper 1.

Giddens, A. (1979) *Central Problems in Social Theory*, Berkeley: University of California.

Gilman, A. (1991) 'Trajectories towards social complexity in the later prehistory of the Mediterranean', in T. Earle (ed.) *Chiefdoms: Power, Economy, and Ideology*, Cambridge: Cambridge University Press: 146–68.

Godelier, M. (1977) *Perspectives in Marxist Anthropology*, Cambridge: Cambridge University Press.

Gregory, C. A. (1982) *Gifts and Commodities*, New York: Academic Press.

Gumerman, G. (1991) 'Subsistence and Complex Societies: Diet between Diverse Socio-Economic Groups in Pacatnamu', Los Angeles: UCLA Department of Anthropology, Ph.D. dissertation.

Haggett, P. (1965) *Locational Analysis in Geography*, London: Edward Arnold.

Hagstrum, M. (1985) 'Measuring prehistoric ceramic craft specialization: a test case in the American Southwest', *Journal of Field Archaeology* 12: 65–76.

Hagstrum, M. (1986) 'The technology of ceramic production of Wanka and Inka wares from the Yanamarca Valley, Peru', in P. Rice (ed.) *Ceramics Notes*, Occasional Papers of Ceramics Technology Laboratory volume 3, Gainesville, Fla.: Florida State Museum: 1–29.

Hagstrum, M. (1989) 'Technological Continuity and Change: Ceramic Ethnoarchaeology in the Peruvian Andes', Los Angeles: UCLA Department of Anthropology, Ph.D. dissertation.

Halstead, P. and O'Shea, J. (eds) (1989) *Bad Year Economics*, Cambridge: Cambridge University Press.

Hansen, U. (1987) *Römischer import im norden*, Lund: University of Lund, Nordiske Fortidsminder.

Harbottle, G. (1982) 'Chemical characterization in archaeology', in J. Ericson and T. Earle (eds) *Contexts for Prehistoric Exchange*, New York: Academic Press, New York: 13–51.

Hårdh, B., Larsson, L., Olausson, D. and Petré, R. (1988) *Trade and Exchange in Prehistoric Europe: Studies in Honour of Berta Stjernquist*, Lund: Lund University Historical Museum.

Hastorf, C. A. (1993) *Agriculture and the Onset of Political Inequality before the Inka*, Cambridge: Cambridge University Press.

Hedeager, L. (1988) 'Money economy and prestige economy in the Roman Iron Age', in B. Hårdh, L. Larsson, D. Olausson and R. Petré (eds) *Trade and Exchange in Prehistoric Europe: Studies in Honour of Berta Stjernquist*, Lund: Lund University Historical Museum: 147–53.

Hedeager, L. (1994) 'Warrior economy and trading economy in Viking-Age Scandinavia', *Journal of European Archaeology* 2: 130–48.

Helms, M. (1979) *Ancient Panama*, Austin: University of Texas Press.

Higgs, E. S. (ed.) (1972) *Papers in Economic Prehistory*, Cambridge: Cambridge University Press.

Hirth, K. (ed.) (1984) *Trade and Exchange in Early Mesoamerica*, Albuquerque, N. Mex.: University of New Mexico Press.

Hodder, I. (1974) 'Regression analysis of some trade and market patterns', *World Archaeology* 6: 172–89.

Hodder, I. (1982a) *Symbols in Action*, Cambridge: Cambridge University Press.

Hodder, I. (1982b) 'Toward a contextual approach to prehistoric exchange', in J. Ericson and T. Earle (eds) *Contexts for Prehistoric Exchange*, New York: Academic Press: 199–211.

Hodder, I. (1984) 'Archaeology in 1984', *Antiquity* 58: 25–34.

Hodder, I. and Lane, P. (1982) 'A contextual examination of neolithic axe distribution in Britain', in J. Ericson and T. Earle (eds) *Contexts for Prehistoric Exchange*, New York: Academic Press: 213–35.

Hodder, I. and Orton, C. (1976) *Spatial Analysis in Archaeology*, Cambridge: Cambridge University Press.

Hodges, R. (1982) *Dark Age Economics: the Origins of Towns and Trade AD 600–1000*, London: Duckworth.

Hughes, R. (1984) 'Obsidian sourcing studies in the Great Basin', *Contributions of the University of California Archaeological Research Facility* 45: 1–19.

Hughes, R. (1994) 'Mosaic pattern in prehistoric California-Great Basin exchange', in T. Baugh and J. Ericson (eds) *Prehistoric Exchange Systems in North America*, New York: Plenum Press: 363–83.

Irwin, G. (1978) 'Pots and entrepôts: a study of settlement, trade and the development of economic specialization in Papuan prehistory', *World Archaeology* 9: 299–319.

Irwin, G. (1985) *The Emergence of Mailu*, Canberra: Australia National University, Terra Australis 10.

Isaac, B. (ed.) (1986) *Economic Aspect of Prehispanic Highland Mexico*, Greenwich, Conn.: JAI Press.

Johnson, A. and Earle, T. (1987) *The Evolution of Human Societies: from Foraging Group to Agrarian State*, Stanford: Stanford University Press.

Johnson, G. (1973) *Local Exchange and Early State Development in South-western Iran*, Anthropological Papers 51, Ann Arbor: University of Michigan, Museum of Anthropology,.

Kaeppler, A. (1978) 'Exchange patterns in goods and spouses: Fiji, Tonga and Samoa', *Mankind* 11: 246–52.

Kirch, P. (1988) 'Long-distance exchange and island colonization: the Lapita case', *Norwegian Archaeological Review* 21: 103–17.

Kirch, P. (1990) 'Specialization and exchange in the Lapita complex of Oceania', *Asian Perspectives* 29: 117–33.

Kirch, P. (1991a) 'Chiefship and competitive involution: the Marquesas Islands of eastern Polynesia', in T. Earle (ed.) *Chiefdoms: Power, Economy, and Ideology*, Cambridge: Cambridge University Press: 119–45.

Kirch, P. (1991b) 'Prehistoric exchange in western Melanesia', *Annual Reviews in Anthropology* 20: 141–65.

Kirch, P. and Hunt, T. (eds) (1988) *Archaeology of the Lapita Cultural Complex: a Critical Review*, Seattle: Burke Museum.

Knapp, B. and Stech, T. (eds) (1995) *Prehistoric Production and Exchange: the Aegean and Eastern Mediterranean*, Los Angeles: UCLA Institute of Archaeology, Monograph 25.

Kristiansen, K. (1984) 'Ideology and material culture: an archaeological perspective', in M. Spriggs (ed.) *Marxist Perspectives in Archaeology*, Cambridge: Cambridge University Press: 72–100.

Kristiansen, K. (1987) 'From stone to bronze: the evolution of social complexity in northern Europe, 2300–1200 BC', in E. Brumfiel and T. Earle (eds) *Specialization, Exchange and Complex Society*, Cambridge: Cambridge University Press: 30–51.

Kristiansen, K. (1991) 'Chiefdoms, states and systems of social evolution in northern Europe', in T. Earle (ed.) *Chiefdoms: Power, Economy, and Ideology*, Cambridge: Cambridge University Press: 16–44.

LaLone, D. (1982) 'The Inca as a nonmarket economy: supply on command versus supply on demand', in J. Ericson and T. Earle (eds) *Contexts for Prehistoric Exchange*, New York: Academic Press: 292–316.

Lass, B. (1994) *Hawaiian Adze Production and Distribution: Implications for the Development of Chiefdoms*, Los Angeles: UCLA Institute of Archaeology, Monograph 37.

LeClair, E. and Schneider, H. (eds) (1968) *Economic Anthropology*, New York: Holt, Rinehart and Winston.

LeVine, T. (ed.) (1992) *Inka Storage Systems*, Norman: University of Oklahoma Press.

Liversage, D. and Liversage, M. (1989) 'A method for the study of the composition of early copper and bronze artifacts: an example from Denmark', *Helinium* 28: 42–76.

Miller, D. and Tilley, C. (eds) (1984) *Ideology, Power and Prehistory*, Cambridge: Cambridge University Press.

Minnis, P. (1985) *Social Adaptation to Food Stress*, Chicago: Chicago University Press.

Morris, C. (1967) 'Storage in Tawantinsuyu', Chicago: University of Chicago, Ph.D. dissertation.

Morrow, C. and Jefferies, R. (1989) 'Trade or embedded procurement?: a test case from southern Illinois', in R. Torrence (ed.) *Time, Energy and Stone Tools*, Cambridge: Cambridge University Press: 27–33.

Muller, J. (1987) 'Salt, chert, and shell: Mississippian exchange and economy', in E. Brumfiel and T. Earle (eds) *Specialization, Exchange and Complex Society*, Cambridge: Cambridge University Press: 10–21.

Murra, J. V. ([1956] 1980) *The Economic Organization of the Inka State*, Greenwich, Conn.: JAI Press.

Neff, H. (1989) 'The effect of interregional distribution on plumbate pottery production', in B. Voorhies (ed.) *Ancient Trade and Tribute: Economies of the Soconusco Region of Mesoamerica*, Salt Lake City: University of Utah Press: 249–67.

Polanyi, K. (1968) *Primitive, Archaic, and Modern Economies*, Garden City, N.J.: Doubleday.

Polanyi, K., Arensberg, M. and Pearson, H. (1957) *Trade and Market in the Early Empires*, Glencoe, Ill.: Free Press.

Randsborg, K. (1989) 'The periods of Danish antiquity', *Acta Archaeologica* 60: 187–92.

Renfrew, C. (1973) 'Monuments, mobilization and social organization in neolithic Wessex', in C. Renfrew (ed.) *The Explanation of Culture Change*, London: Duckworth: 539–58.

Renfrew, C. (1975) 'Trade as action at a distance: questions of integration and communication', in J. Sabloff and C. C. Lamberg-Karlovsky (eds) *Ancient Civilization and Trade*, Albuquerque, N. Mex.: University of New Mexico Press: 3–59.

Renfrew, C. (1977) 'Alternative models for exchange and spatial distribution', in T. Earle and J. Ericson (eds) *Exchange Systems in Prehistory*, New York: Academic Press: 71–90.

Renfrew, C. (1986) 'Varna and the emergence of wealth in prehistoric Europe', in A. Appadurai (ed.) *The Social Life of Things: Commodities in Cultural Perspective*, Cambridge: Cambridge University Press: 141–68.

Renfrew, C. and Cherry, J. (eds) (1986) *Peer Polity Interaction and Socio-Political Change*, Cambridge: Cambridge University Press.

Renfrew, C. and Dixon, J. E. (1976) 'Obsidian in western Asia: a review', in I. L. G. Sieveking and K. Wilson (eds) *Problems in Economic and Social Archaeology*, London: Duckworth: 137–50.

Renfrew, C. and Shennan, S. (eds) (1982) *Ranking, Resources and Exchange*, Cambridge: Cambridge University Press.

Renfrew, C., Dixon, J. E. and Cann, J. R. (1966) 'Obsidian and early culture contact in the Near East', *Proceedings of the Prehistoric Society* 32: 30–72.

Rice, P. (1981) 'Evolution of specialized pottery production: a trial model', *Current Anthropology* 22: 219–40.

Rowlands, M., Larsen, M. and Kristiansen, K. (eds) (1987) *Centre and Periphery in the Ancient World*, Cambridge: Cambridge University Press.

Runnels, C. (1985) 'Trade and the demand for millstones in southern Greece in the Neolithic and Early Bronze Age', in B. Knapp and T. Stech (eds) *Prehistoric Production and Exchange: the Aegean and Eastern Mediterranean*, Los Angeles: UCLA Institute of Archaeology, Monograph 25: 30–43.

Russell, G. (1988) *The Impact of Inka Policy on the Domestic Economy of the Wanka, Peru: Stone Tool Production and Use*, Los Angeles: UCLA Department of Anthropology.

Sabloff, J. and Freidel, D. (1975) 'A model of a pre-Columbian trading center', in J. Sabloff and C. C. Lamberg-Karlovsky (eds) *Ancient Civilization and Trade*, Albuquerque, N. Mex.: University of New Mexico Press: 369–408.

Sabloff, J. and Lamberg-Karlovsky, C. C. (eds) (1975) *Ancient Civilization and Trade*, Albuquerque, N. Mex.: University of New Mexico Press.

Sahlins, M. (1972) *Stone Age Economics*, Chicago: Aldine.

Sanders, W. (1956) 'The central Mexican symbiotic region: a study in prehistoric settlement patterns', in G. Willey (ed.) *Prehistoric Settlement Patterns in the New World*, New York: Wenner-Gren Foundation: 115–27.

Santley, R. S. (1985) 'The political economy of the Aztec empire', *Journal of Anthropological Research* 41: 327–37.

Schneider, J. (1977) 'Was there a pre-capitalist world-system?', *Peasant Studies* 6: 20–29.

Service, E. (1962) *Primitive Social Organization*, New York: Random House.

Shennan, S. (1986) 'Interaction and change in third millennium BC western and central Europe', in C. Renfrew and J. Cherry (eds) *Peer Polity Interaction and Socio-Political Change*, Cambridge: Cambridge University Press: 137–48.

Sidrys, R. (1977) 'Mass-distance measures for the Maya obsidian trade', in T. Earle and J. Ericson (eds) *Exchange Systems in Prehistory*, New York: Academic Press: 91–108.

Singer, C. and Ericson, J. (1977) 'Quarry analysis at Bodie Hills, Mono County, California: a case study', in T. Earle and J. Ericson (eds) *Exchange Systems in Prehistory*, New York: Academic Press: 171–88.

Sørensen, M. L. S. (1987) 'Material order and cultural classification: the role of bronze objects in the transition from Bronze Age to Iron Age in Scandinavia', in I. Hodder (ed.) *The Archaeology of Contextual Meanings*, Cambridge: Cambridge University Press: 90–101.

Spriggs, M. (ed.) (1984) *Marxist Perspectives in Archaeology*, Cambridge: Cambridge University Press.

Stein, G. (1994) 'Economy, ritual, and power in 'Ubaid Mesopotamia', in G. Stein and M. Robinson (eds) *Chiefdoms and Early States in the Near East*, Madison, Wis.: Prehistoric Press: 35–46.

Stjernquist, B. (1967) 'Models of commercial diffusion in prehistoric times', *Scripta Minora* (Lund): 1965–66.

Thrane, H. (1988) 'Import, affluence and cult-interdependent aspects?', in B. Hårdh, L. Larsson, D. Olausson and R. Petré (eds) *Trade and Exchange in Prehistoric Europe: Studies in Honour of Berta Stjernquist*, Lund: Lund University Historical Museum: 187–96.

Torrence, R. (1986) *Production and Exchange of Stone Tools*, Cambridge: Cambridge University Press.

Tosi, M. (1984) 'The notion of craft specialization and its representation in the archaeological record of early states in the Turanian Basin', in M. Spriggs (ed.) *Marxist Perspectives in Archaeology*, Cambridge: Cambridge University Press: 22–52.

Voorhies, B. (ed.) (1989) *Ancient Trade and Tribute: Economies of the Soconusco Region of Mesoamerica*, Salt Lake City: University of Utah Press.

Wallerstein, I. (1974) *The Modern World System*, New York: Academic Press.

Weisler, M. (1993) 'Provenance studies of Polynesian basalt adze material: a review and suggestions for improving regional data bases', *Asian Perspectives* 32: 61–83.

Wheatley, P. (1975) 'Satyanrta in Suvarnadvipa: from reciprocity to redistribution in ancient Southeast Asia', in J. Sabloff and C. C. Lamberg-Karlovsky (eds) *Ancient Civilization and Trade*, Albuquerque, N. Mex.: University of New Mexico Press: 227–83.

Wiessner, P. (1982) 'Beyond willow smoke and dogs' tails: a comment on Binford's analysis of hunter-gatherer settlement systems', *American Anthropologist* 47: 171–78.

Willey, G. and Sabloff, S. (1974) *A History of American Archaeology*, London: Thames and Hudson.

Wilmsen, E. (ed.) (1972) *Social Exchange and Interaction*, Museum of Anthropology Papers 46, Ann Arbor: University of Michigan.

Wright, G. (1969) *Obsidian Analysis and Prehistoric Near Eastern Trade: 7500 to 3500 BC*, Museum of Anthropology Papers 37, Ann Arbor: University of Michigan.

Wright, H. (1972) 'A consideration of interregional exchange in Greater Mesopotamia: 4000–3000 BC', in E. Wilmsen (ed.) *Social Exchange and Interaction*, Museum of Anthropology Papers 46, Ann Arbor: University of Michigan: 95–105.

Wright, H. and Johnson, G. (1975) 'Population, exchange and early state formation in southwestern Iran', *American Anthropologist* 77: 267–89.

Yoffee, N. (1985) 'Perspectives on "Trends towards complex societies in prehistoric Australia and Papua New Guinea"', *Archaeology in Oceania* 20: 40–49.

SELECT BIBLIOGRAPHY

Regrettably no single book deals with the archaeology of prehistoric economies, although the best synthesis of spatial methods is Hodder and Orton (1976). The seminal work on substantivist economics is Karl Polanyi *et al.* (1957) *Trade and Market in the Early Empires*, and the most useful application to archaeology is Renfrew (1975). Starting in the 1970s, processual archaeologists published a series of influential edited books on prehistoric production and exchange that includes many worthwhile chapters dealing with substantial results, research methods, and theoretical implications: Wilmsen (1972), Sabloff and Lamberg-Karlovsky (1975), Earle and Ericson (1977), Ericson and Earle (1982), Renfrew and Shennan (1982), Renfrew and Cherry (1986), Brumfiel and Earle (1987). Broad regional syntheses are available for Mesoamerica (Ericson and Baugh 1993) and North America (Baugh and Ericson 1994). Studies of particular thoroughness focus on Aegean obsidian trade (Torrence 1986), British stone axe trade (Bradley and Edmonds 1993), and Inca imperial finance (D'Altroy 1992; LeVine 1992). A few of the most quoted theoretical articles include D'Altroy and Earle (1985), Earle (1977), Flannery (1968b), Friedman and Rowlands (1977), and Helms (1979).